858.17

WOMEN AND THE "EQUAL RIGHTS" AMENDMENT

WOMEN AND THE "EQUAL RIGHTS" AMENDMENT

SENATE SUBCOMMITTEE HEARINGS ON THE CONSTITUTIONAL AMENDMENT, 91ST CONGRESS

Edited by Dr. Catharine Stimpson, Barnard College,
in conjunction with
the Congressional Information Service,
Washington, D.C.

R. R. BOWKER COMPANY   New York and London   1972

Published by R. R. Bowker Co. (A Xerox Company)
1180 Avenue of the Americas, New York, N.Y. 10036
Copyright © 1972 by Xerox Corporation
All rights reserved.
International Standard Book Number: 0-8352-0532-0
Library of Congress Catalog Card Number: 77-39745
Printed and bound in the United States of America.

CONTENTS

FOREWORD

The Equal Rights Amendment has been introduced in every Congress since 1923, but it has been debated among women's groups for more than 100 years. Many of the early suffragettes were for an equal rights amendment rather than the suffrage amendment. The objections to granting equal rights, however, were so tremendous that women's groups finally settled on the right to vote.

Both political parties in national conventions have endorsed the Equal Rights Amendment for more than 30 years. Yet, until 1970, the amendment never had been discussed on the floor of the House of Representatives, despite the fact it had passed the Senate twice in a restricted form.

When I succeeded in securing the 218 signatures necessary to discharge the House Committee of the Judiciary from further consideration of the amendment in the 91st Congress, it had been more than a generation since a hearing had been held on the amendment in the House. One of the mystifying things to me was the lack of knowledge of the Judiciary Committee on the rights of women, as was exemplified by their arguments on the House floor. A problem in passing any legislation via the infrequently used route of the discharge petition is that usually there has been no in-depth study and analysis in committee of the legislation to foster understanding as to its purpose and intent. Since 1910, for example, out of 25 bills freed from committee through the use of the discharge procedure, only 19 were passed by the House and only 2 eventually became law.

When the Equal Rights Amendment passed the House in August of 1970 and reached the Senate, the lobbying of women's groups ceased. The assumption was that since 82 Senators had introduced resolutions identical with mine, which had secured House approval, they would see it through the Senate. But women's groups did not reckon with the detrimental efforts of the AFL–CIO and others who opposed the amendment. When the moment of truth arrived, Senators refused to vote for their own measure, caving in to the pressures of their friends and betraying the trust which women's organizations had placed in them.

Hopefully, in this 92nd Congress, the Equal Rights Amendment, which passed the House again for the second time, will be successful in the Senate. But, if and when it does secure final approval, there still remains a long road for women to traverse before they really do achieve equal rights.

MARTHA W. GRIFFITHS
Member of Congress

PREFACE

This volume contains both the testimony and documents presented at the Senate Subcommittee hearings on the Equal Rights Amendment (ERA) held in May 1970. Our purpose in publishing this volume is to make accessible to the public in a hardcover edition the record of influential government operations, to make obtainable what might otherwise be ignored. At present only the larger city and university libraries serve as depositories for such government publications, and we have found that to purchase a copy directly from the Government Printing Office (GPO) often takes several months.

In presenting these hearings we have attempted to create a book which is at once readable and informative. None of the oral testimony has been deleted, and only those documents which were either repetitive or easily found in other sources have been deleted. (These have been documented in the Index of Omissions.) The text of this volume has been reproduced from the GPO edition. Therefore, any typographical errors are a part of the original.

Part 1 includes all of the oral testimony. We have edited this material so that, unlike the GPO edition, it reads uninterrupted from beginning to end and will give the reader a sense of the play and flow of the hearings. The many documents which obstruct the testimony in the original edition have been moved to Part 2. The prepared testimonies from which the witnesses read have, with two exceptions, been deleted.

Part 2 contains the documents, and these we have arranged in five sections. Included in the first section are those statements submitted for the record in opposition to the ERA. None has been deleted. The second section is comprised of statements in support. Because of the large number of these and because many were repetitive we have selected statements from the widest possible range of organizations and individuals which are the most representative.

Since the arguments concerning protective legislation were so crucial we have gathered the written statements of organized labor, both for and against, together in the third and fourth sections.

The fifth section contains additional material submitted for the record which neither directly supports nor opposes the amendment but which provides much important information on the present status of women in America.

Following Part 2 are an appendix and three indexes. The appendix consists of excerpts from the House and Senate floor debates on the amendment, taken from the Congressional Record. The Index of Omissions and the Index of Inclusions are designed to be used as a guide to both this and the GPO editions. The Index of Persons and Organizations is intended to be used with this edition only.

I am grateful to the editors at the R. R. Bowker Company and the Congressional Information Service, and I am extremely appreciative of the hard and serious work of Alan Searls, who grasped both the details and the broad purpose of this book unfailingly.

INTRODUCTION

As I write, the Committee on the Judiciary of the United States Senate is considering a proposed amendment to the Constitution of the United States: the Equal Rights Amendment. Once that proposed amendment, which the House of Representatives cheerfully approved on October 12, 1971, had a massive simplicity. "Equality of rights under the law shall not be denied or abridged by the United States or any State on account of sex." For example, I, as a woman, would be able to tell any employer who offered me less pay than he might offer a man for the same job that he was acting unconstitutionally. However, a subcommittee of the Senate Judiciary Committee, led by Senator Sam Ervin, a Democrat from North Carolina, has amended the proposed amendment to read:

Neither the United States nor any State shall make any legal distinction between the rights and responsibilities of male and female persons unless such distinction is based on physiological or functional differences between them.

I do not know if the Judiciary Committee will report out the ERA (the Equal Rights Amendment) in its original form; in Senator Ervin's form; or in still another form. Perhaps it may even fail to ask the Senate to vote on the issue. Many who support the ERA believe that it would be wiser to have no amendment at all than to have one altered as Senator Ervin has proposed.

If the ERA becomes mired in the bogs of Congress, it will not be for the first time. The history of the amendment has been one of frustration for its proponents; condescension and parliamentary evasion on the part of its opponents; and apathy on the part of nearly everyone else. The proponents have been zealous, purposeful, and persistent, a necessary virtue. The opponents may have been as zealous, but among them are persons who might otherwise seem unlikely allies—conservative Southern legislators, liberal Northern labor union officials, and until recently, the Department of Labor.

The ERA was conceived in 1923 at a meeting of the National Woman's Party, whose members were the most radical, the most militant, the most obstreperous workers for the vote for women. They saw, prophetically, that the granting of suffrage to women did not necessarily mean the coming of equality. That same year the amendment was introduced for the first time in Congress. The man performing the service in the House of Representatives was a Republican from Kansas, Daniel Anthony, a nephew of the great feminist Susan B. Anthony. The bill was to be introduced in nearly every subsequent session of Congress, mostly because of the Woman's

Party, and to be supported in the platforms of the major political parties in several campaign years.

In 1950 and in 1953 the Senate passed the amendment. However, on the floor, a venerable Democrat from Arizona, Carl B. Hayden, attached the famous "Hayden rider" to the bill. The rider demanded that the ERA ". . . shall not be construed to impair any rights, benefts or exemptions now or hereafter conferred by law, upon persons of female sex." If women had been either especially favored or especially demeaned in law, by law, they were still to be either especially favored or especially demeaned. In effect, Hayden grafted inequality onto the amendment that was to insure constitutional equality, a neat trick of nullification. More specifically, he guaranteed that any state labor laws protective of women would remain on the books. So doing, he foreshadowed one of the saltiest current arguments about the ERA.

The House of Representatives was more passive. Emanuel D. Cellar, as venerable a Democrat as Hayden, but from New York, the chairman of the House Judiciary Committee, simply refused to hold hearings on any ERA.

Probably neither legislator anticipated the New Feminism. If so, they were not alone. The New Feminism released energies which helped to resuscitate the ERA from the coma to which public opinion had assigned it. In May 1970, the Subcommittee on Constitutional Amendments of the Senate Judiciary Committee, chaired by Birch Bayh, a Democrat from Indiana, held hearings on the ERA. Taking place on May 5, May 6, and May 7, they took down the first formal, legislative testimony on the amendment since 1956. These are the hearings that this book is reprinting.

Bayh's action was a result of a confrontation between his subcommittee and ERA advocates on February 17, 1970. Bayh had been holding hearings on a constitutional amendment giving the vote to eighteen-year-olds. Suddenly, he was interrupted by a group of women, led by Wilma Scott Heide, the chairperson of the Board of Directors of the National Organization for Women, who demanded that he consider the ERA. He did. Those who believe that the passage of time makes polite friends out of political opponents must read the exchange between Ms. Heide and Senator Bayh before she testified in May. Those who believe that the passage of time makes polite friends political opponents must read the opening statements of Senator Hiram Fong, a Republican of Hawaii. The remarks seem to support the ERA. Yet Senator Fong, one year later, was to support Senator Ervin's amendment.

On July 28, 1970, Bayh's subcommittee reported favorably on the ERA. On August 10, Martha Griffiths, a Democratic Representative from Michigan, asked the House to vote to discharge the ERA from its Judiciary Committee. The boldness of the maneuver may have obscured the hard work behind it. The House agreed to detour the Committee. That same day it also approved the amendment. However, the ERA languished back in the Senate, where, on October 14, 1970, the Senate finally declined to support it.[1] It was, obviously, reintroduced again the next year.

The hearings before the Bayh subcommittee are dramatic. They reveal that an authentic source of American theater, at once realistic and ritualistic, active and arcane, often exciting and important, is a Congressional committee room. Among the speakers are persons of stature.

[1]Judith Hole and Ellen Levine, *Rebirth of Feminism* (New York: Quadrangle Books, 1971) offer a useful summary of the history and issues of the ERA.

Take, as only one example, Marguerite Rawalt, a lawyer, a member of President John F. Kennedy's Commission on the Status of Women in 1963, who had kept that Commission from irrevocably opposing the ERA.[2] Or take the officers of the Woman's Party, which had worked so long for the ERA. The testimony, which contains an enormous amount of information about women and their role, is still often witty. Note the women who took the names of their feminist predecessors Angelina Grimké and Emma Goldman. It reveals both human passion and human frailty. Listen to Mortimer Furey, from the Detroit Metropolitan AFL–CIO Council, muttering, "I might call on the indulgence of the committee to say that I cannot help but remember what happened to Andy Warhol who was shot by a feminist," or listen to Margery Leonard, an official of the Woman's Party, slapping out at Communists.

The hearings also show how reformist the ERA is. While it might help to excite radical, or root, change in society, it assumes that change best occurs within a constitutional context. People disagree about the ERA because they disagree on whether distinctions in law may be made because of differences in sex. Is my anatomy really sufficient cause for the state to give me a legal identity separate from that of men? However, the quarrel is one about law in particular, not about the law in general. Ironically, both persons who think of themselves as feminists and persons who shrink from the label rebuke the ERA because they believe law an unreliable instrument of social surgery. Such feminists would say, "Change the Constitution if you want, but just remember that it will never bring Utopia." Such non-feminists would say, "Don't bother to change the law because changing it will never bring the Utopia you seek."

As the hearings provoke a conflict about the efficacy of the law, so do they show how much our sense of the law depends upon our sense of ourselves in a particular historical situation. The men and women who speak about the ERA speak as men and women who live today. Note, if you will, a recurrent theme in the remarks of Senator Marlow Cook, a sympathetic Republican from Kentucky. Why, he wonders, should I bother to put my daughters through college if they are not to have legal and social equality? Yet, he goes on, I am putting my daughters through college. Therefore I should work for their equality and for that of women. His comments are those of a man born after that time when the thought of putting daughters through college was both unthinkable and rarely thought.

Among the specific laws that distinguish between men and women are those governing the draft, jury selection, education, marriage and the family, and labor. The question of protective legislation for working women haunts the hearings. Are protective laws chivalrous or chauvinistic? Do they serve women or inhibit them? Or do they serve men at the expense of women? Most of the testimony from the representatives of organized labor opposes the ERA because it might wipe away protective legislation. However, particularly in the speech of Mrs. Myra K. Wolfgang, the vice president of the Hotel and Restaurant Employees and Bartenders International Union, AFL–CIO, another theme emerges. Mrs. Wolfgang suspects that the women

[2]The Kennedy Commission concluded that the 5th and 14th amendments of the Constitution are good enough guarantees of sexuality equality, giving, as they do, due process and equal protection under law to all citizens. The supporters of ERA argue that one measure, one specific amendment, will help women avoid an endless sequence of court trials and tests of state and local legislation. They also say that the ERA is an important symbolic commitment to sexual equality.

who support the ERA are middle-class women who arrogantly insist upon legislating for lower-class women. Her skepticism symbolizes the class antagonisms that haunt the New Feminism as a political movement and women as a group.

The argument about protective legislation, though serious in itself, often prefaces a profound disagreement about what it means to be a man or a woman. Again and again some opponents of the ERA insist that women are primarily wives and mothers. Even if they work, they have primarily domestic obligations. Without protective legislation, they may lack both the time and the energy to carry through on their two jobs. In brief, the ERA becomes yet another solvent threatening to dissolve the bonds of the traditional family in which men win bread and women breed children. Again and again these opponents of the ERA stress the physical differences between men and women, asserting that biology does indeed destine identity. Perhaps the most famous exegesis of this position emerged, not from the Bayh hearings, but from the floor debate in the House of Representatives three months later. Representative Cellar, in parliamentary defeat, exclaimed:

. . let me say that there is as much difference between a male and a female as between a horse chestnut and a chestnut horse. . . . Any attempt to pass an amendment that promises to wipe out the effects of these differences is about as abortive as trying to fish in a desert—and you cannot do that.

There is no really genuine equality. . . .

Against such beliefs some supporters of ERA pose another moral vision, another ideology of sexuality. Calling for equality of opportunity for everyone, they proclaim that biology need not be synonomous with fate, that the cry of "Vive la difference" between the sexes is an archaic rationale for injustice. After Representative Cellar spoke during the House debate, a short time later, Representative Edith Green, a Democrat from Oregon, got up. She said:

The search for human identity and dignity is not uniquely any one person's. Every man and every woman pursues the search for his and her place in the sun where each may stand with a sense of self-respect and self-worth equal to that of all other human beings. No sex, no nationality, no race of people has a monopoly on this desire for full human fulfillment.

PART 1
TESTIMONY

TUESDAY, MAY 5, 1970

U.S. SENATE,
SUBCOMMITTEE ON CONSTITUTIONAL AMENDMENTS
OF THE COMMITTEE ON THE JUDICIARY,
Washington, D.C.

The subcommittee met, pursuant to notice, at 9:40 a.m., in room 318, Old Senate Office Building, Senator Birch E. Bayh presiding.

Present: Senators Bayh, Fong, and Cook.

Also present: Paul J. Mode, Jr., chief counsel, and Mrs. Dorothy Parker, minority counsel.

Senator BAYH. We will please come to order this morning.

Members of the subcommittee may have some brief statements. I have a few remarks I would like to make as chairman of the subcommittee.

I think it is fair to say that today begins an all-out effort to secure a long overdue objective—equal rights under the law for men and women.

The amendment we are considering provides that "Equality of rights under the law shall not be denied or abridged by the United States or by any State on account of sex." This amendment would outlaw discrimination on account of sex in the same manner and to the same extent that we prohibited discrimination on account of race, religion or national origin in the 14th amendment 100 years ago. This amendment would be a sorely needed step in striking down laws still on the books that deny more than half our population the right of first-class citizenship.

It is hard for many Americans to believe that discrimination against women continues to exist in our country today. Strangely enough, we find that all women do not support the effort that we are undertaking. I hope that this is because of lack of knowledge. But the plain fact is that women have often been left behind in the struggle to make American society a fair and just one. Despite the passage of title VII of the 1964 Civil Rights Act and the Equal Pay Act of 1963, widespread employment discrimination continues throughout the United States. In a recent management survey, for example, 59 percent of the companies admitted that they continue to disqualify women from jobs solely on the basis of sex; 63 percent recruit at men's schools while only 30 percent recruit at women's schools; and 47 percent continue to use separate "male" and "female" classified advertisements despite Equal Employment Opportunity Commission regulations against such placement.

But the range of discrimination against women is not limited to areas of pay and employment. State laws in Illinois and seven other States provide that women attain the age of majority at 21, while men attain majority at 18, despite the fact that science has proven women actually mature earlier than men. Such provisions hamper many mature young women in their efforts to secure employment, sign contracts, lease real property, and conduct other routine activities. Many States impose limitations on jury service. State property laws are a jumble of restrictions, many dating to the 12th century, wholly out of tune with the role of women in modern American society. For example, California and Navada require married women to follow a formal procedure of obtaining court approval before they may engage in independent businesses. Public universities continue to discriminate against women in admissions and in financial assistance. I am hopeful that before these hearings end we will have heard of any other areas in which such discrimination continues to be practiced.

Despite this record of inequality before the law, Congress has repeatedly refused to enact the equal rights amendment, a provision which has been before it since 1923. In every Congress since I have been chairman of this subcommittee, we have reported the equal rights amndment to the judiciary Committee and urged favorable action. In the 88th Congress, in 1964, the Senate Judiciary Committee in turn reported the amendment to the floor, but no further action was taken. In the 89th and 90th Congress, the Judiciary Committee itself failed to act.

But today I believe we have a better chance than ever before to secure passage of the equal rights amendment. We begin this set of hearings with the purpose of incorporating a fundamental change in our Constitution. I realize that there are some, perhaps some of you here who are critical of the very fact that these hearings are being held. But I would like to point out from a practical standpoint there have only been 25 amendments to the Constitution of the United States. Try as we will, we are not going to be successful unless we are able to mount a nationwide effort which recognizes the critical problem which we confront.

It is important, as I see it, for these hearings to stimulate national concern and hopefully to prick the national conscience. If we are successful, as I hope we will be, we can provide the type of grass-roots support which is absolutely indispensable if we are to get two-thirds of the U.S. Senate, two-thirds of the House of Representatives, and perhaps most critically of all, three-fourths of the State legislatures to vote for the equal rights amendment.

I ask that a copy of S.J. Res. 61 be included in the record at this point.

(The material referred to follows:)

[S. J. RES. 61, 91st Cong. First sess.]

JOINT RESOLUTION Proposing an amendment to the Constitution of the United States relative to equal rights for men and women

Resolved by the Senate and House of Representatives of the United States of America in Congress assembled (two-thirds of each House concurring therein), That the following article is proposed as an amendment to the Constitution of the United States, which shall be valid to all intents and purposes as part of the Constitution when ratified by the legislatures of three-fourths of the several States:

"ARTICLE—

"SECTION 1. Equality of rights under the law shall not be denied or abridged by the United States or by any State on account of sex. Congress and the several States shall have power, within their respective jurisdictions, to enforce this article by appropriate legislation.

"SEC. 2. This article shall be inoperative unless it shall have been ratified as an amendment to the Constitution by the legislatures of three-fourths of the several States.

"SEC. 3. This amendment shall take effect one year after the date of ratification."

Senator BAYH. Senator Fong?

Senator FONG. Thank you, Mr. Chairman.

Mr. Chairman, I want to welcome the distinguished Senator from Minnesota and the distinguished witnesses who have come to testify on behalf of S.J. Res. 61 and to thank them for their time, interest, and effort.

I have given considerable thought to the problem of equality for all citizens. Wherever possible, I have activated my firm belief that all people should be considered on their merits and not on extraneous factors such as race, religion or sex.

Of course, the only question we shall be addressing ourselves to at this hearing is the question of equality for women and the elimination of discrimination because of sex. This is a most crucial matter for the entire United States.

In 1968, according to the U.S. Department of Labor, Bureau of Labor Statistics, there were almost 70,000,000 women 16 years of age and over, of whom 28,697,000 were in the labor force.

The Department of Labor, Manpower Administration release entitled "Manpower Report of the President, Including a Report on Manpower Requirements, Resources, Utilization and Training," published January, 1969, shows that in 1968, 81.2 percent of all men ages 16 and over were in the labor force, while 41.6 percent of all women ages 16 and over were in the labor force. Its 1980 projection is that 80.3 percent of men over age 16 will be in the labor force, while 41.9 percent of the women over age 16 will be in the labor force. In the 18 to 64 year range, 49 percent of all women will be in the labor force by 1980.

This rise in women's employment in recent years has been accomplished by an increase in the number and variety of women's occupational opportunities. New fields of employment are being opened up to women—even if they are at present still concentrated in relatively few occupations. But, hopefully, this too will change. Full utilization of all of our human resources, whether manpower or womenpower, is, in my opinion, essential if we are to achieve our maximum national potential.

State laws now affecting employment of men and women are varied in regard to minimum wages, equal pay, fair employment practices, and other subjects.

MINIMUM WAGE LAWS

Minimum wage legislation, first enacted in 1912, was primarily designed for the protection of women and minors. These laws did much to raise the low wages paid women in manufacturing, in trade and in the service industries.

In 1937, the Supreme Court of the United States reversed a 1923 decision and upheld the constitutionality of minimum wage

6

laws. In 1941, long before it became a State, Hawaii became the 30th jurisdiction to enact such legislation.

By now 42 States have minimum wage laws of varying scope and coverage. Of these, 31 States and the District of Columbia extend coverage to men, women, and minors. These States are Alaska, Arkansas, Connecticut, Delaware, Hawaii, Idaho, Indiana, Kentucky, Maine, Maryland, Massachusetts, Michigan, Nebraska, Nevada, New Hampshire, New Jersey, New Mexico, New York, North Carolina, North Dakota, Oklahoma, Oregon, Pennsylvania, Puerto Rico, Rhode Island, South Dakota, Utah, Vermont, Washington, West Virginia and Wyoming.

Thirteen States and Puerto Rico require overtime pay for both men and women. These 13 States are Alaska, Connecticut, Hawaii, Kentucky, Maine, Massachusetts, New Jersey, New York, Oregon, Pennsylvania, Rhode Island, Vermont, and West Virginia.

EQUAL PAY

Equal pay legislation was first given public attention when the National War Labor Board, to get women for employment in war industries during World War I, enforced a policy of "no wage discrimination against women on the grounds of sex." But, unfortunately, it took World War II and a desire to further the war effort for real impetus to be given to this movement.

Thirty-five States now have equal pay laws. These States are Alaska, Arizona, Arkansas, California, Colorado, Connecticut, Florida, Georgia, Hawaii, Idaho, Illinois, Indiana, Kentucky, Maine, Maryland, Massachusetts, Michigan, Minnesota, Missouri, Montana, Nebraska, Nevada, New Hampshire, New Jersey, New York, North Dakota, Ohio, Oklahoma, Oregon, Pennsylvania, Rhode Island, South Dakota, Washington, West Virginia, and Wyoming. Fair employment practices acts accomplish this in five States (Idaho, Nevada, Utah, Vermont, and Wisconsin) and the District of Columbia.

The Federal Equal Pay Act, which I supported, was passed as an amendment to the Fair Labor Standards Act in 1963. This law applies to all employees entitled to the benefits of the minimum wage provisions of the Fair Labor Standards Act, and prohibits employers from discriminating on the basis of sex in the payment of equal wages for equal work.

FAIR EMPLOYMENT PRACTICES ACTS

Prior to the enactment of title VII of the Federal Civil Rights Act of 1964, which I also supported, only the laws of my State of Hawaii and that of Wisconsin prohibited discrimination in employment based on sex.

Now, 22 States and the District of Columbia prohibit discrimination in employment or wages based on sex. These 22 States are Alaska, Arizona, Colorado, Connecticut, Hawaii, Idaho, Maryland, Massachusetts, Michigan, Minnesota, Missouri, Nebraska, Nevada, New Mexico, New York, Oklahoma, Oregon, Pennsylvania, Utah, Vermont, Wisconsin, and Wyoming.

State laws covering maximum hours of work, days of rest, nightwork, industrial homework limitations, limitations on employment before and after childbirth, occupational and weightlifting limitations and similar restrictive legislation have also been enacted. These, unfortunately, all too frequently treat women differently from men. When they do, I submit, in this day and age, such type of legislation constitutes limitations on the equality of and opportunities for women. I can proudly point to the fact that Hawaii is one of the few States which has no different laws for women from those applicable to men in these areas of legislation.

But these laws affecting employment of women are not the only ones we are faced with.

Federal legislation has improved the political status of women. Citizenship rights, voting rights, rights to civil service positions and positions under Federal contracts are the same for women as for men. The Civil Rights Act of 1957 removed the disqualification of women for service on Federal juries in all States.

State legislation followed the Federal lead in these areas. And the U.S. District Court in *White* v. *Cook*, 251 F. Supp. 401, 1966, declared an Alabama law excluding women from State juries unconstitutional as a denial of equal protection to women under the 14th amendment.

At the present time, in 28 States, women serve on juries under the same terms as men, with the same qualifications, disqualifications and exemptions. These 28 States are Alaska, Arizona, California, Colorado, Delaware, Hawaii, Idaho, Illinois, Indiana, Iowa, Kentucky, Maine, Maryland, Michigan, Mississippi, Montana, Nebraska, New Jersey, New Mexico, North Dakota, Ohio, Oregon, Pennsylvania, South Dakota, Vermont, Washington, West Virginia, and Wisconsin.

In the area of martial relations, more differences are found.

As a general rule, the domicile of a married woman is that of her husband. Only five States now permit a married woman to establish a separate domicile for all purposes. Hawaii is one of these five. The others are Alaska, Arkansas, Delaware, and Wisconsin.

Marriage law requirements generally fix lower ages for women than men. When it comes to divorce laws, while the grounds are usually the same for men or women, alimony laws in only 14 States (Alaska, California, Colorado, Hawaii, Illinois, Iowa, North Caroline, North Dakota, Ohio, Oklahoma, Oregon, Utah, Virginia, and West Virginia) permit alimony to the husband, even though seven States (Connecticut, Delaware, Kansas, Mississippi, Nebraska, Pennsylvania, and Wyoming) do provide for holding a wife liable for the support of a husband if the divorce is grounded on his mental illness, and two States (Massachusetts and New Hampshire) allow the husband a portion of the wife's estate in the nature of alimony.

As to the guardianship of a child, most States vest both parents jointly with this right. In case of a divorce, ostensibly the best interests of the child determine custody, but usually it is awarded the mother, with the father primarily liable for support of the minor children.

Unmarried women and unmarried men have the same rights in relation to property management and control, inheritance and enjoyment of their earnings, but when it comes to married women that is not always true, especially as to real property and even a wife's right to contract is limited in at least seven States. These include Georgia, Idaho, and Kentucky which prohibit a woman from becoming a surety; and California, Florida, Nevada, and Pennsylvania which require court sanction for a wife's legal venture into an independent business.

I have outlined some of the differing types of States and Federal law in order to indicate the areas where I believe women can be affected by legislation which affects her differently from the way in which the legislation affects men—when the sole basis of such differentiation is sex.

While I am a cosponsor of Senate Joint Resolution 61, as I was of its precursors, Senate joint resolution 85, 89th Congress, second session (1966) and Senate joint resolution 54, 90th Congress, first session (1967), I am particularly interested in hearing from you whether what is now needed is an amendment to the Constitution or active enforcement and implementation of our present laws or the enactment of such laws, Federal and State, as may be necessary, and then their strict enforcement.

By way of illustration, Executive Order 11375 issued October 13, 1967, strengthened by Executive Order 11478 issued August 8, 1969, explicitly prohibits discrimination on the basis of sex in Federal employment and employment on Federal contracts. When I recently became the senior minority member of this Subcommittee on Constitutional Amendments of the Senate Committee on the Judiciary, it became my privilege to select its minority counsel. I was determined to obtain the services of the best qualified lawyer I could find. I was fortunate in finding a person who is a graduate of Columbia Law School, a member of the bar of the Supreme Court of the United States, and of the bar of the State of New York and of the District of Columbia, among others, who has had a very successful career in the private practice of law in New York and who, for almost 5 years served in a most responsible legal position in the executive branch of the Federal Government. That lawyer has a wide range of experience which serves me well as th snior minority member of this subcommittee and serves this subcommittee well. It happens to be a woman, a gracious lady, I might add. So, Mrs. Dorothy Parker is now serving as minority counsel to this subcommittee—not because she is a woman, but because of her qualifications.

In view of Mrs. Parker's personal interest in this amendment of a fuller record in these meetings, I ask the chairman to allow Mrs. Parker from time to time to participate directly in the questioning of witnesses.

Mr. Chairman, I am most grateful to you for scheduling these hearings so that we may learn what is the best way to tap and to utilize the vast reservoir of strength and ability represented by the women of America and to eliminate the discrimination against women which we all recognize exists.

Thank you, Mr. Chairman.

Senator BAYH. Senator Cook.

Senator COOK. Mr. Chairman, as cosponsor of Senate joint resolution 61, I am pleased to welcome Senator McCarthy and our other distinguished witnesses to this subcommittee. In an era in which emphasis has been properly placed upon equal opportunity for all of our citizens regardless of race, it is only appropriate that we now begin to attempt to remedy the age-old inequities in our society attributable to discrimination on the basis of sex.

I am aware that the history of this legislation, which dates back to 1923, has been characterized by lip service rather than action. I am pleased that the Chairman of our subcommittee has decided that he will not preside over further inaction this year. I pledge to you, Senator McCarthy, and others who support this amendment my energetic efforts to secure Senate passage of this amendment in this session of the 91st Congress.

Senator BAYH. Thank you very much, Senator Cook.

One of the leading knights on a white horse, as far as I am concerned, in this entire area of trying to secure constitutional guarantees of equal treatment of all Americans has been our distinguished colleague from Minnesota. I am pleased he is our first witness this morning.

Senator McCarthy?

STATEMENT OF HON. EUGENE J. McCARTHY, A U.S. SENATOR FROM THE STATE OF MINNESOTA

Senator McCARTHY. Mr. Chairman and members of the committee. I think I might say my white horse has gotten a little gray through the years.

I intend to give a very short statement, and after hearing the members of the commitee, I think I could even shorten what I had intended.

It appears this subcommittee does not need to be persuaded of the necessity or desirability of Senate joint resolution 61, the constitutional amendment with reference to equal rights for men and women.

The presentation has been made by two members, and I am sure essentially the same thing was said in the testimony which the Senator from Kentucky submitted, without reading it, which pretty well makes the case for this particular amendment.

It has been before the Senate on and off, given fair treatment in some cases and shuffled sometimes, since at least 1923.

The chairman, the Senator from Indiana, pointed out nothing happened in the 89th and 90th Congress, even though it had considerable sponsorship in both of those Congresses. We have with us now 78 Senators as sponsors. It seems to me that this indicates the Judiciary Committee can at least take this as a clear indication the Senate is very serious about this amendment.

I commend them for taking it up, especially since the Judiciary Committee has perhaps been the busiest committee, the hardest pressed committee in the entire Senate in the period of the last 2 years.

Not only would we make the Senate honest, but the fact is the three recent Presidents have said they wanted this amendment. This might be the time for us to act to demonstrate that we believe that they wanted the amendment passed through the years at least in their campaigns.

The Senator from Hawaii raised a question about why a constitutional amendment. I am sure he will have that answer in his own mind. The alternative, it seems to me, is to do it in very small steps. This could go on for over 15 or 20 years before you get even close to having more universal standards dealing with reference to the treatment of women in the various areas in which they are now discriminated against.

If we do pass a constitutional amendment it will put general pressure on all the States to conform and make it much easier to proceed to those cases which are very clear, and also permit the State courts to make the kind of proper distinction we know is going to be made, not on the basis of sex, but on the basis of state of life and other conditions that result in differences, not because of sex, but because of the American society.

I can think of no better way to proceed than by way of constitutional amendment.

We have attempted to act by Federal legislation. We can act as far as Federal employment is concerned, but almost immediately we get into jurisdiction disputes with the States in other areas. We can abide and hope the States will proceed, but on the basis of the record, although it has been rather encouraging in recent years, I don't think we can say it has been enough.

Consequently, the way of constitutional amendment, I think, is best.

Finally, I think we ought to acknowledge that as times change the justification for such an amendment has increased. Economic change has taken place in our society as well as change in education and changes in the general structure of society; even psychological changes have taken place. All of these, it seems to me, Mr. Chairman, are justification for the Senate and this committee to recommend passage of Senate joint resolution 61 I hope we can go on from the recommendation of this committee to secure the approval of the Senate by the necessary two-thirds vote and beyond that the two-thirds vote required in the House of Representatives.

Thank you very much.

Senator BAYH. I appreciate very much, Senator, you taking the time, as busy as you are.

I must say if you look at the full committee schedule, as well as our own, we are prepared for an all-out effort, not just the window dressing, which has too often been the type of support this amendment has received in the past.

I am impressed with not only the amount of support, but the necessity of maintaining this kind of support if we are going to be successful with the constitutional amendment. I thus appreciate your opinion relative to the importance of going the constitutional amendment route rather than the statute route.

We have had some moderate success, as you know, with the Equal Employment Opportunity Commission ruling as far as chipping away at some of the discrimination in work practices.

As just one member of this Senate and Chairman of the subcommittee, I want to do the job right and as quickly as possible.

It is your judgment the constitutional amendment route far and away is the best route to pursue?

Senator MCCARTHY. I think it is.

Senator BAYH. I have no further questions, Senator.

Senator Fong?

Senator FONG. Thank you, Senator McCarthy, for making a record showing the constitution amendment route is the type of route to be used.

Thank you for coming and giving us your testimony.

Senator BAYH. Senator Cook?

Senator COOK. Thank you, Senator McCarthy, very much.

Senator MCCARTHY. May I submit the current list of all the Members of the Senate who are sponsoring this amendment and ask it be included?

Senator BAYH. Without objection, so ordered.

(The list follows:)

COSPONSORS OF SENATE JOINT RESOLUTION 61

JOINT RESOLUTION PROPOSING AN AMENDMENT TO THE CONSTITUTION OF THE UNITED STATES RELATIVE TO EQUAL RIGHTS FOR MEN AND WOMEN

By Mr. Allen, Mr. Baker, Mr. Bayh, Mr. Bellmon, Mr. Bible, Mr. Boggs, Mr. Burdick, Mr. Byrd, Mr. Cannon, Mr. Case, Mr. Church, Mr. Cook, Mr Cooper, Mr. Cranston, Mr. Curtis, Mr. Dodd, Mr. Dole, Mr. Dominick, Mr. Eagleton, Mr. Eastland, Mr. Fannin, Mr. Fong, Mr. Fulbright, Mr. Goldwater, Mr. Goodell, Mr. Gravel, Mr. Gurney, Mr. Hansen, Mr. Harris, Mr. Hart, Mr. Hartke, Mr. Hatfield, Mr. Hollings, Mr. Hruska, Mr. Hughes, Mr. Inouye, Mr. Jordan, Mr. Magnuson, Mr. Mathias, Mr. McClellan, Mr. McGee, Mr. McGovern, Mr. McIntyre, Mr. Mondale, Mr. Montoya, Mr. Moss, Mr. Mundt, Mr. Murphy, Mr. Muskie, Mr. Nelson, Mr. Packwood, Mr. Pastore, Mr. Pearson, Mr. Percy, Mr. Prouty, Mr. Proxmire, Mr. Randolph, Mr. Ribicoff, Mr. Saxbe, Mr. Schweiker, Mr. Scott, Mrs. Smith, Mr. Sparkman, Mr. Spong, Mr. Stennis, Mr. Stevens, Mr. Talmadge, Mr. Thurmand, Mr. Tower, Mr. Tydings, Mr. Williams of Delaware, Mr. Williams of New Jersey, Mr. Yarborough, Mr. Young of North Dakota, and Mr. Young of Ohio.

Senator BAYH. We have just received word our next witness, Charles Goodell, is aboard an airplane flying over this city, but he is with us in spirit and, hopefully, he will be with us in person in the very near future.

We placed a call for Congresswoman Griffiths. Has she arrived yet? I don't think she is here yet.

Congresswoman Dwyer?

Is Mrs. Myra Ruth Harmon here?

Fine. We will accept your testimony now, please.

Mrs. Harmon, I am proud to say, is a native of the great State of Indiana, and president of the National Federation of Business and Professional Women's Clubs. She is accompanied by Mrs. Lucille Shriver, federation director, and Dr. Phyllis O'Callaghan, legislation director of the National Federation of Business and Professional Women's Clubs.

I am glad to have you here, Mrs. Harmon and ladies.

STATEMENT OF MRS. MYRA RUTH HARMON, PRESIDENT, THE NATIONAL FEDERATION OF BUSINESS AND PROFESSIONAL WOMEN'S CLUBS, INC.; ACCOMPANIED BY MRS. LUCILLE SHRIVER, FEDERATION DIRECTOR AND DR. PHYLLIS O'CALLAGHAN, LEGISLATION DIRECTOR

Mrs. HARMON. Thank you, Mr. Chairman.

I am Myra Ruth Harmon, president of the National Federation of Business and Professional Women's Clubs. It is a pleasure for me to be here today representing 180,000 members throughout the United States, Puerto Rico, the Virgin Islands, and the District of Columbia.

Our organization has supported the equal rights amendment for more than 30 years and we welcome this opportunity to testify before this committee.

Fifty years ago the Senate had approved and passed on to the States a constitutional amendment enabling women to vote. Now, today, we request the Senate to endorse another constitutional amendment, this one to assure women equal legal rights. We urge passage of the equal rights amendment which essentially provides that "equality of rights under the law shall not be denied or abridged by the United States or by any State on account of sex."

The National Federational of Business and Professsional Women's Clubs, Inc. has no illusion that the equal rights amendment will irrevocably remove the inequities practiced against women; nor that the amendment will elevate women to their proper political and economic role in a democratic society. Neither did passage of the suffrage amendment totally renovate American society, as many reformers had hoped. We do believe, however, that this is a Nation of laws, not men, and that although we cannot change a person's prejudice or ill will, we can and should put this Nation on record in support of woman's right to full economic, legal and social responsibility; to full citizenship. In supporting the equal rights amendment we are not asking for any benefits, assistance or prerogatives. We are asking for the right to be responsible; for the right to be taken out of the minor category.

The equal rights amendment would effectively prevent passage of any new State or Federal laws discriminating between men and women on the basis of sex alone. Significantly the amendment would invalidate current State laws which restrict the contractual and property rights of married women, and remove those ambiguities, uncertainties, and prohibitions regarding a married woman's right to use her own name or choose her domicile (although court tests would probably be required).

My detailed statement distributed to this committee outlines and documents the possible effects of the equal rights amendment on many aspects of our everyday life. In the interest of time I will delete these from my oral testimony.

I would like to concentrate on another matter; namely, the possible effect of the equal rights amendment on State labor laws for women.

A summary of State labor laws for women was published March 1969, by the U.S. Department of Labor. These laws establish maximum daily or weekly working hours, require certain lunch and rest periods and seating facilities, establish weight-lifting limitations, restrict the kinds and places of employment.

Mr. Chairman, we believe that the term "protective" no longer applies to this kind of legislation. Certainly at one time special labor regulations for women were protective because these were the only labor laws on the books; there were no Federal or State laws protcting a worker as to the hours of employment, wages due, or health and safety working conditions. Passage of the equal rights amendment would invalidate these special labor regulations for women. We think today that is important and I will explain why.

In the early 20th century State labor laws for women were enacted not essentially for the protection of women, but for women as bearers of the human race—at a time when there were almost no factory regulations and nothing in the way of Federal wage and hours legislation. The movement for special labor legislation for women was encouraged by the famous *Muller* case in which the Supreme Court upheld Oregon's 1 hour day limitation of working hours for females only, after 3 years before invalidating a New York statute limiting working hours of bakery employees of both sexes to 10 hours a day. Since that time States and the Federal Government have passed comprehensive laws protecting workers.

Today the sweatshop conditions, the dawn to dusk hours, the subsistance level pay are to a large degree sins of the past. Judicious legislation and courageous labor organization have helped to amend that situation. Thus, women do not need protection against oppressive conditions which have ceased to exist. They need the same things men workers need: broad coverage by Federal wage and hour legislation; adequate guarantees against occupational hazards, et cetera.

Consequently today State labor laws for women only impose additional considerations for the employer who hires women; they give him an adequate reason for paying women less for the same work, or refusing to hire a woman who must have a 30 minute lunch hour, must have special seating arrangements, or must depart from the factory without a minute of illegal (for her) overtime regardless of her own financial needs and/or choice.

Increasingly this view of State legislation for women is being adopted. On March 5, 1970, Illinois Bell Telephone filed a suit against the Illinois director of labor regarding the Illinois Maximum Hours Act. A similar suit was filed at the same time by Caterpillar Tractor Co., also a large employer of women. Illinois Bell took that opportunity to explain that such hours legislation for women is discriminatory and means "that if overtime work becomes necessary—at premium pay—it is available to men but not to women, even on identical jobs. Neither can women be promoted or assigned to jobs which regularly require extended hours of work." On March 25, 1970, the Corporation Counsel, District of Columbia described this Federal City's "8 Hour Law for Females" as restrictive and possibly discriminatory in similar terms.

Thus we contend that today, special so-called protective legislation for women has become restrictive, burdensome, and discriminatory.

We support passage of the equal rights amendment to eliminate such laws for women only. These laws will prohibit women from being bartenders but allow them to be barmaids, to serve the drinks they cannot mix, and at a lower pay. In some States women cannot work overtime in factories but laundry, hotel and restaurant workers, agricultural and domestic laborers are often exempt from the hours limitation. At the other end of the scale 27 States (out of 39 with maximum hours laws) exempt some or all women in administrative, executive and professional positions from hours limitation. We emphasize the restrictions imposed on women by this legislation because some continue to oppose the equal rights amendment in order to continue such legislation.

Special labor legislation for women restricts as fully as it was originally intended to protect. These laws operate to prevent millions of women from competing on equal terms with men; they prevent women from providing for themselves and their dependents with the proper support and care. Instead of protecting they impede, they deny equal employment opportunity to those women who need it the most!

The 1969 Handbook on Women Workers reveals that today there are some 29,000,000 women in the labor force—37 percent of the total labor force and that "financial reasons are usually the strongest motivation for work for most women." Widowed, single, and divorced women must support themselves and often dependents. Almost three out of five women workers are married and 38 percent of all women in the labor force are mothers. In 1967, 11 percent of all families were headed by a woman. In 1966, 14 percent of our 48.9 million families had incomes of less than $3,000, sometimes defined as poverty level and 46 percent received less than $7,000, considered a level of "modest adequacy." Thus women work for the same reasons as men, to provide for their families—their educational, housing, health care needs—for themselves and other dependents.

Through special labor legislation for women, employers have been able to deny these women jobs, promotions, seniority benefits, wage increases and overtime; to prevent these women from bing hired, promoted, transferred. Often employers prefer to give overtime to men who are already at the maximum deductible earnings for social security, thus the employer does not contribute more, whereas with women he would have to do so. Special hours legislation protects his interest, not that of the women employees. This means these women are also denied maximum pensions. They lose the chance to pay into social security the payments necessary for maximum pensions while their company pension, based on their earnings, is affected also. These same women may be forced to hold down two jobs instead of one since hours legislation affects employer, not employee.

We must ask, then, Mr. Chairman, whom does such legislation protect? The men who get the jobs unavailable to women due to hours of work or weight lifting requirements or special conditions of employment? If the protections imposed by this labor legislation are so good, we see no reason why they should not cover all workers, not only women. In fact, were the equal rights amendment adopted such legislation would be either nullified or extended to include men. Those laws which actually confer a benefit would be extended to both; those which restrict, voided by the equal rights amendment.

We submit that such legislation creates distinctions between men and women, which in light of prevailing industrial conditions and the contemporary state of medical knowledge, are arbitrary, anachronistic and unreasonable.

The obvious fact that women are different from men does not justify legal restrictions imposed on women. What must be demonstrated is that a particular weakness in women requires the particular kind of restraint which is being imposed. With labor laws for women it should be asked whether the restriction is reasonable, given first, the physical capacity of women, and second, the industrial conditions which prevail in the particular industry to which the law is being applied and in the United States in general. We do not think the restrictions reasonable nor that a need can be demonstrated. We refer you to a study published by the National Safety Council in 1954 which made important observations concerning the ability of women to perform arduous labor.

We would like to point out, Mr. Chairman, that during wartime women loaded and unloaded heavy materials, labored in munition plants, worked at unskilled manual labor. "Rosie the Riveter" was not "protected" from heavy, grueling labor, nor does our population in terms of those women who did this work or their offspring, seem to have been adversely affected by that work.

A recent court decision is pertinent to our statement. In the *Bowe* case, Thelma Bowe and others sued the Jeffersonville, Ind., plant of Colgate-Palmolive on the grounds that they were being excluded from better paying jobs on the excuse that these jobs required the lifting of 35 pounds or more and that women had to be "protected" from such work. The women lost their first round in the Federal District Court for the Southern District of Indiana, but that decision was reversed in their favor September 26, 1969, by the U.S. Court of Appeals for the Seventh District. The court at that time concluded:

If anything is certain in this controversial area, it is that there is no general agreement as to what is a maximum permissible weight which can be safely lifted by women in the course of their employment.

Senator BAYH. Would you yield just a moment at this time?

Is there any scientific evidence as to what is the maximum safe limit to be lifted by men?

Mrs. HARMON. If there is I haven't seen it.

Senator BAYH. This limit is not defined and set up, is it?

Mrs. HARMON. It is not. As the U.S. Court of Appeals also said:

The States which have limits vary considerably. Most of the State limits were enacted many years ago and most, if not all, would be considered clearly unreasonable in light of the average physical development, strength, and stamina of most modern American women who participate in the industrial work force.

Hours and other restrictions for women alone are not only unreasonable but also fundamentally inconsistent with Title VII of the Civil Rights Act of 1964. This title prohibits employment discrimination on account of race, color, religion, nationality origin, or sex. An exception is made whenever sex is a *bona fide* occupational qualification necessary to the normal operation of a particular business or enterprise.

There is in our view, and that of many others, including the Equal Employment Opportunity Commission which is charged with implementing title VII, an irreconcilable conflict between the sex discrimination provisions of title VII and State labor regulations for women. This past August, 1969, the EEOC, after earlier assuming a possible valid purpose for these laws, reversed itself and concluded that these laws which:

Prohibit or limit the employment of females as to certain occupations, night work, maximum weekly hours of work, weight-lifting regulations tend to discriminate rather than protect.

The Commission explained that:

Such State laws and regulations, although originally promulgated for the purpose of protecting females, have ceased to be relevant to our technology or to the expanding value of the female worker in our economy. The Commission has found that such laws and regulations do not take into account the capacities, preferences, and abilities of individual females and tend to discriminate rather than protect. Accordingly, the Commission has concluded that such laws and regulations conflict with Title VII of the Civil Rights Act of 1964 and will not be considered a defense to an otherwise established unlawful employment practice or as a basis for the application of the bona fide occupational qualification exception.

Increasingly women are testing the validity of these laws against the strictures against employment discrimination by sex enunciated in the Civil Rights Act of 1964. The State attorneys general in six States (South Dakoda, North Dakota, Ohio, Pennsylvania, Michigan, Oklahoma) have said they will not enforce hours laws for women in view of that conflict. In the *Rosenfeld* case and the *Richards* case two Federal district courts have rendered decisions against State protective laws (Oregon and California). The hours laws and weight-lifting regulations were deemed superseded by Title VII of the Civil Rights Act of 1964.

When the District of Columbia's chief legal officer ruled this March that the District of Columbia "8 Hour Law for Females" conflicts with the sex discrimination provisions of the Civil Rights Act of 1964, he explained his position in detail:

It is apparent therefore, that Title VII of the Civil Rights Act and the "Female 8 Hour Law" are in conflict—the former among other things, requires that there be no discrimination in employment based on sex; the latter operates to deny to females employment opportunities available to males, with respect to working more than 8 hours a day, 6 days a week, or 48 hours a week.

He concluded with the opinion that to the degree that the 8-hour law results in adverse discrimination by denying to women employment opportunities available to males, it, is superseded by title VII. Thus insofar as the hours law operates in any manner to prevent any adult women from taking advantage of any employment opportunity, that hours law is invalid. Thus for all practical purposes the Minimum Wage and Industrial Safety Board, which enforces this legislation, has determined that the hours law for women is superseded by title VII.

We believe if any of these cases reaches the Supreme Court that body will determine that all such special labor legislation just for women irreconcilably conflicts with title VII and thus is void. For the sake of working women, we profoundly hope this will be forthcoming soon. We need passage of the equal rights amendment however, to speed the process, more than that, to help insure the end result: namely, nullification of special labor legislation for women alone; assurance that labor legislation will affect workers regardless of sex.

I would like to make one last comment, Mr. Chairman. There are some who express the fear that such legislation as the equal rights amendment would disturb the traditional male-female roles, creating grave social, psychological problems for men and women thereby. My answer to this I draw from the last pages of Professor Leo Kanowitz' excellent book, "Women and The Law: The Unfinished Revolution," in which he says, most aptly and to the point:

When women will have achieved true and complete legal and social equality with men, the problem of men or women knowing who or what they are is likely to disappear. For at that time, both men and women will be able to recognize themselves for what they have always been—people. The psychological well-being of our total population may therefore be the most important single reason for getting on with the job of erasing all remaining pockets of legal and social inequality between the sexes.

We respectfully submit, Mr. Chairman, that passage of this equal rights amendment will significantly help to begin the job of erasing all these pockets of legal and social inequality between the sexes. We therefore urge its passage.

Thank you.

Senator BAYH. Thank you very much, Mrs. Harmon.

I wonder if it would be an imposition if we ask you ladies to step aside long enough to let us accommodate two very distinguished Members of the Congress who have arrived and have a busy schedule. There will be some questions we want to ask.

We have an additional problem since the chairman of the Judiciary Committee has called a full committee meeting which is supposed to start at this time. It is my inclination, as chairman, to go ahead with your testimony until we reach the stage of a vote, but some of the committee members may have some business in the full committee.

All of you have waited so long to speak. I think this necessary delay is most unfortunate. We are going to hear everyone's testimony and persevere. We ask you to bear with us because of this inconvenience that has arisen after these hearings have been scheduled, as you know.

Mrs. HARMON. We will be available whenever you want us.

Senator BAYH. We would like now to hear from Congresswoman Martha Griffiths from Michigan, who has been a long-time fighter in the Congress for women's rights as well as full equality for all Americans.

I think her tenure of service in the Congress, not only in this area, but others, is one of merit. In respect of the reluctance of women to brag about tenure of service generally, I will not mention how long she has served in this capacity.

STATEMENT OF HON. MARTHA W. GRIFFITHS, A REPRESENTATIVE IN CONGRESS FROM THE 17TH DISTRICT OF THE STATE OF MICHIGAN

Mrs. GRIFFITHS. Thank you, Mr. Chairman. You are very kind.

It is certainly possible for the courts of this country to interpret the Constitution to make an equal rights amendment. The Supreme Court or any Federal circuit court or any district court must know by now that this is never going to happen. Therefore, as an introducer of the equal rights amendment, I congratulate this committee upon these hearings and urge the passage of the amendment forthwith without so much as adding a comma, for all of those supporters on the status quo, all of those admirers of the rule of stare decisis, those people who believe that the courts have created havoc, those admirers of yesterday, let them look to any decision in any Federal Court that deals with women and they will find almost without exception that as women are treated today by those courts they were treated yesterday and yesterday and yesterday, throughout the life of this Nation.

In a man's view of the world, man worked for many, as I see it. They have mothers, wives, widows, and children. It is a man's duty to love and honor his mother, to support his wife and children, and to provide for his widow and orphans. In this rather simple view of today's world a women is a mother, a wife, or a widow. Laws made and interpreted in this country almost exclusively by man for 180 years have welded the views into the statutory and case law of the country.

Thus, no woman litigant has ever stood up before the Supreme Court and successfully argued that she is entitled to the equal protection of the 14th amendment.

In every instance that I know where a State has enacted so-called protective laws, the courts of this country, including the Supreme Court, has determined that it was well within their powers. As late as 22 years ago in *Gossin* v. *Clarey*, the majority of the Supreme Court in a decision written by Justice Frankfurter, a decision I might say that comes close to being obscene, denied the equal protection clause to possible women bartenders in Michigan.

In November 1961, Justice Harlan was able to determine that a Florida statute which granted women an absolute exception from jury duty, based solely on their sex, but included no similar exception for men, was absolutely within the powers of the State of Florida. He also was unable to distinguish this from cases where Negroes or Mexican-Americans were excluded from juries. He was so engrossed in the rights of women to remain at home that he scarcely bothered to mention the rights of the female defendant, convicted of a capital crime, if indeed he believed she had any, or for that matter even a soul.

Now, what happens when the Congress attempts to equalize rights for women? The 1964 Civil Rights Act gives you a good example of the Federal court system at work. This law, as it relates to women, was first tried, I believe, in *Cooper* v. *Delta Airlines* where Delta Airlines had fired a stewardess for marrying. In an incredible decision Judge Comisky determined that, "Sex just sort of found its way into the Civil Rights Act.

Senator BAYH. If the Congresswoman will yield, the good judge wasn't on the floor of the U.S. Senate when this matter was debated.

Mrs. GRIFFITHS. Nor the House.

Having determined that amendment did not count, he ruled against the stewardess, although Delta admitted that the only question in the case was whether being single was a bona fide occupational exception.

In the case of *Ida Phillips* v. *Martin Marietta Corporation*, the Fifth Circuit Court of Appeals, with Judge Carswell seated, affirmed the decision of the lower court which held that an employer who was willing to hire a man with pre-school age children for a certain position, but would not hire women with pre-school age children for the position did not violate the Civil Rights Act.

Having determined that Martin Marietta hired other women, the court then determined that Martin Marietta had added a qualification other than sex for denying the woman the job.

Senator BAYH. If the Congresswoman will yield, having some familiarity with that particular case through other matters before this committee, I should like to interject at this time that Martin Mariatta did not require men who had children to meet the same tests that women who had children were required to meet.

Mrs. GRIFFITHS. And may I say I hope the three gentlemen sitting here remain forever in the Senate and look over every judge as carefully as you did Carswell.

Senator COOK. Madam Congresswoman, I must say in all fairness that Judge Carswell did not hear the original *Marietta* case. The *Marietta* case was denied by a majority of the judges on the Fifth Circuit.

Mrs. GRIFFITHS. He was on the appeals court, though.

This case is now on appeal to the Supreme Court, and I am happy to say the Attorney General has entered on the side of Mrs. Phillips.

Wouldn't you think that the Fifth Circuit would have considered the results of their action? Couldn't they just once have thought in terms of modern America? What they really were saying was that the children of women can starve or the mother can work for a dollar an hour where no one bothers to ask how many children you have.

Senator BAYH. If the Congresswoman will yield just one more time.

I hate to keep interrupting, but I believe the Supreme Court has granted certiorari in this case, so perhaps we are on the verge of a major breakthrough in terms of protection coming through the courts.

Mrs. GRIFFITHS. The Equal Pay Act has been interpreted recently by the courts in two or three instances for the benefit of women, but there are literally millions of instances in this country where there is unequal pay for the same work. Unions uttering bias platitudes on brotherhood are still willing to set up distinctions without differences in work and negotiate different pay for men and women. It has been suggested that the equal rights of men that would, if enacted, wipe out dower rights. Dower rights were valuable in the Middle Ages for the entailed lands. Any law school freshman can show a husband today how to beat dower rights.

The rights of dowery in today's world are the rights to a job, to a promotion, to pension, to social security, to all of the fringe benefits of any job, and in almost every case rights are either flatly denied to women or are different for women than for men. But, if I died while I sit here my husband has no survivor rights in my pension, but if you die while you listen we will pick up your widow in the morning.

The discrimination against women apply not only to them, but to their husbands and their children. It is in fact a discrimination against families. Law written and enforced by men only have supported the man and his current wife or his widow. They do not really protect the woman in the home unless in some way she currently is connected with a male wage earner.

If the equal rights amendment becomes a law, and I urge its passage, there will be the usual snickering, the usual obscenities, and I would assume a good many court cases.

All this amendment asks could easily be done without the amendment if the Supreme Court were willing to do it, but they are not. The Constitution, written in the time of sailing ships and horse-drawn carriages, has been quite adequate to cover the problems without amendment or mishap of automobiles, submarines, jet takeoffs and trips on the moon. Yet it took a constitutional amendment to change a woman, who was admittedly a citizen, into a voter.

The amendment, if passed, would be like a beacon light which should awaken those nine sleeping Rip Van Winkles to the fact that 20th century is passing into history. It is a different world and they should speak for justice, not prejudice.

I want my education, my effort to buy in the marketplace exactly the same thing your's does. Like Rosa Parks, who was tired of standing up in the back of the bus, I am tired of paying into a pension fund to support your widows, gentlemen, but not my husband. I am tired of forever working wife in America who is paid into a social security fund for an unequal right. I seek justice, not in some distant tomorrow, but by some study commission, but now while I live, and I think the equal rights amendment will help towards that way. Thank you.

Senator BAYH. Thank you very much.

Mrs. GRIFFITHS. If you have some questions I will be glad to answer them.

Senator BAYH. I know how busy you are.

Personally I have no questions. I think you have covered the issues very well.

I think I should say, inasmuch as my better half is presently in the room, she is as anxious to protect your, hopefully never, widower, as she is to be protected herself, and I share this concern.

Mrs. GRIFFITHS. I am sure that we would really change quite a few of these laws if some morning all of you would send your wives out.

Senator BAYH. I think the tremendous service that you and the other ladies have provided in the Congress is indicative of the real contribution that women are making to this country. Given the example some of you ladies have set in the Congress, I have never yet been able to resolve in my own mind why the people of this country have not to a greater extent elected to the Congress the ladies of this land, especially when compared with the number of women that serve their constituencies in other countries. I must conclude that valuable service is not an exclusively masculine domain, but rather belongs equally to both male and female citizens.

Senator Fong.

Senator FONG. Thank you, Congresswoman Griffiths. You have made a very challenging point by saying your husband would not benefit but our wives will benefit.

Mrs. GRIFFITHS. We are paid exactly the same money, and I am paying exactly the same money to the pension fund.

I might say that I pay more for medical insurance than my colleagues pay to protect themselves, their wives and two children. I pay more to protect myself and my husband than they pay, and I have never received a Mother's Day Card from any child.

Senator BAYH. Thank you.

Senator FONG. I have no further questions. Thank you.

Senator BAYH. Senator Cook.

Senator COOK. Congresswoman, there are a number of questions I would like to ask. One question in particular is in regard to women's suffrage. I believe that had this been handled statutorily we would not have needed a constitutional amendment. I wonder if it would be agreeable to you if I pose some of these questions to you in writing so that they can be included in the record.

Mrs. GRIFFITHS. Thank you.

Senator BAYH. Thank you very much, Mrs. Griffiths.

Our next witness is Representative Florence Dwyer, from New Jersey, another pioneer in this field of women's rights.

STATEMENT OF HON. FLORENCE P. DWYER, A REPRESENTATIVE IN CONGRESS FROM THE 12TH DISTRICT OF THE STATE OF NEW JERSEY

Mrs. DWYER. Mr. Chairman and members of the committee, history shows that it took approximately 50 years to secure the adoption of the 19th amendment to the Constitution of the United States guaranteeing to women the right to vote.

History also shows that the equal rights amendment to the Constitution has been pending before Congress for the past 47 years.

I conclude, therefore, that these hearings—for which I want to express my deep appreciation—are both timely and long overdue.

This is not meant to suggest that hearings have not been held before on the equal rights amendment. They have—twice. Nor do I mean to suggest that we still have 3 more years to meet the 50-year deadline for action. We don't.

Never before have women's demands for equal rights and responsibilities been so strong or so widely broadcast. Never before has the fundamental justice of these demands been so manifestly apparent and so generally acknowledged. And the equal rights amendment is an essential objective of these demands.

Gentlemen, now is the time for action.

The immediate nature of the need for action has been well summed up by Miss Virginia Allan, chairman of the Presidential Task Force on Women's Rights and Responsibilities. In her letter to President Nixon last December transmitting the task force report, Miss Allan warned of the—and I think this is a very important quote—she talked about accelerating militancy of the kind of deadening apathy that stills progress and inhibits creativity, unless the leadership necessary to stimulate action is forthcoming.

Since I believe this to be true, it is a fair question to ask why we've waited so long. The same question could be asked about the 50 years it took to adopt the 19th amendment. And I suggest the answer is the same to both questions: fear and uncertainty about the consequences of treating women as responsible citizens coupled with an archaic attitude about the role of women in our society.

Just as it was true, however, of the 19th amendment, so it is true of the equal rights amendment: women want only what is their due. They want to be treated as whole citizens. They want to be recognized as having a full stake in the life of our Nation. Consequently, they also want the means necessary to fulfill this role: the right to earn a living and obtain an education, to make a contribution equal to their talent, to receive the job and promotional opportunities commensurate with their talent, to provide an equal measure of security for themselves and their families, and not only to vote but to participate fully and equitably in the public and political life of their community and country.

To a surprising extent, women do not today enjoy access to these rights and to the related legal protections on which the rights depend. I will not take the committee's time to catalog exhaustively the legal and extra-legal disabilities which women still face today. They range from laws prohibiting women from working in certain occupations and excluding women from certain colleges and universities and scholarship programs, to laws which restrict the rights of married women and which carry heavier criminal penalties for women than for men. The documentation is extensive, and one of the most recent studies is also one of the best. I refer to the memorandum report on the equal rights amendment by the Citizens' Advisory Council on the Status of Women published in March of this year, a report that the committee may want to incorporate as a part of this hearing record.

Most assuredly, Mr. Chairman, adoption of the equal rights amendment will not revolutionize our society. It will not even, by itself, solve the whole problem—no more than did the 19th amendment. What it will do—and this is of fundamental importance—is to remove the ambiguities and repeal the remaining legal discrimination which, together, have placed so many women's rights in a position akin to that of a ping-pong ball being bounced between the courts and the Congress. Legislative remedies could correct this condition, it is true, just as court interpretations of the Fifth and 14th amendments could be extended to prohibit all legal distinctions based on sex. But nothing in this equal rights amendment would preclude any of this from occurring and certainly there is no more valid a way to protect fundamental rights than by an appropriate appeal to the Constitution itself.

With an issue of this kind, so colored by misunderstanding and misinformation, it may be more important to see what adoption of the amendment will not do, rather than what it will do. No more than was true of the 19th amendment, adoption of the equal rights amendment will not destroy the difference between the sexes. It will not require an equal number of women members of the House and Senate. It will not separate women from their time-honored roles as wives and mothers and homemakers.

On a more serious level, other objections to the amendment seem equally unfounded. I do not believe the courts will be flooded by litigation arising from this amendment, but if it happens it will only be because the worst fears of women are borne out and there is massive resistance to compliance. Nor will it impose new burdens or deny new benefits to any group, but rather it will assure that all are protected in the same way and all are held to the same responsibilities. In every respect, the rule of reason and appropriateness and common sense will apply as they do today when, for instance, some men are drafted and some are exempted for a variety of appropriate reasons.

In other words, Mr. Chairman, adoption of the amendment can only add to the Nation's resources since it will help to remove inhibitions which have denied to the country the talents and interests and commitment of millions of citizens who happen to be female.

Not all at once and not automatically—let me add—since women, like other minorities whom they resemble at least in spirit, will require time and experience and confidence in order to utilize fully the new opportunities which adoption of the amendment will open to them. But it will be a new beginning and the country can only profit from it.

I say this in full awareness that a great many women do not now care very much, one way or the other, about the equal rights amendment or about the wider struggle to obtain equal opportunity for women, nor would they use the opportunities once they became available. But this has been historically true of all peoples denied equality, just as it is true that all men do not equally concern themselves with their own rights and responsibilities.

The important thing, I suggest, is that no American—regardless of sex, race, religion, or nationality—should be arbitrarily denied rights and opportunities which are essential components of his humanity and citizenship whether or not anyone else values them or cares to use them. They belong to the person, as a person.

I also acknowledge, Mr. Chairman, that many people—women as well as men—would deny that women are deprived or discriminated against. The mere fact, however, that they do not feel or see in their own lives and experience a pattern of discrimination which has been thoroughly documented over and over again should not blind or deafen us to the claims and rights of those who have, in fact, experienced discrimination.

I am reminded, in this respect, of a story told about the late Senator from New York, Robert Wagner. A leader in the fight for progressive social legislation in the thirties, Senator Wagner was challenged one day by a friend who pointed out that Wagner was living proof that the country didn't need such legislation since he, Wagner, had risen from his position as a poor immigrant boy on the streets of New York to one of the most prominent and powerful places in America.

"If you can do it," the friend said, "so can others."

Senator Wagner replied instantly.

"Make no mistake about it," he said, "I was lucky."

We shouldn't, Mr. Chairman, have to depend on luck when it comes to the fundamental rights and responsibilities of American citizenship.

May I say in closing this amendment has been endorsed by the late Presidents Eisenhower, Kennedy, and today by Johnson and Nixon as well.

I plead with you to do everything in your power to convince the Senators that this is just legislation.

Thank you very much.

Senator BAYH. Thank you Mrs. Dwyer, for a very telling account of the importance of our mission. I know that the measure will be in good hands when, not if, we get it over to the House.

Mrs. DWYER. Thank you very much for your optimism.

Senator BAYH. If I hadn't recognized her when she walked in the door, the applause we have heard speaks well for the fact that another Member of Congress, Mrs. Chisholm, who is effectively battling not just for women's rights, but for all rights for all Americans, is with us today at these hearings. We feel privileged that you are here, Congresswoman Chisholm.

I might bring you up to date as to the two little problems we face. One is the responsibility of the subcommittee chairman to see to the subcommittee and the other is to try to recognize the conflicting responsibility to the full Judiciary Committee, where we are now prepared to vote out a Supreme Court Justice of the U.S. Supreme Court. Inasmuch as I have had great interest in this area over the past 2 months I may be compelled to leave rather hastily. I hope we can conclude with your testimony. I know how busy you are.

Please proceed.

STATEMENT OF HON. SHIRLEY CHISHOLM, A REPRESENTATIVE IN CONGRESS FROM THE 12TH DISTRICT OF THE STATE OF NEW YORK

Mrs. CHISHOLM. Thank you very much.

Mr. Chairman, I had almost decided to forego the opportunity to testify in behalf of Senate Joint Resolution No. 61. There is futility and frustration in testifying for an amendment that has been proposed some 20 times in the last 50 years, and that has passed in the Senate at least twice, only to have my esteemed colleagues on the other side of the Capitol rebut it.

The frustration, the futility is hardly akin to that encountered by Black Americans over the centuries as they watched amendments and civil rights bills swept under the committee's table time after time, as they watched the deliberate and often successful efforts to water down those measures that reach the floor, watch the deliberate circumvention of those that became law.

The Panthers, the NAACP, and other Black organizations have the same frustrations that have created the National Organization of Women, the Women's Liberation Movement, and other women's organizations. The feeling of futility that causes the Republic of New Africa to state that they want five States which all Black Americans may voluntarily rule themselves, thus separating from the Nation is no different than that which causes a Grace Atkinson to refuse to appear with a man except as a matter of class confrontation and to say—"a woman saying men are the enemy with a boyfriend sitting next to her is both humiliating and tragic."

Mr. Chairman, colored minority group Americans are not the only second class citizens in this country. The largest single group of second class citizens is the majority of Americans, American women.

Senator BAYH. If the lady would yield just a moment. I appreciate the fact that you made that observation. I was about to interject it.

Our history has been replete, unfortunately it is nothing to be proud of, with occasions in which we have discriminated against minority groups of one kind or another. This is the first example I know of where we have discriminated against the majority, and I think to the extent that the majority will get up on its—well, rise to the occasion, we can get this inequity corrected.

Mrs. CHISHOLM. According to the 1960 census there were 3½ million more females than males. However, when one examines their representation in the various walks of life we find that they are not adequately represented. More than half of the population of the United States is female, but women occupy only 2 percent of the managerial positions. They have not even reached the level of tokenism yet. No women sit on the AFL–CIO Council or the Supreme Court. There have been only two women who have held Cabinet rank and at present there are none. Only two women now hold ambassadorial rank in the diplomatic corps. In Congress we are down to Senator and 10 Representatives.

The issue before us today, while it seems not to call for the immediate attention that President Nixon's new war on Cambodia calls for, does in fact call for immediate redress of a situation that has hampered this country for 194 years too long. While the Consitution mentioned Black Americans only in the negative term of three-fourths of a man, at least it did refer to them. It does not refer to the inherent rights of women at all.

People have often asked me why I feel that American Blacks and American women have received such treatment. I have always had to respond that I believe it is because American institutions were created by white males and that the freedom, equality, and justice that they mentioned and fought for was intended, albeit consciously, for them and them alone.

This is the reason that I believe that an amendment such as the one presently under consideration has not been passed by the male-dominated Congress in the past. It is also the reason that I feel so terribly futile and frustrated in appearing here today. So may I say that more and more women, because of the futility and frustration, are beginning to realize that Frederick Douglas' words "power concedes nothing without a struggle," are as apropos for women as they are for black Americans today.

May I also remind you, gentlemen, you are the power, and as such you are then the focal point of the struggle. It is not the intention of American women to become a nation of Amazons. We will not longer, however, be denied our rights as human beings equal in all respects to males.

Let me try to refute two of the commonest arguments that are offered against the amendment. One is that women are already protected under the law and do not need legislation. Existing laws are not adequate to secure equal rights for women.

Sufficient proof of this is the concentration of women in lower paying menial unrewarding jobs, and their incredible scarcity in the upper level jobs. It is obvious that discrimination exists. Women do not have the opportunities that men do, and women that do not conform to the system, who try to break with the excepted pattern are stigmatized as odd and unfeminine. The fact is that a woman who aspires to be chairman of a board or Member of the House does so exactly for the same reasons as any man, basically because she thinks she can do the job and she wants to try.

A second argument often heard against the equal rights amendment is that it would eliminate legislation that many States and the Federal Government have enacted giving special protection to women, and that it would throw the marriage and divorce laws into chaos. As for the marriage laws, they are due for sweeping change, and an excellent beginning would be wiping the existing ones off the books.

Regarding special protection for working women, I cannot understand why it should be needed. Women need no protection that men do not need. What we need are laws to protect working people, to guarantee them fair pay, safe working conditions, protection against sickness and layoffs. Men and women need these things equally. That one sex needs protection more than the other is male supremacism and as ridiculous and unworthy of respect as the white supremacism that society is trying to cure itself of at this time.

Senator BAYH. I agree with everything you said.

We appreciate your taking the time to be with us. I might have one reservation with your remarks, which is that although I really cannot blame you for feeling frustrated relative to the task before us, I hope it will not be a futile effort.

Thank you very much.

Mrs. CHISHOLM. Thank you, Senator.

Senator BAYH. Mrs. Harmon, are you brave enough to try it again? Mrs. Shriver, Mrs. O'Callaghan?

I thought your statement was a very inclusive one and I won't belabor you at length.

I know this is really beyond our province, inasmuch as we are weighing a constitutional amendment, but do you have any insight relative to what we can do, in light of the experience of EEOC in this area, to bring about more rapid acceptance in the equity of this and in the enforcement of it?

CONTINUATION OF STATEMENT OF MRS. MYRA RUTH HARMON, NATIONAL FEDERATION OF BUSINESS AND PROFESSIONAL WOMEN'S CLUBS, ACCOMPANIED BY MRS. LUCILLE SHRIVER, FEDERATION DIRECTOR AND DR. PHYLLIS O'CALLAGHAN, LEGISLATION DIRECTOR

Mrs. HARMON. Possibly one aspect of this would be to give the EEOC the right to issue cease and desist orders under this title VII, which would enable them to make a more effective job of enforcement of title VII.

SENATOR BAYH. Just amending that statute to give them more power?

Mrs. HARMON. That would be one way.

Regardless of the amendment, I think we will have probably many court cases that will be necessary to bring this to its full usage.

Senator BAYH. Listening to your statement, it seems to me you make very eloquent testimony to the fact that the Hayden rider, which has traditionally been an albatross around our neck, was not intended to affect those "protective laws" which were, perhaps, designed some years ago with good intentions to deal with specific causes or problems which did in fact exist in the past. Quite contrary to the original intention, these laws now have a reverse effect, prohibiting advancement and the full utilization of the talents of woman; is that an accurate assessment?

Mrs. HARMON. I think this is very true. Perhaps part of this is due to the advanced technology and changing conditions for working people, but I believe that the State so-called "protective laws" are more discriminatory than they are helpful in most instances. These laws regarding working conditions should be for both men and women equally.

Senator BAYH. Are you concerned at all about those laws whose thrust, it seems to me, could not be changed inasmuch as some laws are aimed directly at the attributes of women as distinct from male, such as laws providing maternity benefits or those relating to criminal assault against women? Do you foresee such an impact on this type of law?

MRS. HARMON. It seems to me these are special aspects of our life and would require special laws. For instance the maternity laws are provided to help the extension of the human race and not for— because they are men or women. If a man could bear children he would be under the same law as a woman is and these are entirely different types of laws, in my estimation, than the so-called "protective laws" regarding hours and types of working conditions.

Senator BAYH. I personally do not see any reason why maternity benefits or laws making it a criminal offense to sexually assault a woman should in any way be affected by this type of statute or constitutional amendment, and I wanted to get your thoughts on that subject.

Are you concerned at all with a matter of greatest controversy, that of family case law around the country? Will this affect family law in any way?

Mrs. HARMON. I can't see that it would. I think if the husband and wife were equally responsible for the education and upbringing of a child and the woman should be just as responsible in this area as a man, both in the mental and psychological upbringing of the child as well as the earning power and the support of that child monetarily.

Senator BAYH. Well, two areas that are particularly fraught with controversy are alimony and child custody. Are you prepared to suggest that a judge should consider the custody of the children and the merit of alimony without regard to whether he is dealing with a woman or a man, that each case should be treated individually on its merits?

Mrs. HARMON. I feel it should. It should be based on the individual people involved and the persons themselves and not on whether it is a man or a woman. Each case should be individually assessed in this light.

In regard to alimony, it may very well be that the wife should pay for alimony for the husband if he is unable to support himself or in some particular assistance needs her financial support.

Senator BAYH. As the president of one of the leading women's organizations in the country, would you accept the fact that a man should be paid alimony by a woman, or that a man should be granted custody of the children over a woman or the wife in the case, depending upon the relative marriage?

Mrs. HARMON. I think each case should stand on its own merits in both these instances.

Senator BAYH. Well, thank you very much. I see no reason to burden you further. Your statement was very inclusive, and I appreciate not only your presentation here today, but your willingness and that of your staff to participate in the efforts which I believe necessary at a grassroots level throughout the country if we are to be successful.

We will be calling on you, if we may.

Mrs. HARMON. Thank you very much for your consideration.

It was our pleasure and privilege to appear before your committee today, and you can be assured we will give you every support in this amendment.

Senator BAYH. Thank you very much.

We will recess for about 2 minutes, pending Senator Goodell's arrival.

(A short recess was taken.)

Senator BAYH. May we come to order, please.

I am not certain where Senator Goodell is. I am sure he is on his way.

In light of the witness list, it would be impractical for us to wait further. I noticed that the Congresswoman from Massachusetts, Mrs. Heckler, is here and we will ask her if she will testify at this time, please.

STATEMENT OF HON. MARGARET M. HECKLER, A REPRESENTATIVE IN CONGRESS FROM THE 10TH DISTRICT OF THE STATE OF MASSACHUSETTS

Mrs. HECKLER. Thank you very much, Mr. Chairman and distinguished members of the subcommittee.

It is assumed today by many persons that women were granted equality with the passage of the 14th amendment, ratified in 1868. Only 50 years later, however, was woman suffrage guaranteed by the ratification of the 19th amendment. Half a century of waiting for the vote required a great deal of patience. In the temper of these turbulent times, I do not believe that total equality of opportunity for women can be further postponed.

Thus I speak out in support of the equal rights amendment—a measure that has been before each Congress since 1923. The fast pace of life in the world today fosters impatience. And when much is promised, failure to deliver becomes a matter of critical importance.

I am sure that every woman who has been in the position of "job seeker" identifies in some small measure with the fundamental complaints that have generated the crusade for equality in employment for women. The 42 percent of working women who are heads of household takes a serious economic interest in fair job opportunity, a basic goal in the cause for women's rights. And the women who have contributed their full share to social security, yet who receive the sum allotted widows, certainly have cause for contemplation.

The average woman in America has no seething desire to smoke cigars or to burn the bra—but she does seek equal recognition of her status as a citizen before the courts of law, and she does seek fair and just recognition of her qualifications in the employment market. The American working woman does not want to be limited in advancement by virtue of her sex. She does not want to be prohibited from the job she desires or from the overtime work she needs by "protective" legislation.

These types of discrimination must be stopped, and the forthright means of halting discrimination against women is passage of the equal rights amendment at the earliest possible time. In fact, I have heard it said quite often that the only discrimination that is still fashionable is discrimination against women.

Perhaps, as some say, it is derived from a protective inclination on the part of men. But women seek recognition as individual human beings with abilities useful to society—rather than shelter or protection from the real world.

John Gardner has said that our Nation's most underdeveloped resource is womanpower. The old saying "you can't keep a good man down" might well serve as a warning. It is safe to say, I think, that women are unlikely to stay down and out of the field of competition for much longer.

Legal remedies are clearly in order, and the equal rights amendment is especially timely. Although changes in social attitudes cannot be legislated, they are guided by the formulation of our Federal laws. This constitutional amendment must be passed so that discriminatory legislation will be overturned. That custom and attitude be subject to a faster pace of evolution is essential if we are to avoid revolution on the part of qualified women who seek equality in the employment world.

Time and again I have heard American men question the fact of discrimination against women in America. "American women," they say, "enjoy greater freedom than women of any other nation." This may be true with regard to freedom from kitchen labor—because the average American housewife enjoys a considerable degree of automation in her kitchen. But once she seeks to fill her leisure time gained from automated kitchen equipment by entering the male world of employment, the picture changes. Many countries we consider "underprivileged" far surpass America in quality and availability of child care available to working mothers, in enlightened attitudes about employment leave for pregnancy, and in guiding women into the professions.

Since World War II, nearly 14 million American women have joined the labor force—double the number of men. Forty percent of our Nation's labor force is now comprised of women. Yet less than 3 percent of our Nation's attorneys are women, only about 7 percent of our doctors, and 9 percent of our scientists are women. Only a slightly higher percentage of our graduate students in these fields of study are women, despite the fact that women characteristically score better on entrance examinations. The average woman college graduate's annual earnings ($6,694) exceed by just a fraction the annual earnings of an average male educated only through the eighth grade ($6,580). An average male college graduate, however, may be expected to earn almost twice as much as the female—$11,795. Twenty percent of the women with 4 years of college training can find employment only in clerical, sales, or factory jobs. The equal pay provision of the Fair Labor Standards Act does not include administrative, executive, or professional positions — a loophole which permits the talents and training of highly qualified women to be obtained more cheaply than those of comparable qualified men.

Of the 7.5 million American college students enrolled in 1968, at least 40 percent were women. American parents are struggling to educate their daughters as well as their sons—and are sending them to the best colleges they can possibly afford. As many of these mothers attend commencement exercises this summer, their hearts will swell with pride as their daughters receive college degrees—and these mothers may realize their daughters will have aspirations far exceeding their own horizons.

Few of the fathers or mothers, enrolling their daughters in college several years ago, were at the time aware of the obstacles to opportunity their daughters would face. But today they are becoming aware that opportunity for their daughters is only half of that available to their sons. And they are justifiably indignant. Young women graduating with degrees in business administration take positions as clerks while their male counterparts become management trainees. Women graduating from law school are often forced to become legal secretaries, while male graduates from the same class survey a panorama of exciting possibilities.

To frustrate the aspirations of the competent young women graduating from our institutions of higher learning would be a dangerous and foolish thing. The youth of today are inspired with a passion to improve the quality of life around us—an admirable and essential goal, indeed. The job is a mammoth one, however; and it would be ill-advised to assume that the role of women in the crusade of the future will not be a significant one. To the contrary, never before has our Nation and our world cried out for talent and creative energy with greater need. To deny full participation of the resources of women, who compose over half the population of our country, would be a serious form of neglect. The contributions of women have always been intrinsic in our national development. With the increasing complexity of our world, it becomes all the more essential to tap every conceivable resource at our command.

The time is thus ripe for passage of the equal rights amendment. The women of America are demanding full rights and full responsibilities in developing their individual potential as human beings in relationship to the world as well as to the home and in contributing in an active way to the improvement of society.

In this day of the urban crisis, when we seem to be running out of clean air and water, when the quantity of our rubbish defies our current disposal methods, when crime on the streets is rampant, when our world commitments seem at odds with our obligations here at home, when breaking the cycle of ongoing poverty requires new and innovative approaches, when increased lifespan generates a whole new series of gerontological problems—in these complicated and critical times, our Nation needs the fully developed resources of all our citizens—both men and women—in order to meet the demands of society today.

Women are not requesting special privilege—but rather a full measure of responsibility, a fair share of the load in the effort to improve life in America. The upcoming generation is no longer asking for full opportunity to contribute, however—they are demanding this opportunity.

The equal rights amendment is necessary to establish unequivocally the American commitment to full and equal recognition of the rights of all its citizens. Stopgap measures and delays will no longer be acceptable—firm guarantees are now required. The seventies mark an era of great promise if the untapped resource of womanpower is brought forth into the open and allowed to flourish so that women may take their rightful place in the mainstream of American life. Both men and women have a great deal to gain.

Thank you, Mr. Chairman.

Senator BAYH. Thank you very much, Mrs. Heckler, for your contribution. You spoke eloquently on the point in question, so much so that I see no reason to ask any questions.

Senator Cook.

Senator COOK. Mr. Chairman, I appreciate your statistics concerning the opportunities available to educated women. I presently have a daughter who is a sophomore in college. I also have two daughters who will be entering college in the near future. As a father I know that boards of trustees of colleges throughout the Nation make no distinction in the amount of tuition charged to students on the basis of sex. Therefore your point that large differences exist in opportunities for the educated woman versus the educated man is well made.

There were some questions that I wanted to propose to Congresswoman Griffiths when she was here concerning women's suffrage. Do you feel as a Member of Congress that an issue such as women's suffrage really required a constitutional amendment, especially in view of recent Supreme Court cases? Had the courts taken appropriate and timely action and had we seen the wisdom of equal citizenship, would a constitutional amendment still have been necessary?

Mrs. HECKER. Well, I feel quite the opposite, Senator. In fact, I think the very fact that we are petitioning for an equal rights amendment because of the inequality which has existed and which the States and our Government have tolerated for so long proves that the inequalities in suffrage, the fact that women were not given the right to vote, had to be dramatically achieved through a constitutional amendment.

I regret that such a dramatic step has become necessary, because in the wake of all the attempts to achieve suffrage and the attempts to achieve equal opportunity and a fair share and a fair chance, you have had the frustrations of a loss of terribly talented women, but nonetheless, this is important today.

I think that a good argument can be made that title VII of the Civil Rights Act of 1964 gives great protection to women economically, but the fact of the matter is, in order to actually enjoy the benefits of that protection, a woman would have to bring suit and have the time and the energy and the money to follow the case throughout the many courts which might be involved. In the long run I am quite confident that the woman would be eventually successful, but nevertheless, the less the requirement and the burden of lengthy legal procedures involved in many of these issues—the right to vote on fair employment, in fighting discrimination—the better and more fair. All of these issues are not adequately handled by the availability of the courts because the courts, while they are a great source of just ce to the country, at the same time they mete out justice on very slow terms, and women have waited too long. Justice has been too slow. Consequently, I think an amendment is necessary today.

Senator COOK. I was looking for some congressional support on extending the vote to 18-year-olds by statutory means. It appears that additional work in the conference room is needed, Mr. Chairman.

I think you are right in the essence about the degree of litigation that is necessary under title VII.

The only point I want to make is that often in reading the history of the constitutional amendment procedures it becomes apparent that Congress really could have acted in a forthright manner without creating the need for extensive litigation. Unfortunately, both Congress and the courts have set this slow pattern.

Mrs. HECKLER. Senator, we in the Congress have a good deal to add on this petition. After all, the equal rights petition has been successfully presented every year since 1923, and the question is are we going to live up to this commitment, are we willing to face what will become a growing revolution. I think the urgency of the situation today and the needs of our society are so great that we just can't afford to, in the process of legislation as usual, follow the 1923 precedent on this issue.

Senator COOK. I hope that it will be as convenient to get hearings in the House as it has been to get hearings in the Senate. I say this for the benefit of the chairman. I think we may have some problems in the House.

Mrs. HECKLER. We are always impressed by your forceful leadership, and that will be a factor.

Senator COOK. I think you should give the chairman credit for that.

Mrs. HECKLER. I certainly wish to do so.

Senator COOK. It is nice to know we have so many signatures on a resolution. We may be required to put all of them in a position so that voting on them is mandatory.

Senator BAYH. Let the record show that I think that is the reason we are here.

I want to make one observation, Mrs. Heckler, if I might.

I think we are being a bit naive. I don't suggest that you are. We must recognize the enormous effort that is going to be required to be successful. I don't mean just passing a slip of paper that happens to be appended, whether it is the 26th, 27th, or 28th amendment to the Constitution, but ultimately implementing this at the marketplace, job marketplace, in the court, and at the law office where contracts are written or where divorce proceedings are consummated, I just cannot see how we are really going to escape the need for maximum effort to pursue litigation in the courts, whether it is a constitutional amendment or statute to the 1964 voting rights statute. I think there are going to be those, unfortunately, who are going to stand in the way of a constitutional amendment and test it until it is finally decided. But nevertheless, we must be prepared, in my judgment, to make this effort.

Mrs. HECKLER. I think you are quite right, Senator. I feel that this is a continuing cause. Obviously, the passage of an equal rights amendment to the Constitution would be a very dramatic, long awaited breakthrough and would have a great deal of impact. This would have to be pursued, of course, later in the courts. I would not, as every law does not, and even the Constitution itself does not, in itself implement the opinions it espouses.

Senator BAYH. You see, beginning to tie in is the *Martin Marietta-Phillips* case where the allegations were made successfully to the fifth circuit. As I mentioned before you arrived, the Supreme Court has granted certiorari on this, so perhaps it will be reversed. The contentions which were made there—that it really wasn't a matter of sex at all, but something in addition to sex, namely the fact that there were children involved—will be reexamined. The case shows women with children were treated differently than men with children.

Senator Cook, any questions?

Senator COOK. No.

Senator BAYH. Thank you very much. We appreciate your testimony.

Mrs. HECKLER. Thank you very much.

Senator BAYH. Our next witness this morning is our distinguished colleague, the junior Senator from New York, Senator Charles Goodell.

Thank you for being here this morning.

STATEMENT OF HON. CHARLES E. GOODELL, A U.S. SENATOR FROM THE STATE OF NEW YORK

Senator GOODELL. Thank you, Mr. Chairman, Senator Cook.

I might say to Senator Cook, I don't share the special family interest that he has, since I have five sons and no girls at all. But I am equally devoted to the cause.

I recall about 5 years ago Congressman Bill Widnall of New Jersey, telling me of a visit he made to a third-grade classroom in New Jersey. He invited questions from the class, and a little girl asked him if he thought that some day there could be a woman President of the United States. His reply was "Yes, there could be, certainly. As a matter of fact, if the women got together now, there are more women than men, and they could elect a President of the United

States." And a little male voice came from the back of the room and said, "Now what did you have to go and tell them that for." That, I think, illustrates a bias we build in very early——the male attitude with reference to women's rights.

The constitutional amendment insuring equality of rights regardless of sex has been under consideration by the Congress for almost 50 years.

This committee favorably reported resolutions proposing the amendment in the 80th, 81st, 83rd, 84th, 86th, 87th and 88th Congresses. In addition this subcommittee favorably reported the proposed amendment in the 90th Congress.

Still the Congress has not approved the amendment.

As a cosponsor of the proposed amendment (S.J. Res. 61), I urge the subcommittee to once again exert its leadership and report this measure. I urge you to actively seek adoption by the Senate and House of a constitutional guarantee of equal rights under the law for men and women.

The struggle for women's rights

That a constitutional amendment is needed to guarantee women's rights indicates that we have failed. A constitutional amendment— the 19th amendment—had to be passed to give women the right to vote. At the time this amendment passed, it was assumed that a general revision of laws and practices would follow, ending discrimination against women.

Unfortunately, reality has contradicted that optimistic assumption:

In 1930, 15.4 percent of all Ph. D degrees were conferred upon women, but this percentage declined to 10.8 percent in 1965. The percentage for master's degrees similarly declined from 40.4 to 32.1 percent.

Over 75 percent of working women are employed in nonprofessional clerical, secretarial, service or factory jobs.

About 20 percent of this nonprofessional force consists of women with 4 years of college, and 7 percent of women with 5 years of university study.

The median income of a women was $4,150 in 1967. For comparable work, a man received nearly double that amount—$7,182.

Less than 3 percent of the women earned salaries of $10,000 or more in 1967. The proportion for men was 23 percent.

Although 34 percent of the Federal Government work force is female, less than 2 percent are in executive jobs.

Numerous examples can be cited to confirm that working women mainly occupy low-level, low paying jobs.

The new feminism

The women's rights movement has ben revolutionized by a new feminism—one that is concerned with the underlying social dynamics that have created sex discrimination, not merely with its economic symptoms.

The new feminist is a product of the civil rights movement of the early sixties. Young women, well-educated and well-motivated, volunteered their time and energies to the cause of freedom, equality and dignity for the black people. Too soon, they learned their place in the civil rights movement—doing menial tasks such as cooking, cleaning, typing, filing, but not participating in the decisionmaking.

Their experience reflected the message of Susan B. Anthony when she said:

"Men like to see women pick up the drunken and fallen!—repair the damages of society!—that 'patching business' is a 'woman's proper sphere'—but to be the master of circumstances that is man's sphere!"

These young women witnessed the fruits of a century of resistance to equal rights for blacks, and they witnessed the humiliation and degradation of racial discrimination. And they saw that their enforced roles were also inferior. They could not fight for black equality without recognizing and fighting for their own.

They also soon saw that sex discrimination, like racial discrimination, could not be banished merely by passing laws. They saw that its root cause lay in a state of mind—in fundamental social attitudes concerning the role of women and their relationship to men.

And so they began a campaign to change that state of mind—to change the idea, fixed in the minds of so many men and women, that a woman can have no other role than as a girl friend, a wife, or a mother. They began protesting against forms of advertising and merchandising that, in their view, dehumanize women—that portray women as mere sex objects or glorified housemaids.

Beyond even that, the new feminists perceived that the plight of women stems from still deeper defects in our society—from the dehumanizing, status-seeking and materialistic pressures that deprive so many Americans of both sexes of meaningful lives. And they are determined to change this.

These women are young, articulate, and well-educated. They have become an integral part of the movement of social justice that exists today. Unlike the suffragettes, they are speaking to a more sophisticated and self-analyzing society. They understand their role as political beings. And because of their previous involvement in the civil rights struggle and the antiwar struggle, they well understand the power of organization.

At the same time, a more sophisticated and self-analyzing society can find more excuses for denying equality, more sophisticated ways of denying equality.

The experience with the civil rights movement should have taught us the necessity of immediate action.

As I mentioned earlier, the ratification of the 19th amendment brought hopes that sex discrimination would end.

This has not happened.

The ratification of the amendment embodied in Senate Joint Resolution 61 must be accompanied by implementing legislation which will create the opportunities for choice. Unless such legislation is passed, the new amendment will be devoid of spirit and lasting effect.

One of the most controversial issues before us is the legalization of abortion. Many women are now demanding legalization on such constitutional grounds as the right of privacy and equal protection of the laws.

Restrictive abortion laws, still in force in most States, are killers. They do not prevent abortions—they only increase their risks.

There are about 1 million illegal abortions performed each year. The rich can find doctors to perform these operations—at a cost of anywhere from $500 to $1,000. The poor cannot. They are forced to turn to inept quacks or abortion mills that kill.

Of the maternal deaths in New York City last year, 25 percent of the whites, 49 percent of the blacks, and 56 percent of the Puerto Ricans died from botched abortions. Restrictive abortion laws have become another scourge of the poor.

Restrictive abortion laws are a misguided attempt to legislate matters of private conscience.

Some people believe abortion is morally wrong. I fully respect their views—but their own consciences are sufficient protection. They need no laws to prevent them from obtaining abortions of which they disapprove.

Others have the opposite view about the morality of abortion. They, too, should have the right to follow their consciences. They should not be forced to undergo forced pregnancies, or break the law, because of the moral views of other groups.

This point has been aptly stated by Richard Cardinal Cushing when, speaking of abortion laws, he said:

Catholics do not need the support of civil law to be faithful to their own moral convictions and they do not seek to impose by law their moral views on other members of society.

A number of States—New York, Hawaii, California, Alaska, and the District of Columbia now have liberalized abortion laws either through legislative action or judicial interpretation.

I commend their foresight and courage. But leaving the question to be regulated on a State-by-State basis entails some serious problems.

It means that States that adopt liberal laws risk becoming abortion havens—attracting thousands of women from neighboring States and overburdening their hospitals and medical facilities.

One medical expert in New York State estimated there will be anywhere from 20,000 to 100,000 abortions performed in the State annually. We must think in terms of the effect these figures will have on facilities. We must think in terms of assuring this basic right to the poor who do not have the economic means to avail themselves of the right.

A State-by-State approach also discriminates against the poor who live in States that have restrictive laws and cannot afford to travel to distant jurisdictions that have adopted more rational legislation.

I believe this problem is national in scope and can best be treated on a national level.

Our colleague, Senator Robert Packwood, has attempted to do this by proposing a bill (S. 3746) that would authorize a physician in any State to terminate a pregnancy upon request of the mother.

In his statement introducing the bill, Senator Packwood states that the constitutional basis of such legislation is the right of privacy. The Supreme Court recognized the existence of such a right in *Palko* v. *Connecticut*, when it struck down State legislation restricting the use of contraceptive devices by married couples. Recent lower court decisions have referred to the same right of privacy in striking down restrictive State abortion laws.

The constitutional question bears further examination—but I believe a strong case can be made that national legislation of this nature would be supported by the *Palko* case, and by section 5 of the 14th amendment (see, *Katzenbach* v. *Morgan*, 384 U.S. 641).

Assuming the constitutional power exists, I support the concept of national legislation authorizing an adult mother to obtain on request a medical termination of pregnancy from a licensed physician. The details of such legislation should be studied and developed further.

Another important area is family planning.

Over 5 million women in this country want and need family planning instruction, while only 700,000 are being reached—half by Government and half by private organizations.

Women deprived of family planning information—and these are usually poor women—are often trapped in a vicious cycle of unwanted children, deepening poverty, and, ultimately, welfare dependence.

As I have said elsewhere earlier, Congress should provide adequate funds for the establishment of family planning clinics for those women who desire such assistance.

Day-care centers

Job discrimination still remains a serious problem for women.

The passage of Title VII of the 1964 Civil Rights Act included a ban on discrimination in employment based on sex.

In 1963, while a House Member, I was the author of legislation passed in that year by the Congress providing equal pay for women.

Over half of the Equal Employment Opportunity Commission complaints received are from women.

Still, job equality remains a myth—much like the equality promised to black people after the Civil War.

Euripides said that "A woman should be good for everything at home, but abroad for nothing." Career experiences of women reflect this message. We tell a woman she is entitled to advanced training and a challenging job. Then, however, we deny her this job because it is expected that she will marry and have children. She is effectively taken off the job market before she gets on.

For example, the U.S. Fifth Circuit Court of Appeals in the case of *Phillips* v. *Martin Marietta Corp.*, ruled that a corporation could refuse to employ a woman because she had preschool children. In the minority opinion, Judge John R. Brown stated:

* * * the rankest sort of discrimination against women by employers * * * the average women working earns only 60 percent of the average wage for men * * * our economy depends on women in the labor force.

This case is now on appeal to the Supreme Court.

A Labor Department survey reveals that 50 percent of the Nation's mothers are now employed and that the number is rising. Over 3 million working mothers have children younger than 6 years of age. These children must be left behind to the care of others.

Yet only about 200,000 working women have access to licensed day-care facilities for their children. This lack of day-care facilities remains a serious obstacle to job opportunities for women.

The Federal Government must play a leading role in changing this pattern. It should encourage and fund the establishment of day-care centers for all socioeconomic levels so that women can participate in the search for equal job opportunity. These day-care centers should include an educational component so that the child will have an enriched environment. Day-care centers should be open all day so that women can have their children well-tended while they pursue employment, education, or participation in community affairs.

I do not believe we should allow inequality of women to be perpetuated.

Doubtless many of the expressed inequalities require a fundamental change of basic attitudes in our culture.

Others, however, simply require an updating of antequated law.

We have learned through the civil rights struggle that a piecemeal approach to equality—step by step—is too slow and insufficient.

This amendment, proposed in Senate Joint Resolution 61, must be ratified. But with it must be passed legislation which gives the amendment meaning and strength—legislation which will make a difference.

The deprivation of the rights of women cannot be excused. As long as their creativity is stifled, our whole society suffers.

Thank you, Mr. Chairman.

Senator BAYH. Senator Goodell, we appreciate your very comprehensive statement.

I think that if women are really going to be treated equally under the law it is going to take more than the passage of a constitutional amendment. The statutory provision I am particularly concerned about, a matter which has come to my attention and that of my chief adviser, my wife, is the need for day care centers. We have had the opportunity to view how other nations, such as the Soviet Union, Japan, and Israel provide opportunity for working mothers to adequately care for their children. Certainly, we want to join you in an effort to try to make this a comprehensive effort to see that women are treated equitably.

Senator Cook.

Senator COOK. Thank you, Senator Goodell.

Because you cited *Katzenbach* v. *Morgan*, I want to reiterate a point I previously made, possibly inadequately, to Congresswoman Heckler. It is my opinion that Congress probably has the authority under the equal protection clause and section 5 of the 14th amendment to enact equal rights for women through means other than by constitutional amendment.

I agree with you that the dramatics of the entire problem make action through constitutional amendment appropriate. For the benefit of Congress and the Senate I must state that we have inadequately used our statutory and amendment powers. I think that the Senate has made progress by thinking that action is possible and certainly action can be taken during this session.

Senator GOODELL. I agree with you. I think it is also important a constitutional amendment be passed to symbolize a new approach, a new attitude on the part of not only the Congress of the United States, but by the people of the United States, and I think it is important that the States participate in this because a great many repressive, inequitable laws are State laws. It will be a long process of simply striking down those State laws through the court system. We must pass a constitutional amendment which the States implement and then we must act, implementing legislation in Congress.

Senator COOK. I agree with the Senator. I get the feeling in listening to the testimony that original limitations, such as rules and regulations, were enacted as a degree of protection. But I think in recent years they have been enlarged as a matter of discrimination rather than protection. I think we have to weigh this in regard to our attitude toward legislation as protective of particular groups without necessarily enlarging the rights of other groups.

Senator GOODELL. I agree with you.

Senator COOK. Thank you, Senator, very much.

Senator BAYH. Thank you very much, Senator Goodell. We appreciate your contribution.

Our next witness or witnesses represent the National Organization for Women, Mrs. Aileen Hernandez, the National President, Brenda Fasteau, in charge of the legislative area, and Jean Witter, chairman, Equal Rights Amendment Committee.

Am I right, Mrs. Hernandez, that you were at one time chairman of the Equal Employment Opportunities Commission?

STATEMENT OF MRS. AILEEN HERNANDEZ, PRESIDENT, NATIONAL ORGANIZATION FOR WOMEN; ACCOMPANIED BY JEAN WITTER, CHAIRMAN, EQUAL RIGHTS AMENDMENT COMMITTEE AND BRENDA FASTEAU, VICE PRESIDENT FOR LEGISLATION

Mrs. HERNANDEZ. I was a Commissioner, but I was never the chairman of the Commission.

Senator BAYH. You should have been the chairman.

Mrs. HERNANDEZ. I agree.

Senator BAYH. We are looking forward to your testimony.

Mrs. HERNANDEZ. I would like just to explain the manner in which we are going to testify and to make one correction which I think is significant.

It is the National Organization for Women, not of Women.

Senator COOK. The program was right, the error was made by the chairman.

Mrs. HERNANDEZ. We will proceed by my making an introductory comment; then I will call upon Miss Witter to make her comments, Mrs. Brenda Fasteau afterwards.

My name is Aileen C. Hernandez, and I am the national president of the National Organization for Women, an organization whose acronym NOW expresses forcefully our concept of the timing for equality for women.

I and my sisters in this new feminist organization appear before you today with decidedly mixed emotions. We are infuriated by the cavalier manner in which the gentlemen of the Congress have treated the question of equality for women for 47 years since the Equal Rights Amendment to our Constitution was first introduced. We are saddened by the fact that an amendment is needed, because our male founders and male-dominated courts refuse to accept women as people in setting forth and interpreting the guarantees of freedom in the Bill of Rights.

We are also, however, somewhat indebted to you and to your predecessors in the Senate and the House, because without your dismissal of our petition to you for equality, N.O.W. would never have been born.

In 1966 hundreds of women met in Washington, D.C., to submit and discuss their report on the status of women, reports carefully and intelligently developed in the years of study in the many commissions formed throughout the United States as a result of a gauntlet thrown down by then President John F. Kennedy in his charge to the National Advisory Commission on the status of women, a charge to study and make recommendations on the nature and extent of discrimination against women in the United States. As those delegates attempted to implement their recommendations, they learned that action was not a part of their charge. Out of their frustration came NOW. A group of women met in the hotel room of Betty Friedan, who was then in the process of writing a second book, and decided that a civil rights organization for women was needed if women were to become first-class citizens in this society.

The rage of those women was translated into a program for action, which included as a high priority the passage of the long bottled up in Congress equal rights amendment for women and for men. NOW's program is very easily defined. We believe in equal rights and responsibilities for men and women, and our members, both men and women, are working to bring women into full participation in the mainstream of American society now.

In the short 4 years, or not quite 4 years, since NOW was formed and under the leadership of Betty Friedan, NOW has tallied many gains, chief among which is the fact that new feminists are on the march and that sex discrimination is no longer treated as an obscene joke.

Gentlemen, women are enraged. We are dedicated and we mean to become first-class citizens in this society. We really do not feel that these hearings are necessary. The Congress could and should vote immediately. The issue has been thoroughly defined. Either this Congress recognizes that women, like other oppressed people within our Nation, will wait no longer for equity, and with this recognition moves immediately to redress the many grievances, or like other oppressed groups, women will adjust their tactics to achieve their demands.

Others who testify after us, and some who have testified before us, will address themselves to the technical and legal arguments for passage. This panel for NOW addresses itself to the justness of the cause and the urgency of the demand. We demand the right to assume our roles in every aspect of this society. We demand the right to be heard on all the issues of concern; we demand inclusion in this society NOW so that we may bring all our considerable talents to bear to change those things which need changing in order to achieve full justice for all and to preserve those things which help us to achieve our goal.

Gentlemen, the challenge is directly to you; you have the opportunity to redress the obvious injustices against women by voting immediately to send the amendment to the floor of Congress and to work to achieve its passage in this session of Congress. If you miss this opportunity—and NOW sincerely hopes you do not—the women of America may well see fit to ensure in November that many of you and your colleagues never have another chance to insult the women of America by your failure to act.

I would now like to ask Jean Witter to continue with the testimony.

Senator, Miss Witter.

Miss WITTER. The Equal Rights Amendment has been "the best kept secret of the 20th century." Only this fact has allowed our Congressmen to return to their seats session after session while they are continuing to deny our women constitutional equality and full recognition of first-class citizens. The fact that these hearings are being held in May, when 6 months ago there were more than enough sponsors to pass the amendment, insults every woman voter in the country.

Since 1970 is an election year, Congress will probably adjourn in early August and little action will occur after mid-July. Effectively, there are only 2 short months for the passage—

Senator BAYH. May I interrupt long enough to ask our distinguished witness if she would tell the subcommittee when was the last time Congress adjourned in August?

Miss WITTER. I think it was the last session, wasn't it?

Senator BAYH. No m'am.

Miss WITTER. Well, I hope we have longer.

Senator COOK. It was Christmas eve.

Miss WITTER. Good. I hope that is true.

Senator BAYH. I think your message is clear, but let's not lessen it by aiming at the wrong target date. I am hopeful it will be successful by August. If not, we are going to have to give it a little more time.

Miss WITTER. Very good.

We are determined that the equal rights amendment will not die a quiet death in 1970. If the amendment is not passed this year its ghost will stalk the voting polls in November. If the amendment is not passed in 1970, American women will vote to replace those responsible for its defeat. Let us not be blinded from taking this essential step for the full emanicipation of U.S. women by the fact that some women may not be ready or anxious for full equality.

Certainly after the passage of the 19th amendment some women may not be ready or anxious for full equality.

Certainly after the passage of the 19th amendment some of our older women have never considered voting even to this day. In recent elections, however, the number of women who did vote exceeded the number of men who did so, and the percentage of college educated female voters exceeds the number of college educated male voters.

The fact that some women were not ready to accept suffrage at the time of the passage of the 19th amendment was fortunately not permitted to stand in the way of giving suffrage to their daughters. Our daughters must have constitutional equality, even if some men and women are not able to accept immediately all the implications of constitutional equality for women. Thus the equal rights amendment implies that women should be subject to the draft or compulsory military service as well as men.

Many of us working in the women's rights movement oppose the war as a means of solving international problems, but we believe as long as some citizens are drafted all citizens should be subject to the draft, women equal with men. Congress already has the power to do that. The equal rights amendment would add the requirement that women register for draft.

In the year 1900, to speak of equality of rights under the law for women, would have been almost academic because women are in no position to demand equality and no group has ever received rights without first demanding them. Most women were involved almost continually in the reproductive processes until shortly before their death, which was usually about the age of 48. In 1970 only 40 percent of U.S. women have one or more children under the age of 18, and of these mothers nearly 10 percent are the head of a household.

Today we must recognize that motherhood is usually a temporary condition and encourage our young mothers to realize that, like men, we can expect to do other things besides being parents. The problems of the world today that must be solved are of such magnitude that we cannot continue to waste the talents of half the population. If we do not encourage women to fully utilize their ability to solve the problems of the world today none of us may survive to criticize our present poor judgment and prejudice.

When over 10 million in the world are dying yearly of starvation women must have reason to believe that there are other rewarding endeavors for them besides producing large families.

For the U.S. Congress to kill the equal rights amendment for the 24th time would be a crime, not only against 51 percent of the population who are women, but this would be a crime also against the very survival and well being of our Nation.

Mrs. HERNANDEZ. I would now like to ask Brenda Fasteau to continue.

Mrs. FASTEAU. My name is Brenda Feigen Fasteau. I am legislative vice president of the National Organization for women. I am also a lawyer and recent graduate of Harvard Law School.

Especially since entering law school, I have become increasingly aware of the obstacles which face young women like myself all across the country. The equal rights amendment will go a long way towards eliminating those obstacles. That amendment will have the general legal effect of forcing governmental employers who treat men and women differently to prove that such treatment has a functional justification. The amendment will also prohibit discrimination in all other situations involving Federal and State action.

After the Constitution is amended the presumption will be that every difference in treatment between man and women in prima facie discrimination, rebuttable only by a showing that such treatment is functionally necessary. Men alone may be considered for jobs as attendants in the men's rooms of the Capitol, but not for positions of President of the United States, Secretary of Defense or Justice of the Supreme Court of the United States.

At present, although a woman is theoretically guaranteed against discrimination by the equal protection clause of the 14th amendment, it is she who must prove that the discriminatory treatment about which she is complaining is in fact unjustified and not warranted by the mere fact that she is a woman, she who must prove that laws and practices, which allegedly protect her, in fact harm her and hold her back from using all her talents. Thus, for example, where now a potential female astronaut must show that she is illegally being kept out of the space program and being discriminated against, the equal rights amendment will shift the burden onto the Government to show that there are functional reasons for keeping specific women from journey into space. In a challenge of that kind, I suspect that the Government will lose.

State laws, for example, which deny women the right to bring an action for loss of consortium but grant such rights to men, would be extended to give women these rights or be wiped off the books.

Less tangible, but maybe even more important for the future

of our country, is the effect that the equal rights amendment will have on the general attitudes and beliefs about women that Americans hold. Some people—often employees in powerful positions as well as all the other men in our lives—have reacted to our demands for equal treatment in a joking manner. People who discriminate against women feel that their actions bear the stamp of legitimacy from leaders in Government, industry, law and education. Passage of the equal rights amendment will indicate to the American people that the rampant oppression of women in this country is real, widespread, and not a subject for humor. This amendment will affect much more than the specific areas of the laws about which you Senators will hear in the next few days.

I will tell you a little about my own experience, much of which might never have happened if Congress had acted on this amendment earlier. Being a woman at a professional school (and a supposedly liberal one at that) was an infuriating experience throughout which I was treated like an unwelcome phenomenon. Job interviews conducted through the law school placement office make every other insult, however, mild by comparison. Of the law firms which I interviewed for jobs, four told me that they simply would not hire a woman. Two firms would not hire a woman because their "senior partners" would object, a standard excuse. Several firms stated that women were hired to do only probate, trust, and estate work, the traditional domain of "lady lawyers." Many believe that the toughness of a labor negotiation could not be tolerated by a female attorney. Almost everyone I spoke to felt that women were more suited for work which would never demand that they be available to meet crises at odd hours, i.e. all important work. The reasons given for the kinds of discriminatory behavior which I have described vary. All are illegitimate.

I have been repeatedly told, not asked, that I would have babies and therefore leave my job, that I would follow my husband wherever he may decide to go because his career is presumably more important than mine. Neither I nor my husband agree with these assumptions. Potential employers have laughed, with a slight sneer on their faces, when I tell them that my husband and I make decisions together about where we will live, that he will share childraising as he does cooking and cleaning with me. These men in positions of power are wrong. I am sick of telling them so. I am sick of defending myself from their persistent attacks on my competence and credibility. Men who try to justify their prejudices by these kinds of feeble excuses are really hiding the fact that all they really want is a private male domain to make themselves feel important and reinforce their flagging egos.

I am angry at these men, and I am not the only one. Across the country millions of women and self-confident men are joining together to fight the insidious oppression which has held women back for thousands of years, oppression which results from discrimination disguised as chivalry and protection. I wish that we did not need a constitutional amendment to insure us our freedom. I wish that all men in control today could understand just how cruel and inhuman so many of them have been to us and change themselves, rid themselves of their sense of insecurity which manifests itself in their need to step on women to reinforce that little true masculinity they have.

I, for one, speaking as a young woman of America, will not allow my unborn daughter to be treated the way I have been.

Mrs. HERNANDEZ. I would like to close our formal presentation with three brief comments about the need for this amendment, comments which arise out of my personal experience.

First, as you have indicated, Senator Bayh, I served for 18 months as a Commissioner appointed by President Lyndon Johnson to enforce title VII of the Civil Rights Act of 1964. The number of complaints filed under that law by women convinced me that sex discrimination in employment is an unhappy fact for all kinds of women, professional and nonprofessional. The enforcement of that law was made immeasurably more difficult because there is no clear national policy that women should not be discriminated against. The equal rights amendment will provide that national policy and improve the effectiveness of that law.

Second, for more than 11 years I was an organizer and educational director in California for a nationally known union serving hundreds of thousands of women members but with few women in leadership. The equal rights amendment would help to encourage more women to seek leadership roles in that and other unions.

I am delighted to say that for the first time there appears to be a crack in the solid wall of opposition that the labor movement has always had against the equal rights amendment; that for the first time the United Automobile Workers has indicated that they support the amendment; that at the first Wisconsin conference of trade union women, the group went on record in support of the equal rights amendment. I think that is very, very much long overdue, and I am delighted to welcome them to the fold.

Third, my State, California, has more so-called protective law for women than any other State, and yet the pattern of women's employment is no different than in States without such laws. Women are still found predominantly in the low-paid occupations and predominantly in the lowest categories of any type of occupation. I believe that the passage of the equal rights amendment will do much to change that situation by offering to women the kind of first class citizenship which will permit them early in life to make career choices that are not now available. We therefore urge immediate passage.

Thank you.

Senator BAYH. I appreciate very much the testimony that you have given. I think perhaps the assessment of these hearings, that the very fact that these hearings are being held as an insult to women, is perhaps accurate.

In my judgment, if we are going to be successful, something more has to be done than has been done in the past, something that really pricks the national conscience and calls to the attention of, I think, well-intentioned but misguided males the number and the depth of the discrimination which exist.

I note with a great deal of interest Mrs. Fasteau's assessment of those men who feel that they need to reassert their masculinity by stepping on women. It seems to be this type of masculinity—is——

Mrs. HERNANDEZ. Fragile one.

Senator BAYH. Well, fragile is not exactly the kind of word I was looking for. Perhaps it is unprintable. I think that is a symptom of great insecurity. I believe that many of our male colleagues can be moved by showing the depth of the injustice that does exist, and this is the purpose of these hearings. Hopefully they will be short, and as you know, they are going to be hard-hitting. Then we intend to proceed rapidly before August.

Let me ask you, if I may, Mrs. Hernandez, to give us a little more of the details of your union activity. I would like to know the name of the union.

Mrs. HERNANDEZ. The International Ladies Garment Workers Union.

Senator BAYH. You say there were no women officers at this union?

Mrs. HERNANDEZ. I don't know how many members the union has now. At the time I worked with them there were pretty close to a half million members. At that time, and to my knowledge, still, there is one woman on the National Executive Board.

Senator BAYH. How about the experience in California? Were there any women national officers of the International Garment Workers in California?

Mrs. HERNANDEZ. Not on the national level, no.

Senator BAYH. How about the State level?

Mrs. HERNANDEZ. There were a few women who held positions as business agents with the union.

Senator BAYH. How many business agents were women compared to the total number of business agents in the Government?

Mrs. HERNANDEZ. An infinitesimal number. The last time I looked at them, 8 or 9 years ago, and at that time probably three or four out of a total of about 40 or 50.

Senator BAYH. Is there any reason for this as far as the equality and qualifications necessary to hold a position in a union that is predominantly female?

Mrs. HERNANDEZ. There is no reason for it based on qualification. Again, that has a great deal to do with attitudes about women and whether or not they are able to hold these kinds of jobs, whether or not women are able to work the hours that are necessary or whether they can be involved in the kind of difficult decisions that are made by trade union leaders. I think Brenda indicated, for example, the business of negotiations and labor law. There is an assumption automatically that women are not really fitted for this. I don't think you can put down in writing that there was a purposefully discriminatory approach, but it is based on the attitudes that prevail in our society.

Senator BAYH. We are going to have some testimony later today from union representatives who will be in opposition, and that is why I wanted to have information to compare with the testimony he will have.

Have you actually worked as a dues-paying member of the union?

Mrs. HERNANDEZ. No, I have not. The International Ladies Garment Workers Union in many, many ways is a very socially progressive union, and some 20 years ago they established the first union college. At that college they trained the young people who were just coming out of school to become union organizers and I was a member of that first class of the International Ladies Garment Workers Union and became an organizer and later educational director under that program.

Senator BAYH. I agree with your assessment of the overall policy and social impact of the position taken by the ILGWU.

Mrs. HERNANDEZ. I do, too.

Senator BAYH. We are looking at a specific problem, really an extra-union, all-encompassing one. That is the reason why I asked these questions, not to be critical.

Although you have not been a dues-paying member I suppose you have become very familiar with the duties of the dues-paying members?

Mrs. HERNANDEZ. Oh, yes.

Senator BAYH. Familiar with their qualifications and their characteristics?

Mrs. HERNANDEZ. Well, the qualification for being a dues-paying member is to work in the industry and pay your dues to the union. I think you probably are asking me about officers for business agents or executives.

Senator BAYH. That is the next question.

Given your familiarity with membership in California, is there anything particularly unique about the qualities needed to run a sewing machine or to cut out patterns that would automatically preclude someone from holding down a position, as an officer?

Mrs. HERNANDEZ. I think not, and it is very interesting to note the changes going on in the industry. In the early days of the coat and suit industry, which is the most technical and skilled one, the sewing machine operators were predominantly male and to the extent they are still alive today are still predominantly male.

In the sportswear industry, which is less well organized and also less well paid, the sewing machine operators are predominantly women. As for cutters, the highest paid craft, almost all of the cutters—those are the gentlemen who cut out the patterns—are male.

Senator BAYH. Why is this, please?

Mrs. HERNANDEZ. A custom again, because in the early days I think they probably used as an excuse that the work was difficult because you lifted heavy bolts of material and put them on the table and then had to roll it out and cut the patterns, but with all our labor-saving devices much of this work is done by the kinds of equipment that have been developed and the job no longer requires the kind of heavy work that it used to.

Senator BAYH. Drawing upon your familiarity with the industry, would it be your judgment that all men would be qualified to serve as cutters?

Mrs. HERNANDEZ. Absolutely not. Individual differences among men are as strong as individual differences among women.

Senator BAYH. The person who couldn't cut a pattern hardly could fill the job, whether he is a man or woman?

Mrs. HERNANDEZ. That is correct.

Senator BAYH. But apparently there is a tendency in this aspect of the industry to limit the employment to men and not to women.

Mrs. HERNANDEZ. It has been so.

Senator BAYH. Let me ask you another question about an obstacle that we have confronted until recently concerning our efforts in the passage of this amendment, the so-called Hayden rider which expresses the desire to protect women, to give them a special right, special opportunity.

From what the three of you said, the result, well-intentioned as it might have been, of these various laws has not been to provide special rights and special opportunity, but quite the opposite; is that accurate?

Mrs. HERNANDEZ. It has been very limited in the State of California. I can speak best for that State because that is where I have had most of my work and experience.

Senator BAYH. Can you give us specific examples of women who are unable to get to the top of the ladder to share in an equal paycheck or whatever else the benefits of a job might be with their male counterparts because of a particular type of misguided, perhaps, but well-intentioned protective legislation which has always hovered over our efforts to pass this kind of constitutional amendment?

Mrs. HERNANDEZ. I could probably draw both from my experience in the trade union movement and my experience on the Equal Employment Opportunity Commission, because in the State of California there has been a challenge to the State protective laws particularly as they affect the work day and weight lifting. We have been engaged for a long period of time now in the challenge to those laws by women in the aircraft industry who say that because they are not permitted—flatly by law—in the State of California to work more than 8 hours a day in most industries and recently amended to more than 10 hours a day in some, they may not share the benefits of overtime which occasionally occur in that industry.

So therefore when you total up their work paycheck at the end of the year, since they do not get time and a half for overtime and cannot work the occasional 2 hours or 3 hours more per week, they wind up at the end of the year with considerably less money than the men who work in that industry.

At the same time the employers, because they need the flexibility of occasionally being able to request people to stay overtime, tend not to promote people into these kinds of categories; not to give them the opportunity to move and therefore women do not get the kind of experience which later permits them to become and, incidentally, as supervisors, not protected by the State protective laws.

It is very interesting to me that the areas in which women are most "protected"—and I put that in quotation marks, because I don't believe it is protection—are areas which are not really necessary. Even those women who do not belong to unions—which provide benefits for all their members—it seems to me are not basically benefitted by the State protective laws as they are now operating.

The weight-lifting requirements are ridiculous in some States. I am sure you recognize that across the United States the laws vary significantly. The State of Utah for a while had a 10-pound weight limit for women. Many States have absolutely none, as I have said many times making speeches for the EEOC, my purse weighs more than 10 pounds, and I find that law absolutely ridiculous.

Senator BAYH. Is that all money?

Mrs. HERNANDEZ. No, since I am a woman and being discriminated against, very little is money.

And I think this kind of example is present very many times across the United States. I just don't think in this day and age these laws are currently being used to protect women. I have a tendency to agree with Samuel Gompers who at the turn of the century warned against State protective laws. I am now questioning whether they were ever designed to be protective of women or whether they were really designed to keep women out of the labor market so they could not become productive members of society, and competitive with men in scarce jobs.

Senator BAYH. Let me ask you a question concerning management positions. Does the California time limitation law apply to managerial personnel as well?

Mrs. HERNANDEZ. No, the interesting thing about the State protective laws is how spotty they are in their protection.

For example, they "protect" the women, and I am again putting quotes around this word "protect"—they protect the women in the aircraft industry who want to work the hour and a half for overtime. They do not protect any of the women in domestic service who work all hours of the day and night.

Senator BAYH. Let's look at the aircraft industry. Does the time limitation law apply to all women in the aircraft industry?

Mrs. HERNANDEZ. No, only those women in the manufacturing or production end of that industry. Women who are involved in the managerial end of it are not covered, and frequently work many, many more hours than 8 or 10.

We have a night work law which prohibits women from working in certain kinds of industries at night. The lady who cleans up the office building who works at very low wages is not protected by that law. So I am saying the spotty protection indicates to me the protection is not real and is not warranted.

Senator BAYH. Are any of you ladies at all concerned about the conflict that some people see in the area of domestic law or criminal law pertaining to this act that would apply to specific offenses or specific needs of a woman because she is a woman or mother subject to certain——

Mrs. HERNANDEZ. I heard the two questions you asked earlier, and if I might respond to those specific ones.

You said maternity benefits, and the other one was criminal assault on a woman. It seems to me the maternity benefits are not a sex benefit. They are medical benefits for some women who are about to become mothers, and motherhood, it seems to me, is a different kind of concept and a legitimate benefit—although our organization, the National Organization for Women, is in favor of paternity benefits. We feel there is a great deal to be said for husbands being able to be with their wives at the time when their children are being born.

The second part of it, the criminal assault, it seems to me that that need not be separated by sex either. Criminal assault need not necessarily be upon a woman. It might also be upon a man, so the law could certainly apply to both, and criminal penalties applied whether perpetrated by or against either sex.

Senator BAYH. The criminal statutes in most States look at sexual assault as a more critical problem, with more severe penalties, because of its nature than some of the other types of assault. Do you think this is wrong?

Mrs. HERNANDEZ. I do think it is wrong from a different point of view.

Senator BAYH. I am not contesting that it is right or wrong, because of the manifestations and possible ramifications it has been looked upon by State legislatures as well as this body as a more serious or higher offense against society.

Mrs. HERNANDEZ. I don't feel it is higher than the kind of offenses we perpetrate every day in many ways both as individuals and as a Nation. I think what I am talking about is how sexual assault against women becomes so prevalent. It becomes so prevalent because in this society women are basically conceived of as sexual objects and until we change that attitude and begin to make women full participants in the society I don't think the incidence of sexual assault is going to become any lower.

It is the attitude about women that brings on this kind of assault and we have to address ourselves to that problem.

Senator BAYH. May I say I agree with your point about the shortcoming of prevalent attitudes, but from a pragmatic standpoint I am not sure passage is going to change attitudes. That will take a long time and we will have to continue to work on it and to look at the law after passage. Approaching this from an optimistic point of view, the laws are still going to be necessary, the ones that are necessary now. That is why I asked the question.

But I am glad to have your thoughts.

Let me just direct one other general question to you. I am asking you these specific questions because, as you know, these are the soft spots in our argument.

Mrs. HERNANDEZ. Yes.

Senator BAYH. What about the problems of alimony and child support?

Mrs. HERNANDEZ. I will let Brenda take that. If I need to I will add to her answer.

Mrs. FASTEAU. I think that there is a witness scheduled to testify who will talk in detail about alimony. But I will tell you that in my opinion all alimony laws, to the extent that they talk about "wife" and "husband" as opposed to "spouse," and therefore differentiate between the two, solely because of sex, should be changed to read "spouse" everywhere.

I think that it is obvious that women who are capable of working, who are divorced, should not be getting alimony payments from their husbands, but should be supporting themselves.

There are, of course, some problems when you get into marriages which have been going on for years and years and years, where one of the spouses has been depending on the other to support him or her. I think that in those cases there would probably have to be provisions made for the spouse who is incapable of earning a living because of total lack of experience and preparation to be provided for by the other spouse who has been supporting him or her.

I think that all this ought to be considered on the basis of the specific facts in individual cases as they arise, that there ought not be laws dictating that one person or the other should get alimony.

There are all kinds of fine points in this area, but I think, in general, that is my position.

Senator BAYH. And the same would go as far as—many jurisdictions now, the mother will have the children.

Mrs. FASTEAU. Absolutely. I have talked to a number of people with all kinds of ideas. Obviously the child should go to the parent who will take the best care of him or her, but I think at the moment that there is almost a legal presumption that the mother should get the child unless she is absolutely incapable of taking care of that child.

One possibility, which sounds somewhat more enlightened to me, would be to consider the age and sex of the child along with generally accepted (and respected) psychological theories, in order to help determine which parent should get custody, that is, what is best for the child.

Mrs. HERNANDEZ. As you have already said, Senator, I think the assumption that just passing the Equal Rights Act is going to change things isn't correct, and we are going to have to address ourselves to several things.

Obviously if we operate on present assumptions, it is the women that needs the help. If we simply move on one front, many women are going to be severely disadvantaged. We must do other things in the society—permit women to expand their occupational choices so that they are prepared, in the event of separation or divorce, to take on jobs or to support themselves adequately.

I think we have to do a number of things in the society at the same time. We can't do one little piece at a time. Unless we address the entire gamut we will fail.

Senator BAYH. Thank you. I appreciate all your testimony.

Senator Cook?

Senator COOK. I have very few questions.

Mrs. Fasteau, did you say that attending Harvard was less expensive for you than for the male students?

Mrs. FASTEAU. No, sir, it cost me the same amount of money.

Senator COOK. Did the administration at Harvard Law School give you any indication when you entered or even when you were going to school that it would be much harder for you to find a position in the field of law than it would be for any of the other graduates?

Mrs. FASTEAU. No, nor did they tell me that the law school placement office allowed law firms, which have a flat rule against hiring women, to use their facilities.

Senator COOK. How many women graduated from Harvard Law School, if you know? I am sure you have an alumni organization.

Mrs. FASTEAU. There is an alumni organization for the entire school. I can only say an average of about 30 women out of 550, maybe 40, depending on the draft situation. I don't know, I think women have only been in Harvard since 1950. So the figure [about 600] is not very high, given the——

Senator COOK. Are there any women instructors at the Harvard Law School?

Mrs. FASTEAU. There are none whatsoever, and there is substantial ferment in the law school because of that.

Senator COOK. Since talking to law firms at placement time, do you feel that the administration should have advised you of the problems that you might face as a woman who sought a career in law?

Mrs. FASTEAU. Well, I can only, in answer to that, say that I wasn't prepared to accept that, nor am I now. When I graduated from Vassar College I had no idea that I would run into the sort of thing I did. I think if I had heard it I would only have prepared my fight earlier than I did.

Senator COOK. I didn't mean to offend you as a result of that, and I appreciate your answer very much. The only real point that I was trying to make is that apparently the law school itself would allow law firms to come in and attempt placements and conceivably every one of those law firms would never hire a woman?

Mrs. FASTEAU. That is correct.

Senator Cook. And under those circumstances I am wondering why the administration itself did not feel compelled to tell women students the problem they might have. I do not mean that the administration should have discouraged you in any way from entering law school but rather that they should have informed you of their own discriminatory practices.

Mrs. Fasteau. I agree with that, but the problem is the law school does not acknowledge, as such, that it allows law firms which discriminate to use their facilities. They claim that the minute they hear about it they write letters to such firms.

They also claim, however, that they cannot perform any investigations. I have suggested having tape recorders in rooms where interviews are going on. I have the clearest kind of evidence. All of my female colleagues at the law school have, too. Since this doesn't seem to be enough for the administration, tape recordings of interviews would clinch it.

There is a substantial problem in that the powers that be in the law school won't admit to themselves these firms continue to discriminate. They keep saying they are implementing this policy of not allowing firms to discriminate to use their facilities.

Senator Cook. This is an unfortunate situation.

Mrs. Fasteau. That is right.

I have had several conversations with the Dean on that subject. He has, in effect, admitted just that. I think that I should bring to the attention of everybody who doesn't know that a complaint has been filed with the Office of Federal Contract Compliance against Harvard University which will, if successful, have the effect of keeping $2 million from that University for reasons of discrimination on every basis, including sex, throughout the entire University.

Senator Cook. I am aware of that.

Mrs. Fasteau. I thought you would be.

Senator Cook. My legislative assistant advised me that when he was graduated from the University of Kentucky Law School none of the women in his class of 130 had placements. So I think that the problem you present is one that you not only do by reason of the constitutional amendment, but also by reason of what should be just in this the 20th century.

Thank you very much.

Senator Bayh. Might I ask one question about the qualifications one has to meet, you had to meet, or your contemporaries had to meet for admission?

We have had a number of accusations made, and I hope we can either prove these or lay them to rest, that before admission to certain law schools and medical schools, a higher test has to be met by women than by men, that a quota is applied and that X number of women are admitted despite their qualifications and additional women applicants are denied admission. Have you run into this?

Mrs. Fasteau. Well, I am sorry that I haven't really gotten a clear answer to this question about Harvard. I have heard numbers of times that Harvard and other law schools have quotas. I don't know that for a fact, and I couldn't say it. Women may have to meet no higher technical standards on some one scale—such as grades or law boards—than men, for admission to law schools. I don't think there is a strict number quota for women, but I definitely believe that the admissions office has in its mind the fact that for every place they give to a woman some man who will practice law all of his life will be denied a job, whereas a woman will probably stop her employment when she begins to have a family. Therefore educating women is not considered as great a service to society. No recruitment efforts are made to encourage women to apply and the ratio of men to women remains about sixteen to one.

I am sure the number of women admitted to the law school is limited, but I just don't have any figures.

Senator BAYH. Thank you very much, ladies. We appreciate your testimony.

Our next witnesses represent the Washington Women's Liberation Movement.

I would be grateful if you ladies would identify yourselves for our record, please.

Miss GRIMKÉ. My name is Sarah Grimké.

Miss GOLDMAN. My name is Emma Goldman.

Miss GRIMKÉ. Angelina Grimké.

Senator BAYH. I might make one prior observation. It is rather obvious we are not going to be able to finish all the witnesses before some of us would like to have a short break to dispose of some noontime business.

The plans of the committee now will be to hear the present witness and then to recess for whatever time seems appropriate, depending on the time of recess, and then come back to hear the last three witnesses this afternoon. So please proceed, ladies.

STATEMENT OF EMMA GOLDMAN, WOMEN'S LIBERATION, WASHINGTON, D.C., ACCOMPANIED BY SARAH GRIMKÉ, ANGELINA GRIMKÉ

Miss SARAH GRIMKÉ. We are here representing the Washington D.C. Women's Liberation. We do not use our own names because we are speaking for the group and any three of us could be speaking here today.

We have come here today to support our sisters who have been working since 1923 for the passage of this amendment to guarantee equal constitutional rights.

At the same time we recognize the fears of working women that an equal rights amendment may be used exploitatively against us rather than to guarantee rights. Equal rights under the law will give women the confidence to struggle further for liberation.

The nature of the male supremacist system which viciously discriminates against women in all levels of our society will be exposed. No woman could be against equality under the law, but we know that the amendment cannot guarantee real equality.

For example, the 13th, 14th, and 15th Amendments promised constitutional equality to black men, but now, after 100 years of legalistic doubledealing in the legislatures and the courts, black people have learned that they must struggle in the streets and seize what is rightfully theirs. For women, as for blacks, equal rights are a beginning.

We know, moreover, that the Constitution was written to protect the privilege and status of white men. We do not come here to ask for our freedom. We are going to take it. It is rightfully ours.

As was said more than 100 years ago, I ask no favors for my sex. I surrender not our claim to equality. All I ask our brethren is that they will take their feet from off our necks and permit us to stand upright on the ground on which God has designed us to occupy.

Miss GOLDMAN. These hearings are being held at a time when it is obvious that women are standing up for their rights. We know that this amendment will be passed by Congress in a vain attempt to absorb the growing pressure exerted by women in their own behalf.

The liberation of women has become the issue of the 1970's. The mass media—television, comic strips, magazines from the Atlantic Monthly to Family Circle—has distorted, manipulated and exploited the women's movement. And now the U.S. Congress, close on the heels of Playboy Magazine, manifests its blatant hypocrisy by frantically searching for a way to co-opt a growing women's revolution.

We are aware the system will try to appease us with their paper offerings. We will not be appeased! Our demands can only be met by a total transformation of society which you cannot legislate, you cannot co-opt, you cannot control. The struggle belongs to the people.

Miss ANGELINA GRIMKÉ. That concludes our testimony to the Senate, such as it is represented here, but we still have a few things we would like to say to the people and particularly the women who are here.

So we talk to the people who are here. [Standing and facing the audience.]

At best, they offer women equal jobs with equal pay under this amendment. But we know that this is only an equal right to be exploited in a market economy based on profit and not on human needs; that even then women who work in a home will not be paid for the work that they do. And they still have the responsibility for the home whether they have outside employment or not.

They offer us equal access to higher education, but we know and especially today, that this is an equal opportunity to be shot and slaughtered on the campus.

The amendment will place equal responsibility on men and women for alimony, divorce, and child custody. But it does not deal with the reasons for failed marriages: the nuclear family which cannot meet human emotional needs. The nuclear family which is an isolated unit of the husband, wife and children, in this society takes no responsibility for children. We must, all of us, men and women, take up this responsibility. We are experimenting in new forms of cooperative and communal living. We are working to provide free 24-hour a day child care, community controlled.

The amendment will give us equal social security benefits, but what use are equal social security benefits in a country where all the necessities of life—food, clothes, housing—cost money and inflation is wildly out of control. The health industry makes over $21⁄2 billion profit each year after taxes. At the same time most of our people just simply cannot afford to be sick or old. We are working for free health care, for safe contraception and for abortion on demand.

They offer us an equal chance to kill and to die for the U.S. imperialism. We oppose the draft for both men and women. But like our sisters in Vietnam and Cambodia, we will fight for the liberation of oppressed peoples wherever we are.

Finally, they offer us equal representation on juries and equal criminal penalties within a totally corrupt and repressive judicial system. So-called justice for the Panther women in New Haven means being without bail in solitary confinement, being pregnant with no medical care, giving birth under armed guard, having the baby taken away by the State without the mother's consent, and later being used as a bribe for false testimony.

Constitutional amendments will not make any difference to these things, only revolutionary change can meet the demands that women are making today.

Free our sisters, free ourselves, all power to the people. [Leaving the room.]

Senator BAYH. Will you ladies care to stay for any questions or do you prefer not to?

Would someone like to question these ladies if they would stay for questions?

Senator COOK. Mr. Chairman——

Senator BAYH. I don't think that is indispensable, but I have a question that I think would be appropriate.

I would like them to clarify some of the concerns they have.

Senator COOK?

Senator COOK. Mr. Chairman, I would like to move that the last lady's remarks, be excluded from the record. I so move because of her statement that her testimony had been concluded and because I feel her remarks were intended for the audience rather than for the committee.

I also want to say, as an enthusiastic cosponsor of this amendment, that if I were to make a speech to a comparable group, which was unwilling to be questioned, I may not have extended the courtesy to such a group as you extended to them on this occasion.

I only say this because I think these hearings should be put in true perspective without the use of intimidation by either the witnesses or the committee.

Senator BAYH. I think the Senator from Kentucky, in his own inimical fashion, has put the previous remarks in proper perspective.

If the Senator has no serious objections, and in deference to our previous witnesses, I would like to consult them. If they desire to have their remarks listed in the record, then I see no reason why they should not be in the record. We don't need to agree with all the assumptions and conclusions. If they desire that they be part of the record, whether their position before the committee was just symbolic rather than substantive, I have no objection to these remarks being in the record.

Senator COOK. Obviously I want my remarks to state how I feel about the actions of the previous witness. I think that when witnesses are invited to testify it is because the committee wants to do the best job that it can. If it is the desire of the Chairman to keep those remarks in the record obviously it will be done.

However, I want my remarks to follow her remarks, because I think the record should show that after the first two witnesses concluded their remarks they got up from the witness table, faced the audience, and said that they wished to speak to the audience, not to the committee, for the purpose of the record.

Senator BAYH. We will take the appropriate steps to see that the posture, as well as the postulation of the witnesses, is included in the record.

I, of course, suppose that some committee chairmen and subcommittee chairmen might be concerned about manifestations of support or dissent exhibited in the hearing room. I do not care to follow this policy myself, realizing the extent to which strong feelings are involved in a matter such as this. The reason I was hopeful that the witnesses would permit us to explore their thoughts more fully is that the Chairman has recognized the strong show of support on the part of those who are presently in the hearing room, yet there seems to be significant support for some of the statements of the last witnesses and for the conclusion that the Chair was drawing, that they were opposed to the efforts to amend the Constitution in this fashion.

I am not sure that is a reasonable conclusion, and that is why I wanted these witnesses to clarify whether they were or were not in favor of this; indeed, one following their reasoning would have to conclude they saw no reason for the 13th, 14th, and 15th amendments.

Heaven only knows our history reflects the length of time it took to implement those amendments, but without those amendments it seems we would have been even harder pressed to do the job that was long overdue.

We ask the indulgence of the next witnesses, the three groups remaining, if they would permit us to recess and return at 2:15.

(Thereupon, at 1:15 p.m., the subcommittee took a recess, to reconvene at 2:15 p.m., the same day.)

AFTERNOON SESSION

Senator BAYH. Our next witness is Mr. Mortimer Furay, Metropolitan Detroit AFL–CIO Council.

Mr. Furay.

STATEMENT OF MORTIMER FURAY, METROPOLITAN DETROIT AFL–CIO COUNCIL

Mr. FURAY. I am here today representing the Detroit Metropolitan AFL–CIO Council, the organized labor group of my community.

I have been employed in the labor movement since 1937, most of that time representing women who worked—and worked, I might say, with their hands, not in a professional category, but women who worked with their hands.

I feel it an honor to be the first to speak against adoption of the so-called "Equal Rights Amendment," Senate Joint Resolution 61.

I might call on the indulgence of the committee to say that I cannot help but remember what happened to Andy Warhol who was shot by a feminist.

First of all, I feel the passage of this legislation is unnecessary since women are covered by the provisions of the 14th amendment guaranteeing all persons equal treatment under law. As if, indeed, any legal act of and by itself can guarantee anything. But more to the point, unless this proposal includes the Hayden retention proviso, it will repeal the thousands of laws, rules, regulations, directives, opinions, which now protect women from insidious and destructive working conditions visited upon them largely because of their biological composition and background.

[Voice from the audience.]

Senator BAYH. If the witness will yield, just as we permitted great flexibility this morning and tried to provide the maximum courtesy to all our witnesses, I trust that everyone will proceed accordingly this afternoon.

Please continue.

Mr. FURAY. These laws are the result of years of research, debate, social action of momentous proportion for adoption and years of court testing. They have had subsequent reappraisals and amendments. While many are obsolete and inadequate, they constitute a protective force absolutely mandatory for women's protection.

The proponents of this legislation know not of the havoc they will wreak upon our women workers, their marriages, and familiar obligations. The irony is that this is being done in the name of women's liberation. I want to concentrate my testimony to rebut those who claim the difference between the sexes is minimal and we therefore no longer need protective legislation.

The proponents of pseudo-equality charge that modern industrial and technological methods of production has reduced the need for women's protective legislation. But the opposite is the case. Experts in the field of biomechanics have pointed out that the Second Industrial Revolution of mechanization and automation has created great changes in our workforce. And I would like to cite three of them:

1. Women are far more numerous in the workforce and therefore their safety and well-being constitutes a far greater concern than ever before. We are now talking about more than one-third of our national workforce.

2. Women are more intimately connected with mechanical schedules than they were a decade ago. They spend five to six times as much time of the day, touching, moving, or manipulating something mechanical.

3. For the first time in our history, more than 50 percent of the women in the workforce are married.

Researchers in the field of industrial medicine are beginning to explore the problems of female employment and as a result have uncovered a mass of information that points out the need for special concern, special protective legislation. Certainly, it rebuts those who are recommending the vacating of protective legislation.

Dr. Anna Baetjer in her book "Women in Industry" warns "women should not be required to work more than 55 to 60 hours a week even under very pressing circumstances. Most authorities recommend a maximum of 48 hours." That's why we in Michigan are fighting to retain our present, albeit obsolete, 54-hours maximum workweek law for women.

That's why the AFL–CIO Council of Detroit supported the fight of Stephanie Prociuk, of the United Auto Workers Union, in her suit against the Occupational Safety Standards Commission of the State of Michigan when they attempted to repeal the hours limitation law under the guise of the mistaken notion that the days of female exploitation are over.

It was during that legal battle that the Ad Hoc Committee Against the Repeal of Protective Legislation rallied the women of Michigan to support litigation that would enjoin the State from repealing protective laws.

They induced Dr. Erwin Tichauer, the worldwide authority on biomechanic medical engineering of the New York University

56

Medical Center Institute of Rehabilitation Medicine, to testify as
to his studies on the functional anatomy of the body. His testimony
covered the locomotor performance, efficiency, sources of trauma,
injury, fatigue, accident proneness, and the effects of work places
on the physical health and safety of female workers, all subject
matters of protective legislation.

What he had to say, unchallenged by the attorney-general of the
State of Michigan, led Circuit Court Judge George T. Martin, to
permanently restrain the Occupational Safety Standards Commission from repealing the Michigan maximum hour law. Dr. Tichauer's
testimony induced the following paraphrasing for presentation
here.

He pointed out that while industrial mechanization has improved
conditions for the workers of America, it has created a whole new
set of problems.

While the workload has been consistently lower in industry, a
by-product of that change has been an increase in work stress on
relatively small parts of the anatomy. Previously, people worked
with their arms, back, hands—now they only push buttons and
therefore, the work stress is concentrated, say, on the tip of the
finger.

It is the women who are largely engaged in manipulative work,
in requiring intensive application of effort for the entire working
day. While operations have been simplified, the entire body is no
longer used but certain muscle groups, repetitive movement patterns and certain parts of the anatomy of women are being stressed
intensively for the entire day, while other parts are at rest.

This has lead to an imbalance in work stress in respect to individual body segments in many female occupations. As a result, this
concentrated work stress has created fatigue factors over long periods
of time for women who, because of their structure, are unable to
cope with it from both a medical, as well as from a plain physical
discomfort point of view. This excessive concentrated work strain
appearing after intervals of time is the overriding factor in the
increased hazard to the health and safety of women so involved.

Because of these factors, women now need the protection of State
protective legislation more than ever before—not less. To wipe
out such legislation by enacting the proposed pseudo-equal rights
amendment, as I have said before, without benefit of the Hayden
proviso retaining all such current protection, would be a real blow
to women resulting in further enslavement rather than their liberation.

Those who think equality will be gained by legislation are either
ignorant or naive. My introductory course in sociology at Wayne
University, long ago, dispelled any such belief in that panacea
route. I was cited the passage in Tacitus "Quid leges sine moribus?"
"What are laws without mores?"

I remember the postulation "When the mores are adequate, laws
are unnecessary; and when the mores are inadequate, laws are use-
less." The mores on the status of women are inadequate and un-
reflective of sex equality. All our norms on this subject are designed
by the evil power of male chauvinism. The statutes, the rules and
regulations, the customs and folkways, the taboos and fashions, the
rites and rituals, the ceremonies and conventions, and finally even
etiquette of our society are blocks to accomplishing the objectives

of true sex equality.

Our entire culture is captivated by chauvinism. You can forget the inscription on the pediment of Langdell Hall at Harvard's famous law school "Non sub homine, sed sub Deo et Lege"—"Not under man but under God and Law"—for the corruption on this subject is all pervasive.

Simone de Beauvoir, the French sociologist, correctly reminds us that in all societies:

It is woman who has been subject and slave, man who has been ruler and master. Woman is vassal, receptacle utensil, the nearest tool of man. She is conquered, subdued, vanquished in sexual encounter as in life. Man takes, woman gives. Man acts, woman waits. Man is always the one, woman the other. Always destined to wander in the world of man and never in the world of her own.

There is no genuine equality in the two sexes. Woman is always the other, never the one. Condemned to an eternal alterity and religious platitudes. "Blessed be God that he did not make me a woman," so runs the Hebrew prayer. Among the blessings for which Plato thanked God was first that he had "been born free and not a slave" and second, "that he was a man and not a woman." Herein lies the philosophical basis for male chauvinism supported by Aristotle who also maintained that "a female is a female by virtue of a certain lack of qualities." Do you wonder where the religious basis for our chauvinism comes from? St. Paul said:

The man is not of the woman, but the woman of the man. Neither was the man created for the woman but the woman for the man. For the husband is the head of the wife, as Christ is the head of the church. Let the wives be to their own husband in everything.

And we wonder where our double standard comes from.

John Chrysostom ascertained that "among all savage beasts, none is found so harmful as woman." St. Thomas Aquinas said she "was an imperfect man and an incidental being." The Genesis says that it was Eve who made the man eat the apple and it is she in consequence who is the author of his misfortune. This obvious male chauvinism must be counteracted because it is one of the roots of the evil.

It is man that has made the mores, they are the ones that created religions and philosophies, they occupy the center of the world stage. There has never been equality between the sexes, there is no equality now. The double standards of conduct assuredly still exists even though there has been a constantly narrowing gap between the privileges of the sexes.

Are women the marginal people destined forever to remain on the fringes of history? That condition must be rectified. If there is a woman problem and the intensity of the denials confirms the fact, it exists because biology places certain limitations upon cultural aspirations. To reconcile two careers, one based on physiological fulfillment and the other upon cultural creativity, this was the problem for which our society has found no satisfactory solution, but find one we must.

Women and men alike occupy many different statuses, but for women, the norms attached to these statuses pull them more frequently in two different directions and leave them in conflict caught between contradictory events. A woman can never forget her sex. On the role of sex to women, Margaret Mead has so aptly written:

A woman's life is punctuated by a series of specific events. The beginning of physical maturity at the menarche, end of virginity, pregnancy and birth, finally the menopause, the reproductive period as a woman is definitely over, however zestful she may be as an individual.

Each of these events because once past, can never be retraced, is momentous for a woman, whereas a man's ability to command an army or to discover a new drug is less tied to the way his body functions sexually. Sex in its whole meaning, from courtship through parenthood, means more to a woman than it does to a man although sexual acts may have more urgency for men than for women.

Senator BAYH. Would you yield just a moment?

Mr. FURAY. Yes.

Senator BAYH. Have you had the good fortune to get to know Dr. Mead?

Mr. FURAY. I have met her, I do not know her.

Senator BAYH. How old a lady would you say she is?

Mr. FURAY. I would think she is in her seventies.

Senator BAYH. I suppose from all of these things that she describes for women she is probably beyond that point. Do you suggest that she is not making a significant contribution in many, many ways to this country right now?

Mr. FURAY. I think Margaret Mead has made a greater contribution to the cause of women than any other woman in America, as a sociologist and as an anthropologist. I feel that the remarks she has made relative to this subject bear more listening to than those of any other person in the country.

Senator BAYH. It seems to me that if you take Margaret Mead's contribution and put that in proper perspective, it totally refutes what you are saying. [Applause.]

Please, let us permit our witness to respond.

She testified before our committee when we were discussing the 18-year-old vote. She did not relate the sexual attributes or the physical characteristics of a man or woman's sexual ability to their ability to comprehend, to their ability to contribute.

We are talking about apples and oranges; we are talking about different things.

Mr. FURAY. I think her study, Senator, of the sex behavior and the sex patterns of people both from the primitive and from a modern point of view is unmatched by any other anthropologist in the world.

Senator BAYH. Yes. But with all due respect, I do not see how what she says here pertains to the problem of whether we should pass this amendment or not. She is saying that there are sexual differences between man and women. Can anybody deny that? What we are talking about is her ability to produce and to be treated as an equal in other areas.

Mr. FURAY. That is exactly what I propose in my argument.

Senator BAYH. You may continue. I just wanted to make a point.

Senator Cook?

Senator COOK. Mr. Chairman, I will ask questions at the conclusion of this testimony.

Mr. FURAY. To continue:

It was Mira Komarovsky who had to blast the President of a woman's college for claiming that a knowledge of cooking is more important than a knowledge of Kantian philosophy.

Since the days of Adam and Eve, there has been a sexual division of labor though not determined in any particular way. There is such a division in all societies, and it is fairly uniform because women bear the children in all societies. When we begin to talk about sex this is the one thing that we cannot forget. This is the one thing that Margaret Mead keeps reminding us of. The sexual division of labor is done on a biological base. The differences in the sex status can vary only within the limit of sexual capacities. Among these are the most important—the reproductive functions of the female, the physical strength of the male. The exceptions upon complete examination confirm the rule. These are facts with which we must reckon. These are conditions which we must understand in order to correct.

George Murdock, one of society's most famous anthropologists and sociologists, in a study of 220 nonliterate societies discovered regularities in the sexual division of labor. In those societies, warfare, metal working, hunting and fishing were predominantly male activities. Cooking, the manufacture and repair of clothing, pottery, and firemaking are predominantly female activities. Agriculture, on the contrary, was shared by both sexes.

In civilized society, we similarly find a sexual division of labor, which remains to this day. In view of the slowly growing equality between the sexes, it is somewhat surprising to note the number of voluntary associations still limited to one sex. The Cubs, the Brownies, the Boy Scouts, the Girl Scouts, YMCA, and the YWCA, are but a few examples where men and women do approximately the same things but do them in separate associations.

In spite of the decreasing emphasis on the sexual criteria in many occupations, it still persists. The separation of sexes is both a cultural and social phenomenon. It is deeply ingrained. Culturally speaking, men and women have a different status and conform to different norms, not only in our society but in all societies. This has been a stubborn deterrent to solve the sex equality problem.

Amran Scheinfeld, author of "Women and Men" made this observation:

There is an important difference between the group principle as applied to any two races, two nations or two economic or social classes, and as applied to the two sexes as groups. Given time, individuals of any given race, national or social group can cross over, blend with, or be completely absorbed into another race, nation or society. Biological barriers need not be in the way. But the situation with sexes as a group is entirely different. No other such distinction and unalterable division of mankind exists, where it can never be possible for the two groups to merge and where, with each generation, men and women start off with the same biological dividing line between them and the same general tendencies toward differentiations in their work and social roles.

This kind of differentiation then is destined to last as long as human society will endure, few of us would not have it that way. In no society do male and females do the same thing, occupy the same status, share identical interests, conform to the same norms, or aspire to the same kinds of achievement. All societies channel the conduct of sexes in different directions just as they signalize the difference by a distinction in dress. But this does not mean that we cannot nor should not provide equality of treatment.

It need not be the same, but it should be equal. If the 14th amendment has not brought equality under the law, to our women, how can anyone postulate that an equal rights amendment will do it, an amendment that removes from the statute books the very laws which helps raise women a part way up to the position of male, if only in the marketplace of their hire?

It is going to take the executive, legislative, and judicial branches of our Federal Government, our State, city and county governments combined with all the civic, religious, fraternal, political community, labor organizations to just start the job of bringing equality to women.

All the public media will have to join all of our educational institutions, from nursery school to college, to disseminate our intentions. Our economy must be marshalled, our power structures mandamused and our entire familial structures must be completely reoriented, if the desire for sex equality is to become a reality. It will take, not brassiereless Fridays, nor broom-riding frolics, but the complete mobilization of our social institutions to do that job.

Women must learn John Donne's lesson "no woman is an island" and men must learn the Jeffersonian maxim "freedom is indivisible" if we are to win this fight.

Will the passage of an equal rights amendment prevent the employers of this Nation from subtly discriminating against women by designing their buildings, factories, laundries, furniture, machines, tools, and fixtures for men, as they now do? Of course not. We live in a society so male-oriented that the forms of discrimination assault women every second of their lives. They are discriminated against covertly and overtly, grossly and in the most subtle fashions!

Take the matter of simple tool design. The charts and hard data for body measurements used in determining dimension of tools and hardware which come in contact with workers have been designed in an industrial environment largely-geared to men. As research for design progresses and data for measurement was sought, it came from available statistics.

There is a great amount of data available on men but much less available on women, surprisingly less. Generally speaking, it is a common occurrence that a woman has to adapt herself to a tool or a machine designed for the body contours and body measurement of men. Though the situation is being corrected, it will take from 10 to 15 years for new information to filter through the design process. Most of the information supplied industry for tool, furniture, and machine design comes from the "Measurement of Man," charts published by the Whitney Library of Design or the "Human Factor in Design" published by the Mitre Corp.

What data there is compiled for women deals largely with typewriters. Research now going on is 7 years behind the change in the work force. It takes at least 5 years to get the results of research into production. It will, therefore, be a long time before machines will be properly designed for women. This is a matter of concern about the health and safety of working women.

When Dr. Tichauer was asked the question by the Circuit Court "What is the effect of the extension of the workday beyond 10 hours a day and beyond 54 hours a week for women?" This is a law that would be repealed if the amendment were passed," he answered.

"Considering the normal state of affairs among women, that most have another job to do by looking after household and domestic chores, it would definitely be detrimental to occupational safety and it would certainly not enhance their health and well-being. I would also say that even if they have no domestic work, the length of the work day beyond 10 hours would, in my opinion, increase her accident proneness and would, worst of all, render her more liable to off-the-job accidents such as are caused by erratic movements which would end by her burning herself on the kitchen stove, using an iron, or being involved in traffic accidents."

[Voices from the audience.]

Senator Cook. Mr. Chairman, as a result of having visited some college campuses where I did not have the right to speak I hope that all here today would understand that everyone has a right to speak. I would also hope that every lady in this room would give those of differing opinion an opportunity to be heard.

I am not sure that all of Mr. Furay's statements are relevant to the amendment to the Constitution. I find his point concerning existing equal rights legislation especially irrelevant.

Senator Bayh. The point is well taken.

Mr. Furay, please continue.

Mr. Furay. When asked "Are women more susceptible to injury, to accidents than men because of differences between men and women," he answered:

In certain fields of manufacturing activity or domestic activity, yes. In other fields, no. This cannot be answered categorically. Women are structurally different from men. They have a different anatomy, not only in the quality of their organs, but also by dimensions which affect the mechanical advantage or disadvantage of the muscles employed. The ability to perform mechanically, the ability to produce work output, is related to the lean muscle mass of the body. This is undoubtedly less in the case of women. Women have certain different respiratory characteristics, the vital capacity of respiration in the case of women is lower, so if you compare the physique of women and men, her work tolerance, her endurance, are definitely lower.

When you have a group of people who engage in a task which is heterogeneous, men and women, old and young, all workers of equal efficiency and at equal levels of physiological health and well-being at the beginning, only as the length of the task lengthens, will individual differences become more apparent. In many occupations, there are numerous situations where the efficiency of woman is not impaired for 6, 7, 8, 9, 10 hours, and then all of a sudden, the limit of activity of work tolerance has been reached and efficiency drops, and personal levels of comfort drop and accident risks increase. The first aspect as to the difference between men and women, are many having home duties. The second factor, is the anatomical differences between men and women, the muscle structure, the number, and extent of the muscle structure, also the body measurements with respect to muscle.

When asked if any known statistic indicates a comparison between male and female muscle power, he answered:

The National Safety Council states in its manual that the endurance of women to perform is one-third less than that of men.

He responded to this question, "Do you have any figure indicating the extent to which women have a difference in their respiratory quality?" by testifying:

Most researchers, including myself, have found this vital capacity to be 20 percent less. The operating characteristics of the respiratory system relate to oxygen transport to the tissues, to the muscles, and determines the combustion efficiency. If a woman has less muscle mass, the amount of oxygen she needs to perform will also be less. Like in a motor car, the size of the engine being smaller, her fuel intake and the oxygen intake to burn this fuel will be less. This ability to inhale less of oxygen affects the ability in much the same way as with a motor car. A small engine has difficulties on a long climb that might be performing very well in the city. In the same way, a trained athlete develops large muscle capacity that he must have, and therefore, develops great endurance and greater peak performance levels. It might not always affect their ability to produce average performances, but many examples show that the ability to perform at peaks is impaired in women. Scholars and students of the subject, including myself, ascribe this to the combined effect of less muscle mass and less respiratory capacity.

We learned from Dr. Tichauer's testimony, the real impact of male chauvinist antiquated concepts, deeply rooted superstitutions upon the life of our women. We learned the disastrous effects upon them as wage earners. We were shocked to learn of our ignorance-induced complicity in this matter.

We finally learned to value what protective laws we have and the need to improve them, expand their scope and broaden their coverage. We learned enough to oppose, with determination and resolution, the repeal of any law designed to protect women, whether it be to satisfy the selfish needs of some employer, or the misdirected action of some of our citizenry infatuated with the concept of power unaware of power's awesomeness and responsibility. Under both categories, we place the supporters of the equal rights amendment.

Please do not pass this legislation because you will have contributed to the darkness on the matter and added to the plight of the working women of America.

I have some slides I would like to show to support the testimony. It will take a couple of minutes to show them. And I would like the members of the committee to see these slides.

If we can turn the lights out we will be able to get a better idea of the slides.

These slides will show the differences between men and women are irrevocable and beyond the simple statutory solutions suggested by the passage of a national law.

Senator BAYH. Mr. Furay, if this is going to be a course in elementary biology to show that men and women are different I do not know what is going to be proved by it.

Mr. FURAY. It is going to show you the difference in terms of work, stress, and strain, and the necessity of there being State Legislation that will be repealed by the very nature of the law that you are contemplating.

Senator BAYH. Go ahead. No one is contending that there are not differences between the sexes. I think that is far afield from the issues at hand. But please go ahead. I hope you can enlighten us.

Mr. FURAY. These slides show the spread of body dimensions peculiar to women.

[Showing slide.] The woman on the left is 5 feet 10 and the one on the right is 5 feet 9; interquartile range is 11 inches. The area of difference between man is very much less, one-third less. He runs from 5 feet 8 to 6 foot only, only four inches difference. And yet machines are designed for men.

The problem of adopting equipment to a wide bracket of body measurement as in the case of women is much greater than in the case of men.

[Slide.] Men and women are exposed to machines as seen here in the same interquartile range, and they need not fit body measurements. Excessive bending is required, as pictured in the lower two cases. This is not usually the case as required in men.

[Slide.] Here you see a case where you move to a lower posture. As shown in this slide, the activity abdominally—here we find a woman seated on a chair designed for men, subjecting her breasts to a continuous impact. Will the passage of Senate Resolution 61 change the millions of these chairs that women are forced to sit in?

[Slide.] The height of the chair was too high for the woman's legs. It interferes with the venous flow in the legs and this is shown in the slide.

Will Senate Joint Resolution 61 lower that chair?

Senator BAYH. Sir, when were these pictures taken?

Mr. FURAY. Within the last 10 years. And they are in textbooks, and that is where they come from. And I have already stated the textbooks used in my testimony.

Senator BAYH. In other words, these differences exist today despite all the protective laws you have been referring to?

Mr. FURAY. That is right. They need more laws, not less.

[Slide.] Here is a drill press simulated by sticks and counterweights to record the level of activity of the shoulder muscles shown in the upper myelogram on the right and the muscles of the abdomen as shown in the lower myelogram. The slide shows that when sitting high the abdominal muscles are used, as you can see from the scan.

[Slide.] When moved to a lower position as shown in the next slide, activity of the abdominal muscles is reduced as shown in the lower myelogram. When working essentially with arms there is no pronounced fatigue, while when using abdominal muscles, particularly during the menstrual periods, this causes greater discomfort. The female abdominal cavity containing the reproductive organs is subjected to pressure which would expose the woman to accident hazard if she works excessive hours.

[Slide.] This slide shows the difference between men and women. These differences are due to contours of the spinal and the vertebral columns. Shown on the left is a man lifting identical weight counterbalancing it with his trunk. The female, because of the bulging buttocks and torso on a relatively slim base, counterbalances it with her body mass.

When a woman lifts a load she has to lift her body up, and therefore the amount of physical exertion may be from 10 to 15 percent higher than that of a man. Her metabolic rate and energy expenditure is also higher. If the working day is excessively long her fatigue will be more acute.

[Slide.] Due to the limited number of sizes and heel shapes in safety shoes for women the pelvic angle varies widely. The woman shown on the left without shoes will tire more quickly and will suffer back strain, while the woman wearing the shoes on the right is appropriately balancing. Differences in body structure are affected by heel size. A person with a large pelvis is under lifting stresses before even starting to lift. Women have larger pelvises than men.

[Slide.] This slide represents the measurement of lifting in terms related to time scale. An electrical recording of the muscle and respiration rates is obtained. The electrocardiogram was measured during an hour's interval for almost 4 hours. It shows that in terms of lifting a long time back strain is induced.

[Slide.] The top one is the electrocardiagram and the lower one is the myelogram. This type of testing has only been conducted among women because fatigue signals cannot be secured on men within the 4-hour time set for this experiment. Women produce fatigue signals when lifting even a little load after 2 hours. And men could not produce them until after 6 hours or more. The passage of an equal rights amendment would prohibit laws on weight-lifting for women workers.

[Slide.] Shown here on the right is an old-fashioned pair of pliers used by males for a few minutes doing electric wiring, but which are used today by women in wiring operations for the entire day. Notice the twist bends shown on the left. The pliers are designed to eliminate the wrist. Unfortunately on most assembly jobs for women the pliers provided—are on the right—the effect of this will be shown in the following slide.

[Slide.] Here you see a woman in simulated plier gripping—these with her wrist bent. She is wired for myelogram recording.

[Slide.] Here you see the same woman in a simulated plier gripping test with her wrist straight. In the background observe the myelogram in operation.

[Slide.] In slide 15 here you see the chart showing the effect of each test. On the left you see the results of 40 different subjects using the straight wrist plier grip. Thirty-six divulged no complaint. Four complained of soreness on the portion of the hand. On the right you see the results of 40 different subjects using a 40-degree ulnar-deviation pliers grip. Notice only 15 did not complain. Seven complained of the coporeal tunnel soreness and two complained of a sore elbow. These same tests were given to a man, and the man showed no objective or subjective signs of fatigue under the same load or torque in either case. Why? Because a woman's hand is shaped differently.

The structure is smaller and the muscles weaker. Yet thousands of women are daily put through this ordeal because the tools they used were designed for men.

[Slide.] This slide shows the different effects of increasing the workday from 10 to 12 hours on men and women in respect to accidents per hour. The upper two lines on the left show the sudden increase in accidents among women when they lengthened their day from 10 to 12 hours. It reveals a wide gap increase of over a hundred percent. The bottom two lines, again on the left, show little effect of increasing the work day from 10 to 12 hours on men in respect to accident per hour.

On the right is shown the night shift control example.

Here you see the result of efficiency on women between two plants doing exactly the same work.

On the left is the 8-hour example. Note the efficiency starts off at 89 percent, rises to 97½ percent during the third hour, and tapering off to 94 percent at lunch. After lunch from 96, tapering off to 89. This is a typical work pattern of efficiency.

On the right you see the dramatic results of a prolonged workday on women. They start off with only 82 percent, rise and go up to 97½ in the fourth hour, and then sag down to 90 percent at lunch.

From then on they maintain the same efficiency until the middle of the ninth hour, when it suddenly plummets to 78 percent. This pattern did not prevail for men. The reason for this performance decay was simply fatigue.

[Slide.] This slide shows the increase in the hourly output for women working machine tools in a British war plant when the hours were decreased from 63½ to 55½ per week. While the increase was typically gradual, it ended up by revealing that more was accomplished in 9 hours than had been achieved in 10 hours. This pattern did not prevail for men.

[Slide.] The final slide. This slide relates to the efficiency and output. It was made under the auspices of the National Research Council. And the left half of the graph shows that when the 9-hour day was increased to 10-hours per-day shift women's output and efficiency dropped sharply, even more so on the night shift as revealed on the right side of the graph. This pattern did not prevail for men operators.

We can have the light back on now.

I will conclude.

I hope that by my using these slides that I have not only dramatized the effect of being a woman and a worker, but that I have added to the sum total data on this subject matter. It must be manifestly clear that women are different from men—vive la difference—that they are subject to inequality as a result of their sex, and it is cruel and unjustified.

To correct this injustice you must not add to it by repealing enacted laws, but set in motion forces that will sweep inequality from our lives, not with the sameness of treatment, for the sexes are not the same, but rather by designing equality of treatment with justice of goal.

Voice From the Audience. I question the scientific basis.

Senator Bayh. We appreciate your testimony, Mr. Furay.

Voice. I think this is a good argument for the amendment.

Senator Bayh. If you have any additional information to give us we will be glad to include it in the record. I would be glad to explore some of the thoughts raised by the witness.

I should note that counsel has been conferring with Claudia Lipschultz who is a biologist at the Smithsonian Institution. She takes serious exception to some of the biological hypotheses that have been made, and if she would care to express herself we will include that statement in the record.

(The statement follows:)

STATEMENT BY CLAUDIA LIPSCHULTZ, SILVER SPRING, MI

Dear Senator Bayh: While listening to Mortimer Furay's testimony this afternoon, I felt compelled, as a biologist, to comment on the merits of the scientific arguments for protective legislation for women workers put forth in the first portion of testimony and in a slide show following it.

The conclusions of an experiment or research project are strongly affected by the question one asks and the way in which that question is stated. To this testimony the speaker brought data and conclusions which suggest to me that the question asked was, "How can we show women to be problem workers." Nowhere do I note a denial that men as well as women would benefit from a meticulous and solicitous inquiry into their safety and health on the job— only that their short-comings were not searched for and tested as rigorously. Granted, some data on men was presented but clearly the concern of these researchers was with the "Special problems of female employment," and stress fatigue factors "because of their structure." I can only see these euphemisms as the special vocabulary of, to paraphrase the speaker, a pseudo-scientific discipline.

An aura of authority can grossly and dangerously mislead the ill-informed in any area of life. All jobs entail some safety problems—and perhaps some risk of exploitation. I would not be surprised if it were men who were petitioning for equal rights to protection under the law, for instance, to curtail the hernias and back injuries common to men—in industry and construction work— who routinely lift weights, often too quickly or incorrectly. All that has been demonstrated by the testimony is that people who constantly work long hours (therefore get less sleep and rest) at tedious work which engages only a small aspect of their minds or bodies become fatigued and less efficient.

Mortimer Furay said he sought to rebut "those who claim the difference between the sexes is minimal and we therefore no longer need protective legislation;" his view of the problem was perhaps his chief error. If there be any cogent scientific question in this issue, it is, "What are the tasks of a given job; and, what strength, skills, or stamina do they require." Then ask which individuals can do the job. Jobs have no gender; and no group of persons has exclusive ability.

I hope your committee will recognize my testimony and realize that the testimony to which I refer, quite seriously, was more frightening than laughable in its claim to serious consideration. It was an insult to the intelligence of both women and the committees to which these findings have variously been reported. I hope I may respect your judgment more than that.

Thank you.

Sincerely,

Mr. Furay, you mentioned that the 14th amendment provides equal protection, and you say on page 11:

If the 14th amendment has not brought equality under the law to our women, how can anyone postulate that an equal rights amendment can do it?

Do you know of any one case brought to the highest Court of the land under the 14th amendment that has been successful at all?

Mr. FURAY. No. I think that the 14th amendment is just not enforced. And I do not think that this amendment that you contemplate passing will be enforced, because it is impossible to enforce this law in and by itself.

Senator BAYH. Are you familiar with the legislative history surrounding the 14th amendment, what the basic purpose was for enacting the 14th amendment?

Mr. FURAY. Casually, yes.

Senator BAYH. Did it have anything to do at all with sexual equality?

Mr. FURAY. No.

Senator BAYH. Then is it wrong to assume that the Court would thus not put the same kind of emphasis on sexual equality that it has placed rather successfully on racial equality when determining sex prosecutions under the 14th Amendment?

Mr. FURAY. I think the Court is wrong if they interpret the 14th Amendment to mean that a female is not a "person."

Senator BAYH. Since we have had no action under the 14th amendment, would it not suggest that we need another amendment dealing specifically with the problem of sex?

Mr. FURAY. Not when you are going to remove from the statute books of 50 States laws protecting women.

Senator BAYH. In my judgment, your slides were a bit self-defeating. If you are suggesting that these conditions documented by the slides exist under the present "protective" laws it seems to me that those laws are really not doing the job.

Mr. FURAY. They are not doing the job. And there should be more laws, not repealing the laws we have.

I would like to cite to the Senator a case in Michigan. When the 1954 hours law has been repealed, one of the companies in Detroit, had for years been prohibited to work their women over 54 hours a week suddenly placed their women on a 10 hours a day 7 days a week. And they were working in a refrigeration plant. Now, the women went into court to see to it that this law was put back on the statute books, contending that it was not within the power of the Commission that repealed it to do so. And believe me, those women are grateful that that law is now back on the statute books, because they no longer have to work more than 54 hours a week.

Senator BAYH. I think we are directing our attention at certain conditions that are injurious. It seems to me they are so whether they apply to men or to women. [Applause.]

I have been rather familiar during the last 16 years with the legislative process, working for some of these social programs which have been sponsored by the AFL–CIO.

Am I wrong in suggesting that the AFL–CIO would think it would be wrong for a man to work 10 hours a day 7 days a week in the same refrigeration conditions?

Mr. FURAY. No. We want men covered under the law. But that is not what is being proposed here. The proposal now is to repeal the law.

Senator BAYH. Quite the contrary, that is not accurate, sir. The proposal provides that the laws ought to be applied equally.

Mr. FURAY. But they never are, sir.

Senator BAYH. What is the position of the AFL–CIO as to what the average workweek should be?

Mr. FURAY. I think the position of the AFL–CIO is that all overtime ought to be optional on the part of the employee, that no one should be forced to work more than that.

Senator BAYH. Is there a general acceptance of a 40-hour workweek?

Mr. FURAY. By industries? Unions do not control the workday of the employee, it is industry that controls the work day of the employee, as you well know.

Senator BAYH. What about the legislation that is proposed by your unions?

Mr. FURAY. In Michigan we propose and have fought for optional overtime, that there be no overtime mandatory to hold a job.

Senator BAYH. But in order to have an option of overtime work you have to have a base period of how many hours?

Mr. FURAY. Forty hours.

Senator BAYH. What is the Michigan law?

Mr. FURAY. The basic law now in Michigan is 54 hours, that is, no woman can be asked or directed to work more than 54 hours. There is no maximum law for a man in Michigan. We would like to have the man covered by that 54-hour law too.

Senator BAYH. Why is that, if I may ask?

Mr. FURAY. So that all overtime can be made optional.

Senator BAYH. It sounds to me then that you feel men ought to be treated equally with women?

Mr. FURAY. I think that men ought to be treated equally where there is a question of equality involved. I think that there is need for special legislation to protect women. And I think the contours of their bodies, the shape of their bodies, and the kind of bodies that they have necessitates their being protected by law.

Senator BAYH. Is there a standard workweek by statute in Michigan? You referred to the 54-hour overtime. Is there a 40-hour workweek or a standard similar to that?

Mr. FURAY. No.

Senator BAYH. How does one judge what overtime is?

Mr. FURAY. They are covered by either union contract, or they are covered by the Federal Fair Labor Standards Act.

Senator BAYH. In the union contract, what is the general target, 40 hours, 38 hours?

Mr. FURAY. In the union that I work in it is 40 hours a week, and time and a half beyond 8 hours in any 1 day, and beyond 48 hours in any one week. And in addition in the contracts that we sign all overtime is optional for men and women.

Senator BAYH. The 40-hour period is applied——

Mr. FURAY. Yes, as well as the 6-day, a woman and a man do not have to work 6 days in our industry.

Senator BAYH. So far as the union contract and the collective bargaining effort, men and women are treated equally as far as the 8-hour day?

Mr. FURAY. As far as the premium for over 8 hours a day, certainly.

Senator BAYH. And there is acceptance apparently of that 8 hours as the standard period of labor during any one day?

Mr. FURAY. To determine the overtime.

Senator BAYH. Do you support the premise of equal pay for equal work?

Mr. FURAY. Yes.

Senator BAYH. I remember well in the 1959 session of the Indiana Legislature when I was the Speaker of our Indiana House of Representatives that the one vote I cast was to break a tie in support of this legislation. Do you see any language whereby a woman physicist might get $23 less than a male physicist performing right beside her?

Mr. FURAY. Absolutely none.

Senator BAYH. I suppose it is fair to assume—you stress female exploitation—that you would be equally concerned relative to male exploitation. Is that accurate?

Mr. FURAY. I sure am.

Senator BAYH. I would like to look very quickly at page three of the testimony of Dr. Tichauer, who testified as to studies on the functional anatomy of the body. His testimony covered locomotive performance, efficiency, sources of trauma, injury, fatigue, accident proneness, and the effect of places of work on physical health and the safety of female workers, which are subject matters of protective legislation. Is it fair to assume that a man subject to the trials, tribulations and stresses in work is going to be less efficient and more accident-prone than he would be if he were under normal circumstances? Is this a phenomenon particularly applicable to women? Did Dr. Tichauer have any comparable study relative to men?

Mr. FURAY. Yes. Dr. Tichauer's testimony revealed that in certain kinds of work there was a vast difference between the woman's ability to maintain a regular output over a long period of time.

Now, he definitely showed by his testimony and by his graphs, some of which I have introduced here, that there is a difference in the ability to work beyond 8 hours efficiently.

Senator BAYH. You suggested there was a difference in certain kinds of work and certain kinds of work over long periods of time. Now, we are talking about extremes there, are we not?

Mr. FURAY. We are talking about over 40 hours a week.

Senator BAYH. But by your own contractual arrangement you suggest that we strive for a 40-hour workweek?

Mr. Furay. Yes. I think all people should be protected in working.

Senator Bayh. What I am suggesting—perhaps in a circuitous bit of questioning—is in this day and age I think we have progressed a bit beyond the sweatshop and child labor——

Mr. Furay. They are still around Michigan.

Senator Bayh. Perhaps there is still reason to keep our guard up. But in my judgment it would be foolhardy for any employer to employ women beyond the point at which they could be effective.

Mr. Furay. Apparently they do.

Senator Bayh. How extensive is this?

Mr. Furay. Well, General Motors and the Chrysler Corp. of Detroit, when they felt that the 40-hour had been repealed, immediately placed their women on 6 days a week 10 hours a day.

Senator Bayh. When did this happen?

Mr. Furay. A year and a half or 2 years ago.

Senator Bayh. For how long a period of time?

Mr. Furay. Until we got the law put back on the statute books. And then they reduced their time down to 54 hours.

Senator Bayh. What about the union contract? What is the UAW contract in this area?

Mr. Furay. It does not cover that aspect of their working condition.

Senator Bayh. The union contract does not specify a certain workweek?

Mr. Furay. For the purposes of the payment of overtime, premium pay, but not whether they had to work it or not.

Senator Bayh. Is it voluntary or nonvoluntary?

Mr. Furay. It is nonvoluntary.

Senator Bayh. It is interesting that the UAW recently went on record as in support of this amendment, if indeed it was a problem in Chrysler and General Motors, unless we are suggesting that UAW officials are not sympathetic with the problems of those they represent.

Mr. Furay. I read that resolution they adopted at Atlantic City, and I did not draw the same thing from it that you did, Senator.

Senator Bayh. What did you draw from it?

Mr. Furay. I drew that they were focusing attention of it—you certainly have a copy of the resolution available. I am sure that it was sent here.

Senator Bayh. Yes, I have it. I would be glad to put it in the record at this time.

Senator Bayh. I do not see how one can escape the conclusion that the auto workers in convention a week or two ago did endorse this principle.

Mr. Furay. They did not endorse the equal rights amendment, Senator, that you are now considering.

Senator Bayh. I suppose we can both look at this from our particular standpoint.

Perhaps we should read the resolution.

* * * that we give special attention to a legislative program of more direct concern to women such as a national program for child-care centers, campaigns to end the exploitation of household workers, the repeal or reform of abortion laws, opening up higher paying and skilled trade jobs for women, legislation for a $2.50 national minimum wage law covering all workers, and support for the campaign for enactment of an equal rights amendment to the Constitution of the United States.

Mr. Furay. Then I am wrong. [Applause.]

I read the newspaper reports of the convention. And I read quotes from it, and I did not read that; it was not in the newspaper that I read. I did not attend the convention at Atlantic City.

Senator Bayh. I am sure you were not trying to mislead us at all. But we are just trying to put the record straight.

Mr. Furay. It is the first time—I know that that union until this year had always opposed the passage of equal rights amendments.

Senator Bayh. That is accurate. And hopefully the AFL–CIO in their wisdom, when they have had a chance to study the facts, will also see that things are changing.

I want to call your attention to some practical experiences I have had. You suggest that in Michigan you still have the problems of the sweatshop and this type of thing. I have been in a number of plants in Indiana. I have shaken hands with hundreds of women employed there at the RCA plant in Bloomington; the Westinghouse plant, with 5,000 workers as I recall in Indianapolis; and the Columbia Record plant in Terre Haute, where I would daresay 95 percent or more of the employees are women, because of a unique talent that they have to do the job better than the men. Yet given the situation in which they are denied the right to work more than a certain number of hours in a plant that is comprised almost totally of women, you give the women at work there a difficult time as far as earning promotions because you limit the number of hours that they can work to accomplish the goal.

Mr. Furay. I think this matter could be handled by collective bargaining between the plants and the employees there.

Senator Bayh. But it has not been.

Mr. Furay. But I think that it is absolutely——

Senator Bayh. Excuse me. How are you going to handle it by collective bargaining if you have a State law that prohibits it? That is one of these protective laws that we have in some States, such as California providing that "Thou shalt not work beyond X number of hours." How do you get around that?

Mr. Furay. That law, unless it is changed to include both men and women as far as overtime is concerned of which I am in favor. And we support legislation to include all people under the obligatory overtime aspect of it. But what happens is that you do not include the men, all you do is repeal it for the women. And it is in that area that we are unalterably opposed to it. Under the guise of equality, by removing that amendment, you do not solve the problem for the working women. For that woman who is married and who has got children and has to go home to take care of her household duties, her mother duties, and her wife duties, to be forced to work overtime is wrong. And until men are included under that, it should not be repealed.

Senator Bayh. It seems to me we are suggesting, not that we lessen the protection, but that we protect everybody equally under the circumstances. I do not want to embarrass an individual who is not here now, but I noticed that there was a photographer taking pictures here earlier this morning that was probably shorter than any woman in this room. Now, to suggest that that man would be equally qualified to a fellow like Sam Huff or a professional football player to go into a plant and remove refrigerators I think is rather ridiculous. It seems to me that we need to match the individual to the job.

You might have some women that are perfectly capable of moving refrigerators. You have some men who are not. But to say flatly that no woman is going to move a refrigerator, isn't that unjust?

Mr. FURAY. I do not think so. I think that the law that would protect a person from excessive work is something that ought to be passed for everyone, to prevent people from strain. And if we now have laws on the statute books that protect women, then let us bring the men under them and not repeal them for women. That is all I am saying.

Senator COOK. If all such laws are repealed, is equality attained?

Mr. FURAY. Nobody is protected, that is right. And that is exactly what working women don't want.

Senator BAYH. Well, that is at least what some men representing working women say. And I appreciate your plea. Let us have more perspective. We can have differences of opinion and hopefully still keep our cool.

Let us look a bit further. Apparently there are some jobs that women are more qualified to hold than others because of their dexterity. Working on transistor radios, for example, women perform better than men because of their small fingers.

What about doctors? Should we discriminate against women in the field of medicine?

Mr. FURAY. I do not believe that women ought to be discriminated against in any field.

Senator BAYH. Is it fair to have higher standards of admission set for women for entrance to medical schools than it is for men?

Mr. FURAY. I do not think so.

Senator BAYH. What is your reaction to the testimony given earlier by one of the witnesses relative to her experience trying to get employment with several of the big law firms in New York City? Do you think this is a fair test; fair atmosphere?

Mr. FURAY. It is an outrage.

Senator BAYH. What about women being permitted to serve in the stock market as buyers, brokers?

Mr. FURAY. I think a woman should be permitted to work in any job that she is capable of handling.

Senator BAYH. What about the distinction provided by some statutes which deny women the opportunity to attend Bar? Is that equitable?

Mr. FURAY. I think that is wrong.

Senator BAYH. I have no further questions. I am not sure that I agree with everything that you have said, but I certainly believe that you gave us your testimony with proper motivation. And there is room for differences of opinion.

Senator Cook?

Senator COOK. Mr. Chairman, I agree that his testimony was given in that light, but I disagree with him in many respects.

Mr. Furay, you stated that the executive, legislative, and judicial branches of our Federal Government, our State, city, and county governments, combined with all the civic, religious, fraternal, political, community, and labor organizations will be needed to start the job of bringing equality to women.

Mr. FURAY. That is right.

Senator COOK. What is wrong with that?

Mr. FURAY. There is nothing wrong with it.

Senator COOK. If that is really necessary then what is wrong?

Mr. FURAY. I am in favor of all of that.

Senator COOK. Mr. Furay, your remarks concerning the magnitude of the movement needed to bring "equality to women" could be extended to each of this Nation's major problems. There isn't anything wrong with that.

Mr. FURAY. I think probably the fight to eliminate discrimination against women will be more difficult to accomplish than any of the other things you have just cited.

Senator COOK. After reading your description I say to you, God help the women in this country. And thank God that they did not have that information during World War II, because we would never have won it. [Applause.] During World War II women were working 10 hours a day under inadequate conditions—conditions that probably should have been changed by labor unions years ago. [Applause.]

I am beginning to feel the same way about psychiatrists. I think that the large number of patients in mental institutions today results at least in part because psychiatrists have convinced them that they suffer from more problems now than ever before. American women are not asking you to protect them from the robber barons and inadequate working conditions of this country. They want something else, something which they are not receiving at the present time but which is attainable.

Mrs. Hernandez previously stated that existing special legislation, such as that regulating the number of hours per week women may work, could be repealed. I do not believe this to be necessary. Protection under the law does not have to lead to differential treatment. A constitutional amendment which says that the rights of the sexes are equal does not necessarily negate legislation designed to protect women.

If the women in the State of Massachusetts want to repeal the law which established a 40-hour workweek because they want to earn as much money as some of the men your union represents, let them go to the State Legislature and repeal the law. But it seems to me that we have many men in this country, particularly in your position, that are in effect saying, now, ladies behave yourselves, we are trying to protect you." I must say to you again, they are not looking for your help in that respect. Your remarks included a citation from Amran Scheinfeld in reference to the only unalterable division of mankind, sex. I feel that Scheinfeld's observation lacked courage.

Mr. FURAY. No, but it is good information, and it is correct.

Senator COOK. But don't we all know that that difference exists? You said in your last remarks, vive la difference. The point I am making is, it did not take any courage to say that there is a difference between the sexes and yet not between the races.

Mr. FURAY. He was not writing it to display his courage, he was writing it to make a point. And he made the point, and adequately made the point. That is the reason I cited it.

Senator COOK. Maybe so, Mr. Furay. Possibly I misunderstood what I read. But it just seems that you are trying, apparently from the standpoint of the AFL–CIO, to equate the rights of women to specific job requirements and working conditions. For example, do you agree with a law of the State of Nevada which says that a woman should not lift anything over 10 pounds in weight?

Mr. FURAY. No.

Senator COOK. I would guess that labor organizations in Nevada were responsible for promoting the 10-pound bill in the State Legislature.

Mr. FURAY. It could be. I am not familiar with the facts.

Senator COOK. It appears that you are trying to justify your position by saying that a person who happens to be different is not entitled to have complete and absolute equal rights in this Nation. I will present your position to my three daughters when I go home tonight and I know they will reject it, as they should. For instance, I think it is wrong for the young lady from Harvard to maintain an "A" average during law school and subsequently earn $6,000 a year while a male student may maintain a "B" average and later receive $11,000 a year. To extend this to the labor field, I could visualize men and women doing the same amount of work but due to existing legislation the two sexes are placed in separate categories with the result that women receive less salary. Such a situation could result under Nevada's "ten-pound" law.

Mr. FURAY. But the passage of this law would not guarantee it.

Senator COOK. It would not guarantee it at all, Mr. Furay. It will only guarantee it if the executive, legislative and judicial branches of our Federal Government, State, city and county governments, combined with civic, religious, fraternal, political, community and labor organizations, get together and see to it that the long neglected inequality between the sexes is ended. The bad feature about your saying that all these governments and groups are needed to insure equality between the sexes is that all of these bodies are controlled by men. You are saying that all of these men need to get together and realize that women are equal to men. It should have been said a long time ago. [Applause.]

Mr. FURAY. I will say it.

Senator COOK. I am really not preaching to you. I am just saying that I think you tried to prove your point with nuts and bolts. And I think where it fails is that the proof of the point that is being made in these hearings is an establishment of mentality, not nuts and bolts and chairs. It is a matter of accomplishment. I think it is a matter of where everyone stands and this is the difference.

Mr. FURAY. If I may in conclusion paraphrase what I have said before to answer you, Senator, I came here to see to it that current legislation on the statute books of the various States that are kept there to protect people—you may call it nuts and bolts——

Senator COOK. I believe that most of the existing legislation on the topic can remain because it is within the police power of any given State to solve a particular situation. For example, under your union contracts you treat workers differently according to age, whether that age be 17 or 30. Various States differ on voting-age requirements, my own State extending the vote to 18-year-olds. The point I am trying to make to you is that this equation is unsolvable to me. We say that 18-year-olds in our State are responsible citizens and are entitled to vote, yet in your State you say they are not entitled to vote. That is the same thing as saying that a woman is not entitled to do something, and therefore legislation exists to forbid her from doing it.

Mr. FURAY. If a Federal piece of legislation is designed to eliminate that right for the 18, 19 and 20-year-old people to vote in that State you would fight it. That is exactly what I am down here doing now.

Senator COOK. This is where you and I disagree, because I do not think this amendment is relevant to the law of the State of Michigan. You seem to take the position that it repeals all of the police powers of a State to regulate whether a person 5 feet 2 or five feet 8 should be given a particular job, i.e., a woman or a man. If the existing legislation is in fact within the police power why do you think the "equal rights" amendment will repeal all this legislation? You treat women differently than men in your labor contracts. You are afraid that more women will enter the labor market with a resulting effect on the union.

Mr. FURAY. I work in a union where 85 percent of the members are women.

Senator COOK. And I will make you a bet that the leadership includes only men.

Mr. FURAY. That is not true.

Senator COOK. What is the percentage?

Mr. FURAY. Over 50 percent of the people working in the group that I work for are women.

Senator COOK. If 85 percent of your members are women and only 50 percent of the leadership positions are held by women, then women to some extent have been cheated. Which sex occupies the top position?

Mr. FURAY. The top position in our union is held by a woman. She will testify tomorrow.

Senator COOK. That is good. I commend you.

Senator BAYH. Thank you very much, Mr. Furay. We appreciate your testimony.

Our next witness is Miss Marguerite Rawalt, from the Women's Bar Association of the District of Columbia, accompanied by Mrs. Lee Berger Anderson, president of the Women's Bar Association of the District of Columbia.

STATEMENT OF MARGUERITE RAWALT, WOMEN'S BAR ASSOCIATION OF THE DISTRICT OF COLUMBIA; ACCOMPANIED BY LEE BERGER ANDERSON, PRESIDENT

Miss RAWALT. Senator Bayh, Senator Cook, you have just stated my name, Marguerite Rawalt. I am a member of the bar. I have served as president of two national bar associations. But more importantly to this hearing, I think, I served on the President's Commission on the Status of Women and on the succeeding citizens advisory council on the status of women from 1961 to 1968.

And as I said, my appearance here today is for the women's bar association, along with Mrs. Lee Berger Anderson, our president.

Now, the lawyers of our women's bar association, which is one of the largest local bar associations in the country, are in full and wholehearted support of the equal rights amendment.

I would point out that the equal rights amendment calls for equality of rights for men or women. There are few laws on the books that discriminate against men. But because most of the restrictive laws, as we prefer to call them, operate to restrict and limit the rights of women, we are still accustomed to speaking of it as equal rights for women. But it would cover equal rights for men.

We are filing a long statement here today in the nature of a legal brief. And I shall not attempt to read it, time would not permit it.

Senator BAYH. I will ask that it be put in the record in toto.

Miss RAWALT. Thank you, sir. I will abridge it and hit the high points of it.

This brief supports the thesis that American women as of today are without equal protection of law under the present Constitution, under the 14th and Fifth amendments, particularly, as interpreted by our U.S. Supreme Court. And as Justice Holmes said, the Constitution means what the Court says it means.

The points I made are supported by citations, particularly of the Supreme Court, as set out in the footnotes.

And we are here to invite the Congress to tell the Court that women are a part of the Constitution by enacting an equal rights amendment.

The 14th amendment reads:

No State shall make or enforce any law which shall abridge the privileges and immunities of the citizens of the United States; nor deprive any person of life, liberty, or property without due process of law; nor deny to any person within its jurisdiction the equal protection of the laws.

Point one, the 14th amendment did not give women the right to vote. Susan B. Anthony thought so, and went to court, but they soon found out that this was not so. And so it took a constitutional amendment, the 19th, to give women the right to vote. It took very little time for a court to announce that the 19th amendment gave women the right to vote, and that is all that it gave them. And we know that is true today.

Point two, the 14th amendment did not give women the right to practice a lawful profession. In 1872, the U.S. Supreme Court upheld the denial to a woman of the right to practice law in Illinois, and in doing so affirmed a decision of the Illinois Supreme Court which said, "That it belonged to men to make, apply and execute the laws," and this "was regarded at common law as an almost axiomatic truth."

Third, the 14th amendment has not been held to extend to women the right to work at any lawful occupation of an individual's choice. There is a long line of decisions of the Supreme Court. The Court has applied the 14th amendment, the equal protection clause, to strike down a San Francisco ordinance which denied licenses to operate laundries to Chinese. In 1914 it outlawed a Texas statute which operated to deny the job of freight train conductor to a fireman-engineer.

In 1915, the Supreme Court voided an Arizona statute which restricted an alien Austrian cook from working in a restaurant.

These cases are cited in footnotes. I will not take the time to give their names.

In 1918, the State of California was told that it could not deny a license to a commercial fisherman, Japanese nationality. To this day, research has failed to disclose a single case decided under our Constitution in which our High Court has upheld the right of an individual female to work at any lawful occupation of her choice. To the contrary, the Supreme Court has applied the 14th amendment and the equal protection clause thereof to limit and restrict women, as I see it.

In the case of *Muller* v. *Oregon*, decided in 1908, the Court upheld the hours limitation for women workers by declaring the principle that: "Sex is a valid basis for classification." Women as a class could be denied equal protection under the 14th amendment. This decision has supported and undergirded the whole structure of restrictive labor laws on women workers, and stood unchallenged until congressional action of 1964.

Sex as a "valid classification" has marched down through the years to deny women all sorts of rights. And I will point out as one of the later ones in 1960 to deny the rights of Miss Allred to matriculate and attend Texas University A&M College for a degree in horticulture which she could not obtain in any other State college. Sex was ruled a valid classification for keeping her out of the University.

Back to the *Muller* v. *Oregon* case, that case was supported by a very comprehensive brief written by Brandeis, who later became a Supreme Court Justice, at the behest of the National Consumers League and other representing sentiments of numerous labor unions. I wonder if some of the charts displayed today were from that brief.

Title VII of the Civil Rights Act of 1964 raised the hopes of women high in the field of employment, because as we all know, as it has been discussed today, it forbids discrimination in an employment on account of sex.

The Equal Employment Opportunity Commission created thereunder as its rulings stand today, requires that virtually all jobs must be open to men and women based upon qualifications only.

And then we have been in the courts under title VII since 1967. Individual women working on the assembly line had to go into court at their own expense and at the risk of their jobs, let me say, to challenge the hours laws in California, the weight-lifting laws in Georgia, and the weight-lifting laws in Indiana. And out of all this we have two landmark decisions. The first by the U.S. Court of Appeals of the Fifth Circuit, and one by the U.S. Court of Appeals in the Seventh Circuit in *Weeks* v. *Southern Bell Telephone and Telegraph Co.*, and in the case of *Bowe* v. *Colgate-Palmolive*, which has been discussed here today.

I want to point out that at one time these cases were a total loss, the first three cases put into the court by these women were lost cases, until the National Organization for Women, which was a newly formed civil rights for women organization, of whose legal committee I became chairman, came to the fore, to these women who had lost their cases, and offered to take their appeals up—which was done—furnishing financial support and legal counsel.

Senator Cook. May I interrupt at this point?

Miss Rawalt. Yes, Senator.

Senator Cook. In essence, Miss Rawalt, what you are saying is that in recent years the predominant action on the part of women plaintiffs has been to have certain pieces of State "protective legislation" declared in violation of either the Constitution or title VII of the Civil Rights Act; is that not correct?

Miss Rawalt. Precisely so. The first case challenged was the lifting laws in Georgia and in Indiana, and the case that is still undecided in the ninth circuit which challenges the hours law of the State of California for women only.

Now, title VII therefore has not opened wide the doors of employment opportunity. And I would like to quote from a 1-month old authentic survey published by the Bureau of National Affairs which provided a reply. This is a first survey of 150 executives made jointly by ASPA and the BNA—the American Society of Personnel Administration and the Bureau of National Affairs.

The employers were represented by these executives who were divided about 60 percent representing larger companies employing 1,000 or more, and 40 percent executives in smaller companies from every part of the United States. The survey revealed that today 59 percent of employers still disqualify women on the basis of sex; 51 percent still apply the State "protective" laws, notwithstanding EEOC rulings, and even recent rulings of State attorneys general that Federal law supersedes; 49 percent apply State maximum hours laws for women.

Senator BAYH. Excuse me.

Is it fair to ask if you, or the Bureau of National Affairs, or anyone else had similar information, inquiries, or responses thereto prior to the passage of the 1964 Right Act with the title VII provision, to see whether—we have gotten it down from 100 percent to 51 percent, or down to 54 hours? That is far from perfect, but it shows that the door is opening, and perhaps with a little more religious enforcement, we are going to be able to significantly help the problem.

Miss RAWALT. Yes, Senator Bayh. The Women's Bureau publications contain those data, of course, over the years, they are published periodically, as you know.

Senator BAYH. What is your judgment? The statistics indicate that it is far from totally successful. Has there been significant progress since 1964?

Miss RAWALT. I would say there has been significant progress. There has been some progress, but not significant.

Senator BAYH. We have been led to believe——

Miss RAWALT. In other words, not 100 percent of the employers disqualified women purely on the basis of sex, perhaps, before. But still today, after all these laws and decisions, we have 59 percent of all of them admitting that they still disqualify women on the basis of sex.

Senator BAYH. You may proceed.

Miss RAWALT. The next point I would like to make which hasn't been covered is that the 14th amendment does not insure fair and equitable property rights to married women. In every State in the Union, there is one or another kind of legal disability or restriction which limits the property rights of married women, as reported by the President's Commission on the Status of Women.

And I think it is all summed up very nicely in a 1944 court opinion of the Florida Supreme Court:

* * * a woman's responsibilities and faculties remain intact from age of maturity until she finds her mate; whereupon, incompetency seizes her and she needs protection in an extreme degree.

Senator BAYH. The court could have said that her mate needs protection also.

Miss RAWALT. Not from the standpoint of property rights.

Senator BAYH. Not from the standpoint of property rights?

Let the record show that there was great laughter, and that the Chairman asked the question facetiously.

Miss RAWALT. "Upon the advent of widowhood she is reinvested with all her capabilities which had been dormant during her marriage, only to lose them again upon remarriage. Intermittently, she is protected and benefited accordingly as she is married or single."

Now, the property rights, I can't take time to go into. But there are 42 common-law States and eight community-property States. And they have limitations upon the married woman's right to convey property.

The laws of Denmark, Sweden, and the Federal Republic of Germany provide a sort of formula that considers an equitable division of property upon termination of marriage. It provides:

That there first be deducted from each spouse's property the debts of that spouse. Inherited or separate property would then be excluded. The remaining properties, the marital property, would then be divided equally 50-50, between husband and wife.

I think that the proposed constitutional amendment would crystallize a 50–50 marital partnership principle and set up a controlling legal test for eliminating the remaining inequities as to the ownership or control of property.

The next point—the 14th amendment has not opened the doors to jury service to women. Although the Civil Rights Act of 1957 provided that women were entitled to sit on all Federal juries, there is a whole variety of restrictions on other juries still on the books of the States supported by the U.S. Supreme Court decision in *Hoyt* v. *Florida*, in 1961, which provides that no female person shall be taken for jury service unless that person has registered with the clerk of the court her desire to be placed on the jury list.

There are still not less than 20 States and the District of Columbia which provide different treatment for men and women as jurors. And, again, a constitutional amendment is needed which cannot be twisted into a ruling that "sex is a reasonable classification."

The 14th amendment through the decades was not applied to abrogate longer prison sentences for women criminals than for men.

It was not until 1968 that the Supreme Court of Pennsylvania voided that State's Muncy Act in a case in which a woman convicted of robbery was sentenced to prison for a term of up to 10 years, instead of the 1- to 4-year term which would have been the maximum sentence for a man for the same offense. I am glad my name appeared on that brief.

Now, I turn to congressional treatment.

Senator BAYH. May I interrupt here.

Miss RAWALT. Yes, sir.

Senator BAYH. The fact that until 1968 one of our great States continued to permit this kind of treatment reflects the modern fact of such discrimination which I hope you will bring graphically into focus. There is still this type of discrimination concerning housing and how woman are treated before the courts in this land. I am reminded of the assessment made by Simone de Beauvoir, as quoted by our previous witness, who said:

It is a woman who has been subject and slave, man who has been ruler and master. Woman is a vassal, receptacle utensil, the mearest tool of man. She is conquered, subdued, vanquished in sexual encounter as in life. A man takes, a woman gives. A man acts, a woman waits.

This sounds like something that may have happened when a man was dragging a woman around by the scruff of her neck, or carrying a limb to subdue her with. But it certainly doesn't happen in my house, and I am sure it doesn't happen in Senator Cook's house.

Senator Cook. No, it does not. But Simone de Beauvoir said that a long time ago.

In all good conscience, haven't we left the Dark Ages, and haven't our desires to shed some light on these inequities brought us together in an attempt to solve the situation?

I would pose one question to you based on the knowledge that you, Senator Bayh, and I have all worked on statutory law. You spoke of a prison term that was unequal. But you are not really saying that the courts of Pennsylvania adhered to this and gave both males and females the maximum sentence for their sex—10 years for females and 4 years for males.

The point I am trying to make to you is that as a member of the State Legislature I always contended that one of the greatest sessions we could have would be a repealing session rather than a creative session. My feelings stemmed from the need to remove much legislation from the books. I am delighted that your name was on a brief that concerned equal sentencing for men and women in Pennsylvania. But, in essence, we are saying only that the maximum sentence for an offense, such as robbery, differed between the sexes. We are not saying that the sentences actually handed down to both sexes were of maximum length.

Miss Rawalt. No. The situation was that the Muncy Act provided that if a female criminal received under the indeterminate sentence a sentence longer than 3 years, she must then receive the maximum allowable under the law. The judge sentenced her for 1 to 4 years. The sentence was entered that way.

And then it was reopened at the instance of the district attorney, who pointed to the Muncy Act, and she was resentenced for the maximum of 10 years. And two courts in Pennsylvania affirmed that before it got to the Supreme Court of Pennsylvania.

I might just say that the rationale behind the Pennsylvania act was, "It requires longer to rehabilitate a female criminal than a male."

[Laughter.]

Now, a word, if I may, on the congressional treatment of the equal rights amendment. All Congress is asked to do, as you gentlemen know, is to submit a proposed constitutional amendment to the States for their ratification. And at least 110 States have already taken official action memorializing the Congress to do so. But in the many recent years since 1923 the House of Representatives has never taken a vote on the resolution. It has never had an opportunity to since the present chairman of the Judiciary Committee was named. Its 435 Members have had no opportunity to vote on it because it has been bottled up in the House Judiciary Committee. And I quote the chairman who is an eminent lawyer, saying in 1956:

Distinctions based on sex had never been considered within the purview of the equal protection clause of the 14th amendment.

I want to note that. I agree with him.

Then in the U.S. Senate, the Senate has voted on this proposal on four occasions, but not, gentlemen, without first nullifying it by putting on an amendment and a rider which was known as the Hayden amendment. And as one Senator put it in 1956:

In one paragraph it would grant women equality and in the second, wipe out that equality by granting special benefits.

And so it is that the Senate has never truly passed the resolution for the equal rights amendment to go to the States as it is proposed. We hope it will do so soon.

We have had a great break in the news recently. And the Women's Bar Association is happy to applaud the action of the present Citizens Advisory Council on the Status of Women for its endorsement of the equal rights amendment on February 7, 1970, and its recommendation that the President request its immediate passage. And I am attaching to this paper——

Senator BAYH. Would you repeat that? The Commission recommends that the President request its immediate passage?

Miss RAWALT. The Citizens Advisory Council on the Status of Women appointed by President Nixon has recommended to him that he give his full support.

I attach to this paper a letter addressed to me dated April 28 from Mrs. Stuart, staff director to Mrs. Nixon, giving assurance of President Nixon's support of the equal rights amendment, and today's newspaper carrying the welcome declaration that Mrs. Nixon has declared her support of the equal rights amendment.

Senator BAYH. If I might interrupt, I hope that we get full cooperation from the Justice Department, because the committee staff has been requesting an unqualified position, which I hope will be forthcoming. I think the President's prestige and his influence would be extremely helpful to us.

I am glad to see that Mrs. Nixon has lent her support. If that is any indication of the way things operate in our household, that means that the President is probably going to be coming forth very soon.

Miss RAWALT. That leads me to make one comment that I think should be made here. Many references have been made to the *Martin-Marietta* case in the Supreme Court which has been accepted for decision; it was accepted March 2. And the Court did so, perhaps motivated or influenced by the Justice Department, the Solicitor General's request that it do so. But it must be borne in mind that the *Martin-Marietta* case does not present a constitutional issue. It does not present an equal protection under the 14th amendment issue, as I have seen the briefs so far.

It simply presents the question of the application of title VII of the Federal law and not the constitutional issue. We have several in the future—I hope not too far future—on the constitutional issue.

The AFL-CIO has repeatedly voted against the equal rights amendment, and in 1963 filed a statement to the Commission on the Status of Women saying that:

Exactment of the equal rights amendment would jeopardize existing State legislation establishing minimum wages, maximum hours, and other special provisions for the protection of working women against substandard conditions of employment.

That is their view.

But a great breakthrough has come through the United Automobile Workers.

Senator COOK. May I interrupt you? In that one paragraph there is a tremendous discrepancy. If the AFL-CIO filed a statement with your Commission the status of women saying that enactment of the equal rights amendment would jeopardize existing State legislation establishing minimum wage, maximum hours, and other special provisions for the protection of working women then again they are telling a woman that she can't work beyond a specific period of time even if she so desires. Do you interpret the AFL–CIO's statement similarly?

Miss RAWALT. Absolutely. Mrs. Mengelkoch, who is in the Ninth Circuit Court of Appeals, and Mrs. Rosenfeld, who is in the Ninth Circuit Court of Appeals, challenged the maximum working hours of California.

Senator COOK. May I say that they also could have included after "maximum hours," "maximum reimbursement."

Miss RAWALT. That is true. Not only does it deny them premium overtime, one and a half or twice the pay, but it keeps them from getting promoted, because the North American Aviation said to Mrs. Mengelkoch, we would like to have more women—I wrote a brief in that case, too—we would like to have more women working for North American, but we have to meet NASA contracts, and we have to put in overtime, and we must therefore have somebody who can work overtime without having the Attorney General of California breathing down our necks.

Senator COOK. In essence. what they are saying, then, is that when you limit women's hours you not only limit their total pay, but you also limit their ability to advance. This results because supervisory personnel are often required to work long hours and since women are not allowed to work such hours, they are prevented from holding supervisory positions.

Miss RAWALT. Right—which is a perfectly reasonable thing on the part of the employer.

Senator COOK. So that it works for the majority members of the Union, not the minority.

Miss RAWALT. For the male majority.

I was saying, a great breakthrough occurred in labor ranks when one of the progressive and powerful unions, the United Automobile Workers, changed its policy. It did not wait until 2 weeks ago to change it. The United Automobile Workers came before the Equal Employment Opportunity Commission at hearings held in May 1967 and there testified that they felt that these maximum hours laws for women, weight-lifting laws, laws barring them from certain occupations, should be repealed, that they were outmoded in today's economy.

And they backed it up 10 days ago in Atlantic City by voting for the equal rights amendment as a way to do that.

So caught up as the pawns in this trade union discrimination still in force in most of the labor organizations are the individual women, paying the same union dues as the men members. And I want to quote from a 1969 study published in the American Academy of Political Science:

The hard fact of the late 1960's is that less attention is being paid by the unions today to the special needs and problems of their women union members than was the case earlier in the century. Even at national level in the unions, where women make up more than one-half the membership, "tokenism" is the standard practice in placing one or two women on the national boards. The International Ladies Garment Workers Union has one woman thereon.

Now, we have made a lot of progress in 1960. I think we started off with the President's Commission on the Status of Women, and followed up by State commissions in every State, and by many other women's organizations coming into being and expressing their views.

In summary, this 14th amendment ratified almost 100 years ago has never yet been applied by the Supreme Court to guarantee to an individual female the right to work at any lawful occupation of her choice, although the Court has applied its guarantees of equal protection to insure the right to work at any lawful occupation to Chinese lanndrymen, Japanese fishermen, a train conductor, and an Austrian cook.

Its guarantees were early (1872) denied to insure the right of a woman to practice law.

Secondly, the Supreme Court has applied the 14th amendment to limit, restrain and deny freedom to work to women by upholding maximum hours limitations, upholding exclusion from certain occupations, and has rationalized denial of equal protection to women by lumping them into a class. It declared in 1908 that "sex is a valid classification" for limiting hours of work. And I hope to live to see the day when we modify that. And all the courts in the land are bound by this precedent which stands today, 62 years later.

Thirdly, title VII of the Civil Rights Act passed by Congress in 1964 forbids discrimination in employment, but after 5 years of operation it has not received consideration by the High Court. The case it agreed to take on March 2, 1970, does not involve constitutional equal protection. The petition that we filed in the *Mengelkoch* case asking it to take direct appeal from a three-judge court in the middle district of California was denied in 1968.

The 14th amendment does not insure equitable property rights to married women. Every State in the Union has some kind of legal disability as to ownership, management, and inheritance rights in respect thereto.

The 14th amendment has not fully opened doors to jury service by women.

Through the decades, the 14th amendment failed to abrogate longer prison terms for women criminals than for men, imposed by State law.

We urge this committee to stop further delay, to recommend passage to the Senate and proper submission of this act to the House. And we would call upon the members of the House Judiciary Committtee to eliminate the bottleneck they have maintained over the years in that committee and let the people of this Nation vote women into full citizenship.

Somebody spoke of the inscription over the entrance to the Supreme Court, "Equal justice under law." We hope that that will shortly and immediately be made a reality for the female members of our population, and that the Senate will submit the equal rights amendment without, as Martha Griffiths said, one comma added.

Thank you.

[Applause.]

Senator BAYH. Thank you very much, Miss Rawalt. I know of no one who has provided a more thorough background in the legal ramifications of this proposed amendment than you.

Let me ask you to expand your thoughts in several other problem areas in which I addressed questions to some of the other witnesses.

How is this going to affect, in your judgment, the whole area of family law in the matter of alimony, child custody, and this type of thing?

Miss RAWALT. I would point out that there are two reports on family law, one filed with the Commission on the Status of Women, and one filed as a Task Force Report on family law with the Citizens' Advisory Council. I had the task of being a chairman of both those committee reports, in which we analyzed all the State laws. As to the alimony, I don't have those task force reports in front of me, but I am sure they are in this record.

Some States now grant alimony to either spouse.

Senator BAYH. Excuse me. It would be helpful if you do have at your fingertips a compilation of the various ways different States treat this question. If you could let us have this, we would like to put it in the record at this time.

Miss RAWALT. I can see it on a page, it is all set out. And we will put those in the record.

Senator BAYH. Thank you.

Miss RAWALT. In some States alimony already runs either way. It could run against either spouse. If a tobacco heiress or a dimestore heiress wishes to be divorced, she may well be the one who should pay the alimony. The alimony laws vary terrifically in the States. There is no uniformity. But the recommendations of the task force, and adopted by the council, were that the matter of alimony must be left to the discretion of the courts, looking upon the individual case and the circumstances in that case.

You asked about child support,

Senator BAYH. Alimony, and child custody.

Miss RAWALT. Child custody.

Senator BAYH. And the questions of maternity benefits and criminal assault against women, this whole area.

Miss RAWALT. As to child custody, the State laws have a variety of provisions. In one State that I am familiar with, the husband has a preference as to custody of a son in the event of divorce, for example. And the custody laws, likewise we feel, are still a matter of decision in the individual case by the court which has before it the facts in the individual case. We speak generally of divorce, of course.

As to maternity benefits, I am going to ask Mrs. Anderson.

Mrs. ANDERSON. I think you can answer the question.

Miss RAWALT. Go ahead, Mrs. Anderson.

Mrs. ANDERSON. I can only speak for my thinking. I am not an authority as Miss Rawalt is. My thinking about the maternity benefit is that that is a benefit to the family. It is a benefit to the husband as well as to the children and to the prospective mother or wife.

Senator BAYH. Primarily, it is to the benefit of the children, is it not? You call that a maternity benefit, but it is primarily to help the children.

Mrs. ANDERSON. Primarily, to benefit the children.

Senator BAYH. Senator Cook, do you have questions?

Senator COOK. No. I have interrupted many times, for which I apologize. It is a tremendous brief. I want to read all of it in depth.

Your brief is very interesting because it refutes the testimony of the last witness who contended that women want to be protected by men. Also that the real movement is for women to rid themselves of certain protective laws passed by State legislatures as a result of the imagination of men.

It may not be as imaginary as we think, Miss Rawalt, because probably their original intention was one of protection. Conceivably it has moved from protection to discrimination and to the extent that it has moved it should be eliminated.

We see, for instance, that much of this legislation came into existence while women were denied the right to vote. Therefore, maybe she was entitled to a degree of expression legislatively.

Certainly, your brief establishes the point that the movement today contains women who came to organizations such as yours on their own initiative, rather than through union membership to eliminate discriminatory practices.

Your brief comes at a very opportune time, following the testimony of a representative of a major organization who, in essence, feels that whether women like it or not, should be protected. Being in a household of four daughters and a wife, there are times when I would like to have protection but I find I have very little.

Miss RAWALT. Loving protection.

Mrs. ANDERSON. May I take this opportunity to thank you for permitting the women's bar association to have Miss Rawalt testify as our representative.

Senator BAYH. Quite the contrary, we are indebted to you for making this study available to us.

I might point out that we have received a little bit of additional information from Catherine East, which has been provided to her by Mrs. Carolyn Teiner, the legal aid attorney in the case in connection with the Muncy Act. Apparently, the sentences of 200 women prisoners were reviewed as a result of the Supreme Court decision invalidating the Muncy Act.

Most of them were released from prison, having already served longer than a man convicted of the same offense would have served.

Miss RAWALT. We went into another case, but the Attorney General of the State decided not to appeal from the lower court, which had invalidated the law under the 14th amendment. There are still some laws on the books.

Mr. Chairman and Senator Cook, may I be permitted to put into the record also an account of resolutions and actions of the First National Conference of Women Law Students which was held April 3d and 4th, 1970, at the New York University School of Law. The meeting was attended by women law students from 17 law schools. And as two practitioners of law, we were delighted to see that women law students are awakened to the situation. And I would like to place the account of that first meeting in the record.

Senator BAYH. We would be glad to put that in the record. [Applause.]

Senator BAYH. Thank you very much.

Our next and last witness today is Dr. Elizabeth Farians, professor of theology, Loyola University.

STATEMENT OF DR. ELIZABETH FARIANS, PROFESSOR OF THEOLOGY, LOYOLA UNIVERSITY

Dr. FARIANS. My comment will be very brief. I am sure you will all be very happy.

Despite the separation of church and state, religion exercises a significant influence in this country. This should not be a startling statement. Anyone who ignores the influence is apt to find himself, or herself, in possession of less than a total picture of the de facto situation.

This is especially true of the way in which religion has influenced the position of women in our society.

That religion influences our society is inevitable at this time in our history and in fact it is probably good as long as true religious values are put forth. It is good because in a free society light from as many sources as possible should play on the landscape of human consciousness and radiate a rainbow of beautiful new freedoms for all of humanity.

In the past, some have said or implied that their religious views do not allow equality for women at all. Or some have said that it is not according to divine law for women to have their freedom. In fact, these persons have said that it is divinely ordained that woman's only role in society is as wife and mother.

Some of these people, among them some women, have also said that to give women full economic, political, or educational equality would interfere with the divinely ordained role of women and is therefore to be opposed.

In a free society we should receive all views, but we should do so in a critical way. This critical stance also applies to religion. We must try to determine if any particular religious view is of true value to our society, if it really fosters the welfare of humanity. If the view does, then we can welcome its support but if the view does not foster the welfare of humanity, it seems to me that the harm and defect of the view should be made clear. I am saying nothing new here; I am merely describing how we do, in fact, operate.

I asked to testify at these hearings so that I could have a chance to show that there is every indication that true religious principles do call for the total equality of women.

To cite two brief statements:

As you know, the Church is proud to have glorified and liberated woman and in the course of the centuries in diversity of characters to have brought into relief her basic equality with man but the hour is coming, in fact, has come, when the vocation of woman is being achieved in its fullness, the hour in which woman acquires in the world an influence, an effect and a power never hitherto achieved. (Second Vatican Council, Closing Messages, Paul, VI. Dec. 8, 1965.)

Since women are becoming even more conscious of their human dignity, they will not tolerate being treated as mere material instruments but demand rights befitting a human person both in domestic and public life. (Pacem in Terris, No. 41, John XXIII, Apr. 11, 1963.)

Besides the Roman Church, other religious groups are also calling for total equality for women. As you know, a woman was recently elected president of the National Council of Churches. The fact that over 80 denominations ordain women is also an indication of positive religious influence on the total equality of women. There is even a woman studying to be a rabbi.

I think it is important for this assembly to know that many Catholic women actively support the equal rights amendment and their numbers are rapidly increasing. In fact, a number of Catholic women have recently formed a coalition of their organizations so that their voices could be more forcefully heard regarding the equality for women.

Among these are the Ecumenical Task Force on Women and Religion—Catholic caucus; The Women's Committee on Freedom in the Church—The National Association of Laymen (Chairwoman), a group of women aspiring to be deaconesses; Women Theologians United; and the Coalition of American Nuns. St. Joan International Alliance also supports the equal rights amendment and is sending in separate testimony.

These women want the equal rights amendment passed and they want it now. They understand this amendment and they want the legal protection it will afford them. They are tired of waiting. They demand their God-given rights and they say to this committee and to the Congress and to the people of this country that they have no right to continue to keep women in a state of childhood and subjection.

I have not tried to prove anything here, because I think a theological disputation would be out of place. I have simply tried to describe the situations.

Women are persons. It is ridiculous that we have to keep on saying this. The very fact that I have to come to Washington, prepared testimony on this subject, and then find myself faced by an all-male committee shows how badly we need this amendment. I could go on and on but it is late in the day. The others before me have documented the case in every conceivable way.

I finish by saying that I can think of no more fitting way to celebrate the fiftieth anniversary of women's suffrage than to pass this amendment now and to pass it in honor of Alice Paul, the beautiful woman feminist who has given her entire adult life to this cause. We have heard enough. Let us get on with the vote. [Applause.]

Senator BAYH. Thank you, Dr. Farians.

I noticed with a great deal of interest the theological basis for your testimony, in the light of past objections raised by some religions. Does this portend a change—perhaps the word "enlightenment" is too prejudiced, but at least a change generally in theological circles as far as women are concerned?

Dr. FARIANS. No, I don't think so. I think that the problem here is one of having misinterpreted really basic true religious values; in other words, religion discriminates against women and understands women in some of the same kinds of ways that the general society does, and in fact reinforces and sometimes causes this kind of reciprocal interaction. And although we have these pious statements, we haven't always had the actions that follow them in the church either.

What we really need in the church is a civil and equal rights amendment also, you see. Because in one place it says all you have to do to have all your rights and responsibilities in the church is to be baptized, and then in another canon later on it says that only a male "vir", very definitely a male man, can be ordained. And in another canon it says that women can't have their rights, and many other things, and then they are classified with the idiots and the imbeciles and the children.

So, again, we need a special law which says a person is going to have all her rights and responsibilities which pertain to women as well as men. That is exactly the same kind of problem.

Senator BAYH. I notice a previous witness who opposed the amendment went to some length to quote Hebrew Prayers, St. Thomas Aquinas, and St. Paul relative to the inferior status of women. What would be your response to those quotations?

Dr. FARIANS. Well, there has been quite a breakthrough in Temple and Scripture study in the last 50 years, let's say, and it is filtering down to the Roman Catholic Church now, and it has been for the last 10 years. You will find that most Scripture scholars are interpreting Scripture in such a way that shows that when it was written it was written by those who reflected the prejudices of their own times.

So we must see these statements in that light and not as a matter of divine law which is unalterable for all time.

Senator BAYH. Thank you very much.

Senator Cook, do you have any questions?

Senator COOK. Yes.

I note with great interest your testimony on the historical influence of religion on the rights of women. I think that Mr. Furay was merly quoting from St. Thomas Aquinas and Jewish Prayers as to the servile position of women at that time. However, we cannot equate the inequality of women to religion when it becomes legal practice. Rather we must equate it to the attitudes of men toward women. Your paper, although supporting the distinction between church and state, indicates the influence of the church upon the actions of the state regarding women.

Dr. FARIANS. That is right. And that is why I was very anxious to testify, because I think that not enough people understand how religion has influenced our present situation. And we see a great many of the reasons why women are in a situation which is due to religion, and especially a religion that has been falsely interpreted.

When we realize this, then we realize that we don't have to consider these as laws with which we cannot tamper. We realize that they aren't divine laws. And that is why I was so anxious to testify.

Senator COOK. For instance, there is no divine law that allows the males of one religious sect in this country to practice polygamy. Rather polygamy probably resulted from attitudes of male supremacy and the obligation of men to care for the "relegated portion" of society.

You stated that you felt badly about appearing today because this committee included no women. Although the House includes a number of women members, I am unsure concerning the membership of Congresswomen on the House Judiciary Committee.

Dr. FARIANS. This simply proves my point. In other words, if women were equal and didn't need a special amendment, more than likely there would be more women than men on the committee.

Senator COOK. My point being that when the time arrives that committee assignments are no longer chosen purely from the standpoint of best serving constituents, it would be in the best interest of women for women legislators to serve on the Judiciary Committee. I state this in view of the nature of the legislation which the Judiciary Committee handles.

Dr. FARIANS. I would like to add one other thing as an aside.

When I was in Connecticut a couple of years ago, it came to our attention that there was a law which stated that a female child could be put into prison even though she had not committed a crime. And at that time there was a female minor child put into prison under that law. And, of course, some of us were outraged, and we began to work on trying to get it changed.

And while we were doing that, the State legislature was in session, and they were taking up the taxpayers' time and money, and so on, to enact another law which said that a woman need not reveal her age when she is arrested.

And I just wanted to point out again, the reason why we need equal rights, because State laws come and go, and some of them are really very ridiculous. And the equal rights amendment would stop this kind of offense.

Senator COOK. Also in reference to New England, I am unable to recall a single instance of a male witch being burned at the stake.

Dr. FARIANS. Thank you very much.

Senator BAYH. Thank you very much, Doctor.

We will recess now, to reconvene in the morning at 9:30 in the same place.

(Whereupon, at 4:50 p.m., the subcommittee adjourned, to reconvene at 9:30 a.m., Wednesday, May 6, 1970.)

WEDNESDAY, MAY 6, 1970

U.S. Senate,
Subcommittee on Constitutional Amendments
of the Committee on the Judiciary,
Washington, D.C.

The subcommittee met, pursuant to recess, at 9:40 a.m., in room 318, Old Senate Office Building, Senator Birch E. Bayh presiding.

Present: Senators Bayh, Thurmond, and Cook.

Also Present: Paul J. Mode, Jr., chief counsel, and Mrs. Dorothy Parker, minority counsel.

Senator Bayh. May we please come to order this morning.

Our first witnesses are Mrs. Betty Finegan and Mrs. Myra Wolfgang of the Michigan Women's Commission.

What I am about to say is not directed at the present witnesses alone. From the standpoint of absolute necessity, we are not going to be able to allow these hearings to go as late in the afternoon today as they did yesterday. I will ask all of our witnesses if they will try to go straight to the heart of their testimony. We will put any prepared statements that are available in the record as if they had been read in full.

I am sorry to have to make that type of a suggestion, but from a practical standpoint that is the only way we are going to complete these hearings. I think we are all anxious to place the testimony on the record, but not to overly delay the hearing.

Now, ladies, we are glad to have you with us.

STATEMENT OF MRS. BETTY FINEGAN, MICHIGAN WOMEN'S COMMISSION

Mrs. Finegan. I am Mrs. John Finegan, and I am chairman of the Michigan Women's Commission. Mrs. Wolfgang is a member of the women's commission, but is also representing the hotel and restaurant workers, in the State of Michigan.

The Michigan Women's Commission is a statutory body consisting of 15 members from all over the State plus four ex-officio members who are directors of the department of labor, education, social service and civil service. Members are appointed by the Governor of the State.

Our charges are to study and review the status of women, strengthen home life, direct our attention to the critical problems facing women as homemakers, wives, mothers, and workers, and to

89

secure appropriate recognition of the contribution women have made.

We are concerned with the multidimensional role women have as wives, mothers, homemakers, and workers in today's complicated society. We are concerned with women realizing their potential and we are seeking means to enable them to do this. We are concerned with utilizing more fully the huge resources of womenpower in this country. We want to have a choice in what course their lives will follow.

The Michigan Women's Commission has gone on record as opposing the equal rights amendment. Our opposition is fundamental and deals with matters that are basic to our social structure. There are real differences both physical and social between men and women. Nature cannot be amended. Women still bear children and will continue to give them the majority of care. They will still need maternity benefits and maternal care. Our society today still recognizes that the wife and mother is the center of the family. We firmly believe this should be so. The legal position of women cannot be stated in a single formula as their relationships are so varied. Absolute legal equality is impossible. Where there are real physical or social differences, identity of treatment is itself a form of discrimination.

Secondly, we believe women already have the protection of the laws because of the fifth and 14th amendments which guarantee to all persons due process and equal protection of the laws without arbitrary discrimination. We are confident that the courts today will interpret these laws to give full recognition to this principle.

Certainly, there are injustices in the treatment of women. We recognize the discrimination in employment, in promotions, in training opportunities, in admission to universities, in access to public accommodations, in the social security system and in many other areas. We wish to correct these inequities by specific legislation. Orderly legislative revision, by means of specific legislations is the practical way to erase such unwise discrimination as still exists in the laws. Discrimination exists in the laws relating to property, personal status, marriage and employment. Legal discriminations in State laws and constitutions will be changed as fast as enough women in those States want them changed.

Michigan's law limiting the number of hours a woman could be forced to work would be threatened. Unfortunately, our law applies to women only. Passage of the equal rights amendment would nullify it. And there is no guarantee that new legislation would be enacted to provide protection for both sexes. Therefore, there would be no protection for either sex. The women's commission has gone on the record as favoring protective legislation for both men and women.

We want equal opportunities and responsibilities and equal status for women. We do not think that the equal rights amendment will accomplish this.

It is our conviction that: First, the amendment is unnecessary. The fifth and 14th amendments guarantee to all persons due process and equal protection of the laws without arbitrary discrimination. Most of the inequalities about which its advocates complain are due to custom and tradition and not to law;

Second, the adoption of the amendment would nullify Michigan's labor laws for the protection of women. This legislation is perhaps more necessary than before because of the number and proportion of women in the labor force;

And finally, adoption of the amendment would cause great confusion in the wide field of laws relating to property, personal status and marriage.

We ask the committee's consideration of the position of the Michigan Women's Commission.

STATEMENT OF MRS. MYRA K. WOLFGANG, VICE PRESIDENT, HOTEL AND RESTAURANT EMPLOYEES AND BARTENDERS INTERNATIONAL UNION, AFL–CIO, IN BEHALF OF MICHIGAN WOMEN'S COMMISSION

Mrs. WOLFGANG. My name is Myra Wolfgang. I reside in the city of Detroit. I am the international vice president of the Hotel and Restaurant Employees Union, AFL–CIO, and also the secretary-treasurer of its Detroit local. I bring to this hearing 35 years of experience in representing the interests of service workers, both organized, and may I hasten to add, unorganized as well. I am a member of the Michigan Minimum Wage Board representing service employees thereon. I have been a member of the mayor's committee on human relations, and as Mrs. Finegan, chairman of our commission, indicated, I am a member of the current Governor's commission on the status of women and was a member of the Governor's commission under the previous two administrations. I am quite proud of the fact that I made the suggestion to Gov. John Swainson that we have a commission on the status of women, and Michigan was the first State to have such a commission.

The service industries which I represent comprise more than 5.5 million women workers. There are an additional 5 million women employed in the wholesale and retail trades industries. I represent unskilled and untrained women workers, the majority of whom are not organized into trade unions. They also are not burdened with the necessity of holding philosophical discussions on whether women should or should not be in the work force. They are in the work force because of dire, economic necessity and have no choice in the matter.

My concern with the equal rights amendment, Senator, is not an academic one. It embodies the problems that I work with day in and day out, year in and year out. My concern is for the widowed, divorced mothers of children who are the heads of their families and earn less than $3,500 a year working as maids, laundry workers, hospital cleaners, or dishwashers. And there are millions of such women in the work force. Now is as good a time as any to remind you that only one out of 10 women in the work force have had 4 or more years of college, so I am not speaking of, or representing the illusive "bird in the gilded cage." I speak for "Tillie the Toiler."

I am opposed to enactment of the equal rights amendment. I recognize that the impetus for the passage of the equal rights amendment is the result of a growing anger amongst women over job discrimination, social and political discrimination, and many outmoded cultural habits of our way of life.

And the anger is justified, for certainly discrimination against women exists. I do not believe, however, that passage of the equal rights amendment will satisfy, or is the solution to the problem. The problem of discrimination against women will not be solved by an equal rights amendment to the Constitution, conversely, the amendment will create a whole new series of problems. It will neither bring about equal pay for equal work, nor guarantee job promotion free from discrimination. It will not compel the partner of a senior law firm to hire a woman lawyer if he has prejudice against a woman lawyer. And may I point out at this time that if that law firm employs less than 25 persons, they are not even covered by the title VII of the Civil Rights Act. And I would suggest that would be a good place to start a fight against law firms that won't hire lady lawyers.

The amendment is excessively sweeping in scope, reaching into the work force, into family and social relationships, and other institutions, in which, incidentally, "equality" cannot always be achieved through "identity." Differences in laws are not necessarily discriminatory, nor should all laws containing different provisions for men and women be abolished, as the equal rights amendment would do.

Opposed, as I am, to the equal rights amendment, certainly does not mean that I am opposed to equality. The campaign for an equal rights amendment, in many instances, has become a field day for sloganeers and has become as jingoistic as the "right to work" law campaign did. The "right to work" laws do not guarantee a job, anymore than the equal rights amendment will guarantee equality. To assume that it would is as invalid as to assume that because women have suffrage they are independent.

Representing service workers gives me a special concern over the threat that an equal rights amendment would present to minimum labor standards legislation. I am sure you are aware of the influence of such legislation upon working conditions. And I am sure you are aware that many such laws apply to women only.

They are varied and they are in the field of minimum wages, hours of work, rest periods, weight lifting, childbirth legislation, et cetera.

These State laws are outmoded and many of them are discriminatory. They should be amended where they are. They should be strengthened and they should be handled on a case-by-case basis.

It is difficult to unite women against vague philosophies, so the new feminists look for a focus in the law. Thus, the revived interest in the equal rights amendment. The feminists movement in the main is middle class, professional woman, college girl oriented, as is the list of your testifiers, Senator.

Senator BAYH. May I interrupt just a minute, please?

Mrs. WOLFGANG. This should be obvious to you.

Senator BAYH. I don't think any of us are going to suggest that if a person happens to be fortunate enough to have a college education and is discriminated against, that is good?

Mrs. WOLFGANG. I think it is bad and I don't think that the equal rights amendment will correct that. And if you will permit me to continue testifying, I will try to show you what my position is.

Senator BAYH. I would be happy to let you continue but the whole thrust of this intimation that there is some devious means of——

Mrs. WOLFGANG. Well, why don't you wait until I conclude my testimony, and let me assure you I don't think it is devious. I think it is unfortunate that the women who are working washing dishes or working in the laundry can't afford to be here while the rest of us can. And I list myself amongst the fortunate.

Senator BAYH. I will try not to interrupt anymore.

Mrs. WOLFGANG. Thank you.

Some feminist groups have concluded that since only females reproduce—and to be a mother is to be a "slave eternal"—that nothing short of the destruction of the family and the end of internal reproduction will do. Having discovered "artificial insemination" all that is missing now, in order to do away with women, entirely, is discovering an artificial womb.

You will be hearing, I am sure, from many who will contend that there are no real differences between men and women, other than those enforced by culture. Has culture created the differences in the size of the hands, in muscular mass, in respiratory capacity? Of course not. The differences are physical.

Let me add some more. Women on the average—these are averages, Senator—are 85 percent as heavy as men and have only 60 percent as much physical strength. Therefore, they cannot lift as heavy weights. They cannot direct as much weight or have the same strength for pushing or pulling of loads.

One can take any cell from a human being and determine whether it came from a male or a female. This does not suggest superiority or inferiority among the sexes, it emphasizes differences. Because of the physical—and I emphasize physical—differences between men and women, the question of protective legislation for women must be reviewed. In addition, the dual role of women in our modern society makes protective legislation necessary.

The working mother has no "wife" to care for her or her children. She assumes the role of home maker and worker and must perform both these roles in a 24-hour period. Even in the two-parent households, there is an unequal division of domestic chores. While much could be done to ease the burden of the working women by men assuming the fair and equal share of domestic chores, they are not prepared to do so. And I am not prepared to become confused with what should be and what is.

If the community does not take action through protective legislation to enable women to work outside the home, then the expressed desire for equal rights is an empty promise and a myth. The equal rights amendment would make it unconstitutional to enact, and would repeal legislation embodying this protection for working women. You must ask yourself this question: Should women workers be left without any legislation because of State legislature's failure and unwillingness to enact such legislation for men?

The elimination of laws regulating hours women may work permits employers to force them to work excessive overtime, endangering not only their health and safety, but disrupting the entire family relationship.

The women in the work force who are in the greatest need of the protection of maximum hour legislation are in no position to fight for themselves.

Do you want me to wait, Senator? Would you want me to pause?

Senator BAYH. No, ma'am. I didn't want to interrupt. Go right ahead.

Mrs. WOLFGANG. Well, I noticed that you were in a conference.

Senator BAYH. That is quite all right. I will try to do my job and I know you will try to do yours.

Mrs. WOLFGANG. Thank you.

Let me emphasize again that the majority of them are not represented by labor unions (working as they do in organized industries); thousands are not covered by the Fair Labor Standards Act since their employers do not gross $500,000 a year, which is the definition of interstate commerce. And may I point out that as a result of that, that all of these women who are not covered by the Fair Labor Standards Act do not even get premium pay when they are compelled to work overtime. Nor are they covered by title VII of the Equal Employment Opportunities Act, or of the Civil Rights Act. As you well know, that act only applies to employers of 25 persons or more. So we find that the woman worker, particularly the service worker, is not covered by the Fair Labor Standards Act; therefore, will not receive overtime when she works it, is not covered by the Equal Employment Opportunities, or by title VII, and gets neither protections.

Yet, we are told that the decision of the Equal Employment Opportunity Commission stating that State laws are superseded by the Federal law, should remove objection to enactment of the equal rights amendment. The Equal Employment Opportunity Commission, in setting guidelines on the question of labor standards law applying to women only, stated that:

Such laws and regulations conflict with Title VII of the Civil Rights Act of 1964 and will not be considered a "defense" to an otherwise established unlawful employment practice or as a basis for the application of the bona fide occupational qualification exception.

The new guidelines, as such, give protection to a small minority—and I emphasize minority—of working women who wish to work overtime by saying that the employer can no longer refuse—refuse them such work because of the State laws. It says can no longer be a defense in not giving women overtime.

However, I must remind you that those thousands of women who are not covered by the Equal Employment Opportunities provisions who do not want to work excessive overtime, regardless of what their reasons may be would have only a State law to protect them, and there are thousands of them who consider overtime a punishment, not a privilege.

I think, Senator, that the fair way to approach that question would be to amend State laws to permit those who wish to work overtime to work overtime, and politically I suppose we may as well say that the best way to accomplish that would be to exclude professional women, administrators, and executives, but the approach that I am suggesting is that the specific problem—and I am only using hours as an example now—can be more equitably handled by amending, repealing, strengthening State laws where it is rquired, than by having an amendment to the Constitution which would make it impossible to do such things unless they are applied equally to men and women.

In this mad whirl toward equality and sameness one question remains unanswered: Who will take care of the children, the home, cleaning, the laundry, and the cooking? Can we extend this equality into the home? Obviously not, since the proponents of the equal rights amendment are quick to point out the amendment would restrict only governmental action and would not apply to purely private action.

I would like to point out that this was a statement made by my good friend Congresswoman Martha Griffiths. It was inserted in the Congressional Record, and on that subject I agree that the social security laws are discriminatory, and I respectfully suggest that the way to correct that would be by amending the social security laws. And it seems to me that if it cannot be amended as a result of an intelligent discussion even with the powerful voice of Congresswoman Griffiths in the Ways and Means Committee that perhaps there are issues involved in the entire social security picture which makes it appear that what was stated here yesterday is an oversimplification of the facts.

Unfortunately, I am a widow. I pay the same amount of social security as do all other persons, male or female. I have no husband to leave it to. But let me assure you I do not feel that my social security taxes are being used to support your widows.·as is felt by Congresswoman Griffiths, according to her testimony given yesterday. I feel my social security taxes are being used to support ADC mothers, and I hope that they can get more support. I am much more concerned, Senator, about my tax dollars being sent to Cambodia, than I am whether it supports your widow or not.

Senator BAYH. Well, at the risk of interrupting again, if it were possible for this committee to consider that issue and to pass it out, at least this morning, we would have a unanimous vote to bring the troops back from Cambodia. But unfortunately, that isn't before us and I think we have to deal with the specific question. I think you said a moment ago, did you not, that you realized the inequities that exist in social security relative to women?

Mrs. WOLFGANG. Oh, yes. I recognize them, but I think they should be corrected by amending the Social Security Act. And I venture to say—that is my point, Senator, that if it can't be done there, even though it is so very, very unfair that there must be some reasoning there—in other words, what we are trying to get in correcting social security through an equal rights amendment is we are trying to get something through the back door that we can't get through the front door.

Incidentally, Cambodia is not so far removed from us when we are told that with an equal rights amendment that women will serve in Armed Forces the same as men.

I know the pressures upon you have been great, and I am aware of the recent position taken by the Citizens Advisory Council on the Status of Women in support of the equal rights amendment. Since it differs with the report of President Kennedy Commission on the Status of Women, what has occurred to explain this change? You know, as it is said, in order to know the players, you have to have a scorecard. Well, have women changed since 1963? No. Have the fifth and 14th amendments to the Constitution been changed, repealed, or amended since 1963? The only thing that has changed is the personnel of the Citizens Advisory Council. The new Council was appointed last August and consists of business and professional women whose knowledge of proper labor standards for workers is negligible. And if you don't believe me, ask the domestics that work in their homes. Not one labor representative is on that Council.

You have been reminded in strong and ominous tones, and I was here yesterday and heard it, that women represent the majority of the voters. That is true. But there is no more unanimity of opinion among women than there is amongst men. Indeed, a woman on welfare in Harlem, and a unionized laundryworker in California, an elderly socialite from Philadelphia may be of the same sex and they may be wives and mothers, but they have little in common to cause them to be of one opinion.

Whatever happens to the structure of opportunity, women are increasingly motivated to work—and they want to work short hours on schedules that meet their needs as wives and mothers. They want fewer hours a week because emancipation, while it has released them for work, has not released them from home and family responsibilities.

I oppose the equal rights amendment since the equality it may achieve, may well be, equality of mistreatment.

I would be very happy to answer any question that you direct.

Senator BAYH. Well, being a member of a minority group in this country——

Mrs. WOLFGANG. Aren't you glad the majority isn't of one mind?

Senator BAYH. I was just about to say that is the most heartening bit of evidence so far. It is proved conclusively by the testimony today that indeed proof is needed.

I would like to look at this very quickly just to try to clarify some of the things that both of you ladies have said. I think you said them very well, although I am not sure that I agree or disagree with what you said.

You mentioned that legal equality is impossible. Is that really accurate? Is it possible to recognize our lives are not really created identical, but that as far as legal equality and doors of opportunity they ought to be open equally wide regardless of our race, color, creed, or sex?

Mrs. WOLFGANG. Of course. And the equal rights amendment, Senator, does not accomplish that. I believe that the important thing in that area is to strengthen title VII and, incidentally, to give it more enforcement provisions.

Senator BAYH. May I ask why it doesn't accomplish that?

Mrs. WOLFGANG. The expressions were mine.

Senator BAYH. Excuse me. You were here yesterday and you heard me suggest that I disagreed with some of the ladies who were on the other side of this issue with you. I said then that I didn't feel the passage of this amendment was going to be a panacea such that all of a sudden discrimination was going to disappear, but rather that it was going to take active pursuit of the rights given under this Constitutional amendment to bring about changes in due course. But you stress now the equalities provided under the Fifth and 14th amendments. Can you specify one court case that has reached the Supreme Court today in all these years of history that has been based on the fifth and 14th amendments that has been successful for women's rights?

Mrs. WOLFGANG. I believe the trial on the question of serving on an Alabama jury raised the question of the 14th amendment and as a result of that litigation women can now serve on juries in Alabama.

However, Senator, I also heard yesterday——

Senator BAYH. That was——

Mrs. WOLFGANG. Just a minute. You asked me a question. Let me answer it.

Senator BAYH. Yes, but you were not accurate; that was not a Supreme Court case. That was a district court case.

Mrs. WOLFGANG. I thought you were talking about the validity of the application of the 14th amendment. Because I know there were many instances where the lower courts didn't uphold it, and therefore it was said that the 14th amendment does apply. And that was said yesterday and you interrogated them so I assumed you meant both areas of the court. However, the expression was mine there when I spoke of legal equality. What I mean, and let me elaborate, is that equality will not be achieved by legislation. Perhaps the word "legal" is not used in the correct context there. I do not believe that you can legislate equality no more than you can legislate antidiscrimination. You have antidiscrimination laws on your books, but the way people feel on the question of race relations is indicated by the flight to suburbia all over this country, and there isn't any law you can put on the books that is going to change that. There isn't any law that is going to alter the fact that people where they live even determines the schools their children go to, and yet, you cannot stop that exodus.

Senator BAYH. Granted that you are not going to legislate equality. But according to your testimony, and you are where the action is literally on the floor representing women who clean and wash dishes——

Mrs. WOLFGANG. I venture to say the dishwasher in Gary, Ind., doesn't like to work more than 10 hours a day.

Senator BAYH. The efforts we have made to date to legislate have not been successful because they have applied to large numbers of people and they have not been enforced. The question we have to ask ourselves is this: If we are going to try to change attitudes and estblish a movement in a certain direction to give, for example, cleaning women, high school dropouts, grade school dropouts, an equal piece of the action and an equal opportunity is a broad principle stated in a constitutional amendment going to be able to create the attitude and aura of movement in this direction more than a piece by piece statute?

Mrs. WOLFGANG. Well, Senator, I am inclined to agree with you an equal rights amendment would do that. If you recall from my testimony I said my opposition to it is based only on the fact of its impact on protective labor legislation because I am aware of the fact that the majority of the women in this country, and incidentally, you know, when they speak of the women's median wage being so much less than the men's, there are factors other than the fact that the majority of them are in the unskilled occupations. Whether we like it or not in Government service in spite of Presidential orders going all the way back to President Kennedy, you have this wide range of the average earnings of the women and men because you know women do not achieve the same tenure. They are in the work force and they are out of it, and they return to it, and that is as it should be if that is the way the individual woman wants it to be.

Senator BAYH. But I think you would be the first to suggest that that is not the only reason why there is this discrepancy between a woman executive working in Government and a man executive.

Mrs. WOLFGANG. Of course not. Amongst the executives it is now assumed that there are laws to protect that. I would suggest that either the laws be enforced or that the women fight more aggressively to see that they get what they are entitled to under law, not to pass an amendment to the Constitution that will take the rights away from that woman who is making less than $3,000 a year, leave her without any legislation that says her employer can make her work 10 and 12 hours a day and then go home to a day of housework. That is where a majority of the working women are.

Senator BAYH. Let me look at several specific areas. Is it accurate that the Michigan attorney general has held that State labor laws applicable only to women are invalid under title VII?

Mrs. WOLFGANG. This will take—would you like to know the whole situation on the hours question in Michigan? Because the attorney general gave three different opinions. We had him in court twice and beat him both times. But what the present situation is, the attorney general interprets the recent guidelines set by EEOC in August to mean that the 54-hour-limit law in Michigan is repealed for those women who are working for covered employers. In other words, those women who are working for employers of 25 or more according to our attorney general are not now covered by the 54-hour law.

It is our intention to take this matter into courts, because we feel that the guidelines say that the employer cannot use this as a defense for refusing to give overtime, which suggests two things: that a women requested overtime, and that it was denied her because of the State law.

Unfortunately, right now in Michigan the whole issue is not being tested because we are confronted with layoffs. Right now it isn't a question of anyone working more than 54 hours. Right now it is a question of them working, period.

Incidentally, I would like to emphasize that the court case that we had in Michigan was started by the women of the Dodge local of the UAW. The action was supported by the UAW women in the Rawsonville Ford Motor plant, the Ac Spark Plug plant from Flint, Mich., Chrysler Corp. in Lyons, Mich. This just wasn't service workers. The women who are covered by EEOC equally as concerned with the impact of excessive overtime.

There was a 5-month period when the law was not on our books.

Now, that is a wild situation there. Our legislature passed two pieces of legislation. One repealed the law. The other referred it to an occupational safety standards commission. The attorney general ruled that one that repealed the law was invalid, but during that period there was three months' time when we did not have the hours law on our books. The result was so catastrophic that women actually in this day and age, even though we were told here yesterday that the days of exploitation are over, were working 12 hours a day, 7 days a week. In the Chrysler Motor Co. Chrysler Vernor-North plant in the city of Detroit, they were put on a schedule of 12 hours a day, 7 days a week, and women were compelled to quit their jobs because they could not work those hours and go home afterward and do their housework. And that is why we took them to court and that is why I think we will again.

Senator BAYH. Let me ask you if you think it is a good practice to have men working 12 hours a day, 7 days a week.

Mrs. WOLFGANG. I think it is a very bad practice for a man to have to work 12 hours a day, and I think this legislation should aply to both. The question that I asked in my statement, and that may have been at the moment when you were discussing something else, was what do we do until legislatures amend the law to include both men and women? That is the question that is before us.

Senator BAYH. Let me suggest to you that I am very sensitive to criticism that I would be in favor of or consider legislation that would lessen the standards and working conditions of the labor force.

Mrs. WOLFGANG. I am sure you would, Senator. That is why I am testifying the way I am.

Senator BAYH. In most instances I think my legislative record has shown I have been on the other side of such issues. I am not convinced yet that supporting the equal rights amendment puts one on the side of taking away this protection. The amendment is subject to different interpretations, I am sure, but it is entirely possible to interpret this that if there is a 54-hour law in Michigan in which a woman is not permitted to work more than 54 hours, that under the proposed amendment it would be just as reasonable to conclude that the 54-hour law would be applied to men and women, not that it would be repealed as it applies to women.

Mrs. WOLFGANG. Senator, are you aware of the fact that every State that has repealed its hours law for women only in the last few months has done so based upon the EEOC's decision and guidelines of August, including the attorney general in Michigan, Pennsylvania. He tried to get away with it in Ohio. He did that in Ohio. He couldn't get away with it in the legislature. When the question of hours came up there, the legislature there wanted their hours law on the books, but he has now ruled that the Federal law supersedes the State and the State department of labor will not enforce their hours laws. And if that were the fact that what is good for women will remain for men, I have to ask the question, and I hope one of the proponents of this bill will answer it in their testimony; they haven't yet—why are they opposed to the Hayden amendment, which would do just that? I can't answer it. Somebody else will have to.

Senator BAYH. I can answer that myself.

Mrs. WOLFGANG. Well, good.

Senator BAYH. I am not sure that I can answer it to your satisfaction.

Mrs. WOLFGANG. No, no. I just want to know what the answer is.

Senator BAYH. Anyone who is familiar with the Hayden amendment, can argue the merits of this amendment: the whole question of whether we should have an amendment to the Constitution, is answered by the amending the Constitution on the one hand saying one thing and then on the other hand saying that we really didn't mean anything we said——

Mrs. WOLFGANG. No, no. I agree with you there.

Senator BAYH. It is just totally ridiculous to suggest we go through this overture. It is just a political ploy, it seems to me, to do it, and I think the Congress has been guilty of this.

Mrs. WOLFGANG. Well, I don't think we ought to attribute motives to anyone else. I don't. I think that the—I hope that proponents of the equal rights amendment will recognize my sincerity and commitment to labor legislation for the unskilled, untrained women workers who are my primary concern. By the same token I wouldn't say that this a ploy.

Senator BAYH. I don't think—all right.

Mrs. WOLFGANG. That it was a ploy. I think that the contribution that was made there at least made a lot of people aware of the fact that the equal rights amendment is a possible threat to protective legislation. We both concede that the courts are going to have to make the determination. And I am not a lawyer, so I won't discuss it.

Senator BAYH. Is it reasonable to assume that passing an equal rights amendment with the Hayden rider would leave us exactly where we are today?

Mrs. WOLFGANG. That is reasonable to assume, and I think as far as the equal rights amendment in this type of legislation, that is where I would like to be. I believe that the laws have to be amended and strengthened on a case-by-case basis. I am not prepared to throw the baby out with the wash.

Mrs. FINEGAN. Senator, you made a statement that you thought the protective legislation might be interpreted so that the hours would be the same for men; in other words, they would have a 54-hour week, but I think that is an unrealistic approach because of the trend that has been happening across the country, that the hours have been removed, not extended to cover men, but have been removed so that women who have these dual or multiple roles are not protected. And I feel very strongly that this is a necessity in today's society. I don't think that we can assume that the other interpretation would take place.

Senator BAYH. But neither can we assume that, at least we cannot accurately say that this amendment would prohibit that from happening.

Mrs. WOLFGANG. That is correct. So our statement that this would be decided by the courts is a correct one.

Senator BAYH. Let me ask just one last general question here.

What has been accomplished by your commission, Mrs. Finegan? The reason I ask is not to be critical of your efforts or the commission's efforts, but to try to point out the fact that what is being done now for some reason or another is not doing the job.

Mrs. Wolfgang pointed out a number of areas in which under present "protective" laws, there are large numbers of people that are being discriminated against. Now, it seems this is totally contradictory if we don't want to repeal those laws or we don't want to pass a constitutional amendment because we might affect those laws which provide protection which in essence doesn't exist.

Mrs. FINEGAN. You are talking about passing a law without an amendment, isn't that correct?

Senator BAYH. Yes, ma'am.

Mrs. FINEGAN. And isn't the Hayden rider——

Senator BAYH. You see I asked Mr. Furay this yesterday. He went through a very well documented graphic presentation of the shortcomings, the work conditions, the strains on various parts of the body, all of which are going on today. And yet, he suggests that to pass the amendment, and you suggested to pass it, is going to take away this protection which apprently isn't effective.

Mrs. WOLFGANG. That is why it should be strengthened, those laws. Even EEOC should be strengthened so it has enforcement provision.

Mrs. FINEGAN. You might be interested to know that at a public hearing in Michigan there was one representative from industry and everybody else represented the labor force. I think this indicates the lack of concern on the part of industry if they are permitted to force people. if they can force people to work beyond the normal working week. I think this indicates that they are certainly going to take advantage of this?

But you did ask what our commission had accomplished, and the present commission has been in existence just a year. We have taken a stand on the abortion laws in Michigan. We have published a pamphlet on laws applying to women. We are at the present time engaged in four ongoing programs dealing with household employees, with family planning, with parttime employment opportunities for women, and these are ongoing projects at the present time. Since we have only been in existence a year I would say that our stand on the abortion issue and our fight on the abortion issue has been the most significant contribution of this commission.

Mrs. WOLFGANG. Senator, Mrs. Finegan has been very modest. Our commission didn't just take a stand on the abortion hearing. Mrs. Finegan as our chairman has been one of the leaders of the struggle for abortion reform in Michigan.

Senator BAYH. Well, thank you. I am glad of that for the record.

Mrs. WOLFGANG. Senator, in closing may I make a short statement. There was a great deal of questioning yesterday of one of the witnesses here on the organized labor movement, and the employment of women officials. Incidentally, you were interrogating a non-elected official of the labor movement, a trade union functionary. As an elected official of one of the five largest unions in the AFO–CIO and its international vice president, I would like to point out that in my way of thinking there are three reasons why there aren't more women leadership positions in the labor movement, and you expressed a concern about it yesterday. As a matter of fact, I thought the labor movement was on trial yesterday. The first one is that the men in the labor movement——

Senator BAYH. Let me suggest I think that is patently fair. There is nobody more sympathetic with the labor movement than I, and I suggest it is reasonable to ask if you have a union comprised of women who run sewing machines why you don't have a preponderance of female leaders at the higher levels as well as at the local level?

Now, I don't see how that puts anybody on trial. That is trying to get some facts on the record.

Mrs. WOLFGANG. I think that is a very reasonable question to ask and I would like to answer you have a preponderance of women in the country, 53 percent of them, and one woman in the U.S. Senate, but I would like to continue that there are three reasons for this, Senator, and I do respect your sincerity. I think you really want to know. In my way of thinking the first one is male chauvinism. I think the men in the labor movement are not different than any other men.

But the second and the more important reason is that the women in the labor movement who are members of the trade unions who are in the work force in the main have to go home to domestic and household duties when they get through work and can't go to a union meeting to participate in the union politics to the same extent that men do.

And the third explanation I would like to give is that the record is infinitely better in the labor movement than it is, the record of the democratic process in electing women to high office in our country.

Senator BAYH. Well, let me suggest to you that——

Mrs. WOLFGANG. And look to the Congress.

Senator BAYH (continuing). That may be partially a compliment, but I hope that the labor movement is not satisfied with a 10 percent success. I have been to many labor meetings at which time there have been many women present and I don't suppose——

Mrs. WOLFGANG. Have any of them run for office?

Senator BAYH. Excuse me, if I may suggest we not interrupt each other, since that has been suggested earlier—but I don't suppose there is a male union official who works more hours than the woman he represents in the shop. He just puts in a little different time and in a little different way. And I am not saying we are going to snap our fingers and solve this, but I still must say I am not fully able to understand why there is not a larger percentage of women officials in those unions that are predominantly female. Now, that is——

Mrs. WOLFGANG. Well, I can't understand the country either. I think we are both raising the same question. I am saying, I gave as my No. 1 reason male chauvinism. Yet, nevertheless, I have no intention, for instance, just to vote for a woman because she happens to be a woman. I will always vote for who I consider to be the best candidate. I mean we have a secret ballot but everybody may as well know I will vote for Senator Hart rather than Mrs. Romney even though Lenore Romney is a charming woman and a personal friend of mine. I will vote for the man because I happen to think he is a better candidate for office.

Senator BAYH. Perhaps that is a good note to thank you for your testimony and ask for the next witness.

Thank you very much, ladies.

Our next witnesses are Miss Gloria Steinem and Miss Caroline Bird, Miss Steinem, a writer and critic of some renown, and Miss Bird, author of "Born Female." What was the other title, "The High Cost of Keeping Women Down"—is that the one?

Miss BIRD. I happen to have it with me.

Senator BAYH. We won't call that commercialism. You go right ahead.

Make sure you get a picture of that book.

Thank you, ladies, for taking your time to be with us. We are looking forward to hearing your testimony.

STATEMENT OF GLORIA STEINEM, WRITER AND CRITIC

Miss STEINEM. My name is Gloria Steinem. I am a writer and editor, and I am currently a member of the policy council of the Democratic committee. And I work regularly with the lowest-paid workers in the country, the migrant workers, men, women, and children both in California and in my own State of New York.

I am here in support of the equal rights amendment. Before I get on with the statement I would like to point out that Mrs. Wolfgang does not disavow the principle of equality only disagrees on the matter of tactic. I believe that she is giving up a long-term gain for a short-term holding action. Some protective legislation is gradually proving to be unenforceable or contrary to title VII. It gives poor women jobs but serves to keep them poor. Restrictions on working hours, for instance, may keep women in the assembly line from becoming foremen. No one is trying to say that there is no difference between men and women, only as I will discuss more in my statement that the differences between, the differences within the groups, male and female, are much, much greater than the differences between the two groups. Therefore, requirements can only be sensibly suited to the requirements of the job itself.

During 12 years of working for a living, I have experienced much of the legal and social discrimination reserved for women in this country. I have been refused service in public restaurants, ordered out of public gathering places, and turned away from apartment rentals; all for the clearly-stated, sole reason that I am a woman. And all without the legal remedies available to blacks and other minorities. I have been excluded from professional groups, writing assignments on so-called "unfeminine" subjects such as politics, full participation in the Democratic Party, jury duty, and even from such small male privileges as discounts on airline fares. Most important to me, I have been denied a society in which women are encouraged, or even allowed to think of themselves as first-class citizens and responsible human beings.

However, after 2 years of researching the status of American women, I have discovered that in reality, I am very, very lucky. Most women, both wage-earners and housewives, routinely suffer more humiliation and injustice than I do.

As a freelance writer, I don't work in the male-dominated hierarchy of an office. (Women, like blacks and other visibly different minorities, do better in individual professions such as the arts, sports, or domestic work; anything in which they don't have authority over white males.) I am not one of the millions of women who must support a family. Therefore, I haven't had to go on welfare because there are no day-care centers for my children while I work, and I haven't had to submit to the humiliating welfare inquiries about my private and sexual life, inquiries from which men are exempt. I haven't had to brave the sex bias of labor unions and employers, only to see my family subsist on a median salary 40 percent less than the male medial salary.

I hope this committee will hear the personal, daily injustices suffered by many women—professionals and day laborers, women housebound by welfare as well as by suburbia. We have all been silent for too long. But we won't be silent anymore.

The truth is that all our problems stem from the same sex based myths. We may appear before you as white radicals or the middle-aged middleclass or black soul sisters, but we are all sisters in fighting against these outdated myths. Like racial myths, they have been reflected in our laws. Let me list a few.

That men are biologically inferior to men. In fact, an equally good case can be made for the reverse. Women live longer than men, even when the men are not subject to business pressures. Women survived Nazi concentration camps better, keep cooler heads in emergencies currently studied by disaster-researchers, are protected against heart attacks by their female sex hormones, and are so much move durable at every stage of life that nature must conceive 20 to 50 percent more males in order to keep the balance going.

Man's hunting activities are forever being pointed to as tribal proof of superiority. But while he was hunting, women built houses, tilled the fields, developed animal husbandry, and perfected language. Men, being all alone in the bush, often developed into a creature as strong as women, fleeter of foot, but not very bright.

However, I don't want to prove the superiority of one sex to another. That would only be repeating a male mistake. English scientists once definitively proved, after all, that the English were descended from the angels, while the Irish were descended from the apes; it was the rationale for England's domination of Ireland for more than a century. The point is that science is used to support current myth and economics almost as much as the church was.

What we do know is that the difference between two races or two sexes is much smaller than the differences to be found within each group. Therefore, in spite of the slide show on female inferiorities that I understand was shown to you yesterday, the law makes much more sense when it treats individuals, not groups bundled together by some condition of birth.

A word should be said about Dr. Freud, the great 19th century perpetuator of female inferiority. Many of the differences he assumed to be biological, and therefore changeless, have turned out to be societal, and have already changed. Penis envy, for instance, is clinically disappearing. Just as black people envied white skins, 19th century women envied penises. A second-class group envies whatever it is that makes the first-class groups first class.

Another myth, that women are already treated equally in this society. I am sure there has been ample testimony to prove that equal pay for equal work, equal chance for advancement, and equal training or encouragement is obscenely scare in every field, even those—like food and fashion industries—that are supposedly "feminine."

A deeper result of social and legal injustice, however, is what sociologists refer to as "Internalized Aggression." Victims of aggression absorb the myth of their own inferiority, and come to believe that their group is in fact second class. Even when they themselves realize they are not second class, they may still think their group is, thus the tendency to be the only Jew in the club, the only black woman on the block, the only woman in the office.

Women suffer this second class treatment from the moment they are born. They are expected to be, rather than achieve, to function biologically rather than learn. A brother, whatever his intellect, is more likely to get the family's encouragement and education money, while girls are often pressured to conceal ambition and intelligence, to "Uncle Tom."

I interviewed a New York public school teacher who told me about a black teenager's desire to be a doctor. With all the barriers in mind, she suggested kindly that he be a veterinarian instead.

The same day, a high school teacher mentioned a girl who wanted to be a doctor. The teacher said, "How about a nurse?"

Teachers, parents, and the Supreme Court may exude a protective, well-meaning rationale, but limiting the individual's ambition is doing no one a favor. Certainly not this country; it needs all the talent it can get.

Another myth, that American women hold great economic power. Fifty-one percent of all shareholders in this country are women. That is a favorite male-chauvinist statistic. However, the number of shares they hold is so small that the total is only 18 percent of all the shares. Even those holdings are often controlled by men.

Similarly, only 5 percent of all the people in the country who receive $10,000 a year or more, earned or otherwise, are women. And that includes the famous rich widows.

The constantly repeated myth of our economic power seems less tetimony to our real power than to the resentment of what little power we do have.

Another myth, that children must have full-time mothers. American mothers spend more time with their homes and children than those of any other society we know about. In the past, joint families, servants, a prevalent system in which grandparents raised the children, or family field work in the agrarian systems—all these factors contributed more to child care than the labor-saving devices of which we are so proud.

The truth is that most American children seem to be suffering from too much mother, and too little father. Part of the program of Women's Liberation is a return of fathers to their children. If laws permit women equal work and pay opportunities, men will then be relieved of their role as sole breadwinner. Fewer ulcers, fewer hours of meaningless work, equal responsibility for his own children: these are a few of the reasons that Women's Liberation is Men's Liberation too.

As for psychic health of the children, studies show that the quality of time spent by parents is more important than the quantity. The most damaged children were not those whose mothers worked, but those whose mothers preferred to work but stayed home out of the role-playing desire to be a "good mother."

Another myth, that the women's movement is not political, won't last, or is somehow not "serious."

When black people leave their 19th century roles, they are feared. When women dare to leave theirs, they are ridiculed. We understand this; we accept the burden of ridicule. It won't keep us quiet anymore.

Similarly, it shouldn't deceive male observers into thinking that this is somehow a joke. We are 51 percent of the population; we are essentially united on these issues across boundaries of class or race or age; and we may well end by changing this society more than the civil rights movement. That is an apt parallel. We, too, have our right wing and left wing, our separatists, gradualists, and Uncle Toms. But we are changing our own consciousness, and that of the country. Engels noted the relationship of the authoritarian, nuclear family to capitalism: the father as capitalist, the mother as means of production, and the children as labor. He said the family would change as the economic system did, and that seems to have happened, whether we want to admit it or not. Women's bodies will no longer be owned by the state for the production of workers and soldiers; birth control and abortion are facts of everyday life. The new family is an egalitarian family.

Gunnar Myrdal noted 30 years ago the parallel between women and Negroes in this country. Both suffered from such restricting social myths as: smaller brains, passive natures, inability to govern themselves (and certainly not white men), sex objects only, childlike natures, special skills, and the like. When evaluating a general statement about women, it might be valuable to substitute "black people" for "women"—just to test the prejudice at work.

And it might be valuable to do this constitutionally as well. Neither group is going to be content as a cheap labor pool anymore. And neither is going to be content without full constitutional rights.

Finally, I would like to say one thing about this time in which I am testifying.

I had deep misgivings about discussing this topic when National Guardsmen are occupying our campuses, the country is being turned against itself in a terrible polarization, and America is enlarging an already inhuman and unjustifiable war. But it seems to me that much of the trouble in this country has to do with the "masculine mystique"; with the myth that masculinity somehow depends on the subjugation of other people. It is a bipartisan problem; both our past and current Presidents seem to be victims of this myth, and to behave accordingly.

Women are not more moral than men. We are only uncorrupted by power. But we do not want to imitate men, to join this country as it is, and I think our very participation will change it. Perhaps women elected leaders—and there will be many of them—will not be so likely to dominate black people or yellow people or men; anybody who looks different from us.

After all, we won't have our masculinity to prove. [Applause.]

Senator BAYH. Thank you very much, Miss Steinem.

STATEMENT OF MISS CAROLINE BIRD, AUTHOR OF "BORN FEMALE"

Miss BIRD. My name is Caroline Bird, and I have supported myself as a magazine writer for nearly 25 years. I appear to support the equal rights amendment. I want to tell you what I have learned firsthand about the anger in every woman, but first I want to draw your attention to an article I wrote called "Let's Draft Women, Too" that appeared in the June 18, 1966, issue of the Saturday Evening Post, and an article by Margaret Mead, the distinguished anthropologist, "A Case for Drafting All Boys—And Girls" in Redbook of September 1966.

At that time, I was not a practicing or overt feminist. I was more interested in questioning the morality of forcing anyone to fight. We don't make women fight because we say fighting is unfeminine.

My point is that forcing anyone to fight is inhuman, which is more important than being unfeminine. No one should have to do it. If it has to be done, then women should do their share of the dirty work.

I is relevant to the amendment here because some people say women should not have the privileges of male citizens because they do not fight wars.

We have never added the guarantee of equal rights to our Constitution the way it has appeared in other constitutions, I think, because our legislators have made two assumptions about American women.

One. We don't need any more rights. We have got everything. We are happy, or at least we are quiet.

Two. If we do not like our lot, it is something that laws cannot change. If there are inequities, they are based on the sex role of women, and that is too deep for the law. We have made the assumption that laws cannot change morals, laws cannot change customs.

Now, I used to believe both of these assumptions, as recently as 1966, but things have changed in the past few years. In 1970 neither assumption is a safe premise for ignoring the equal rights amendment once again.

First, women do care—all women. We have all been mistaken about the apathy of women about their legal rights. That includes women themselves. Most women shrug off or smile at talk about their rights. They say they don't care.

But hidden deep in every woman there is a well of anger. Women don't like to think of all the little slights, put downs, and limitations they have learned to accept under the name of being a woman. It makes them too angry. They fear that this anger will damage their relations with the men on whom they depend, so they repress it.

But when a woman is forced to take a situation seriously, to look at all those slights, limitations, putdowns, and restrictions that other witnesses have documented, then she cannot contain her anger. Once she admits to herself that she is a victim, she can never go back to the Garden of Eden. When one woman admits it, she makes it harder for the woman next to her to ignore it.

That is why you find most ardent opposition to equal rights from women themselves.

Now, in 1970 the lid is off the volcano. All over the country women are gathering in each other's living rooms to tell each other about the way they really feel about their vaunted role. They are saying out loud to each other things they never said out loud before, that they do not like losing their names when they marry, for instance, that they do care about getting promoted at work, that sometimes they really don't like children or don't want to have children. They don't like being put down. They don't like being used.

I think it is very significant that women's liberation girls do not smile: they do not have these little feminine characteristics. They look you straight in the face like Gloria Steinem, and tell you just as it is.

Senator BAYH. I noticed Miss Steinem smiling right now. I think it adds a great deal.

Miss BIRD. But she doesn't sort of giggle and use feminine smiles in an artificial way to put over points, and I think that is a big change in mood.

Miss STEINEM. That is Uncle Tomming.

Miss BIRD. It means taking yourself seriously as a person. I think that is really happening, and this is the important thing that is happening, the big change in young women, and I think it is important for men to realize this.

As for the rest of us, like me, who have been around for a while, I am astounded to discover how strongly I actually feel about this matter. So what I want to say today, there is all sorts of evidence about how women are discriminated against. All these putdowns are well documented. They have been around for a long time. But what I think you should know is the way women really feel about them. This is what is so mysterious to men. They say, "what do women really want?"

It seems to me what they really want is to be taken seriously. They keep saying this but nobody seems to believe it.

So let me tell you a little bit about how I got liberated by recognizing some of these things.

In 1966, after I did that article on the draft, an editor of the Saturday Evening Post asked me to find out whether women were really discriminated against. And I will never forget the moment. I said, "Gee, I guess they are discriminated against, but I have never really had any trouble, you know. I have just gone as far as my own talents could carry me."

But I said, "sure, I will go out and find out." I was very cool and professional about this, and I tackled it by doing more work than necessary, which I still do. And I think that women probably are good at detail because they do not have the self-confidence to ignore it.

But I got a little Russell Sage grant, and I went tearing around the country and I talked to women in a dozen cities who had succeeded by earning $10,000 a year or more. I discovered that none of them were very angry about their lot. They all started out by saying what I said, that they really had no trouble. Many of them begged me not to stir men up. "Don't talk rights. Don't talk like Betty Friedean because it will just make it harder for women to get ahead. We want to forget about this whole women's rights business."

When I asked, "why don't more women get ahead," they'd answer, "because most women won't work hard enough and long enough. Sure there is discrimination. But I am sick and tired of hearing about it, because you can get around it."

They told me about all sorts of ploys and situations that made it easier for a woman to do something than if she were a man. I concluded that the women who have succeeded in this country have taken advantage of their sex in many of the same ways that Negroes have used their subservience to get into policymaking places.

But then even as I interviewed these women a very funny thing happened. The more they talked about their careers the more you could see resentment beginning to dawn. A woman stockbroker would say, "Well, now, of course, I don't earn as much as the men, but, you see, I run the office. The men are all too busy out selling clients." She would start out as if it were a plausible explanation, but by the time she heard what she said you could see she was wondering, "Why am I not out making money, too."

I would ask a woman why she couldn't be president of her company and she would say, "Well, you see, my work has been on the inside. I just don't know all the big customers." I did not have to ask her, "How come that your work was all on the inside?"

Women generally have taken their situation for granted.

When I got two or three of these women together they reminded each other of the little things they usually put out of mind. One would say, "They don't invite me to the meetings," and another would say, "Come to think of it, they don't invite me either." One would say, "I never thought of asking for a business card. I suppose I really do need one, don't I."

After sessions like this, women sometimes called me up the next morning to say "I had never thought of it that way before, and please don't use my name."

I must have gone through this in two or three cities before it dawned on me that I had been discriminated against myself. I began as a researcher at Newsweek and Fortune, and I spent World War II putting red dots over names and dates on copy written by men to be sure in their great creativity they had not spelled the name wrong. At the end of World War II I was fired for incompetence, and I believed it. I believed I was incompetent. It never occurred to me to question that verdict. And I was sort of crushed and just wished I was better qualified. But I luckily had a father who said, "You know, Caroline, I think you can write." And I said, "Oh, go on." But I tried it and I have earned a living ever since at writing.

A couple of years ago there was a Fortune editor who said I made Caroline Bird a writer by getting her fired from Fortune magazine.

Now, the point of this story is not that I made it. The real point is that 20 years later in 1966 I could say in all honesty that I had never suffered any discrimination. Women get so used to their role that they don't question it. But once you do, once you see it, you can never go back to that state of innocence in which you can put up with all this stuff.

So on that story I began to question this whole situation, and my report was a resounding "yes," women are discriminated against, and I likened the role of women in business to the role of Negroes.

It was soon very clear that this was not what the Saturday Evening Post wanted. They wrote long memos about my piece. They questioned my facts, my logic, my style. Editors said women don't get ahead because it's only the dregs who are in offices working. Some editors thought women didn't get ahead because the best ones were hauled off to the suburbs to have babies, so only the inferior women were left working. And they said, "Of course, now, Miss Bird doesn't understand how hard it is for a man to sit next to a woman in an office, and women really don't understand how it is to be men." My editor kept saying, "We are not questioning your conclusions. We are not questioning your data. It's just the way you say it. If you could only say it better."

And once again I accepted this verdict—if only I could write better; if I were more clever; if only I were more graceful in the way I said it, then I could put the point across.

I rewrote that piece three times. When it was turned down, I was crushed. I was also furious by this time, absolutely furious. And when I went to bed, I don't mind telling you for a week I was just unable to move.

Finally I looked at this material and I said something has to be done with it. Luckily I had just done a book "The Invisible Scar" that was well received, so I had a sympathetic publisher and editor in Eleanor Rawson of David McKay, but some of the people around the office said, "Well, you know, women don't really care about getting ahead in business. However, if Caroline really wants to do this book." So I did it.

In 1967 women's liberation was a kaffeeklatch of women in the radical movement who claimed that they hadn't joined the revolution to tote coffee.

In 1967, airline stewardesses could be fired for getting married or for attaining the great age of 30, and if you suggested that they fire the stewards for getting married or attaining the great age of 30, people just giggled and laughed at you.

In 1967, women were excluded from some of the best colleges and professional schools. The sex provision of Title VII of the Civil Rights Act of 1964 was widely regarded as a joke.

Now 3 short years have passed and things have changed. You can get an abortion on demand in New York State. You can get a divorce practically on demand in California. Women are now on every major college campus in the country, not on an equal basis with men but some arrangement has been made so that they are not totally excluded by virtue of sex. The pay gap between the starting salary of men and women college graduates is narrowing, and the percentage of Ph.D.'s awarded to women is rising. I rather imagine that when the 1970 census is in it will show that women have made some progress over 1960. While there was a decline between 1950 and 1960, I think the economic outlook for women is improving.

I am not about to say that discrimination has ended, but I think that we have turned the corner, and it's fair to ask: How did it happen? Why do we have women's liberation in every single city of this country? Why do we have people more aware of the plight of women? So I go around asking the sociologists: "How did this come about?" And they say, "It started with this law—this law against discrimination—back in 1964."

Well, now, you and I know that Title VII was just about the weakest law that you could possibly imagine. You remember that it was added to the Civil Rights Act of 1964 as a joke. The people who put it in hoped it would serve to laugh the whole idea of a law against discrimination out of court. Many who voted for it thought it would never be applied. The EEOC charged with enforcing it publicly said it was embarrassing. Lawyers said it was as full of holes as a sieve. Personnel people said women don't care. There is one thing women don't care about—their jobs. They said they will never complain. They are too timid to complain. They don't want to assert themselves. The newspapers had a wonderful time laughing at title VII. But it was the law of the land. Some women did complain, and then others complained. In some times and places there were almost as many complaints on the basis of sex as of race. There were no real teeth in title VII but it was a law and it had an enormous effect. It got people to thinking, both employers and women. Sometimes that is all that is needed. I do not believe that men are trying to hold women down. I do not think that there is a real hostility. We are just brought up in a culture that makes this difference. Everybody accepts it. Both men and women accept it. And so when discrimination is inadvertent and covert, it just rankles along inside poisoning the relations of men and women and undermining the confidence of women.

I do not want to imply that title VII has ended discrimination, but it has begun the fight and it shows that laws do matter even in this day and age in which we assume that there is no respect for law. I believe that a law that states a high moral purpose, especially one that most people deep down can agree with, starts thought, makes people recognize inequities that they have passed over in silence, and ultimately will do more good toward equalizing the roles of men and women in this country than any specific correction of a specific disability.

Even if the equal rights amendment did nothing but state the principle, it would be worth it. I think the time has come when this equal rights amendment is both needed and politically feasible. Women are beginning to see their situation. They can never go back so we must all go forward. To paraphrase a great magazine: "Never underestimate the anger of a woman."

Thank you.

[Applause.]

Senator BAYH. Thank you very much, Miss Bird, We appreciate the fact that you and Miss Steinem have taken your time to come here.

As a man, I cannot really answer a question, which I think is the most important one. Namely, inasmuch as I think most proponents as well as opponents of the equal rights amendment have suggested this is not going to be a panacea in which things all of a sudden change as if the sun is rising and darkness disappears, do women as you see it, ladies, really care enough that they are willing to bite the bullet and pursue the enforcement of a constitutional amendment through the courts?

There are a number of instances, let me say very frankly, where they have not been willing to pursue the rights to which they are entitled under certain statutes.

Now, you suggest, Miss Bird, that you think things are changing. I am hopeful that that is the case. That has nothing to do with this amendment. I think we are losing a tremendous amount of talent.

We had some disagreement, at least a friendly discussion with the previous witnesses, and the response to one of the observations made was that there was only one Member of the United States Senate who was a woman. I think that is wrong. I think it is unfortunate we are losing potential creativity because some women, more women are not in the Congress.

Do women really care? Has this changed? Is it real?

Miss BIRD. I think they all care once they look at it, and I think that the young women are an entirely different breed and that they have grown up and expect to take themselves seriously in a way that was never possible before. I think it is an exciting new kind of thing coming up, and Gloria is really on to it and an exponent of it. The people who are coming out of college now are so different. The freshmen are even different from the seniors. And I think also that women do spark each other. It is a contagious grass fire kind of thing. I think it is important. I think it is growing.

Miss STEINEM. Unfortunately, I am not that much of an Evaner. I am a little too old to be an Evaner. I think I am a bridge in between. But I have not yet gone to a town where there is not a group of activist women, including Dayton, Ohio. I went there for a television show on this subject and was told as I faced this audience full of women, who actually had curlers in their hair and were all working class women, that they would hate me, that they would not want to listen to this, and it simply is not true. They have all been discriminated against and it all comes pouring out as if you had opened a floodgate. In fact, I think it is a very valuable political bridge. I think perhaps politicians should view it politically as one of the few issues that cuts into the silent majority as well as the white radicals and the black women.

Miss Bird. You cannot go by what they say. You cannot go by what they say overtly. I mean they kind of reluctantly come to it. But I think there is support there, and it is becoming much more articulate which makes it more useful.

Senator Bayh. Well, each one of us finds ourselves under our own circumstances. Some circumstances are self-made, some are accidental. But in light of the previous discussion that I had with Mrs. Wolfgang on this point, I think an accurate observation would be that both of you ladies fit in the category of women, because of your background and your education in a professional category, where she suggests that the large number of workingwomen that they represented, the service employees and others, did not feel this way.

Now, do you have any experience that can shed som light on your opinion of that attitude or that assessment?

Miss Bird. I think that workingwomen are even more bitter about the limitations of being women because they are right down there where they mop the floors. They have the kids at home and they have fewer outs. And if we are talking about sex hostility, the feeling that men are putting upon you, I think that there is more of it in working class women, for very good reasons.

Miss Steinem. I have been giving a few lectures on this subject to women, some of them working class women, and they all respond in a very deep and, to me, unexpected way. I think it really is a political bridge and it is one that should not be overlooked, because the students who are being treated with more equality than they ever will be again in their lives have come to understand that the situation of the suburban or working class women, who they would not normally speak to as a former SDS girl, is worse than theirs. They are picking these alliances, and there is going to be a political structure. In fact, there are already rather large movements and what-not to work for any candidate, hopefully for women candidates, and not to work for a candidate who merely offers a statement of his intention, but only for a candidate who has women in positions of power in his campaign.

The women in New York State are seriously considering withdrawing from the Democratic Party on this issue.

Senator Bayh. What about the protective features in some of the laws you have heard discussed? I think we were discussing the 54-hour law in Michigan before you got here. Are you concerned about the fact that this amendment might cause the repeal of this and thus return women to the sweatshop conditions?

Miss Steinem. Yes. I think that is a big concern and is one we were discussing very seriously before we came to testify. I feel deeply, though, that one should not give up a long-term gain for a short-term holding action, and that those kinds of protective laws are not going to hold up, and in many cases they are not enforced. Certainly in the case of the protective legislation of children it is not enforced, much less of women. It is much more important that we make the deep basic fundamental change and at the same time take the individual instances and try to guarantee the protection they already have in other ways.

Senator BAYH. Senator Cook?

Senator COOK. Mr. Chairman, I want to apologize. I have been testifying before a committee this morning. We spent many hours here yesterday.

Senator BAYH. Let me suggest, if the Senator will yield, there is no need for the Senator from Kentucky to apologize because there is not a single member of this committee who has been more faithful in his attendance, not just yesterday but for all of the hearings. It is sort of a duet, a soft shoe between the two of us.

Senator COOK. You see, there might be something very political about it after all.

Miss STEINEM. The women may avoid you.

Senator COOK. I did not hear your earlier remarks, but I see a great legal distinction between a constitutional amendment and police powers, those laws that regulate, regardless of the nature of the group. I cannot understand why all of this legislation that now is to be considered as protective legislation, and we are beginning to consider that maybe it is discriminatory legislation, must be repealed or that it automatically will be repealed. Unlike Mr. Furay, who testified yesterday, I fail to see the correlation between the passage of such a constitutional amendment and the repeal of existing protective legislation, such as that regulating the maximum number of working hours for women.

Miss BIRD. I believe that there have been studies showing that there is practically no law that you cannot write without mentioning sex. If it is a lifting law, the issue is the physical competence. Some women can lift 35 pounds, for heaven's sake—most women who are mothers do. If you want to legislate, do it on the basis of the specific thing that is at issue. You have to pass a driver's license test to drive a car. You do not assume that because you are a man you can drive a car. And so it should be with all these things. And as far as the hours laws go, I don't think that men should work long hours either.

Senator COOK. It is possible that many of the so-called protective legislative actions have intentionally been passed to limit the availability and ability of women to attain supervisory positions. I cite as an example the dilemma of women attempting to gain supervisory positions, which demand longer hours than they, under the State law, are allowed to work.

Miss BIRD. I am concerned though about the lowest paid workers. If it is true that women who have to work long hours are compelled —you know, I was impressed by the testimony that they made women work 12 hours a day or face being fired. I have given a great deal of thought to this. But it seems to me that the remedy is in other directions.

Senator COOK. Absolutely.

Miss BIRD. I am not a lawyer, but it would seem to me that there are other remedies.

Senator COOK. Certainly, other remedies exist.

Miss Steinem. The point I was trying to make earlier was that the difference between the two groups, male and female, is much less great whatever it may be, and we do not know exactly what it is, than the difference is internally in each group, so that it really only makes sense to legislate according to the needs of the particular job.

Senator Cook. Absolutely.

Miss Bird. Some women can lift just as well as men. I mean, there are wide variations. Sex is a bad classification really.

Senator Cook. Another example of protective legislation creating inequities concerns a Nevada law which limits the amount of weight which women may lift to 10 pounds. No doubt, this law was strongly supported by organized labor in the name of protection for female workers. This means that organized labor wanted the lifting of weight to become a specific classification possibly to discriminate against females.

Miss Bird. That was discriminatory. Some of them are not discriminatory. Some of them were intended to keep women out in the beginning in the early history. A lot of good labor law got on the books by utilizing the feminine role, and I suppose in a way you are willing to do anything you can to help people who are grossly underprivileged, but I really think that by now we do not need it.

Senator Cook. I feel that protective legislation was enacted as a manifestation of the desire of males to protect females but since, has become a tool for discrimination.

Miss Steinem. Mrs. Wolfgang was talking about college-educated women and I meant then to make the point and I forgot, that even at the upper levels that we think are equal or superior there turns out to be a very great difference. The Gorman Report of the Chicago Institute of Higher Education took the top five men's colleges and the top five women's colleges and rated them for everything: Course selection, teacher quality, and so forth, and came to the conclusion that the worst men's college was considerably better than the best women's college. Either we are educating the ruling class or we are not, and segregation does not work there either.

Senator Cook. I will repeat what I said yesterday. This fall I will have two girls in college and three the following fall. I am disturbed at these differentials because no university has yet advised me that the tuition for my daughters will be less than the tuition for men, because of the inequities between the sexes in earning power after graduation.

[Applause.]

Senator Cook. Thank you very much.

Senator Bayh. Thank you very much for letting us have your thoughts.

Our next witness is Mrs. John Basto, special representative, Communications Workers of America, District Four.

Mrs. Basto, glad to have you with us this morning.

STATEMENT OF MRS. ELOISE M. BASTO, SPECIAL REPRESENTATIVE, COMMUNICATIONS WORKERS OF AMERICA, DISTRICT FOUR

Mrs. Basto. I am glad you let me come this morning to testify on the subject before us.

My name is Eloise Basto, and I reside in Williamston, Mich. I am employed as a special representative of the Communications Workers of America in the district 4 office in Lansing. The Communications Workers represent approximately 520,000 members, and over 55 percent of these people are women.

My background includes serving on the Michigan Status of Women Commission, appointed by Governor Romney, and the Michigan Women's Commission, appointed by Governor Milliken, and 20 years as an international representative and working for Michigan Bell Telephone Co.

Now, I have become aware of problems caused by the conflict between title VII and various State laws designed to protect the health of women who are employed. And the problems become somewhat complicated due to the nature of the telephone industry, which, of course, provides 24-hour continuous service, 7 days a week. During the busy hours, the women who place the long-distance calls and render other kinds of service are under nerve-wracking pressures.

Title VII was written to break down discrimination in employment, and the title was and is necessary. However, the carrying out of the law's provisions I think can result in a form of discrimination never intended by the Congress. According to the strict interpretation of title VII, a woman may not be denied the opportunity for advancement or for consideration to fill any job which she can perform.

In the telephone industry, the strict interpretation has resulted within the last few years in placing a few women in various "craft" positions. Many of these are technical jobs held only by men. Some of these craft positions require lifting of weights and other tasks in which physical strength is needed. In Michigan, we have about 10,000 women employed by Michigan Bell, and of these approximately 400 are in "craft" positions; the others are in the traffic operator group, clerical groups and related work. Some of these 400 women have been promoted into "craft" jobs following the enactment of the Civil Rights Act, and during the same period I might point out that the Michigan State Labor law was in effect and did not serve as a deterrent to the advancement of these qualified women.

With the apparent nullification of State protective legislation, employers now feel free to assign excessive overtime, which they will freely admit is cheaper than hiring sufficient personnel to accomplish the normal workload without resorting to overtime. The Michigan State Law had a 9-hour daily average and a 54-hour weekly limit on work for women; the maximum limit for any single day was 10 hours. However, in light of the interpretation of title VII, Michigan Bell is acting to discontinue restrictions on the hours any woman can work.

As a matter of clarification, I point out that the job of telephone operator in a company central office is not performed under what is normally thought of as relaxed working conditions. It is noisy and it is hectic. The operator herself is in a small work space, nearly elbow-to-elbow with the operators at her right and left. The operator's vision consists of a tall switchboard directly in front of herself, with lights constantly coming on to signal a customer demanding attention. At her fingertips is the equipment needed to establish most connections. The near-universal use of dial systems has markedly changed the concept of a telephone operator's job. The operator's main function used to be helping one customer reach another. Now that the dial system has replaced all except the very smallest manual exchanges, the operator is called on for more specialized and difficult services, such as directory assistance, placing person-to-person and conference calls, emergency calls, and reporting of line troubles.

And I think you have all experienced occasionally the voice of a smile gets tired.

The women themselves are not agreed at all on the subject of overtime. Some would object to working more than the standard 40-hour week. Others would want to work overtime frequently, and still others only occasionally.

I am here today to ask that the Federal laws contain at least enough flexibility to allow the States to continue setting and enforcing maximum hours of work for women. The Michigan women's commission, on which I am now serving, has gone on record in opposition to repeal of the hours-limitation laws, but urges amendment of these laws so that professional, supervisory and executive personnel be excluded.

And I might point out here that we all agree in making our recommendation "employee." We scratched the words "woman" or "female" anywhere they appeared and said "any employee" be limited to 54 hours a week and that overtime beyond 54 be voluntary for men and women.

Mr. Chairman, you and your subcommittee may justifiably ask me why I am here in support of "yes-but" equality for women. I think women should be given the same consideration for any role in society that is now open to men. But working women in the United States can be called on to play a number of difficult roles. A mother who works on a job often has only half of her day's tasks finished when she punches out; normally she goes home to prepare the evening meal, supervise or do the normal household tasks, and otherwise make her unique contribution to her family's well-being.

The mother who must work needs maximum-hours protection, if only for her own health. She can least afford to be turned down at the "hiring gate," the employing office.

When the employer says can you work, can you work overtime? And she has to say no based on family responsibilities, she is eliminated. She does not get on the payroll to refuse overtime.

Many of the State protective laws were enacted to help end the sweatshop era of American labor groups. One of the most tragic single events in our labor history was the March 1911 fire at the Triangle Shirtwaist Co. in New York. The Triangle fire killed more than 140 employees, most of them young women from Italian and Jewish immigrant families. That fire so shocked the Nation that major reforms were enacted.

And I think you will recall there were strikes, there was picketing, there were demands for protective legislation for women by these garment groups very unsuccessfully until the fire, lives were lost, and then came the protective legislation.

The Congress presently is considering what may be the final step in worker protection—the Occupational Safety and Health Act of

1970. This act hopefully will be effective in requiring safe and healthy working conditions for all Americans. I would suggest that one working condition necessary is maximum hours; a fatigued employee is a possibly accident-prone employee. The Congress and other legislative bodies customarily have enacted special bills for special ills.

I believe these problems can be handled this way, too.

The Communication Workers of America, and the AFL–CIO, to which the union belongs, have traditionally opposed the "Equal Rights" amendments proposals because of their potential effects on laws to protect working women. The main reason for opposition is the threat that equal employment opportunity provisions could be applied contrary to the intent of the Congress, as set forth in title VII. I believe elimination of employment discrimination against women does not require jettisoning of economic and social gains for women simply because they do not apply to men.

At its 1967 convention, the Communications Workers of America went on record in support of the legal right of any worker to refuse to work overtime without jeopardy to his or her job or the opportunity to be considered for advancement. The convention sentiment overwhelmingly supported the idea that hours beyond the normal workweek should be on a voluntary basis.

The Seventh Constitutional Convention of the AFO–CIO, in December 1967, adopted a similar position. I am providing for the subcommittee's use a copy of that policy resolution. The position was reffirmed by the AFL–CIO's Eighth Constutional Convention, in December 1969.

Mr. Chairman, unemployed individuals do not benefit when additional hours are piled on those already employed. And an employed worker, who is required to spend excessive hours on the job, hardly benefits when some of his or her premium time earnings are consumed by payments for health care necessitated by the physically wearing effect of extra-long hours.

I believe the equal rights amendment would contribute to both of those unfavorable situations.

I thank you again for the opportunity to appear here today.

Senator BAYH. Thank you very much, Mrs. Basto. We appreciate your taking time to be with us. And certainly I have a warm feeling in my heart for the many friends that I have in the Communications Workers. I appreciate the service that they render, and most of the time the voices are smiling.

The argument that passing this amendment will cause longer hours to be heaped upon the backs of the women is a matter of some concern to me.

Could you expand your thoughts concerning the possibility that this amendment could be passed and still have reasonable limitations beyond which men and women could not work involuntarily?

Mrs. BASTO. Well, I believe, of course, that would be the answer, to establish a maximum number of hours beyond which no employee could work.

Senator BAYH. Unless they wanted to. Unless it was voluntary.

Mrs. BASTO. That is right, voluntary.

I have had some firsthand experience with this. In Michigan we had a bill, bill 2310, which was being considered by the senate-house committee for passage which was to establish voluntary overtime. We testified on it, as did all labor on that bill.

Now, we found it unique, and the reason I say professional and executive people should be exempt, those groups and the UAW, should I say UAW Women's Division testified yes, voluntary, but in the event you cannot have it, remove all restrictions.

The working people from all the unions complained, the men complained bitterly of the abuse that they had suffered and the hours that they had worked, and the male UAW International reps complained at the excessive hours in the Flint plants where the men had been terribly abused by overtime and the companies unwilling to negotiate anything near reasonable for the number of hours.

Now, what I interpret this to be is our saying let's give the women equal abuse to what the men are getting, and I think it is wrong. I think you try and bring the men up to share what the women have so that everybody as a group is better off.

Senator BAYH. This would be my intention.

Mrs. BASTO. And then anybody can volunteer for any number of hours they would like to work.

Senator BAYH. I would like to think that would be the best way to proceed rather than to suggest we are going to continue to allow this inequity to exist.

Mrs. BASTO. Companies testified that they were in dire straits if they had to limit their overtime.

Senator BAYH. Thank you.

Senator Cook.

Senator COOK. I have no questions. I am trying to equate the respective police powers of the state to the language of the resolution, "shall not be denied or abridged," and the question arises how do we legislate concerning the health and safety of all employees and not run into a conflict with the language, "shall not be denied or abridged"? I think this is what we have to answer in this testimony and in preparing our report for submission to the full committee.

Thank you, Mr. Chairman.

Senator BAYH. Thank you very much. We appreciate your contribution and your thoughts on the subject.

I am advised that Mrs. Jacqueline Gutwillig representing the Citizens' Advisory Council on the Status of Women has to catch an airplane. If it would be helpful to her, we would be glad to take her next.

I understand you are the Chairman of that organization, is that accurate?

Mrs. GUTWILLIG. Yes, sir.

STATEMENT OF MRS. JACQUELINE G. GUTWILLIG, CHAIRMAN, CITIZENS' ADVISORY COUNCIL ON THE STATUS OF WOMEN

Mrs. GUTWILLIG. Mr. Chairman, members of the subcommittee, I am, as you said, Jacqueline Gutwillig, chairman of the Citizens' Advisory Council on the Status of Women and I consider it a privilege indeed to be a part of this history-making hearing.

I should like to provide you with a brief personal background as it relates to my remarks particularly those concerning the military.

I am a retired lieutenant colonel, Women's Army Corps, with service as executive officer in Psychological Warfare Division of Supreme Headquarters Allied Expeditionary Forces in England, France, and Germany. I was awarded the Bronze Star Medal and was decorated an honorary member of the Most Excellent Order of the British Empire for Meritorious Service. Later, I served as a Reserve officer and logistical staff officer in the Logistics Division of the United States Army General Staff in the Pentagon.

I have been a member of the National Foundation March of Dimes as assistant national director for women's activities. Volunteer activities include service as a member and officer in the League of Women Voters and the March of Dimes; national codirector for veterans affairs in the 1952 Citizens for Eisenhower Campaign; campaign manager for the Women's National Republican Club in the 1956 Eisenhower campaign and in 1968 a member of the Women's National Advisory Committee for Nixon-Agnew.

I relate these activities not to draw attention to myself but to provide background.

The Citizens' Advisory Council on the Status of Women was established by Executive Order 11126 November 1, 1963. The Council consists of 20 members who serve without compensation for an indeterminate period. Each of us was appointed by President Nixon on August 15, 1969.

The Council is assigned the responsibilities of review and evaluation of progress in furthering the full participation of women in American life. The Council serves as a means for suggesting and stimulating action with private institutions, labor, civic, service groups, and individuals working for improvement of conditions of special concern to women.

At the Council's first meeting in this administration a project committee was appointed to study equal legal status for women. The project committee, chaired by Miss Sarah Jane Cunningham, recommended that the Council endorse the equal rights amendment. The Council did so and has published a memorandum on the equal rights amendment which I am submitting for the record.

I regret Miss Cunningham is unable to be with us today. She is a lawyer in private practice in McCook, Nebr., and is an expert on the legal status of women.

I wish to emphasize that the proposed equal rights amendment might more appropriately be titled the "Equal Legal Rights and Responsibilities Amendment," since it relates only to legal rights and since it would impose responsibilities as well as rights on women.

Some may interpret the equal rights amendment as "more words." You have already heard that, and declare again that the fifth and 14th amendments and title VII of the Civil Rights Act prohibit sex distinctions in the law.

Maybe so—but the courts are the final arbiters of the meaning of the Constitution and our laws. And the Supreme Court has not, thus far, acknowledged the protection of the amendments to female citizens, per se, although under the fifth and 14th amendments the Supreme Court has ruled on cases involving racial bias there are still many inequities in our States, such as women criminals serving longer prison sentences than men for the same crime, which was mentioned also yesterday.

We believe the proposed equal rights amendment offers the best assurance to secure the rights of all persons—both men and women—to equal treatment under the law.

I shall not read our memorandum which you have at hand and which sets forth in detail these and additional views on the legal issues. But I wish to note that the equal rights amendment would also equalize the responsibilities for jury service and military service.

Presently, young women volunteering for military service must have high school diplomas and must achieve higher scores on the educational tests than the regular scores for men who are drafted. Incidentally, I remind you as was said in testimony yesterday, the Congress has the power to draft women as well as men but has not done so. However, near the end of World War II, a law drafting nurses was passed by the House of Representatives and had been reported favorable in the Senate. The end of the war was in sight at that time so the bill was not acted on by the Senate.

Today, many young women when asked their views on drafting women have in the majority concurred that it is fair to share this responsibility of citizenship with young men.

Should our country's policies of recruitment change to voluntary military service—of which there is a very great likelihood—females under the equal rights amendment could volunteer and be accepted under the same standards as set for males.

Females in the armed services could expect to be selected to serve in positions for which they are qualified as men are now so selected. Opportunities for training, education, and self-improvement through military service, now available to young women. This service would be an avenue for a rising quality of life for many girls, particularly those whose opportunities in life have been denied.

My own military experiences benefited me personally—if I may use myself as an example. I received advanced training at command and general staff college and achieved a better understanding of governmental affairs during my years of duty. I know that I am a better contributor as a citizen and a better human being as a result of my military service. In the quest for equality of opportunity and social justice for women there is a need for public awareness and understanding, which the discussion and debate about this amendment will help to promote.

And I should like to bring to your attention an example of awareness, although its relationship is a little indirect. The American Council on Education undertook a study of campus tensions. This special study committee consisted of 18 members, only one of whom was a woman—even though 40 percent of college students are women, even though the Women's Liberation movement on college campuses is the most rapidly growing protest movement in the United States, and even though 24 percent of the teaching staff in colleges and universities are women.

The campus tensions committee sponsored a 3-day workshop of student leaders; of the 19 participants, six were women selected by the student representatives. The committee published a 79-page report which is very excellent, but direct reference to the participation of women students in campus unrest and the cause of their dissatisfactions were disposed of in about four sentences. Basically, these sentences dealt with discriminations; some students asserted that they were the victims of both institutional and individual discrimination although most colleges and universities, by policy and regulations, prohibit discrimination.

The ratification of the equal rights amendment would not directly influence social attitudes either but it would most certainly have indirect effects.

Leo Kanowitz points out in his book, "Women and the Law: The Unfinished Revolution" that:

Rules of law that treat of the sexes per se inevitably produce far-reaching effects upon social, psychological, and economic aspects of male-female relationships beyond the limited confines of legislative chambers and courtrooms. As long as organized legal systems, at once the most respected and most feared of social institutions, continue to differentiate sharply, in our treatment or in words, between men and women on the basis of irrelevant and artificially created distinctions, the likelihood of men and women coming to regard one another primarily as fellow human beings and only secondarily as representatives of another sex will continue to be remote.

The public discussion growing out of the legislative process in the Congress and the State legislative bodies must lead to greater awareness of the economic, social, and psychological discriminations against women, as well as legal differences.

Men generally are not antiwomen—I say this hopefully—and may not consciously discriminate, but also may not be mindful of the effects on women of outmoded attitudes and pressures. The biggest obstacle to improvement in the status of women is lack of knowledge. I look to these and future hearings on State levels to advance us beyond merely securing the equal protection of the law, important as that is.

Mr. Chairman, ratification of the equal rights amendment is the most effective and expeditious method of securing for women equal protection of the law. Laws for women are 40 years behind laws for minority groups in achieving constitutional guarantees. Passage by the Congress in 1970 of the equal rights amendment would be a most appropriate commemoration of the 50th anniversary of the suffrage movement.

This would be good for women; this would be good for men, and it would be good for America.

I kept my remarks brief to avoid repetition, but I wish to commend you again, Mr. Chairman, and your subcommittee for holding these hearings and for your efforts in furthering the proposed equal rights amendment.

Thank you. And may I add that I have brought with me the Report of the Task Force on Family Law and Policy. Questions were asked several times yesterday and this morning of the effect on family law of ratification of the equal rights amendment, and I would like to enter in the record the report of the Task Force on Family Law and Policy of the Citizens' Advisory Council. All the recommendations are in accord with the equal rights amendment. This report covers alimony, support, divorce, child custody, age of marriage, property law, and domicile. It includes tables of marriage and divorce law. We have additional copies. They are available from the Citizens' Advisory Council in the Department of Labor.

Senator BAYH. Thank you very much. I appreciate not only your testimony, but the report.

I trust you have listened to some of the discussion that has transpired here this morning. Do you have any further observation on the legitimate concern that some women have expressed about the length of work controversy, nullification of these laws and the fact that this could be a regression to the sweat shop. You have heard me state that we ought to keep men as well as women out of the sweat shop and that perhaps this would be the best way to do it. Would you give us your frank judgment on the dangers, possible dangers of this?

Mrs. GUTWILLIG. I would be very happy to.

Times have changed. Laws that were good 150 years ago do not necessarily serve the same purposes today. Women have changed. Women want to be where the action is. They want to be contributors today. They are not necessarily the ones who just sit back and do not contribute and be part of their community. We are 51 percent of the population.

Senator BAYH. I wish you ladies would stop emphasizing that.

Mrs. GUTWILLIG. Well, then, I think you gentlemen ought to do more about having more male babies.

Senator BAYH. We will see if we can't add an amendment to the amendment to do something about that.

Mrs. GUTWILLIG. This might help.

Senator BAYH. But is it not fair to say that even though women want a piece of the action that perhaps they should be subjected to the 12 hour a day, 7 day a week treatment that was earlier described?

Mrs. GUTWILLIG. Well, we still have laws and always will limiting the hours of work for people.

Senator BAYH. Couldn't this be applied to men and women.

Mrs. GUTWILLIG. Yes, it could be applied to men and women. There is no reason why the same laws shouldn't apply for both men and women. Men don't want to work 60 or 80, or 90 hours either because it's not necessary in our economy, and I am sure the union people themselves try to keep hours down so that people can live and work and enjoy life also. There is no reason why if there is overtime and if a woman wants to work that overtime, she should not have the opportunity to do so. It doesn't mean that everybody wants to do it, but if a woman is in the type of job where overtime is required, she knows that before she takes the job and she should have the same opportunity as a man. Every human being should have the same opportunity regardless of race, color, creed, origin, sex, to pursue life in their own way.

Senator BAYH. I certainly appreciate your testimony. I would like to emphasize again for the record your past service to your country in the military. This reflects on another question which is often raised in the context of the equal rights movement.

Senator Cook?

Senator COOK. I notice your remark that the equal rights amendment would also equalize the responsibilities of jury service and military service.

The matter of jury service is a hodge podge situation. There is much difference among the States in jury participation by women.

To further comment on your testimony I wish to remind you that Miss Rawalt, who testified yesterday, was instrumental in overturning the discriminatory Pennsylvania law which allowed for longer prison sentences for women than men.

I am interested in finding the bill which deals with the drafting of nurses because it concerns the matter at hand, that is the responsibilities and obligations of every individual. Had each citizen of this Nation possessed equality and had we called fully on each citizen rather than stifling some, a portion of today's problems might have been averted.

Mrs. GUTWILLIG. Senator Cook, may I offer to get that bill for you?

Senator COOK. I would appreciate it very much.

(See letter following:)

CITIZENS' ADVISORY COUNCIL ON THE STATUS OF WOMEN,
Washington, D.C., May 13, 1970.

Hon. BIRCH BAYH,
U.S. Senate,
Washington, D.C.

DEAR SENATOR BAYH: The Council appreciates very much the holding of the hearings on the Equal Rights Amendment. I am sure they will serve a very valuable purpose in educating the public to the facts about discrimination against women. I feel you are to be complimented on your courteous and firm conduct of the hearings.

Senator Cook asked for more details concerning Congressional action to draft nurses during World War II. The House Commmittee, after hearings, reported H.R. 2277 on February 22, 1945 (House Report No. 194). The bill was debated in the House on March 5th and 6th and passed on the 7th. The Senate Military Affairs Committee held hearings on March 19, 21, 23, and 26, and reported the bill to the Senate on March 28th (Senate Report No. 130). On May 25, 1945, shortly after V.E. Day, Acting Secretary of War Patterson wrote that the Army could get along without drafting nurses.

Please feel free to call upon this office if there is any further help we can render.

With warm regards,

JACQUELINE G. GUTWILLIG, *Chairman.*

Mrs. GUTWILLIG. I am sure that our office could get the number and provide you with the information. I don't have the number in hand, the number of the bill.

Senator COOK. Again I return to the correlation between protective legislation and an "equal rights" amendment. I feel the two can not be equated and that certain protective legislation, such as that dealing with maximum working hours for women, actually grants privileges to women. I am unable to imagine women wanting such legislation abolished, in fact many men would like to be so protected.

Mrs. GUTWILLIG. Senator Cook, if I may make a remark to that, these laws are restrictive. They prohibit a woman from pursuing the job in the same equal manner that a man can. Therefore, it is stopping them from being promoted, very often from even getting the job that they want to have and are capable of performing. This is the important crux of the whole thing, I think. It is the restrictive part of it. Let a woman have the opportunity of applying, being heard and given the opportunity to do the job. And she will not have the opportunity if she cannot fulfill the requirements of the job.

Senator COOK. I am inclined to wholeheartedly agree with you.

To continue my questioning, did a particular time period occur in which several labor classification laws were enacted? For example,

124

was such legislation enacted during a given time period, such as the depression, when some people might have felt the need to exclude certain groups, such as women, from the labor pool? I ask this in light of the fact that what once was termed protective legislation is now referred to by some as discriminatory legislation.

Mrs. GUTWILLIG. Senator Cook. in our memo, "The Proposed Equal Rights Amendment to the United States Constitution," which you have had and which I have referred to, these things are covered in detail in there. I don't have the exact dates in hand, but over the years passed—well, it's got 1908, 1937. In many cases, it was—and this is my own personal observation on this—they wanted the jobs for men, and by instituting so-called protective phases the jobs then were off limits to women. They could not apply for them or be accepted for them. Also, it was an attitude of the times. Women themselves felt they should be protected. Women were brought up on the old-fashioned way that they had to be more careful of themselves, that their bodies were less able to take things than men.

We have grown up now. Life and times have changed. We know that we can do things. And I can take myself for example. I have a husband who has a heart condition and for years I am the one who lifts suitcases and drives the car. I am the one who moves the furniture around the house and it hasn't hurt me one bit.

I am physically capable and so is the majority of women who want to do something. Did that answer your question, sir?

Senator COOK. Yes.

[Applause.]

Senator COOK. Having had spinal fusions, your last remark was very meaningful.

Mrs. GUTWILLIG. Thank you.

Senator COOK. Thank you, Mr. Chairman.

Senator BAYH. The record might show that the chairman of the subcommittee was an interested observer to that last response.

I would like to ask that the Proposed Equal Rights Amendment to the Constitution Memorandum of your Citizens' Advisory Council be placed in the record at this point.

Senator BAYH. We appreciate very much your being here with us.

Mrs. GUTWILLIG. Thank you, sir, for the opportunity.

Senator BAYH. We have here an article which deals at some length with one of the problems that has been discussed repeatedly, entitled, "Sex Discrimination and 'Protective' Labor Legislation," which I think would be beneficial for our record and anyone who might care to pursue it. If my distinguished colleague from Kentucky has no objection I would like to put it in the record at this time.

Senator BAYH. Our next witnesses are Dr. Bernice Sandler, and Dr. Elizabeth Boyer, Women's Equity Action League.

STATEMENT OF DR. BERNICE SANDLER, WOMEN'S EQUITY ACTION LEAGUE

Dr. SANDLER. I am Dr. Bernice Sandler of the Women's Equity Action League (WEAL) where I am chairman of the Action Committee for Federal Contract Compliance in Education. I am also a psychologist with the Department of Health, Education, and Welfare, and a visiting lecturer at the University of Maryland in the Department of Counseling and Personnel Services, but I am not speaking on behalf of HEW or the University of Maryland. I am speaking as an individual and as a representative of WEAL. I have submitted a statement for the record on behalf of the amendment and I would like to summarize the highlights of that statement.

Senator BAYH. We will ask without objection that the entire statement be put in the record as if it were presented.

Dr. SANDLER. Thank you. I will limit my testimony to the crucial area of sex discrimination in our universities and colleges, and to how the equal rights amendment will begin to alleviate some of the terrible injustices and inequities suffered by women on the campus.

Since Januaary 1970, formal charges of sex discrimination under Executive Order 11246, as amended, have been filed against 43 universities and colleges with the Department of Labor. The Women's Equity Action League (WEAL) initiated 41 of these formal charges. The Executive order forbids Federal contractors from discriminating against race, creed, color, national origin, or sex. As Federal contractors who receive about $3.3 billion per year, universities and colleges are subject to the provisions of this order. WEAL submitted about 80 pages of materials documenting our charges of an industry-wide pattern of sex discrimination in the academic community.

Half of the brightest people in our country—half of the most talented people with the potential for the highest intellectual endeavor are women. These women will encounter discrimination after discrimination as they try to use their talents in the university world. They will be discriminated against when they first apply for admission. They will be discriminated against when they apply for financial and scholarship aid. They will be discriminated against when they apply for positions on faculty. If they are hired, they will be promoted far more slowly than their male counterparts, and furthermore if hired at all, women will most likely receive far less money than their male counterparts on the campus. And all of this is legal.

Columbia University violates no law when only 2 percent of its tenured faculty are women, although 25 percent of its doctorates go to women. Harvard violates no law, when, of the 411 tenured professors in its Graduate School of Arts and Sciences not one—not one, is a woman, despite that fact that 22 percent of the graduate students are women. The University of Maryland, my own university, violates no law when only one professor in the Department of Psychology, 3 percent of the faculty, has tenure, while nationally women earn 23 percent of the doctorates in psychology. It is legal for the University of California at Berkeley to simply hire no women at all in its Department of Psychology. Statistics like this cross my desk almost daily. The position of women on our campuses is steadily worsening. It is not getting better. The proportion of women graduate students is less now than it was in 1930. The University of Chicago has a lower proportion of women on its faculty now than it did in 1899.

Somehow, women qualified to earn doctoral degrees are not considered qualified to teach. And women, qualified enought to teach in the university or college, are not considered qualified enough for promotion and tenure.

It is completely within the law to discriminate against women on the campus. There is no law forbidding the University of North Carolina from maintaining its quota system for the admission of women, and I quote from an official publication of that university: "Admission will be restricted to those who are especially well qualified."

Such official, and unofficial, quota systems restrict the number of women entering our colleges, but they break no law. Section 702 of the Civil Rights Act of 1964 exempts educational institutions. Title VI of the same Civil Rights Act forbids discrimination but only applies to discrimination based on race, religion, and national origin—not sex.

The Equal Pay Act excludes "executive, administrative, or professional employees". Even the U.S. Commission on Civil Rights has no jurisdiction whatsoever concerning sex discrimination—it is limited by law to matters pertaining to race, color, religion, or national origin—not sex.

At best, Executive Order 11246 under which WEAL is filing its charges of sex discrimination, is an administrative remedy for such discrimination in our universities and colleges. Unfortunately, as you well know, the Executive order does not have the status of law; it can be amended or suspended at the pleasure of a particular administration. And any institution that wanted to continue discrimination is legally free to do so if it gives up its Government contracts. The very rules and regulations of the Executive order require far less of State-supported institutions than they do of private institutions. In contrast, the equal rights amendment would have a direct effect on all State schools at all levels of education. It would forbid laws or official practices that currently exclude women from State colleges and institutions, including higher admission standards for women, and it would end many of the discriminatory practices now legally engaged in by universities and colleges. While the amendment would not have a direct effect on private institutions, the State universities and colleges would undoubtedly serve as a model for the private institutions.

The psychological effect of such an amendment would be enormous. Women have been loath to complain about discrimination in their institution because they risk academic suicide if they do so. I know of two women who did protest this year and who were promptly and officially censured. They may well lose their tenure, if not their jobs.

Senator. BAYH. Did they have any recourse through the courts or a similar appeal mechanism?

Dr. SANDLER. We are exploring this now to see what can be done.

We have filed charges under the Executive order against that particular university system. I have been asked not to mention the particular university's name because the women understandably do not want this kind of publicity. They are frightened.

Senator COOK. Is there no recourse through the National Association of University Professors?

Dr. SANDLER. I think the women are exploring that. The American Association of University Professors doesn't keep statistics by sex anymore. We have trouble even getting the data from them.

Senator BAYH. The basic problem we still will have if we are successful with this amendment is that we cannot change things unless the women who are discriminated against will seek redress for their grievances in the courts.

Dr. SANDLER. Yes, I quite agree. What women need is moral and legal support to carry on this struggle. If they don't have the legal support, there is very little they can do except complain. I have been amazed because since we started filing complaints women all over the country are suddenly writing and saying, "We want to complain now, too, legitimately. We want to use the Executive order and open this up on our campus."

Senator COOK. The loopholes that exist in the dismissal procedures for college students disturb me, especially with today's rapport between faculty and students. This morning on television the president of New York University, in answer to the question, "Whyy aren't more students dismissed?", listed a long and detailed procedure for the dismissal of students. In addition he cited the rights of students to counsel, to a hearing and to petition for a rehearing.

Dr. SANDLER. Well, part of the problem is that sex discrimination on the campus has really gone unnoticed for years.

Senator BAYH. I suppose that it is part of the problem—excuse me for interrupting again. It is part of this whole attitude that we have discussed in which it is "the thing" to protest against a person being discriminated against because he (or she) is black or because he is dressed wrong or because he may want to teach or preach a certain philosophy, but it is still not in vogue to demonstrate against discrimination of the basis of sex.

Dr. SANDLER. Yes. It is the last socially acceptable prejudice you can have.

Senator COOK. Maybe one of the problems that we are facing is that even though most universities ascribe to the doctrine of academic freedom, certain faculty members feel that this does not include women. I speak in reference to one of your colleagues at the University of Maryland who insists that 'women should not be professionals'. Undoubtedly, more cooperation is needed from your fellow faculty members.

Dr. SANDLER. Not very much cooperation in my own department on this.

Dr. BOYER. I just happen to have a fact on this.

You inquired about the American Association of University Professors having a procedure when professors are fired. Yes, they do, but while it covers some people without tenure, it does not cover temporary or special appointments, or part-time appointments, many of which are filled primarily by women. That is the technicality. I am sorry I interrupted.

Senator COOK. I think that is a big technicality.

Dr. BOYER. I am sorry I interrupted.

Dr. SANDLER. Sex prejudice is so ingrained in our society that many who practice it are simply unaware that they are hurting women. Let me reiterate,—it is the last socially acceptable prejudice. The chairman of a department sees nothing wrong in paying a woman less because "she is married and therefore doesn't need as much" or paying her less because "she is not married and therefore doesn't need as much."

Many of the most ardent supporters of civil rights for blacks, Indians, Spanish-speaking Americans and other minority groups simply do not view sex discrimination as discrimination. No university today would advertise for a "white assistant professor" yet these same concerned humanitarians see nothing wrong with advertising for a "male assistant professor." These same humanitarians fail to notice that half of each minority group are women. Both Congresswoman Shirley Chisholm and Pauli Murray, a noted lawyer, have both stated that they have suffered far more from being a woman than from being a Negro.

In a little noted development, all over the country, on both small and large campuses, women have begun to form groups across departmental and professional lines. They are beginning to do more than complain; they are examining the role of women on their campus, and the university's treatment of them. In various professional groups, such as the American Psychological Association, the American Sociological Association, the Modern Language Association, the American Political Science Association, the American Historical Association, women are forming pressure groups and demanding an end to discrimination within their respective professions. Women are tired of second class citizenship on the campus.

We live in a rapidly changing world, one which is threatened by the problems of population growth. There is little reason to expect a woman to limit her family if the only realistic alternative to childbearing is a job far below her capacities, coupled with extensive educational and occupational discrimination. Extensive reform in our abortion laws, and the dissemination of birth control information will have little impact unless women have something else to do with their lives. The education of women is crucial if we are to achieve this.

Women have been discriminated against in many areas of life, of which the university is but one. We need to begin to redress these wrongs. The equal rights amendment is a symbolic and actual beginning. It will give hope and dignity to women, the second class citizens of the Nation. As a member of the women's equity action league, as an educator of counselors, and as a psychologist, as a teacher, as a woman, a wife and a mother, and above all as a human being, I urge you to support this amendment.

[Applause.]

STATEMENT OF DR. ELIZABETH BOYER, WOMEN'S EQUITY ACTION LEAGUE

Senator BAYH. Dr. Boyer.

Dr. BOYER. Members of Congress and friends, I am Elizabeth Boyer of Cleveland, immediate past president of the Women's Equity Action League. I too will abridge my remarks in view of the time. And I ask that they be included in the record as written.

If every woman who is tired of working could quit her job, and go home and do needlepoint, many would consider it a cause for rejoicing. We sympathize with the women who are serving life sentences in uninteresting and poorly paid jobs, with little hope of advancement.

Opponents of this amendment often point to the duties of homemaking and motherhood as woman's highest destiny. But let us examine the facts for a moment.

If women stopped work business and industry would be at a loss to replace them. Women's brains and skills still come cheap, and are an economical factor in company budgets. So business and industry don't really want the ladies to go home—they just want them to work cheap, and not to expect too much advancement.

If women stopped work, their income tax payments would cease. A large proportion of the tax total is collected from the lower earnings brackets. During the recent revision of the tax structure, it was apparently found unfeasible to excuse persons earning, for example, $3,000 a year, from paying tax, for this reason. Therefore, I don't suppose that Congress really wants the ladies to retreat en masse to the home, either.

If women stopped work, who would support them? A vastly increased number of women, whether married or not, are in fact responsible for their own support, and often for that of dependents. Could they all be supported by Federal subsidies? Additional taxes to be paid by working males? Impossible. Increasingly fewer men can support and educate their own children without mother going back to work. Voters are increasingly reluctant to support other people's children, as witness the failure of school and welfare levies. A recent Gallup poll disclosed that 64 percent of the men interviewed wanted their wives to go back to work. No, men don't want their women to stay home, really. The ironic truth is that from now on many women are going to have to deny or abridge their motherhood functions if a reasonable population balance is to be maintained.

Therefore, we are now confronted with a situation where the majority of our women have to work. Our political, economic and military commitments over the past 50 years or so have landed us in a situation which the Founding Fathers certainly never contemplated: We are dependent on the economic productivity and financial responsibility of women.

The inescapable corollary is that we must give women equality of rights under the law, to counterbalance this responsibility so that they may more equitably share in the fruits of their labor.

Until recently, the predicament of workingwomen was not a subject for open discussion. Each woman was too proud to admit that she was in a low-paid, deadend job, and that her father, or husband, had not made her financially independent. Only a relatively few women understood, and were willing to discuss, the disabilities of women under the law, and the discriminations against them which held sway.

The pressures of inflation and the widening salary gap have ended this suffer-in-silence era. Women are in rebellion, and there is little doubt that the rebellion is economically based. In my opinion, the equal rights amendment, at this time, is an economic issue.

It is notable that opposition to the amendment has been withdrawn by most of the groups who historically opposed it and whose interests were sociological. Opposition is still evinced by those groups whose interest is economic, and who benefit by keeping women as a cheap labor pool.

The standard prediction of opponents of the amendment used to be that if it were passed, "a veritable Pandora's box" of litigation and statutory redrafting would ensue.

I believe that a consideration of the problems predicted in past years will show something very interesting: Most of their dire predictions have come about without passage of the amendment. Unfortunately, the benefits for which its proponents hoped have been slower in evolving.

To enumerate: Opponents predicted that the State so-called protective laws would be eliminated. These laws are now on their way out, which we could go into great detail about, because of the conflict with the provisions of title VII of the Civil Rights Act of 1964, and the various States are slowly drawing their laws into conformity with that act—largely eliminating the hours and weight-lifting regulations.

I would like to interpolate something in response to a previous speaker. I have been invited twice to testify in Ohio on hearings on regularizing protective laws to bring them into conformity with title VII. The members of the very labor union which came down there and testified and came here and testified supporting the protective laws, that union's own women members came in force in Ohio, they brought 50 members up from Dayton to object to their own union's stand on this matter and to say that they needed the overtime just as much as the men did. And my mail supports this, as does the stand of the industrially employed members of WEAL of whom we have a great many. This is their stand. They say their experience has been, as members and as union stewards, that their women need the overtime and want it.

Our point of view of course is that protective legislation should be applied to both men and women.

It is interesting to note that most women's organizations have supported the elimination of protective laws, having found them more discriminatory then protective.

A Pandora's box of legislation has been opened in a proliferation of cases on discrimination against women. At this time passage of the amendment could only reduce the number and simplify the case precedents, by furnishing a sound constitutional base.

Opponents formerly predicted that equality of rights under the law would throw into confusion the husband's duty to support his wife and children.

Well, this would bear investigation now.

Runaway mothers are a rarity; runaway fathers a commonplace. Alimony awards are seldom made now to women who can possibly go back to work, and child-support allowances are usually pretty austere—based on the mother's participation in supporting the children. And any lawyer can testify to the impractibility of forcing an unwilling man to support his children. So families are finding their own solutions to these problems, irrespective of who is theoretically the "head of the house."

The benefits for which its proponents hoped have been slower in arriving. The salary gap between men and women is widening; the economic pinch in which workingwomen find themselves is increasing in severity; opportunities for women in education and the professions have declined. Over half the children whose mothers head the household, are living at or below poverty level, and nearly 60 percent of retired women live at or below poverty level.

If we are in a position where women must take responsibility for themselves, we must give them equal powers of economic self-determinism.

The passage of the equal rights amendment at this time would serve many purposes. It would show that Congress is cognizant of the productive efforts and tax contributions of women, which are needed now as never before, as well as of their voting potential.

It would demonstrate a serious effort at readjustment of our system of jurisprudence, in an orderly way, to meet the economic and social changes that have taken place, thrusting responsibilities upon women which the drafters of the Constitution never contemplated.

A sound and unequivocal constitutional base is needed to bring uniformity to the laws of the various States, and to undergird the various legal actions now in progress and in preparation in this area of law. The question of "legislative intent," always a concern in construing laws which are general or ambiguous would thus be clarified as to the rights of women under the law.

At the time of the drafting of our Constitution four groups had no legal status and were not represented—slaves, indentured servants, men of no property, and women. The Negro's rights have been insured by amendment, indentured servants are no more, and various conflicts of interest on property rights eliminated early discriminations against "men of no property." Women remain, nearly 200 years later, with their legal status unresolved. The suffrage amendment gave them the vote, but their rights are subject to common law interpretations and the laws of the various States, and a confusion of case decisions leaves them in an intolerably anomalous position. As a lawyer involved in a number of cases concerning the rights of women under the law, I am sorely conscious of the need for a sound constitutional base.

Reliance on the case decisions of the Supreme Court has proved difficult. It is probably fair to say that the due process cases under the 14th amendment which concerned women's freedom to contract, reflected the sociological attitudes of the judges sitting at the time. In the absence of legislative clarification this will thus continue to be an unpredictable area, according to the attitudes of whatever judges hear the cases.

Because of the present pressures, cases involving the employment rights of women are on the increase. Economic and social trends, such as Government debt, overpopulation, increased longevity, and the increasing number of broken homes, will make the economic self-sufficiency of women an increasing problem. In view of our national commitments, these pressures will increase for the forseeable future.

Women at large may not have the technical insight to analyze exactly where the law is failing them, but, increasingly, they are becoming aware that "the times are out of joint" so far as women are concerned. If respect for the law is to survive, laws must meet the present needs of the governed. A patchwork of inclusion of women in a hodgepodge of State and Federal statutes does not seem to be an orderly approach. A number of cases are presently in the courts where employers and newspaper publishers are seeking to avoid conforming with various such statutes. Government agencies are delaying issuance of supporting enforcement guidelines, and even the White House is holding back the issuance of a much-heralded task force report submitted last December 15.

Everyone is apparently hoping the problem will "go away." The problem will not go away, simply because women cannot afford to acquiesce in their own economic suicide.

I receive a great deal of mail from women throughout the country, since the organization I represent, the Women's Equity Action League, commonly known as WEAL has as its purpose obtaining equity for women in jobs and education. Although we are not much over a year old as an organization, we already have representation in 34 States, and our mail points up problems which will eventually reach the courts. The difficulty seems to be that many employers, Government officials, and even some of our elected representatives, do not seem to realize that in this matter women have finally reached a state of great determination. The problem is not going to go away, it is going to become worse.

The quality of a system of jurisprudence, and of a political system is displayed by its ability to meet the legitimate needs of those it governs. I therefore urge the reporting out of committee, and the early passage, of the equal rights amendment as a first logical step in meeting the legitimate needs of the women of this country.

I thank you.

[Applause.]

Senator BAYH. Thank you, both of you, Dr. Boyer and Dr. Sandler. I have a number of questions I intended to ask you, but I think you already answered them quite well. Your work in pointing out discriminatory practices in the field of education which serve to deny young women the chance to totally develop their talents is particularly helpful to us.

Senator Cook.

Senator COOK. The bell you just heard designates a vote. I would like to ask you what your analysis is of the phrase "under the law shall not be denied or abridged" in relation to a wide variety of statutes that are now on the books.

If these statutes were designated specifically for women, don't you feel that these statutes could be redesigned according to capability rather than sex? In other words, there are many people, in the labor pool other than females who cannot lift 35 pounds, and I think we should designate capabilities only.

Mrs. BOYER. Exactly.

Senator COOK. Designating qualifications and capabilities is more equitable than designating sex because the entire working force is included. Protective legislation, such as that governing the number of working hours in a week, is then applicable to all.

Mrs. BOYER. Very true.

Senator COOK. I am disturbed by those witnesses who speak at a 54-hour-workweek while the organization they represent supports a 3-day-workweek. I cannot equate this proposed constitutional amendment with the basic police power of a State or local agency to care for people, not men or women, but people.

Mrs. BOYER. I quite agree.

Senator COOK. If it is done on this basis, then we violate nothing, but we do exercise the right as a nation to care for a category of people which, because of this amendment, no longer is based on sex.

Mrs. Boyer. This is exactly the way our legal staff sees it; exactly what you have stated so much better than I would have. It is just exactly our view of the matter. As a matter of fact, also as a practical matter, we think that if the women's rulings are ruled out, they will be more likely to get passed for men and women both because hen both men and women will be pressing for the legislation. To get a law for both men and women will be more practical, in other words.

Senator Cook. Then the application would be more uniform within the labor force.

Mrs. Boyer. Absolutely. By the way, could I make one more observation.

Senator Cook. Absolutely.

Mrs. Boyer. I am telling tales out of school here, but in view of some of the previous testimony I would like to remark that some of our legal staff is examining the question of whether some of the unions are fairly representing women. We have had many complaints from women in the labor movement who would like us to look into this matter and we are looking into it. We are a great birddogging group. Most of what we are doing is like the iceberg under the surface, digging things out and that is one of the ones we are digging on.

Senator Cook. Thank you, Mr. Chairman.

(Short interval.)

Senator Cook. Thank you, ladies. I apologize for keeping you waiting. Thank you for your contributions. I would like to observe that we are behind schedule and because of this vote perhaps we should recess until 2 o'clock. I am advised by our staff that we have a logistical problem. At that time we will reconvene in room 457, which is on the fourth floor, up and to the left. Room 457 at 2 o'clock to hear the last two witnesses. I am sorry that this has lasted so long.

(Whereupon, at 12:30, the committee recessed, to reconvene at 2 p.m., in room 457; this date.)

AFTERNOON SESSION

Senator Bayh (presiding). If we could please come to order. I would like to proceed as rapidly as we can, knowing that you as well as we have many places to be and things to do. I appreciate the patience that all of you have expressed.

Our next witnesses are Margery Leonard and Mrs. Butler Franklin of the National Women's Party.

STATEMENT OF MISS MARGERY LEONARD, NATIONAL VICE CHAIRMAN, NATIONAL WOMEN'S PARTY

Miss Leonard. Mr. Chairman and members of the Senate Judiciary Subcommittee on Constitutional Amendments——

Senator Bayh. We are going to have to ask the witnesses to speak as loudly as they can and everybody else to be quiet. These are not the best circumstances, but we have been evicted from the other room.

Miss LEONARD. My name is Margery Leonard. I am an attorney from Boston. I edited the pamphlet which was printed by the Senate Judiciary Committee Several years ago, entitled "Equal Rights Amendment—Questions and Answers."

The question is frequently asked, "Why do we need the equal rights amendment?" I shall attempt to answer that question. The purpose of the amendment is to lift the women of the United States out of the state of inferiority imposed by the ancient English common law and the French and Spanish civil law brought here by the colonists. It would complete the equal suffrage amendment by giving constitutional equality in the fields not covered by the 19th amendment. It would place the principle of equality of the sexes at the basis of the legal system of the United States. For more than three centuries have women yearned for this, patiently and without violence.

The Supreme Court has held that the Constitution created no new rights, it merely guaranteed those already in existence when the Constitution was adopted in 1789. What were the rights of women at that time? We find in Blackstone's "Commentaries of the Laws of England," printed in 1756, that when a man and woman married, they became one and he was the one. Upon marriage, all her property including furniture, clothes, jewelry, and even her hair became his property. She had nothing to say about her children; in fact, the husband could take them away from her. She could not vote nor hold office. Neither could she serve on a jury. She could not contract nor make a will.

Blackstone went on to say that the husband had the right to beat his wife for her protection. Incidentally, this appears to be the first use of the phrase "protection of women." She was a chattel and her husband's servant. The husband could even sue for the loss of her services resulting from the tortious act of a third person. This was called the loss of consortium. This is a very sketchy outline of the basic law of our country in respect to women, as it was in 1789.

The opponents of the equal rights amendment maintain that there is no reason for the adoption of the equal rights amendment because the principle of equality of the sexes is embodied in the 14th amendment to the Constitution. We maintain this is not true, by the decisions of the Supreme Court. When the 14th amendment was adopted, the word "male" was inserted three times in section 2. Thus, for the first time, discrimination on the basis of sex was written into our Constitution. George Gordon Battle, illustrious constitutional lawyer, submitted a brief on this subject to the Senate Judiciary Committee in 1941 and summarized the situation:

It soon became evident that the right to redress this injustice against women was not to be found in the 14th Amendment.

The Supreme Court has found in the 14th amendment protection for the alien, the powerful and ruthless corporation, the criminal of the most vicious type, and the Communists who would destroy our country, but it has never, with one short-lived exception, found protection therein for one-half of our people, the women. After more than a century, it is inconceivable that the Supreme Court will reverse its position, which is in fact historically correct.

In reading the debates in the Congress before passage of the 14th amendment, it is terribly clear that the proponents never intended that it should apply to women. After receiving thousands of petitions for women that they be included in the 14th and 15th amendments, the Abolitionists shouted at the women, "Stand back. This is the Negro's hour."

In a long line of cases, the Supreme Court has held that many statutes restricting women are not repugnant to the 14th amendment. That is the phrase used. The States still had the power to restrict to men the right to vote. The States still had the power to restrict to men the right to practice law. The States still had the power to regulate and limit the hours of labor for women. That was the decision in *Muller* v. *Oregon* in 1908, and this is the decision which the Federal District Court in California, in 1968, 60 years later, used to defeat enforcement of Title VII.

In employment, the Supreme Court has upheld the right of the State to regulate working hours for women, minimum wages, and professions and occupations in which they might enter. The only time the Supreme Court found these discriminations against women unconstitutional was in the case of *Adkins* v. *Children's Hospital*, which was speedily reversed by the decision in *West Coast Hotel Co.* v. *Parrish*.

In education, the Supreme Court refused to review the two Texas cases, so it is now constitutional to bar women from tax-supported State colleges and universities. The ramifications are frightening, because if it is constitutional to bar women from state colleges, then it would be constitutional to bar them from public high schools and even primary schools. There would be nothing to prevent such action on the part of the States. Texas A. & M. the college involved in the two decisions, is one of the original land grant colleges made possible by the Morrill Act passed by Congress, and it is supported by taxation. Women pay their just share of the taxes.

Women are being kept out of tax-supported colleges all over the land. There is much comment on certain colleges. For example, the University of Virginia, the University of North Carolina at Chapel Hill, the University of Maryland et cetera. A quota system is used to keep the women out.

In respect to jury service, the Supreme Court has stated that it is constitutional to keep women off juries in the State courts. The last decision on this point was *Hoyt* v. *Florida* in 1961. This decision cited the original Supreme Court decision of *Strauder* v. *West Virginia*, which specifically stated that it is unconstitutional to keep Negroes off State juries, but it is constitutional to keep women off State juries.

In respect to women doctors, it took an act of Congress to enable women doctors to serve their country in World War II.

In respect to confessions, in a case involving a woman who murdered her husband because she was mentally deranged because of his brutality, she was not provided with an attorney at any time before the trial. The Supreme Court in a shocking decision said it could not see how this was prejudicial. Contrast that decision with the one in the famous Escobedo case, where the conviction of a vicious murderer was overturned because he did not have an attorney when he made his confession. Thus freed, he was able to commit other serious crimes, for which he was convicted.

The Constitution makes it crystal clear that the power to say the final word as to the validity of a statute assailed as being unconstitutional was given to the Supreme Court. As you well know, there is no appeal from a decision of the Supreme Court. Eighty years after the adoption of the 15th amendment, the grant of the franchise was given to women by the 19th. The only right which women have which is guaranteed by the Constitution and enforceable by the Supreme Court is the right to vote and hold office as granted by the suffrage amendment. And that is all we have. This was tersely stated by the late Justice Robert Jackson in *Fay* v. *State of New York* in 1947.

Many distinguished Senators have supported the equal rights amendment. Senator Warren Austin, in his favorable judiciary report of May 28, 1943, recommended the present wording of the amendment. Surely he would not have done this had he not firmly believed the amendment was just and necessary. Other favorable reports were presented by distinguished Senators: James A. Hughes, Carl A. Hatch, Homer Ferguson, Pat McCarran, Herbert R. O'Conor, William Langer, James O. Eastland, Estes Kefauver, and Birch Bayh.

William Draper Lewis, one of the America's most distinguished jurists, a director of the American Law Institute and dean of the University of Pennsylvania Law School, said—

It is a comment on the immaturity of civilization that the recognition of woman's political equality with man did not come in the United States until 1920. The fight to gain for her full legal recognition as a human being has neared its culmination in the presentation to Congress of the equal rights amendment.

One further point. The United Nations Charter, adopted in 1945 and ratified by the United States, opens with the affirmation of "faith in fundamental human rights, in the dignity and worth of the human person, in the equal rights of men and women." As the world's greatest democracy, we should lead in securing the equal rights of men and women in our country by the adoption of the equal rights amendment. It will be an inspiration to the entire world. [Applause.]

Senator BAYH. Thank you very much.

Do you care to testify, Mrs. Franklin?

STATEMENT OF MRS. BUTLER FRANKLIN, VICE PRESIDENT, NATIONAL WOMEN'S PARTY

Mrs. FRANKLIN. Under the circumstances, may I stand up? I think I would be a little louder.

My name is Butler Franklin. I am a vice president of the National Women's Party. I come from our honorary chairman, Dr. Alice Paul, who founded this party after she got out of jail, having helped get the vote for women in 1920. She asked me to remind you of Margaret Brent.*

---

*I wish to join my colleague from National Woman's Party, Dr. Margery Leonard in the arguments she has just presented in support of the pending Equal Rights for Women Amendment (S. J. Res. 61). We ask your committee to issue a favorable report on this amendment as your committee has done so many times in the past; and we trust that you will take this action without further delay so that there will be time for both Houses of Congress to pass the amendment before the adjournment of the present 91st Congress.

Now, Margaret Brent was a Maryland lady who asked for the vote in 1648, but she asked for two things: the vote and place. Three hundred years later, we got the vote. Today we are arguing still about the place. And we ask you for it.

She was a middle-aged, handsome spinster and student of law who had settled in Maryland from England 10 years before, with a sister and brothers, 20 indentured servants of her own, and a note from Lord Baltimore bringing the servants, she might claim 1,000 acres of land as Mistress Margaret Brent, adventurer gentleman.

The House of Delegates was not fooled. They gave her 78 acres as a woman and never any more. However, Governor Leonard Calvert, Lord Baltimore's brother, recognized her ability and named her executrix of his will should he die and attorney in fact for Lord Baltimore.

A vote of confidence was given her by the local Indian chief of the Pescetores, Kittinamquuñd. He brought his little daughter to her for adoption and to live in her household to become the Pocahontas of Maryland and to keep the peace with the Indians.

But disaster struck from elsewhere. A pirate named Engalls, operating with a warship from Kent Island, invaded the colony in what was known as Engalls Rebellion. Margaret raised a thousand settler-soldiers and promised pay if they would save the colony. They did, but the struggle exhausted the treasury. There was no pay.

Meanwhile, the Governor died and Margaret was in charge. The soldiers threatened to take over the Government if pay was not forthcoming. Margaret sold the Government cattle and paid the soldiers, restoring peace.

A letter arrived from Lord Baltimore in England accusing Margaret of stealing his cattle. The five delegates sent an answer titled "Letter of Assembly to Lord Baltimore, 1649:

We do verily believe and in conscience report that it was better for the colony's safety at that time in her hands than in any man's else in the whole province after your brother's death.

Margaret thereupon rose in the little log statehouse in Saint Marys— it is there yet, and her picture is on the wall in a mural doing this—and she asked for voice and place. Five of the six delegates would have given it to her. But a new Governor, William Green, a Puritan said "no," and the vote was denied. The whole Brent family moved to Virginia, where Margaret was granted 2,000 acres of land and on one-half of its stands the city of Alexandria and on the other half stands the city of Fredericksburg, where I live.

She was of great service to the State and would have been to Maryland if they had kept her there.

Now, in her memory and as a sort of result of these remarkably clever and moving testimonies that I have heard, I should like to quote a modern scientist and philosopher who would have delighted in these hearings and the progressive and just spirit of modern woman. I quote from Pierre Teilhard de Chardin, his essay, "Building the Earth."

Stimulated by consecutive discoveries which in the space of a hundred years have successively revealed to our generation * * * the power of living beings acting in association, it seems that our psychology is in the process of changing. A conquering passion begins to show itself which will sweep away or transform what has hitherto been the immaturity of the earth. And its salutary action comes just at the right moment to control, to awaken, or to order the emancipating forces of live, the dormant forces of human unity, and the hesitant forces of research.

* * * It is really the universe which, through woman, is advancing towards man * * *.

In isolation, men suffer and stagnate without fully realizing it. They have need of a higher impulse from without to force them from the immobility of their dead point and bring them on to the beam of their profound affinity with women.

I thank you.

[Applause.]

Senator BAYH. Thank you very much, ladies, for your testimony, which recorded rather dramatically some of the historic inequities of the problem which brings us together. Senator Cook?

Senator COOK. I might say to Miss Franklin in regard to women having vote and not the place, it reminds me of hearings held before this very committee on a constitutional amendment to establish 18 as the voting age. A right which has been enjoyed by those over 18 in Kentucky since 1954. We were trying to make comparisons on the privilege of voting and we were given an example of the election that was just conducted in the State of Ohio last year in which the right of 18, 19, and 20-year-olds to vote was denied. We felt the problem was that they had not only included on the ballot the right to vote but also the right of 18, 19, and 20-year-olds to hold office, to sit on juries, to consume alcoholic beverages, and to do several other things. We as members of the committee were never able to determine why this legislation was defeated. We were not able to pinpoint whether the people of Ohio did not want this age group to have the right to vote, or to hold public office, to consume alcoholic beverages, or to something else. So we felt that the Ohio Legislature should have limited the legislation to voting rights for 18, 19 and 20-year-olds and by adding the other proposed rights did an injustice to these young citizens. I believe this situation to be similar to your remarks.

Mrs. FRANKLIN. Thank you.

Senator BAYH. Our last witness today is Mr. Stanley McFarland, Assistant Secretary for Legislation and Federal Relations of the National Education Association.

Senator COOK. Mr. McFarland, you have much courage.

STATEMENT OF STANLEY J. MCFARLAND, ASSISTANT SECRETARY FOR LEGISLATION AND FEDERAL RELATIONS OF THE NATIONAL EDUCATION ASSOCIATION

Mr. McFARLAND. Mr. Chairman, Senator, I am Stanley J. McFarland, Assistant Secretary for Legislation and Federal Relations of the National Education Association. The NEA is an indepedent professional association of educators, 95 percent of whom are classroom teachers. Our membership totals 1.1 million with an additional 900,000 members in our affiliated State and local associations. We appreciate the opportunity to speak in support of Senator Joint Resolution 61 which would amend the Constitution to guarantee equal rights for women.

In the interest of saving the committee's time, we shall confine our remarks to the matter of discrimination against women in the education field, particularly in the fields of elementary and secondary education.

While women make up 67.6 percent of the public elementary and secondary school teachers of the country, they comprise only a small fraction of the administrative staffs of the public schools. In the top local public school position, district superintendent, we have found only two women out of 13,000. There are a few rural counties in which women hold the elected office of county superintendent of schools. Of the 50 chief State school officers, only one is a woman, Dolores Colburg of Montana. In 1950, there were six women holding this position in the 48 States—all of whom were elected in general elections. As the States switched from election to appointment, every woman was replaced by a man. Montana still elects its chief State school officer. The electorate is apparently more appreciative of women than are the appointed boards.

There are approximately 78,000 school principals in the United States. Of the elementary principals, 78 percent are male. Of the high school principals, 96 percent are male. In 1928, 55 percent of the elementary school principals were women.

The attached article by John Hoyle, Assistant Professor of Educational Administration of Texas Christian University, Fort Worth, from the January 1969 issue of the "National Elementary Principal" indicates that research shows no valid reason for the decrease in the number of women principals—except the attitude of the boards of education. Note that Dr. Hoyle, in January 1969, states that 69 percent of the principals are men. His statement was based on 1965 data. Today, the percentage of men is 78 percent.

Discrimination against women is a consistent pattern in the academic world. The American Council on Education's annual freshman class survey indicates that in both public and private colleges girls admitted ranked higher in their classes and came from high schools rated as academically superior. In the fall of 1968, over 40 percent of the girls admitted to public 4-year colleges had B plus or better averages in high school. Only 18 percent of the boys had such grades. It seems clear that it is easier for a young man to enter college, despite his grades, than for a young woman to do so. In graduate school the discrimination intensifies. In 1966 two-thirds of the master's degrees and 88 percent of all doctorates were awarded to men. In professional schools—law, medicine, engineering, et cetera—78 percent of all students were men.

Before the G.I. bills of World War II and the Korean conflict, the picture was not so one-sided. With the influx of veterans into institutions of higher education, the opportunities for women in graduate schools decreased sharply. While the U.S. Office of Education reported in August of 1968 that women received 40 percent of all degrees conferred, men received 64 percent of the master's degrees and 87 percent of the doctorates. The vast majority of women's degrees was in education—equipping them to teach, but not permitting them to enter educational administration.

With the latest improvements in subsistence payments under the "Cold War G.I. bill," it can be expected that men will again edge women further out of the picture—at least in public institutions—unless women can legally assert their rights.

For several decades the NEA has by resolution been committed to the principle of the single salary schedule. While the vast majority of school systems follow this practice, it is interesting to note that in Salina, Kans. the salary schedule provides $250 extra for male teachers. In Biloxi, Miss., $200 extra is provided for men. In Kansas

City, Kans., men are paid $400 extra for extra duties. Women with extra duties are not so rewarded, according to available information.

NEA Resolution Ca–32, adopted by the association's representative assembly in July 1969, states:

The National Education Association insists that all educators, regardless of sex, who are qualified, be given equal consideration for any assignment by boards of education. Local affiliates are urged to launch a program to remove existing discriminatory practices against women.

It must be emphasized that discrimination as to teachers' salary schedules is rare—but it does exist in public schools. It is far more prevalent in higher education. The median for women college teachers' salaries, according to a University of Pennsylvania study, is $1,000 below that of men in comparable positions. Since women are increasingly shut out of opportunities for advanced degrees, this situation will likely worsen. Women in college positions predominate in the part-time, nontenured positions where they are expendable—they are added or dropped in response to budgetary or enrollment changes.

With the present oversupply of some Ph. D.'s the gap between men and women faculty members will widen unless some protective measure is provided.

We do not contend that the amendment proposed in Senate Joint Resolution 61 will cure a bad situation overnight. But the clear statement of national policy which the amendment embodies can only have a good effect. Boards of education will be more aware that appointments to administrative positions must be defensible on the basis of qualifications rather than sex. Public colleges and universities will of necessity stop discriminating against women in admission policies in both undergraduate and graduate programs.

Of course, we also share the concerns of others who support Senate Joint Resolution 61. And we believe that all persons, regardless of sex, race, color, creed, age, or political affiliation, should be guaranteed equal opportunity under the law of the land.

Thank you very much, Mr. Chairman.

[Applause.]

Senator BAYH. Thank you very much, Mr. McFarland.

The statistics that you provide prove even further the indictment against some of the male members of the population.

I notice the distinction the system of education makes between appointive and elective. This suggests that the country is undoubtedly willing if they are given the chance to solve this inequity and would accept such an amendment.

Mr. McFARLAND. I do not know whether sex determines a good politician or not.

Senator BAYH. At least it does not prove a bad one.

Mr. McFARLAND. That is right, sir.

Senator COOK. Mr. McFarland, I note your statistics with great interest. It would be helpful to see the figures of the U.S. Office of Education in about 1 year. You may have noticed a lengthy article recently published in the Sunday New York Times concerning the current overabundance of Ph.D.'s. With many Ph.D.'s unable to secure employment it would be interesting to know what percentage of the positions filled in the coming months is filled by each sex. Mr. Chairman, I hope we can obtain this information. It is both unfortunate and a waste of educational achievement when people with advanced degrees are unable to find employment. It is my hope that women are not forced to bear the brunt of this situation.

Thank you, Mr. Chairman.

UNIDENTIFIED. If I might please mention that this might prove a clue for the information that you are trying to find, that my mother-in-law during the depression got out of school and had wanted to teach high school mathematics but was not allowed to take the exam in order to do so because she was a woman.

Senator COOK. In what state?

UNIDENTIFIED. New York.

Senator COOK. New York is a progressive State. I had much fun on the hearings concerning lowering the voting age to 18 when people from New York, Pennsylvania and other progressive States testified. I informed them that 18-year-olds have been allowed to vote in Kentucky since 1954 and in Georgia since 1952. It is time for these progressive States to act on both voting rights and women's rights.

Senator BAYH. We will reconvene tomorrow morning at 9:30 a.m. in room 318, Old Senate Office Building.

(Whereupon, at 3:10 p.m., the committee recessed, to reconvene Thursday, May 7, 1970, at 9:30 a.m.)

THURSDAY, MAY 7, 1970

U.S. SENATE,
SUBCOMMITTEE ON CONSTITUTIONAL AMENDMENTS
OF THE COMMITTEE ON THE JUDICIARY,
Washington, D.C.

The subcommittee met, pursuant to recess, at 9:50 a.m., in room 318, Old Senate Office Building, Senator Birch E. Bayh, presiding.

Present: Senators Bayh and Cook.

Also Present: Paul J. Mode, Jr., chief counsel, Mrs. Dorothy Parker, minority counsel, and Andrea Gilligan, secretary.

Senator BAYH (presiding). May we come to order, please.

Our first witness this morning is Mr. Kenneth A. Meiklejohn of the AFL–CIO, who is their legislative representative.

Mr. MEIKLEJOHN. Thank you, Senator.

Senator BAYH. Glad to have you with us this morning.

STATEMENT OF KENNETH A. MEIKLEJOHN, LEGISLATIVE REPRESENTATIVE, AFL–CIO; ACCOMPANIED BY MISS ANNE DRAPER, ECONOMIST, AFL–CIO

Mr. MEIKLEJOHN. Mr. Chairman, I want first to express Mr. Biemiller's regrets that he is not able to be here. He is unavoidably detained, and he wished me to tell you that he is very sorry he was unable to come.

He has asked me to read his statement in his absence, and I will read it as his statement. I should add that I am accompanied here by Miss Anne Draper of our Research Department.

Senator BAYH. Fine.

Mr. MEIKLEJOHN. We appreciate very much, Mr. Chairman, this opportunity to present the views of the AFL–CIO on the proposed equal rights amendment to the Constitution. About 2.7 million, or approximately 20 percent, of our 13.5 million union members are women.

We are opposed to the equal rights amendment, as set forth in our most recent policy resolution on women workers adopted by the Eighth Constitutional Convention of the AFL–CIO in October 1969. The pertinent portion of the resolution reads as follows:

We continue our opposition to the long-pending Equal Rights Amendment to the Constitution because of its potentially destructive impact on women's labor legislation.

I have attached or submitted for the record a copy of this resolution which I would like to ask be included in the record at this point.

Senator BAYH. Without objection, we will put it in the record.

Mr. MEIKLEJOHN. The pros and cons of the equal rights amendment have been debated and considered over a period of 47 years and need not be debated at any length here. Probably due to congressional doubts about the need for and the implications of the amendment, however, no congressional action has been taken in recent years. Congressional hearings on this subject have not been held since 1956.

The principal events since that time are: (1) The report of President Kennedy's Commission on the Status of Women, "American Women," October 1963 and (2) the enactment of title VII of the Civil Rights Act of 1964 which includes provisions forbidding discrimination in employment on account of sex.

I might interpolate there, Mr. Chairman, there was of course the equal pay amendment which was added to the Fair Labor Standards Act in 1963.

More recently, President Nixon's Citizens' Advisory Council on the Status of Women issued an endorsement of the equal rights amendment and released an analytical memorandum supporting the amendment. On April 23, there were newspaper reports that another presidential committee, The President's Task Force on Women's Rights and Responsibilities, had also endorsed the amendment.

President Kennedy's commission considered the amendment and other aspects of the status of women with great care in the course of a study lasting approximately 2 years. Its Committee on Civil and Political Rights held open hearings on the amendment, as well as on alternative proposals to seek reinterpretations of the present Constitution in particular instances where existing interpretations are unfavorable to women. A third means of rectifying discriminatory legislation that came under consideration was that of seeking legislative amendments to existing laws and the promotion of positive legislation to advance the status of women in situations where public law does not apply.

The AFL–CIO presented formal testimony at that time.

I am attaching a copy of the AFL–CIO statement submitted to the 1963 commission.

And I would like to ask that this be included in the record.

Senator BAYH. Without objection, so ordered.

Mr. MEIKLEJOHN. In brief, Mr. Chairman, we opposed the amendment on the following principal grounds:

(1) The amendment could destroy more rights than it creates by attempting to create equality through "sameness";

(2) Many State labor standards laws on wages, hours and other conditions of employment apply only to women. The practical effect of the amendment therefore could be to destroy these laws for women rather than to accomplish extension of coverage to men.

In a separate memorandum, we set out these considerations in somewhat more detail, pointing out that most working women do not have the protection afforded by trade union membership and must therefore rely on safeguards provided by law. We also pointed out that the existence of special labor standards legislation for women is a positive offset to discriminatory disadvantages they suffer in the marketplace.

Further we noted that the equal rights amendment is essentially negative in its impact. It creates no positive law in itself to combat discrimination against women where private employment or other discriminatory practices are concerned. Finally we noted the myriad of legal relationships in every area of life which eventually might be affected by the equal rights amendment, with uncertain and possibly inequitable results in particular situations where identity of treatment might not yield true equality of treatment between the sexes.

The preferred route for remedying legal discrimination against women, we believed, was through specific legislative remedies to particular legal inequities plus specific positive antidiscrimination legislation such as the Equal Pay Act, to which I have already referred, which was later enacted into law on June 10, 1963, with our full support.

President Kennedy's commission, in its final report, rejected the equal rights amendment in the following words:

Since the Commission is convinced that the U.S. Constitution now embodies equality of rights for men and women, we conclude that a constitutional amendment need not now be sought in order to establish this principle.

We believe that the commission's conclusion was and is essentially sound and that is represented a fair conclusion based on consideration of many divergent viewpoints, both within the commission itself and among the groups testifying before it.

In the year following the commission's report, Congress enacted the Civil Rights Act which included sex in its title VII provisions prohibiting discrimination in the terms and conditions of employment, effective June 1965.

The status of State labor legislation for women under title VII, however, became a controversial issue. Eventually the Equal Employment Opportunity Commission issued an administrative guidelines (August 19, 1969) holding that State laws which "prohibit or limit" the employment of women are in conflict with title VII and would be disregarded by the commission. Specific types of "restrictive" legislation which the commission ruled against were listed as maximum hour laws, laws prohibiting nightwork, laws setting maximums on weights to be lifted by women, and laws barring women from certain types of occupations (usually bartending and coal mining).

Over the past 5 years, States have, in fact, been modifying their women's labor laws in a number of different ways. But total repeal has been the exception, not the rule. The principal adaptation has been to exempt women whose employers are in compliance with the Federal Fair Labor Standards Act as to minimum wage and overtime premium pay provisions. In other cases, permitted hours of work have been lengthened, or provision made that overtime work be on a voluntary basis.

A document listing these laws and explaining them briefly is included as exhibit 3, which I would again like to ask be included in the record.

Senator BAYH. Without objection, so ordered.

Mr. MEIKLEJOHN. Our own view, as expressed in our 1969 convention resolution, is that the commission's ruling is much too sweeping and that it makes no allowance for women who may need the protective laws the most, namely those not covered by union contract or by alternative forms of labor standards legislation providing substitutes for the safeguards the commission seeks to abolish.

Because of developments under title VII, which have been essentially hostile to certain types of women's labor legislation, it has been suggested that there is no reason for the labor movement to continue its opposition to the equal rights amendment. We must respectfully disagree. While the EEOC has dealt a severe blow to certain types of such laws, it has not completely destroyed them, nor has it attacked every form of women's labor legislation. If the commission can be persuaded to a less doctrinaire viewpoint, allowing for situations where the laws clearly continue to serve a protective function, the worst aspects of its attack could be blunted. Of course, the Congress and the courts could in future actions also serve as a moderating influence.

The equal rights amendment, on the other hand, permits of no negotiation or compromise, no matter what the circumstances. It would simply become unconstitutional for any law to distinguish in its application between men and women. It makes no guarantee of extension of labor law protections to men. Enemies of labor legislation powered by a combination of middle-class feminists and employers, could speedily wipe out all forms of protections afforded specifically to women whether "restrictive" or not—minimum wage laws, for example, rest period, meal periods, seating requirements, transportation at night, and other provisions.

Finally, with regard to the recommendations and analysis released by President Nixon's Citizens' Advisory Council on the Status of Women, this Council was officially appointed only last August. Unlike the original Presidential Commission and successive advisory councils, it is notably unrepresentative of any group except business and professional women. The prior bodies were broadly representative of all areas of American life, including labor. The council held no public hearings and rather speedily came out with an endorsement of the equal rights amendment in February of this year. This endorsement cannot, therefore, be said to represent a broad consensus of opinion as did the original President's Commission of 1963, and succeeding advisory councils.

We have carefully reviewed the arguments presented in the analytical memorandum of the new Citizens' Advisory Council. We would like to point out certain areas of our own disagreement and what we consider important omissions and mistaken assumptions:

1. We basically take exception to the proposition that "constitutional protection" is needed "against laws and official practices that treat men and women differently." We do not agree that every difference is a discrimination by definition. We do subscribe to elimination of discriminatory differentials of treatment and believe this can be achieved under the present Constitution and through appropriate and specific legislative enactments.

2. The section entitled "Laws Which Discriminate on the Basis of Sex" fails to identify the basis of past opposition to the equal rights amendment, casually dismissing it as "based in part on 'fear of the unknown'; that is, lack of information concerning the types of laws

which distinguish on the basis of sex and would therefore be affected by the amendment." Totally ignored is the history of opposition by labor, women's reform groups, and Government agencies seeking to improve the conditions of work for women through women's labor legislation. The memorandum then lists several types of invidious distinctions, including what the EEOC has ruled are "restrictive" labor laws.

The numerous other types of labor standards laws which apply only to women are not mentioned, but they also would be affected, as pointed out earlier in our statement. The memorandum is clearly inadequate due to its obvious lack of information and lack of understanding of the purposes and necessities of labor legislation.

It may also be fairly concluded that the list of invidious "examples" by no means exhausts the types of laws which would be affected, good, bad, and indifferent. More humble legal authorities than the authors of this document do not presume to foresee these in their entirety. A much-quoted memorandum prepared by Prof. Paul Freund of Harvard Law School and introduced into earlier hearings makes this point very succinctly:

If anything about this proposed amendment is clear, it is that it would transform every provision of law concerning women into a constitutional issue to be ultimately resolved by the Supreme Court of the United States. Every statutory and common-law provision dealing with the manifold relation of women in society would be forced to run the gauntlet of attack on Constitutional grounds. The range of such potential litigation is too great to be readily foreseen * * *

3. No persuasive case is made that adequate protection against invidious legal discriminations cannot be secured under the present Constitution through its fifth and 14th amendments. The argument for the additional amendment in reality is reduced to (1) a feeling of "anxiety" on the part of its proponents and (2) the proposition that "no harm would be done" if the equal rights amendment turned out simply to be duplicative of present constitutional protections.

4. The section entitled "Effect the Equal Rights Amendment Would Have on Laws Differentiating on the Basis of Sex" is an exercise in wishful thinking rather than a sober assessment of the possible ramifications of the equal rights amendment.

(a) Particularly unrealistic is the assumption that laws "conferring a benefit, privilege, or obligation of citizenship" would automatically be extended to the opposite sex by striking the words of "sex identification." Legislatures are under no obligation to retain existing legislation for either sex, let alone extend it to both. This issue would be particularly serious in the field of State labor legislation. It is true that any of the existing seven State minimum wage laws that apply only to women could readily be adjusted by striking the sex identification in the law. But it is equally true that the legislature could strike the laws altogether. Labor legislation is highly vulnerable to the "least common denominator" approach. Nothing in the amendment prohibits the reduction of present benefits and privileges as a means of complying with the equality standard set out by the amendment.

As an example of downward equalization, we are attaching a copy of a recent opinion of the Attorney General of Pennsylvania, dated November 14, 1969.

And here again I would like to ask that this be included as part of our testimony.

Senator BAYH. Without objection, so ordered.

(The opinion follows:)

Hon. CLIFFORD L. JONES,   NOVEMBER 14, 1969.
Secretary of Labor and Industry,
Commonwealth of Pennsylvania,
Harrisburg, Pa.

Dear SECRETARY JONES: We have your request for advice as to the resolution of an apparent conflict between the Act of July 25, 1913, P.L. 1024, as amended, 43 P.S. 101 *et seq.* (Women's Labor Law), and the Pennsylvania Human Relations Act of October 27, 1955, P.L. 744, as amended, 43 P.S. 951 *et seq.* insofar as the two acts apply to the employment of females.

The Women's Labor Law was originally enacted in 1913 to alleviate the oppressive circumstances relative to hours and conditions of employment of females. The statute was an outgrowth of flagrant sweat-shop conditions which impaired the health and welfare of female employes.

That Law regulates the hours and conditions of employment of females in any establishment where work is done for compensation of any sort. It also deals with such items as intervals between work periods, suitable facilities for seating females, washrooms, dressing rooms, lavatories, lunch rooms, and drinking water. Criminal penalties are provided for any violations of its provisions. The effect of the statute is to accord preferential treatment and status to female employes.

The Pennsylvania Human Relations Act was enacted in 1955 to proscribe discriminatory activities in the fields of housing, public accommodations and employment. That statute was amended by Act No. 56 of 1969 to include discrimination in the named areas on account of sex of the individual. Specifically, it provides that it shall be an unlawful discriminatory practice for an employer to refuse to hire or employ any person because of sex unless based on a bona fide occupational classification. (Section 5(a)). The statute eliminates the need and justification for preferential treatment in the field of employment because of sex by placing males and females on a equal footing.

Recent social and economic changes have improved the status of females so that they now enjoy a status substantially equally to that of males in all areas of employment opportunities. Thus, the conditions prompting the enactment of the 1913 statute no longer exist. As a matter of fact, females now enjoy the freedom to be employed under conditions and hours of employment equivalent to that of males. The Human Relations Act reflects the change in the social and economic attitude which required protective and preferential legislation for females. It nullified the reasons which existed for the Women's Labor Law.

The effect which a later law has on a prior law dealing with the same or similar subject matter, where the former is intended as a substitute therefore, it is treated in a Statutory Construction Act of May 28, 1937, P.L. 1019, as amended, 46 P.S. 591. That Act provides that the later law, in such an instance, shall be construed to impliedly repeal a former law upon the same subject. This implied repealer arises where the intent and language used in the later statute discloses an irreconcilable repugnancy between its provisions and those of the earlier statute so inconsistent as not to admit of any fair consonant construction of the two. *Parisi v. Philadelphia Zoning Board of Adjustment,* 393 Pa. 458 (1958) ; *Kelly v. City of Philadelphia,* 382 Pa. 459 (1955).

In view of the sex discrimination provision of the Pennsylvania Human Relations Act and its repugnancy to the 1913 law, we must conclude that an implied repealer of the earlier statute was intended by this later amendment.

Your attention is also directed to the Federal Civil Rights Act of 1964, which makes it an unlawful practice to discriminate based on sex. It is consistent with the Pennsylvania Human Relations Act in that regard. Rules and regulations were promulgated under the Federal statute to provide guidlines for employers and, recently, these regulations were amended to provide that no defense can be maintained based on a state statute which may be in conflict with the federal law and regulations.

Therefore, it is our opinion, and you are advised, that the Women's Labor Law, to the extent that it conflicts with the Pennsylvania Human Relations Act, has been impliedly repealed.

Very truly yours,

WILLIAM C. SENNETT,
Attorney General.

Mr. MEIKLEJOHN. This opinion abrogates the State women's labor law because of sex discrimination provisions added to the Pennsylvania Human Relations Act in 1969. The women's labor law provisions covering hours and conditions of work, rest periods, seating requirements, washrooms, dressing rooms, lavatories, and drinking water, were held to "accord preferential treatment and status to female employees." Rather than extend the "preferential treatment" to men, the attorney general declared it removed for women.

I would point out that the so-called Hayden rider to the equal rights amendment, which was incorporated into it in 1950 and 1953, the only two occasions when the amendment passed in the Senate by the necessary two-thirds majority, was an attempt to correct this fundamental defect in the amendment that I have been discussing. It provided that the amendment "shall not be construed to impair any rights, benefits, or exemptions now or hereafter conferred by law, upon persons of the female sex." If feminists find, as has apparently been the case in the past, that the Hayden amendment would violate the amendment's beneficial effects—and I find this a rather curious point of view—we challenge them to produce new language that would in fact prevent equalization through a reduction of rights. An analogous provision appears, for example, in the Equal Pay Act of 1963. It reads as follows:

Provided, That an employer who is paying a wage rate differential in violation of this subsection shall not, in order to comply with the provisions of this subsection, reduce the wage rate of any employee.

The inclusion of this proviso in the Equal Pay Act was brought about by the insistence of the labor movement.

(b) We question the simplistic distinction made between "opportunities" and "restrictions." The authors of the memorandum assume that "restrictions" in the field of labor law are automatically an invidious invasion of individual liberty. They give no weight to the fact that the restraints are upon employers in relation to their workers, in recognition of the power of the employer to compel excessive hours of work on the part of employees to the detriment of their health and their well-being; or to condition employment upon the acceptance, without protest, of substandard conditions of work.

Freedom of unlimited weight-lifting appears to be sought as a constitutional right, no matter what the consequences to the individual. Labor organizations throughout the world have sought restraints on weight-lifting, for the protection of the worker. I attach a copy of ILO convention No. 127, which deals with this subject, and I ask that that be included in the record as another exhibit, exhibit 5.

Senator BAYH. Without objection, so ordered.

Mr. MEIKLEJOHN. It includes provision for lower limits on weights to be lifted by women than by men. Presumably the equal rights amendment would preclude ratification of such an international convention by the United States and would render it completely inapplicable in this country. Admittedly, a requirement that weight-lifting limits be geared to each individual worker would be the ideal solution, but this millennium is unlikely to occur in the foreseeable future. Other reasonable means of dealing with the problem should not be rendered unconstitutional.

The authors of the memorandum could as easily have put "restrictive" laws in the category to be extended to both sexes as a means of worker protection. But they have chosen instead to render these laws simply unconstitutional in their own system of values.

We would anticipate that "rights," "opportunities," and "restrictions" in various other areas of law would also develop into controversy rather than neatly falling into place under the far-from-immutable principles of right and wrong postulated in this document, reflecting the particular values of the women whose views are represented in it.

Finally, Mr. Chairman, we hope this statement will be of assistance to the committee in reaching a judgment on the equal rights amendment. We sincerely believe that the amendment will produce more problems than it solves, that it is a threat to labor standards legislation for women and for labor generally, and that adequate and more fruitful means of eliminating discrimination against women are available through the legislative process and through the judicial process under the present Constitution.

Thank you very much, Mr. Chairman.

Senator BAYH. Thank you very much, Mr. Meiklejohn. The record should show that Miss Anne Draper——

Miss DRAPER. Yes.

Senator BAYH. I am not certain what her official capacity is unless she keeps some of you fellows in line down there at the AFL–CIO headquarters.

Miss DRAPER. I am an economist in the research department.

Senator BAYH. Fine. I thought that that was your area, but I was not certain.

We appreciate your taking time to be here. I think you are another of two individuals who want to accomplish the same purposes as the rest of us here, but disagree as to the roadway which should be traveled and the vehicle which should be used.

Let me ask you, if I may, to expand your thinking a little bit.

Mr. MEIKLEJOHN. There is much more a problem of means rather than ends, Senator.

Senator BAYH. Yes, I think we are all trying to accomplish the same ends.

Mr. MEIKLEJOHN. Right.

Senator BAYH. The question is means.

Am I accurate in reading your statement and that of Mr. Biemiller that you feel the Constitution now provides under the 14th amendment adequate guarantee for all women to enable them to successfully challenge instances of discrimination against them in the courts?

Mr. MEIKLEJOHN. I think that would be a fair statement of the way we feel, Senator. I think that the Constitution as it is presently written does clearly require equality of treatment under the law. It does not say, of course, that everybody must be treated alike, but it does say everyone must be treated equally.

Senator COOK. May I interrupt right there?

Senator BAYH. Please.

Senator COOK. I am in complete disagreement with Mr. Meiklejohn concerning his last statement.

Senator BAYH. Yes, I am, too. I do not want to interrupt the Senator from Kentucky, but let me just put this next question and then yield to my friend from Kentucky.

Senator Cook. All right.

Senator Bayh. It seems to me that if we are saying that the woman's right to be treated equitably, if not equally—and I think perhaps we are involved in a semantical argument there—is a constitutional right, then this means these rights are going to have to be pursued through the courts. In the first place we have no record of success through the courts in this area. Second, I find a great inconsistency between that thought and another expressed by my good friend, Paul Freund, who suggests that if this amendment passes, the rights are going to have to be tested in the courts.

Now, if on the one hand you argue that these rights are already guaranteed in the Constitution, and then on the other say that this amendment will pass and the right will have to be tested through the courts to assert their constitutionality, it seems to me you are being rather inconsistent.

Senator Cook. I agree with the point made by the Senator from Indiana. Mr. Meiklejohn, I return to your testimony which quoted Professor Freund of Harvard as stating that with the passage of this constitutional amendment:

Every statutory and common law provision dealing with the manifold relation of women in society would be forced to run the gauntlet of attack on constitutional grounds;

And your later point that:

No persuasive case is made that adequate protection against invidious legal discriminations cannot be secured under the present constitution through its fifth and 14th amendments. In effect, you are saying that while your group and Professor Freund are unwilling to fight these contests on a constitutional basis, the women of this Nation who feel discriminated against must exercise their rights under the fifth and 14th amendments or under title VII.

Mr. Meiklejohn. Senator, Miss Draper would like to answer this.

Miss Draper. I think the seeming paradox is explained in another part of our statement. The equal rights amendment really provides for identical treatment. Sex would never be a reasonable classification under any circumstances. Under the fifth and 14th amendments, sex can be a reasonable classification under some circumstances.

Senator Cook. By reason of the interpretation of the courts?

Miss Draper. That is right. This would be done away with. Under the equal rights amendment there would never be any reasonable classification. Therefore, you would have an additional scope of litigation because of this identity aspect of the equal rights amendment. What you get at is discrimination, discriminatory, unfair treatment on the basis of any kind of classification rather than a l'teral identity of treatment, so that you can attack invidious discrimination without having to go through all the precise specifics of whether a law is exactly the same and comes out the same on the basis of sex.

And I wanted to further say that in recent interpretations in the courts under the 14th amendment that are bginning to come down, the batting average is getting a little bit better. Back in 1874, 1895, you did not get very good decisions, but they are beginning to get them. I think some of them are listed in the citizens' advisory council memorandum. It is not 100 percent, but the batting average is much better. I think as women's status is evolving, you are going to get better decisions in the court system.

Mr. MEIKLEJOHN. Let me add one thing to it, Senator. The amendment reads, "Equality of rights under the law shall not be denied or abridged by the United States or any State on account of sex." I think our big problem is just exactly the scope of that phrase "on account of sex."

Senator BAYH. Well, this is the exact point I wanted to bring out.

Mr. MEIKLEJOHN. This is similar to the language which we have in our civil rights statutes, and I think that whereas we were after identity of treatment there, the question of whether that same identity of treatment is appropriate here is a very difficult question——

Senator BAYH. This is a point——

Mr. MEIKLEJOHN (continuing). That I thought you were getting at.

Senator BAYH. As a result of these hearings we will be able to point out some very real areas where discrimination which neither you, nor I, nor the Senator from Kentucky likes, does exist. But we have not been able to deal with them yet. Perhaps we will be able to clarify some of these concerns that we have.

I see great similarity between the language of the 14th amendment which says that no State shall make or enforce any laws which shall abridge the privileges or immunities of the United States nor shall any State deprive any person of life, liberty, or property without due process of law, nor deny to any person within its jurisdiction the equal protection of the law—I see great similarity between that and the words that you just quoted. And the fact that we have included similar language in various civil rights bills leads me to suggest that we do not say that a person who is a minority group member, say a black man, is going to get absolutely identical treatment with any white man or any other black man. I am wondering if some of the laws that involve the ability of a woman to do a job well would not be tolerated under this amendment.

If they go—if there are laws which actually deal with the competence of a woman or a man, a 110-pound man might have a real problem moving a refrigerator around. I think we can suggest that there is room for legislation that relates to the ability to do a job and that some women may be qualified and some women may not be qualified. And we are not saying here that everyone is being treated equally. We are asking for equality of rights.

I do not know whether I make myself clear as far as the distinction is concerned.

Miss DRAPER. In that case, why do you need an additional amendment?

Senator BAYH. Well, I have not yet read your memoranda, but I am sure they are well documented as far as discrimination that does exist today.

Senator COOK. I reject the distinction made in your testimony.

For instance, on page 6—go ahead, Birch. Go ahead.

Senator BAYH. No, go ahead.

Senator COOK. There are many inconsistencies in this testimony, for example in item 4 you state:

Particularly unrealistic is the assumption that laws "conferring a benefit privilege, or obligation of citizenship" would automatically be extended to the oposite sex by striking the words of sex identification. Legislatures are under no obligation to retain existing legislation for either sex, let alone extend it to both.

Legislation is for the sexes. You are trying to make the point that we cannot solve this problem merely by striking the words of sex identification partially because of the existing legislation that differentiates between the sexes. But you visualize the elimination of all such legislation.

Miss DRAPER. This is not saying what happened to it because there are pressures against labor legislation. There are enemies of labor legislation beyond sex.

Senator COOK. My major concern with your paper is the conclusion in which you state that this amendment will upset existing labor standards legislation. You sense that this amendment will create work for the labor movement.

I realize that the hierarchy of the labor movement has traditionally attempted to solve part of its problems by negotiation and part by statutory amendment. A significant percentage of the problems that you have solved by statutory amendment have been in the field of apparent "protective legislation for women". Have you done this to avert negotiation? I ask this question especially since you still negotiate these matters for men.

Miss DRAPER. Mr. Cook, do you know anything about the history of these women's labor laws? They were not started by the labor movement. They were started by women. They were started by women, and these people here who have never read anything——

Senator COOK. Wait a minute. I have read some of it.

Ladies, I wish we would have order, seriously. I wish we would have order.

Many of the women's labor laws were not created by women but rather by the labor movement during major depressions or recessions. For instance, can you sincerely tell me that the women at Nevada went to their state legislature and pressed for the passage of a statute that would bar them from those jobs which required that more than 10 pounds be lifted?

Miss DRAPER. It was not 10 for one thing. It was Utah for another.

Senator COOK. Excuse me, I was referring to the Western State having a limit of 10 pounds.

Miss DRAPER. There is no State with a 10-pound limit. It is 15. I am afraid the next time we hear it, it is going to be down to 5. The State of Utah, is the horrible example everybody brings up.

Senator COOK. Who gets that legislation passed in the State?

Miss DRAPER. It is not labor. The labor movement is very weak in Utah. But at any rate, the Utah statute provides a 25-pound limit on carrying. It provides a 15-pound—I mean—excuse me. It is the other way around. It provides a 25-pound limit on lifting and a 15-pound limit on carrying. I do not know where the 10 pounds came from.

Senator COOK. I apologize to you. I believe that you are correct about the State being Utah but someone testified previously that the limit was 10 pounds. We must check the statute.

You stated your approval of title VII; is that correct?

Mr. MEIKLEJOHN. That is correct.

Senator COOK. Do you agree with the Civil Rights Act?

154

Mr. MEIKLEJOHN. Yes.

Senator COOK. Title VII disallows discrimination. Do you agree with title VII because of the extensive regulation to which it is subject?

Mr. MEIKLEJOHN. We believe that title VII can be construed in such a way, Senator, that it will not interfere and destroy those laws in the States and localities which provide necessary protection for women workers.

Senator COOK. You and I disagree about some very basic points. I cite your statement, "We basically take exception to the proposition that constitutional protection is needed."

Women are not looking for constitutional protection, but rather constitutional equality.

Miss DRAPER. It is their word.

Senator COOK. Excuse me.

Miss DRAPER. It is their word. That was a direct quote?

Senator COOK. The point remains, Miss Draper, that women want constitutional equality not protection. You also state that:

The amendment could destroy more rights than it creates by attempting to create equality through "sameness."

Later you quote from President Kennedy's Commission:

Since the Commission is convinced that the United States Constitution now embodies equality of rights for men and women, we conclude that a constitutional amendment need not now be sought in order to establish this principle.

That is sameness.

I find these statements to be inconsistent.

Mr. MEIKLEJOHN. First, you are reading from a Commission report which is a little different from a constitutional provision.

Senator COOK. If you believe the wording of President Kennedy's Commission why don't you say that this amendment would be redundant instead of saying that this amendment would threaten existing labor laws?

Mr. MEIKLEJOHN. I believe at some point in the statement, as I read it, we did say almost exactly that, that it really was not necessary under the provisions of the Fifth and 14th amendments to the Constitution.

Senator COOK. You are desirous that existing labor laws be maintained but I am desirous that women, feeling the sting of discrimination, not be forced in all instances to seek a constitutional judgment.

Mr. MEIKLEJOHN. Senator, I do not believe it is going to be that easy to determine in every situation whether or not a discrimination, a distinction, a difference is one that is "on account of sex." That is exactly what this amendment would provide. And unless a determination were made that a particular discrimination, distinction, or difference were "on account of sex," this amendment would not protect them.

Senator BAYH. If I might interrupt here——

Senator COOK. Go ahead.

Senator BAYH (continuing). I agree with that assessment. As much as I am inclined to think passage of this amendment is important now—I respectfully differ with your evaluation here—I have tried to suggest to some of the enthusiastic supporters of this legislation that this is not going to be a panacea. It is going to have to be pursued through the courts. But it gives us a stronger basis from which to attack this discrimination from the standpoint of equity and equality, but not sameness. I think a distinction can be made there.

Mr. MEIKLEJOHN. I think one of our other areas of concern, Senator, is—excuse me.

Senator BAYH. No, excuse me. I just want to add one other thought there. The record that has been brought to us—and if you good folks have any other information, we certainly are looking for all the facts—shows that success in the courts is nonexistent. The only example that has been given to us was provided yesterday by a witness from the labor movement that shared your opposition. That example was a case in Alabama which said that it was unconstitutional to deny women the right of sitting on juries, if we are talking about the law of the land. And that was a Federal district court, and the brief survey that we have had a chance to make since then is that the Supreme Court has ruled contrariwise. So even that step has not been decided on a national basis but only applies to that one district in Alabama.

Now, we do have the court taking this one case, *Phillips v. Martin Marietta*, over which you and Mr. Biemiller, I am sure, are concerned. But there again if you look at the briefs that have been filed —and "cert" has been accepted—the thrust of the argument there, even the Attorney General's argument who interceded on the part of Mrs. Phillips, is not on a constitutional question. So I just do not think the present Constitution has given us much reason for comfort here.

Excuse me.

Mr. MEIKLEJOHN. I was going to respond simply by saying that we have in our testimony today discussed basically only the effect that this amendment might have in the field of labor standards legislation as it applies to women. Historically labor standards legislation began through laws which were designed to provide certain protections to women. They were not designed to take anything away from women. They were primarily designed to provide protection. It is our concern that protection where it is needed should not be taken away, and it is our very great fear that the breadth and sweep of this proposed constitutional amendment could very well do that. It might accomplish—in fact, we know it will accomplish— very beneficial effects in certain areas. But we also feel that with the complexity of the problem insofar as these protective laws are concerned in the labor field that there are—that this problem would be increased many times when you get into other fields of law. We have not tried to discuss those, and I do not know that I am particularly qualified to discuss them in any detail.

But I do suggest that the complexity of the problem here in the labor law field indicates that the problem in these other fields would be equally great, if not much greater.

Senator BAYH. We have been searching for a way—and I have not had a chance to discuss this with my distinguished colleague—to create laws which deal with legitimate distinctions without letting some of the laws which have no direct relationship to qualitative performance serve as a hindrance to advancement and freedom of choice. And this language that I suggest has been drafted here by staff as they have listened to this, and I just toss this out as a possibility. I am not even certain after I slept on it I would be for it, but would it be possible to add some words to this bill—that do not do what I am concerned about with the Hayden amendment—which say something to the effect that "any law respecting wages, hours, or conditions of employment for members of one sex shall be applied equally to both sexes?" I mean what you are concerned about is that when the attorney general of a State is faced with the law that says in Michigan you cannot work more than 54 hours, that instead of involuntarily saying that law applies to men and women equally, they strike out the law altogether.

Now, knowing the general philosophy of trying to improve working conditions that exists in the minds of most of the people, I know the AFL–CIO knows no water cooler or poor restroom facilities is contrary to the belief of equality for men and women as far as you are concerned.

Mr. MEIKLEJOHN. Certainly.

Senator BAYH. So if we had something like this addition, we would provide a guideline to that man who has to administer it, saying, "do not strike out that law but see that everyone is treated equally."

Mr. MEIKLEJOHN. Senator, in reference to the language which was included in the Equal Pay Act of 1963. That act, as you know, prohibits discrimination insofar as payment of wages is concerned on the basis of sex. We supported that provision of law with the proviso which we have quoted here on page 7 of our statement and which prohibited the reduction of any wage in order to achieve equality. We have no—we would certainly have no objection to working with anybody in trying to devise language which would accomplish both the objective that you have, and which we share, and the objective which we have which is to make sure that these laws that do extend protection to women are continued where they are needed.

I am sure that there are areas in these laws where such protections are not needed. But there are others where they are urgently needed. And I am sure that language could be worked out. The Hayden amendment was an attempt to do that.

Senator BAYH. But you see, if I might interrupt you——

Mr. MEIKLEJOHN. One of the difficulties with the Hayden amendment was that the proponents of the amendment found too much difficulty with it.

Senator BAYH. But you see, where you say we are going to provide equality of rights under the law, and then you say this amendment "shall not be construed to impair any rights, benefits or exemptions now or hereafter conferred by law upon persons"—you are giving with one and you are taking away with the other. I am not too sure——

Mr. MEIKLEJOHN. We are not in here advocating that the Hayden amendment be put on here, although——

Senator BAYH. Maybe when we examine this language that I have just read to you, we will come to the conclusion we are doing the same thing.

Mr. MEIKLEJOHN. I refrained from commenting on it because I would really like to see it, and I am not sure how far it goes or whether it does what we would like to see done or whether it might not go a great deal further than you might want it to go.

Senator COOK. I think we should end this discussion; I did not intend to be argumentive. I cite the laws regulating working hours to illustrate my point. It is my contention that a strong argument can be presented for and against laws that regulate working hours. One side might describe such legislation as a privilege while the other side might view such legislation as a denial of rights. If such legislation was passed as a privilege, I am confident the women of this Nation would support it.

Additionally, I am unable to equate the language of this amendment to the repeal of those statutes that were created within the police powers of the respective states in regard to considerations such as safety and health. A distinction other than sex must be used in formulating protective legislation.

This amendment would also cover those areas of citizenship in which women are not allowed full participation, such as jury service. I feel this dimension of the amendment to be very important.

Mr. MEIKLEJOHN. I think, Senator, there is no question about the repeal of the point of view that you are expressing. We share that point of view as well. And I think the record of the labor movement has been a fairly clear record as far as the protection of equality of rights is concerned. We have been in the forefront. We would have no title 7 in the law and the Civil Rights Act if it had not been for the labor movement. And make no mistake about that.

Senator COOK. I reiterate the necessity of changing a situation or climate which, for example, would allow differential treatment of the sexes in punishment for the same offense. Such a statute was recently declared unconstitutional in Pennsylvania but the point remains, how many other such discriminatory practices still exist throughout the Nation?

Mr. MEIKLEJOHN. I think the problem is going to be one pretty much along the lines that Senator Bayh indicated, and that is to see whether or not it is possible to work out language to preserve what is good in the State labor laws and in other beneficial statutes and still retain—and still promote, rather, the objective of this amendment which is assure equality of rights without discrimination based on sex.

Our biggest problem with the proposed amendment is the breadth of its language. I do not believe it is going to be quite so easy as some of its proponents think to find out, when the cases go to court asking for an interpretation, what that rather broad sentence means and what the phrase "on account of sex" means.

If this language can be pinned down and can be made more clear, then there may be no difference of opinion on this. But our experience has been that when we try to do this and where we try to protect these laws where they are needed, then we run into objection and opposition from those who want this amendment.

Senator COOK. Thank you, Mr. Chairman.

Senator BAYH. Thanks to both of you. You have been very thought-provoking.

Mr. MEIKLEJOHN. Thank you, Senator.

Senator BAYH. We are glad to have your thoughts and I hope you will search for that magic language.

Mr. MEIKLEJOHN. We would be very happy and glad to work with the subcommittee, with you, Senator, and Senator Cook, in trying to work out such language if you would like.

Senator BAYH. Thank you very much.

Mr. MEIKLEJOHN. Thank you.

Senator BAYH. Our next witness is Miss Betty Freidan, the author of "Feminine Mystique" and founder of the National Organization for Women. [Applause.]

Miss Freidan, glad to have you with us here this morning.

STATEMENT OF MISS BETTY FREIDAN, AUTHOR OF "FEMININE MYSTIQUE" AND FOUNDER OF NOW

Miss FREIDAN. Glad to be with you, Senator.

I speak in the sense of history for the women's liberation movement which my words and actions are credited or blamed for having brought into conscious being. I speak with a sense of historical urgency at this moment and unprecedented national crisis and torment of enacting after so many years of delay the equal rights amendment to the Constitution which would finally assert women's full equality and inalienable human right, her personal finding under the Constitution, and help bring to an end the war between the sexes which is so closely linked to the violence that is becoming associated with our Nation and which our Nation is perpetrating on the world.

There is a historical urgency to getting on with this. I take grave exception to any man today who professes to speak in the name of women, although I do not think that men are the enemy of the women's liberation movement. They are the fellow victims of the sex discrimination in equality between the sexes that binds us both. And I especially accuse those male leaders of labor, the male labor establishment, and the "Aunt Toms" who do not identify with their sisters in the working force, of not spelling correctly our name as women.

As James Baldwin said in a letter to his nephew, to a young black boy:

Whitey has spelled your name too long, and until you start spelling your own name, you won't know the truth about anything.

Well, I and the millions of women young and old who have emerged in the new feminism insist on our right to spell our own name. And for the 30 million women who work in this country, the real women who work in this country, the name of the game is equality, not protection. What we want and urgently need is equality of opportunity and protection, not a special protectiveness that masks discrimination.

Senator BAYH. May I interrupt here, and I will not interrupt further, both because I do not want to interrupt your thoughts and because of the necessity to keep moving here. But if you in your statement could deal with the point raised in the questioning of our previous witnesses concerning other wording that might more clearly indicate that we are not desirous of striking off the books legislation that goes to specific competence that would see that all laws are applied equally to men and women relative to wages, hours, working conditions, whether you feel this is necessary or whether it is self-defeating, I would appreciate that.

Miss FREIDAN. I am about to, Senator.

I do not think that any tampering with the language of the equal rights amendment is necessary. And, in fact, I think that there is a great deal of hypocrisy here. I am going to mince no words about this. There are 30 million women who work today. We have to start now because women who work in trying to get the protection guaranteed to them under title VII of the Civil Rights Act, in trying to fight sex discrimination in employment, we are getting no help from the unions which are almost completely dominated by men.

I accuse the male labor establishment of gross neglect and blindness to the problems of women workers, for only 3.5 million of 30 million women who work have been organized into labor unions. And furthermore, there is something grossly wrong with a male-dominated labor movement that has brought about or acquiesced in a condition whereby the wages of women who work today are 40 percent less than wages of men who work on the same job, and where 89 percent of women who work earn less than $5,000 a year, where only 40 percent of men who work earn less than $5,000 a year.

We have been asked to take case after case where the labor union was blind to the fact of sex discrimination or actually colluded with management in perpetuating the separate seniority lists that were accepted by the male labor leaders even though they were in violation of the law. And time and again the excuse for the sex discrimination was not necessarily the State where the case was but the fact that some States had laws protecting women from lifting weights of 12, 30, or 35 pounds, and this was invoked, for instance, to keep women from the opportunity of getting into better paid jobs or to excuse the fact that women despite their seniority or the necessity of their wages to support families were fired while men were hired from the streets.

And I accuse the male labor leadership of hypocrisy here, and this is not a mild hypocrisy in a time of recession when again women are going to be the last fired, I mean the last hired and the first fired and yet there is no kitchen for them to go back to when most women who work, work because their wages are needed to support or help support themselves and their family. And furthermore, it is hypocrisy to talk about protecting women from lifting weights when technology as we know it is eliminating that muscular work from most jobs and when in fact the good jobs that are going to continue and not be eliminated from the machine are ones for which women migh qualify equal with men and the special State protective laws only deny women the opportunity to move into these jobs.

And it is hypocrisy, it is hypocrisy in a time of recession and great technological change such as today for the male labor establishment to invoke questions of hours and overtime when in fact the interests of all workers, men and women, would indicate that too much overtime should be illegal for either men or women, so that whatever work there is be spread to both in the interest of all who need it having a chance to earn what is needed, you know, to eat and live today and in the sense that both men and women are equally needed at home some hours of the day and evening with their children and to shoulder equally the responsibilities of home and family life.

So that because we have this resolution and technological change, what I am saying we really need is the protection of absolutely assured equal opportunity, equal protection of the Constitution and amendments of this country. And title VII of the Civil Rights Act with its final assertion that equal employment opportunity must be abridged on account of sex has been a greater boon to women than any of these special protective laws which mask discrimination.

The only full special protection that women need is in the matter of maternity and childbering and none of the so-called protective laws cover this. And furthermore, that is a functional distinction that the equal rights amendment wouldn't touch because men don't bear babies.

So that there is an economic urgency at the moment in enacting the equal rights amendment. There is also a psychological and political urgency. The hostility between the sexes, the war between the sexes, if you will, is linked to the sociological problems of the people of this country and to the political turmoil in this country today. Anthropologists have noted that in societies where women are kept from whatever the society defines as human, where women are kept from the mainstream of action and participation, where the role of the sexes is most polarized, as for instance, it is in a kind of pedestal definition of woman or the kind of protective definition or anything that denies women full equality and personhood, in most cases they are most obsessed with sex. In this country today, the definition of sex is dirty where man acts by the old Victorian prudery or the new sort of Playboy pornography, and there is the most violence.

And at this particular time when the entire generation of our young are in the streets in revolution against the violence that we unleashed in Cambodia, when this violence has unleashed a world-wide wave of revolution against America, this violence finally where we are murdering our own children at Kent State, and who knows where next, it is not irrelevant but germane to say we cannot further delay in getting on with this unfinished revolution of sexual equality.

I do not think that the equal rights amendment is sufficient to complete this revolution, but it is necessary. It is necessary because the Constitution which is the document that embodies our conscience, our American conscience, our morality and governs in many ways other than the actual punishment by law our behavior and our institutions, our Constitution has not yet been unequivocally interpreted to include women as people, to define women as people. And there is no delay. There is no delay now to getting on with this, bcause otherwise the impotent rage of women which has as its other mirror coin, its mirror image the rage of men, the lowliness, the alienation, the frustration, the sexual torment bred by inequality between the sexes, finally has its outlet in violence, in repression. And this is true when we think in terms of the obsolete masculine mystique, if you will, the crewcutted, tightlipped, bear-killing heman definition that can only assert manhood by dominance, you know, by Napoleoning children and facesaving spoiling of nations and people in the name of a false, a brutality of dominance to which our young men are finally saying no, or whether we speak of the exploding rage of women that is evidencing itself today in my movement, the Women's Liberation Movement which I think is being recognized as the biggest force for basing change in America and let either be recognized politically in restructuring institutions and re-interpreting our Constitution and adding unequivocally to it for instance, the equal rights amendment or will I think explode against, again men—an armed Armageddon between the sexes which is almost, it is inconceivable but it is happening on the fringes, and I don't like it and you can't like it either.

I don't think man is the enemy. I don't think love is the enemy. I think woman's liberation is necessary to liberate men and women to make love not war. But we must get on with. And after nearly 50 years of bottling up this equal rights amendment it seems it is your responsibility now to bring it out of committee, to bring it to the Senate for a vote and get it to the House and get it to the States for ratification. And as you know, I have called for a general strike of women on Wednesday, August 26, 50 years after the amendment giving women the right to vote was ratified by the final State. We have had history but not "herstory", too much in this country and so this day has been chosen for the general strike of women.

And I would tell you in my recent travels around the country women everywhere are reacting to this, are going to join in on this, from secretaries and nurses and telephone operators to women in the home and women in your offices and I would think your wives and daughters and the students in the schools. And I would warn you that in addition to confronting the unfinished business of equality in our offices and homes and our march on city hall that if by Wednesday, August 26 you and your fellow Congressmen in the House have not sent the equal rights amendment to the states for ratification, we are going to track you down in your offices here, or on the beaches or in the mountains and we are going to stay with you, our most eager scouts, night and day, until this amendment is passed because we mean business. The militance of women today crosses lines of generation, of race, of color, of class. We are not stopping now. There is no turning us backward. And we are 53 percent of the adult voting population of this country. And we are not being stopped any longer by manmade political divisions.

And we know also the value of our own labor and what is needed to protect our own labor and we are not being dissuaded or diverted by the hypocrisy of the male labor leaders. We speak for ourselves, and I speak for all my sisters, young and old, in saying to you heed us seriously because we mean it, and this equal rights amendment which we now insist on passing, though it's been nearly 50 years since the torch was passed on to us by our predecessors who won the vote, we will not tolerate any tampering with the language, any further delay.

We want constitutional equality for the women of the United States now. [Applause.]

Senator Cook. First of all, let me say that if there is a battle between the sexes, I want to be in a rowboat in the middle of the Potomac River. Secondly, if we are not successful by late August, I will neither be in the mountains nor on the beach and you certainly may contact me.

I note with interest your indictment of male labor leaders especially after having heard their testimony before this subcommittee. The point was raised to some of the labor officials testifying before this subcommittee, that the so-called protective legislation they are earnestly trying to uphold is actually discriminatory. I cite as reference those laws which govern the number of hours per week women are allowed to work. Such legislation eliminates women from those positions, often of a supervisory nature, which require a lengthy workweek. Do you consider such legislation to be protective?

Miss FREIDAN. This is discriminatory because it hasn't worked to protect women. I have known many cases——

Senator COOK. Who has it worked to protect?

Miss FREIDAN. Men. It has worked to protect men on the jobs that are the good jobs. The same with the weights. You know, if it is a question of real protection on weights, men are more susceptible to hernias than women, and 30 pounds—little children that we lift all the time weigh that; briefcases; often in the rush of my travels my own pocketbook has weighed 30 pounds, I think. It is very interesting how all the good jobs, the high-paying jobs which men want domination in, exclusive access to, those factors aren't involved. And it is just to keep women from getting to those jobs.

Yes, let's get rid of those special sex protective laws that protect men against the competition of women workers.

Senator COOK. Do you feel that universities have an obligation to their women students to advise them of the discrimination they are likely to encounter after graduation?

Miss FREIDAN. Well, more than that; a great many colleges and universities have completely different standards for women and men in the professional schools, and sometimes, you know, in the colleges, the undergraduate colleges they have different standards for women and men in giving them fellowships and scholarships.

And in the case of the law school you mentioned until there was actual pressure they didn't even, the law school didn't even send women out to apply for certain jobs and accepted job bids from firms which would say they didn't want women.

Now, if we have the equal rights amendment, this kind of educational discrimination against women would be unconstitutional, and I think that it's simply an elementary American right of women who are more than half the population to get equal educational opportunity.

Senator COOK. Mr. Chairman.

Senator BAYH. Well, I want to apologize, Miss Freidan. One of these unexpected emergencies arose, and I was trying to listen on the telephone with one ear and listen to you with the other.

Senator COOK. You must have received an earful from both sides.

Senator BAYH. I am not sure it did anything to fill up the vacuum in between my ears. That's the problem.

You mentioned that the only special protection that women need is maternity benefits. I think I heard that. Were you emphasizing the word "special?"

Miss FREIDAN. It is special because it is simply functional, shall we say——

Senator BAYH. What I mean is, when you said the only special protection women need, is it fair to suggest that the working force as a whole, men and women, need certain protections from the sweatshop, from excessively long hours, from unsatisfactory working conditions, and that this should be applied across the board to men and women?

Miss FREIDAN. Right. And I said when you were out, Senator, that it is very hypocritical at a time of recession to speak as if the big issue is 54 hours—protecting women from working more than 54 hours. The big issue at a time of recession is whether women are again going to be the last hired and above all the first fired at this moment. And the big issue to perhaps more men and women alike is that excessive overtime may not be a good thing for anybody, you know, to feed all of our families and ourselves.

The work should be spread around, whatever work there is. And furthermore, that from the point of view of the family, men and women are equally needed, you know, at home at certain hours of the day. And just as the weight-lifting protection is hypocritical at a time when labor leaders know, as well as you do, and I do, that the blue-collar jobs requiring heavy muscular strength and all that are being eliminated very rapidly—you can see this in studies of Government jobs, and the same is true in private industry—these are not the issues at the moment. I would be the last to want woman ever used as a force to undermine the necessary protection of working conditions, you know, or labor working conditions.

But this is not what is going to happen. The only way that can happen is when women are there as a low-paid—a force that you can pay less and that you can use, you know, to bring wages down. This hypocritical kind of thing disguises what the real situation is.

And as far as the maternity benefits are concerned, that is what everybody is talking about when they talk about these hypocritical, these protective laws.

Senator BAYH. Do not the statistics which you gave earlier in your statement of average income of women versus men and the number of men versus women earning over $5,000 a year, could that not go beyond normal job discrimination and be a direct result of discrimination in the educational process?

Miss FREIDAN. Yes. And that is what Senator Cook——

Senator BAYH. Did he tell you he has two daughters that are in college and that he has to pay the same tuitions?

Senator COOK. Wait until you are faced with the same situation.

Senator BAYH. I just wanted——

Miss FREIDAN. Senator, I think your daughter should go to battle against this discrimination.

Senator COOK. As a matter of fact, it is going to get worse because this fall I will have two daughters in college and three the following year.

Senator BAYH. You see what he is doing, he is rubbing it in because I am not fortunate in having a daughter. I say that in jest, let the record show.

Miss FREIDAN. The educational discrimination on the basis of sex is the only kind of educational discrimination—you know, as I have often said sex discrimination is the only kind of discrimination still considered legal except for title II and it is still considered a joke in this country.

It is not a joke. It has not been necessary to use mace and tear gas to keep women down. As you know they have been kept down by treating it as a joke or this kind of invisibility. I have often said, women have been visible to the degree that they were too visible as the sort of sex objects, or for false pedestalling that we must protect the poor little dears from.

Well, you know at this moment we are making ourselves visible and I commend you Senators for really, you know, opening your own eyes to this. It is a tribute to the speed of the chain reaction of the women's liberation movement, which has reached critical mass in the 1970's, that 47 years of traditional, you know, blindness to the necessity of an equal rights amendment has at least been broken by you and by these hearings. But I think there is an urgency of really getting on with it and of not being delayed. I remember that in the civil rights legislation of 1964 no one who was committed to enactment of the Civil Rights Act would listen to any tampering amendments because they understood clearly the intent of them. This would be the same case. There is no need to change the word. The simplicity of this amendment, "equality of rights under the law shall not be denied by the United States on account of sex," that covers the waterfront.

Senator BAYH. Well, let me say that I hope you don't feel I suggested that language as a delaying tactic or as an effort to water it down, because I think I have expressed myself rather equivocally as to the Hayden rider type of approach. I am very pragmatic. I want to get 67 votes in the U.S. Senate. I want to get them as quickly as possible. And if by a little change in the language we can get this job done without materially affecting the substance of the amendment, then I think we are moving forward. I don't know whether there is any language that can do one without doing the other, and I don't want to diminish the forward thrust of the liberation movement. I have no questions. I appreciate your being here with us.

Senator COOK. Mr. Chairman, I did not mention my daughters attending college to solicit sympathy but rather to establish a point. I am disturbed that the same university presidents and administrators who constantly criticize members of Congress also operate institutions which charge the same tuition for both sexes yet contribute little to ending discrimination against women. [Applause.]

Institutions of higher learning can and must begin to solve this problem. It is inexcusable for these institutions to allow recruiters who discriminate on the basis of sex on campus.

Mis FREIDAN. It is like taxation without representation. You know, we are taxed equally with men and yet we are not even, under our old Constitution, considered people. So I think, you know, if we don't get constitutional equality we might wonder what kind of citizenship we actually have.

Thank you.

Senator BAYH. Thank you very much. [Applause.]

Our next witness is Adele Weaver, president of the National Association of Lawyers. Did I slip and leave out the "Women"?

STATEMENT OF MRS. ADELE T. WEAVER, PRESIDENT-ELECT, NATIONAL ASSOCIATION OF WOMEN LAWYERS

Mrs. WEAVER. Well, Senator, if you did, I will accept your correction.

Senator Bayh, Chairman Bayh and Senator Cook, on behalf of the National Association of Women Lawyers I speak with deepest conviction on behalf of the equal rights amendment. The thrust of my remarks will be on the legal impact of the proposed equal rights amendment and will be aimed at areas other than labor law because I feel that that field has been sufficiently covered. These areas will be political rights of women, disabilities of women, family law, divorce, alimony and custody, and military service for women.

I eliminate the areas of equal opportunity in employment and equal pay for equal work, although that is a subject dear to my heart having helped the Florida Legislature pass an equal pay for equal work bill in their last session.

My statement is directed to those opponents of the equal rights amendment who take the view that women will be adversely affected by the amendment. It is my position that the equal rights amendment will correct legal deficiencies that exist and assure women the rights that they are intitled to legally in order to cope with their responsibilities in today's changing world.

I first refer to the political rights of women and historically to the right of suffrage.

It is noteworthy that the 15th amendment to the U.S. Constitution ratified 100 years ago on March 30, 1870, provided that the right of the citizens of the United States to vote shall not be denied or abridged by the United States or by any State on account of race, color, or previous condition of servitude.

It is certainly further worthy of comment that the political, social, and legal rights of women are running generations behind the rights of black people.

Prior to the 19th amendment, 50 years later, the courts had taken the view that the status of women as citizens did not confer upon them the right to vote and that that right could be constitutionally limited to males. This first recognition of women as a person and citizen was only achieved by a constitutional amendment.

JURY DUTY, A POLITICAL RIGHT OF WOMAN

At common law women were not eligible to serve as jurors; however, there is no doubt that States have the power to make them eligible, and in most jurisdictions women are now qualified to be jurors, although the view has been taken that the 19th amendment to the U.S. Constitution guaranteeing the right of suffrage, does not require States to admit women as jurors.

Therefore, though most States have now enacted jury duty statutes automatically qualifying women for jury duty and have eliminated the necessity of women having to volunteer for jury duty as was the case in my State of Florida until 1967, but not now, the proposed equal rights amendment to the U.S. Constitution would make unconstitutional any discrimination against women in that regard so that any State not yet having provided for automatic selection of persons for jury duty without discrimination as to sex would be obliged to enact such legislation. In fact any legislation to the contrary would be automatically voided.

Since jurors are consistently excused for hardship reasons already, there is no legal problem involved in a statutory provision excusing the mothers of children under a certain age from jury duty upon their application to be excused.

The need for women to be called consistently to fulfill this primary duty of citizenship is obvious; so long as we retain the jury system, the jury should be representative of the entire population, and not just 50 percent or less of it, thus neglecting a tremendous potential source of capable jurors.

I refer now to the disabilities of women, and in particular at this moment to the disability of a minority of single women.

The legal disability of single women is generally related to the age requirement for marriage, voting, and entering into legal contracts. At the present time, influenced by the common law, most States allow a girl to marry without parental consent at a younger age than boys. Now, here, the discrimination is actually against the male sex. The effect of the proposed equal rights amendment prohibiting discrimination as to sex would be to lower the age requirement to that of the female. It follows that State Legislatures might well wish to enact legislation advancing the age requirement for marriage without parental consent for both the girl and boy, if this be deemed desirable. The equal rights amendment would not affect a State's right to legislate age requirements for voting, for marriage without parental consent, or for attaining majority, so long as there is no discrimination as to sex in such legislation.

MARRIED WOMEN

The real impact of the equal rights amendment would be felt by the married woman. It is in the area of the disabilities of married women, particularly in the handling of property, and in the areas of family law and divorce that great discrimination exists; and I must add that this discrimination is not always directed toward woman, but frequently toward the man.

I testified in Florida before one of the committees of our Florida Legislature on a divorce reform bill, and many questions were thrust at me regarding the field of alimony, and here is where the discrimination does exist.

The disabilities of marriage are generally the result of the common law under which a married woman lost her identity and husband and wife became legally only one person; that is, the person of the husband.

The married woman under the common law lost her right to contract, and except as that right was remedied or was granted to her by the legislature, her attempted contract was void. Under the common law she could not acquire or dispose of property without consent of her husband and she could not contract with her husband.

The husband, as head of the family alone established the family domicile and still does generally and is primarily obligated for support of the family. The wife, even where the common law has been modified, is limited to her own earnings in employment separate from her husband's and in many States still must obtain joinder of her husband in any conveyance or encumbrance of her separate property.

Now, these common law restrictions and their many statutory modifications have resulted in the enactment of "Free Dealer" laws and their equivalents. Such free dealer laws would become unnecessary and would be eliminated by the equal rights amendment. The necessity for free dealership or free agent statutes is an anachronism in this era when the majority of married women work, generally to contribute to the support of the family, and many of them being in professions and businesses requiring them to contract, to bind themselves legally, to sue and be sued.

Heretofore, only under these free dealer laws or specific legislalation has a woman been able to convey or encumber her own separate property without joinder by her husband. The equal rights amendment would eliminate the discrimination against either sex in this regard; naturally, if the constitutional or statutory requirements of a given State were identical as to conveyancing or encumbering of their separate property by either sex, the proposed equal rights amendment would not affect such requirements.

We have had a good example in my State of Florida of this. Our new 1968 constitution provides that there shall be no distinction between married women and married men in the holding, controlling, disposition, and encumbering of their property. However, we have had statutes in existence for quite some time requiring a married woman to join her husband in the conveyance or encumbrance of his own separate property in order to release her inchoate dower right to that property, and which also required the joinder of a husband in any conveyance or encumbrance by a woman of her own separate property and these statutes are in conflict with the new constitution. Bills have been introduced and passed by the House in our current legislative session putting into effect the policy and intent of the new constitution. The bills, if passed, will first, eliminate the necessity for a woman to secure the joinder of her husband in any conveyance of encumbrance of her own separate property, and also eliminate the necessity of joinder by the wife in the conveyance or encumbrance by a husband of his own separate property by elimination of the inchoate right of dower, that is, limiting the right of dower to that property owned by the husband at the time of death. I give this simply as an example of what can be done with regard to dower rights.

In this regard, therefore, the equal rights amendment would affect dower laws or their counterparts where the equivalent right of courtesy or its counterpart is not given the husband. There is no reason whatsoever why a married man should not have at the moment of his wife's death a right to a portion of her property equivalent to the right of dower which she has in his property. I, of course, refer here only to those States having dower statutes. In other States, the statutory share of the spouse's property to which the surviving spouse is entitled should be identical. In the community property States there would appear to be no problem that cannot be solved by some form of the community system of property, assuming that there is no discrimination as to sex. Generally, the effect of the proposed equal rights amendment would be to eliminate any discrimination whatsoever in the area of the right to convey or encumber one's separate property and the right to dower, courtesy, community property or an equivalent right of inheritance between the spouses.

I go now to the field of family law and touch upon the fact of domicile.

As we know in common law, the husband establishes the domicile in most jurisdictions. The legal effect of the proposed equal rights amendment would be to affect the automatic establishment of the domicile by the husband as head of the family. From a practical point of view, since marriages are established for the purpose of living together and it is generally desirable from the woman's point of view to be domiciled in the area most conducive to the welfare and business or professional activity of the husband, the equal rights amendment would have little or no effect. Statutes that follow the common law could be modified to hold that the breadwinner of the family determines the domicile for the family or in those cases where neither one party or the other is predominantly the breadwinner, the domicile could be established by either party. The concept of domicile has lost its importance in family law, except as a basis for the right of one party or the other to come into the courts of any particular State for solution of domestic or family matters. Domicile is now primarily concerned with the establishment of the right to vote and other civil rights.

Support of the wife and child: This has been the legal duty and is the legal duty of the husband and father, and some States even make it a criminal offense for a husband to withhold support from his wife and child. Yet, our courts have consistently interpreted the obligation of the husband to support his wife with due regard to financial conditions, earning capacities, and other circumstances of either spouse that bear upon the discharge of his obligation. Therefore, the legal effect of the equal rights amendment would be to make the obligation of the husband to support the wife consistent with actual practice. Obviously, it should be the legal duty of either spouse to support the other more dependent spouse.

I believe the words of the marriage vows imply such a moral obligation already.

The argument of some opponents of the equal rights amendment that it would allow a man to escape from his obligation to support is not a valid argument. So long as the wife contributes in services to the family, in the duties of homemaking, of rearing children, of being a social hostess for her husband, and so on, she is contributing equally to the marriage, and with each year that she makes such contribution to the marriage her ability to earn an independent income from the outside world diminishes while her contribution to the marriage increases.

It is conceivable that there may be a few cases where the spouse contributing the services to the home or caring for small children would be the husband. This may sound a bit ludicrous but the possibility exists, and the equal rights amendment should result in State legislation making the support of one spouse by the other dependent upon the circumstances of those spouses, and their respective contributions to the marriage—the contribution of homemaking and related duties being as vitally important a contribution as that of earning the family income.

It follows that both spouses should be responsible for the support of their children, and pursuing this thought, and along this line, who has ever seen a mother who would not go out to work, or even to beg, borrow, or steal to support her children when they were not being supported by the father? The legal effect of the equal rights amendment in this area of support for the spouse and the children of the marriage would be to place the responsibility upon both spouses with due regard to their respective contributions to the marriage and their respective abilities to be self-supporting.

I have already mentioned the effect of the proposed equal rights amendment upon the concept of dower which would be either to eliminate dower or to establish an equivalent right of curtesy and legislation might be necessary in those instances to establish the latter or to eliminate the former. The necessity for married women who have dedicated their lives to the occupation of homemaking to share in the fruits of the marriage partnership can be established in any one of several ways, by dower and the equivalent curtesy, by one of the community property systems, by inheritance laws, and/or by alimony awards in the event of divorce.

The nature of the particular measure will depend in each jurisdiction upon existing laws and the circumstances involved.

Now I get to the area of divorce and its related alimony and custody matters.

It is not in the grounds or procedures for divorce that the impact of an equal rights amendment will be felt; it is rather in the determination of the rights of the parties as to alimony, support, and cutody of children that the greatest thrust of the equal rights amendment will be seen.

While the amendment would make unconstitutional the award of alimony to a wife based simply on the ground of sex there would be no deterrent to an award of alimony on grounds such as the following: the wife's financial contributions or their equivalent in homemaking services to the marriage partnership, the years of duration of the marriage, the need for support based on the inability to be self-supporting, age, lack of education or training, lack of availability or need for the services that the dependent spouse is capable of performing.

Using these or similar guidelines, it is obvious that either spouse who, having dedicated many years to the marriage partnership without remuneration and with resulting depreciation of value in the labor market, is entitled to support by the other spouse; such support or alimony should, of course, be commensurate with the need of the dependent spouse and should be based upon the employed spouse's ability to pay. As a matter of fact, these are the guidelines generally used in our courts today by judges accustomed to hearing and deciding matters of support and alimony in divorce cases.

The need of the one spouse against the other spouse's ability to pay is the guideline and the equal rights amendment would simply give a constitutional basis for sensible judicial decisionmaking as it exists.

As to custody of children, it has been said, well, custody of children would automatically be taken away from the wife. She would no longer be entitled to custody. We know that at common law, the husband was automatically entitled to custody of his child. But gradually the concept of making a determination of custody solely "for the best interests of the child or children * * *" came into effect. Generally, neither parent has priority as to custody today although many courts follow the rule that the best interests of a child of tender years are served by granting custody to the mother, with reasonable rights of visitation to the father. Now, an equal rights amendment should have no effect whatsoever, I feel, upon the existing law and practice in our courts.

I finally touch upon an area that has been discussed as one of the possible legal effects of the proposed equal rights amendment, and that is the eligibility of young women for military service.

While it may seem at first impression a bit shocking to think of the young girl of 18 being drafted, the fact is that many thousands of our young women went into military service in World War II. They wore their uniforms with pride and rendered immeasurable service to this Nation. There is no reason whatsoever why any healthy young woman should not serve her country for a year or two in any capacity for which she is physically, mentally, and emotionally suited. No young man today is required to do more. While we may not wish for our young women to be placed in hazardous battle areas, the fact remains that our military nurses are and have been subjected to such hazards. We may not wish to follow the example set by the Israeli Army—but there are thousands of activities by which our young military female could give service to her country.

There are, no doubt, many other areas of concern to the American woman today which would eventually be affected by the proposed equal rights amendment. Certainly one cannot be omniscient and predict the outcome of such an evolutionary, not revolutionary, but evolutionary measure as the proposed equal rights amendment. The legal effects would seem, however, to be beneficial not only to woman, but to society generally. It is my humble contention on behalf of the National Association of Women Lawyers that the American woman today really does not recognize her own value as a person and a human being, and until she is accorded the constitutional right to equality under the law in every respect, she will not begin to free herself from the bondage of centuries of self-depreciation. She must assume the full responsibilities as well as the full rights of citizenship and until she does this, this great country of ours will be deprived of the benefit of the service, the brains, and the talent of a half of our population—women.

The National Association of Women Lawyers urges this committee to report out the equal rights amendment favorably as a first most important step toward achievement of woman's full status as a citizen.

Thank you. [Applause.]

Senator BAYH. Thank you very much, Mrs. Weaver. It has not come as a surprise to me that you have presented such an excellent discussion of this whole picture with particular emphasis on those legal aspects and legal concerns which have been brought before us by some opponents and which are general concerns and questions existing in the country.

You have done such an excellent job here I find it difficult to ask questions that haven't already been covered.

Is it fair to suggest that the experience that you have had in Florida with the positive response of the legislature to the constitutional mandate is the same type of response we would see from other legislatures and indeed the Congress of the United States itself relative to a Federal constitutional requirement?

Mrs. WEAVER. I certainly would hope so. As a matter of fact, our Florida Legislature I think one could describe as rather conservative, so certainly if our Florida Legislature responds affirmatively, I would think that we would see this same type of response all over.

I don't want to mislead you. These changes have not yet taken place; they have only passed the House and as yet I do not think

that our Senate has taken up these two measures that would conform
our statutes with our Florida constitution. We do expect them to be
passed, however.

Senator BAYH. But your general impression is that passage of the
constitutional amendment demanding equality of the sexes would
not necessarily mean that protective legislation would be wiped from
the books but rather it would be given to all members of the work
force, all members of our society who are writing contracts who are
establishing domicile?

Mrs. WEAVER. This is precisely what I interpret the amendment
to mean, that any protective legislation would apply to both sexes.
If you don't mind, I would like to note here, the thought occurred
to me as we were discussing this protective legislation that I
believe this type of legislation originated way, way back at the time
of or prior to the Fair Labor Standards Act, and back in those days
when women were working, little children were working in sweat-
shops, worked, I don't know how many hours a day, 15, 18 hours
a day perhaps and under atrocious working conditions; no doubt
that protective legislation was needed at that time. But since that
time labor conditions have changed. And the laws that we do have
today should apply equally to men and women.

Now, I think at the time this equal rights amendment was first
introduced, at least about the time the Hayden rider was tacked on
I believe that our late and revered Eleanor Roosevelt had a great
deal to do with being for the rider on protective legislation.

With due respect to her memory, I feel that this type of thinking
does not, is not to the advantage of women today and it is not to the
advantage of women in this world today. The world has changed.
Labor conditions have changed. We don't need that protective
legislation except as it applies to all people in the labor field.

Senator BAYH. Thank you very much.

Senator Cook.

Senator COOK. Mrs. Weaver, I congratulate you on the presentation
of an excellent paper and note that the National Association of
Women Lawyers should be extremely proud to have you as its head.
I would assume that you will have little problem in securing the
passage of your constitutional mandate in the Florida Senate. The
Florida Senate in doing otherwise would be rather derelict in its
duties, wouldn't it?

Mrs. WEAVER. It certainly would.

Senator COOK. I want to thank you. You elaborated on several
points that are of extreme importance such as jury service, the
property rights of married women, child support and child custody.
You mentioned the participation of young women in military service
and I wish to add that legislative history concerning this matter
has been established. I cite the bill, passed by the House in the
final days of World War II, that called for the drafting of qualified
female nurses. It is my desire that this Nation fully utilize the talents
of all of its citizens in the future.

I want to thank you again.

Mrs. WEAVER. Thank you. May I add one word. Senator Cook
spoke along the line of the educational disadvantages of our young
women in colleges. The National Association of Women Lawyers and

its current president Mrs. Jettie Selvig, has just held a regional meeting in Las Vegas, Nev., and the subject of that conference was discrimination against women in law schools and in placement by the law schools.

So that this matter is being seriously considered by the law school deans, by our association and by the American Law Schools Association. And a committee of the American Bar Association has been set up. It is a subcommittee called Equal Rights for Women, and it is under the Individual Rights and Responsibilities Section of the American Bar Association. So that a great many different committees and different organizations are looking into this area of discrimination against women.

Thank you so much for this opportunity.

Senator COOK. Thank you very much.

Senator BAYH. Mrs. Weaver, if you have any statistical evidence relative to this type of discrimination that is going on in law schools or in hiring practices of law firms after graduation, it would be very helpful to have this information for our file.

Mrs. WEAVER. I would be most happy to send it to you.

Senator BAYH. Thank you very much. We appreciate your contribution.

Mrs. WEAVER. Thank you. [Applause.]

Senator BAYH. Our next witnesses are Miss Virginia Allan, Chairman of the President's Task Force on Women's Rights and Responsibilities. And I understand she is accompanied by Dr. Laurine E. Fitzgerald, professor and associate dean of students at Michigan State University, and Miss P. Dee Boersma, a graduate student at Ohio State University.

We appreciate you ladies taking the time to let us have your thoughts on this subject.

STATEMENT OF VIRGINIA R. ALLAN, CHAIRMAN, PRESIDENT'S TASK FORCE ON WOMEN'S RIGHTS AND RESPONSIBILITIES; ACCOMPANIED BY DR. LAURINE E. FITZGERALD, PROFESSOR AND ASSOCIATE DEAN OF STUDENTS, MICHIGAN STATE UNIVERSITY, AND MISS P. DEE BOERSMA, GRADUATE STUDENT

Miss ALLAN. Thank you.

Senator BAYH. You are the graduate student?

Miss ALLAN. Thank you very much.

We are from Michigan, and we are honored and pleased to be with you today to testify in favor of the equal rights amendment. It's already been noted that I am accompanied by Dr. Laurine E. Fitzgerald, who is the associate dean of students at Michigan State University and professor of administration and higher education. Dee Boersma is a graduate of Central Michigan University and is a graduate student at Ohio State University at the present time.

Last year I was appointed Chairman of a special study Task Force on Women's Rights and Responsibilities by President Nixon. The work of the task force was completed on December 15, 1969. Thus the task force terminated its job of recommendations on that date and I, my chairmanship. So I come today to speak to you as an individual, one with special interest in the subject of women's rights and responsibilities.

It is my firm conviction that passage of the equal rights amendment would eliminate impediments to women's rights (which rights are or should be the same as those of men) and enable women to share with men the responsibilities of family, community, and nation. Too long have men borne the total burden themselves without the full partnership of that other half of the human population. Men and women should share alike in the full range of family, economic, and political responsibilities.

There have been many learned expositions in this hall these past two days clearly defining the extent of the equal rights amendment and the effects of passage of that amendment on various aspects of our national life. I come to you today to add my statement in support of the equal rights amendment, concentrating my remarks in the field of education.

My experience in the last 7 years as regent of Eastern Michigan University has increased my knowledge of the problems women face in discrimination in our universities and colleges.

Mr. Chairman, I will touch upon various aspects of the problem as they have been impressed upon me and then indicate what ameliorating effects would occur with the pasage of the equal rights amendment.

I think we can all be proud of the fact that the level of education attained by women has risen steadily since the turn of the century. High school graduations increased from a ratio of 7 per 100 girls 17 years of age in the population in 1900 to 32 per 100 in 1930, to 67 per 100 in 1960, and to 78 per 100 in 1968. College graduations have increased as well. Whereas only 5,237 women received a college degree equivalent in 1900, there were 278,761 joining them in 1968; there were 303 M.A.'s conferred on women in 1900 and 63,401 in 1968; 23 Ph.D.'s in 1900 and 2,906 in 1968.

However important and encouraging these statistics may be, there are others less promising, less encouraging and of equal relevance. Just recently, the Women's Bureau of the United States Department of Labor published a "Fact Sheet on the Earnings Gap" which compared the median wage or salary incomes of women and men who work fulltime year round, revealing not only that the salaries of women are considerably less than those of men but also that the gap has widened in recent years. In 1955, for example, women's median wage or salary income of $2,719 was 64 percent of the $4,252 received by men. In 1968 women's median earnings of $4,457 were only 58 percent of the $7,664 received by men.

The gap appears in the fact that 20 percent of the women but only 8 percent of the men earned less than $3,000 and 60 percent of the women but only 20 percent of the men earned less than $5,000. While, on the other hand, only 3 percent of the women but 28 percent of the men had earnings of $10,000 or more.

There is a definite correlation between educational accomplishment and income among both men and women: those with the least schooling have the lowest income, those with more formal education, higher income. Yet, the gap between the earning power of men and women is repeated all along the line. With a chart verifying the statement, the 1969 Handbook on Women Workers concluded that "at all levels of educational attainment the median income received by women is substantially below the median income of men." Thus regardless of education that "earnings gap" remains.

The reason seems to be that women are more likely than men to be employed in lower-skilled, lower-paying jobs even if they are as highly educated as men. Despite the fact that the United States has been in the forefront in opening higher education to women, today the proportion of women in the professions is lower in this country than in most countries throughout the world; 9 percent of all full professors; 8 percent of all scientists; 6.7 percent of all physicians; 3.5 percent of all lawyers, and 1 percent of those listed in Who's Who in America for 1967.

Actually, before careers are launched, the discrimination begins with experiences in educational institutions. Nowhere, Mr. Chairman, is the gap in earning power, in professional status and administrative responsibility more noticeable than in the field of education. Nowhere does it influence more people, affect more careers and job opportunities. And, I might add, nowhere is it more deplorable. One of the basic concepts upon which our democracy was founded was the idea that people can only be free and equal where there is equality of opportunity. In today's increasingly technological world, real equality of opportunity requires a significant amount of education. Whether, as student or teacher, women today do not have equal educational opportunity with men in admissions policies, in fellowships, in leadership activities, in professional appointments, promotions, in accessibility to the positions of dean and president. In proportion to the numbers who go to graduate school there are actually fewer women on college faculties today. The few in higher education are seldom department heads, full professors, or chairman of committees. Thus women students are denied what today are called "role models." They are also subtly influenced against pursuing careers in education or careers that depend upon advanced degrees, the access to which is impeded by financial problems, by child care responsibilities, by stereotypes concerning their sex.

Admissions policies for graduates and undergraduates keep women separate and unequal. The manual of "Freshmen Class Profiles" published by the College Entrance Examination Board reveals that colleges discriminate in admissions policies between men and women. Some schools accept both men and women scoring high on the verbal portion of the scholastic ability test, commonly known as the "College Boards," but accept more of the men applying although both men and women are of the same scholastic ability level. With variations, this is the pattern that emerges, whether colleges make this kind of discrimination among the top, middle, or lower level of student. At the same scholastic achievement level, men are preferred.

Many, perhaps most, State colleges and universities apply higher standards to girls than to boys. The American Council on Education annually surveys the freshmen class admitted to a large sample of institutions of higher education. This survey indicates that in both public and private schools, the young women admitted as freshmen are younger, had higher grades in high school, ranked higher in their class, came from high schools of higher academic standing, and are more apt to have been high achievers in high school extracurricular activities, except in varsity sports and in science contests.

For example, 41 percent of the girls admitted to public 4-year colleges in the fall of 1968 had average grades in high schools of B plus or better, whereas only 17.8 percent of boys had such grades. When Mr. Gayle C. Wilson, the president of the American Association of Collegiate Registrars and Admissions Officers and a past president of the Association of College Admissions Counselors, was asked by the National Observer in an interview last year whether a student's sex has any bearing on how his application is considered, Mr. Wilson answered "yes." When asked if girls are qualified for admission he replied: "Various studies have shown that generally two-thirds of the top third of high school graduates nationally are women."

What happens to these intelligent women achievers before and during college that they do not equal men in careers? I would like to try and offer some tentative answers.

While in college women students find subtle discrimination in various ways. Take the matter of counseling. Two recent studies by the U.S. Department of Labor indicate that women college graduates are discontent with their vocational counseling while in college. And with little wonder. Women students are sometimes openly discouraged from pursuing graduate education. It is assumed they will marry, raise a family and that this precludes a profesional interest for them. The same is not assumed with male students, nor need it be. Thus inadequate attention and assistance are offered to solving the real problems many women face who choose both a profession and family life. In a special report on women and graduate study of June 1968 four significant factors were listed which would induce more women to enter graduate study in the fields of science and medicine. They are: (1) Greater availability of part-time training and employment, (2) establishment of child-care centers or allowances, (3) increased number of stipends, and (4) greater recognition of women who have been successful in these fields.

These same factors would apply to any field.

Women undergraduates and graduate students find discrimination in scholarship and fellowship awards. As late as 1967 Congresswoman Edith Green, member of the House Committee on Education and Labor, noted that women do not get their proportionate share of the guaranteed loans provided for in the Higher Education Act. She also noted that only one out of five graduate fellowships under NDEA goes to a woman; that about one in four teaching fellowships goes to a woman. Sometimes overt, sometimes covert, the hesitancy to award grants to women results from the fact that the dispensers of funds perfer to invest in men who will make a career of whatever field they choose. They assume women may well abandon the field.

Discrimination filters down even into the nonacademic life of the student. Seldom do we find women elected student body president or student union president or student newspaper editor, in a coeducational institution. How many women students become presidents of coeducational professional, social or honorary societies on campus? When women so seldom see themselves in these positions, what are they to expect of themselves and their sisters?

Recruitment and placement discrimination operate in multiple ways: In the absence of certain recruiters at women's colleges, in the clear preferance for men, in the type of jobs suggested to women on the one hand (secretarial and clerk) and to men on the other hand (management or management training positions).

The kind of company and the type of job offered to men and women are not the only differences. There is the accompanying matter of salary and promotion. In a survey conducted in November of 1969, jobs and salaries expected to be offered by 206 companies to June 1970 college graduates were reported. There was a significant difference in the offers to be made to men and women with the same college majors. This is not an isolated case but a recurring example.

I am gratified to note one promising recent development. Some recruiters and some universities are becoming aware of the fact that in the process of placement they are acting as employment agencies and therefore must conform to title VII of the Civil Rights Act which prohibits discrimination. Others are becoming aware of the moral and humane values attached as well to equal employment opportunity.

The University of Michigan Law School faculty barred a prestigious New York and Washington law firm from using job recruiting facilities at the University during the 1970-71 academic year because of charges that that firm discriminated against employment of women. This followed charges by members of the local chapter of the legal sorority that a recruiter had made statements indicating that the firm would hire fewer female law graduates than men and that those women hired would need higher qualifications. As universities become sensitive to sex discrimination in the lives of their women graduates we can expect greater attention to equal placement policies by all concerned.

So far I have talked more of women as students than women as professors. Their problems are clearly related. What do these women students observe of their teachers? How many are female? How many of them are full professors? Dr. Lawrence A. Simpson, who is currently a placement director and whose doctoral research analyzed academic discrimination regarding the women has reached the followiing conclusions regarding the present-day woman college teacher:

More than 50 percent of all academic women are in the broad fields of English, fine arts, health, education, and physical education.

Academic women are most frequently employed in private 4-year colleges with small faculties.

Women are predominantly at lower academic ranks—instructor or assistant profesor.

Women are more likely to teach beginning undergraduate students—freshmen and sophomores.

Women earn substantially less than men in the academic world.

In institutions of higher education in 1965-66 women full professors had a median salary of only $11,649 as compared with $12,768 for men. Comparable differences were found at the other three levels as shown in the followinng table:

MEDIAN ANNUAL SALARIES OF TEACHING STAFF IN COLLEGES AND UNIVERSITIES BY SEX, 1965–66

Teaching staff	Number		Median annual salary	
	Woman	Men	Women	Men
Total_____	26,734	118,641	$7,732	$9,275
Professors_____	3,149	32,873	11,649	12,768
Associate professors_____	5,148	28,892	9,322	10,064
Assistant professors_____	8,893	37,232	7,870	8,446
Instructors_____	9,454	19,644	6,454	6,864

Where are women college presidents? If it were not for the Catholic women's colleges we could numebr them on one hand. It is not at all unusual to have men as presidents of women's colleges but how many women presidents are there of all male schools or even of major coed universities? Women outnumber men 7 or 8 to 1 as teachers in our elementary and secondary schools. Yet in recent years women have been all but eliminated as public secondary school administrators. Between 1950–51 and 1961–62 the 12.0 percent women junior high principals and 6.0 percent senior high principals fell to 3.8 percent for all secondary schools. The ratio of women elementary principals sank from 56 percent to 37 percent.

A declining status of women also appears in superintendencies of education. In 1925 eight of the 48 State superintendents of education were women. In 1964, there was only one in the 50 States. On all levels in 1939 there were 765 women superintendents and assistant superintendents of schools. In 1962 there were 222 women superintendents and assistants—3.3 percent of the total for the whole United States. Are we retrogressing?

Mr. Chairman, I now turn to the role of the equal rights amendment in relation to educational discrimination toward women.

I believe that ratification of the equal rights amendment would have widespread effects on education. It would mean that all public schools must be open to girls on the same basis as boys. There could be no separate public high schools (where the boys learn science, mathematics and the girls something else) and no courses closed to girls (or boys either). Sex would not be the determinant of these matters but inidividual interest and ability.

If the equal rights amendment is passed, or when it is, State colleges and universities could not apply higher admission standards to girls, either at the undergraduate or graduate level.

The equal rights amendment would prohibit discrimination by Federal, State, and local government in employment. Thus, teachers and professors in public institutions would be legally protected against discrimination because of sex. They do not have this protection at this time. Educational personnel in schools and colleges are exempt from Title VII of the Civil Rights Act of 1964. There is a movement to remove this exemption, but at this time, such legislation has not been passed. The resultant discriminatory policies I have tried to detail.

Mr. Chairman, all universities which are recipients of Federal contracts are prohibited from discriminating in employment by Executive Order 11246 and specifically as to sex by the amendment to that executive order in the form of Executive Order 11375. This policy has been reaffirmed by President Nixon, who also has issued his own Executive Order 11478 calling for additional steps to strengthen equal employment opportunity in the Federal Government. The Office of Federal Contract Compliance is the agency directed to carry out this order which includes prohibition of discrimination in employment by colleges and universities under their Government contracts. I am sorry to report that the OFCC has been very slow in devising guidelines to prevent sex discrimination. Repeatedly they have been asked when these would be forthcoming and the promise is always for the future. We are waiting and hoping on this front.

Passage of the equal rights amendment would greatly assist us to impress upon the colleges and universities the illegality of the discrimination they practice.

We also believe, Mr. Chairman, that passage of the equal rights amendment would help to eliminate discrimination as to sex in education by the fact that it woud once and for all nullify the 1908 *Muller* decision which established women as a recognizable class, subject to special legislation. I believe that with this accomplished the full force of the *Brown* decision could be directed toward equality of educational opportunity for women. In the words of the court at that time:

Today, education is perhaps the most important function of State and local governments * * *. Such an opportunity, where the State has undertaken to provide it, is a right which must be available to all on equal terms * * * in the field of public education the doctrine of "separate but equal" has no place.

Separate educational facilities are inherently inequal * * * segregation is a denial of the equal protection of the laws.

I thank you, Mr. Chairman, and Senators of this committee for your interest in this proposed legislation, and your attention during this presentation.

I have two authorities with me, and I am going to spread the microphones now and they will have to answer for what I have said.

Senator BAYH. I think the two individuals who are accompanying you, Dr. Fitzgerald and Miss Boersma, could answer for you in all good conscience and with little danger stand on just about everything you have said.

Miss ALLAN. It has not been released by the White House. No, sir.

Senator BAYH. Could you tell us why—what we could do to get it released? I don't want to put anybody in an embarrassing position. I am anxious to get everybody on record and get this——

Miss ALLAN. The women of this country are very much interested in this report. Many, many letters I know have been written to the White House about the report.

Let me say this, that there were 17 task forces created by the President in the fall of 1969. As you know, we had 2 months to do our work. We were appointed around the 25th of September and our report had to be in December 15. The reasons for the task forces are for the guidance of the President. He was looking for information for his state of the Union address, and so that is why the December 15 deadline. Those reports were in. As I said, there were 17 of them. But to date, two have been released.

Senator BAYH. In your report do you ask, have you asked, do you officially ask, or have you personally asked the President to throw his moral support behind this effort?

Miss ALLEN. Mr. Chairman, I, as Chairman of the task force—and it was in the guidelines—was asked not to reveal the content of that report. The White House has that prerogative because it was for the information of the President. And so let's chalk one up for women. We have kept quiet 4 months, and I think we have exploded the myth that women can't keep a secret.

Senator BAYH. Are you familiar with the report that was in the Miami Herald about that report?

Miss ALLAN. Yes, sir.

Senator BAYH. Would it be a violation of your pledge to maintain silence to suggest whether that report is relatively accurate?

Miss ALLAN. Yes, sir, it would be in violation of my pledge of silence.

Senator BAYH. Is it unfair to suggest that if you felt strongly, as I am sure you do, about what you said that it may be somewhat inconsistent to give this committee the benefit of the information in this report and advise us as to how we could increase the incentive for those who received it to respond to what it contains or is alleged to contain?

Miss ALLAN. We would appreciate it if you would ask for the report. It is my understanding it is at the Government Printing Office now. You know better than I do how these things work. And so I have just told people that I think it will be a matter of a couple of weeks. I don't really know. And I am sure that there isn't a woman in this room that when the report is released they won't be interested in some respect, and I am sure that the men of this country as well will be interested. And I am sure that there will be action on many fronts by both men and women when the report is released.

Senator BAYH. You are very diplomatic in handling that without saying anything.

Miss ALLAN. I have had 4 months to learn that art.

Senator BAYH. Did you ask, or anybody on the Commission ask the administration to take a position or to testify before our committee?

Miss ALLAN. Not that I know of, no.

Senator BAYH. Would you?

Miss ALLAN. Would I testify?

Senator BAYH. No, would you ask that someone from the administration take a position on it?

Miss ALLAN. I will be happy to ask; yes, sir.

Senator BAYH. You don't need to make that request public. You can still maintain your silence by private request.

Well, I wish you would do that because we are trying to mobilize all of the forces we can, and certainly the White House would be a valuable ally in this effort.

Thank you very much.

Senator Cook?

Senator COOK. I have no questions, Miss Allan. However, the statistics you presented buttress the complaints which I have voiced earlier in these hearings. Having served as chairman of the board of trustees of a women's college and a member of the board of trustees of a coeducational college, 1 consider your remarks to be very apt.

I note with interest that in recent years the desire of excellent female students to attend the better women's colleges has lessened as these students are attracted by the competitive aspect of coeducational universities. I raise this point as a result of family experience and I would ask Miss Boersma to elaborate on this new competitive attitude in coeducational universities.

Miss Boersma. Well, I am very glad, needless to say, more units opened up to coeducational standards. However, Martha Griffiths, Congresswoman Griffiths reported in the March 9 Congressional Record of this year that the State of Virginia last year had people applying for higher education and 21,000 women were turned down for higher education and not one male, which I think is a very interesting commentary still on the state of higher education in many States, one reason why the equal rights amendment would be very helpful for educational institutions, not that it will certainly end discrimination but that it will be a step in the right direction to at least advocating that women are equal in many areas of our society; they should start taking an active role in furthering the Nation.

And right now, I don't think that we are perpetuating this type of philosophy.

Senator Cook. I agree completely.

Thank you, Mr. Chairman.

Senator Bayh. Ladies, thank you very much for your contribution to our committee.

Miss Allan. Thank you, Mr. Chairman. [Applause.]

Senator Bayh. Our next witness is Mr. John Mack Carter, publisher and editor of Ladies Home Journal, American Home, and Family Weekly.

Certainly, Mr. Carter, I know of no one who has a greater avenue of entry to the minds and boudoirs of American women than you.

Senator Cook. I don't know, John. Do you feel safe here?

STATEMENT OF JOHN MACK CARTER, EDITOR AND PUBLISHER, LADIES' HOME JOURNAL; AND PRESIDENT, DOWNE PUBLISHING

Mr. Carter. Mr. Chairman, Senator Cook, I am pleased and honored to be here today. My only recent public statement on women's rights had to be delivered under some harassment before an uninvited audience that dropped into my office for 11 hours recently. The women of the liberation movement presented their viewpoints and plans in many carefully prepared papers. But my own statements were somewhat inhibited at the time. Surrounded by a group of angry women who had already prejudged the Journal as degrading and prejudged me a sexist, chauvinist oppressor, I was not about to discuss whether I stopped beating my wife. In a television interview later, I labeled that date "the most interesting of my career." Instead, I believe I should have called it most educational, for in the long run it helped to clarify my mind and judgments about the plight of American women, and therefore of American men, in the changing framework of our contemporary society.

The committee no doubt saw fit to invite me here today because as editor and publisher of the Ladies' Home Journal, a man in the communications medium addressed to the needs of American women, I possibly could add another perspective to your range of testimony.

I wish there were more time to go into the history of the magazine to do a countdown on how it has reflected the changing roles of women through 87 years, only 5 of which have come under my supervision.

If I may be permitted a bit of personal history, much shorter than that, relevant to the opinions I will express, I was born 42 years ago in Kentucky. I happened to be the male half of fraternal twins, and my twin sister with whom I shared a prenatal coeducational dorm, has never expressed any resentment of the fact that I was born first. She does, however, urge me to stop the press from publicizing my age—our age. My father and mother were both teachers; and neither of them seemed to worry much about who was the most successful. My grandparents had a small farm in Kentucky, and as with most farmers, leaned heavily on their children to help them. They were blessed—and they felt blessed—with five daughters.

In the fevered feminine liberation thrust of today, we cannot completely forget that the American heritage has not completely ignored the strengths and courage of American women. Sometimes it has exploited them; sometimes it has only begrudgingly recognized them. But the picture is not totally one of oppression and omission.

At the Journal as on all the other magazines where I have had primary responsibility, the majority of my staff has always been women, with many of them in top editorial positions. I had lunch the other day with George Delacorte, who heads the Dell Publishing complex, and he said that he has always preferred women in top executive jobs because—and these are his words—"They're just as smart as men, if not smarter; they work harder and they tend to be more loyal."

As far as any generalization can be said to be true, I agree with him. At the same time, I realize that in the communications industry, the statistics reveal that this truth is far from being recognized.

And not only in that industry. My experience this morning in listening to the other witnesses has led me to the belated recognition that we have to move even faster in the communications industry.

Enough of the personal aspects. We meet here today in a week that quakes with crisis, and our national anguish, female and male, is focused on what has happened in Cambodia and in Ohio. Perhaps these other troubles make the questions we ask here seem peripheral, but I think not so. This is an important hearing about an important amendment. And I am fully in favor of the adoption into the U.S. Constitution of an amendment which states that equality of rights under the law shall not be denied or abridged by the United States or by any State on, of sex.

I always take the view that in the climate of today this amendment should not be burdened by the additional Hayden rider since this would limit the effectiveness of the amendment by imposing restrictions on it.

I am not taking this stand lightly, or condescendingly, or as I undoubtedly will be accused, with commercial motivation. I am not a constitutional lawyer, so I will not be able to discuss the fine points of whether the fifth or the 14th already includes women, making this amendment unnecessary from a legalistic point of view.

Miss Weaver has taken care of that quite well this morning. But I believe that women today are entering a new era of participation in the total national scene, and it is time for men to put themselves on the line to provide women with every chance to prove their abilities and responsibilities. It is not a matter of atoning for the past but of building for the future.

There has been much publicity given to the occupation of the Journal's office by Women's Lib. None has been given to the letter-writing campaign which has recently deluged our offices from members of another movement called Fascinating Womanhood, centered in Santa Barbara, Calif. It is very nearly the exact opposite of feminine liberation, and the women who write in its behalf are as vocal and loyal to its precepts as are the women of NOW and Redstockings. Helen B. Andelin, its leader has written its text, a book called "Fascinating Womanhood," which in most simplistic terms urges that men be given their rightful place as the heads of homes as God intended man to be. In the most simplistic terms, it urges women to become more feminine—that is, to subjugate themselves to their husbands, to be—to use their words, "a goddess," to be adorable when angry, to accept men's leadership and superiority . . . to be weak, suppliant, and arouse male chivalry.

The Fascinating Womanhood movement, to many of the people in this room, may seem out of another century, and indeed out of another civilization. But it should not be overlooked, for it is also obviously a growing ideology, with its own form of consciousness-raising. It is the right wing of women's thinking today. To quote the book:

It is only in his role as a man that he longs for supremacy over women. * * * Nothing gives him a more enjoyable sense of power and manliness than does this supremacy. Therefore, if he does not feel superior now, women must make him feel so.

Well, Fascinating Womanhood is here. Along with garden clubs, sewing circles, and women's auxiliaries of all kinds, they represent the extreme polarization that is occuring even in the field of women's attitudes.

And so, although I favor the constitutional amendment for equal rights, I ask, "Will a constitutional amendment really solve the problem?" It is a necessary start.

Pearl S. Buck, a long-time defender of woman's causes, wrote in 1941:

Equality, of course, is no easy matter except for talk. Only careful education can make people equal. There is no equality in individuals. That we know. But how can man be persuaded that woman is his equal until he is educated in that knowledge.

I feel that along with the constitutional amendment, men and women of good will everywhere had better start educating themselves to live in this rapidly changing world of sex roles in transition, or we face the most devastating division possible in our society. We have already built chasms between the haves and the have-nots;

between the young and the old at the magic line of thirty; and, of course, between the blacks and the whites. Must we now escalate the awakening of women to their past put-downs and their need for fuller opportunity into a real war between the sexes? Can't we find an enlightened way to come together as whole human beings and find a way to move forward without destroying ourselves?

I return to that word "education," for both females and males. In 1968, I was invited to give a talk at the University Club in New York, which does not admit women as members, and indeed has a separate dining room for visiting women. I gave a speech on women in business, quoting all the statistics which emphasized that there were not enough women at the top levels, and examining the need for utilizing woman power at every level. It wasn't a speech which would completely please Betty Freidan or Caroline Bird today, but it might have surprised them at the time. I had special research done by mail and telephone among 600 business and professional women across the country. Only 32 percent of the women felt that they had encountered career roadblocks because of prejudice against women—or at least, only 32 percent of the women dared to admit it, in 1968. When asked why women had not reached the upper and middle echelons of business and professions, 58 percent checked discriminatory practices, but 71 percent noted the lack of interest or motivation on the part of women. And when, upon learning that the University Club does not accept women members and relegates them to separate dining facilities. I did a rapid personal survey to find out if any of our staff or the wives of my personal family friends thought this an affront. Most of them shrugged and laughed. That was in 1968 when Fascinating Womanhood was still in flower in New York.

I wish I had the time before this statement to go back to the same women and ask their opinions. I suspect, and it is a suspicion based on male intuition, that the very same women today would have different reactions. If today's women's movement has been born of the black liberation struggle, as some say, if the radical dialectic is suspiciously prevalent in what too many of the far-out feminists shout about, if the media have exaggerated the numbers and impact of this rebirth of feminism, so be it. The militant feminists are causing trouble because they have a real point. They are making women look at their condition honestly. And that can be frightening to women and to men.

One of our senior editors is our public affairs editor, Margaret Hickey, long associated with the Journal in its campaigns for women's causes, and former chairman of the Citizens' Advisory Council on the Status of Women. I asked Margaret how she felt about this new amendment, and her answer was that ERA is premised on the concept that equality is an absolute thing, and that equality in terms of law will not necessarily establish equality in fact. "Many women who have studied its implications, as I have since 1923, believe that the principles of equality and the dignity of the man-woman relationship can be advanced far more by improvement of specific situations."

Margaret, who is a lawyer, went on to say that one of the improvements which should be instituted is "a new advocacy on the part of men for higher status of women." She was talking to me.

Which is why, although this prominent woman adviser and friend indicated she was not fully in favor of this constitutional amendment. I go a step further. If we are to move out of the Fascinating Womanhood stone age and into a new era—let's start by putting our belief into the Constitution. If it has some legal red-tape involved, let's iron it out.

And statements I have heard from both Senator Bayh and Senator Cook show that this can indeed be good. And then let's get this new male advocacy launched. Can the men of 1970 in business, in the professions, in politics, in education, in their personal lives afford not to reexamine the existing dishonesties and discriminations that have been traditionally accepted as part of our society? I have a sneaking suspicion that the present crop of college boys— jocks as well as the so-called bums—will not be thinking of sex roles in the same way we did, just as they look at everything else in different light.

I am in favor of the amendment. But I would like to add a few personal amendments to the support of my view, addressed chiefly to males.

1. I propose that every man examine his fascinating manhood to see if he is a strong enough human being to share life with women without damanding that they be slaves. Warm, reassurring, loving, feminine partners, yes. But intelligent, capable, and achieving, too, as individuals in their own right, free to make their own choices. If a man insists on servitude, there probably will be women to meet his needs. But under the docile surface there will be increasing hostility. So beware. Slavery is not only out of date; it is out of fashion.

I see that Betty Freidan and I agree on that point at least.

2. I propose that men in authority in business, education, the professions, politics, and even in the executive branch of government reexamine their policies about women. It is more than a case of adjusting inequities; it is a necessity for humanizing American society. I am not recommending the overthrow of existing power structures, but improving them by adding a whole new element to the mix. Even in the church, the pressure is on to allow women more participation; no longer is the feminine aspect of religious participation limited to church suppers. It is their time for ministry.

3. Such restrictive establishments as men's bars, men's clubs, men's entrances, and men's restaurants may be pleasant, muscle-flexing retreats. But as long as these seem to be philosophical or denigrating insults to large groups of women—even if not to all women—men should at least pay women the humanistic respect of considering an alternative.

I know when this happened recently, as some of the women in this group have said, it produced for them a great deal of ridicule and very few, to this date, results.

4. Just as we have sharpened out sensitivities to Jewish, Italian, and other racial jokes and stereotypes, we should alert our sympathies for the patronizing condescending pejorative skits and remarks that portray women as lovable, stupid, conniving, and somewhat useful inferiors. Television situation comedies should acknowledge that there are new situations in American families. And in our advertising

and marketing, we would do well to remember that there is a growing group of educated women who find those ladies rapidly discussing whiteness around the clothesline out-of-date and nonidentifying. Women will respond to updated images of individualistic womanhood just as they have responded to contemporary visual presentations and the new music.

And this is one I take well to heart.

5. As the upsurge of the women's rights movement continues, and more and more women get the training and the opportunity to move into supervisory and·management positions, we should be flexible enough to meet the competition. The economic side of the picture has not been overly discussed. The same thing applies to women as it does to black workers in the unions; there may just not be enough jobs to go around. But industry and Government together should be able to build expanding economy with room for everyone. And labor unions should be able to do this, too.

6. Let us be done with cliches that women cry in the office. They sometimes do, but **men also** get ulcers, which are worse for the personnel departments than tears. Women take special time off to have babies and sometimes at the turn of the moon, but the men are missing at world's series and round the water cooler. We should discard the old shibboleths.

Girls should not automatically be given typing tests while men get the management aptitude exams. And incidentally, when new corporate structures are being built, the need for part-time and full-time woman workers will be greatly helped by the growing trend toward day-care centers.

7. Let us keep the lines of communication open. When 125 liberation movement women stormed into my office on March 18 and turned my desk into a barricade, I was, of course, tempted to call the police and turn them out. I did not. As you know, the liberationists asked to have the magazine turned over to them. I refused. But I did feel that a magazine published for women should present to its audience at least a sample of this point of view. It is a laborious and difficult way to put out a magazine, by negotiation, and counter-negotiation, and counter-counter negotiation. It has all taken much patience, and a great deal of the time of our staff, but it was all worth the struggle. We are glad the liberation women chose the Journal for their historic visit; we will be pleased if the section they produce is appropriate for our pages. We expect many of our readers to disagree with it, and many of our male business friends to take umbrage at it. But that is communications, 1970, and unless one is willing to take some chances, he—or she—might well retire.

8. There is another outmoded stereotype that can be tossed out: that behind every successful man there is a woman. First of all, there is usually more than one woman in the background. Secondly, she (or they) should not be allowed to lurk back there anonymously, even if she (or they) profess to shun the limelight, because of the rules we have made. Which gives me the opportunity to point out that I could not have done this position paper today without the help of two women; one, in this room—Managing Editor Lenore Hershey and the Journal's Washington Bureau Chief, Mary Finch Hoyt. Not to mention a great many more of the women on my staff,

women contributors, and my supportive, but not submissive wife, Sharlyn.

9. I would like to close with one more rather pointed personal plea. The 20th century has been created largely by men, and by some yardsticks we have made things work, and by others we have created a frightening mess. Now women are demanding equality, and with equality responsibility. Every person, male or female, has his own potential in terms of achievement and in service. The awareness of that potential is the discovery of purpose; the fulfillment of that potential is the discovery of strength.

And we need it.

Thank you.

Senator BAYH. Mr. Carter, I am extremely impressed by your statement, not only because of what it outlines in the form of a basic attack on this problem, but especially because it evidences what I have read between the lines, the fact that you have yourself put these practices into use. I compliment you for it.

The key, it seems to me, to not only passing this amendment but, as you point out very accurately, as I have tried to point out before, to ultimately having these goals consummated, whether it is through general recognition or through the courtroom, is education and the knowledge that some of the shibboleths are totally out of date and totally irrelevant to what we are trying to do in the space age.

You point out the fact that in this survey 71 percent of the women were disinterested. In my judgment if we are able to turn that around it will be a great impact on the men in the country.

Mr. CARTER. Yes, sir. I quite agree with you. You know, this statement, Senator, is more of a commitment on my part than any I have made in this regard to date; certainly, any that I made to March 18 at the women's liberation movement.

This thing has changed; this disinterest. It is indeed lessening; I can assure you of that. It must have been about 7 years ago, when I was editor of McCall's, I ran part of the book that was referred to earlier by Betty Freidan, the "Feminine Mystique." I didn't understand that book when I ran it, but I want to say that I understand it now.

Senator BAYH. Well, I think there are a lot of ways of describing your testimony which helps to portray the side of the problem which, of course, is one of the major reasons for these hearings. One could describe it, I suppose, as brave, courageous—perhaps the best way to describe it is right, and I appreciate your taking the time to let us have your thoughts. They have been very helpful.

Mr. CARTER. Thank you, Senator.

Senator BAYH. Senator Cook?

Senator COOK. Thank you, Mr. Chairman. I want the record to include that Mr. Carter who is from Murray, Ky., attended Murray State College. That institution, which probably had 2,000 or 3,000 students then, has approximately 10,000 students today.

Mr. CARTER. 1,500.

Senator COOK. 1,500

In 1963, John was one of the 10 outstanding young men in the United States as listed by the U.S. Junior Chamber of Commerce. I am also pleased to report that tomorrow John will receive the

University of Missouri's award for distinguished service in journalism. John earned a master's degree at the University of Missouri.

I was amazed in reading your remarks to learn of the statement by Helen B. Andelin of California that "it is only his role as a man that he longs for supremacy over women, nothing gives him a more enjoyable sense of power and manliness than does this supremacy. Therefore, if he does not feel superior now, women must make him feel so." I dislike having women telling other women what men want and men telling other men what women want.

[Applause.]

Hopefully those men who seek to protect women, such as by means of legislation, will realize that women do not want to be protected.

I am delighted to have you here, John. Thank you.

Mr. CARTER. Thank you, Senator.

Senator BAYH. Thank you very much.

Mr. CARTER. Thank you, Senator Bayh.

[Applause.]

Senator BAYH. I am going to suggest that we recess now and reconvene at 2 o'clock. We will then have four witnesses, and Carl Megel, representing the American Federation of Teachers, will be our first witness.

(Whereupon, at 12:45 p.m., the committee recessed, to reconvene at 2 p.m., this date.)

AFTERNOON SESSION

Senator COOK (presiding). Mr. Carl J. Megel, legislative director of the American Federation of Teachers.

We will get started.

Mr. Megel, Senator Bayh will be detained briefly.

STATEMENT OF CARL J. MEGEL, LEGISLATIVE DIRECTOR, AMERICAN FEDERATION OF TEACHERS

Mr. MEGEL. Thank you very much, Senator.

Mr. Chairman and members of the committee, my name is Carl J. Megel.

I am legislative director of the American Federation of Teachers, a national teachers' union of more than 200,000 classroom teachers affiliated with the AFL–CIO.

I am appearing before this committee in support of Senate joint resolution 61 proposing an amendment to the Constitution of the United States relative to equal rights for men and women. The purpose of the proposed amendment is to provide constitutional protection against laws and official practices which treat men and women differently.

On July 28, 1945, the U.S. Senate gave its advice and consent to the Charter of the United Nations and statute to the International Court of Justice by a vote of 89 to 2. Chapter 9, article 55, of the Charter of the United Nations pledges, "Universal respect for, and observance of, human rights and fundamental freedoms for all without distinction as to race, sex, language, or religion.

Subsequently thereto, the United Nations proposed for ratification, nine conventions relating to human rights. The American Federation of Teachers supports the ratification of these nine conventions, only one of which has been ratified by the United States Senate.

Our support of the proposed Joint Resolution 61 can be sustained by centering our attention upon the inequities which are evidenced within the following four conventions:

1. Equal remuneration;
2. Employment discrimination;
3. Discrimination in education; and
4. Political rights of women.

Referring to equal remuneration, there are slightly more than 2 million teachers actively engaged in the classrooms of our Nation's schools.

Of this number, at the present time, slightly more than 50 percent are women. This percentage was considerably higher only a few years ago.

The starvation wages paid schoolteachers was actually a discriminatory practice which accounted for the predominance of women teachers.

The American Federation of Teachers for more than twenty years has fought vigorously for increased teachers' salaries, as a first requisite to improved educational opportunities for the children we teach.

These efforts, together with assistance from other organizations at a time of critical teacher shortages have advanced teachers' salaries to some extent. Higher salaries attracted more men into the teaching professions.

However, since our salary increase efforts have always been based upon equal pay for equal work, provided experience and training are similar, little discrimination exists in remuneration because of sex at the elementary-secondary classroom level.

This situation is not true for women in other professions. The Women's Bureau of the Department of Labor, in its report, stated that in 1968 the median salary of the male wage earner was $75.64 per week; whereas the median salary of women wage earners was only $44.57 or 58.2 percent of that of the male worker.

More significant is the fact that the gap between the earnings of men and women workers is widening. In 1955, the median wage for women was 63.9 percent of that of men workers. Ten years later, in 1965, the income median had decreased to 60 percent.

The report further pointed out that the wage gap varied widely by occupation. In sales work, women earned only 40 percent of what men earned. The salary of a woman scientist ranged from $1,700 to $4,500 less than that of all civilian scientists. Women chemists led the gap with a differential of minus $4,500 per year.

Employment discrimination is point No. 2: While differential between the salaries of men and women in education is more nearly stabilized on the basis of equal pay, for equal work, employment discrimination in the higher administrative areas are quite evident. There are in the United States 751 school districts with an enrollment of 10,000 or more students. In these 751 school districts, 749 superintendents are men and only two women. In the principalships, the discrimination is only slightly less percentage-wise.

Clifford Alexander, former head of the Equal Employment Opportunities Commission, reported that in a survey of 100 major corporations, 18 percent had not a single woman in a managerial position. He stated that of the 32,000 top level jobs in these 100 corporations, only 3.8 percent of these jobs were filled by women.

In 1949, 28 percent of the faculty and professional staff in our colleges and universities were women. Nevertheless, this percentage decreased to 22 percent in 1960.

In other categories, 10 percent of all scientists are women; 7 percent of all physicians are women; and 3 percent of all engineers are women.

Discrimination in education is point No. 3. It is well known that a quota system in our medical schools is maintained by rigid entrance requirement.

In chemical and scientific education departments, the discrimination is easier to maintain for another reason.

Technical high schools throughout the Nation which may enroll as many as 7,000 students refuse to admit girls. Without this high school training, it is almost impossible for a superior young lady with exceptional mathematical or scientific talents to enter a college or university. Even some federally funded opportunity schools enrolled only male students.

Political rights of women is point No. 4. Women struggled for more than 50 years to secure the right to vote in our Nation. Nevertheless, women still lack full opportunity to participate on an equal basis with men in the full exercise of their political rights.

There are few women in the legislatures of our States and even a smaller percentage are mayors of our cities.

Of 435 Congressmen in our Nation's Capital, only 10 are women; and of our 100 Senators, only the voice of one woman is heard. No woman has ever sat on or been nominated to the Supreme Court of the United States.

In our organization, out of the 13 AFT presidents during our 54 years of existence, two have been women. A larger percentage have been members of our executive council. There are at the present eight women on our 21 member executive board.

Certain other labor affiliates have a lesser percentage of women on their boards.

Few women are presidents of corporations and only a slightly larger percentage are members of the board of directors.

A larger percentage of women are members of boards of education but seldom is a woman board of education member appointed to the negotiating committee to work out a collective bargaining agreement with the representative of the teachers' bargaining unit.

In conclusion, Mr. Chairman, we do not overlook the physiological difference between men and women nor do we discount other factors which may negate complete parity with men.

However, the inability of women to compete with men in securing higher echelon positions in education, in Government and in industry are certain signs that discrimination still exists.

A woman wage earner, head of the family, has greater difficulty securing a mortgage to buy a home than would a man who was earning the same salary.

To be accepted in her own right is the purpose of this amendment which we support and endorse.

Mr. Chairman, I am here in support of this amendment, but in doing so I am not here to raise my voice in support of any criticism of the labor movement or of any labor leader.

For 12 years I served as president of American Federation of Teachers and know firsthand the continuous effort of the labor movement to improve the salaries and working conditions of those who work for a living. Many waitresses here in Washington, D.C., earned only 33 cents an hour until the passage of the Minimum Wage Act, which could not have been passed in all probability without the help of the labor movement.

Advances made by the labor movement were made largely by men since nearly 40 percent of the working force of men are organized as against less than 1 percent of the female working force.

I believe that fear and insecurity have had much to do with organizational reluctance on the part of women. I know from my own experience whenever we were invited to go into a school and to try to organize teachers into a teachers' union, men were much more ready to join than women. And I believe that fear and insecurity were the main reasons for this fact. Therefore I believe that the passage of this resolution would eliminate fear and make it possible for women through unionization to secure many benefits for themselves that they have not now been able to do.

The AFL–CIO is composed of 137 separate internationals which within their own jurisdiction are autonomous. It is in this context that I am here to support Senate Resolution 61, since we are an autonomous international of the AFL–CIO.

Mr. Chairman, we thank you for the opportunity to appear before this committee. We sincerely thank the chairman for the courtesy he has given us here. We want to urge support of this resolution.

Senator COOK. Thank you, Mr. Megel. It is my sincere wish that you do not conclude as a result of hearing previous testimony that I am here to demean the labor movement. Rather I consider it important to determine the motivation behind much of the so-called protective legislation we are discussing. Also that the aspects of full participation in society, such as jury service and the right to dispose of personal property, possibly are more important than certain employment regulations such as the number of pounds of weight women may lift.

Let me ask you——

Mr. MEGEL. Yes, sir.

Senator COOK (continuing). You have stated that, "The technical high schools throughout the Nation which may enroll as many as 7,000 students refuse to admit girls."

It appears to me that a strong position by your organization in opposition to this unfair practice might be helpful in correcting the situation.

Considering the tremendous amount of Federal assistance given to technical schools, it is my contention that such discrimination probably violates title VII of the Civil Rights Act and the stipulation of the Federal educational programs in which these schools participate. Do you agree?

Mr. MEGEL. There is probably no question about that, Senator. The purpose of the technical high schools when they were begun, was to train for skills, to enable young men to secure jobs. Therefore boys only were admitted. This situation has not been challenged.

Senator COOK. Are you of the opinion that one of the reasons for the reluctance of many State legislatures to create new sources of revenue for the teaching profession is due to a presumption by these bodies that most of the teaching profession is composed of women?

Mr. MEGEL. I think that has something to do with it, but I don't think that is it entirely.

Senator COOK. Oh, no. I agree with that.

Mr. MEGEL. The competition for the dollar today, the tax dollar, since 73 cents of every tax dollar comes to Washington is intense. Accordingly the States are in financial difficulty. There are many, many forces exerting their energies to secure part of that tax dollar at a State level.

Senator COOK. I thank you very much, Mr. Megel. I appreciate your testimony.

Hopefully the Senate will be as gracious and responsible in passing this amendment as it was in sanctioning the entrance of the United States into the United Nations. I wonder whether all of the Senators knew when they sanctioned this Nation's membership in the United Nations that its charter pledges "Universal respect for and observance of, human rights and fundamental freedoms for all, without distinction to race, sex, language, or religion." After tacitly approving a charter containing such language, the Senate should have little difficulty in passing this amendment.

Thank you very much.

Mr. MEGEL. Thank you very much.

[Applause.]

Senator COOK. Mrs. Wilma Scott Heide.

We have been talking about Pennsylvania at some length.

STATEMENT OF WILMA SCOTT HEIDE, CHAIRMAN, BOARD OF DIRECTORS, NATIONAL ORGANIZATION FOR WOMEN, INC., NOW?

Mrs. HEIDE. I bet we could.

Would you mind if I pulled my chair around here to the side?

Senator COOK. No, please do.

Mrs. HEIDE. I don't like to sit with my back to everyone who might be interested. This way I can see everyone.

"Equality of rights under the law shall not be denied nor abridged by the United States or by an State on account of sex."

This is, contrary to what was mentioned earlier by one person who testified, not the equal rights for women amendment, but the equal rights amendment.

I am Wilma Scott Heide. I am a behavioral scientist by profession, chairman of the Education Committee of the Pennsylvania Human Relations Commission, the only woman commissioner, as usual and also chairman of the Board of Directors of the National Organization for Women, Inc., NOW.

My primary identities for today are those of behavioral and human relations educator. NOW was ably represented by other officers. I will testify in favor of the equal rights amendment hopefully so that the next great moment in history—although I think we perhaps should say her story—may be ours.

It is with considerable ambivalence that I do testify today.

All of my social conditioning teaches me to be grateful for the opportunity to speak in a public forum convened by Senators. Yet I am really outraged to even consider gratitude as an appropriate response for a chance to plead for what is the birthright of every male in the United States. My credentials for testifying today were scrutinized; yet perhaps the only relevant credential is that I am a person denied my personhood by law, by legal interpretation, and by practice. This, of course, is not to deny my sex but to affirm my personhood which transcends gender.

To demand to be equal to men under the law is not to state or imply sameness of biology; but biology is not relevant to human equity.

Interestingly, I was asked to quantitatively document especially the educational inequities to women that a ratified equal rights amendment would rectify. And certainly, I can quote statistics if that is necessary, to establish communications.

For instance, in Pennsylvania, two at least partly publicly-supported institutions: Pennsylvania State University and the University of Pennsylvania, have publicly documented quotas that limit the number of women admitted regardless of their superior or equal educational qualifications.

I am prepared to supply documentation of these statements if requested.

The unpublished quota systems in admissions, recruitment, promotion, guidance, and so forth, at every level of these and other institutions in Pennsylvania and every other State are a national disgrace.

The statistical documentation, case histories, research studies of sex discrimination in academia are available from The Business and Professional Women's Foundation; Jessie Bernard's "*Academic Women*;" the Association for Women Psychologists; the Women's Caucus of the American Sociological Association; American Political Science Association; the Modern Language Association; and most other professional associations, as well as from the proceedings of the recent National Professional Women's Caucus held at New York University Law School.

These data sources are just for openers; there are more than I can detail today, let alone citing the enormous antifemale bias evident in the content of their findings.

Back to the numbers game: In 1930, women earned 40 percent of the master's degrees, in 1969, women earned 34 percent of the master's degrees; in 1930, women earned 15 percent of the doctoral degrees, in 1969, women earned only 12 percent of doctoral degrees; in 1930 women formed 30 percent of college faculties and at higher ranks than the mere 22 percent of women on college faculties in 1969.

Significantly, women's participation in the "prestigious" professions reflects this loss of ground: 3 percent of lawyers, 7 percent of physicians, less than 10 percent of scientists and token numbers of executives are women in the United States.

In other countries, propagandized in the United States to be less advanced, actually have women represented in these professions in percentages ranging from 25 to 75 percent.

One must wonder if the women in European and other countries are somehow biologically, that is innately, different from U.S. women.

Such, of course, is not the case. What is different is the laws, practices and behavioral attitudes outside the United States.

It is the laws or their absence, the practices and attitudes that guarantee that the tip of the iceberg reflected in the documented educational exclusion and dwindling attainment of U.S. women will indeed be manifest.

Education is the sine qua non of significant participation in public life and employed work in our society.

Genuine education must finally begin right here in the Congress and with this administration. The first lesson is that I—and I think every other woman—was insulted to be told that "we'll have lots of 'emotional' testimony from women's organizations. You document the objective facts of educational discrimination."

First of all, women and black people have always been called "emotional" when outraged by our oppression; this is a genuine put-down attempt by white male-oriented people.

Second, I think Congress and the administration needs sensitized about its own emotional conservatism in even considering constitutional equality as debatable. But most importantly, I would assert that the instructions to stick to so-called "objective quantification" denies my significant behavioral insights the total reality of social problems including human inequity.

In pretending to some fantasied objectivity, presumed logic and implied supremacy of the male-oriented facts—that is, numbers—as more valuable than emotional/social implications predicted to come from "women's organizations" is a fairly typical devaluation of emotions and, by association, of women.

We must put the need for this amendment precisely in its place and stop trying "to keep women in their place," as decided by someone else.

Its place should be at the top of the congressional agenda for immediate positive action. That top priority is necessary because this society, this Nation is antifemale in its laws, its expressions, its value systems, its language, everything. Ours is an androcentric, that is, male-oriented, male-dominated—culture, however subtle, and never mind the mythology to the contrary.

Any society so structured, biased and value-oriented is unhealthily balanced. It takes enormous individual and national resources to support and sustain the fragile male ego that male supremacy values dictate. The psychological crippling of most girls and women from their inferior legal, political, educational, religious, familial, economic status, will never be cured by consumership, more sexist Freudian psychotherapy, or one more child.

The fact that some women do not want equal rights is some

measure of the depth of their psychological enslavement.

Is it not possible that human aggression may have its roots in the young child's perception of the amonymity impotence, and alienation of voiceless, imageless women whose identity is determined almost solely from their sexuality, and its products?

If children see few or no women as authentic persons heading all our social institutions, will they not devalue and have contempt for that half the population and the values women are told we uniquely cherish?

The answer is, I think, and has been "Yes." It is everywhere evident in the denial by many men of those traits labeled as "feminine." This is changing some with our long-haired, more colorfully dressed males, some of whom protest: "Make peace, not war," once considered only the interest of women. Yet antifemale bias is evident in the comic strips and comedians who still capitalize on the woman driver—statistically safer—and the mother-in-law jokes.

If we analyze the antifemale bias in this sometimes cruel humor, perhaps we will find that the only error of the mother-in-law is that she never really found anything else to do with her time except be a mother.

We find the ridicule of feminists even by people otherwise liberal. Antifeminism is the last stronghold of sanctioned prejudice.

The Vice President of the United States gets laughs when he states: "Three things we've tried to tame—the ocean, fools, and women. We're making progress with the first two, but having trouble with the last one." This insensitive misogynist calls women "things" and classifies us with fools.

We might note that Mother's Day is a few days away and suggest what we want and need is fewer roses and more rights. Mother's Day has been like a day of symbolic atonement for the lack of attention generally given women as people. But unlike most other days of atonement, there is no promise to do better or differently afterwards.

Women, like all oppressed groups, bear the marks of oppression in very deep and abiding ways. Many behaviors considered "feminine" are actually survival techniques not unlike the behavior of oppressed blacks. I refer you to the appendix of Gunnar Myrdal's "American Dilemma" for the striking analogy.

The United States is the best armed, most violent Nation in the world and I submit to you it will continue to be as long as we sanction violence as the final assertion of manhood and nationhood, which turn out to be synonymous.

It will continue to be as long as constitutional equality is denied to over half its population. The passage and ratification of the equal rights amendment is no panacea. But in education alone, no State or Federal law forbids sex discrimination in education and the amendment would at least guarantee equal protection of the law; for instance, the 14th amendment, to all persons including women.

If we would look to limiting our population and to the quality of our total environment, then legislative actions and policy decisions must be forthcoming.

First, our Government must understand that no matter how safe, and universally available is any contraceptive method for women or men, that if women have no viable significant alternatives to motherhood, they will continue to overproduce children instead of being producers of ideas, literature, art, policy, inventions, and leadership.

The problem is one of identity, motivation, social climate, legal inequality and psychological oppression.

Furthermore, most girls from day one, will not expect or be expected to have a commitment to life beyond their sexuality and dilettantism if their legal equality both reflects and guarantees their secondary status.

Such has been their sex role stereotyped socialization that it guarantees aborted aspirations if indeed they are ever conceived.

The sex role stereotyped socialization of boys is such that they must exhibit "masculine" traits or be branded sissy or effeminate and pretend to characteristics that presume unchallenged virility. Well, there are no social-psychological traits that are "feminine" or "masculine," whatever that is.

Feminity is often a euphemism for immaturity. Masculinity is often an excuse for brutality. There are only human traits. There are no men's roles or women's roles beyond the biological.

There are no women's interests and men's interests. There are only human interests and human roles. My possession of a uterus does not uniquely qualify me for child care, housework, secretarial work or nursing.

Men's biology does not disqualify them for child care and housework or qualify them for leadership or scientific analysis or any particular courage.

The continuation of sex-stereotyped, sex-caste laws that deny the individuality and humanity of women and men to the distinct mutilation of women is simply intolerable.

I have come to Washington, D.C. on previous occasions to demonstrate for, participate in press conferences about, visited congressional offices to persuade, contacted countless people to advocate, and once interrupted this Subcommittee on Constitutional Amendments to dramatize the need for this equal rights amendment.

Now, I am testifying at hearings finally pressed to this subcommittee whose chairman said on February 17, 1969, that he could have released this amendment from the subcommittee a year ago and yes, could have 2½ years ago, but didn't. And I would say let us worry about the other things like the Judiciary Committee and the House of Representatives. Your responsibility is in this subcommittee.

The delay on hearings or action once again comes near the end of Congress. This has been happening for 47 years.

I, for one, predict the equal rights amendment will pass this session of Congress or the increasingly aware, outraged women of this Nation will take more dramatic measures to gain our birthright and I will be in the vanguard. This is not a threat; it is a promise.

We know Congress can pass in a few weeks or days any legislation it wants to pass and I trust you want to pass this one to finally, and unequivocally, declare the constitutional equality of women and men.

As Senators representing women and men, you can do no less.

As leaders of the cradle of democracy, you should want to do more. The hand that has rocked the cradle now needs to rock the boat so that we may share in the guiding of the ship of state. Just as the hand that has led the state from war to war needs the civilizing influencing of nurturing a human infant to maturity.

A male must free himself from his mother before he can accept another woman—any woman—as an equal. Women imprisoned at home by conditioning, not by free choice from viable options, have no outlet for themselves as people and they very often do work out their frustrations particularly on their sons, who therefore cannot develop healthy attitudes toward women and thus perpetuate the cycle of inequality.

The double standard assures men unearned prerogatives throughout our society and outrages women. Women want the right and the expectation to grow up, to define ourselves and contribute our underutilized talents. The home is not our world. The world is our home.

The problem with the young, I think, is really the problem of the old. The problem of the poor is the problem of the insensitive rich. The problem of the blacks has been the problem of the whites. The problems of the women, I think, are the problems of men.

Therefore, I think that it is the young who are freeing the old, the poor who are freeing the rich, the blacks who are freeing the white, and so it will be the women who will emancipate men so that all can come to see our common humanity that transcends all else.

This women's liberation, actually human liberation is, I think, the most profound social movement ever. It promises to inject some massive new insights into the bloodstream of our culture, not because women are so different, but because it will bring the life experience of the other half of the population to bear on our common problems and opportunities. (Standing.)

And now I would like to do something that I have considered very carefully. I would ask that every woman and man in this room who believes that women are people and that constitutional equality is fundamental to a viable democracy, please stand with me, as a symbolic act. No woman ever again should have to stand alone in speaking for the first-class citizenship of all women.

Your standing with me will be no tribute to me but a behavioral action to continue or begin, if necessary, your involvement in the personhood of all women.

I would ask that the Senators and others who are for this stand with us. It is a small request to publicly affirm what I have never been privately convinced of—that this subcommittee not only sponsors but publicly advocates the prompt passage of the equal rights amendment to the United States Constitution.

Senator Cook. Mrs. Heide, I don't mind standing. You were present at this subcommittee the first time it was interrupted and I being a new member of the Senate, felt shocked. I am confident that you remember the ocassion. I was not offended by your request but I maintain that these hearings are tremendously serious. I mention this because during earlier sessions a few disruptions occurred, for instance, a witness rose, faced the audience and proceeded to address the audience exclusively.

I shall begin the questioning by asking you why you think this nation is antifemale.

Mrs. Heide. Well, first let me say I never previously interrupted a subcommittee of the Senate, and I don't do it every day.

To answer your question why this Nation is antifemale, I do

not mean to imply that it is necessarily a conscious or a vicious or evil thing that is plotted out although I suppose some of that happens in order for people to support or defend what they have already done.

I do think that we do not know the origins of human inequality, but I think probably we have enough evidence to suggest that the first human inequality was probably a sexual one, and it may have been reasoned to be necessary for survival, and that having the priority of physical survival in terms of the necessity to get food, some priority was given to that which the man did.

As a matter of fact though, when we look more closely we find that women have been food gatherers and not only nurtured the young, but have actually obtained the food. Perhaps we did not have as good a press agent as the men have had. But from what we do know, and we may never know fully—I would suggest that given the interests of physical survival, given the amount of time women had to give to childbearing and child rearing just in terms of the number of children that survived, that patterns and practices came about that gave priority to the man getting the food. His generally superior musculature gave him enforcement power that he developed with experience.

And what we know is once a sanctioned practice is supported, it becomes supported in codified ways through the laws and then people begin to internalize, to belive that indeed this is natural, the status quo.

And I think that most of us are educated to analyze that these are social practices developed and created by people, they are not natural. And if they are developed and created by people, they can be changed by people, as conditions and circumstances change.

Now, I am sure that is an oversimplified answer, but I think that would be some of the substance of my approach.

Senator Cook. To what extent has religion been a motivating factor, throughout history, in creating anti-female attitudes?

Mrs. Heide. It is quite a paradox. Perhaps the simplest way I can answer that is that some of us who have a tendency for low blood pressure only need to read the scriptures to raise our blood pressures. I think this has been a part of it. Whatever the rationalization is, the point in time when the scriptures were really written we don't know, but I suspect it is not unrelated to the kinds of things I said before.

We also know that once a group of people have certain prerogatives and advantages, it seems to be part of the human condition to retain them. No group ever gained any rights by doing much of anything except demanding them. And I think that is one of the reasons why many groups of activists say yes, we prefer other kinds of channels but if they don't get results, we will do dramatic kinds of things, because humans do not easily give up prerogatives and advantages, particularly if they have had them all their lives.

And if they have been told it is indeed right and proper and justified that they have them.

To more precisely answer your question: I think all our social institutions, including the religious institutions, have been part of the problem and not part of the solution.

Senator Cook. My question stemmed from a realization that religion has been a great historical influence on society. Therefore, I was soliciting an answer based on your research in the behavioral sciences.

Mrs. Heide. I think so. I think that is part of it. But I would not put it on any one social institution. They all reinforce each other and all derive from a kind of "masculine mystique" that preoccupies.

Senator Cook. Mr. Chairman, I am sure you remember Mrs. Heide. She met with us last February.

Senator Bayh (presiding). I remember Mrs. Heide.

Senator Cook. This off the record, please.

(Discussion off the record.)

So, Mr. Chairman, I wish to again introduce Mrs. Heide.

Senator Bayh. Well, Mrs. Heide, I want to apologize. It was one of those unexpected committee meetings, a policy meeting, that came up literally while we were sitting here. Because of this, I asked Senator Cook if he would be kind enough to preside. Of course, in his usual gracious manner he complied. I apologize for not being here. I read part of your testimony—not all of it. I am sorry I was not here when you gave us the chance to stand up with the rest of the audience.

Mrs. Heide. May I say I suspect there may be other chances to stand on the issue.

[Applause.]

Mrs. Heide. I am sure you realize we have a completely unbiased audience.

I wonder if I may, and I am going to, if you do not stop me, I wonder if Dorothy Parker, who is minority counsel, has any comments or questions, understanding, of course, that if she has any questions, I would have all the answers.

Senator Cook. Dorothy, we have been somewhat remiss but I recall Senator Fong requesting that you be allowed to ask questions. I assumed Dorothy would ask questions if she so desired.

Senator Bayh. Her presence is hovering over us in a very beneficial way.

Senator Cook. She could be my counsel any day.

Mrs. Parker. Thank you, Senator.

I appreciate your efforts, but I do want to make it clear that the chairman runs the committee hearing, and I think he should.

Thank you.

Senator Cook. Mr. Chairman, do you have anything?

Senator Bayh. You made reference to the University of Pennsylvania State University.

Mrs. Heide. That is right.

Senator Cook. I am anxious to obtain all the statistics and other information you used in writing your testimony for placement in the record. Your testimony was excellent and I feel that the Office of Education should be made aware of this discrimination against women.

Mrs. Heide. I will be glad to.

Senator Bayh. Thank you very much, Mrs. Heide. We appreciate your contribution.

Senator Cook. Additionally, Mr. Chairman, I request that the Office of Education be asked to place in the record any pertinent information they might possess. I am especially interested in that information which concerns discrimination against women in entering college and in receiving scholarships subsidized by the Federal Government.

Senator BAYH. We would be glad to make that request.

[Applause.]

(The request and response follow:)

U.S. SENATE,
COMMITTEE ON THE JUDICIARY,
Washington, D.C., May 19, 1970.

HON. ROBERT H. FINCH,
Secretary of Health, Education, and Welfare, Department of HEW,
Washington, D.C.

DEAR MR. SECRETARY: As you may know, our Subcommittee on Constitutional Amendments has recently concluded three days of hearings on the "Equal Rights" Amendment, Senate Joint Resolution 61, which would provide that "Equality of rights under the law shall not be denied or abridged by the United States or by any State on account of sex." We were disappointed and surprised that, despite our repeated invitations to the Justice Department, the Administration chose neither to send a witness nor to give us a written statement of its position on the Equal Rights Amendment.

I am writing to call your attention to one particular series of questions which arose during our hearings, and to elicit whatever information you may have available. During our hearings on Thursday afternoon, May 7, Senator Cook asked: "Mr. Chairman, I would like to ask if the Department of Education of HEW could be asked to put a statement in this record relative to any studies that they have made, relative to any efforts that they have made to determine whether there is discrimination against women in the receipt of scholarships that are paid for and subsidized by the Federal Governments." I agreed with Senator Cook that this would indeed be valuable information and that we would seek it for the Record. To this end, I would appreciate having your answers to the following questions:

(1) Which public colleges and universities admit only members of one sex? How many public secondary schools are still restricted to members of one sex?

(2) Of those colleges and universities which admit members of both sexes, please identify those institutions that apply different admission standards to men and women in undergraduate schools and graduate schools. We are particularly interested in graduate schools of law and medicine.

(3) What proportion of federal educational grants and loans is awarded to women, and how does that figure relate to the proportion of women eligible for such assistance? Please indicate any discrimination against women in the award of educational assistance by public agencies other than the Federal Government.

We are particularly interested in any studies made by the Department in these areas, and we would appreciate your forwarding such studies to us for inclusion in the Record.

I look forward to your prompt reply.

Sincerely,

BIRCH BAYH,
Chairman, Subcommittee on Constitutional Amendments.

THE SECRETARY OF HEALTH, EDUCATON, AND WELFARE, *Washington, D.C.,*

June 25, 1970.

HON. BIRCH BAYH,
U.S. SENATE,
Washington. D.C.

DEAR SENATOR BAYH: Thank you for your letter of May 19 concerning discrimination against women.

In response to the questions contained in your letter, I have asked the Bureau of Higher Education in the Office of Education to respond and they have provided the following answers to your questions.

Replying to your first question, a chart is enclosed showing those public institutions of higher education which are not coed. The data for this chart was compiled from the latest edition of the *Education Directory 1967-68, Part 3, Higher Education.* The Office of Education does not collect similar information concerning secondary schools.

Your second question concerns variances in admissions standards by sex. Information concerning admission standards of this sort is not collected by the Office of Education. Traditionally, as you know, the Federal Government has left the matter of admissions standards to the colleges and universities. It is also felt that the variance in admissions standards across the country would make them nearly impossible to quantify.

Also enclosed is a table showing the percentage of students by sex participating in the Bureau of Higher Education's programs of student financial aid. This data is compiled from the most recent available information. We are not aware of any discrimination against women by other public agencies.

I hope these responses provide some of the information you are seeking.

Sincerely,

EDWIN R. MARKHAM,
Secretary.

ATTACHMENT I—PUBLIC INSTITUTIONS OF HIGHER EDUCATION

FOR MEN ONLY

1. U.S. Air Force Academy
2. U.S. Coast Guard Academy
3. Georgia Military College
4. Maine Maritime Academy
5. U.S. Naval Academy
6. Massachusetts Maritime Academy
7. New Mexico Military Institute
8. State University of New York Maritime College
9. U.S. Merchant Marine Academy
10. U.S. Military Academy
11. Air Force Institute of Technology (Ohio)
12. Oklahoma Military Academy
13. The Citadel
14. The Judge Advocate General's School
15. Virginia Military Institute

FOR WOMEN ONLY

1. Mississippi State College for Women
2. Winthrop College (S.C.)
3. Texas Woman's University
4. Longwood College (Va.)
5. Mary Washington College (Va.)

ATTACHMENT II—PERCENTAGE OF STUDENTS BY SEX PARTICIPATING IN PROGRAMS OF STUDENT FINANCIAL AID

	Male	Female	No response
National defense student loan program	56.7	43.3	--------
College work-study program	51.0	49.0	--------
Educational opportunity grants program	N.A.	N.A.	N.A.
Guaranteed loans program	62.1	37.2	7

N.A. = not available.

Senator BAYH. We will make that request, and also ask once again to get the officials downtown to send someone up here to give us their opinion on this whole issue. So far we have not been successful, and I think perhaps my friend from Kentucky might be more influential there than I.

Our next witness is Georgianna Sellers, representing the League for American Working Women.

We are fortunate to have Mrs. Sellers here with us.

STATEMENT OF GEORGIANNA SELLERS, ON BEHALF OF THE INDIANA AND KENTUCKY UNIT OF THE LEAGUE FOR AMERICAN WORKING WOMEN

Mrs. SELLERS. Thank you, sir.

I am Georgianna Sellers of Clarksville, Ind., speaking on behalf of the Indiana and Kentucky unit of the League for American Working Women, known as LAWW.

I am acting chairman of this organization. LAWW is a new organization. Its basic purpose is to work for and achieve equality of rights for women. While our organization is not confined to working women, most of our members are employed as factory workers.

The members of our organization wholeheartedly support the equal rights amendment—and for many reasons. It would eliminate injustices to women in employment, educational opportunities, and other areas.

Since our major efforts have been directed toward achieving equality for women in employment, one of our strongest reasons for supporting the equal rights amendment is that it would nullify all State restrictive laws that limit women as to what work they can do, how long they can work, and what they can lift.

It is an insult to women that such laws or rules are referred to as "protective" when their sole function is to exclude women from the higher-paying jobs.

The experience of the women employees at the plant where I am employed, demonstrates the urgent need for the equal rights amendment.

Most of us working women are employed in factories on high-speed production lines. Some of us—including myself, are working for the Colgate-Palmolive Co. which has arbitrarily refused to concede that there is a Civil Rights Act of 1964, which prohibits discrimination in employment on the basis of sex.

The union supposedly representing the employees at this plant fails to see why it should recognize the minority group—women—and has made contracts since the advent of Title VII of the Civil Rights Act of 1964 that were just as discriminatory as were the previous contracts.

The women working for Colgate were denied the right to work on the better-paying jobs to which their seniority entitled them, simply because they were women and the jobs might occasionally require the lifting of over 35 pounds.

As a matter of fact, some women employees on the low-paying jobs lifted as much as 17 tons per day while men employees thumped buttons on automatic machinery. While Indiana has no so-called "protective" laws prohibiting women employees from lifting 35 pounds, the mere existence of such laws in other States was used as a phony excuse for this discrimination.

"Oh, no", our employer would say, "you are a woman. You can't do this job. You have to lift 35 pounds. Let George do it."

We were kept off of higher paying easier jobs for years because the company wanted to "protect" us. I say it did not protect, but exploited women. Used their hard labor for low pay, just as employers treated the Negroes for years. Keep them under foot, not on top."

Incidentally, the record that we sent to the Seventh Circuit Court of Appeals weighed 38.6 pounds. We did not have a man to carry it for us.

As a result of the employment discriminations practiced by the company and union at the Colgate plant, some other women employees and I filed a class action under Title VII of the Civil Rights Act against the Colgate Palmolive Co. in the U.S. district court, and then we had to appeal the district court's decision against us to the Court of Appeals for the Seventh Circuit before we won our case.

However, we are still being discriminated against because we are women although our complaint against this type of discrimination was filed with the Equal Employment Opportunity Commission in 1965.

The officials of Local No. 15, International Chemical Workers Union—our union—tell us that we should not fight for our rights because we are a minority. There are about 1,100 men employees and only 145 women employees at this plant. We need the equal rights amendment to eliminate restrictive laws and practices and to give us quicker and surer relief against both employers and unions.

The male representatives of the AFL–CIO who have appeared before the committee and argued that women should not be given their equality, should not be heard—they have no right to claim they represent working women.

[Applause.]

Mrs. SELLERS. There is not one single woman in the AFL–CIO executive council. Even the predominantly women's unions are governed and controlled by men. It is insulting for these males to use State restrictive laws as a gimmick for exploiting us by claiming they are protecting us. These males running the labor unions are merely trying to monopolize better jobs for themselves.

The women union representatives who testified yesterday that they preferred the State restrictive laws to equality are obviously sick.

Any human being who has no desire for equality has lost his or her self-respect. Women who have lost the urge to be free individuals have no right to speak for those who still are willing to fight for their human and civil rights.

American working women have learned the lesson that the black people have learned. There is no such thing as separate but equal. We do not want separate little unequal, unfair laws and separate little unequal, low-paid jobs. We want full equality.

I say that if a woman has to spend her time, her money, and give of herself to defend herself in court through long, drawn-out litigation, that there is no law that we now have that protects us or will do anything to protect our rights.

Therefore, we further support the equal rights amendment because it would have a restraining effect on those who abuse and discriminate against women. It would help to dispel the myth of women's inferiority.

We are meeting in public life and public offices the male of the species who refuses to recognize a woman as an individual with her own peculiar sense of values, freedoms, and faults.

Even the most docile female in the United States has her "weaker" moments when she'd much prefer to stand on her own two feet and say, "I have my rights, too, you know!"

Who she tells this to is not important. The important thing is that she is an individual wanting her ideas respected and her abilities recognized. This does not mean that because a woman wants equal rights she is a "man hater," nor a radical who wishes only her own rights to be recognized.

On the contrary, there is no stronger advocate of equal rights than I, and yet I have raised five wonderful sons, one lovely daughter, and have a devoted husband.

All my family respect and believe in me as an individual person with every right to say for whom my vote shall be cast and how I will live my own life.

I realize that the fifth and 14th amendments should have been enough to give women equal rights, but these amendments have been in effect over 100 years, and women are still discriminated against in every important phase of human life.

We need the equal rights amendment to further implement the present constitutional provisions and to strengthen the language so no one, no how, nowhere, can ever misinterpret the correct language which says that women as individuals must have equal rights.

It is my own personal viewpoint that any Senator or Congressman that wants to be elected or reelected must support the equal rights amendment. There is another unit of LAWW in California, and we intend to establish other units throughout the United States.

In Indiana we have gone from door to door during the past 6 months, and I still say that women are well enough organized to give anyone pussyfooting around with the amendment or dragging his feet and delaying passage a run for his money.

There is no one more aware of the power of woman than women—especially working women.

We are knowledgeable enough to know who is for us, who is against us, and who is using delaying tactics. There will be no acceptable alibi for failure to pass the amendment this term of Congress.

We are determined to fight for passage of the amendment on a day-by-day, week-by-week, and if necessary, year-by-year basis until we have won the passage of the equal rights amendment, and achieved complete equality.

Thank you .

[Applause.]

Senator BAYH. Thank you very much, Mrs. Sellers. You present a very convincing story.

I would take partial issue with one observation you made. That was toward the close of your testimony when you said there is no one more aware of the power of a woman than women. May I suggest that perhaps also man—politicians—are certainly aware.

Mrs. SELLERS. That is right. I will agree with you.

Senator BAYH. Hopefully. Hopefully.

Mrs. SELLERS. That is right.

Senator BAYH. You work for Colgate. What union?

Mrs. SELLERS. I work on the production lines.

Senator BAYH. But what union is organized at Colgate?

Mrs. SELLERS. That is the International Chemical Workers Union, Local No. 15.

Senator BAYH. Chemical Union. Now, you mentioned the weight discrimination. Are there other aspects of discrimination in the contract? As I understand it, this is a matter of contractural agreement between representatives of your union and management.

Mrs. SELLERS. Yes, there are. They have what they call a grandfather clause that so-called protects the women from overwork loads.

Senator BAYH. What are the specifics of that? I am trying to get those in the record.

If you don't have them with you today, you could find out what they are and send it to us in short order. We would be glad to put it in the record. I think it would be helpful to us.

Mrs. SELLERS. Well, I can give that to you. I have it with me but not here right now. But it is in the contract, yes.

Senator BAYH. If you could get that to us. We don't want to violate any confidences as to what the contract may or may not say except that it would be helpful if we could have specific examples of a private agreement between management and labor that is discriminatory.

[Relevant aspects of the contract are set out and described in *Bowe* v. *Colgate-Palmolive Co.*, 272 F. Supp. 332, 340–60 (S.D. Ind. 1967) and the decision on appeal, reproduced above.]

Mrs. SELLERS. Naturally, they have opened up the jobs to us since the Seventh Circuit Court of Appeals has ruled that they should.

Senator BAYH. Now, was the Seventh Circuit case specifically limited to the weight issue?

Mrs. SELLERS. Oh, no.

Senator BAYH. Or the whole contract?

Mrs. SELLERS. It was on the basis of—see, we have been restricted from these jobs. They have hired, I believe during the testimony in 1966 they had hired in a period from May until August 228 men and no women, and some of these men were hired before some of the women were called back that were on layoff.

Senator BAYH. Was that the issue then, seniority?

Mrs. SELLERS. Well, we filed this lawsuit because we were illegally laid off under title VII.

Senator BAYH. Just women were laid off?

Mrs. SELLERS. Just laid off the women because they were women.

Senator BAYH. Well, thank you. If you could give us those specifics of the contract, we would like to have them.

Mrs. SELLERS. Thank you.

Senator BAYH. Senator Cook?

Senator COOK. Mrs. Sellers, I appreciate your testimony.

The case is presently in the Seventh Circuit?

Mrs. SELLERS. Well, it has been remanded to the Southern District of Indiana.

Senator COOK. For a judgment in accordance with the decision?

Mrs. SELLERS. Yes.

Senator COOK. Now, on that basis you had to carry this case yourself?

Mrs. SELLERS. Yes.

Senator COOK. The union offered no assistance?

Mrs. SELLERS. No.

Senator Cook. Did you start out by filing a grievance with the union?

Mrs. Sellers. We filed a grievance under the normal procedure and we were laid off. The union refused to recognize it saying that it was not a grievance procedure.

We contacted a member of the EEOC. They sent us some forms but in the meantime the union found out that we were going to file charges with the EEOC, so they very conveniently told us that they would take us to a lawyer and file our complaints for us, which they did. But we were delayed in a hearing on those charges until our time had run out.

And if we had not contacted the EEOC and got an extension of time, we would not have been able to have filed this lawsuit and naturally would have lost everything that we had hoped to gain.

Senator Cook. In other words, the statute of limitations almost negated your case?

Mrs. Sellers. That is right.

Senator Cook. You are still a dues-paying member of the union?

Mrs. Sellers. Oh, yes.

Senator Cook. How long have you been a dues-paying member of the union?

Mrs. Sellers. I have been there 23 years.

Senator Cook. Twenty-three years?

Mrs. Sellers. Yes.

Senator Cook. How many employees were laid off?

Mrs. Sellers. There were 35 of us.

Senator Cook. When was the last female worker hired?

Mrs. Sellers. I believe I made a mistake on that. Last month they hired about 89 men. They hired one white woman and one Negro.

Senator Cook. But prior to that——

Mrs. Sellers. Whether they are still there, or not, I don't know.

Senator Cook. But prior to that time, when did they hire the last female worker?

Mrs. Sellers. 1947.

Senator Cook. So you 35 ladies had been employed since at least 1947 and the union denied you the right of a hearing.

Mrs. Sellers. Well, we approached the union on this grievance procedure and then we called them because we protested being laid off while there were younger people in the plant. They told us if we did not like it to sue, that there wasn't anything they could do about it.

Senator Cook. When was this suit filed?

Mrs. Sellers. March 30, 1966.

Senator Cook. 1966?

Mrs. Sellers. Yes.

Senator Cook. You ladies had paid union dues for a period of about 20 years?

Mrs. Sellers. Yes.

Senator Cook. And your union refused to participate with you in this suit?

Mrs. Sellers. That is right.

Senator Cook. I note with interest that previously today a labor representative testified that unions had tried strenuously to insure the inclusion of title VII in the Civil Rights Act. Yet, your union refused to assist your case.

Mrs. SELLERS. This is right.

That is why we are so very interested in having equal rights, because we feel like—see, Indiana does not have a weight limitation law, no protective laws for women at all. But Colgate has their other plants in California and in Jersey City, and in Kansas City. Two of those states do have weight limitations, so they imposed them on the people working in the Clarksville plant in Indiana.

And a lot of these people were from Kentucky, these women were from Kentucky, too.

Senator COOK. And there is no weight-lifting law in the State of Indiana?

Mrs. SELLERS. No, none at all.

Senator COOK. Therefore, these laws were arbitrarily imposed?

Mrs. SELLERS. Yes.

Senator COOK. What is your impression of so-called protective legislation?

Mrs. SELLERS. I feel like if the State of Delaware could repeal all of its so-called protective laws and let men and women have the same legal protection, whatever that might be, under whatever circumstances that might be, I see no reason why it could not apply to all the other States. I don't feel that we need a restrictive law, because it is only used—we have a plant manager who testified in court, and said that during the time that we had asked for these jobs, the opening up of all the jobs, rather than be laid off—there was jobs in the plant that the women could have performed, rather than be laid off, and we asked for these jobs and he said, "Well, we can't let them have them. We are protecting our women."

They were protecting us by laying us off.

Senator BAYH. That is what you call being protected to death.

Mrs. SELLERS. That certainly is. We certainly do not need that kind of protection.

Senator BAYH. You know, I get back to that 14th amendment, Senator Cook, and if you read the language of this amendment which we are considering, I really don't see how the passage of this amendment is going to prevent that type of private agreement.

This is just the type of thing that ought to be prevented now because what we are talking about is how we prevent discrimination by the United States or by States. It does not say anything in here about discrimination on a private basis. What we would do, of course, would be to strike down those State laws on which Colgate was relying, but that still does not get to this unconscionable type of treatment you have experienced.

Mrs. SELLERS. I think it would, Senator Bayh, because I do not belief that even Colgate would go up against an amendment to the Constitution.

Senator BAYH. But you see, the amendment to the Constitution is not directed at Colgate the way it is worded now. It talks about the United States—the equality of rights under the law shall not be denied or abridged by the United States or by any State.

This is a private——

Mrs. SELLERS. It is not a contractural thing, if that is what you are talking about. It goes much further than that.

Senator BAYH. But we would take away the basis, the crutch that they are relying on; namely, other State laws.

Mrs. SELLERS. Well, I am not against the unions. Don't misunderstand me. I think that we need them. I am not against unions at all. I am against them when they refuse to represent a minority group. And I say that the equal rights amendment would further implement whatever laws we have that would protect our rights.

And it is the only thing I see that would protect our rights.

Senator BAYH. Fine. Well, I really appreciate your taking time to let us have the benefit of your personal experience concerning the way equal rights has been pursued in the courts in Indiana. If you would get the other items in the contract, it would be very helpful to us.

Mrs. SELLERS. I would be glad to.

Senator BAYH. Here again, what we are hoping to be able to do do in these hearings is to paint a picture of the size, the scope of the discrimination which is presently going on. I think many, many Americans, men and women, are not familiar with the discrimination that exists in this area.

Mrs. SELLERS. I don't believe they are, either.

Senator BAYH. Thank you very much.

Mrs. SELLERS. Thank you, sir.

Senator BAYH. Our next witness is Olga Madar, vice president of the United Auto Workers.

Mrs. Madar, glad to have you here to tell us all about how these unions are discriminating against women.

STATEMENT OF OLGA M. MADAR, VICE PRESIDENT OF THE UNITED AUTO WORKERS

Mrs. MADAR. First, let me thank the Senators for making it possible to arrange the schedule so that I could testify here today.

As the past case was being described, it sounded familiar to me, and I suddenly realized why it sounded familiar. It is because the UAW filed an amicus curiae brief in this particular case, supporting the position of the workers there.

I wanted to thank you for accommodating your schedule for me to appear, because frankly about three weeks ago in Atlantic City 3,000 delegates representing over 1,700,000 men and women of the United Auto Workers took action in adopting a very comprehensive resolution which put us four-square on the record not only for opposing all discriminatory patterns as far as women are concerned and for programs which would provide additional opportunities for them to participate at an equal level with all other individuals, but also put us squarely on record favoring the equal rights amendment.

[Applause.]

That received considerable publicity for which we were grateful, and I know we are in the process of, if we have not already done so, making available to all of the Congressmen copies of that resolution. For these reasons and because my schedule was extremely heavy, I had not planned to appear personally before this Committee. Newspaper articles about the hearing, however, made me realize that people were getting the impression that all unionized workers were opposed to the equal rights amendment, and I am here to tell you that that is not so.

I was very much interested in the unions which were represented here in opposition to the equal rights amendment, particularly those labor leaders who represent the waitresses in the Detroit area.

I do have an opportunity to eat out occasionally. I sometimes go to what is commonly referred to as the better restaurants as well as those which are not so good, and I find that many times in the restaurants where the salaries are higher and the gratuities greater, that there are very few women employed.

And I would hope that this concern for the interests of the women on the part of the waitresses' union would spread to seeing to it that they have placement opportunities at these other places where they could make higher income as well as opening up some of the job opportunities, such as being able to tend bar as well as wait on tables and carry the heavy trays of dishes.

But primarily I wanted to appear before you because I think it is very important that we remove all obstacles to expediting the process of democratizing our society, because there has never been any time in the history of our country when we need as we do now, the full involvement of all individuals. We need as many people as possible to help solve the many problems that we face.

And I am sure the two Senators here, as well as others are aware of these problems—our environmental problems which not only exist where we live and where we recreate but are also at the work place and involve both males and females. The question of economic deprivation, of violence, of racial conflict, none of these issues will be resolved until we get the fullest participation of all members of our society. The addition of the equal rights amendment will help to remove an obstacle that we have had in the past in terms of the utilization of all of the members of society.

That, gentlemen, was extemporaneous. I cannot not match the eloquence which I have heard here today but I share the viewpoints expressed. And I further want to say to you that the 3,000 delegates who were at that convention represent a union with predominantly a male membership. We would never have been able to improve our programs and our policies, adopt the resolution, and now to go ahead and implement it if it wasn't that we also have many males who believe that something ought to be done about this.

And now if I might for my prepared statement.

These hearings take place on the eve of Mother's Day, a ritual observance which celebrates not so much mothers and motherhood as the American genius for wedding sentimentality and profitable commercialism. It is one of the axioms of American politics that nobody is against motherhood. Congressmen and even Presidents have established their careers by consistently defending it against its detractors. But Mother's Day 1970 may usher in a new era, for it comes at a time when a very strong tide is running in behalf of the proposition that American women, while they may like candy and roses, really need basic rights still denied them. Rights not roses is the watchword for an increasing number of American women, and the UAW believes unequivocally and unreservedly that the equal rights amendment to the Constitution is essential in any serious effort to make equal rights for women a reality.

Senator BAYH. May I just interrupt to say there have been a

great many eloquent phrases given here today but that phrase has to be at the top or close to the top of all those phrases—rights not roses.

Mrs. MADAR. Thank you.

The UAW supports the equal rights amendment for women for a number of reasons. We seek its enactment because it will reinforce Title VII of the Civil Rights Act and make it more difficult for employers to circumvent the Equal Employment Opportunity Commission.

The amendment will also reinforce the "equal pay for equal work" principle, which is so often disregarded by employers, especially in small plants.

The equal rights amendmt is also needed because the 14th amendment has proven to be vague and inadequate in assuring women of equal protection of the laws. In case after case over the years, the Supreme Court has failed to find ground in the 14th amendment to find unconstitutional laws which classify persons on the basis of sex.

Despite the 14th amendment and in the absence of the equal rights amendment for women, most states still have laws regarding property rights, inheritance rights, and marriage, which make women if not indentured servants then certainly second-class citizens vis-a-vis their husbands.

In a number of States, unequal treatment adds absurdity to injustice in criminal statutes which provide for harsher sentences for women than for men upon conviction for identical crimes.

In the course of events, the Supreme Court will have to re-examine the whole matter of "sex as a basis for legislative classification" and to separate the reasonable from the unreasonable with regard to laws and practices.

This will be done sooner rather than later if the equal rights amendment is enacted. What is more, it will be done in a manner excluding discrimination but without endangering special treatment for persons in special circumstances which is non-discriminatory with respect to sex if the High Court undertakes such examination in the new light provided through enactment of the equal rights amendment.

Opponents of the equal rights amendment have played upon fears that certain social legislation would be endangered if the amendment were enacted. Such fears, however, are groundless. Maternity laws, for example, would not be affected because such laws do not apply to women as a class (not all women, as exemplified by me, incidentally, are mothers). Nor would special legislation for mothers with dependent children be invalidated by enactment of the amendment.

It should also be stressed that with enactment of the equal rights amendment, benefits such as a minimum wage or guarantees of seating facilities and lunch periods which cover women workers could also be extended to men. The position of the UAW regarding laws limiting and restricting the employment of female workers is as outlined by the attached documents by President Reuther in administrative letter No. 10, volume 21, November 6, 1969, and the statement of UAW General Counsel Steve Schlossberg before the EEOC.

And I would like to have those two included in the record.

Senator BAYH. Without objection, so ordered.

Mrs. MADAR. There is a larger and fundamental point, apart from all the detailed considerations regarding the equal rights amendment which argues eloquently and imperatively for its enactment.

And if I just might say that I would concur with the previous speaker this afternoon you apparently at one point in time did demonstrate before your committee that the question of immediacy is really a very important one. And I would hope that this would be the session of Congress in which we could see it enacted.

The point is that six years short of our 200th anniversary as an independent Nation, and over 180 years since the ratification of the Constitution of the United States, American women are still second-class citizens.

This year, we celebrate the 50th anniversary of the 19th amendment which gave women the right to vote. Yet the democratic process is demonstratively impaired and must be regarded as more frustrating than fulfilling for many women—and not only women—as long as it fails to strike away all the legal impediments to the equal treatment of Americans, regardless of sex.

The equal rights amendment is not a panacea, but it will bring us closer to the goal of equal justice under law. We in the UAW know no valid reason why this amendment, which proposes equal treatment for men and women, should not be incorporated into the U.S. Constitution. [Applause.]

Senator BAYH. Well, thank you very much. You dealt with some of the fears that have been expressed about particular kinds of legislation that are directed to unique characteristics of women as persons and individuals, biological and otherwise.

Are there areas where you feel there can legitimately be laws to protect not just women but human beings, all members of the work force, that would not be struck down by this type of legislation?

Mrs. MADAR. Yes, I believe so. In fact, I believe we probably need to have them in many areas.

Senator BAYH. What kind of laws?

Mrs. MADAR. One of the problems that we have is the lack of physically handicapped persons having opportunities for work. Currently in civil service tests, for instance, I know in the city of Detroit you cannot be employed if you have some impairment of vision even though it is corrected by glasses. And I would think in terms of providing physically handicapped as well as other specialized groups of people, particularly in regard to certain kinds of jobs and tasks, we need to have specialized legislation.

Senator BAYH. What about the hours limitations?

Mrs. MADAR. Now, that is one that I think we really have gone at in the wrong way for a long time. I think it is because of the so-called protective legislation for women that we have been unable to move faster in terms of getting legislation for voluntary overtime provisions not only in State legislation but on a Federal level. I know that stemming out of Michigan, for instance, there has been much controversy over the fact, supposedly, the women were forced to work longer hours because of the removal of the hours law. The fact of the matter is that in our organization the complaints about excessive overtime came primarily from the men.

Overtime in this country has been excessive in many cases and not necessary. It is as bad for the men as it is for the women. It makes chattel of all people, not just females. And what we need to have is Federal legislation making the right of determining the whole question of overtime hours on a voluntary basis by the employee rather than in terms of the employer regulating that proposition.

Incidentally, we have moved faster in Michigan in terms of introduction of legislation for voluntary overtime with the enactment of title VII and now that we have a ruling from the Attorney General that title VII supersedes our protective State legislation.

And interestingly enough, some of our friends who testified here contrary to the way we are testifying, did join with us in supporting that voluntary overtime legislation. And I think if they did not get so hung up on the protective legislation we might even have a better chance of getting voluntary overtime in Michigan in this next session.

Senator BAYH. One last question which I think has been answered by everything you said, but I want to deal with it specifically one more time.

Is it your judgment that the vast number of working women who are the recipients of the so-called benefits of these protective laws really do not feel they need them and that these working women would support the proposed amendment as a step forward?

Mrs. MADAR. Yes. Well, let me put it this way, though, Senator. I think the kind of protective legislation that we have now that supposedly protects women has not protected them, as you have heard many times, and discriminates against them. I do think that we do need to have protective legislation for people at the work place, and this is one of the issues, for instance, that we are dealing with right now as we are talking about bringing the whole question of in-plant environmental pollution to the collective bargaining table. We need to have protective legislation in certain kinds of instances but the kind of legislation that we have had as far as the women are concerned has not really protected them. It has worked against them.

And I think you have to deal with specic legislation that has application for the general population in order to get the kind of protection that workers need which sometimes we cannot get just through contractual provisions. If we in the UAW, for instance, are able to get these kinds of contractual provisions in terms of health and safety in our contracts, they do not even apply to all of our UAW membership and may indeed only apply in some of the larger plants such as the Big Three.

So that what I am saying in effect is that we can do things through collective bargaining but what we need is Federal legislation. We need it to deal with specific problems which have general

212

application to the entire working population.

Senator BAYH. Thank you.

Senator Cook?

Senator COOK. I enjoyed your testimony. I must reveal to you that I agree with your remarks concerning the number of hours per week people are obligated to work.

Secondly, do you have any other ideas, other than those you have expressed, why the unions that have been represented here, are so opposed to this amendment. Is it simply a desire to preserve protective legislation or would you rather not say?

Mrs. MADAR. Well, let's put it this way: There are some things I would rather not say. I will say this, however, that it is true, as in any other segment of society, that quite often the leadership of the union may misinterpret what the membership wants.

And I think we get the same kind of thing in unions as you do in terms of the Government.

Senator COOK. I appreciate your answer and I applaud your choice of the word "misinterpret." In looking back at the testimony of the past few days I think it is fair to say that many new ideas and attitudes have been presented here. It is my hope that those people who have worked several years to secure protective legislation are today able to objectively evaluate that legislation in terms of equal rights for women.

Mrs. MADAR. And I wonder if I just might comment on your remarks because I think, again, in all fairness that we ought to say this, particularly as it applies in terms of the leadership of the unions in the past.

It has been true that many of the men leaders moved out for good motivation to develop strategy under a certain set of circumstances to assure women some kind of protection in terms of employment. They used that approach because that is all at the time they had to use.

And as you have said so well, Senator Cook, the problem is that we did not move up to date fast enough in the realization that a new type of strategy was possible to get the whole loaf of bread rather than just a half loaf of breaf. And I do want to say this to my friends here: Those of us in the union movement who have been way out front on many social causes over a great number of years, including the whole question of fighting for women's rights, welcome the kinds of things that are occurring, including the women's liberation movement. We now know that we have a lot of company in trying to achieve the objectives for which all of us are fighting, and we welcome this upsurge We know and we have moved, and our convention delegates indicated that at the convention. And we know that this is now the time to move faster. And maybe that is the difference between our union and some of the other unions from whom you have heard.

Senator COOK. Thank you.

Thank you, Mr. Chairman. [Applause.]

Senator BAYH. Thank you very much, Mrs. Madar.

Thank you very much. You have, I think, made a very significant contribution to our record.

This will be the end of our hearings. We have had a number of requests from individuals as well as organizations whom we have been unable to fit into our hearing schedule due to time limitations.

We regret this, and without prolonging and delaying the final consideration of this issue which is of significant importance to so many, let me suggest that we will keep the record open for 1 week for anyone who wants to submit an individual statement or one representing the views of an organization which could not be heard. At that time we will close the record and proceed as rapidly as we can to implement the legislative process.

Thank you for your patience. [Applause.]

(Thereupon, at 4 p.m. the hearing was adjourned.)

PART 2
DOCUMENTS

STATEMENTS IN OPPOSITION

NATIONAL COUNCIL OF JEWISH WOMEN, INC.,
NEW YORK, N.Y.

STATEMENT IN OPPOSITION TO S.J. RES. 61—THE "EQUAL RIGHTS" AMENDMENT SUBMITTED TO THE CONSTITUTIONAL AMENDMENTS SUBCOMMITTEE OF THE COMMITTEE ON THE JUDICIARY, U.S. SENATE, MAY 14, 1970

The National Council of Jewish Women, an organization established in 1893, with a membership of over 100,000 in local units throughout the United States, has throughout its existence actively supported measures to improve the legal status of women. To this end we actively campaigned for an equal pay for equal work law, we supported repeal of state laws which clearly discriminated against women, such as the prohibition on jury service for women, and other measures which were vestiges of earlier times and were no longer relevant to present day society.

The National Council of Jewish Women was also in the midst of the struggle for woman suffrage. After the passage of the 19th Amendment we, together the preponderant majority of those in the forefront of the struggle, rejected the proposal of a splinter group to support another constitutional amendment, the so-called Equal Rights Amendment. Delegates to our conventions have consistently opposed the Amendment and at our last biennial convention held in April 1969, the following resolution was reaffirmed:

"The National Council of Jewish Women believes that the freedom, dignity, and security of the individual are basic to American democracy, and that discrimination because of race, creed, national origin, color, age or sex undermines that democracy.

"It therefore resolves:

To endorse measures which establish the principles and equality of the legal status for women, while opposing any so-called "Equal Rights" amendment which may destroy protective legislation for women."

When the Amendment was introduced, some 47 years ago, it did not have much validity, but it has even less now. For during the 47-year period many changes in the status of women come about which have made the proposal obsolete. The enactment of an Equal Pay law in 1963, title VII of the Civil Rights Act of 1964, and the issuance of a series of Executive orders that prohibit discrimination on the basis of sex by Federal contractors, in Federal Emploment, and in employment on Federally assisted construction projects, have rendered the argument for the Amendment as a means of removing this type of discrimination invalid. The States have also acted in this area quite extensively. Equal pay is now required by law in 35 states and 21 states and the District of Columbia have fair employment practices laws which prohibit discrimination in employment on the basis of sex.

There also have been significant developments in the civil and political status of women. At the present time there are no restrictions on voting, holding of public office, jury service, both Federal and State, or any other political activity. Women are now permitted to bring legal action in their own name, make contracts, own property, and collect their earnings. There are no restrictions with respect to property rights which apply to married women that do not also apply to married men. In a very few states there remain some restrictions on the right of married women to enter into their separate

217

business. In a number of jurisdictions the question of domicile is considered a discrimination against women.

In reviewing the vestiges of legal discriminations against women the question arises whether a constitutional amendment, which may place in doubt a body of law found to be socially desirable, is the most efficient means of removing the very few legal discriminations. The effect of the Equal Rights Amendment upon our law poses a great many questions to which the proponents have given no answers and to which no one probably can respond in any definitive manner until the courts have had an opportunity to interpret the very vague wording of the amendment. For the sake of a few legal discriminations, which can be eliminated by simple repeal, should we jeopardize a whole body of law dealing with complex personal and family relationships, military service, age of consent, etc. And what would be the status of laws which cannot possibly apply to both sexes, such as maternity benefits and laws prohibiting rape. The answer is obviously in the negative.

The greatest difficulty the amendment poses is the definition of "equal rights" and "discrimination." Some years ago proponents of the amendment compiled a list of State laws which discriminate against women. The preponderant majority of the laws listed were family support laws. It is very doubtful that the majority of the women in the United States would agree that a family support law is a curtailment of their rights.

The proponents of the amendment view the issue primarily from their personal perspective as economically independent professional women, who may be subject to discrimination. Very likely these discriminations are not necessarily legal, but rooted in custom and prejudice. To these women other considerations, so important to an orderly society, seem unrelated. But it is necessary to point out that in the United States there are some 70 million women above the age of 16 and only about 25 million are in the labor force. It must be therefore assumed that the majority in this age group do not choose to be in the labor force and their right to this choice must also be given some consideration.

In spite of their single-minded drive for the Equal Rights Amendment the proponents have not been able to ignore the safeguards in our present Constitution, namely the Fourteenth Amendment which provides that "no State shall deprive any person of life, liberty, or property, without due process of law; nor deny to any person within its jurisdiction the equal protection of the laws," and the "due process clause" of the Fifth Amendment. Nevertheless they claim that because in cases brought under the Fourteenth Amendment the Court did not always agree that any differentiation is per se unconstitutional, we must reiterate these safeguards in another amendment. This position makes it clear that the proponents of the Equal Rights Amendment are not seeking equality under the law, but identity of treatment. Since it is impossible to predict how a given court will interpret a given constitutional amendment, the proponents are not really assured of the objective they seek, that is, identity of treatment. Under these circumstances it would seem that such an amendment does not fit in very well with sound constitutional principles, and that it may not be wise to rush to amend the constitution in order to correct disabilities, real or imaginary, which can more simply be eliminated through other governmental action.

Some years ago a professor of history and a well-known lecturer and writer on the Constitution, Henry Steele Commager, in opposing the Twenty-Second Amendment to the Constitution, commented on the amendment process in general and wrote:

". . . To confuse limitations on the realm or scope of government with limitations on the authority of government when it operates in its proper field, is a fundamental error. From time to time we have committed this error in our law-making, but heretofore—with the possible exception of the Prohibition Amendment—we have not committed it in the Constitution. The original Constitution set careful limits to the realm of government, but when authority was granted it was granted fully. And that is the interpretation which John Marshall and most of his successors placed upon the Constitution . . . We are confusing what belongs in a Constitution with what belongs in administration or ordinary politics."

We can only conclude that the "Equal Rights" Amendment is not the proper vehicle for the elimination of whatever discriminations against women may still exist and we agree with Professor Paul Freund of the Harvard Law School who stated in an analysis of the Amendment:

"The basic fallacy in the proposed Amendment is that it attempts to deal with complicated and highly concrete problems arising out of a diversity of human relationships in terms of a single and simple abstraction. This abstraction is undoubtedly a worthy ideal for mobilizing legislative forces in order to remedy particular deficiencies in the law. But as a constitutional standard, it is hopelessly inept. That the proposed equal rights amendment would open up an era of regrettable consequences for the legal status of women in this country is highly probable. That it would open up a period of extreme confusion in constitutional law is a certainty."

We urge the Committee to reject the so-called "Equal Rights Amendment."

NATIONAL COUNCIL OF CATHOLIC WOMEN,
Washington, D.C., May 13, 1970.

The National Council of Catholic Women, a federation of local, diocesan, State and National organizations of Catholic women, whose combined membership totals about ten million, wishes to present for inclusion in the hearings of the proposed Equal Rights Amendment, the following statement based on resolutions passed at National Conventions of the National Council of Catholic Women:

"Again we strongly reiterate our opposition to the proposed 'Equal Rights' Amendment to the U.S. Constitution as a threat to the nature of woman which individuates her from man in God's plan for His creation.

"Under the guise of equality, the proposed 'Equal Rights' Amendment would in reality wipe out the many legal safeguards which protect woman's position in the family. Under the proposed amendment maximum hours and minimum wage laws for women, widows' allowances, alimony and support payments, and the basic responsibility of man to provide for his family would be placed in jeopardy.

"Because it proposes an idea of woman foreign to the Christian concept of woman's co-equal, but individual, dignity with man, and because it would destroy the legal safeguards women have secured through the years, we oppose the proposed 'Equal Rights' amendment."

"We reaffirm our opposition to the proposed Equal Rights Amendment to the Constitution of the United States."

Similar resolutions have been passed at successive conventions and Board Meetings.

We would appreciate your entering this letter in the record of the hearings on the proposed Equal Rights Amedment.

Respectfully yours,

MRS. NORMA FOLDA, *President.*

STATEMENTS IN SUPPORT

B'NAI B'RITH WOMEN,
Washington, D.C.

PREPARED STATEMENT OF B'NAI B'RITH WOMEN ON EQUAL RIGHTS
AMENDMENT

B'nai B'rith Women, a major Jewish women's organization of 135,000 members, welcomes this opportunity to submit a statement supporting ratification of an equal rights for women amendment to the United States Constitution. A major goal of the organization in initiating social action is to insure that every citizen enjoys all the privileges of participation in a democratic society. B'nai B'rith Women's continuing commitment to securing guaranteed equality for citizens in any area affected by law prompts this testimony in favor of the amendment under consideration.

The very nature of our organization has influenced our support for equal rights for women in all areas of life—politically, culturally, economically and socially. Delegates to our national conventions have passed resolutions calling for equal pay for equal work; the placement of capable women in positions of trust and responsibility in the government; and stricter enforcement of Title VII of the Civil Rights Act of 1964.

However, we feel that existing federal and state legislation is neither comprehensive nor consistent throughout the nation. Although much progress has been made in recent years, there is still discrimination against women in business, education, the professions, and in the government. Women receive lower pay while performing in the same capacity as men. Women are not considered—much less hired—for certain positions. Women are prohibited from earning overtime pay by some states' so-called protective statutes.

Over 1,000 civil and criminal state laws discriminate against women. They are denied the right to own real estate or stocks and bonds. They cannot institute divorce proceedings. They are treated differently in cases of homicide or other criminal acts. These instances, and many others, create a status of second-class citizenship for over 51% of our population.

Such conditions, and the attitudes which created them, are extremely difficult to change on a state-by-state, law-by-law basis. It is unfortunate that when women try to effect change in these laws, they are forced into an adversary position against the very government they support and honor. The equal rights amendment now being considered would eliminate the need for such unnecessary litigation .

It is now fifty years since the 19th Amendment to the Constitution, granting women suffrage, was adopted. In that time women have made creative, constructive contributions to American society. They are willing and able to continue to work, on an equal basis, to insure the growth and realize the potential of this great nation.

B'nai B'rith urges the Subcommittee on Constitutional Amendments to recommend to the United States Senate passage of the Equal Rights Amendment. The ideals of this nation demand justice and fair treatment for all our citizens. The women of this country are a vitally significant group. They are entitled to the same Constitutional rights accorded to any citizen of the United States.

MAY 1970.   MRS. MICHAEL SHAPIRO, *President.*

STATEMENT BY ST. JOAN'S ALLIANCE

Although I regret that you were unable to schedule me to testify during the May 5, 6 and 7 Hearings of your Sub-Committee I am following your suggestion and presenting a written statement of the views of St. Joan's Alliance with respect to the proposed Equal Rights Amendment.

St. Joan's Alliance (U.S. Section) was formed in 1965 and is affiliated with St. Joan's International Alliance whose headquarters are in London. The Alliance was founded in England in 1911 at the time British women were struggling for voting rights. It was the only Catholic organization which participated in that struggle. After suffrage was won the Alliance continued its efforts to eradicate injustices and inequalities suffered by women in the political, economic and social areas. We have been working on the national level and through international organizations (League of Nations, United Nations, ILO, UNESCO). The encyclical *Pacem in Terris* of John XXIII inspired us to extend our egalitarian endeavors to the Church itself. True to the teachings of her Founder, the Church should, we feel, be a leader in all human rights crusades.

Support of the Equal Rights Amendment is well within our terms of reference and the text of the Amendment is consonant with the spirit and letter of the Second Vatican Council documents, which were drafted by the world's Bishops and promulgated by Pope Paul VI.

"There is therefore, in the Church no inequality on the basis of race or nationality, social condition or *SEX* because 'there is neither Jew nor Greek; there is neither slave nor freeman; there is neither male nor female. For you are all one in Christ Jesus.' (Gal. 3:28)" *Constitution on the Church* No. 32 (Emphasis added)

Addressing an Italian women's meeting in Rome in 1965 Pope Paul said: "You should remind women that perfect equality in their nature and dignity, and therefore in rights, is assured to them from the first page of the sacred scriptures." (Cited by Mary Daly: *The Church and the Second Sex* p. 60)

It usually comes as a shock to most Americans—men and women—to learn that the United States Constitution does not outlaw inequality between men and women, or discrimination on the basis of sex. The more knowledgeable cite the Fourteenth Amendment, but that Amendment has frequently been interpreted as not guaranteeing women's rights. A few cite Title VII of the Civil Rights Act of 1964, but under Title VII only equality in employment is assured. We all know how Title VII happens to include the word "sex". However, its inclusion, in addition to its more tangible fruits has proved to be of educational value in that it draws public attention to the prevalence and degree of discrimination against women in the labor market. This law, however, can easily be superseded by other less favorable legislation. Within eight months of the entry in effect of the Civil Rights Act of 1964, a bill was introduced into the Senate (S. 3077) which would repeal Title VII and limit the protection against discrimination in employment to the grounds of race, color, religion, or national origin. While an amendment to the Constitution could be repealed this process is difficult.

Ironically, if not hypocritically, many who oppose the Equal Rights Amendment claim to be motivated by a desire to "protect" women. From long and sometimes costly experience women have learned that "protection" and "discrimination" can be in effect synonymous. Statistics supporting this conclusion are abundant and well publicized. They have been cited no doubt by persons testifying before this Sub-Committee.

Discriminations, which if practiced against other groups of citizens would—and rightly so—provoke indignation and vehement protest are considered trivial if the victims are women. Some time ago, for example, as a matter of principle, we protested exclusion from a regularly scheduled, non-chartered air flight between Newark and Chicago because the flight was "for men only." In reply to our query as to whether the airline scheduled flights "for Whites only" or "for Christians only" the reply was "Of course not, that would be illegal." The Director of the New Jersey Human Rights Commission wrote, "New Jersey's law against discrimination does not prohibit any kind of discrimination based on sex. The Federal Civil Rights Act of 1964 prohibits discrimination based on sex only in its coverage of employment (Title VII)." Is it not high time that all manner of discrimination against women be rendered illegal once and for all in every State? The Equal Rights Amendment would do exactly that.

Mr. Chairman, when in 1966 St. Joan's Alliance voted to support the Equal Rights Amendment we expressed the hope (unfulfilled) that the Amendment would be adopted prior to the celebration of International Human Rights Year (1968). The United Nations Charter, the *Universal Declaration of Human Rights* and other international documents included the word "sex" in enumerating the grounds on which discrimination is condemned. Representatives of the United States participated in drafting these documents and voted for their adoption. One could quote each of the eleven articles of the *Declaration on the Elimination of Discrimination Against Women as* pertinent to the enactment of the Equal Rights Amendment to the Constitution of the United States. We shall quote only those immediately applicable.

ARTICLE 1

"Discrimination against women, denying or limiting as it does their equality of rights with men, is fundamentally unjust and constitutes an offense against human dignity."

ARTICLE 2

"All appropriate measures shall be taken to abolish existing laws, customs, regulations and practices which are discriminatory against women, and to establish adequate legal protection for equal rights of men and women: in particular:

(a) The principle of equality of rights shall be embodied in the constitution or otherwise guaranteed by law:

(b) The international instruments of the United Nations and the specialized agencies relating to the elimination of discrimination against women shall be ratified or acceded to and fully implemented as soon as practicable."

ARTICLE 10

"1. All appropriate measures shall be taken to ensure to women, married or unmarried, equal rights with men in the field of economic and social life. . . ."

ARTICLE 11

"1. The principle of equality of rights of men and women demands implementation in all States in accordance with the principles of the United Nations and of the Universal Declaration of Human Rights . . ."

Mr. Chairman, we have learned with great satisfaction that the Citizen's Advisory Council on the Status of Women has endorsed the Equal Rights Amendment and has requested the Interdepartmental Committee on the Status of Women "to urge the President to immediately request the passage of the proposed Equal Rights Amendment by the Congress of the United States."

The Council adopted its resolution we hear by a vote of 19 to 1. Our information indicates that the one dissenting vote was cast by the representative of a Catholic organization. It is for this reason that we particularly wished to testify at the Hearing and why in the opening portion of our statement we stressed the harmony between the spirit and text of the proposed Amendment and basic Catholic teaching.

Not only because we are Americans but also because we are Catholics we believe that all God's children are created equal.

Nearly twenty-five years ago Cardinal Dougherty, the Archbishop of Philadelphia at that time, endorsed the Equal Rights Amendment in a letter addressed to the officers of the National Women's Party.

". . . My dear Ladies:

Apropos of the Equal Rights Amendment to our Constitution, according to which it is proposed to give women full constitutional rights, I am glad to hear from you that his Excellency, President Truman, and also the Judiciary Committee of the House of Representatives are heartily in favor of this Amendment. Personally I agree with them in this matter.

Respectfully yours

(Signed) D. CARD. DOUGHERTY,
Abp. of Philadelphia."

Senator Bayh, we appreciate this opportunity to record our views.

Very sincerely yours,

FRANCIS LEE McGILLICUDDY,
President, St. Joan's International Alliance (U.S. Section).

STATEMENT OF THE UNITARIAN UNIVERSALIST WOMEN'S FEDERATION ON THE EQUAL RIGHTS AMENDMENT FOR THE SUBCOMMITTEE ON CONSTITUTIONAL AMENDMENTS, SENATE JUDICIARY COMMITTEE

The Unitarian Universalist Women's Federation has 480 affiliated units in the United States with a membership of 17,000 women. Under its stated purpose of working for universal human dignity, freedom, and peace, it adopted as a program priority at its 1969 biennial convention "the civil rights of women."

One of the basic tenets of Unitarian Universalist belief is the inherent worth of every human being without regard to color, race, creed or SEX. Therefore all rights under law should be equalized for women and men. Since there has been considerable ambiguity in the interpretations of the Fifth and Fourteenth Amendments in respect to the rights of women, it is essential that a clear statement on the equal rights of men and women should be incorporated in our constitution.

The argument that is used most frequently against the Equal Rights Amendment is that it would void certain protective legislation applying to the working woman. For instance, in the Commonwealth of Massachusetts, where our Unitarian Universalist Women's Federation has its national headquarters, there is legislation prohibiting the employment of women for more than 9 hours a day or 48 hours a week, which in a 5-day work week in practice works out to 45 hours a week. A woman cannot be required to lift a weight of more than 40 pounds. This seemingly protective legislation does in fact have a very adverse effect on the working woman, for it can be used to prevent the promotion of women to better jobs. A sexually prejudiced manager, in order to prevent a woman from being promoted or moved to some higher-paying job can write into the specification for the job that it might occasionally require lifting more than 40 pounds or working occasionally more than 48 hours.

Only 10 states have such weight-lifting laws.* There is no consistency in their specifications. They vary from 50 pounds lifting and 10 pounds up and down stairs in California, to 15 pounds carrying in Utah or to 40 pounds lifting in Massachusetts. But, what about the women workers in the other 40 states? How have they been managing without protective weight-lifting laws? As a matter of fact, several states have repealed weight-lifting laws. They have been declared unconstitutional in court cases under Title 7 of the Civil Rights Act of 1964, which prohibits discrimination in employment on the basis of race, creed, color, religion, and sex.

It would seem that any protective laws on weight-lifting should apply to men as well as women, since there are physiological factors which make many men even more prone to injury from lifting than women.

As to restrictions on hours of work, should not women as well as men be free to decide whether or not they are able to take on extra hours of work? Not all women have families which require their attention. In 1967, 36% of working women were single, widowed, or divorced.* There are a number of single, widowed, or divorced women who might occasionally welcome the extra income from over 48 hours of work.

An argument might also be made that if hours of work for women need to be restricted, men should also be protected by restrictions, since in the case of the family man, overtime, or moonlighting, prevents him from fulfilling his role as father.

We are also told that because some women are in need of extra money, and are prohibited under law from working substantial overtime hours on one job, they are flouting the law by carrying two jobs, expecting that it will not come to the attention of their state labor regulatory agencies.

Again, not all states have protective hours legislation. In Alabama, Alaska, Delaware, Florida, Hawaii, Idaho, Indiana, Iowa, and West Virginia women manage their working lives without such protection.**

It is true that in federal courts state protective laws have been held invalid under Title 7 of the Civil Rights Act of 1964, and it has been ruled that weight-lifting restrictions cannot be used to prevent the promotion of women to higher-paying jobs. However, this law does not apply to intra-state business and industry. State commissions on discrimination must consider state laws in responding to complaints from women workers.

To carry a case through the courts is a long and costly process, far beyond the means of the average woman worker who feels she has suffered discrimination in hiring, promotion, or pay. The passage of the Equal Rights Amendment would discourage employers from using "protective" state laws as loopholes for discriminatory practices, establish the principle of equality and

---

* *Handbook on Women Workers,* Women's Bureau Bulletin 294, U.S. Department of Labor, p. 279.

* *Handbook on Women Workers,* Women's Bureau Bulletin 294, U.S. Dept. of Labor, p. 23.

** *Ibid.,* p. 271.

make possible a strengthening of such legislation as is now on the books, such as Title 7 of the Civil Rights Act of 1964.

Under the Equal Rights Amendment, injustices to women under criminal law could be prevented. As recently as 1968, the states of Connecticut and Pennsylvania were found to have laws providing for longer prison sentences for women than for men committing the same crime. While these particular laws were found to be unconstitutional, there are doubtless other states where more litigation would have to be employed to establish their unconstitutionality. An Equal Rights Amendment would automatically wipe such laws off the books.

We believe that there are some areas in which men would benefit from this Amendment as well as women. A woman would no longer be granted alimony regardless of need. A divorced wife might have to pay alimony to a dependent husband. The custody of children in a divorce would not so automatically go to the mother, but the welfare of the children would be the important factor for the court in making a decision. The financial status of both the mother and father would be considered in allocating responsibility for support.

In other areas of family law, there are further benefits to be derived from the Equal Rights Amendment. State laws restricting property rights of married women would be invalidated; they would have the same rights of contract as men and inheritance rights would be the same as for men.

Women are ready to accept the implication that Equal Rights Amendment would make them subject, also, to the draft, though we would hope the Congress and Administration would move toward an all-volunteer armed force, as recommended by the Gates Commission. Too, we believe that too many of the decisions in the armed forces and in the Defense Department are being made exclusively by men and that women should also have responsibility in the military establishment. Certainly over 50% of the population by sex should have a voice in life and death decisions.

In the long struggle for equal rights, women have made some important gains in the United States, but there still exists a jumble of state laws in effect discriminating against women. There is much yet to be attained. Consider the fact that the median wage of women in 1968 was still only 58.2% of men's. Consider the fact that only 2.5% of women, compared to 19.5% of men, earned over $10,000 a year in 1968, and only .4% of women $15,000 or over as contrasted with 8.2% of men. Clearly women are far from attaining equal rights. In this time of accelerating change, the Equal Rights for Women Amendment would have a tremendous psychological as well as legal value in improving the lot of women.

As a member nation of the United Nations, the United States by its signature to the Charter, has affirmed its "faith in fundamental human rights, in the dignity and worth of the human person, in the equal rights of men and women." The world will take note of the fate of the Equal Rights Amendment in 1970." Let us say to the women and men of all nations that in the United States the human rights of women is on the agenda for endorsement by Congress in its 91st session.

ALICE H. KIMBALL, *President.*
CONSTANCE H. BURGESS, *Executive Director.*

LUELLA A. HUGGINS,
ATTORNEY AT LAW,
Altadena, Calif., June 24, 1970.

Re: Article—Equal Rights Amendment.
HON. BIRCH BAYH,
Senate Office Bldg.,
Washington, D.C.

DEAR SENATOR BAYH: I was sorry I had court cases to attend to and could not stop to write an article for the hearings at the time of the request. But I think your very fine letter which cheered many in his area was an inspiration and as soon as a little time could be found I tried to do something. I love to write but am never satisfied with what I put out, but if you like it and there is still time to insert it into the Record then it will serve its purpose and pay for the effort.

I could write an article on a lifetime of frustration in my desire as a youth to do something of value for society and for my country and meeting only prejudice and discrimination and apathy. I could have done much, and to some extent still can if the way is opened.

226

I would much like to meet you if and when I come to Washington this year as it is my custom to come there during the summer but have been delayed this year. If you can spare a little time I would like to see to what extent we may agree on many problems before the country, and perhaps I can then do my stint in helping with them.

Will you let me know the result of this letter and the article enclosed, whether you could find time to read it, or liked it, or had time still to use it, and whether you will see me when I come that way.

I thank you again for myself and all the women of the country for your efforts in our behalf.

Sincere yours,

LUELLA A. HUGGINS, (Miss).

SHOULD THE EQUAL RIGHTS AMENDMENT BE PASSED?

It is incongruous in this day and age when science can send an Apollo II to the moon, guide its every action and return it to the earth safely, that it has never been able to guide mankind safely in his journey through life with its many intricacies and experiences and bring him individually and collective to full fruition and fulfillment to his intended destiny. What is lacking is his knowledge and application of the natural laws that govern man and his well-being the same as he does other fields of science, and his refusal to seek and use the rich resources he has available to bring that result about.

And nowhere is this attitude more clearly shown than in treatment of women throughout the ages. Future generations will talk of the struggle of women to be heard and have a place in society and in their own public affairs and the constant blocking of their efforts as a symptom of the vextigals of former barbarism when there began the custom of treating women as inferior beings subject to men because men were in fact physically stronger and could enforce their customs and decrees upon women when in the earlier days of history and of mankind, great physical strength was the greatest need of man, for fighting, for protection, for hunting, and for other duties and needs of precivilization. Women were naturally delegated to the lighter tasks and man found it pleasing and a natural desire at that time to feel superior which he carried through later centuries and to this age when such delegation and customs are no longer needed nor consistent today, but she is still in partial bondage and victim to his ancient whims, decrees, customs, traditions and laws and his inner need of belief in his own superiority.

Advances in this day and age has almost erased the need of physical superiority and the partial civilization in which we live has lessened the need for physical strength only, and has evolved until more important needs are paramount and which modern needs require the contribution of women as much as that of men, and more than that of men alone, for the natures of the two are supplementary, neither one the superior of the other, excepting in a few rare instances, which makes the need of both even more important, and this supplementary need covers all phases of social and public life.

It is true that many women will not avail themselves of any greater spheres of life or greater freedom, for they are content as they are, and no one would want to disturb their contentment, but many are not content, they have sought and obtained training and have the desire for a wider sphere in life, interested in other channels of expression the same as men are, and should not be barred from that greater expression and opportunities simply because they are women, without being given a chance to prove their competence, altho seeing many unqualified men appointed, elected or otherwise involved in private and public affairs whose competence cannot match that of many of the barred and rejected women.

The destinies of mankind are not superficial, nor can they be controlled or attained through simple means or laws. They are controlled by natural laws just as the Apollo II was when it was sent to the moon and came back safely. When it did not function correctly the scientists knew that some natural law had been neglected, ignored, violated, or had developed, and they set it right. When men and society do not function positively and constructively it is because society (and men are in control) has violated or ignored some basic natural law or laws. This is true in their educational processes today, in their conduct of government, in their private lives, in all phenomena, and in all phases of life and of action. Thousands of years ago a shepherd of Tokea said "My people are destroyed for lack of knowledge," and the statement is as true now as it was then. There have been minor and major eruptions at various periods of history, and these eruptions are growing more articulate today, not because the contenders are always right in their contentions, any more than many of those who try to remedy the situations are right in their presumed remedies, but because much is wrong or there would never been general eruptions. Too many natural laws have been violated, which subject it is not possible to pursue further in detail at this time and place.

The same fact is true concerning the traditional treatment of women throughout the ages. Some allowance might be made for it in past ages, for man had not evolved very high on any level but it is inexcusable now when he has gone so far in other advances and still treats women in many respects as inferior creatures. While the Equal Rights Amendment will not bring about a full correction, it will be a step in that direction. The next step, and even more important, will be its observance in spirit as well as in fact and in law. If it had been observed it would not be necessary to have the Amendment. Mature people do not need a law or laws to govern their conduct or control their actions. But our society is not mature, even in training its young to live positively and constructively and be an asset to society instead of so many a liability, or there would not be these many problems among and with youth today. We are tied down by our own inadequacies of understanding, of thought and of action. It is easier to travel in well-defined ruts than to seek and find and follow a better and higher way. It may be yet that women will have to save this country and the world from its folly and errors. Who knows?

Beliefs and prejudices will have to recede in the presence of facts. When man began to keep statistics of his various aspects of life, he found some of his aged beliefs showing up badly. He had barred girls from even the primary grades of school on the ground that they did not have the same mentality as boys and could not take or profit by the studies. He later barred them from schools of higher learning on the same ground but later because of their persistence and inner urgings to be more than a recluse in a home. when men admitted girls to a limited degree to higher schools they were often found more apt and quicker to learn and earned better grades than the boys. Although they were generally barred from using that knowledge and training for the benefit of themselves and for society because of strong prejudice and discrimination, which custom still persists today.

Men called women the "weaker sex" for centuries, because of their lesser physical strength, but that charge is not heard much any more, again because of statistics, for while men have greater strength on the short haul women have greater strength and endurance on the long haul for they live longer than men. This was formerly stated to be due to the occupational hazards of men, but when women got out into the same occupations, and there were strict safeguards around dangerous machinery, men got rather "weak" on that charge.

Then the charge is made that women are too emotional to be competent or deal soundly with momentous questions and make decisions of value. Again the facts dispute their claim. Who is it that commits the most murders, many through jealousy or resentment, who fills most of the jails, mental institutions, patronizes the most psychiatrists, has the most heart attacks and strokes, not always due to emotions but often to mental strain? As to male emotions—have you ever listened to a long drawn-out bitter election campaign, with its charges and countercharges?

The fact that women are better able to stand these fatalities is that they are far better *natural* philosophers than men. They have had to be to take what they have had to put up with throughout the centuries. For they have been subject to the edicts of men with no hope or possibilities of changing them over so long a period of them. They had to bear them, and philosophically, or break under them as men more often break under pressures.

Akin to being far better *natural* philosophers making it possible to better stand their problems and troubles, women are of a deeper spiritual nature. Enter the average church and it will be seen that most of the congregation is comprised of women. They go to renew their spiritual strength to carry them on in their everyday needs and tasks, which they have learned to take better than men ever have learned. Women have their own remedies for their tensions and disappointments largely within themselves. They are far more loyal to their obligations to their offspring than men are. There are thousands of men each year who desert their children and throw the support of them on the taxpayers while they earn and spend on themselves what they have. Yet it is rare that a women deserts her children. True, today she usually gets helped for their support but she rarely deserted them when she did not receive aid of any kind.

Men have decreed by custom, tradition, law, superior physical strength and every other means to hold control of women in his own hands, and pigeonhole them and their nature, what they should be and do into certain narrow and prescribed channels and keep them therein, ignoring, violating, and perverting and failing to understand and recognize the natural laws that govern her being. His ancient cry that "women's place is in the home" still resounds in the public forum when it denies the fact that each person is born with certain abilities and talents according to their genes, and it is no more consistent with nature for *every* women to confine herself in a home as it is for every man to be confined to carpenter work in a shop and be decreed to do nothing else.

It is the plan of nature to round out the needs and capacities and abilities of mankind so as to serve and complete a whole. And while some women choose the home life and it is well that they do, many women who do not so choose and have a destiny to fill outside the home are needed to do it. All persons should be and do what nature intended, and that includes women. Men and women are not exactly alike. They are supplementary and the one-half of the whole is needed as badly as the other half, and what women can do and be for the benefit of the whole should be recognized as quickly and as fully as what men and do and be for the good of the whole. There is not enough recognition in this respect for the men but it is far worse for the women, and society and posterity suffer because of this failure to know, appreciate and appropriate each person's contribution.

Men had been in control of the affairs of society and of the world from time immemorial, and what a mess they have made of it with all their advances. The facts speak for themselves. These might be much better if there was more involvement of women in public and world affairs, or if there had been in the past. Many other nations have recognized this fact, and acted accordingly. They have taken women into full partnership in their country's affairs and those women have acquitted themselves with great credit, which cannot be said the same for many male leaders. Many more women have become heads of state and have served well, while this nation has never had a women on the Chief Executive's personal staff with the same status as the men, not considering their counsel as much needed or of value as that of the men, the women comprise the greater number of the population and have much to give in all affairs of government, both as counsel and in charge in some instances. While there are few women highly trained there are plenty of them considering the posts available, and those which should be available. This nation, the most progressive in many respects, is still far behind many others in its acceptance of women at their full value.

Two writers a few years ago authored books along the same line: Montagu Ashley-Montagu wrote The Natural Superiority of Women, and Richard G. Levy's book was titled Women Should Rule the World. Perhaps both were unduly optimistic, but they saw what not many today see—the value of women's place and voice in society's and the world's affairs, and in all phases of life to which women could have added much had they not been barred by prejudice and discrimination. Women have been too long barred from the important decisions on matters pertaining to their own welfare and the welfare of other members of society for whom they are partly responsible and taxed heavily on programs for which often they have no voice and are not consulted, and it is time they took their place far more in number in and with the highest echelons of our government and in its social needs and ministrations for all society for progress and posterity have suffered because of their absence.

The Equal Rights Amendment should have passed a century ago. Its passage is largely under control of men for women yet are not numerous for their voices to be heard in numbers. Their better wisdom along many lines is desperately needed at this time.

To those men who still live in centuries past one can only say to them to come into the 20th century or there may not be another century for this country or for the world for those we know are fast destroying themselves from inside and from without. Medieval prejudices and attitudes are not consistent with an atomic age. Let us try together to make this country what our forefathers envisioned and what it once was—the hope and inspiration of all mankind.

Statement of Jean Faust
417 Riverside Drive
New York, N. Y. 10025

Assistant on Women's Rights
to Congressman William F. Ryan

For the Senate Sub-Committee Hearings
on the Equal Rights Amendment
May 5,6,7, 1970

WHY THE EQUAL RIGHTS AMENDMENT?

1970 marks the Fiftieth Anniversary of the Suffrage Amendment--an appropriate occasion for presenting the Equal Rights Amendment to the States for ratification.

The first organized meeting of women to demand equality of rights in the United States was held at Seneca Falls, N. Y., in 1848--one hundred and twenty-two years ago. It was organized by Lucretia Mott, Elizabeth Cady Stanton and other pioneers in the Women's Movement, both men and women.

But it was not until seventy-two years later that women won the right to vote (but no other rights) through the passage of the Nineteenth Amendment in 1920 (fifty years after the Fifteenth Amendment had given the right to vote to former slaves--but males only).

Unfortunately, the right to vote has had little effect on the status of women. A much broader measure is required to eliminate the widespread inequalities that oppress American women.

In 1923, Senator Charles Curtis, of Kansas, proposed an Amendment to the United States Constitution to provide that
> "Equality of Rights under the law shall not
> be denied or abridged on account of sex."

An identical resolution was introduced in the House of Representatives by Representative Daniel Anthony (nephew of Susan B. Anthony), also of Kansas.

Forty-seven years later, the Equal Rights Amendment still has not been enacted.
This failure of the American Congress to bring women under the protection of the constitution (from which they were deliberately excluded[1]) is a symbol of the discrimination practiced in every level of American society.

There exist in the various States over one thousand State laws that discriminate against women. These cover the areas of bond making, contracts, criminal laws, marriage and divorce, educational opportunities, access to employer records, employment opportunities, guardianship of children, health and medical care, property management, right to sue, right to run for public office, limitation of hours to be worked, weights to be lifted, etc., etc. These restrictions prevent women from pursuing the full, productive lives of which they are capable.

Some legislators still contend that these are "States' Rights" issues; but any congressman who attempted to use the states' rights argument in the case of civil rights for black people would be booed off the floor. Nevertheless, oppression of women is still so acceptable that this most unacceptable of arguments is still posed.

Why should a citizen in one state be less equal, less protected by the constitution than a citizen in another state? Why should the United States permit prejudice and "tradition", in the names of states' rights, to maintain outmoded laws on marriage, divorce, abortion, etc. when the United Nations, in the cause of human dignity, is attempting to establish uniform laws all over this globe.

Another argument against the Equal Rights Amendment, that it would threaten State Protective Legislation (concerning hours and weight limitations for women workers), has already fallen: the Equal Employment Opportunity Commission declared, on August 19, 1969, that Title VII of the Civil Rights Act of 1964 supercedes these state laws. Years ago, the United States Civil Service Commission had declared all women employed by the United States Government exempt from these laws.

Recently, several United States District Court decisions have declared State laws in violation of the Civil Rights Act:

> U. S. 5th Circuit Court recently ruled,
> in Weeks v. Southern Bell Telephone,
> that Title VII of the 1964 Civil Rights
> Act superceded the State's rule.

> A district court in California, in Rosenfeld
> v. Southern Pacific Company, struck down
> State laws limiting working hours and weight
> lifting laws affecting women.

> A district court in Oregon, in Richards v.
> Griffith Rubber Mills, ruled that a State
> law re: rest periods and bans on weight
> lifting could not be used to deprive an
> individual woman of her rights under Title VII.

Some people complacently assume that "women have it made" and that American women, particularly, "have all the rights they need." They also assume that girls have no needs or aspirations beyond marriage and family; but the Department of Labor has found that 9 out of 10 girls will work some time during their lives. And the flowering of a vigorous, militant new women's movement, from 1966 to 1970, has demonstrated that American women bitterly resent the roles offered to them by society.

The new feminist movement, sparked by the founding of the National Organization for Women (NOW) in 1966, has grown so rapidly that it is second only to ecology in the public interest and attention of the mass media.

Why has this movement grown so rapidly? The President's Commission on the Status of Women, the various States' Commissions on the Status of Women, and the Women's Bureau of

the Department of Labor has patiently collected data that
illustrate only too vividly the low status of women in American society. The question should be, why have women been
patient so long?

Nearly half the women in the population between the
ages of 18 and 65 are IN THE LABOR FORCE and the percentage
continues to rise rapidly.

THERE WAS NO OCCUPATION LISTED IN THE LAST CENSUS AS
OCCUPIED SOLELY BY MEN OR SOLELY BY WOMEN.
                                    women
    Nearly thirty-two million/16 years of age and over
were in the labor force in February, 1970, (comprising
nearly 40% of the total labor force--up from 33% in 1969).
And, the number of women working is increasing faster than
men. Further, another two million women want to work, but
cannot find a job. Unemployment among women is far greater
than among men: for 1969, the average for men was 2.8%;
for women, 4.7%.

    Because of prejudice and discrimination, female workers
are heavily concentrated in low-status, low-pay jobs. In
April 1969, the largest number (9.8 million) were employed
in clerical jobs. 4.7 million were service workers (NOT
including private household). 4.4 million were operatives
and 4.1 million were in professional and technical occu-
pations--nearly always at lower pay than men for the same
job.

    The wage gap between male and female workers has always
been large--and IS STEADILY INCREASING, despite the Equal
Pay laws. In 1967, women workers (14 years and over) had
median wage and salary incomes of $3,139 compared with
$6,584 for men. The median for full-time year-round women
workers in 1967 was $4,273 compared with $7,298 for men;
in 1968, $4,457 for women, $7,664 for men.

    To dispel some of the myths and prejudices that deny
women employment, Prentice-Hall recently prepared a bulletin advising employers how to avoid violating the 1964
Civil Rights Law, the Equal Pay Law and the proposed
Office of Federal Contract Compliance guidelines on sex
discrimination.

    Prentice-Hall reported a 35% drop-out rate for MALE
college grads during their first three years of employment--
NOT COUNTING THE DRAFT. Not only were girls not dropping
out sooner; they were also not getting married at the
rate expected: less than 25% of 1968 grads had married.
AND, newly-married grads were helping their husbands
through school and were therefore likely to remain in
the work force.

    Colleges surveyed reported that 54.4% of their female
grads were working.
    Northwestern University reported to Prentice-Hall
that starting salaries for women were lower than for men
IN ALL FIELDS.

    Only 40.1% of female grads surveyed were enrolled in
graduate schools. Those who were enrolled had chosen aca-

demic fields leading to a master's or a Ph.D. rather than
professional programs leading to degrees in law, medicine,
or business: 4.5% law school, 2.2% medical school; 2.1%
studying for the MBA.

These figures reflect the discrimination practiced
against girls in the American educational system. Because
of automatic and traditional, but unjustified, assumptions
that women are not interested in education or will not use
it in their lives, the educational system provides less
stimulus for girls, pushes girls into service occupations
and favors boys in scholarships, fellowships and sends boys
to be trained as "leaders" in segregated schools.

Discrimination in education starts with circumstances
such as a family spending more money on the education of
sons and training them for a profession while sending girls
to finishing schools, trade schools or two-year colleges
(even if the girls are brighter); girls marrying early
and working to help put young husbands through graduate
school; and sisters going to work early to help the family
put brothers through medical school, law school, etc. etc.

Girls finish last in the career race because they are
excluded from the finest schools (although a few of the
leading universities such as Yale and Princeton in 1969
began admitting a limited quota of girls). Girls are
further victimized by denial of scholarship aid or fellowships on the dubious grounds that education is wasted on
women because "they'll only get married." In high schools
guidance counselors follow "tradition" and counsel girls
into teaching, secretarial and service occupations. Young
men are sent to medical schools to become doctors; young
girls are sent to hospital training programs to become
nurses. (In toy stores, "Doctor Kits" are for boys--girls
get "Nurse Kits.")

The following figures, showing percentage of degrees
earned by women, are an interesting illustration of the ups
and downs in women's higher education:

	1900	1930	1967	
Bachelor or first professional	19%	40%	40%	
Master's	19%	40%	35%	(note decline)
Doctorates	6%	15%	12%	(note decline)

One cause of the decline in higher degrees for women
was the "Back to the NURSERY Movement" of the late forties
and early fifties, when women gave up higher education for
themselves in order to help returning GI husbands through
school. Women were ejected from factories, corporations
and graduate schools and sent back to the nurseries and
kitchens, creating the baby boom that is threatening our
environment and draining our resources--seriously handi-
capping the women, who were thus deprived of full educational attainment. Much as slave masters used to contend
that slaves were happy down on the plantation because they
had no responsibilities, men insisted that women didn't
want to struggle with careers or higher education, that
all women wanted was husband, family and home.

The patterns begun then are still in operation today.
Girls are still working their husband's way through graduate
school./ Scholarships and fellowships are more available
to boys than to girls (even if the girls have higher IQs
and better grades). Girls who apply for graduate school
are denied a space so that it can be given to a boy to
keep him out of the draft and out of Vietnam.

So the education gap continues and the employment
gap continues.

This trend is inviting serious trouble for the future.
Herbert Bienstock, of the U.S. Bureau of Labor Statistics,
recently reported to the New York City Council on Economic
Education that in the 1965-75 decade, the number of working
women in the city will increase by 121,000 while male workers will decline by about 10,000. Something should be done
immediately to see that every possible opportunity be given
to training women for the role they must play in our technological society.

Labor-saving appliances, food preparation industries
and changing living styles have released women from many
of their traditional duties. Radical changes must be made
in the expected life patterns of women in order to accommodate the rising aspirations and the changing plans of
young women who are looking forward to a life completely
different from that of their mothers.

The young woman of today has little interest in going
quietly mad in her own private ghetto (known to a man as
"home").

More important, it is not even in the interest of
society to continue programming women into narrow pre-
occupation with home and family. Over-population is no
longer a shadow threatening the future but a very real
threat to our resources, our environment and the quality
of life. At the same time that masses of people are
demanding an ever-rising standard of living, we are faced
with the possibility that our resources may not support
even minimum standards for the numbers that unchecked population growth might produce.

How then can we afford to continue channeling women
into the role of child-bearer and carer? Today's woman,
with an ever-lengthening life expectancy, devotes hardly
one-third of her life to rearing her family, even today's
large families. Under changing family structures and
reduced family-size, even less of her life will be given
to bearing and caring.

The life expectancy of a girl born in 1967 is 74 years.
This forces us to recognize that women will need to fill
many years--perhaps as much as three-fourths of their
lives--in occupations other than "mother".

And, since the number of women in the population
exceeds the number of men, millions of women will never
even be married. Further, since the grim fact is that
males have a shorter life expectancy, it is clear that

even women who list their occupation as "housewife" will eventually find themselves alone--unemployed and unneeded-- for a large portion of their lives.

But, completely aside from any problems that discrimi- nation against women causes, simple human dignity demands that women must be educated to their fullest potential and that they must be extended every opportunity to function in society to the limit of their ability. Instead of being cast in sex=stereotyped roles, they must be encouraged to become fully contributing persons. No society can afford to waste the talents of half its members.

In this period of revolutionary fervor, this Age of the Individual, women may not be denied their share of opportunity.

The Congress must see that the doors are thrown wide to the aspirations of one half the human race.

1. In THE MALE ATTITUDE (Little, Brown; Boston, 1966) Charles Ferguson discusses Abigail Adams' request of John Adams that rights for women be included in the constitution. In a letter of April, 1776, she says:
    "In the new code of laws which I suppose it will be necessary for you to make, I desire you would remember the ladies and be more generous and favor- able to them than your ancestors. Do not put such unlimited power in the hands of the husbands. Remem- ber, all men would be tyrants if they could. If par- ticular care and attention is not paid to the ladies, we are determined to foment a rebellion, and will not hold ourselves bound by any laws in which we have no voice of representation."

John answered:
    "As to your extraordinary code of laws, I cannot but laugh. We have been told that our struggle has loosened the bonds of government everywhere; that children and apprentices were disobedient; that schools and colleges were grown turbulent; that Indians slighted their guardians, and negroes grew insolent to their mas- ter. But your letter was the first intimation that another tribe, more numerous and powerful than all the rest, were grown discontented...
    Depend upon it, we know better than to repeal our masculine systems."

Most of us are aware today that children are rebelling and schools and colleges are turbulent; Indians are demanding that old treaties be upheld; "negroes" no longer even have masters---and Abigail's spiritual des- cendants are indeed refusing to hold themselves bound by laws in which they had no voice of representation.

The revolution is here.

The EQUAL RIGHTS AMENDMENT is supported by the following groups:

Alpha Iota Sorority
American Association of Women Ministers
American Federation of Soroptimist Clubs
American Medical Women's Association
American Women's Society of Certified
       Public Accountants
American Society of Women Accountants
American Association of Women Dentists
Congress to Unite Women
General Federation of Women's Clubs
National Association of Colored Women
National Association of Women Lawyers
National Council of Women Chiropractors
National Federation of Business and Professional
       Women's Clubs
National Organization for Women (NOW)
National Women's Party
Osteopathic Women's National Association
Susan B. Anthony Memorial, Inc.
Women's Auxiliary to American Osteopathic Assoc.
Women's Auxiliary to National Chiropractic Assoc.
Women's Circle, Woodmen of the World
Women's International Association of Aeronautics

STATEMENT OF HON. CATHERINE MAY, M.C., ON S.J. RES. 61 AND OTHER LEGISLATION PROPOSING AN AMENDMENT TO THE CONSTITUTION TO PROVIDE EQUALITY SHALL NOT BE DENIED BECAUSE OF SEX

Mr. Chairman: Thank you for holding these hearings.

This equal rights amendment has been before Congress since 1928. This Subcommittee favorably reported identical legislation in 1968 and, in 1964, it was even favorably reported by the full Senate Judiciary Committee. That's as far as it progressed in previous Congresses.

As one who has been a sponsor of legislation proposing an amendment to the Constitution of the United States relative to equal rights for men and women since coming to Congress in 1958, I can only say that it is way past time for action to protect women's rights as citizens and human beings, to eliminate discrimination against women, to recognize women's ability to contribute to the economic, social and political life of this Nation.

The history of this Nation, the first government based upon the proposition that government derive their just powers by consent of the governed, could not have been written without the contributions of women. Still, the road to emancipation was long and heartbreaking.

Then, when the 19th Amendment was ratified, fifty years ago this year, it was hoped that there would follow a general revision of laws and practices so that legal discrimination against women would end. As you well know, though, as recently as 1964 we found it necessary to include in Title VII of the Civil Rights Act a provision to prohibit discrimination on the basis of sex as well as race.

We must make every effort to achieve equal status for women, guaranteeing to them opportunity to choose from a wide range of alternatives in economic and public life. Prevailing laws in both private and public sectors do not, at this point in time, permit women to have such freedom of choice.

No one would argue that there hasn't been substantial improvement in the status of women during this century—but the statistics speak for themselves, and they have all been made available to you—there is sexual discrimination in our society.

Women ask only that they be judged on merit as human beings, not as special and separate classifications. And, let's face it, the now and future United States depends upon the women, their contributions and, yes, their leadership.

The 19th Amendment to our Constitution was ratified on August 26, 1920. Understandably, then, we are anxious that committee and floor action in both Senate and House take place in this Congress, making this 91st Congress historic as the champion of justice and equality for women.

Thank you, Mr. Chairman, for letting me have this opportunity to speak in support of the legislation proposing an amendment to the Constitution to provide that equality of rights shall not be denied because of sex.

STATEMENT BY SENATOR WILLIAM PROXMIRE SUBMITTED TO SENATOR BAYH'S CONSTITUTIONAL AMENDMENTS SUBCOMMITTEE IN SUPPORT OF THE EQUAL RIGHTS FOR WOMEN AMENDMENT

Mr. Chairman, I am pleased to submit testimony to this Subcommittee in support of the Equal Rights for Women Amendment, S.J. Res. 61. Both as a co-sponsor of this Amendment and as a Senator deeply concerned with the full protection of human rights, I feel that the passage of this Resolution by the Senate is of great importance.

This Amendment embraces a fundamental precept set down in the 19th Amendment to the Constitution and reaffirmed in much of the civil rights legislation passed in the last 40 years. This precept, of course, is that women are entitled to and must receive the equal protection and benefits of the law. Nothing could be more basic to Democracy than this vital concept. And yet few ideals have been so difficult to put into practice. This Amendment would finally guarantee long-overdue rights to women on an equal basis with men.

And certainly, this Amendment has sound practical justification as well. The advent of the technical age and higher education have dramatically removed the last vestiges of the belief that women are not capable of performance on a par with men. Today, in all segments of our society, women have shown conclusively that they are able to handle the same responsibilities as men. And they have demonstrated this in every imaginable field—in government, education, industry, science, and the professions.

Thus, there are compelling reasons—both moral and practical—for passage of this Amendment.

In connection with this Amendment, I would also like to mention the United Nations Convention on the Political Rights of Women. This vital international agreement guarantees women the right to vote, to hold public office and exercise all public functions, and to be elegible for election to all publicly elected bodies. Although this important human rights treaty has been signed by 42 nations, it has not as yet been ratified by the Senate.

The provisions of this convention are entirely consonant with our present national laws. And yet, we have failed to act on this treaty, thus creating the false impression we have something to fear from Senate ratification.

I would hope that prompt, affirmative action by the Senate on the Equal Rights Amendment will set the stage for ratification of the Political Rights for Women Convention.

In the field of women's rights, we have failed to move decisively. This unjustified situation must be corrected immediately. Securing equal rights for women is a cause whose advancement is crucial to our society, and is an area in which we cannot and must not tolerate any further delay.

STATEMENT BY COMMISSION ON THE STATUS OF WOMEN, IOWA STATE HOUSE, DES MOINES, IOWA

On April 18, 1970, the Iowa Governor's Commission on the Status of Women endoresd the proposed amendment to the Constitution of the United States relative to equal rights under the law for men and women. The Commission voted to prepare this statement for inclusion in the record of your public hearings.

By way of background on the Commission, in September of 1969 Governor Robert D. Ray asked the heads of all women's organizations in the State of Iowa to make recommendations of women they believed to be qualified to discuss and to advance the status of women. From these many recommendations, the Governor selected 24 women, plus eight men, from all parts of the State to serve for a one-year term on the Commission.

The proposed amendment under consideration by your Sub-committee is co-sponsored by Congress Fred Schwengel and Senator Harold E. Hughes of

Iowa. The Commission joins these members of Congress in urging that the Congress adopt the amendment and submit it in for approval by three-fourths of the States.

Failure to pass the equal rights amendment acts to deter equal rights for women, and for men as well, and permits individual states to keep laws on their books that are discriminatory because of sex.

Theoretically, women should already be entitled to "equal protection" under the 14th Amendment to the Constitution. and to "due process" under the 5th Amendment. But in actual fact the Supreme Court has never rendered a decision holding that laws classifying persons on the basis of sex are unreasonable and unconstitutional.

Until we define the legal status of women on the constitutional level, we shall have no means of preventing its varying interpretation from state to state. And until then, we will have no means of wiping out the many vestiges of ancient rules of law that treat women as inferiors.

When the Constitution was written, women were not considered persons under the old English common law. The Constitution uses words such as "people" "persons" "citizens", but at that time these words did not include women. It was not until 1920 that women's suffrage became a matter of law throughout the United States. The equal rights amendment has been before the Congress since the 1920's, but has not been acted upon.

Many states have labor restrictions; women are prevented from working overtime and enjoying the high overtime pay men get; women are restricted from lifting weights in excess of a specified weight. These restrictions, while purporting to protect women, actually result in discrimination against women in certain jobs. Such "protective" restrictions hinder women in their competition with men for supervisory, technical, and professional job opportunities.

In some states, penalties for the exact same crime are higher for women.

Take the domicile law. In many states, if a woman chooses not to live where her husband decides, he has grounds for divorce. A woman should have equal rights in the decision.

Men would benefit from the amendment because it would mean that, in divorce cases, men would not be discriminated against in custody of the children; it would also give them a fairer shake in alimony. Awarding alimony is called for when wives are divorced late in life and have no equality in the labor market, but it is not fair in many other situations.

An example of discrimination in the professional world is the dirth of women principals and superintendents in our school systems. The administrative position in education used to be filled almost entirely by women. But then the pay scale changed and men flocked into the profession.

The gap between the earnings of men and women workers is widening. In 1955, women's median wage or salary income for the year was 63.9% of men's; women's median being $2,719 and men's $4,252.

According to the latest figures reported by the Women's Bureau of the United States Department of Labor, the median male wage earner in 1968 made $7,664 and the median woman made only 58.2% of that, or $4,457. The wage study based on Bureau of the Census figures dealt only with full-time workers.

College students who graduate this June will find that a man can make $1,032 more annually in accounting than a woman beginner. In Liberal Arts, he will have a lead of $804; in Chemistry a lead of $508; in Engineering, $336; in mathematics or statistics, $324.

The proposed amendment, would ensure equal pay-rate for the job without regard to sex, in the factory—in the school—in the office—in the store—and in all other places where men and women perform work of comparable character.

The unequal rights which are today more obvious than ever had their beginnings in 1940's when American women went to work in every job imaginable because so many men were serving in World War II. Women were desperately needed and they proved themselves beyond anyone's anticipation, then stepped aside when the men returned. They had risen to the challenge and were forever after dissatisfied with just staying home.

Many women are talented, educated and bored. They are no longer needed all day long by their children or to keep house, and many are not content to twiddle their thumbs or take the bridge party routine. Discrimination, especially in the business world, prevents these women from leading a happy and satisfactory life.

Women in the business world should be looked upon, not just as women trying to do something, but as trained and qualified persons. What difference does it make if you're a man or woman, if you can do the job? If women were meant to be maternity machines, they would not have been given minds.

Some states have taken steps to eliminate inequality under the law for men and women. On July 1, 1970, a new Iowa law will go into effect that amends the Iowa Civil Rights Act to make discrimination on the basis of sex unlawful. The ban on discrimination by sex extends to employment, housing and public accommodations. Women, who feel they are discriminated against in these areas because they are women, may now take their case to the Iowa Civil Rights Commission for ajudication.

Some states have varying laws regarding equality under the law. Other states have no laws. Only through the enactment of this proposed Constitutional Amendment can women everywhere be assured of equality under the law. Our Commission strongly urges its adoption by the Congress and its submission to the several states.

Respectfully submitted,

(MRS.) BETTY J. DURDEN,
Chairman, Governor's Commission on the Status of Women.

OTHER MEMBERS OF THE COMMISSION

Mrs. Dorothy M. Goettsch, Davenport (Vice-Chairman).
Mrs. Linda Archibald, Des Moines (Secretary).
Ralph R. Brown, Davenport.
Mrs. Shirley Clark, Waukon.
Mrs. Jacqueline Day, Des Moines.
Mrs. John Dayhoff, Cedar Rapids.
Mrs. Beverly Everett, New Sharon.
Mrs. Georgia Gohring, Marshalltown.
Mrs. Phyllis M. Henderson, Des Moines.
Honorable Edgar Holden, Davenport.
Dr. Mavis L. Holmes, Cedar Falls.
Mrs. Ruth S. Hoover, Newton.
Miss Jeannie Hoosman, Cedar Falls.
Mrs. Leone K. Hopson, Des Moines.
Senator Ernest Kosek, Cedar Rapids.
Miss Hazel O. Larson, Des Moines.
Dr. Helen R. LeBaron, Ames.
Dr. Edwin C. Lewis, Ames.
Senator J. Henry Luckens, LeMars, Iowa.
Mr. George Lundberg, Des Moines.
Honorable Floyd Millen, Farmington.
Miss Cheryl A. Miller, Wellman.
Mrs. Evelyn M. Oujiri, Cedar Rapids.
Mrs. Betty M. Page, Waterloo.
Mrs. Vera N. Pedersen, Sioux City.
Miss Helen Reich, Iowa City.
Sister Madeleine Marie Schmidt, Ottumwa.
Robert F. Tyson, Des Moines.
Mrs. Evelyn Villines, Des Moines.
Mrs. Hilda Weingart, Des Moines.
Mrs. Cristine Wittgraf, Des Moines.

Statement of

Mrs. Walter Varney Magee
President
General Federation of Women's Clubs

Submitted to the
Subcommittee on Constitutional Amendments
Judiciary Committee
United States Senate
Washington, D. C.

May 6, 1970

During your consideration of the proposal to amend the Constitution of the United States in order to guarantee to women the same rights as those enjoyed by men and the same responsibilities as those borne by men, we would appreciate your considering the views of the General Federation of Women's Clubs, which is the largest organization of women in the world.

We are not an organization of "militants" nor are we in any way connected with the so-called "women's liberation movement". We urge ratification of the Equal Rights Amendment only because it would achieve what is fair. It is truly unfortunate that we must resort to amending the Constitution to secure equality - when those rights ought to be as automatic for women as they are for men. Surely, women, like men who are born or naturalized in the United States, are citizens and are governed by the same laws. The Constitution does not specifically exclude women. If it did, it would probably be easier to correct it. But, as it is, we are attempting to secure rights which ought to be ours without asking. We are persons, we are citizens, we are taxpayers, we vote and we are responsible but we are not "legally" considered "equal" to the male in numerous ways of which you need not be reminded. This is not fair and this is what we seek to change. We are not seeking special favors. We seek only equal treatment for men and women and, in many instances, an Equal Rights Amendment would be of particular benefit to men.

You will note that we readily acknowledge and accept the fact that along with the rights must come the responsibilities. This, too, is only fair.

The Resolution adopted in 1944 by the General Federation of Women's Clubs which expresses our support of the Equal Rights Amendment says only that. It does not mention all the discriminations on account of sex and the injustices which would be corrected by ratification of an Equal Rights Amendment. To correct them all on a piecemeal basis, if that were possible, would be a formidable undertaking indeed - and though an Equal Rights Amendment would not correct them all overnight, the task would be greatly lightened. Reduced to the very basics, what is being sought through an Equal Rights Amendment is that men and women be considered as persons - and without regard to whether they are male or female. We urge you to act favorably on the proposal to amend the Constitution of the United States so that equality of status for women will be guaranteed. Thank you for giving consideration to our views.

TESTIMONY OF THE NATIONAL ORGANIZATION FOR WOMEN, MAY 5, 1970, IN SUPPORT OF THE EQUAL RIGHTS AMENDMENT TO THE U.S. CONSTITUTION

(By Jean Witter, Chairman, Equal Rights Amendment Committee, National Organization for Women)

INTRODUCTION

The U.S. Congress finds itself increasingly in the position of having to answer the question, "Why are you still beating your wife?" Further delay in the passage of the Equal Rights Amendment is indefensible. To deny Constitutional Equality to over half the U.S. population in 1970, in an era when people are becoming increasingly aware of human rights and human dignity, is incomprehensible, inexcusable, and will in fact become tantamount to political suicide before long.

Only the fact that the Equal Rights Amendment has been "the best kept secret of the 20th century" has allowed Congressmen to return to their seats session after session, while they have denied our women Constitutional Equality and the full recognition as first class citizens. The fact that Senate hearings are being held in May, when six months ago there were more than enough sponsors to pass the amendment insults every woman voter in the country. Since 1970 is an election year Congress will probably adjourn in early August and little action will occur after mid-July. Effectively, there are only two short months for the passage of the Equal Rights Amendment. One cannot help but to surmise that the members of Congress expect the Amendment to die a quiet death and to be quietly resurrected to start from scratch again in the new Congress in 1971. American women have better things to do with their time, even if Congress appears not to.

The Equal Rights Amendment will not die a quiet death in 1970! If the Equal Rights Amendment is not passed in 1970, its ghost will stalk the voting polls in November! If the Amendment is not passed in 1970, American women must de-seat the present Congress and replace them with legislators who are responsive to the electorate.

STATUS OF WOMEN COUNCIL FAVORS THE AMENDMENT

I do not intend to repeat the arguments so ably presented in the March 1970 Memorandum, "The Proposed Equal Rights Amendment to the U.S. Constitution" prepared by the study group on equal legal rights for the Citizen's Advisory Council on the Status of Women.[1] The Council as you know in Feb. 1970 declared in favor of the Equal Rights Amendment. [A copy of this later memorandum appears in the hearing record in connection with the testimony of Mrs. Gutwillig.]

Rather than to repeat the material presented by the Council, I intend to build onto the material and arguments presented in the Council's thorough study.

DISCRIMINATORY LAWS

It is well-known that many laws discriminate on the basis of sex. It has not not been emphasized, however, that nearly every form of discriminatory law has been either repealed or never existed in some states.

Some states do have:

Separate legal domicile for either spouse.
Inheritance laws that are identical for both men and women.
The same lower limit to the marriage age for both sexes.
The same jury duty obligations for both men and women.
Child support laws applying equally to both parents.
Property laws that apply equally for men and women.
Joint guardianship of children.
Labor standards that apply equally to men and women.

. . . and so on, in nearly every area of discriminatory law.

The fact that a condition of non-discrimination on account of sex does exist in some states in nearly every area of disputable legislation, does prove that the system of sex discrimination under the law is not essential and that people living under the equal situation find that situation not a problem and not a hardship. The argument that the Equal Rights Amendment should not be passed because of the many changes that would be required in state laws is a poor one; on the contrary, the Equal Rights Amendment may be of great benefit to the states in helping them to up-date their laws, and encouraging more uniformity in family law from state to state.

PROTECTIVE LEGISLATION

The Equal Rights Amendment was once opposed by some groups because it was a threat to protective legislation, or protective labor laws for women. In recent years protective legislation has proven to be restrictive legislation. In the past five years 17 states have repealed all or part of their protective laws. Delaware, for example, repealed its protective labor laws in 1965 with no ill effects.

Ohio has announced recently that it will no longer enforce the protective labor laws since they are in conflict with Title VII of the Civil Rights Act of 1964.

In Pennsylvania the new Sex Amendment to the Pa. Human Relations Act has, by the statement of Pennsylvania's Attorney General, impliedly repealed the Pa. Protective Labor Laws.[2] The staff and machinery for the enforcement of these laws no longer exists. There have been no complaints.

Protective labor laws can no longer stand in the way of the passage of the Equal Rights Amendment; they are on the way out of existence even without the Amendment. The strict enforcement of Title VII of the Civil Rights Act of 1964 would eventually supersede the protective labor laws.

Similarly, the strict enforcement of Title VII would supersede many other state laws that may discriminate in employment situations.

STOP DISCRIMINATORY LAWS

When the Equal Rights Amendment is a part of the U.S. Constitution, laws that discriminate on the basis of sex will not be passed since they would be unconstitutional. The Amendment will thus protect both men and woman from injustice on account of their sex.

THE OLD ENGLISH COMMON LAW V. MODERN COMMON LAW

When our U.S. Constitution was written in 1787, the Old English Common Law was then in use in the English speaking world, including our thirteen colonies. Under the Old English common law, women were not regarded as persons under the law; women were regarded as chattel, as property. Consequently, when a legal document or constitution contained words such as people or person, these words did not mean women and men, but men only.

Bearing in mind that words like people and person did not originally mean women in a legal document, such as a constitution, if we read again our Constitution looking particularly for changes which were made to give our women coverage under the Constitution, we find only one such change; namely, our 19th Amendment gave our women the right to vote. Women are covered by our U.S. Constitution for three minutes twice a year in the voting booth. Other than this our women are covered by our State laws and by a few specific Federal laws, but not by the U.S. Constitution. Only our men have the full protection of the U.S. Constitution. The Equal Rights Amendment is needed to rectify this situation—and the sooner, the better!

With the advent of woman suffrage, state constitutions have gradually come to be interpreted that words such as person and people do mean both men and women. In other words, under the present common law, state constitutions are gradually being interpreted as protecting both sexes equally. Why then, hasn't the U.S. Constitution gradually come to include both sexes under the common law? If it were not for the 10th Amendment, this probably would happen. The 10th Amendment states: "The powers not delegated to the U.S. by the Constitution" . . . "the reserves to the States" . . . "or to the people."

Therefore, when women are admitted into a state legislature, it is because words like citizen or person in the state constitution are being interpreted by the common law to include women. The common law is allowing the legal meaning of such words to change to mean both men and women in state law.

However, when women were admitted into Congress, it was not because the word person in the U.S. Constitution was being interpreted by the common law to include women. It was because the method of selecting state representatives to Congress is determined by the states and is a matter of States' Rights as protected by the 10th Amendment, a power reserved to the States. Not to admit Jeannette Rankin, the first woman Representative, in 1917 as the Representative from Montana, would have been an abridgement of States' Rights as protected by the 10th Amendment.

Since all laws regarding women were originally regarded as being in the realm of "powers reserved to the States," a constitutional amendment is needed in order to clearly give to U.S. women the equal protection of the U.S. Constitution. The Equal Rights Amendment is needed because the 10th Amendment cannot allow this change in intepretation of the U.S. Constitution to come about by common law interpretation. Neither can it be denied that such a basic right as equality under the law between the sexes, should be clearly spelled out in the words of a Constitutional Amendment.

SOME WOMEN DID NOT WANT SUFFRAGE

"Equality of rights under the law" for both men and women in the form of the Equal Rights Amendment is an essential step, but full enforcement may take up to a century. Certainly, not every eligible woman registered to vote after the passage of the 19th Amendment, and some of our older women have never considered voting. In recent elections, however, the number of women who voted exceeded the number of men who voted; and the percentage of college educated female voters exceeded the percentage of college educated male voters.[3] The fact that some women were not ready to accept suffrage at the time of the passage of the 19th Amendment was fortunately not permitted to stand in the way of giving suffrage to their daughters.

Similarly, let us now not be blinded from taking this essential step in the full emancipation of U.S. women by the fact that some women are not yet ready or anxious for full equality. We must not continue to deny our daughters equal opportunity. Our daughters must have Constitutional Equality even if many older women and men are not able to accept immediately all of the implications and manifestations of Constitutional Equality for women.

THREE ROUTES TO CONSTITUTIONAL EQUALITY

U.S. women could possibly achieve Constitutional Equality by two routes in addition to the route of the Equal Rights Amendment. Neither of the other two methods would assure the immutable protection to both men and women that will be assured by the Equal Rights Amendment.

THE SUPREME COURT ROUTE

Women could eventually achieve Constitutional Equality by Supreme Court decision. If the Supreme Court ruled that several sex discrimination laws were unconstitutional according to the 14th Amendment, women would then have the "equal protection of the law."[4] However, there is no assurance that the next Supreme Court decision would not reverse the previous decisions, thereby again denying Constitutional Equality to our women again. The Supreme Court in one case, Adkins v. Children's Hospital, 261 U.S. 525 (1923), held an act of Congress fixing minimum wage standards for women to be unconstitutional.[5] The doctrine expressed in the Adkins case was soon reversed by subsequent Supreme Court rulings.[6] All other Supreme Court rulings before and after the Adkins case have held that differences in the law based on sex are not unreasonable and therefore, constitutional.

It may be a long, arduous and expensive route for women to achieve Constitutional equality by Supreme Court interpretation of the 14th Amendment. Since it was not the original intent of Congress that women should have the "equal protection of the laws" when the 14th Amendment was passed in 1868, the Supreme Court could justify excluding women from coverage under the 14th Amendment indefinitely. It is after all the function of the Supreme Court to interpret the Constitution and its amendments according to the original intent of Congress and not to change the Constitution or its intent. The Constitution states in Article I: "ALL legislative Powers herein granted shall be vested in a Congress of the U.S." It is therefore the function of the Congress, and not of the Supreme Court, to change the law of the land. The U.S. Congress should not abdicate its legislative power to the Supreme Court by taking the stand the Supreme Court should change the original meaning of the 14th Amendment to include women. It is clearly the responsibility of the Congress under the Constitution to pass the Equal Rights Amendment; men and women must have the equal protection of the Constitution, and it is the duty of the Congress to bring this about by exercise of its Constitutionally ensured legislative powers.

Further, the Constitution in Article V states: "The Congress, whenever two-thirds of both Houses shall deem it necessary, shall propose Amendments to this Constitution." Since 75 Senators are sponsors for the Equal Rights Amendment, far more than two-thirds of the Senate, there would appear to be a clear mandate from the Constitution for the immediate passage of the Equal Rights Amendment, without change, by the U.S. Senate.

The U.S. Constitution as a Model for the World.—The Constitution of the U.S. has long been considered a model document; it has been read and studied by political science students throughout the world. To not include within the Constitution or its Amendments the provision for equality of rights under the law regardless of sex, would be a serious omission of a right which is basic to every citizen. Such a basic right should not be left to the Supreme Court to take away as the times change. The U.S. Constitution is incomplete as a model document without the Equal Rights Amendment.

"Appropriate Legislation" Route.—Constitutional Equality for women could also be accomplished by "appropriate legislation" under the 14th Amendment, Section 5.[7] Recently, such "appropriate legislation" was passed to reduce the voting age to 18 (See H. R. 4249).[8] But the best age at which citizens should start voting may change over the centuries, and is not the subject for a constitutional amendment, although an amendment was thought by some to be necessary. The rights guaranteed in the Equal Rights Amendment are basic human rights and should be clearly and unequivocally stated as part of the U.S. Constitution.

I have considered having a bill introduced in Congress to clearly extend "the equal protection of the law" in the 14th Amendment to cover both men and women, specifically stating that sex shall not be considered a reasonable ground for discrimination under the law. Such a bill is provided for in the 14th Amendment, Section 5: "this amendment may be enforced by appropriate legislation."

Such a bill could pass with only a majority vote in each House. It would certainly be quicker than a constitutional amendment and could possibly accomplish the purpose. However, a similar bill could repeal or qualify the bill at a later date. And of course, the Supreme Court may eventually declare the law unconstitutional in that it was not the original intent of the 14th Amendment to give women "the equal protection of the laws." While I believe such a bill should be considered as a temporary measure to extend the 14th Amendment to women immediately, the Equal Rights Amendment must become a part of our Constitution to protect both men and women for all time.

THE DRAFT FOR WOMEN

Does the Equal Rights Amendment imply that women should be subject to the draft or compulsory military service as well as men? Many older and middle aged people in the U.S. seem much against the draft for women, mostly I believe, because it was something they never considered for themselves when they were draft age. It is interesting that the young people who are draft age are very open to the idea of drafting women. They realize that women in some countries are already subject to military service and do serve in the armed forces on the same basis as men.

Many of those working for women's rights, myself included, very much oppose war as a way of solving international problems. As an individual, I favor a well-funded Dept. of Peace and a national peace program equivalent in scope and intensity to our present defense and space programs. But in spite of such aspirations, we must recognize that equality of responsibility does imply that as long as men are being drafted, women should be drafted as well.

However, a valid question can be raised as to whether women do indeed have any obligation to serve in the armed forces. Since women in practice have been denied access to policy-making position, they have not been involved in the decisions leading to military involvement. One can argue that women, as a group, have no responsibility to risk their lives to carry out policy decisions from which they as a group are barred. This is a valid point.

However, the same argument can be made on the basis of age; that is, the young should not be asked to implement the decisions of the old. Perhaps it is equally unfair, and even uncivilized, to draft the young men to carry out the military decisions of the old men. The fact remains that we have always done this, and we are still doing it today. The case can be made that the draft is just as unfair to young men as it would be to young women. Therefore, we must consider drafting women as long as we draft anyone.

While certainly the disadvantages of being subject to the draft outweigh the advantages, it should be noted that there are certain advantages. Women who are not drafted do not share the following benefits:

Valuable in-service training (even for high school drop-outs).
Correction of physical problems.
Opportunity to travel.
Learning to live and cooperate with others.
Opportunity to learn leadership.
Additional benefits after discharge from service:
Educational opportunities, scholarships.
Veterans bonuses.
Veterans loans.
Continuation of G.I. Insurance.
Medical treatment in V.A. hospitals.
Veterans preference in federal and state employment:
Civil Service lists.
Extra points on Civil Service tests.
Much less likely to lose government job during Reduction-In-Force.
Life-long respect due to those who have served the nation.
Women who are not drafted share neither the disadvantages or the benefits.

CONGRESS HAS THE POWER TO DRAFT WOMEN NOW

It should be emphasized that not passing the Equal Rights Amendment will not ensure that women will not be drafted in the future. Congress already has the power to include women in any conscription and the Equal Rights Amendment would not affect the power of Congress.[11] The Equal Rights Amendment, however, would imply that women would be required to register for military service and would be called for induction on the same basis as men.

THE EFFECT OF DRAFTING WOMEN

A number of countries already do draft women.[12] Women are drafted and serve in the armed forces on the same basis as men in Israel, Cuba, Red China. In countries where women do serve in the armed forces on the same basis as men, the status of women is very high. The young women in Israel are not aware of a "women problem"—they are completely equal with men.[12]

Of course, just as men are exempt from the draft for reasons of health or responsibility, many women would also be exempt for like reasons.

On the whole the advantages to American women because of being subject to the draft are greater than the disadvantages. If American women are to step into their rightful place in the nation, they must accept full responsibility as well as rights. At this point in history, a part of full responsibility includes the draft.[9, 10]

If some do object to people, male or female, being drafted, then it is up to those of us who object to the draft to change the world so that the draft can become a part of our primitive history. Until that time, women and men must share equal responsibility in being subjected to the draft.

WOMEN CANNOT BE DENIED CONSTITUTIONAL EQUALITY BECAUSE THEY BEAR THE BURDEN OF REPRODUCTION

In the year 1900 to speak of "equality of rights under the law" for women would have been a purely academic, if not meaningless, consideration because women were in no position to demand equality of rights, and no group has ever received rights without first demanding them. Most women were involved almost continuously in the reproductive processes throughout their adult years, until shortly before their death—on the average at the age of 48 years.

In 1970 only 40% of U.S. women have one or more children under age eighteen, and of these mothers nearly 10% are also the head of a house hold.[18] Who is to say that these women and U.S. women of past generations should not share the "equal protection of the laws" under our Constitution? Who is to say that the bearing of rifles in the past by our men was more important to the nation than the bearing of children? And who is to say that the men of our nation deserved full Constitutional protection for carrying their share of the burdens, but the women did not? It is a grave miscarriage of justice that has denied U.S. women Constitutional Equality until 1970! Certainly women are human beings and deserve to be accorded equal treatment under the law. Women cannot be denied Constitutional Equality because they bear the burden of reproduction!

In 1970 60% of U.S. women do not have a child under age eighteen.[13] To deny equal opportunity to 60% of U.S. women who do not have a child under 18 years of age, because of biological sex differences is senseless, as well as unconscionable. Indeed, we must recognize motherhood as a temporary condition and encourage our young mothers to realize that they can expect to do other things in addition to being a parent, just as men do.

INTERNATIONAL IMPLICATIONS

Women in Pakistan have Constitutional Equality.[16] Many nations of the world have Constitutional Equality for their women. It is internationally embarrassing that U.S. purports to be a leader among nations and yet continues to deny Constitutional Equality to over half of its citizens.

Senator Eugene McCarthy, recent presidential candidate and chief sponsor of the Equal Rights Amendment, found it necessary to vote against the U.N. Convention on the Political Rights of Women in 1967.[14, 15] Senator McCarthy, in so voting, recognized that it would be inconsistent for the U.S. to ratify the U.N. Convention on the Political Rights for Women because U.S. women have only the right to vote under the U.S. Constitution (the right to vote is covered in Article I of the U.N. Convention).

While the ratification by the Senate of the U.N. Convention would not give full Constitutional Equality to U.S. women, it would extend Federal coverage into areas now covered only by State law, and for this reason may even be unconstitutional. Quoting from the U.N. Convention on the Political Rights for Women:

"Article II. Women shall be eligible for election to all publicly elected bodies, established by national law, on equal terms with men, and without discrimination.

"Article III. Women shall be entitled to hold public office and to exercise all public functions, established by national law, on equal terms with men, without discrimination."

Ratification of a U.N. Convention has the force of an international treaty and under the Constitution would become the law of the land. Ratification of the U.N. Convention on the Political Rights for Women would not be just a statement that U.S. favors rights for women in other countries, but since our own women have only the right to vote under the U.S. Constitution, it would extend the rights of U.S. women under Federal law into the two areas covered by Article II and Article III, which are now covered for women only by State law.

Until the Equal Rights Amendment is passed, the U.N. Convention on the Political Rights for Women cannot be passed; to do so would be to infringe on States rights as guaranteed by the 10th Amendment; namely, that "the powers not delegated to the U.S. by the Constitution" . . . "are reserved to the States" . . . "or to the people."

If the U.S. is to retain its place of leadership among the nations, the Equal Rights Amendment must be passed. The Equal Rights Amendment as part of the U.S. Constitution would then delegate certain powers to the U.S. (that were formerly reserved to the States), and subsequently the ratification of the U.N. Convention on the Political Rights for Women would then be possible under this new constitutional amendment.

WORLD CRISIS

The problems of the world today that must be solved *soon* are of such a magnitude that we cannot continue to waste our human talent. If we do not encourage our women to fully utilize their talents to help to solve the critical problems of the world today, none of us may survive to criticize our present poor judgment or prejudice. The clear statement of Constitutional Equality for U.S. women in an amendment to the U.S. Constitution can serve as a mandate and a challenge to our women. The Equal Rights Amendment is needed NOW! Please act with all due haste.

The Amendment must pass both Houses in the next two months or it will die again. The U.S. Congress cannot afford to take upon themselves the responsi-

246

bility of further penalizing the nation by continuing to discourage our women at this time; a time when the population explosion is already a reality. At a time when over 10 million people in the world die yearly from starvation, our women must be encouraged to participate in the mainstream; they must have reason to believe that there are other rewarding endeavours for women besides producing a large family.[17]

For the U.S. Congress to kill the Equal Rights Amendment for the 24th time would be a crime not only against the 51% of the population who are women, but against the survival and well-being of the nation as a whole.

FOOTNOTES

1. Citizen's Advisory Council on the Status of Women, "The Proposed Equal Rights Amendment to the U.S. Constitution, A. Memorandum," March 1970
2. Pa. Manufacturers Assn., Legislative Bulletin, No. 31, Harrisburg, Pa., Nov. 28, 1969
3. U.S. Dept. of Commerce, "Voter Participation in the National Election Nov. 1964," Series P–20, No. 143, Oct. 25, 1965
   1966 Supplement, Series P–20, No. 160, Feb. 2, 1967
4. President's Commission on the Status of Women, AMERICAN WOMEN, 1963
5. ENCYCLOPEDIA BRITANICA, "Women, Legal Position of," 1945
6. President's Commission on the Status of Women, REPORT OF THE COMMITTEE ON CIVIL AND POLITICAL RIGHTS, GPO, 1963
7. N. Y. Times, "Lowering Voting Age Is an Idea Whose Time Has Come," p. 12, March 29, 1970
8. 91st Congress, 2nd Sess., H. R. 4249, "Voting Rights Act Amendments of 1970," Title III, passed by the House, Dec. 11, 1969, passed by the Senate, April 2, 1970
9. Hughes, Judge Sarah T., "Should Women Be Left Behind?", National Business Woman, Oct. 1969
10. Mead, Margaret, "The Case for Drafting All Boys—and Girls," Redbook Magazine, Sept. 1966
11. National Federation of Business and Professional Women, "Some Questions and Answers on Equal Rights Amendment," Nov. 1968
12. Borgese, Elisabeth Mann, ASCENT OF WOMAN, Braziller, N.Y., 1963
13. U.S. Dept. of Commerce, STATISTICAL ABSTRACT OF THE U.S., 1968
14. 90th Cong., 1st Sess., Senate Foreign Relations Committee, "Hearings on Human Rights Conventions," 1967
15. Swayzee, Elizabeth N., "Action Needed in Human Rights Year," THE BRIDGE, Jan. 1968 (?)
16. Senate Reports, most recent, 87th Cong., 2nd Sess., Rept. No. 2192, 1962
17. Ehrlich, Paul R., THE POPULATION BOMB, Ballantine Books, N.Y., 1968

Statement of Dr. Bernice Sandler †

before the

Senate Judiciary Committee

Subcommittee on Constitutional Amendments

May 6, 1970

Re: S.J. Res. 61 (Equal Rights Amendment)

I am Dr. Bernice Sandler of the Women's Equity Action League* (WEAL), where I

----

*The Women's Equity Action League was incorporated in 1968 in Ohio to promote greater economic progress on the part of American women and to seek solutions to economic, educational, tax, and employment problems affecting women. There are members in more than thirty states. National headquarters are at 22414 Fairlawn Circle, Fairview Park, Ohio 44126. Information regarding Federal contract compliance should be addressed to Dr. B. Sandler, 10700 Lockridge Drive, Silver Spring, Md. 20901.

†EDITOR'S NOTE: This article was retyped for clarity.

am Chairman of the Action Committee for Federal Contract Compliance in Education.
I am also a psychologist with the Department of Health, Education and Welfare,
and a Visiting Lecturer in the Department of Counseling and Personnel Services
at the University of Maryland.

I come before this distinguished committee on behalf of S.J. Res. 61, the Equal
Rights Amendment. You have already heard, and will be hearing from many witnesses who address themselves to many aspects of this question. I will limit
my testimony to the crucial area of sex discrimination in our universities and colleges, and to how the Equal Rights Amendment will begin to alleviate some of
the dreadful injustices suffered by American women on the campus.

Since January 31, 1970, formal charges of sex discrimination under Executive
Order 11246 as amended, have been filed against 43 universities and colleges.
The Women's Equity Action League (WEAL) initiated 41 of these formal complaints.
This Executive Order forbids Federal contractors from discriminating against race,
creed, color, national origin, and sex. According to the National Science Foundation report entitled "Federal Support to Universities and Colleges, Fiscal Year
1968," universities and colleges receive about 3.3 billion dollars of Federal
contracts per year. As Federal contractors, universities and colleges are subject to the provisions of the Order.

In its initial complaint, WEAL charged an industry-wide pattern of sex discrimination and asked for a class action and compliance review of all universities
and colleges holding Federal contracts. At that time WEAL submitted to the
Secretary of Labor, George P. Shultz, more than 80 pages of documents sub-
stantiating its charges of sex discrimination in the academic community.

Half of the brightest people in our country -- half of the most talented
people with the potential for the highest intellectual endeavor are women.
Yet these gifted women will find it very difficult to obtain the same kind
of quality education that is so readily available to their brothers. These
women will encounter discrimination after discrimination -- not once, not
twice but time after time in the very academic institutions which claim to
preach the tenets of democracy and fair play. The women will face discrimination in admission where they will encounter both official and unofficial
quotas; they will face discrimination when they apply for scholarships and
financial assistance. When they graduate, their own university will discriminate against them in helping them find jobs. They will be discriminated

against in hiring for the faculty. If hired at all, they will be promoted far more slowly than their male counterparts, and they will most likely receive far less money than their colleagues of the other sex.

In a speech on the floor of the House of Representatives on March 9, 1970, Congresswoman Martha W. Griffiths stated:

> Yet most of these institutions discriminate outrageously against half of our citizens -- women. They neglect and disregard their potential talent. They place innumerable obstacles and hurdles in the way of academic women. Is our nation so rich in talent that we can afford to have our universities penalize the aspirations of half of our population? Should the Federal Government close its eyes to such unjust discrimination and continue to provide the billions of dollars that help to support those unjust practices?

The position of women in higher education has been worsening; women are slowly being pushed out of the university world. For example, in 1870, women were one-third of the faculty in our nation's institutions of higher learning. A hundred years later, women hold less than one-fourth of the positions. In the prestigious Big Ten universities they hold 10% or less of the faculty positions. The proportion of women graduate students is less now than it was in 1930. The University of Chicago, for example, has a lower proportion of women on its faculty now than it did in 1899.

Women are 22% of the graduate students in the Graduate School of Arts and Sciences at Harvard University. Of the 411 tenured professors at the Graduate School of Arts and Sciences at Harvard University, not one is a woman. Let me repeat that. Of the 411 tenured professors at the Graduate School of Arts and Sciences at Harvard University, the number of women is: ZERO. At the University of Connecticut, a state supported institution, women are 33% of the instructors but only 4.8% of the full professors. On the University of Massachusetts campus at Boston, also a state-supported institution, there are 65 women faculty but only 2 of those have tenure.

Even when women are hired they generally remain at the bottom of the academic hierarchy. The higher the rank, the lower the percentage of women. In a typical study of 188 major departments of sociology, Dr. Alice Rossi, a noted sociologist at Goucher College found that women accounted for:

30% of the doctoral candidates	9% of the associate professors
27% of the full-time instructors	4% of the full professors
14% of the assistant professors	less than 1% of the departmental chairmen

Figures like these cross my desk almost daily; they are by no means unusual. They can readily be duplicated in most departments and most universities throughout the country merely by reading the college catalogue. In
many places, the figures are worse, for in some departments and institutions
women are simply not hired at all.

One typical rationale -- excuse, if you will -- for justification of figures
such as these appears as: "Isn't the simple truth that there just aren't
enough qualified women to fill these posts?" The so-called "shortage of
qualified women" is an academic myth. A higher percentage of women with
doctorates go into college teaching than do men with doctorates. Let me
give you some examples of the so-called shortage of qualified women.
Columbia University awards 24% of its doctorates to women, but only 2% of
it's tenured graduate faculty are women. Using a particular field as an
example, nationally women earn 23% of the doctorates in psychology. At
Rutgers, the State University of New Jersey, only 9% of the graduate faculty
in psychology are women. At the University of Maryland Dept. of Psychology,
another state-supported institution, there are only 2 women on a faculty of
35 -- less than 6%. At the University of California at Berkeley, the percentage
of women in the Dept. of Psychology is zero; not one of the 42 faculty members
is female. The same is true at Columbia University; there are simply no women
"qualified" to teach there, despite the fact that the Dept. of Psychology at
Columbia grants 36% of its doctorates to women. Apparently women are somehow
qualified to earn doctoral degrees but are not considered "qualified" to teach
once they have earned these degrees. How does one explain such large discrepancies?
Indeed, it would be more accurate to ask how the universities and colleges of the
United States can explain these discrepancies.

Where do these women go, for it is clear that very few of them will teach
in the major universities and colleges. Do they marry and give up their
careers? This is another academic myth: 90% of the women with doctorates
are working. Many end up teaching on the faculty of junior colleges and
community colleges where they comprise about 40% of the faculty, and where
the pay, status, and research opportunities are substantially less than in
the major universities. I have appended to this report a selected list of
various academic disciplines and the percentages of doctorates awarded to
women. In virtually every major institution the percentage of women on
the faculty is far below the percentage expected on the basis of the number

of doctorates awarded in particular fields.

Undoubtedly the percentage of degrees awarded to women would still be higher if the discriminations based on sex were eliminated. Official and unofficial quota systems for women are widespread. Just a few weeks ago WEAL filed against the University of North Carolina - a publicly supported institution -- which states quite openly in a publication by the Office of Undergraduate Admissions: "admission of women on the freshman level will be restricted to those who are especially well-qualified." And indeed, in the freshman class at the General College at the University of North Carolina, for this current year, there are 1893 men, and only 426 women. Girls need higher grades for admission to many colleges and universities. Unofficial quotas exist in many graduate and professional schools. The percentage of women with M.D. degrees is the same today as it was 50 years ago when women first won the right to vote. In the Soviet Union 75% of the physicians are women; in our country it is barely 7%.

Women are denied admission to graduate and professional training programs because of the rather odd and illogical reasoning on the part of university decision makers: if a woman is not married, she'll get married. If she is married, she'll probably have children. If she has children, she can't possibly be committed to a profession. If she has older children, she's too old to begin training. It is true that she may very well marry. Many of her fellow male students will do likewise. She may very well have children. Men also become parents, but we do not as a society punish them by limiting their professional development and professional opportunities.

Essentially, our universities punish women for being women. They punish women not only for having children, but even for having the potential to bear children. Such blatent discrimination against women has gone virtually unchecked for years. In every sector of university life women are losing ground.

Women who are actually hired to teach have not crossed over the last barriers of discrimination. They will be promoted far more slowly than their male counterparts. 90% of the men with doctorates and 20 years of academic experience will be full professors; for women with the same qualifications barely half will be full professors. In other words, women have about half the chance that men have to become a full professor. And this is after 20 years of full time dedicated service. The figures at specific universities tell the story. At Stanford University, for example, 50% of the men have the rank of associate or full professor. Only 10% of the women are at these ranks. Somehow, many of the women who are "qualified" enough to be hired, are not "qualified" enough to be promoted.

Salary discrepancies abound. Deans of men make far more money than deans of women, even in the same institution. Numerous national studies have documented the pay differences between men and women with the same academic position and qualifications. Women instructors make less than men instructors; women assistant professors make less than men assistant professors; women associate professors earn less than men associate professors; and women full professors earn less than men full professors. Indicative of the widening gap between salaries of men and women is the extreme difficulty in getting salary information from practically all institutions, including the publicly supported ones.

I know of one full professor who is earning less than a newly hired male assistant professor in her department fresh out of graduate school. I know of another woman, an associate professor for more than 10 years who discovered she was earning more than $1000 below the bottom of her university's scale for associate professors. I know of a third woman, at what must surely be the world's wealthiest and most prestigious university, who is teaching without any pay, because there is "not enough money" to pay her.

At the administrative level, women are most conspicuous by their absence. The number of women college presidents is decreasing, even at women's colleges. Women rarely head departments. Even in fields where women predominate, such as in education, women do not move to the top. At the University of Maryland, for example, in the College of Education, only one department -- Special Education -- is headed by a woman. Even in women's colleges there has been a decline in the number of high administrative posts held by women. At Smith College, for example, (and Smith was a noted pioneer in the education of women), the percentage of women in high administrative posts has declined from nearly 70% in 1962 to less than 50% in 1969.

Many of the best scholarships are limited to men only. It took a highly active and sophisticated group of New York University Law School students earlier this year to get women to be considered elegible for some highly coveted $10,000 law scholarships. Practically all Federal scholarship and loan aid is for full-time study -- a practice that works to virtually eliminate married women with families from receiving such aid, since they may need a part-time schedule. Indeed, many schools forbid or discourage part-

time study, particularly at the graduate level, thus punishing women who
attempt to combine professional training and home responsibilities simul-
taneously.

Whether by design or accident, women are second class citizens on the
campus. As students they are often excluded and often actively discouraged
from entering professional fields. (One member of my own department at the
University of Maryland feels strongly that "women shouldn't be professionals"
and tells this to his women students.) As faculty, women can look forward
to low pay, low status, and little or no opportunity for promotion.

Why has this massive discrimination gone virtually unchecked and unnoticed
for so long? The reasons are many. Sex prejudice is so ingrained in our
society that many who practice it are simply unaware that they are hurting
women. It is the last socially acceptable prejudice. The Chairman of a
department sees nothing wrong in paying a woman less because "she is married
and therefore doesn't need as much" or paying her less because "she is not
married and therefore doesn't need as much." Many of the most ardent supporters of civil rights for blacks, Indians, Spanish-speaking Americans and
other minority groups simply do not view sex discrimination as discrimination. No university would today advertise for a "white assistant professor";
yet these same concerned humanitarians see nothing wrong with advertising
for a "male assistant professor." These same humanitarians fail to notice
that half of each minority group are women. Both Congresswoman Shirley
Chisholm and Pauli Murray, a noted Negro lawyer, have both stated that they
have suffered far more from being a woman than from being a Negro.

It is also very dangerous for women students or a faculty member to openly
complain of sex discrimination on their campus. Each day, in my role as
Chairman of the Action Committee for Federal Contract Compliance in Education,
my mail includes letters from women who want WEAL to file a formal complaint
of sex discrimination against their university. With practically no exceptions
these women plead for anonymity. Even the Head of a department in one major
state supported university, as well as numerous other women with tenure, ask
that their names be kept confidential. And well they might. I know of two
women who protested against sex discrimination recently in a large publicly
supported university system, and they were promptly and officially censured
by the university for their actions. In effect they stand to lose their

253

tenure if not their jobs. Unless women band together and protest as a group
it is virtual academic suicide to protest sex discrimination on practically
all campuses.

Mr. Chairman, believe it or not, it is completely within the law to discriminate
against women in universities and colleges. Section 702 of Title VII of the
Civil Rights Act of 1964 exempts every "educational institution with respect
to the employment of individuals to perform work connected with the educational activities of such institution." Title VI of the same Civil Rights
Act forbids discrimination in programs or activities which receive Federal
assistance, but it only applies to discrimination based on race, religion
or national origin. It does not forbid sex discrimination. The Equal Pay
Act of 1963 specifically excludes "executive, administrative, or professional employees." Even the U.S. Commission on Civil Rights has no jurisdiction whatsoever concerning sex discrimination; it is limited by law
to matters pertaining to race, color, religion or national origin.

Executive Order 11246 as amended, under which WEAL is filing its charges
of sex discrimination, is at best an administrative remedy for such discrimination in academia. Unfortunately, the rules and regulation under
that Executive Order require far less of state supported universities and
colleges than that required of private institutions. It is incredible that
such rules and regulations expect far less from the public institutions.
This inequity must be corrected immediately.

Moreover, let us not forget that an Executive Order does not have the
status of law. It can be amended or suspended at the pleasure of a particular administration.* Furthermore, any institution that wanted to continue discrimination is legally free to do so if it gives up its government contracts. There are simply no laws that forbid universities and
colleges from continuing their vicious patterns of sex discrimination
and their violation of the human rights of women.

*Until WEAL's complaints were filed, all compliance agencies of the U.S.
government including the Office of Federal Contract Compliance of the Dept.
of Labor, for all intents and purposes shamelessly ignored those aspects
of the Executive Order that pertained to sex discrimination.

It is perhaps instructive to compare race discrimination and sex discrimination in this context. Racial segregation of our educational system was outlawed by the Supreme Court in 1954, yet as recently as 10 years ago, the
Supreme Court declined to hear a case in which the Texas Court of Civil
Appeals upheld the exclusion of women from a state college, Texas A and
M. In another, court case, under the 14th Amendment, in February 1970 a three
judge Federal court dismissed as "moot" a class action in which women sought
to desegregate all male and female public institutions in Virginia. The
Court had previous ordered the University to consider without regard to
sex the women plaintiffs' applications for admission to the University of
Virginia at Charlottesville, and to submit a three year plan for desegregating the University of Virginia at Charlottesville. To give you an idea of
the results of a sex segregated university and college system* let me quote
from a Report of the Virginia Commission for the Study of Educational Facilities in the State of Virginia, 1964· "21,000 women were turned down for
college entrance in the State of Virginia; during the same period of time,
NOT ONE application of a male student was rejected."

In general, the 14th Amendment has not been applied in any meaningful fashion
concerning women's rights. No case has ever reached the Supreme Court where
the Court ruled that a woman was a "person" within the meaning of the Equal
Protection clause of the 14th Amendment. Corporations have been declared
as "persons." Negroes are considered "persons." But not women. As long
as there is no Equal Rights Amendment women can only rely on the possibility
of enlightened court interpretations of the 14th Amendment, and history
has shown that this is clearly insufficient.

The Equal Rights Amendment is vitally needed if we are to begin to correct
many of the inequities women face. Such an amendment would have a direct
effect on all state schools at all levels of education. It would forbid
laws or official practices that currently exclude women from state col-

---

*Sex segregated colleges, particularly when operated by the same governing
body are particularly reminiscent of race segregated facilities: they are
separate, but hardly equal. Dr. Kate Millett of Barnard College recently
analyzed a series of coordinate "brother-and-sister" colleges, and demonstrated
that the women students were given a vastly inferior education compared to
that of their "brothers." The course offerings are less varied, facilities are
inferior, faculty are paid less, etc.

leges and universities (including higher admission standards for women,
and in the administration of scholarship programs.) It would end many of
the discriminatory practices now legally engaged in by universities and
colleges today. While the Amendment would not have a direct effect on
private institutions, the state universities and colleges would undoubtedly
serve as models for private schools such as Harvard University.

Moreover, the psychological effect that such an amendment would have on
women is enormous. Women need moral and legal support if they are to
have the courage to fight for their rights in the academic community.
We need to undo the wrongs that have been done. Too many women already
have had their academic careers stunted by the effects of sex discrimination.
The Equal Rights Amendment will state loudly and clearly that the time has
come for sex discrimination to end in America's colleges and universities.

Women on campuses all over the country have begun to form groups, across
departmental and professional lines. They are beginning to do more than
complain; they are examining their own university's commitment and treatment of women. Women faculty, women staff, and women students are all
participating. Women's rights are even being included in a variety of
student protest activities. In January, 1969, at the University of Chicago
the first demonstration concerning equal rights for women took place.
In February, 1970, a group of women students from Yale University seized
the microphone at a Yale Alumni dinner and made several complaints and
demands concerning the treatment of women at Yale. We need to give women
alternate and better ways of combatting sex discrimination than seizing a
microphone or taking over a building. It is within the power and responsibility of this Committee and of the Congress to make such change possible
by passing the Equal Rights Amendment.

Women in the professions are becoming highly sensitive to the need for
the recognition of the inequities within their professions. At the Fall
1969 meeting of the American Psychological Association, women psychologists
charged that organization with accepting "male" job openings. (WEAL has
since filed formal charges against the American Psychological Association
and the American Personnel and Guidance Association for this very reason.)
The women psychologists proceded to form a new group, the Association for
Women Psychologists. In other professional organizations such as the

American Sociological Association, the Modern Language Association, the
American Historical Association, the American Political Science Association,
and the American Association for the Advancement of Science, women have begun to form caucuses and organize as pressure groups to end discrimination
within their respective professions. In April 1970, a Professional Women's
Caucus emerged which will represent all professional women. These are but
a few examples of activity by women in the academic and professional worlds.
They will not accept second class citizenship any longer.

We live in a rapidly changing world. The roles and responsibilities of
both women and men are changing. No longer do women need to choose between
a career or marriage; now the choice for most women is: what is the best
way to combine career and marriage. If we are to come to grips with the
problem of population growth it is vital that women have alternate life
styles other than extensive child bearing. There is little reason for a
woman to limit her family if the only realistic alternative is a job far
below her capacities, coupled with extensive educational and occupational
discrimination. Extensive reform in our abortion laws, and the dissemination of the Pill and other birth control information will not have much
impact if there is no other style of life for a woman to pursue. Dr.
Roger Revelle, Director of the Center for Population Studies at Harvard
University recently stated in hearings before a Subcommittee of the Committee on Government Operations, House of Representatives, 91st Congress:

> One way to influence them (individual families) is to make alterna-
> tive careers available for women, careers other than parenthood,
> other than the domestic pattern which is the norm of American life.
> If you look at our college and university enrollment, I think it is
> nothing short of disgraceful that there are about twice as many men
> as women in our colleges and universities. We will never persuade
> women to play their full role in society, let alone to have fewer
> children, unless we give them opportunities for something else to
> do -- something meaningful and important to do. This means, among
> other things, a much greater opportunity for higher education than
> they have at the present time.

Women have been discriminated against in the past in many areas of life,
of which the university is but one. We need to begin to redress these
wrongs. The Equal Rights Amendment is a symbolic and actual beginning.
It will give hope and dignity to women, the second class citizens of
the nation. As a member of the Women's Equity Action League, as an educa-

tor of counselors and as a psychologist, as a teacher, as a woman, a wife

and a mother, and above all as a human being, I urge you to support this

Amendment.

***

The 80 page WEAL Sex Discrimination Report submitted to the Secretary of

Labor, George P. Shultz, has been made available to Senator Birch Bayh,

Chairman of the Subcommittee on Constitutional Amendments of the Senate

Judiciary Committee.

STATEMENT

To: Constitutional Amendments Subcommittee of the Judiciary Committee.
From: Mrs. Gladys O'Donnell, President, National Federation of Republican
    Women.
Subject: Equal Rights Amendment.

On behalf of our Board of Directors and half million members I express appreciation for the opportunity to present the following statement for the National Federation of Republican Women.

The Equal Rights Amendment has long been supported by our organization, and on January 23rd, 1970, to reemphasize our endorsement, it was again approved by a unanimous vote of our Board of Directors.

The extraordinary anachronism of this hearing is that it is taking place in the early twilight of the twentieth century; that it finds women still struggling for equality in an enlightened, libertarian society. One hundred and ninety-four years ago the Declaration of Independence set forth the philosophical tenets of a young nation—"we hold these truths to be self-evident, that all me are created equal, . . ."

Beyond all doubt the word "men" is used in its generic sense and women were not excluded, but we must admit that men are much more "equal" than women.

It has been my privilege to hear two days of testimony in this hearing. Witnesses established with professional skill and clarity the framework for legal and economic consideration of the Equal Rights Amendment. The women who made the presentations deserve profound admiration.

The hearings also provided an unbelievable defense of discrimination against women, first through Biblical quotations to prove their inferiority, and secondly by a slide presentation of chairs, tools, and other industrial devices to show that they are not suitable for women's anatomy. Neither quality nor excellence is a matter of size or shape. The opposite poles of this argument could be the late, great Babe Didrickson and Tiny Tim.

In this presentation it is my wish to approach the subject as a matter of the heart and spirit and then as a political reality.

This year we celebrate the 50th Anniversary of the 19th Amendment which gave American women the right to vote. Last year we honored the State of Wyoming which, as a territory, gave this recognition to women 100 years ago. Mrs. Esther Hobart Morris of South Pass, Wyoming, guided the victory. Shorty thereafter she was appointed justice of the peace of South Pass, the highest honor the West could bestow for a quality it admires most—true grit.

As we prepared a suitable tribute to the women pioneers who carried the crusade for the right to vote, we did considerable research. To know their story is to be acutely aware of the enormity of their legacy; the unwavering, single-minded purpose; the courage of heroic measure. Will we ever know women like this again—magnificent women who bring a lump to our throats?

The settlement of the west, or any other part of this country for that matter, owes more to the endless toil of these pioneer women than to all other factors in its history. A character in Edna Ferber's *Cimarron* tells it this way:

"You can't read the history of the United States, my friend . . . without learning of the great story of those thousands of unnamed women . . . women in mud caked boots and calico dresses and sunbonnets, crossing the prairie and the desert and mountains, enduring hardship and privation. Good women with a terrible and rigid goodness that comes of work and self-denial. Nothing picturesque or romantic about them, I suppose. . . . No, their story's never really been told, but it's there just the same. And if it's ever told straight, you'll know it's the sunbonnet and not the sombrero that's settled this country.

The greatest of all observers of the American scene mid-nineteenth century, Alexis de Toqueville, said, "If I were asked . . . to what the singular prosperity and growing strength of the United States ought mainly to be attributed, I should have to reply 'To the superiority of its women.'"

The first national convention for women's suffrage was held in Seneca, New York, in 1948. Seventy-two years later, in 1920, the 19th Amendment was passed. It was just a step in a long journey—the struggle continues.

Granddaughters and great grand-daughters of the pioneers are now in the forefront. Their quest is for the Equal Rights Amendment. It has been before Congress for 47 years. In this interim women have been more quiescent, but now the tide is rising and the mood changing. Predictably the old bromides and cliches are being dusted off. We have heard many of them at this meeting. There is a very special concern about legislation protecting women. If I read the evidence correctly there is a large question about *who* is getting the protection. Too often it turns out to be not protection but insulation—a buffer between women and opportunity, higher wages, faster promotion and positions of leadership.

This is not what women want. We reject it. Women want to be accepted as people, free independent human beings. As such we would have the coinciding benefits—equal opportunity, compensation, recognition and inclusion at policy-making levels. Collectively and individually we would like to be in on some of the take-offs since we are always there for the crash landings.

Women do not desire to dominate what man has so long considered his private domain, and which he is loathe to share. We just wonder why man needs so much defense of his masculinity. The great majority of women are happy as homemakers. But those of who choose a career want to be accepted and treated as equals.

Women make up 40% of the workforce, represent 51% of the population. We have expanded beyond the four walls and roof that once defined our province, and are escaping the psychological conditioning of inferiority that has been imposed upon us since time began.

Varying figures place the preponderance of women over men in the United States at 4½ to 7 millions (voting age). These are politically significant figures and it is ironic that we are here today endeavoring to justify a plea for an Equal Rights Amendment that we should have had long ago as a matter of simple justice. We are tired of being the silenced majority.

Looking back across the years since the 19th Amendment we can see where women erred. Winning the vote was accepted as an end in itself, which it was not. Having won political power, women have never used it. Therein lies our failure.

It is the opinion of many astute women in politics that we will not get any place until we elect more women to high office. This is a major goal of our Federation. We are urging State Federations to seek out qualified women of character, stability and training to become candidates. Once they have been nominated, either by primary election or convention, we will assist in every way in the general election.

Where we do not have women candidates we will screen the potential men who are anxious to run and encourage those who are sympathetic in matters of concern to women. This is in the best political tradition—the way in which every group achieves its political objectives. It is time that women used a little of their abundant political moxie.

The proliferation of women's activist groups across the nation speaks eloquently and sometimes stridently for itself. Approaches vary widely, as at this hearing, but the goal is the same—equal rights and protection under the law, acceptance as persons, and recognition based on individual merit.

How little this is to ask after centuries of patient, enduring servitude and imposed inferiority.

Women can be a powerful force, acting collectively on an issue generating as much heat and polarization as the Equal Rights Amendment. A determined mood long absent from women's groups is spreading—its emotional logic is that nothing less than militancy is effective. We hope this is not true.

Years of experience and costly legal procedures have proved that the 5th and 14th Amendments and Title VII of the Civil Rights Act are not the answer to our need. The void in our Constitution concerning women should be bridged by an Amendment in clear, simple language which recognizes us as first class citizens with equal rights and protection under the Constitution.

Favorable action on this simple request could bring historic distinction to this Congress and earn for it the lasting gratitude of American women. And how wise and ingenious it would be to magnanimously grant this recognition now—while there is still time!

In closing there should be no clearer summation of the objectives of proponents of the Equal Rights Amendment than the slogan of those early pioneers in the movement for women's right—"Principles, not policy; justice, not favor; men, their rights and nothing more; women, their rights and nothing less."

STATEMENT OF THE EQUAL RIGHTS AMENDMENT TO THE CONSTITUTION (SUBMITTED BY MARJORIE R. LONGWELL, CALIFORNIA CHAIRMAN, AND NATIONAL CHAIRMAN—NATIONAL WOMAN'S PARTY)

TEXT OF AMENDMENT

"Equality of rights under the law shall not be denied or abridged by the United States or by States on account of sex."

The U.S. Supreme Court has ruled that women enjoy only ONE right under the Constitution—THE RIGHT TO VOTE. In all other respects, women live under State laws, and these contain more than 1,000 legal discriminations against women as to property and inheritance rights, guardianship rights, management of earnings, etc. Such discriminations contrast surprisingly with the rights of men under Federal and State laws.

Today it should not be difficult to find a man or woman who does not believe that women should enjoy, with men, the full protection of the U.S. Constitution.

Former Presidents Eisenhower, Truman, Kennedy, Johnson, all supported the Equal Rights Amendment. President Nixon recently said: *"It is my hope that there will be widespread support for the Equal Rights for Women Amendment to our Constitution, which would add equality between the sexes to freedom and liberties guaranteed to all Americans."* Many Senators and Congressmen support this bill. TEN STATES HAVE MEMORIALIZED THE CONGRESS TO PASS THE EQUAL RIGHTS AMENDMENT.

The Equal Rights Amendment has been endorsed by the Business and Professional Women's Clubs, the National Federation of Women's Clubs, the National Associations of Women Lawyers, Doctors, Ministers; the National Association of Colored Women, the Ladies' Auxiliary of Veterans of Foreign Wars, the Catholic Daughters of America, the National Association of Railway Business Women, N.O.W., the W.C.T.U., the National Woman's Party, and hundreds of State and local groups.

The Amendment would give women no special privileges, for the word *women* is not used in the text. It merely forbids discrimination on the basis of sex. Special laws still may be enacted for citizens in need of special laws. No one today questions special laws for Veterans, the Blind, etc. Thus, under the Amendment, women may still enjoy special laws for mothers or for mothers-to-be.

It would be a time-consuming procedure to bring under Supreme Court Review each discriminatory law against women. How long does the Supreme court take to act upon one State Statute? How long would it take to act upon one thousand?

Be assured that each of the 1,000 discriminations, is felt and experienced by certain American women citizens. In one State a wife's clothing belongs, legally, to her hubsand. In another State a husband may obtain a divorce on mere suspicion of unfaithfulness on his wife's part, while the wife must not only prove his unfaithfulness, but *must prove that it was habitual* before she may win a divorce. In every state the employed woman is eased out of the better jobs by discriminations against her in upgrading, transfer, and many normal conditions of employment.

The Founding Fathers may have left women out of the Constitution because their world of 1780 so little resembled today's world. But Modern Woman has earned her right to be included, 100%, in that great document. Don't you agree?

Won't you, as a "committee-of-one" do what you can to get the Equal Rights Amendment passed favorably through Congress, then ratified by ¾ of the State Legislatures, and made part of the Constitution?

With your help *it can be done.*

THE PROPOSED EQUAL RIGHTS AMENDMENT

TO THE

UNITED STATES CONSTITUTION

A Memorandum

CITIZENS' ADVISORY COUNCIL ON THE STATUS OF WOMEN
Washington, D.C. 20210
March 1970

CITIZENS' ADVISORY COUNCIL ON THE STATUS OF WOMEN
Washington, D.C. 20210

Honorable Jacqueline G. Gutwillig, Chairman

Miss Virginia R. Allan
Executive Vice-President
Cahalan Drug Stores, Inc.
Former President, National
 Federation of Business and
 Professional Women's Clubs

Miss Nola Allen
Attorney at Law

Dr. Margaret Long Arnold
Honorary President, General
 Federation of Women's Clubs

Mrs. Paul Bethel, Executive Assistant
U.S. Citizens Committee for Free Cuba

Mrs. Lorraine L. Blair, President
Lorraine Blair, Inc., Founder President
Finance Forum of America

Dr. Rita Ricardo Campbell
Senior Fellow, Hoover Institution
Vice Chairman, Western Interstate
 Commission for Higher Education

Mrs. Julie Casterman Connor
Folk Music Entertainer & School Teacher

Miss Sarah Jane Cunningham
Attorney at Law
Vice-President, International Federation
 of Business and Professional Women's
 Clubs

Mrs. Robert A. Griffin
Civic Leader and Businesswoman

Miss Maxine R. Hacke, Executive
Warren Petroleum Corp.

Mrs. Charles M. Hamel
Vice-President, Hamel's Dairy &
 Ice Cream Company, Inc.

Mrs. Mary J. Kyle
Editor & Publisher
Twin Cities Courier
Television Editorial Commentator

Miss Margaret J. Mealey
Executive Director
National Council of Catholic Women

Miss Hazel Palmer
Attorney at Law
Former President, National Federation
 of Business and Professional Women's
 Clubs

Mrs. Chapman Revercomb
Civic Leader & Former School Teacher

Honorable Patricia Saiki, Member
Hawaii State Legislature

Miss Rachel E. Scott
Research Department
Department of Pediatrics
Johns Hopkins University

Mrs. Daniel H. Wasserman
Civic Leader & Past President
Cleveland Section, National Council
 of Jewish Women

Mrs. Irene Wischer, President
Paladin Pipeline Co.
Sr. Director & Executive Officer
Panhandle Producing Co.

Mrs. Catherine East
Executive Secretary

CONTENTS

- -

This paper was presented to the Council by its study group on equal legal rights: Sarah Jane Cunningham, Chairman, Virginia R. Allan, Lorraine L. Blair, Rachel E. Scott, Irene Wischer; Mary Eastwood, Technical Staff.

A MEMORANDUM ON
THE PROPOSED EQUAL RIGHTS AMENDMENT
TO THE UNITED STATES CONSTITUTION

The proposed equal rights amendment to the U.S. Constitution would provide that "Equality of rights under the law shall not be denied or abridged by the United States or by any State on account of sex," and would authorize the Congress and the States to enforce the amendment by appropriate legislation.[1]

The purpose of the proposed amendment would be to provide constitutional protection against laws and official practices that treat men and women differently. At the present time, the extent to which women may invoke the protection of the Constitution against laws which discriminate on the basis of sex is unclear. The equal rights amendment would insure equal rights under the law for men and women and would secure the right of all persons to equal treatment under the laws and official practices without differentiation based on sex.

Joint resolutions proposing that the equal rights amendment be approved for submission to the States for ratification have been sponsored by 75 Senators and 225 Members of the House of Representatives in this (91st) Congress (as of March 11, 1970). Adoption of the amendment would require a 2/3 vote of both Houses of Congress and ratification by 3/4 of the States. Thus there are already more than the necessary number of Senators who are committed to support the amendment for its approval by the Senate. These joint resolutions are currently pending in the respective Senate and House Judiciary Committees.

The Citizens' Advisory Council on the Status of Women, at its meeting February 7, 1970, endorsed the equal rights amendment, adopting the following resolution:

> The Citizens' Advisory Council on the Status of Women
> endorses the proposed Equal Rights Amendment to the
> United States Constitution and recommends that the
> Interdepartmental Committee on the Status of Women
> urge the President to immediately request the passage of

---

[1] See, e.g., S.J. Res. 61, 91st Cong., 1st Sess.

- 1 -

the proposed Equal Rights Amendment by the Congress of
the United States.

The Council's recommendation was transmitted to the President on February
13, 1970.

History of the Equal Rights Amendment

Resolutions proposing an equal rights amendment have been introduced in
every Congress since 1923. Hearings were held by the House and Senate
Judiciary Committees in 1948 and 1956, respectively. [2] The amendment
has been repeatedly reported favorably by the Senate Judiciary Committee,
most recently in 1964 (S. Rept. No. 1558, 88th Cong., 2d Sess.), and has
twice passed the Senate, in 1950 and 1953.

Both times it was passed, however, with the so-called "Hayden rider",
which provided that the equal rights amendment "shall not be construed to
impair any rights, benefits, or exemptions now or hereafter conferred by
law, upon persons of the female sex." [3] Both times the rider accomplished
its purpose of killing the proposed amendment since, as the Senate Judiciary
Committee has noted, the rider's "qualification is not acceptable to women
who want equal rights under the law. It is under the guise of so-called 'rights'
or 'benefits' that women have been treated unequally and denied opportunities
which are available to men." (S. Rept. No. 1558, supra)

Since the proposed equal rights amendment has failed to pass Congress for the
past 47 years, it may appear to be a "loser", although admittedly it took women
more than 50 years to secure the adoption of the 19th amendment. However, a
revival of the feminist movement has occurred during the past four years and
it is greatly increasing in momentum, especially among younger women. Thus
the demand for equal rights and support for the amendment is becoming more
widespread, with a corresponding increase in likelihood of early adoption of
the amendment.

---

[2] Hearings on the Equal Rights Amendment to the Constitution and Com-
mission on the Legal Status of Women, House Committee on the Judiciary,
Subcommittee No. 1, 80th Cong., 2d Sess. (1948); Hearings on Equal
Rights, Senate Committee on the Judiciary, Subcommittee on Constitutional
Amendments, 84th Cong., 2d Sess. (1956).

[3] See 96 Cong. Rec. 872-3 (1950); 99 Cong. Rec. 8954-5 (1953).

Laws Which Discriminate on the Basis of Sex

A number of studies have been made in recent years by the President's Commission on the Status of Women, the Citizens' Advisory Council on the Status of Women, and State commissions on the status of women concerning the various types of laws which distinguish on the basis of sex. [4] Opposition to the equal rights amendment in the past has been based in part on "fear of the unknown," i.e., lack of information concerning the types of laws which distinguish on the basis of sex and would therefore be affected by the amendment. Further delay in approving the amendment thus need not await any further study of the kinds of laws that discriminate on the basis of sex.

These studies have shown that numerous distinctions based on sex still exist in the law. For example:

1. State laws placing special restrictions on women with respect to hours of work and weightlifting on the job;

2. State laws prohibiting women from working in certain occupations;

3. Laws or practices operating to exclude women from State colleges and universities (including higher standards required for women applicants to institutions of higher learning and in the administration of scholarship programs);

4. Discrimination in employment by State and local governments;

5. Dual pay schedules for men and women public school teachers;

6. State laws providing for alimony to be awarded, under certain circumstances, to ex-wives but not to ex-husbands;

7. State laws placing special restrictions on the legal capacity of married women or on their right to establish a legal domicile;

8. State laws that require married women but not married men to go through a formal procedure and obtain court approval before they may engage in an independent business. [5]

---

[4] See especially, Report of the Committee on Civil and Political Rights, President's Commission on the Status of Women (GPO, 1963); Report of the Task Force on Labor Standards, Citizens' Advisory Council on the Status of Women (GPO, 1968); Report of the Task Force on Family Law and Policy, CACSW (GPO, 1968). See also, Kanowitz, Women and the Law: The Unfinished Revolution, U. of N.M. Press, 1969.

[5] See, e.g., Calif. Code Civ. Proc., §§ 1811-1819; Nev. Rev. Stats., §§ 124.010--124.050.

9. Social Security and other social benefits legislation which give greater benefits to one sex than to the other;

10. Discriminatory preferences, based on sex, in child custody cases;

11. State laws providing that the <u>father</u> is the natural guardian of the minor children;[6]

12. Different ages for males and females in (a) child labor laws, (b) age for marriage, (c) cutoff of the right to parental support, and (d) juvenile court jurisdiction;

13. Exclusion of women from the requirements of the Military Selective Service Act of 1967;

14. Special sex-based exemptions for women in selection of State juries;

15. Heavier criminal penalties for female offenders than for male offenders committing the same crime.

Although it is possible that these and other discriminations might eventually be corrected by legislation, legislative remedies are <u>not</u> adequate substitutes for fundamental constitutional protection against discrimination. Any class of persons (i.e., women) which cannot successfully invoke the protection of the Constitution against discriminatory treatment is by definition comprised of "second class citizens" and is inferior in the eyes of the law.

The Position of Women Under Existing
Constitutional Provisions

The Fourteenth Amendment to the U.S. Constitution provides that no State shall "deprive any person of life, liberty, or property, without due process of law; nor deny to any person within its jurisdiction the equal protection of the laws." The Federal government is similarly restricted from interfering with these individual rights, under the "due process clause" of the Fifth Amendment.

6/ See, e.g., Code of Ga. Annot., §§ 49-102--49-104; Okla. Stats. Annot., tit. 10, § 5.

During the past century, women have been largely unsuccessful in seeking judicial relief from sex discrimination in cases challenging the constitutionality of discriminatory laws under these provisions. As the Committee on Civil and Political Rights, President's Commission on the Status of Women, noted in its 1963 Report,

> In no 14th amendment case alleging discrimination on account of sex has the United States Supreme Court held that a law classifying persons on the basis of sex is unreasonable and therefore unconstitutional. [7]

In 1874, the Supreme Court held that the privileges and immunities of citizens of the United States, protected from abridgment by the States under the Fourteenth Amendment, did not confer upon women the right to vote, although the Court conceded that women were persons and citizens within the meaning of the amendment. [8] Similarly, the privileges and immunities clause was held not to confer on women the right to practice law. [9]

The constitutionality of State laws regulating the employment of women (but not men) was upheld in a number of cases brought between 1908 and 1937: maximum hours laws, [10] laws prohibiting night work for women, [11] and laws requiring a minimum wage for women. [12] In 1948, the Court upheld a Michigan law prohibiting (with certain exceptions) the licensing of women as bartenders. [13]

A Florida law providing that women not be called for jury service unless she registers with the clerk of court her desire to serve was held not violative of the Fourteenth Amendment in 1961. [14] However, more recently, a three-judge Federal court in Alabama held that State's law excluding women from

---

[7] GPO, 1963, p. 34.

[8] Minor v. Happersett, 21 Wall. 162, 168.

[9] Bradwell v. State, 16 Wall. 130 (1872); In re Lockwood, 154 U.S. 116 (1894).

[10] Muller v. Oregon, 208 U.S. 412 (1908); Riley v. Massachusetts, 232 U.S. 671 (1914); Miller v. Wilson, 236 U.S. 373 (1915); Busley v. McLaughlin, 236 U.S. 385 (1915).

[11] Radice v. New York, 264 U.S. 292 (1924).

[12] West Coast Hotel Co. v. Parrish, 300 U.S. 379 (1937), overruling Adkins v. Children's Hospital, 261 U.S. 525 (1923).

[13] Goesaert v. Cleary, 335 U.S. 464 (1948).

[14] Hoyt v. Florida, 368 U.S. 57 (1961).

jury service violated the rights of women under the Fourteenth Amendment, stating:

> The Constitution of the United States must be read as embody-
> ing general principles meant to govern society and the institutions
> of government as they evolve through time. It is therefore this
> Court's function to apply the Constitution as a living document
> to the legal cases and controversies of contemporary society.
>
> . . . .
>
> . . . The Alabama statute that denies women the right to serve
> on juries . . . violates that provision of the Fourteenth Amend-
> ment to the Constitution of the United States that forbids any
> state to "deny to any person within its jurisdiction the equal
> protection of the laws." The plain effect of this constitutional
> provision is to prohibit prejudicial disparities before the law.
> This means prejudicial disparities for all citizens -- including
> women. White v. Crook, 251 F. Supp. 401, 408 (M.D. Ala., 1966).

In Abbot v. Mines, 411 F. 2d 353 (C.A. 6, 1969) the Court reversed a case in which the trial judge had dismissed women jurors from the panel because the evidence in the case required testimony concerning cancer of the male genitals. The Court of Appeals stated:

> It is common knowledge that society no longer coddles women
> from the very real and sometimes brutal facts of life. Women,
> moreover, do not seek such oblivion. . . .
>
> The District Judge's desire to avoid embarrassment to the women
> jurors is understandable and commendable but such sentiments
> must be subordinated to constitutional mandates. 411 F. 2d at 355.

As recently as ten years ago, the Supreme Court declined to hear a case in which the Texas Court of Civil Appeals had upheld the exclusion of women from a State college, Texas A. & M. [15]/

In February 1970 a three-judge Federal court dismissed as "moot" a class action in which women sought to desegregate various all male and all female public institutions of higher learning in the State of Virginia. However, the

---

15/ Allred v. Heaton, 336 S.W. 2d 251 (1960), appeal dismissed and cert.
    denied, 364 U.S. 517, rehearing denied, 364 U.S. 944; see also Heaton
    v. Bristol, 317 S.W. 2d 86 (1958), appeal dismissed and cert. denied,
    359 U.S. 230, rehearing denied, 359 U.S. 999.

Court had previously ordered the University to consider without regard to sex the women plaintiffs' applications for admission to the University of Virginia at Charlottesville and to submit a three-year plan for desegregating the University at Charlottesville. Kirstein et al v. The Rector and Visitors of the University of Virginia, etc., et al. (E. D. Va., Richmond Div. Civil No. 220-69-R).

Although there are very few female criminals as compared to male criminals, some laws provide for longer prison terms for women than for men committing the same crime. Such laws in Pennsylvania and Connecticut have been held to be inconsistent with the equal protection guarantees of the Fourteenth Amendment.[16]

Thus, in at least two areas -- jury service and criminal penalties -- women appear to have made progress in invoking the protection of the Fourteenth Amendment. Although jury service is important as a practical matter it is hardly central to the lives of women. Criminal penalties are of real significance to only a very few women. Moreover, the court decisions have not wiped out discrimination even in these areas. The Kirstein case noted above represents some progress in an area vital to women -- education, but the extent to which women may insist on equal educational opportunities under the Constitution still remains unclear.

Different treatment of men and women for purposes of computing social security benefits has been held not to violate the right to due process and equal protection of the laws. Gruenwald v. Gardner, 390 F. 2d 591 (C.A. 2, 1968), cert. denied, 393 U.S. 982. The Court of Appeals stated that "the trend of authority makes it clear that the variation in amounts of retirement benefits based upon differences in the attributes of men and women is constitutionally valid." The Court also stated:

> There is here a reasonable relationship between the objective sought by the classification, which is to reduce the disparity between the economic and physical capabilities of a man and a woman -- and the means used to achieve that objective in affording to women more favorable benefit computations. There is, moreover, nothing arbitrary or unreasonable about the application of the principle underlying the statutory differences in the computations for men and women. Notwithstanding the

16/ Commonwealth v. Daniel, 430 Pa. 642, 243 A. 2d 400 (1968); U.S. ex rel. Robinson v. York, 281 F. Supp. 8 (D. Conn., 1968).

favorable treatment granted to women in computing their
benefits, the average monthly payments to men retiring at age
62 still exceeds those awarded women retiring at that age.
390 F. 2d at 592. (emphasis supplied)

In a case involving a violation of the Military Selective Service Act of 1967,
the defendant raised the issue of sex discrimination, charging that since men
but not women are compelled to serve in the Armed Forces, his rights to
due process of law under the Fifth Amendment were violated. United States
v. St. Clair, 291 F. Supp. 122 (S. D. N. Y. , 1968). The Court stated:

In the Act and its predecessors, Congress made a legislative
judgment that men should be subject to involuntary induction
but that women, presumably because they are "still regarded
as the center of home and family life" (Hoyt v. State of Florida,
...), should not. Women may constitutionally be afforded
"special recognition" (cf. Gruenwald v. Gardner, ...) particularly since women are not excluded from service in the Armed
Forces....

In providing for involuntary service for men and voluntary
service for women, Congress followed the teachings of history
that if a nation is to survive, men must provide the first line of
defense while women keep the home fires burning. 291 F. Supp.
at 124-5. (Emphasis supplied)

In two recent cases, women sought to enjoin State officials from enforcing
special restrictions on the hours of work of women on the ground that such
laws violate their rights to due process and equal protection of the law under
the Fourteenth Amendment. The three-judge Federal courts (convened pursuant to 28 U.S. C. 2281, 2284) held that the constitutional issue was insub-
stantial and that the three-judge court lacked jurisdiction.[17] The women
argued that because of the State restrictive laws, they were deprived of
opportunities for better paying jobs and overtime pay.

The President's Commission on the Status of Women stated in its 1963 report,
American Women, that it was --

convinced that the U. S. Constitution now embodies equality
of rights for men and women.... But judicial clarification
is imperative in order that remaining ambiguities with respect

---

[17] Mengelkoch v. Industrial Welfare Commission, 284 F. Supp. 950, 956
(C. D. Calif. , 1968), three-judge order vacated, 393 U. S. 83, rehearing
denied, 393 U. S. 993, appeal pending in the Ninth Circuit; Ward v. Luttrell,
292 F. Supp. 162, 165 (E. D. La. 1968).

to the constitutional protection of women's rights be eliminated.
Early and definitive court pronouncement, particularly by the
U.S. Supreme Court, is urgently needed with regard to the
validity under the 5th and 14th amendments of laws and official
practices discriminating against women, to the end that the
principle of equality become firmly established in constitutional
doctrine. (GPO, page 45)

The position of women under the Constitution remains ambiguous in 1970.

Relationship Between the Equal Rights Amendment and Existing Constitutional Provisions

It is, of course, possible that the 5th and 14th amendments will in the future
be interpreted by the courts as prohibiting all sex distinctions in the law. Nothing
in the proposed equal rights amendment would preclude this from occurring;
the amendment would in no way cut back, modify, or qualify any protection
against discrimination based on sex which may be afforded by the 5th and 14th
amdnements. As pointed out in Story, Commentaries on the Constitution of the
United States (5th Edit, §§ 1938, 1939):

> The securities of individual rights, it has often been observed,
> cannot be too frequently declared, nor in too many forms of
> words; nor is it possible to guard too vigilantly against the
> encroachments of power, nor to watch with too lively a suspicion
> the propensity of persons in authority to break through the
> "cobweb chains of paper constitutions."...
>
> . . . .
>
> Conceding, therefore, that if correctly construed, and applied
> according to their true intent and meaning, other constitutional
> provisions, State and national, might afford ample security for
> individual rights, we may nevertheless pardon the anxiety for
> further prohibitions, and concede that, even if wholly needless,
> the repetition of such securities may well be excused so long
> as the slightest doubt of their having been already sufficiently
> declared shall anywhere be found to exist.

The proposed amendment would secure the right of all persons to equal treatment under the law without any distinction as to sex. If the protection against
sex discrimination provided by the equal rights amendment should prove to be
duplicative of protections afforded by enlightened interpretations of the 5th
and 14th amendments, no harm would be done.

Supporters of the equal rights amendment believe that the potential of the 14th amendment is too unclear and that women's constitutional rights to equality are too insecure to rely exclusively on the possibility of getting more enlightened court decisions under that amendment.

In a 1963 case, the Supreme Court stated:

> The Fifteenth Amendment prohibits a State from denying or abridging a Negro's right to vote. The Nineteenth Amendment does the same for women . . . . Once a geographical unit for which a representative is to be chosen is designated, all who participate in the election are to have an equal vote -- whatever their race, whatever their sex. . . . This is required by the Equal Protection Clause of the Fourteenth Amendment. Gray v. Sanders, 372 U.S. 368, 379.

This interpretation of the 14th amendment reinforced and made doubly secure the right to vote. There are numerous cases in which the Supreme Court has interpreted the 14th amendment to reinforce or to extend rights guaranteed by earlier or, as in the above case, later amendments to the Constitution. For example, the more general due process and equal protection concepts of the 5th and 14th amendments have been used to strengthen more specific rights of individuals to freedom of speech, assembly and religion guaranteed by the First Amendment; and the right to a speedy trial and the right to counsel guaranteed by the Sixth.

If the equal rights amendment is adopted, the courts might well subsequently interpret the Fourteenth Amendment as reinforcing constitutional equality for women. Certainly this possibility does not justify further delay in approving the amendment.

Effect the Equal Rights Amendment Would Have on Laws Differentiating on the Basis of Sex

Constitutional amendments, like statutes, are interpreted by the courts in the light of intent of Congress. Committee reports on a proposal are regarded by the courts as the most persuasive evidence of the intended meaning of a provision. Therefore, the probable meaning and effect of the equal rights amendment can be ascertained from the Senate Judiciary Committee reports (which have been the same in recent years):

1. The amendment would restrict only governmental action, and would not apply to purely private action. What

constitutes "State action" would be the same as under the
14th amendment and as developed in 14th amendment
litigation on other subjects.

2. Special restrictions on property rights of married women
    would be unconstitutional; married women could engage in
    business as freely as a member of the male sex; inheritance
    rights of widows would be same as for widowers.

3. Women would be equally subject to jury service and to
    military service, but women would not be required to serve
    (in the Armed Forces) where they are not fitted any more
    than men are required to so serve.

4. Restrictive work laws for women only would be unconsti-
    tutional   (e.g. maximum hours, night work and weight-
    lifting restrictions on women).

5. Alimony laws would not favor women solely because of their
    sex, but a divorce decree could award support to a mother
    if she was granted custody of the children. Matters concern-
    ing custody and support of children would be determined in
    accordance with the welfare of the children and without
    favoring either parent because of sex.

6. Laws granting maternity benefits to mothers would not be
    affected by the amendment, nor would criminal laws governing
    sexual offenses become unconstitutional   (e.g. rape,
    prostitution).

Although the proposed amendment would specifically authorize the Congress and
the States to enact implementing legislation, the amendment would be largely
self-operative. The amendment is patterned after the 15th and 19th amendments,
which required equal voting rights for Negroes and women, respectively. The
15th and 19th amendments did not render unconstitutional all State voting laws;
they simply required the extension of voting rights to Negroes and women.
The equal rights amendment would simply require that men and women be treated
the same under the law. In some instances, like the 15th and 19th amendment,
the effect of the amendment would be to strike the words of sex identification in
the law rather than render it unconstitutional, thereby extending the rights under
the law to both sexes. In other cases, where the law serves only to restrict,
deny or limit the freedoms or rights of one sex, such restrictions would not be
extended to both sexes; the law would be rendered unconstitutional. In still

other cases, the law is partially restrictive to persons of one sex in that age limitations are imposed differently on males and females.

Following is a five-point analysis of the impact the equal rights amendment will have on the various types of Federal and State laws which distinguish on the basis of sex:

1. Strike the Words of Sex Identification and Apply the Law to Both Sexes.

    Where the law confers a benefit, privilege or obligation of citizenship, such would be extended to the other sex, i.e. the effect of the amendment would be to strike the words of sex identification. Thus, such laws would not be rendered unconstitutional but would be extended to apply to both sexes by operation of the amendment, in the same way that laws pertaining to voting were extended to Negroes and women under the 15th and 19th amendments.

Examples of such laws include: laws which permit alimony to be awarded under certain circumstances to wives but not to husbands; social security and other social benefits legislation which give greater benefits to one sex than the other; exclusion of women from the requirements of the Military Selective Service Act of 1967 (i.e., women would be equally subject to military conscription).

Any expression of preference in the law for the mother in child custody cases would be extended to both parents (as against claims of third parties). Children are entitled to support from both parents under the existing laws of most States.[18] Child support laws would be affected only if they discriminate on the basis of sex. The amendment would not prohibit the requiring of one parent to provide financial support for children who are in the custody of the other.

2. Laws Rendered Unconstitutional by the Amendment.

    Where a law restricts or denies opportunities of women or men, as the case may be, the effect of the equal rights amendment would be to render such laws unconstitutional.

Examples are: the exclusion of women from State universities or other public schools; State laws placing special restrictions on the hours of work for women or the weights women may lift on the job; laws prohibiting women from working

---

18/ Reciprocal State Legislation to Enforce the Support of Dependents, Council of State Governments, 1964, page 20.

in certain occupations, such as bartenders; laws placing special restrictions on the legal capacity of married women, such as making contracts or establishing a legal domicile.

3. **Removal of Age Distinctions Based on Sex.**

Some laws which apply to both sexes make an age distinction by sex and thereby discriminate as to persons between the ages specified for males and females. Under the foregoing analysis, the ages specified in such laws would be equalized by the amendment by extending the benefits, privileges or opportunities under the law to both sexes. This would mean that as to some such laws, the _lower_ age would apply to both sexes. For example: a lower minimum age for marriage for women would apply to both sexes; a lower age for boys under child labor laws would apply to girls as well. In other words, the _privileges_ of marrying or working would be _extended_ and the sex discrimination removed.

As to other laws, the _higher_ age would apply to both sexes. For example: a higher cut-off age for the right to paternal support for boys would apply to girls as well; a higher age for girls for juvenile court jurisdiction would apply also to boys. In these cases, the _benefits_ of paternal support or juvenile court jurisdiction would be _extended_ to both sexes.

Thus, the test in determining whether these laws are to be equalized by applying the lower age or by applying the higher age to both sexes is as follows:

> If the age limitation restricts individual liberty and freedom the lower age applies; if the age limitation confers a right, benefit or privilege to the individuals concerned and does not limit individual freedom, the higher age applies.

4. **Laws Which Could Not Possibly Apply to Both Sexes Because of the Difference in Reproductive Capacity.**

Laws which, as a practical matter, can apply to only one sex no matter how they are phrased, such as laws providing maternity benefits and laws prohibiting rape, would not be affected by the amendment. The extension of these laws to both sexes would be purely academic, since such laws would not apply differently if they were phrased in terms of both sexes. In these situations, the terminology of sex identification is of no consequence.[19/]

19/ See Murray and Eastwood, "Jane Crow and the Law: Sex Discrimination and Title VII" 34 G. W. L. Rev. 232, 240-241 (1965).

5. Separation of the Sexes.

    Separation of the sexes by law would be forbidden under the amendment except in situations where the separation is shown to be necessary because of an overriding and compelling public interest and does not deny individual rights and liberties.

For example, in our present culture the recognition of the right to privacy would justify separate restroom facilities in public buildings.

As shown above, the amendment would not change the substance of existing laws, except that those which restrict and deny opportunities to women would be rendered unconstitutional under the standard of point two of the analysis. In all other cases, the laws presently on the books would simply be equalized, and this includes the entire body of family law. Moreover, the amendment in no way would restrict the State legislature or the Congress in enacting legislation on any subject, since its only purpose and effect is to prohibit any distinction based on sex classification.

Objections to the Proposed Equal Rights Amendment

Objection: The equal rights amendment is not needed because women already have equal rights under the 5th and 14th amendments.

Answer: The extent to which women may invoke the protection of the due process and equal protection guarantees of the 5th and 14th amendments is unclear. In fact, some recent court decisions have upheld sex distinctions in the law, in spite of these constitutional provisions. Even if the 5th and 14th amendments are in future cases construed so as to eliminate all sex distinctions in the law, the equal rights amendment would simply make the individual's right to equal treatment doubly secure.

Objection: If the amendment were adopted the courts would be flooded with litigation because the meaning of the amendment is not clear; e.g., what are the various "rights" that would be protected? What does "equality" mean?

Answer: The equal rights amendment would not cause excessive litigation unless there were massive resistance to compliance with the amendment's requirement of equal treatment of men and women. If that happened, it would only prove the great need for the amendment. The "right" protected by the amendment is the right to equal treatment under the law, whatever the subject of the law may be, without distinction based on sex.

Objection: The amendment would render unconstitutional a wide variety of State laws which now treat men and women differently.

Answer: Some State laws -- those which deny rights or restrict freedoms of one sex -- would be violative of the equal rights amendment and rendered unconstitutional. Laws which confer rights, benefits and privileges on one sex would have to apply to both sexes equally, but would not be rendered unconstitutional by the amendment.

Objection: The amendment would require sweeping changes in laws pertaining to the family.

Answer: The amendment would simply require equality. In States where the law provides for alimony only for wives, courts could award alimony to husbands as well, under the same conditions as apply with respect to wives. (More than 1/3 of the States now permit alimony to be awarded to either spouse.) Mothers and fathers would both be legally responsible for the support of their children, as is generally the case under existing law.

Objection: The amendment would nullify special State protective labor laws for women, such as those governing limitations on hours of work, weightlifting on the job, and prohibitions against night work, for women employees only.

Answer: This issue is fast becoming moot, because the Federal law (Title VII of the Civil Rights Act of 1964) prohibits sex discrimination in employment and requires employers covered by the Act to treat men and women equally. A number of States have already conceded that special restrictions on women may no longer be enforced.

Objection: Women would be equally subject to the draft.

Answer: This is true. Women do serve in the Armed Forces now, but on a volunteer basis. The amendment would also prohibit more stringent eligibility standards for women than for men volunteers.

Objection: The equal rights amendment would require equal rights and responsibilities for women under the law.

Answer: True.

[Where the term GPO is mentioned in the text or in footnotes, the documents are available from the Superintendent of Documents, Government Printing Office, Washington, D.C. 20402]

Executive Order 11126

ESTABLISHING A COMMITTEE AND A COUNCIL RELATING TO THE STATUS OF WOMEN

The President's Commission on the Status of Women, established by Executive Order No. 10980 of December 14, 1961, has in fulfillment of its responsibilities, submitted a report concerning the steps that should be taken to further the effort to achieve the full participation of women in American life.

Enhancement of the quality of American life, as envisioned by the Commission's report can be accomplished only through concerted action by both public and private groups, through coordinated action within the Federal Government, and through action by States, communities, educational institutions, voluntary organizations, employers, unions, and individual citizens.

In order to assure effective and continuing leadership in advancing the status of women, it is deemed appropriate to establish an interdepartmental committee and a citizens' advisory council on the status of women.

NOW, THEREFORE, by virtue of the authority vested in me as President of the United States, it is ordered as follows:

Part I---Interdepartmental Committee on the Status of Women

Section 101 (a) There is hereby established the Interdepartmental Committee on the Status of Women (hereinafter referred to as the "Committee"), which shall be composed of the Secretary of Labor, who shall be the Chairman of the Committee, the Secretary of State, the Secretary of Defense, the Attorney General, the Secretary of Agriculture, the Secretary of Commerce, the Secretary of Health, Education, and Welfare, the Chairman of the Civil Service Commission, the Chairman of the Equal Employment Opportunity Commission, the Director of the Office of Economic Opportunity, and an Assistant Secretary of Labor to be designated by the Secretary of Labor, all ex officio. The Chairman may designate a Vice-Chairman of the Committee from its membership, and the Director of the Women's Bureau of the Department of Labor shall serve as Executive Vice-Chairman of the Committee, and shall be an ex officio member thereof. [1]/

(b) When any matter especially related to the area of responsibility of any Federal Department or agency, the head of which is not a member of the Committee, is to be considered by the Committee, the Chairman of the Committee shall invite the head of such department or agency to participate in the deliberations of the Committee with respect to such matter and to be a temporary member of the Committee during such deliberations.

---

[1]/ As amended by Executive Order 11221 of May 6, 1965, 30 F. R. 6427.

Sec. 102. The Committee shall--

(1) Maintain a continuing review and evaluation of the progress of Federal departments and agencies in advancing the status of women.

(2) Serve as a clearing house for information as to the activities being directed toward, and the progress being made in, improving conditions of special interest to women.

(3) Stimulate cooperation and the sharing of data, views, and information among Federal agencies, State and local governments, State commissions on the status of women, and public and private organizations having responsibilities and interests in areas of special concern to women.

(4) Encourage research on factors affecting the status of women in the areas of education, home and community activities, employment, social insurance, taxes, civil and political rights, labor legislation, and related matters.

(5) Exchange information with the Citizens' Advisory Council on the Status of Women, established by Part II of this order, on progress toward advancing the status of womeh and on new developments requiring consideration by the Council and the Committee.

Sec. 103. Annually the Committee, after consultation with the Citizens' Advisory Council, shall transmit a report to the President concerning the status of women. 1/

Part II---Citizens' Advisory Council on the Status of Women

Sec. 201. There is hereby established the Citizens' Advisory Council on the Status of Women (hereinafter referred to as the "Council"), which shall be composed of 20 members appointed by the President, one of whom he shall designate to serve as Chairman. The Council shall meet at the call of the Chairman of the Committee, but not less than twice a year. Members of the Council shall serve without compensation from the United States. 1/

Sec. 202. The Council shall--

(1) Serve as a primary means for suggesting and stimulating action with private institutions, organizations, and individuals working for improvement of conditions of special concern to women.

(2) Review and evaluate progress of organizations in furthering the full participation of women in American life.

1/ As amended by Executive Order 11221 of May 6, 1965, 30 F.R. 6427.

(3) Advise and assist the Committee in the evaluation of total progress made and recommend to the Committee, as necessary, action to accelerate such progress.

(4) Consider the effect of new developments on methods of advancing the status of women and recommend appropriate action to the Committee.

Part III---Financing and Administration

Sec. 301. The departments the heads of which are, under Section 101 (a) of this order, members of the Committee and the Civil Service Commission shall, as may be necessary, furnish assistance to the Committee in accordance with Section 214 of the Act of May 3, 1945, 59 Stat. 134 (31 U.S.C. 691). To the extent practical and not inconsistent with the law, (1) all Federal departments and agencies shall cooperate with the Committee and the Council and furnish them such information and assistance as may be necessary for the performance of their functions, and (2) the Secretary of Labor shall furnish staff, office space, office facilities and supplies and other necessary assistance, facilities, and services for the Committee and Council (including travel expenses and per diem in lieu of subsistence for members of the Council).

/s/ John F. Kennedy

The White House,
    November 1, 1963.

(3 CFR 1959-1963 Comp., p. 791; 28 F.R. 11717.)

C
  O
    P
      Y

C
  O
    P
      Y

STATEMENT BY JACK R. COWLES, BROOKLYN, N.Y.

The benefits to women of the proposed Equal Rights Amendment have been well covered elsewhere. Now, I wish to show how the ERA also would be of considerable benefit to men.

Being specially aware of the need for divorce law reform, I see clearly that the ERA would bring more equity into the divorce, child custody and alimony laws in the various states and thereby help bring about sorely needed improvements in these laws. As Robert Veit Sherwin, an attorney, says in his book, "Compatible Divorce": "Let us say at the very start that the laws concerning separation and divorce are inadequate, inappropriate, archaic, unworkable, barbaric and whatever adjectives you wish to apply . . . There always seems to be enough money to update the laws concerning corporations, trusts, patents, and other laws concerning the earning of money. But laws concerning humans in their behavior toward each other are seldom brought up to date." Therefore, I have brought to the attention of the 31 divorce law reform organizations in the U.S. the reasons why men—particularly men who have already been under the guns of the divorce, custody and alimony laws in this country—should support the ERA. Obviously, the ever decreasing fraction of men who have not yet been divorced would also do well to support the ERA for the following reasons:

First—Men who believed women needed "special protective legislation" passed many such laws, primarily in the area of employment. However, this "protective" attitude has spilled over into the divorce laws as well.

Second—equal rights for women also means equal responsibility. As women gain equality in jobs, education and similar areas, they will become more self-supporting and more able to assume equal responsibility.

Third—and most important—equality under the law for both sexes means a more sound legal basis to fight discrimination against men in the divorce, custody and alimony laws.

By acting in their own self-interest in helping women attain passage of the ERA, men have an opportunity to bring to the attention of women that it is to the self-interest of women to help men in revising he divorce laws. Men and women would do well to work together to revise divorce laws which encourage hypocrisy and are predicated on the guilt of one party. Better laws would permit unsuccessful marriages to be terminated without hypocrisy and new marriages to be contracted without undue financial hardship to either men or women. In "The Disgrace of Our Divorce Laws" (Good Housekeeping, April 1970) Evan McLeod Wylie, a woman herself, makes a strong appeal to women to help in exposing the injustices of divorce and its high cost to society. It is apparent that mutual cooperation will help provide the voting strength needed to attain the mutual objectives of men and women.

Other specific ways in which the ERA would eliminate discrimination against men have been covered adequately elsewhere.

In conclusion, I wish to point out that in a more general sense—and therefore even more importantly—nearly all men would benefit indirectly by the long run benefits to women which passage of the ERA would bring about. As women more fully develop their potential as human beings, the relationship between men and women in our society would continually improve thereby benefiting men as well as women—and reducing the divorce rate as well. For, what is truly in the long range interests of women, is also in the long range best interests of men.

ORGANIZED LABOR IN OPPOSITION

STATEMENT IN OPPOSITION TO THE PROPOSED EQUAL RIGHTS AMENDMENT TO THE CONSTITUTION BY JACOB S. POTOFSKY, GENERAL PRESIDENT, AMALGAMATED CLOTHING WORKERS OF AMERICA

I am submitting this statement on behalf of the more than 390,000 members of the Amalgamated Clothing Workers of America, AFL–CIO. They are employed primarily in the men's and boys' apparel and related industries, in the laundry and cleaning and dyeing industries, and in retail trade, in hundreds of communities throughout the United States.

Our organization has been deeply concerned with recent developments affecting women workers as a result of the confusion surrounding the application of Title VII of the Civil Rights Act of 1964 and, specifically, the onslaught against state protective legislation. We view the proposed Equal Rights Amendment to the Constitution as an immeasurably grave threat to women workers, almost entirely negative in effect, and we, therefore, urge this Subcommittee on Constitutional Amendments to oppose its adoption. We are particularly alarmed by the totally sweeping, indiscriminate, destructive effect it would have on state protective legislation.

Three-fourths of the members of the Amalgamated Clothing Workers of America are women. The apparel industries have always been major employers of women workers. From the inception of our Union, more than 55 years ago, the Amalgamated has considered the problems of women workers one of its basic concerns. The principle of equal pay was established in our industries long ago; rates have always been set for the job, without regard to sex. At the same time, we have been aware that many women workers really have two jobs—the job in the shop and the job at home, the latter often involving the care of children. As a result, we recently established the first labor-sponsored program of day-care centers, so that our women members in the areas which have these centers can work, secure in the knowledge that their children are properly supervised.

While we have done, and are continuing to do, what we can to secure the welfare of our women members, the Amalgamated has also been aware that the vast majority of women workers are not protected by union contracts and have been subjected to severe exploitation. When women began entering the labor force in substantial numbers at the turn of the century, working conditions were, in general, deplorable. Individual workers had no bargaining power, and the few trade unions were largely craft unions in occupations filled by men. The exploitation of women, many of them recently arrived immigrants, was the rule of the day and was so striking that their cause was taken up by many prominent social reformers. The historic Triangle Shirtwaist Company fire in 1911—in which 150 workers, mostly women needle-trades workers, were burned to death—was a deeply shocking tragedy that aroused the public conscience and gave impetus to the enactment of protective legislation.

The labor movement was instrumental in achieving these early minimum standards, just as the labor movement played a major role in the passage of the Fair Labor Standards Act in 1938. The leading part of the Amalgamated Clothing Workers in these efforts is well known, and I refer to it merely to reaffirm the commitment of our Union to these positive advances for American workers.

284

There is nothing new about the so-called Equal Rights Amendment, except the "new look" the latter-day "women's liberation" groups have attempted to give it. It has been introduced in every session of the Congress since 1923. We are well acquainted with it. Throughout the years, those of us in the mainstream of the fundamental struggle for the advancement of labor standards—aware of the threat the Amendment poses to the status of women workers because it would negate state protective standards—preferred to fight for *positive* measures and, in its stead, repeatedly supported equal pay proposals, which were finally adopted by the Congress as the equal pay amendment to the Fair Labor Standards Act in 1963.

The legislative history of the Civil Rights Act of 1964 indicates that the inclusion of the word, "sex," in Title VII was introduced in order to defeat the entire Act and that its inclusion was not intended to undermine state protective legislation for women. In its positive application, Title VII can be an effective instrumentality for overcoming discrimination against women in employment and can contribute substantially to their progress.

Unfortunately, Title VII also invited a major assault on state protective legislation, without distinguishing between those provisions might be viewed as discriminatory and those which are not, in fact, discriminatory. A number of adverse court decisions and the invalidation by a few states of their protective provisions have already undermined these important protective measures. The Equal Rights Amendment would automatically wipe out the existing protective provisions. Since one of our primary objections to the Amendment is its destructive effect on state protective legislation, it appears to be necessary to review, briefly, the situation with regard to state protective legislation and why such protection is not obsolete at all—as is claimed by some—but still very much needed by millions of women workers.

There are various kinds of protection provided by state laws and regulations—minimum wage, overtime compensation, equal pay, fair employment practices, hours, industrial homework, employment before and after childbirth, occupational limitations, and others, including seating and weight-lifting. Not all of these are considered to be discriminatory in their effect on employment. It is doubtful that serious objection would be raised if state provisions were confined to employment for periods before and after childbirth, seating, rest periods, days of rest, and meal periods. Except for the first, these provisions could be extended to men as well as women, thus advancing labor standards for all workers. The Equal Rights Amendment would not have this effect, however; it would wipe them all out.

With regard to weight-lifting—the subject of some of the recent litigation—the existing state regulations do appear to be obsolete and in need of revision. Obviously, there are women who can more easily lift heavy weights than some men. In this field, standards could be set by medical experts for *individuals* of various heights, weights, and other physical characteristics, with regard to sex, which would protect men and women equally. The Equal Rights Amendment would prevent the revision of *existing* provisions to extend them to protect all workers from excessive demands by employers with regard to weight-lifting. On this important point, we would have to start from scratch.

But the heart of the matter is really the hours limitations—not only the maximum hours to be worked but the prohibition on night work. When state hours limitations were enacted, protection was deemed necessary partly for two major reasons, the severe and extensive exploitation of women workers and their domestic responsibilities. It is important to examine the extent to which these two basic factors are still relevant.

At the time state protective legislation was initiated, there were relatively few women in the labor force. At present, there are more than 31,000,000 women in the civilian labor force, almost 30,000,000 of whom are employed. Almost 60 percent of all women workers are married and living with their husbands. Working mothers constitute 38 percent of all working women. Obviously, the majority of women workers have domestic responsibilities, and a very substantial number of them, almost 11,000,000, have children under the age of 18 years. Even with a 40-hour workweek, such women—between their paid employment and their many hours of cooking, cleaning, shopping, child care, and other household duties—have arduously long hours.

Large numbers of women workers are employed in traditionally low-paying occupations and low-wage industries. Full-time women workers had a median income of only $4,026 a year in 1966. Families in which the head of the family was a female had a median income of only $4,010, scarcely above the poverty level.

What kind of protection do women workers have, apart from state protective legislation? To begin with, more than one-fourth of them are not even covered by the Fair Labor Standards Act. In addition, only 12 percent of them are unionized and working under the protection of collective bargaining agreements. If state protection is outlawed, most women workers will be completely at the mercy of their employers.

Who will benefit from the repeal of state protective legislation? A relatively small number of women workers who want to work overtime beyond the hours set forth in the state regulations will benefit. (Ironically, many of the business and professional women most vocal in advocating the overthrow of hours limitations would not be affected at all, since a majority of the states with hours limitations already exempt them from these restrictions.) Those who would benefit are largely women in fairly high-paying (but not, for the most part, executive, administrative, or professional) jobs, usually protected by union contracts. Also benefiting will be non-union and anti-union employers who would prefer no limitations at all on their conditions of employment.

Who will suffer from the repeal of state protective legislation? Much has justifiably been made of the fact unorganized women not covered by the Fair Labor Standards Act—numbering several million—could be required to work excessively long hours. In many cases, this would make it impossible for them to meet their home responsibilities and might force them to become unemployed because they are unable to meet their home responsibilities and continue to work in jobs where long hours are required. This is most likely to happen in service industries and in certain types of retail trade and would be essentially true in times of recession and labor surplus. No recourse would be open to such women. It is a tribute to the social-mindedness of some labor unions that they fought for state protective legislation for these largely unorganized women.

The question then is one of assessing the discrimination against a relatively small proportion of women workers by virtue of denying them overtime or the far greater, potentially cruel discrimination against the vast majority of women workers for whom excessive overtime would be a great hardship and possibly the cause of their having to abandon employment altogether because of their domestic responsibilities. It is a question of the advancement of a few or the welfare of many.

A timely footnote consideration which should be noted is the fact that the Nixon Administration's welfare proposal would require recipients who are mothers of school-age children and are deemed employable to accept training or employment or lose their portion of family benefits. Such women are usually among the least skilled, and the added pressure of employment in occupations with unduly long hours—which could result from the repeal of state protective legislation—is unconscionable.

I have set forth the importance of state protective legislation in originally advancing and now maintaining the status of the vast majority of women workers because I truly believe that the impact of the Equal Rights Amendment on this vital field will be retrogressive and can set back the progress made against the exploitation of low-paid women workers by many decades, perhaps irretrievably.

There are, however, other—and very basic—objections to the Equal Rights Amendment. In and of itself, it will wipe out much that has been gained without, in other ways, specifically advancing the status of women. Apart from the issues relevant to state protective legislation, there are other areas in which women have been discriminated against. In connection with the important area of equal employment opportunity, we now have Title VII of the Civil Rights Act of 1964—and the Equal Rights Amendment will do nothing beyond Title VII to further equal employment opportunity. What is needed here is simply implementation and enforcement of Title VII and not a constitutional amendment of a general and sweeping nature. Similarly, with regard to equal pay, what we need is enforcement of the equal pay amendment to the Fair Labor Standards Act and not a constitutional amendment. In these two basic areas, the Equal Pay Amendment would achieve nothing.

In the same way, in other areas in which women suffer discrimination, redress must be sought through specific remedial measures. In the field of education, women are still not equally considered for admission to state colleges and universities and other institutions of higher learning. There are also a number of state laws which restrict married women with regard to the establishment of a legal domicile or the undertaking of an independent business. There are some exemptions of women in the selection of juries, and, in some states, their are heavier criminal penalties for women than for men committing the same crimes. Undoubtedly, there are other specific areas in which there is discrimination against women.

I maintain that, on the legislative front, discrimination against women can be attacked effectively only through *specific* legislative provisions. This view is supported by the weight of our entire experience with civil rights for minority groups. It is best evidenced by the fact that, despite the enactment of the Fourteenth and Fifteenth Amendments to the Constitution a hundred years ago, discrimination against minorities remained practically intransigent until, only within the last few years, we effectuated, on the legislative front, the intent of these amendments by a series of specific laws dealing with voting rights, public accommodations, education, housing, and equal employment opportunity.

If we want to remove discrimination against women, it must be done in the same way. We must legislate in the areas in which the problem still exists—just as we did with regard to equal pay and equal employment opportunity and just as we did in many of the areas involved in civil rights for minority groups. Legislation to eliminate discrimination against women does not require the Equal Rights Amendment. Such legislation is already constitutional. The immediate effect of the Equal Rights Amendment would be to destroy what has been built up over many years of struggle—in the name of empty rhetoric—without contributing anything positive to the advancement of the status of women. The specific and positive measures called for do not require a special constitutional amendment. They require the formulation, enactment, and enforcement of specific legislation which can deal with the problems effectively—all of which would be constitutional. Admittedly, this is a more difficult task than the enactment of a single, sweeping, broad-side amendment. But it is the only way to do the job without destroying what we have already gained.

I, therefore, respectfully urge this Subcommittee on Constitutional Amendments to reject the Equal Rights Amendment.

STATEMENT ON THE EQUAL RIGHTS AMENDMENT TO THE CONSTITUTION SUBMITTED BY EVELYN DUBROW, LEGISLATIVE REPRESENTATIVE, ON BEHALF OF THE INTERNATIONAL LADIES' GARMENT WORKERS' UNION, AFL–CIO

On behalf of the International Ladies' Garment Workers' Union and its more than 420,000 members in the United States—80 percent of whom are women—I welcome this opportunity to make known our views in opposition to the Equal Rights Amendment to the Constitution.

The Constitution of the United States already fully guarantees equal rights to all persons regardless of sex, age, race, religion or national origin. Laws to accomplish this end have also been adopted by the Congress on numerous occasions and have been upheld by our courts. Thus, no Constitutional amendment is required to achieve equality of the sexes.

Of course, the existence of a right under the Constitution does not automatically guarantee that discrimination will not exist. More than 100 years after the adoption of the 15th Amendment guaranteeing suffrage regardless of race, there is still inequality to be eliminated at the polls. And more than 100 years after adoption of the 14th Amendment, the federal courts had to rule unconstitutional a state law barring women from jury service. In such circumstances, legislative or judicial intervention often becomes necessary to achieve broad constitutional objectives.

Although women faced discrimination in many areas of society—economic, political and social—the most serious deprivation of their rights occurs in their role as employees. From the time women began to enter the labor force in substantial numbers, their substantially weaker bargaining power made them the target of many discriminatory practices. Sub-standard wages, inhuman working conditions, long hours, unsanitary factories, jobs that threatened health and safety—all of these were forced on women and minors by circumstances they could not control. They had no alternative—accept or starve.

Under pressure from an aroused and irate citizenry, state and federal governments enacted legislation to alleviate the discrimination to which working women were subject. Laws set minimum wages and maximum hours; they provided rest periods, sanitary facilities, ventilation, seating and limited work before and after childbirth. All of these laws have been upheld as proper actions of the states and the federal government. The continued right of local and federal governments to provide appropriate safeguards to every segment of our population that need them should not be destroyed.

Under the proposed Amendment, a number of essential legislative safeguards of women's rights as industrial citizens would be wiped out. This should not be permitted to happen.

The proposed "Equal Rights" Amendment is unnecessary. However, if in its wisdom, Congress deems it desirable, it should specifically and explicitly provide that it would not act as a waiver of paragraphs 1 and 3 of Article I, Section 8 of the Constitution.

EIGHTH CONSTITUTIONAL CONVENTION, AFL–CIO, OCTOBER 1969

WOMEN WORKERS

Nearly 31 million working women play an important part in the nation's labor force. Organized labor, with about 4 million women in its ranks, has traditionally sought to protect and promote the interests of women workers, to eliminate discrimination on the job and to be responsive to the special needs of women workers carrying the double responsibilities of job and home.

The labor movement has historically promoted the interests of women through trade union objectives of raising wages, shortening working hours, promoting job security, and improving the conditions of work. Particular needs and aspirations of women workers have been recognized in efforts to eliminate job discrimination, to obtain full enforcement of equal pay for equal work and to secure enlightened public policy in the fields of labor standards legislation, education and training, social benefit programs and taxation.

A continuing major concern of working mothers is the need for expanded provision of day-care facilities and more adequate federal income tax deductions for women who must pay for child-care services at their own expense in order to work.

Heightened emphasis on equal employment opportunity for women under Title VII of the Civil Rights Act has placed special strains on the long-standing state protective labor laws for women. These laws have traditionally had the support of organized labor and of women's groups concerned to prevent the exploitation of female workers, concentrated in low paying jobs and in unorganized industries.

The Equal Employment Opportunity Commission has recently issued an opinion that state laws which "prohibit or limit" the employment of women are in conflict with Title VII. Such laws include, but are not limited to such protective legislation as occupational prohibitions, maximum hours, night work, and weight-lifting.

We regard the EEOC position as too sweeping, in that it applies to reasonable limits as well as unreasonable ones, fails to recognize the interests of women who rely upon such laws as a protection against employers, and ignores the needs of those women workers for whom alternative forms of protection either by public law or union contract are not available. Until adequate protection for all workers can be secured under general legislation, reasonable legal safeguards should be available for those women who are most in need of them. Therefore, be it

Resolved: Trade unions should expand their efforts to organize the unorganized among women workers, to design programs that reflect the interests of women workers, and to encourage more women to participate fully in union activities and policy-making, as many outstanding women are now doing.

All possible steps should be taken to expand the availability of day-care centers. Federal law should be amended to permit employer contributions to trust funds established under collective bargaining for day-care centers. States should be encouraged to take advantage of federal funds now available to them under the Social Security Act. Federal funds should be appropriated so that public or non-profit agencies, including trade unions, can be enabled to operate day-care centers.

We urge liberalized tax deductions for child care-expenses of women workers, under federal income tax provisions.

We support equal pay and equal employment opportunities for women, adequate maternity leave and benefit plans, and expanded educational and training programs in which women can upgrade their job qualifications.

We call upon the Equal Employment Opportunity Commission, as well as the courts and legislatures, to seek reconciliation of conflicts between Title VII and women's state labor laws, without abandonment of necessary safeguards. We urge appropriate extensions of the benefits of women's labor legislation to men and the enactment of improved federal wage-hour legislation for both sexes.

We continue our opposition to the long-pending Equal Rights Amendment to the Constitution because of its potentially destructive impact on women's labor legislation.

STATEMENT OF THE AFL–CIO ON METHODS OF REMOVING LEGAL DISCRIMINATION AGAINST WOMEN

In accordance with the recent invitation of the Committee on Civil and Political Rights to submit our views on various methods of correcting legal inequities affecting women, we are pleased to offer our observations in this statement. The three methods under consideration by the Committee and (1) securing an Equal Rights Amendment to the Constitution (2) challenging the validity of discriminatory provisions through litigation under the present 14th Amendment to the Constitution and (3) improving laws through State action.

1. EQUAL RIGHTS AMENDMENT TO THE CONSTITUTION

As previously indicated to the Committee, the AFL–CIO has traditionally opposed attacking the problem through the device of an Equal Rights Amendment.

In a recent letter to the Committee from Secretary-Treasurer William F. Schnitzer, our general position was set forth as follows:

"Despite our positive interest in advancing women's rights, we have found it necessary to oppose this particular method of doing so, since it could well destroy more rights than it creates. The Amendment is excessively sweeping in scope, reaching into a very complex set of legal family, and social relationships, in which equality cannot always be achieved through sameness. We do not think that all differences in law are necessarily discriminatory, nor that all laws containing different provisions for men and women should be abolished.

"As a labor organization we have had a special concern over the threat that a simple Equal Rights Amendment would present to minimum labor standards legislation. Many state labor standards laws on wages, hours and other conditions of employment apply only to women. It may be desirable for such laws to be extended to men, but the practical fact is that an Equal Rights Amendment is likely to destroy the laws altogether rather than bring about coverage for both sexes."

On February 7, 1963 a special "Memorandum on Objections to the Equal Rights Amendment" was sent by the AFL–CIO Director of Legislation to all members of the Congress of the United States. (This memorandum is based on an earlier one circulated to the Congress in February 1959.) A copy of the current memorandum, with the covering letters, is attached for the Committee's convenient reference.

We would add further that an Equal Rights Amendment offers not even the advantage of a speedy resolution of the inequities and discriminations against which it is directed. Not only is it highly controversial on a substantive basis, so as to make its actual adoption highly unlikely, but in the opinion of many authorities it would lead to a new era of confusion and litigation through the courts, while rights and duties were adjudicated on a piecemeal basis under the new and impracticable rule of mechanistic equality.

This prospect was stressed, for example, by former Secretary of Labor James P. Mitchell in his letter to the House Committee on the Judiciary on April 24, 1954. The Secretary wrote:

"The uncertainties and unsettling effects created by S.J. Res. 49 would remain until removed by years of litigation in every state. For this primary reason, I cannot recommend favorable action on the proposal."

It would appear therefore, that the Equal Rights Amendment would at best accomplish only confusion in the rights of women in the foreseeable future and at worst it would destroy many valuable rights and benefits now accorded by particular types of laws, especially in the labor legislation field.

2. THE "PAULI MURRAY PROPOSAL"

Essentially the Pauli Murray approach is to challenge the constitutionality of various types of discriminatory legislation through appeal to the "equal protection clause" of the Fourteenth Amendment. The proposal contemplates the setting up of a specialized body of experts to give direction to a concerted effort through the courts, making a careful selection of cases to be undertaken and laying the groundwork for briefs based on modern economic and sociological data.

In our view, this approach has obvious advantages over the Equal Rights Amendments as a means of liquidating outmoded legal discrimination against women. A the same time, we have certain reservations as to its possible ramifications and so cannot give it unqualified endorsement at present.

The major advantages are that this approach is evolutionary in nature and does not contemplate a sweeping nullifcation or confusion of existing laws which deal differently with men and women. Under ideal circumstances, it would permit an orderly resolution of specific injustices or classes of injustice on which there is a broad consensus and on which the arguments are especially well grounded.

Court actions could be selective, concentrating upon particular issues, for example, anachronistic property laws, exclusion from state educational institutions or occupations licensed by the state under certain circumstances, etc. Furthermore, in judging the validity of state legislative classifications under the equal protection clause, the courts would be able to apply the broad standard of "reasonableness" rather than being bound by a mechanical rule that there must always be identity of treatment.

There is a danger however, of securing too broad a constitutional rule on sex discrimination.

Miss Murray's formulation of a constitutional principle would strike down laws differentiating on the basis of sex unless it can be shown that a law is justified as (1) a necessary protection for that group of women performing family functions, or (2) a valid health regulation based on some scientifically demonstrated need that women have and men do not, or (3) a measure intended to promote women's rights that have been curtailed because of women's traditionally disadvantaged position in society. In addition it must be shown that the differential treatment does not imply an inferior status for women.

This formulation may be intended to reach only invidious distinctions, but it could reach legal provisions advantageous to women (and potentially of advantage to all workers), though not supported by conclusive demonstration of special requirements of women as compared to men. For example, legislation setting minimum wages was applied first to women and later extended to men. Frequently, the enactment of labor standards legislation limited to women is largely a matter of practical politics—a half loaf if better than nothing, and sometimes is a step toward the whole. But at a certain point it might be impossible, for example, to say that the special health needs of women justified any distinction, and employers might be able to use this argument to invalidate labor standards legislation where it applies only to women.

Also, to the extent that women's labor legislation has been grounded on the protection of the maternal and family functions of women, labor laws could be thrown into doubt as to their applicability for women who do not individually perform these functions.

Obviously, the greatest care would have to be exercised in selecting the targets of any court test of discriminatory state laws. To minimize the danger to protective or humane labor legislation, the targets might have to be all outside the labor field. Even so, however, litigation in a totally different field could produce some sweeping judicial pronouncements that employers might seize upon to turn against protective labor legislation. Miss Murray's standards would need further refinement before the AFL–CIO could endorse them, even in the abstract.

Finally, if a litigation approach should be adopted, what are the chances of its success?

Most major constitutional developments occur after a particular issue has become "ripe" for decision. The Supreme Court likes to have a certain body of judicial decisions and scholarly writing to work with when it takes up a problem. Miss Murray indicates there is a dearth of law review writing on the subject, although in time this could be remedied.

Progress through the courts would in most instances require initial testing in the state courts and reverses could be anticipated since state courts are generally reluctant to hold enactments of their own state legislatures unconstitutional. In some situations however, there might be the possiblity of seeking injunctions against the enforcement of state statutes before a 3-judge federal court, thereby avoiding the state courts.

The litigation route would involve much preparation on a long term basis and a sustained effort in carrying it out.

The present composition of the Supreme Court itself would not appear to be an unfavorable factor.

3. IMPROVING LAWS THROUGH STATE ACTION

Despite the varying opinions upon the desirability of remedying legal inequities through the Constitutional route, most interested parties undoubtedly agree in principle on the repeal or amendment of specific outmoded state statutes adversely affecting women's rights. Labor fully supports such efforts, since they can more readily be isolated from attacks upon labor standards legislation. This route also is slow, but it is one by which concrete advances have actually been achieved over the past half century.

CONCLUDING OBSERVATIONS

Historically the emancipation of women as to civil and political rights and the growth of social legislation to protect and promote the welfare and economic security of women have proceeded hand in hand. The Nineteenth Amendment was ratified at the height of the movement to establish protective legislation for women as to maximum hours and minimum wages. The advancement in both sectors has continued and broadened since 1919, despite the divisive controversy brought about by the proposal for an Equal Rights Amendment, first introduced into the Congress in 1923.

In the future the abolition of legal restrictions on women's rights will become of less importance than positive action to promote the expansion of rights not now protected by law. It has often been observed that today the major problems of discriminatory treatment on the basis of sex lie far less in the provisions of public law than in private practices not dealt with by law. Chief among these is discrimination in private employment. Action against private discriminatory practices will in many instances require new laws, of which statutes requiring equal pay for equal work are a good example. The gaining of substantive rights will require not only the abolition of old laws, but the enactment of new ones.

AMERICAN FEDERATION OF LABOR AND CONGRESS OF INDUSTRIAL ORGANIZATIONS

MEMORANDUM ON OBJECTIONS TO PROPOSED EQUAL RIGHTS AMENDMENT

1.   Lowering of labor standards for women

Enactment of the Equal Rights Amendment would jeopardize existing state legislation establishing minimum wages, maximum hours, and other special provisions for the protection of working women against substandard conditions of employment.

Most working women do not have the protection afforded by trade union membership and must perforce rely upon the safeguards provided by public law.

Should legislation enforcing minimum employment standards for women be cancelled under the Amendment, there is no assurance that new legislation would be enacted providing appropriate protection for both men and women. Rather, the result is only too likely to be no protection for either sex. There might be "equality", but it would be an equality without "rights."

2.   New opportunities for discrimination against women

        The Equal Rights Amendment does not deal substantively with the
real problems of discrimination against women, which today lie largely outside
of formal provisions of law. Much of the special labor legislation for women
which Equal Rights proponents vigorously decry as "unequal", represents a
positive advance in the reduction of discriminatory disadvantages which women
suffer in employment, through being required, for example, to work longer
hours at lower pay than men. The opportunity for employers to play off one
group against another in the lowering of labor standards would be aggravated
in the absence of the legislative restraints which the Equal Rights Amendment
would remove.

        The AFL-CIO has supported and continues to support positive legis-
lation to advance the rights of women, including the enactment of equal pay
legislation to establish the legal rights of women to receive no less pay than
men when they perform work equal with that of men. By contrast. the Equal
Rights Amendment would do nothing to eliminate pay discrimination against
women by private employers.

3.   Sweeping scope of Amendment

        The Equal Rights Amendment threatens not only laws protecting
women's labor standards, but also all other laws which make any distinction,
however reasonable, between men and women. These laws encompass every department of life, ranging from marriage and support laws, inheritance and property
rights, to pension laws and health and welfare systems. Differences in their
provisions cannot in all cases automatically be construed as discriminations
against women, for true equality is not always achieved through exact and
unvarying identity of treatment. The Equal Rights Amendment is an oversimplified approach to what is actually a complex problem in the achievement
of real justice which must necessarily take account of the special and sometimes
differing needs and responsibilities of men and women in particular circumstances.

4.   Specific inequities better remedied by other means

        Anachronistic and inappropriate legal restrictions on women's
rights as citizens property owners, and wage earners have been rapidly
disappearing under the steady pressure of social and economic change, even
while the Equal Rights Amendment has failed of passage in every year since
1923. Remaining legal inequities can be most fruitfully attacked in the
particular situations where they continue to exist. Such efforts have the
full support of the AFL-CIO. The evolutionary process of increasing freedom
and equality for women properly contemplates a more realistic notion of
"discrimination" than is impled by a Constitutional amendment which proclaims
all differences in the treatment of men and women, as automatically unfair
and discriminatory.

5.   AFL-CIO position

        In view of the genuine rights which women stand to lose under the
Equal Rights Amendment, with respect both to labor standards and other provisions of law. the AFL-CIO opposes the Equal Rights Amendment. At the very
least, the Amendment should include appropriate language to insure that it
will not be used to destroy substantive and appropriate rights and benefits
accorded to women now and hereafter by state and federal laws. Such has been
vigorously opposed by Equal Rights proponents. This opposition dramatically
underlines the very real danger that the Equal Rights Amendment presents to
the welfare and advancement of women.

AFL-CIO Research Department
February 1963

AMERICAN FEDERATION OF LABOR AND CONGRESS OF INDUSTRIAL ORGANIZATIONS

815 SIXTEENTH STREET, N.W.
WASHINGTON 6, D.C.   NATIONAL 8-3870

February 7, 1963

TO ALL MEMBERS OF THE UNITED STATES SENATE

Dear Senator:

Proponents of the so-called Equal Rights Amendment have been contacting Members of the Congress urging them to sponsor the amendment.

The AFL-CIO opposes the so-called Equal Rights Amendment. In order to make the position of the AFL-CIO absolutely clear, I quote the pertinent paragrah from the resolution on "Women Workers" adopted by the 4th Constitutional Convention of the AFL-CIO in December 1961:

"We reaffirm our opposition to the so-called Equal Rights Amendment to the Constitution, which would wipe out hard-won gains in the field of special labor legislation for the protection of women, as well as all other laws, no matter how reasonably based, which in any way differ in provisions for men and women."

To clarify further the position of the AFL-CIO, I am transmitting to you with this letter a memorandum outlining in greater detail the objections of the AFL-CIO to an Equal Rights Amendment.

Sincerely yours,

Andrew J. Biemiller, Director
DEPARTMENT OF LEGISLATION

enclosure

293

INTERNATIONAL LABOUR CONFERENCE

CONVENTION CONCERNING THE MAXIMUM PERMISSIBLE
WEIGHT TO BE CARRIED BY ONE WORKER

The General Conference of the International Labour Organisation, having been convened at Geneva by the Governing Body of the International Labour Office, and having met in its Fifty-first Session on 7 June 1967, and having decided upon the adoption of certain proposals with regard to maximum permissible weight to be carried by one worker, which is the sixth item on the agenda of the session, and having determined that these proposals shall take the form of an international Convention, adopts this twenty-eighth day of June of the year one thousand nine hundred and sixty-seven the following Convention, which may be cited as the Maximum Weight Convention, 1967:

Article 1

For the purpose of this Convention—
(a) The term "manual transport of loads" means any transport in which the weight of the load is wholly borne by one worker; it covers the lifting and putting down of loads;
(b) The term "regular manual transport of loads" means any activity which is continuously or principally devoted to the manual transport of loads, or which normally includes, even though intermittently, the manual transport of loads; and
(c) The term "young worker" means a worker under 18 years of age.

Article 2

1. This Convention applies to regular manual transport of loads.
2. This Convention applies to all branches of economic activity in respect of which the Member concerned maintains a system of labour inspection.

Article 3

No worker shall be required or permitted to engage in the manual transport of a load which, by reason of its weight, is likely to jeopardise his health or safety.

Article 4

In the application of the principle set forth in Article 3, Members shall take account of all the conditions in which the work is to be performed.

Article 5

Each Member shall take appropriate steps to ensure that any worker assigned to manual transport of loads other than light loads receives, prior to such assignment, adequate training or instruction in working techniques, with a view to safeguarding health and preventing accidents.

Article 6

In order to limit or to facilitate the manual transport of loads, suitable technical devices shall be used as much as possible.

Article 7

1. The assignment of women and young workers to manual transport of loads other than light loads shall be limited.
2. Where women and young workers are engaged in the manual transport of loads, the maximum weight of such loads shall be substantially less than that permitted for adult male workers.

Article 8

Each Member shall, by laws or regulations or any other method consistent with national practice and conditions and in consultation with the most representative organisations of employers and workers concerned, take such steps as may be necessary to give effect to the provisions of this Convention.

Article 9

The formal ratifications of this Convention shall be communicated to the Director-General of the International Labour Office for registration.

Article 10

1. This Convention shall be binding only upon those Members of the Interntional Labour Organisation whose ratifications have been registered with the Director-General.

2. It shall come into force twelve months after the date on which the ratifications of two Members have been registered with the Director-General.

3. Thereafter, this Convention shall come into force for any Member twelve months after the date on which its ratification has been registered.

Article 11

1. A Member which has ratified this Convention may denounce it after the expiration of ten years from the date on which the Convention first comes into force, by an act communicated to the Director-General of the International Labour Office for registration. Such denunciation shall not take effect until one year after the date on which it is registered.

2. Each Member which has ratified this Convention and which does not, within the year following the expiration of the period of ten years mentioned in the preceding paragraph, exercise the right of denunciation provided for in this Article, will be bound for another period of ten years and, thereafter, may denounce this Convention at the expiration of each period of ten years under the terms provided for in this Article.

Article 12

1. The Director-General of the International Labour Office shall notify all Members of the International Labour Organisation of the registration of all ratifications and denunciations communicated to him by the Members of the Organisation.

2. When notifying the Members of the Organisation of the registration of the second ratification communicated to him, the Director-General shall draw the attention of the Members of the Organisation to the date upon which the Convention will come into force.

Article 13

The Director-General of the International Labour Office shall communicate to the Secretary-General of the United Nations for registration in accordance with Article 102 of the Charter of the United Nations full particulars of all ratifications and acts of denunciation registered by him in accordance with the provisions of the preceding Articles.

Article 14

At such times as it may consider necessary the Governing Body of the International Labour Office shall present to the General Conference a report on the working of this Convention and shall examine the desirability of placing on the agenda of the Conference the question of its revision in whole or in part.

Article 15

1. Should the Conference adopt a new Convention revising this Convention in whole or in part, then, unless the new Convention otherwise provides—

(*a*) The ratification by a Member of the new revising Convention shall *ipso jure* involve the immediate denunciation of this Convention, notwithstanding the provisions of Article 11 above, if and when the new revising Convention shall have come into force;

(*b*) As from the date when the new revising Convention comes into force this Convention shall cease to be open to ratification by the Members.

2. This Convention shall in any case remain in force in its actual form and content for those Members which have ratified it but have not ratified the revising Convention.

Article 16

The English and French versions of the text of this Convention are equally authoritative.

ORGANIZED LABOR IN SUPPORT

EXCERPT FROM : REPORT NUMBER ONE, RESOLUTIONS COMMITTEE
22ND CONSTITUTIONAL CONVENTION, UAW

THE WOMAN IN SOCIETY

(Adopted April 23, 1970)

President John F. Kennedy, in establishing the President's Commission on the Status of Women in 1961 said:

". . . prejudices and outmoded customs act as barriers to the full realization of women's basic rights which should be respected and fostered as part of our Nation's commitment to human dignity, freedom, and democracy . . .

It is my hope that the Commission's Report will indicate what remains to be done to demolish prejudices and out-moded customs which act as barriers to the full partnership of women in our democracy . . ."

The Commission's recommendations fell short of expectations. However, the ferment which the Report created resulted in procedures to eliminate some aspects of discriminatory treatment and has provided the impetus for further progress.

During President Kennedy's Administration, "The Equal Pay Act," as an amendment to the Fair Labor Standards Act, which was introduced in every session of Congress for over 16 years, was enacted into law. The law represents the only legislation enacted in this century affecting primarily women since the voting rights law was passed in 1920.

Under the Johnson Administration, the 1964 Civil Rights Act was passed with the term "sex" included in Title VII, the Fair Employment Section. The term "sex" was also included under President Johnson's executive order on nondiscrimination in government contracts.

The marked increase in the participation of women in the work force is not noted by a similar increase in economic gain. Indeed, as a result of continuing sex discrimination, women are receiving an ever lesser share of the economic pie as indicated by some of the following statistics.

In 1968, 52.9 percent of all families headed by a nonwhite woman and 25.2 percent of all families headed by a white woman had incomes below the poverty line. Comparable figures for families headed by a white or nonwhite male respectively are 6.3 percent and 18.9 percent. The number of families headed by white and nonwhite males living below the official poverty level declined by 48.6 percent between 1959 and 1968. During this same period, there was a 17.2 percent decline in families headed by white women and a 7.5 percent increase in the number of poor families headed by nonwhite women.

Among adults, unemployment currently is more severe for women. Families headed by a woman worker are also more often poor, despite her participation in the labor force. Among families headed by a woman worker, 45 percent of the nonwhite families and 16 percent of the white families lived in poverty in 1968. The comparable percentages for families headed by a male worker were 16 percent for nonwhite families and 4 percent for white families. Of all adults 16 years of age and over living in poverty in 1966, 6.9 million were men and 11.2 were women.

Part of the problem of poverty among women is that by custom and their own acceptance they are almost always regulated to the lowest-paying jobs. For instance, in 1968, of the estimated 2.2 million employees in "domestic" service, most of whom were women, 86 percent earned less than $1.00 per hour. Such work, which pays rock bottom wages is essentially work that no one really wants to do. Yet when much of the same job content is labeled "sweepers" or "janitors" and performed by men, it becomes respectable and better paid.

The concentration of women in the lower-paying occupations is reflected in the gap between the median earnings of women and men. (The median is the figure that divides any group of figures so that half are above it and half are below it.)

The median income of year-round full-time workers in 1968 was: white men, $7,870; nonwhite men, $5,314; white women, $4,580; and nonwhite women, $3,487.

When the incomes and earnings of women and men are compared on the basis of educational attainment, the median income received by women at all levels is substantially below the median income of men.

Basic to the solution of the problem of low wages earned by women is increasing the Federal Minimum Wage under the Fair Labor Standards Act to at least $2.50 per hour and extending its coverage without exception to every job within the reach of federal authority. A $2.50 per hour minimum would provide a full time worker with an annual income of $5,200, still substantially below the $5,500 guaranteed income recommended by President Nixon's White House Conference on Food, Nutrition, and Health. Extension of the Fair Labor Standards Act to all workers would also provide them with the protection of the Equal Pay amendment. The same universal minimum should be set at state levels for jobs within state jurisdiction.

The ferment on the issue of women's rights in the last decade has produced an eruption of new militant women's groups and reactivated old ones. Women caucuses have been formed and strong resolutions adopted by numerous national and professional organizations. The purpose—full equality now.

In over 30 years of existence, the UAW has always been in the vanguard in the fight to eliminate discrimination wherever it exists, and can document its record with pride. Past convention resolutions show the UAW historically out in front, waging the fight for equality of wages and opportunity for women— in the labor agreements, in the law, by administrative policy. The UAW has always been in the forefront of the fight for equal pay for equal work, full seniority protection, maternity leave, and strong enforcement of the sex discrimination provisions of the 1964 Civil Rights Act. To assist in realizing these goals and help solve the special problems of women, the UAW established a Women's Department. Women's committees, special women's meetings, educational classes, regional and area conferences, have educated UAW women in the total program of our Union and motivated them to engage in leadership activity. A high proportion of UAW women are active and hold elective and appointed positions in their locals, communities and regions.

Most women workers find jobs for the same reason that most men do: because they need to support themselves and their families. In many cases, women work because they are the sole support of a family. or because their husbands earn less than is required to meet family needs. Many families get into the middle income bracket only because both the husband and wife work.

The UAW deplores the economic inequity which forces many women to work when they would prefer to stay home and take care of their families. However, we insist, without reservation or qualification, first, on the right of every woman to work, if she so chooses, second, on the right of every woman who does work to be paid for her labors on the same scale as men doing the same or comparable work and, third, on the right of equal opportunity for advancement.

We share the grave doubts which many have expressed regarding the social desirability and wisdom of any blanket welfare measure which would compel mothers of school-age children to work or undergo work training. Projects and surveys in various parts of the country have demonstrated clearly that where adequate jobs, training and child care centers are available, there is a backlog of mothers awaiting openings. New York City, for instance, has reported just such a situation.

The financial independence and dignity possible through work provide a positive incentive. It is, therefore, neither necessary nor desirable to make such work mandatory.

The need for increased family income to help meet the higher costs of educating children, health care and the wider variety of goods and services considered essential to the American standard of living also lead more and more women to seek paid employment. Increasingly women are seeking the right to choose how they will make their contribution to their family and community.

A problem in documenting discrimination based on sex is the fact that most government grants and studies of discrimination do not require a breakdown by sex. This should be corrected on both the federal and state levels. For instance, the Equal Employment Opportunity Commission, the agency charged with enforcement of legislation forbidding discrimination in employment under the 1964 Civil Rights Act, has published a three-volume report based on a survey of numbers of persons employed in the private sector by industry, occupation, sex, and race. Upon examination, not a table or narrative statement can be found in the report that compares the employment situation for white men, Negro men, white women, and Negro women. There are not even any tables comparing white women with white men or Negro women with Negro men. Yet roughly 25 percent of the complaints filed with this Commission claim discrimination based on sex.

Essential justice requires the government on both the state and federal levels to give greater attention to the elimination of sex discrimination and to the needs of women living in poverty. Priorities should be established as sensitive to sex in discrimination as to any other form in manpower training programs and in referrals to training and employment.

President Reuther pointed out in an Administrative Letter regarding UAW procedures relating to possible violations of the Sex Discrimination provisions of the Civil Rights Act of 1964:

"Many states have statutes which prohibit or limit the employment of females, e.g., the employment of females in certain occupations, in jobs requiring the lifting or carrying of weights exceeding certain prescribed limits, during certain hours of the night or for more than a 'specified number of hours per day or per week. The Equal Employment Opportunity Commission (EEOC), the federal agency charged with enforcing Title VII, has now unequivocally ruled with court approval, that Title VII supersedes such and abilities of individual females, and tend to discriminate against them rather than to protect them. This has been the position of the International Union since the enactment of Title VII. Now that the intent of the law has been clarified by administrative ruling as well as judicial decisions, it is imperative that we conscientiously and vigorously comply with its requirements."

The EEOC continues to be thwarted in its efforts to enforce the law by an inadequate budget and lack of authority to issue cease and desist orders and enforce them through the courts. The backlog is such that it presently takes about 18 months to 2 years for the Commission to finally dispose of a case after a charge is first filed. Its conciliation efforts have been unsuccessful in more than half of the cases in which it has found that discrimination has occurred. Under these circumstances, if the Commission is given additional authority without additional resources to carry out its responsibilities under Title VII of the Civil Rights Act, the federal government's commitment to equal employment opportunity will become a farce.

Since the first Executive Order on Government Contracts was issued in 1941, the UAW has been on record urging the inclusion of the word "sex" in this non discrimination clause. This was finally done in a Presidential Executive Order issued in 1967 and became effective October 13, 1968. However, the Office of Federal Contract Compliance, which held hearings on proposed sex discrimination guidelines in August 1969, has not yet issued these guidelines or moved to enforce this order. Affirmative action should be taken immediately by the Office.

Many union contracts (and some employers acting unilaterally) do provide (some) temporary disability protection for their workers. The fact that a far smaller percentage of women than of men are organized in unions means that statutory protection against temporary disability is of particular concern to women workers, even aside from the question of maternity benefits.

Maternity benefits, in the form of cash payments to replace the lost wages of women workers, are a logical part of a broader program of replacement of wages lost because of short-term illness. The cost of this would not be exorbitant. Public Health Service reports have shown that in three of the last four years studied, men actually lost more days from work per year on the average because of disability than women (including days lost by women because of pregnancy and childbirth).

When a married woman works full time, she probably contributes between thirty-five and forty percent of her family's income. Most states have arbitrary time limits in regard to collecting unemployment compensation before and after childbirth which do not reflect the variation in physical ability of women workers, their health, or the demands of the job. Federal standards should be enacted permitting women to collect unemployment compensation before and after childbirth whenever they are physically able to work and to guarantee job protection for women who desire to return to work after pregnancy.

In February, 1965, 47 percent of the children of working mothers under 6 years of age were looked after in their own homes, 30 percent were cared for in someone else's home, and 23 percent were cared for by other arrangements. Only 6 percent received group care in day care centers or similar facilities. Of the children 6 to 11 years of age, 47 percent were looked after in their own homes, 11 percent received care in someone else's home, and about 42 percent were cared for by other arrangements. At least 8 percent of the older children looked after themselves, and only 1 percent received group care.

Mothers who are widowed, separated, or divorced are more likely to work than other mothers. In March, 1967, 51 percent of the mothers in these categories worked, even when there were children under 6 years in the family. In homes where the husband was present, only 27 percent of the mothers with young children worked.

The development of child care facilities available on all-day, all-year basis, adequate to the needs of children from the pre-school years to early adolescence, should be available for all parents who require them.

As of this date, however, the relatively modest day-care provisions contained in the Social Security Amendments of 1967 have not been realized. Substantial funding as well as new and imaginative approaches are basic to overcoming the shortage of trained personnel and adequate child care facilities. Together with the provisions made for remodeling existing structures, such funds could provide new jobs for ghetto residents and add to model cities and other important programs for rehabilitating urban areas.

Our experience during the second World War with a federal supported child care program, and more recently with the Head Start Program, has demonstrated that nursery school care for children provides opportunity for physical, mental and emotional growth and development, and is beneficial to the child, the parent and the home.

There has been no change in the amount allowed as an income tax deduction since the Revenue Act of 1954 was amended to permit a deduction of up to $600 for the care of one child and up to $900 for two or more children under 13 years of age, provided the child care enables a working woman and other specified persons to be gainfully employed. Widows, widowers, separated and divorced persons may deduct up to these amounts regardless of income. However, a married woman or a husband whose wife is incapacitated must file a joint return with the spouse in order to claim the deduction; if the combined adjusted gross income exceeds $6,000, the deduction is reduced $1 for each $1 of income above that amount. The amount allowed for two or more ought to be increased to at least $1,800, and the combined adjusted gross income below which these deductions are allowed ought to increase to at least three times the annually adjusted minimal subsistence level identified by the United States Bureau of Labor Statistics.

The emergence of a new pattern of family economic interdependence has been accompanied by an awareness of inequities in the Social Security Program as they apply to families in which the wife works. The family protection provisions of the Social Security Program were based on the sociological conditions and climate of the 1930's. The percentage of two-income families is increasing. Yet a wife who has worked for many years and contributed to the Social Security Program system may in some cases receive no larger benefit than if she had never worked.

The present provisions result in situations where a retired couple who have both worked receive less in benefits than a couple where only the husband worked and had the same earnings as the combined earnings of the working couple. If, for example, only the husband had worked and had average earnings of $650 a month—$7,800 a year—the benefits paid to the couple at age 65 would be $323 ($218 to the husband and $105 to the wife). By contrast, if the husband and wife each had average earnings of $325 a month, or $3,900 a year—combined annual earnings of $7,800—their benefits will be only $134.30 each, or a total of $268.60. More equitable recognition should be given to working wives for their Social Security contributions.

Resolved; 1. That the EEOC budget be increased to allow sufficient staff and funds to operate effectively and eliminate the backlog of cases, and that the 1964 Civil Rights Law be amended to (1) give the EEOC authority to issue cease and desist orders and enforce them through the courts; (2) extend coverage to (a) employers of 8 or more (b) state and local government employees and (c) individuals in educational institutions performing work connected with educational activities.

2. That the Fair Labor Standards Act be amended to (1) provide coverage under minimum wage without exception for every worker within the reach of federal authority and (2) provide equal pay for comparable work under the Equal Pay Act and extend the provisions of that Act to all workers without exception; and further, that the UAW work for equal protective state legislation to cover workers who come under state jurisdiction.

3. That on the state level, the UAW continue its policy of repudiating certain so-called "protective" state laws which are used by employers to deny women workers rights and benefits to which they are entitled, and the UAW give support to updated, uniform application and strict enforcement of state laws which protect both men and women from unacceptable work practices.

4. That the UAW make every effort to have maximum hours of work and voluntary overtime provisions extended to all workers by legislation on the federal and state level.

5. That a general system of basic statutory protection for men and women against wage loss due to temporary disability, including illness, pregnancy and maternity, be provided in one insurance program.

6. That statutory regulations be enacted and in the meantime contract clauses be negotiated establishing job security during maternity leave, with standards that encompass reasonable tests for the ability and capacity of the individual to work, recognize the physical health of the woman and the nature of her occupation, and which would not deny either employment, or unemployment compensation, when these standards are met.

7. That we press for more comprehensive federal legislation and immediate implementation of existing establishing child care centers and nursery schools for the use of all parents, and the liberalization of income tax deductions or provision of tax credit for the cost of child care.

8. That more equitable retirement benefits be provided under Social Security for families with working wives.

9. That we urge the Office of Federal Contract Compliance to issue immediately guidelines on the inclusion of the word "sex" in the President's Executive Order on government contracts, that they require strong affirmative action and be in harmony with those of the EEOC.

10. That governments on both the federal and state level be required to establish priorities as sensitive to sex discrimination as to any other form in all manpower training programs, in referrals to training and employment and in studies regarding discrimination in employment under federal or state auspices, both directly or by grants to independent institutions.

11. That all Local Unions continue to police UAW procedures relating to possible violations of the sex discrimination provisions of the Civil Rights Act of 1964, particularly as outlined in the Administrative Letter No. 10 of November 6, 1969.

12. That those companies which have discontinued hiring women and have work which could be performed by women be urged to discontinue such discrimination, and if those companies cannot thus be persuaded that the Local Unions process complaints through the proper governmental agencies responsible for enforcing Civil Rights statutes.

13. That Local Unions which have not yet done so establish Women's Committees in compliance with Article 43 of the International Constitution on Standing Committees, which requires that a Women's Committee be established in every Local Union having women in its membership.

14. That we continue holding Regional UAW Women's Conferences on an annual basis in all regions, and that area conferences also be held, in particular in those regions covering broad geographic areas.

15. That women be encouraged to employ their talents and capabilities toward the advancement of the social, political and economic well-being of the nation and the enhancement of its culture, and be it

Further resolved; That the commemoration of American women's 50th anniversary of their right to vote be reflected in increasing efforts by our Union to involve women members, wives of members, mothers, sisters and daughters in all levels of political activity during this most crucial election year; that special efforts be developed through our Citizenship-Legislative Department, through our Education Department, through our Organizing Department, through our entire CAP structure and especially through our Local Unions to expand our influence among our women's members as well as women throughout the country by:

Including women in strategic positions throughout our Union,

The advancement of women candidates projecting and supporting the UAW ideals,

The organization of distinctive events such as family institutes, leadership training, family events in Local Unions and special legislative activities,

The greater use of women in registration and get-out-the-vote activities and in the planning of such activities,

Caravans of UAW women and their families in support of key issues to Washington and to their state capitols, and be it

Finally resolved; That we give special attention to a legislative program of more direct concern to women such as a national program for child care centers, campaigns to end the exploitation of household workers, the repeal or reform of abortion laws, opening up higher paying and skilled trades jobs for women, legislation for a $2.50 national minimum wage law covering all workers, and support for the campaign for enactment of an equal rights amendment to the Constitution of the United States.

50TH ANNIVERSARY OF WOMEN'S RIGHT TO VOTE

Whereas: This year marks the 50th anniversary of the woman's right to vote. In the years that followed the liberation of the woman at the ballot box, she has become a powerful force in the continuing development of democracy in the country. It is not alone that politicians vie for the woman's vote; it is that she has entered politics and influences its direction and its results.

We in the UAW, who have always stood for and fought for equal rights for all, pay tribute this year to the women of our nation and share with them in celebrating this first half century of their political emancipation.

Political emancipation however is not yet the guarantee of social and economic emancipation. Women suffer from flagrant discriminatory treatment which shames a society which declares its adherence to the principal of equal opportunity.

While women have made significant gains in many sectors of our national life, the patterns of discrimination which continue to exist remain a stain on our national conscience. Unfortunately moreover too many women have themselves held back from the full expression of their convictions and their active participation in the political process and in community and union affairs.

Women today represent a majority of the voting strength in the United States. We must mobilize their power and direct it toward the liberal, progressive objectives for which our Union stands and we must join our efforts with the efforts of women's groups in the nation whose goals and aspirations are consonant with ours to help move America forward. Therefore be it

Resolved: that the 50th anniversary commemoration of American women's winning of their right to vote be reflected in increasing efforts by our Union to involve women members and wives, mothers, sisters and daughters of members in all levels of political and community activity. And be it further

Resolved: That the delegates of the 22nd UAW Constitutional Convention pay special tribute to the women of our nation on this 50th anniversary of their right to vote.

UAW
Administrative Letter

Walter P. Reuther..............President
Emil Mazey........Secretary-Treasurer
Leonard Woodcock....Vice-President
Pat Greathouse..........Vice-President

Volume 21	November 6, 1969	Printed in USA	Letter No. 10

IN THIS ISSUE:

UAW Procedures Relating to Possible Violations of the Sex Discrimination Provisions of the Civil Rights Act of 1964.

To All Local Unions:

GREETINGS:

In 1964 the Congress enacted and the President signed into law the Civil Rights Act of 1964. Title VII of that Act prohibits employers, employment agencies and labor organizations from discriminating against employees or union members because of race, color, religion, sex, or national origin.

Title VII became effective on July 2, 1965. Thus, it has been in effect for over four years. Because of the attitude of the various states and employers across the country, as well as the shifting views of the EEOC, there has been, necessarily, some confusion with respect to possible violations of Title VII regarding sex discrimination, particularly where based on state laws limiting women's hours and weight lifting. The purpose of this Administrative Letter is to set forth the policies of the International Union and the procedures recommended to Local Unions and Local Union officials for resolving sex discrimination issues.

Policy Regarding Challenge To State Protective Laws

Many states have statutes which prohibit or limit the employment of females, e.g., the employment of females in certain occupations, in jobs requiring the lifting or carrying of weights exceeding certain prescribed limits, during certain hours of the night or for more than a specified number of hours per day or per week. The Equal Employment Opportunity Commission (EEOC), the federal agency charged with enforcing Title VII, has now unequivocally ruled, with Court approval, that Title VII supersedes such state laws because they do not take into account the capacities, preferences, and abilities of individual females, and tend to discriminate against them rather than to protect them. This has been the position of the International Union since the enactment of Title VII. Now that the intent of the law has been clarified by administrative ruling as well as judicial decisions, it is imperative that we conscientiously and vigorously comply with its requirements.

Many employers have utilized the so-called "state protective laws" to deny women as a class, opportunities to work overtime, for recall, to bid on certain jobs, work in certain departments and on certain shifts, notwithstanding the fact that an individual woman might have had the seniority, skill and ability which should have been recognized in any of these situations. Employers have followed this course despite the absence of any contract language requiring women to be treated any differently than men. WHEREVER SUCH A PRACTICE STILL EXISTS, THE LOCAL UNION SHOULD CHALLENGE IT BOTH IN THE GRIEVANCE MACHINERY AND WITH THE EEOC.

When in Doubt About International Policy . . . Contact Your Regional Director

302

If the contract contains a clause prohibiting discrimination on the basis of sex, the grievance should allege a violation of that provision. Where the contract does not contain such a provision, the grievance should allege a violation of the seniority, job bidding, layoff and recall provisions of the contract. Additionally, a charge should be filed against the employer with the EEOC alleging that the employer is discriminating against its employees on the basis of sex. COPIES OF THE GRIEVANCE AND THE CHARGE SHOULD BE FORWARDED TO YOUR REGIONAL DIRECTOR AND THE WOMEN'S DEPARTMENT OF THE UAW.

Policy Regarding Contract Clauses Treating Female Employees Different From Male Employees

Title VII. THE GENERAL PRINCIPLE TO BE FOLLOWED IS THAT WITH RESPECT TO WAGES, HOURS AND OTHER TERMS AND CONDITIONS OF EMPLOYMENT MEN AND WOMEN ARE TO BE TREATED IDENTICALLY. Every effort should be made to eliminate any contract language which does not comply with this principle.

Conclusion

It is impossible to enumerate all of the varied situations which will constitute a violation of Title VII. UAW policy is, however, to challenge such discrimination whatever form it may take. It must be challenged by the International and Local Unions, and eliminated. Whenever a question arises as to whether a particular situation violates the prohibition against sex discrimination, or any of the other prohibited discriminations, of Title VII, the Regional Director's Office will provide advice and assistance to the Local Union.

For the convenience of the Local Unions we have attached as Appendix A, a listing of the EEOC offices and their addresses. The charge form used by EEOC may be obtained by writing to the EEOC office covering the area where your local union is located. However, a letter to EEOC detailing the discrimination is sufficient to start an investigation by that agency.

Local Unions desiring any additional information or assistance in connection with Title VII problems should contact their Regional Director.

With all good wishes.

Fraternally yours,

Walter P. Reuther, President
INTERNATIONAL UNION, UAW

WPR:bdm
opeiu42

STATEMENT OF THE INTERNATIONAL UNION, UAW TO THE EQUAL
EMPLOYMENT OPPORTUNITY COMMISSION AT PUBLIC HEARING ON
May 2, 1967

My name is Stephen Schlossberg. I am General Counsel of the
International Union, UAW, and I appreciate the opportunity to be here to give
you our position on the very troublesome area of so-called state "protective"
laws with respect to the employment of women.

The UAW's record in fighting all forms of discrimination is outstanding,
both within the labor movement and within the community. Our efforts to secure equal
job opportunity by way of collective bargaining or by way of legislation have
continued since we formed our union thirty years ago.

The number of women workers who are members of UAW is now
approaching 200,000. Under our Constitution they are completely equal with
respect to the right to exercise all of the rights, privileges and responsibilities
of any union member. Over 800 women have been elected to top positions in
their local unions by the men and women members of those locals. Thousands
of women serve as stewards or committeemen and handle the daily on-the-job
problems which plague workers of both sexes.

On the International staff there are three department directors who
are women and one who is an Executive Board Member; another sixteen women
are International Representatives working in various departments and regions
of the union. All of these women, whether working for the local union or for the
International, carry out their assignments and their responsibilities with the
same energy and dedication as their brother unionists and none of them ask for
or receive special privileges.

I give you this background because I think it's important to understand
that we are not just in the wings crying advice to others. We take our Constitution
seriously, and we practice what we preach.

The contracts we negotiate with employers provide for equal pay,
equal job opportunity, equal seniority, training, etc., but I couldn't begin to
estimate the number of grievances we have taken all the way to arbitration in an
effort to enforce a contract only to be stymied by one or another of the so-called

state "protective" laws.

Because employers have used these laws to circumvent our collective bargaining contracts and to discriminate against the women who are members of our union, the UAW has taken the position that so-called "protective" state laws-- that is, those based on sterotypes as to sex rather than true biological factors-- are undesirable relics of the past.

At the end of World War II and the Korean conflict we first encountered the management practice of invoking state laws in order to bypass women's job rights. During war periods, management had been more than happy to employ females in practically any capacity and to ignore these state laws. They were honored only in the breach. Yet, when men were again available, the employers resorted to the technique of combining two jobs into one so that it was beyond the state maximum weight law, or scheduling hours of work beyond the statutory limit for women in order to avoid hiring women employees. Delegates to our biennial convention in 1946 spoke out against these practices.

In 1949, again, delegates went on record "opposing eight hour laws affecting only women workers" and supporting a National Equal Pay Law.

And so it has been through the years. Our membership has demanded equal treatment for women. In 1966 this demand was reaffirmed in a Convention Resolution which stated in part:

> "With regard to women workers strict enforcement of the Equal Pay Act and all other federal legislation bearing on discrimination in employment on the basis of sex; extending the coverage of the Equal Pay Act now limited to approximately one-third of the working women; repudiation of state laws which unjustifiably treat women as a separate group; updating, uniform application, and strict enforcement of state labor laws which cover both men and women..."
> (Emphasis supplied)

For the women who work in the United States, Title VII has turned out to be a cruel hoax--a bad joke on women. Cocktail party conversation with respect to the Civil Rights Acts provisions against sex discrimination is familiar to everyone. It usually goes something like this: 1. "The sex thing was thrown in by reactionaries to kill any chance for an FEPC." 2. "There is no legislative history on the sex thing so it really doesn't mean anything." 3. "The sex part creates more problems than it solves." 4. "The Act is part of the Civil Rights revolution and the Commission should stick to racial discrimination and avoid getting bogged down in sex cases."

We reject out of hand this kind of unenlightened comment.

The point is that Congress did bar employment discrimination on sex grounds, and that bar should be vigorously enforced by the Commission.

Now what has happened since Title VII became law? More and more employers have been able to discriminate against women because of anachronistic, so-called "protective" state laws regulating the employment of women. Because of state laws and regulations limiting the weights a woman may lift, or the hours a woman may work, employers have been able to deprive women of jobs, promotions and overtime. Provisions in UAW collective bargaining contracts prohibiting discrimination and regulating seniority are avoided and evaded through employer reliance on these outmoded laws.

It has been our experience that women work because they need the money--to making a living or to supplement a too meager family income. They are entitled to the same breaks in employment as men--a chance-- 1. to share equally in overtime; 2. to bid on the basis of seniority for any job they can perform, and 3. to the same promotion opportunities as men.

It is axiomatic that some women can lift more than some men. So it is that some women can work longer hours than some men. In Japan, the pearl divers who dive six hours a day to depths of 40 feet or more in icy waters are almost all women because, in that culture, women are thought to be stronger than men. A nostalgic view of women may seem romantic but when that societal view, enforced by law, operates to the economic detriment of women, it is nothing more than a state operated system of discrimination,

Any law regulating weight lifting or hours of employment should affect all workers equally instead of being based on an arbitrary, sterotyped and prejudicial view as to the sexes. We urge that the Congress meant to supersede such state laws and we urge the Commission to adopt that view forthrightly and forcefully and to support it in appropriate court tests.

Now, clearly, some state laws really are protective -- those dealing with pregnancy, maternity leaves and the like. They are not based on a sterotype but on biological facts and they need to be preserved. We must distinguish between prejudice and fact. Presumed differences in the stamina and strength of the two sexes is a far cry from actual physiological differences.

With the advent of Title VII, we believed that the goals of equality in employment would become a reality. Disappointingly, however, this did not happen. Despite the clearly expressed language of the statute, the so-called state "protective" legislation has become even more a millstone around the neck of women at work.

We are unhappy with the EEOC's performance in this area of the law. Its lack of courage here has brought long neglected laws and regulations out of the woodwork. This Commission's interpretation of "bona fide occupational qualifications" in Section 703 (e) of Title VII is too broad. The states are even worse. They pass new civil rights legislation dealing with sex and add caveats that employer may, nevertheless, discriminate if they use the cover of a discriminatory state law. It is a vicious cycle.

Michigan, for example, in 1966 prohibited discrimination in employment on the basis of sex except where it was "based on law, regulation, the requirements of any federal or state training program or on a bona fide occupational qualification." Left to its own devices, the state would, under this statute, justify an employer's refusal to hire a woman because she cannot work more than ten hours in any one day, an average of nine hours per day in any one week, and no more than 54 hours per week as a permitted discrimination because it was "based on law". Other states have followed a similar pattern. See, for example, the laws or rulings of the States of Maryland, Missouri, New York, Utah and Wisconsin.

States which have no laws prohibiting discrimination in employment on the basis of sex, of which there are 34, have hidden behind the Commission's refusal, up to now, not to challenge directly state "protective" legislation as a justification for their continued and renewed enforcement, resulting in a denial of many job opportunities to women. Thus, in California, for example, the women we represent are denied jobs, overtime and promotions because they cannot work more than eight hours a day, 48 hours a week, or lift more than 25 pounds; in

Ohio the law says they cannot lift more than 25 pounds, work more than 48 hours

per week, or work with certain machinery; in 38 other states the number of hours

they can work is limited; in 25 states there are occupations from which they

are excluded.

The Commission's requirement that where exceptions are available

under these state "protective" statutes an employer is obligated to seek them to

avoid a finding of reasonable cause has had a very limited effect, if any. In Ohio,

for example, the interpretation of what constitutes "frequent and repeated" lifting

is more restrictive than it was six years ago; in California, the Industrial Welfare

Commission's weight lifting limitation is 25 pounds less than that in the California

statute.

There is presently developing a hodge-podge of decisions with respect

to these state "protective" laws. As a result of the Commission's present refusal to

face these laws on their merits, suits have been filed in California, Illinois, Indiana,

and Kentucky to, hopefully, eliminate these discriminatory statutes. Such a scattered

approach, we believe, is unnecessary in the face of the existence of a clearly

enunciated federal policy.

Among the provisions of Title XI of the 1964 Civil Rights Act is Section

1104 which reads:

> "Nothing contained in any title of this Act shall be construed as indicat-
> ing an intent on the part of Congress to occupy the field in which any
> such title operates to the exclusion of State laws on the same subject
> matter, nor shall any provision of this Act be construed as invalidating
> any provision of State law unless such provision is inconsistent with any
> of the purposes of this Act, or any provision thereof. (July 2, 1964, P.L.
> 88-352, Title XI 1104, 78 Stat. 268, 42 USC 2000h-4.)" (Emphasis supplied)

It is clear that any state statute in conflict with the purposes of any provi-

sion of the 1964 Civil Rights Act is superseded by that Act. As far as we have been

able to determine, only two states have recognized this principle -- Delaware, which

has repealed its protective legislation and Arizona, which in a courageous and

enlightened opinion by its civil rights commission ruled:

> "The legislative history surrounding the enactment of Title VII of
> the Civil Rights Act of 1964 does not disclose what effect Congress
> intended that title to have upon protective legislation for women, but
> the spirit of the legislation is clear. It was enacted to provide equal
> employment opportunity for all persons including women. That op-

portunity is restricted and prevented by ARS 23-281(a). We believe that Congress was not unmindful of the effect of protective legislation on employment opportunities for women and that it was the intent of Congress that legislation such as ARS 23-281(A) yield to Title VII. We similarly believe that the same spirit motivated the Arizona legislature and that the intent of the legislature was that the Arizona Civil Rights Act be controlling over ARS 23-281(A) to the extent they are inconsistent."

Section 1104 of the Act provides the vehicle through which this Commission must give guidance in the area of conflicts between the state protective laws and the purposes of Title VII. To permit a morass of conflicting interpretations reflecting local biases and attitudes rather than the uniformity the statute was intended to create is a sin of omission, and nonfeasance. The Commission must take firm control in this area because no other forum has the expertise or the duty to step up to this problem and meet it squarely. We need practical and enlightened enforcement of the federal law to cure the pernicious ills of these unfair state laws.

The UAW has found the grievance provisions of our contracts inadequate to meet this national problem. Employer's generally deny such grievances on the ground that they are bound by the state laws. Arbitrators who have dealt with the problems of female employment rights have ruled that the various state "protective" laws constitute bona fide occupational qualifications, or that, as private arbitrators they are without the power to resolve conflicts between state and federal law. Even, where arbitrators have resolved these conflicts the Courts have been reluctant to enforce their awards.

The effect on collective bargaining agreements of diverse state limitations, flouts the Supreme Court's decisions requiring uniform federal law under Section 301 of the Labor Act. In Textile Workers Union v. Lincoln Mills, 353 U.S. 448, the Court definitely ruled that courts are to fashion a body of substantive federal law in implementation of the statute. Subsequently, in Charles Dowd Box Co. v. Courtney, 368 US 502, the Court extended the substantive law of Section 301 to state litigation. And in Local 174, Teamsters Union v. Lucas Flour Co., 369 US 95, 102, it ruled that in 301 cases "incompatible doctrines of local law must give way to principles of federal labor law." In the latter decision, which rejects the survival of "individualized local rules" in litigation of collective bargaining agreement rights, the Court emphasized (at p. 103) the underlying uniformity goal, in terms applicable to the present question:

> "Comprehensiveness is inherent in the process by which the law is to
> be formulated under the mandate of Lincoln Mills, requiring issues
> raised in suits of a kind covered by 301 to be decided according to the
> precepts of federal labor policy. More important, the subject matter
> of 301(a) 'is peculiarly one that calls for uniform law.' . . . The
> possibility that individual contract terms might have different meanings
> under state and federal law would inevitably exert a disruptive influence
> upon both the negotiation and administration of collective agreements. . . .

Thus, the position we urge would prevent the erratic, state-by-state
interpretation of women's rights under a single national collective bargaining agreement and, thereby promote, rather than offend, national policy.

It is a plain fact of life that the discrimination against women in the
employment market is class discrimination almost as gross and as evil as race
discrimination. It cannot be rectified through a faint-hearted approach. We urge
the Commission to take a more positive approach to the problems presented by
state "protective" legislation and to cause Title VII to have real meaning for the
women of America.

We strongly recommend that the Commission:

1. Reconsider its interpretation of Congressional intent
   with respect to state "protective" laws to make it clear
   that state laws that provide an umbrella for the protection
   of employers who discriminate are superseded.

2. Revise its guidelines and its definition of "bona fide occupational
   qualification" to prohibit reliance on state "protective" laws as
   a means of denying employment opportunities to women.

3. Rule on the merits of cases presenting conflicts between Title VII
   and state "protective" legislation, particularly where the legislation
   contains no exceptions.

4. Prepare and publish recommendations on appropriate revisions in
   state laws to achieve equal employment opportunity.

5. Encourage the repeal of archaic statutes which have no relevance in
   the modern industrial world.

6. Use the provisions of Title VII to attack in the Courts the patterns
   of sex discrimination in the various industries.

7 Make clear that the only protective legislation compatible with

Title VII is that based on real biological factors, such as that dealing with maternity leaves, separate rest rooms, pregnancy, and the like.

We believe the attitude of this Commission can be the paramount influence in the alteration of attitudes among unions, employers, arbitrators, courts and legislators.

The UAW's stand against racial discrimination is a matter of public record. This Commission can take official notice of that stand and the courageous and vigorous implementation of it. Moreover, we realize that racial discrimination is currently the most compelling problem in our society.

But all of that does not mean that this country, in this day and age, cannot protect women from discrimination at the same time it moves against the bigots. Only a square confrontation with these so-called "protective" state laws can do the job. The point is, very simply, they do not protect women, they injure them.

Nor is it an answer to cite ancient court decisions from out of America's past. Court approval of legislation regulating the conditions of women's work pioneered true social legislation designed to protect all workers. We do not criticize those decisions. We applaud them. But it is 1967. Just as Brown v. Board of Education laid to rest the separate but equal doctrine of Plessy v. Ferguson, it is time now to guarantee the true equality of workers in this nation.

Thank you for permitting us to appear here today to express our views. We hope they will be helpful to the Commission.

Respectfully submitted,
/s/ Stephen I. Schlossberg

Stephen I. Schlossberg
General Counsel, UAW

opeiu42aflcio/rms

THE
NATIONAL
FEDERATION
OF

BUSINESS AND PROFESSIONAL WOMEN'S CLUBS, INC.
of the United States of America

2012 MASSACHUSETTS AVENUE, N. W.
WASHINGTON, D. C., 20036
293-1100

May 22, 1970

The Honorable Birch Bayh
United States Senate
363 Old Senate Office Building
Washington, D. C. 20510

My dear Senator Bayh:

During the hearings certain questions were raised regarding the effect of the
Equal Rights Amendment on state labor laws for women. At the time we indicated in our testimony that passage of the Equal Rights Amendment would not
necessarily nullify those laws, but possibly require their extension to men as
well.

I thought you might be interested in the enclosed memorandum drawn up by our
legal counsel at our request on this question.

Sincerely,

Myra Ruth Harmon

(Mrs.) Myra Ruth Harmon
National President

MRH:tes
Enclosure

MEMORANDUM

May 27, 1970

TO: PHYLLIS O'CALLAGHAN

FROM: WILLIAM W. SCOTT

RE: EQUAL RIGHTS AMENDMENT

During the course of the hearing before the Constitutional
Amendment Subcommittee of the Senate Committee on the Judiciary, a
question arose as to the impact of the Equal Rights Amendment on
various state labor laws. Specially the issue was raised as to whether
state labor laws which confer special benefits or privileges to one sex
would be nullified by the passage of the amendment or would they be
extended to persons of both sexes. Andrew J. Biemiller, the legislation director of the AFL/CIO, took the position that all laws which
distinguish between men and women, including state labor laws which
confer some form of benefit on women workers, would be nullified. He
stated:

> The Equal Rights Amendment, on the other hand
> permits of no negotiation or compromise, no
> matter what the circumstances. It would simply
> become unconstitutional for any law to distinguish
> in its application between men and women. It
> makes no guarantee of extension of labor law pro-
> tections to men. Enemies of labor legislation
> powered by a combination of middle-class feminists
> and employers, could speedily wipe out all forms of
> protections afforded specifically to women whether
> "restrictive" or not -- minimum wage laws, rest
> periods, meal periods, seating requirements, trans-
> portation at night, and other provisions

The AFL/CIO further notes:

> Particularly unrealistic is the assumption that laws
> "conferring a benefit, privilege or obligation of
> citizenship" would automatically be extended to the
> opposite sex by striking the words of sex identifica-
> tion. Legislatures are under no obligation to retain

existing legislation for either sex, let alone extend
it to both. This issue would be particularly serious
in the field of state labor legislation. It is true that
any of the existing seven state minimum wage laws
that apply only to women could readily be adjusted
by striking the sex identification in the law. But it
is equally true that the legislature could strike the
laws altogether. Labor legislation is highly vulnerable to the "least common denominator" approach.
Nothing in the amendment prohibits the reduction of
present benefits and privileges as a means of complying with the equality standard set out by the
Amendment.

This view is contrary to the position taken by the

Citizens' Advisory Council on the Status of Women. In its memo-

randum of March 1970 entitled "The Proposed Equal Rights Amend-

ment to the United States Constitution" which was presented to

the Subcommittee, it is stated:

> Where the law [state or federal which distinguish
> on the basis of sex] confers a benefit, privilege
> or obligation of citizenship such would be extended
> to the other sex, i.e., the effect of the amendment
> would be to strike the words of sex identification.
> Thus, such laws would not be rendered unconstitu-
> tional but would be extended to apply to both sexes
> by operation of the amendment, in the same way that
> laws pertaining to voting were extended to Negroes
> and women under the Fifteenth and Nineteenth Amendments.

We believe the view of the Citizens' Advisory Council

is the more sound one and although there is no conclusive precedent

we believe Congress has available tools to insure that those laws

which extend certain benefits to women are not nullified by the

passage of the amendment but extended to men.

It is appropriate prior to noting the precedent that does

exist and suggesting a means of securing the result to identify the

type law at issue.

State laws which restrict the number of hours a woman may

work, the weight she may lift, the position she may hold and the

time of day during which she may work are in our opinion clearly
restrictive. They confer no benefits or privileges and it would be
completely unrealistic and unreasonable to argue that such laws
could or should be extended to men. In some states this would
mean that an employer might have to discontinue overtime employment entirely, close his business during certain hours of the night,
or reduce the weight of his equipment or product. Clearly such
laws should be nullified.

Yet those laws which confer recognizable benefits to
women could be extended. Examples of such laws would be those
which require rest periods and special facilities, such as seats,
dressing rooms, or restrooms. These laws could simply be extended
to persons of both sexes thereby obviating the need for nullification.

Precedent for such action is found in the adoption of
the Fifteenth and Nineteenth Amendments to the Constitution. The
adoption of the Fifteenth Amendment which required that all citizens
would have the right to vote regardless of race, color, or previous
condition of servitude and the Nineteenth Amendment which required
that all citizens would have the right to vote regardless of sex
resulted in having those state laws pertaining to voting simply
extended to Negroes and women. This was done by striking the
qualifying criteria in the state law, caucasion with regard to the
Fifteenth Amendment and male with regard to the Nineteenth Amendment.

The effect of the Nineteenth Amendment has been considered
by the courts and the results indicate that instead of nullifying the
laws in question and discriminatory aspects were struck and the law
made applicable to both sexes.

In the case of <u>Graves v. Eubank</u>, 87 So. 587, 205 Ala. 174

(1921), the Alabama Supreme Court reasoned:

> This amendment automatically strikes from the
> state laws, organic and statutory, all discrimina-
> tory features authorizing one sex to vote and
> excluding the other, or placing conditions or
> burdens upon one not placed upon the other as a
> condition precedent to the right to vote, but in
> no wise interferes with, changes, or alters state
> laws with reference to elections that cannot and
> do not amount to a discrimination in favor of one
> sex against the other. It protects the man and
> woman alike, and a burden cannot be placed upon
> one sex that is not put upon the other, nor can a
> privilege, benefit, or exemption be given one to
> the exclusion of the other . . . The result is that
> upon the final ratification of the Nineteenth Amend-
> ment it had the effect of making our organic as well
> as statutory laws applicable to men and women alike,
> and placed all women in the state upon the same
> footing with men.

Similarly the Massachusetts Supreme Court took the same tact

in <u>Re Opinion of the Justices</u>, 135 N.E. 173, 240 Mass. 601 (1922), wherein

it stated:

> This amendment struck the work "male" from the
> Massachusetts Constitution wherever it appeared
> therein as a qualification of the right of a citizen
> to vote, and that in view of the provisions of
> article 9 of the Massachusetts Bill of Rights and
> art. 2, ch. 1, §2, giving all inhabitants the right
> to elect and be elected to office, women were
> placed on the same basis as men with regard to
> their eligibility for election to office.

It is our opinion that these two cases indicate the approach

which should result with the adoption of the Equal Rights Amendment.

Very simply this would mean that those state laws which confer benefits

or privileges to women would, rather than be nullified, be extended to men.

To make this an absolute certainty, a very simple approach is

all that is required. The Judiciary Subcommittee in its report on Amendment

could state that such laws would be extended to men and thus through

the vehicle of legislative history such a result would be achieved.

316

STATEMENT IN SUPPORT OF S.J. RES. 61—THE "EQUAL RIGHTS AMENDMENT"
FILED WITH THE SUBCOMMITTEE ON CONSTITUTIONAL AMENDMENTS OF THE
SENATE JUDICIARY COMMITTEE BY BARBARA IRETON—MAY 13, 1970

My name is Barbara Ireton, private citizen, of Falls Church, Virginia. I had not originally intended to file a statement before the recently held hearings of May 6–8, 1970, on S.J. Res. 61, since I had presupposed that other witnesses would more than adequately cover the need for the Amendment. However, testimony attempting to establish that women are physically incapable of arduous or repetitious physical labor, and thus should be excluded from protections afforded by the United States Constitution, has encouraged me to present this statement.

For three years, from December 1965 through December 1968, I held the position of Director of Women's Activities with the American Trucking Association, Inc., Washington, D.C. This job brought me into much contact with women truck drivers in this country through research I conducted, materials I requested from Federal and State government bureaus, and through personal interviews. I did not appreciate the extent of knowledge I had gained in this area until, without mentioning my name, I made a phone inquiry about women truck drivers, to the New York State Department of Labor and was told to "contact Barbara Ireton at ATA—she knows more about women truck drivers than anyone else in the country!" I surely do not know if such is fact, but I probably do have more specialized information on women truck drivers than any one other source in this country.

In 1968, there were approximately 8,000 women in the United States who earned their livings by driving trucks, from single-axle "van" types to five-axle tractor-trailers—logging trucks, livestock haulers, refrigerated trailers, moving vans, and automobile carriers, to mention but a few. This number excludes women who have driven family-owned camper trucks, panel trucks, and farm vehicles in the course of their normal recreational or family duties for which they were, of course, not paid.

Every woman truck driver I have met and interviewed was every bit a "lady" according to current definition by even the most critical person. All have appeared dainty and feminine and extremely proud of their careers. I have never been able to get one of them to say that she found truck driving arduous or physically overtaxing for her, even when I have asked leading questions to encourage these women to answer critically. None appeared to understand the possibility that truck driving could be considered a physical hardship for her, or for any other woman in normal health.

While job opportunities for women truck drivers are increasing, much is dependent upon local labor demand and the willingness of men to permit women entry into this job market. Medium wage for employees in motor freight transportation, based on Department of Commerce figures, was $8,030 in 1965. Many interstate truck drivers earn $10,000 or more a year.

For a person to qualify for interstate trucking, he or she must pass the Interstate Commerce Commission's stringent physical examination and must conform to driving standards outlined in the ICC's 50-page booklet. Truck drivers must also have complete knowledge of the safe operation of trucks, be able to check out on pre-trip safety inspections, and know how to make certain minor repairs.

The driver must also have sufficient strength to couple the truck's cab to a trailer although hydraulic systems on newer models makes this task easier for both men and women.

Whether one drives interstate or only in local delivery, most employers in the trucking industry maintain rigid company training and safety rules. Some require at least one year driving experience on the type of vehicles they own. Others may also require graduation from a truck driving school. Since most trucks represent investments of up to $100,000 when loaded, truck company officials feel money invested in driver training well spent. Because of these economic considerations, qualifications of women truck drivers must be as rigid as those for men drivers.

Rather than represent women truck drivers from a statistical standpoint, I believe a series of thumbnail descriptions can best show what kind of women are doing what sort of work other witnesses before your Subcommittee infer women are unable to do. The fact that women are now operating, by choice, 40-, 55-, and 60-foot long trucks, with up to 15-gear transmissions, should illustrates that interesting as is expert opinion. It is strictly secondary to day-to-day reality.

Lucy Peters of Louisville, Kentucky (only four feet, 10 inches tall), is a truck driver. She tells it this way:

"When I bought the business—a refuse and garbage hauling firm—16 years ago, I was about the same height but only weighed 99 pounds. I learned the knack of picking up a 20-gallon garbage can and tossing it, from my dad who owned the business for a good number of years.

"The early going was rough because I had a 49-foot truck with a 14-foot open bed, and every inch counted. In 1955, a new ordinance called for closed garbage trucks, so I bought a closed packer and lading became a dream.

"When I first started, I ran 10 hours a day, seven days a week. I gave the customers twice-weekly collections, then ran six times a week.

"My first week, I cleared $2.50 after expenses. I worked to really make a go of it and I sure did. It wasn't climbing the hill but one day I started coasting and with God's help, I've made it all pay off.

"Today, I have two fine daughters, a grand husband, and a nice-going business. I guess my slogan should be 'Never underestimate the power of a woman.'"

Mrs. I. B. Jackson is a petite brunette housewife, mother, and former school teacher. She has worked since 1959 for a motor truck dealer, driving trucks between Michigan and Virginia. Her boss reflected early skepticism when Mrs. Jackson's husband urged him to hire her. "My answer to that was an emphatic 'No!'" he recalled. "I wasn't about to have any woman responsible for my trucks. But Jackson persisted and finally convinced me that his wife was qualified. Since that time, she has been as far west as Dallas and Denver. She's never been late and has had only one breakdown on the road."

"Sam" Ballard of Dallas drives as half of a husband and wife team. She is a second generation driver—her parents also worked as a driving team. Gloria Lewis, mother of five, started driving in 1963 and was honored, along with another woman logging truck driver, by Senator Mike Mansfield in the CONGRESSIONAL RECORD. Jessie Brewer of Montana owns her own truck and transports livestock and lumber to markets in Iowa, Nebraska, South Dakota, and Montana. Mrs. Marcella Chaney was an office worker for 17 years before she became a truck driver because it "pays better than office work."

There are so many others—the Wyatts family, father, mother, and daughter, all truck drivers; Wanda R. Wolke, a widow with four children, who is a truck driver for the U.S. Army; and Bernice MacDonald, Ripon, Wisconsin, with more than 20 years of truck driving, entirely accident-free, married, mother of two daughters, active in her church, and a skilled amateur musician. In March, 1968, THE WISCONSIN MOTOR CARRIER magazine wrote: "She has excelled in a profession generally open only to men, thus it has been even tougher for her and makes her achievements even more impressive."

A few men in the trucking industry have encouraged women to enter the field. Director Paul Roy Brown of the Walker County (Alabama) State Trade School which conducts truck driver training, said: "We wish that we had more ladies in truck driver training. . . ." Robert Klabacka of the Diesel Truck Driver Training School, Madison, Wisconsin, said: "The (School) has incorporated a program designed for women, and in particular. husband and wife teams. The Diesel School has found that the safest drivers on the road are females." Mr. Klabacka advised me that his school's course for women is no less stringent than that for men.

Tom Lavin, General Manager, Truck Driver Training School, Inc., Huntley, Illinois, wrote:

"You might be interested to know that we have trained over 20 "Lady" drivers. After our first experience about three years ago, we were reluctant to try again. After about 10 requests from the ladies, we decided to try again—and are we glad we did. The ladies have achieved remarkable grades and on several occasions had the highest score. Another interesting feature is that in each class where women are training, the men have above average grades and seem to try a lot harder. We have separate lounge facilities for the fairer sex and have made adjustments in the equipment so they can easily reach the vehicle controls. We recently trained a lady who has the Black Belt in Judo, has her Masters in Economics, and is a Licensed Pilot. Our most recent female graduate is driving a Diamond T with a Cummings 250 and 15-speed Road Ranger transmission for a company near Milwaukee."

Clayton J. Logan, Operations Manager, Clay Hyder Trucking Lines, Inc., Auburndale, Florida, wrote in 1967: "In the fall of 1966, our company embarked upon a program of experimenting with man and wife truck driving teams. Our experiment has proven successful in our operations, enough that we are now advertising for husband and wife driving teams."

However, neither unions nor the management side of the trucking industry has welcomed women truck drivers with open arms. Stated in kindest terms, I would say they are greeted with extreme disinterest by the industry as a whole. Thus, it was not unusual for me to receive letters from women similar to the following:

"I have been trying to get a job as a truck driver, but to no avail. I have a full-time job as a dictaphone typist in a law office and during the past years, I have been driving a taxicab part-time. I have a Chauffer's license with both an "A" and "C" classification. I received an Illinois Highway Safety Citation in August, 1968, for safe driving, and I am in excellent physical condition. However, the companies to which I have applied appeared never to have heard of women truck drivers and refuse to hire them."

All women truck drivers with whom I have spoken have told me they drive for two basic reasons; one, because they love the work, or they like the work and wish to be with their truck-driving husbands; and two, they want to earn more money than that usually available in occupations that are open to women.

These women have never stopped to consider that someone may have interpreted St. Paul, Aristotle, Plato, the intent of the Constitution, or State and Federal legislators as saying women are physically, morally, or intellectually less capable than men to pursue the vocations of their choice.

Until this time, I have never given thought to how state "protective" laws could possibly be applied to women truck drivers, particularly to interstate drivers. I rather assume that women truck drivers, like most women who are determined to succeed at what they want to do, simply ignore these discriminatory laws.

Passage of S.J. Res. 61 would not result in women rushing to become truck drivers, or lawyers, or mothers. It would not automatically overturn every outdated piece of "protective" legislation that now discriminates against women. It would not change public opinion overnight by eliminating the hidden and erroneous sexual prejudices held by so many men.

It would make women equal citizens with men under the United States Constitution. It would serve notice that this country considers women seriously, as full citizens under our form of government.

I ask the Subcommittee a short time for me to very quickly recount past personal experiences, which are certainly not unique for women who head households.

I am the mother of two draft-aged sons and one teenaged daughter. I have supported them without assistance from any source for the past 14 years and I may add, without receiving any benefit from any kind of special "woman only" law.

My *only* right under the Constitution—that of voting—has been taken away from me because, although separated from my husband, I am still legally married to a nonresident alien and thus have no "legal residence" in the country of my birth (Lucretia Mott, Benjamin Franklin, and a couple of Iroquois are supposed to be installed in my family tree).

I have been told by employers that I have been paid less than men for the same kind of work, even though they also told me I did the work better than the men who had done it previously. I have been denied promotions and told by by an employer that it was solely because I was a woman (only he used the term "girl," as insulting to a 38-year-old woman as it would be to a black man to be called "boy.")

Because my income has been less, since I am a woman, my children have received fewer of the necessities of life and because I have been unable to save money and feed my children both, they have no opportunities for college education even though two of them test in the "bright" category of intelligence. I have been denied the right to rent apartments and houses many times over the years simply because I am a woman (the rationale being that a woman would be less likely to pay rent month after month). In one case, the owner of a house I wished to rent insisted that surely I must be a prostitute to want to live in a house rather an apartment, since I am a woman. If I were to divorce and remarry, I would lose almost all of my right to money I have paid into the Social Security program because of course, here also women's rights are not protected by treating them equally with men.

My daughter has experienced many open prejudices because of her sex, as

I am sure, the daughters of members of the Subcommittee have also felt. Upon entry into the seventh grade, her science teacher, a man, surveyed the class which was composed largely of girls, and assured them that they need not be proficient in the study of science since they were girls. Another teacher instructed a class my daughter attended that hurricanes are named after women because they are destructive and unpredictable. Certainly, this sort of thing is given in a joking (and belittling) manner, rather like the attitude that says "Nigras are just so marvelous; they have such a *natural* sense of rythm. Just give 'em a watermelon, and they're happy to sit under a shade tree all day long." A little more pointed perhaps was the new math principle of "the empty set," compared with "The number of women who have been president of the United States." This statement appeared on large printed posters distributed by a well-known educational printing house. I could continue with many like examples but they are so common to women they are not surprising to them.

The big surprise is that so many women are not embittered from the many discriminatory experiences they suffer. It surely is not easy to remain patient, especially if, as a woman, one reads the Constitution, or sings the National Anthem, or recites the Pledge of Allegiance—"the right of the people," "all persons born or naturalized in the United States," "land of the free," and "with liberty and just for all" doesn't quite ring true to many women who are faced with reality.

Surely, if Congress wants women to contribute the best of their talents, pay their full share of taxes, sacrifice their sons and daughters in Vietnam and on American campuses, it must also be willing to recognize these same women as persons under the Constitution. Otherwise, it is most difficult for a women not to feel thoroughly "used" by the system—Constitutional rape.

It would appear that American women today have more responsibilities with fewer rights. Surely, the very *least* the Congress can do is recognize women as human beings under the Constitution through passage of S.J. Res. 61.

Thank you for permitting me this opportunity to present the above views.

ADDITIONAL MATERIAL

[From Newsweek Magazine, Mar. 23, 1970]

ON PREJUDICE

(By Paul A. Samuelson)

As Mayor La Guardia once said after a gaffe, "When I make a mistake it's a beaut." I know what he meant. In the course of a recent interview for The New York Times I made some derogatory remarks about the caliber of students at Sweet Briar.

If I sinned, I have been made to pay for it. My mail has been full of denunciatory letters from female liberationists who are under no vow to be ladylike. What hurts more though are the well-merited reproaches from Sweet Briar, which happens to have a strong offering in economics and rightly resents being characterized as a frivolous finishing school.

I wish I could say that I was misquoted. But even though I was woefully ignorant about Sweet Briar and used its name as a surrogate for any girl's school, that did not keep me from opening my big mouth and slurring its good name.

So *mea culpa*. There is nought to do but make humble apology, both to the institution in particular and to the feminine sex in general.

IN JOCO NON VERITAS

The incident, however, has set me to pondering. Freud claimed that much is revealed by the jests we make, and I must ask myself why, in an unguarded moment, I found myself expressing a stereotype concerning the implied inferiority of women. Since I am an economist, that naturally raises the question of why women have an economic status so unfavorable relative to that of men.

That they do have such an inferior status there can be no doubt. On the occasion that my wife's class at Radcliffe celebrated its 25th anniversary, I was able to examine the range of their incomes and to compare them with the distribution of the same class at Harvard. Although I am an experienced man of the world, I must confess to shock when I saw the cold numbers before me. The top women's salaries literally ended about where the bottom men's began.

I know you will say that many college women become wives and mothers. That you must not compare part-time earnings with those from full-time work. That one must allow for the fact that many women return to the labor market after a hiatus of many years years spent in the home, and that their loss of momentum explains their pauper-like wages.

But I reply that these explanations will not wash. A class at Radcliffe has long been, if anything, even more select in such qualities as IQ and erudition that the contemporaneous class at Harvard. And many Radcliffe graduates have pursued full-time careers. Why then do *they* turn out to have the incomes of librarians and of teachers rather than the incomes of corporation lawyers, NEWSWEEK editors, and machine-tool salesmen?

Confronted with these undoubted facts, a defender of the status quo will say, "Women get less because they are worth less." In its usual formulation this becomes little more than a tautology, deserving of the same reply that

Hemingway gave to F. Scott Fitzgerald's remark, "The rich are different from us." "Yes," said Hemingway, "they have more money." (And exactly this reply is warranted to the assertion that the poor are different; experiments with the negative income tax in New Jersey show that the poor differ primarily in the fact that they are under the Biblical curse of poverty, and in not much else.)

Somebody has written an essay with the fascinating title: "The Student as Nigger." It makes the point that students are men with boys' incomes, who are expected to remove their hats and shuffle their feet in the presence of their superiors (if not their betters).

A woman would understand that essay. How many of them have climbed the executive ladder up to the rung marked assistant vice president only to be barred, Moses-like, from the Promised Land.

REDEMPTION

Tokenism has begun to rear its head. One or two blacks or females or French-Canadians look good on the organization chart. But do not knock it. Tokenism is the tribute that bigotry pays to conscience. If you feign a virtue, you may end up having it.

But I digress to philosophy from my task as an economist. What would be the effects of wiping out, or say for the sake of the argument, halving the earnings and productivity differentials between men and women?

Will the extra affluence of women have to come at the expense of the surplus value earned by men? Economics suggests that the removal of discriminations will pay its own way, adding to GNP about what it costs.

RECENT DATA RE. THE EQUAL RIGHTS AMENDMENT TO THE U.S. CONSTITUTION
BY MARJORIE R. LONGWELL, NATIONAL CHAIRMAN, NATIONAL WOMAN'S PARTY

On October 1, 1969, President Nixon announced the establishment of the Task Force on Women's Rights and Responsibilities. This Task Force was to review the present Status of women and recommend what might be done to further advance their opportunities. Recently their recommendations were made public, and at the TOP of their list was the passage of the EQUAL RIGHTS AMENDMENT.

President Nixon appointed a CITIZENS' ADVISORY COUNCIL ON THE STATUS OF WOMEN, and on Feb. 7, 1970 this Council announced that it had endorsed the equal Rights Amendment.

As of today, April 30, 1970, 245 U.S. Congressmen have introduced on the Floor of the House of Representatives 245 Equal Rights Amendment Resolutions, and 79 Senators have become Sponsors.

The famous and powerful Walter Reuther has endorsed the Amendment.

The YWCA has endorsed the Equal Rights Amendment recently.

The First Lady, Mrs. Nixon, has stated in the Washington Post on April 28th that she agrees with her husband's endorsement of the Equal Rights Amendment.

I am enclosing a copy of my article: THE AMERICAN WOMAN—THEN AND NOW, in the Fall, 1969 issue of the Delta Kappa Gamma Magazine.

THE AMERICAN WOMAN THEN AND NOW ...

(By Marjorie Longwell, *Member of Phi Chapter, Chi State*)

Serving as California chairman and national vice-president of the National Woman's Party, Mrs. Longwell has been interested for a long period of time in the role of women in America. She has written various articles that have been published in previous issues of the *Bulletin* and has authored a book on women in America. Her pertinent comments on "women, past and present" were given at a recent meeting of Phi Chapter.

Nearly two hundred years ago, when our Founding Fathers were drawing up a code of laws, one Founding Father, John Adams, received a letter from his wife, Abigail, saying:

My dear John: By the way, in the new code of laws, I desire you would remember the ladies and be more generous and favorable to them than were your ancestors. Do not put such unlimited power in the hands of husbands. Remember, all men would be tyrants if they could.

YOUR LOVING WIFE, ABIGAIL.

Not many people are aware of John Adams' answer. He wrote: "Depend upon it, my dear, we men know better than to repeal our masculine systems."

Thus were women left out of the Constitution, and have been left out ever since, except on voting days. In 1920 women of the U.S.A. were given the right to vote.

As someone has wisely said: "Behind every man, as a man stands the Constitution; but behind every women stands the Old English Common Law which places upon her the stigma of inferiority and bondage."

It is vitally important to remember that our Founding Fathers wrote the U.S. Constitution in THE LIGHT OF THE OLD ENGLISH COMMON LAW, and the OLD ENGLISH COMMON LAW *did not recognize women as PERSONS*.

But lest we tend to blame our Founding Fathers unjustly, we must remember that their world of almost 200 years ago no more resembled today's world than an ox cart resembles a rocket ship.

The 1786 woman, spinning and weaving by candlelight, cooking at an open hearth, making clothes for all 14 of her children, could scarcely read or write. Her daughters, attending a hickory stick school, were not taught long division—that mathematical area being reserved for boys.

Daily needs in 1786 were woman-supplied. Did the family need a new blanket? She wove it. Did a child have an aching tooth? She rode with him on horseback to the doctor who, by dint of pliers, turned dentist. Was a neighbor ill? The 1786 woman willingly shouldered the duty of nurse.

To the 1786 woman, gazing out her curtained window at horsedrawn carriages on cobbled streets, our modern woman would have seemed more improbable than Gulliver's tallest tale. How could she visualize 30 million women marching each morning to jobs outside the home, attending college, becoming lawyers, doctors, scientists? How could she know that women would someday drive their own cars, fly their own planes?

The point to remember is that our Constitution, written in 1786 for men and women, STILL SERVES TODAY FOR MEN AND WOMEN, with the exception of the 19th amendment which gives women voting rights.

The 14th and 15th amendments, written in 1868 and 1870, said: "ALL PERSONS BORN OR NATURALIZED IN THE U.S. ARE CITIZENS AND HAVE THE RIGHT TO VOTE."

Susan B. Anthony, considering herself to be a person, registered and voted in 1872. She was arrested, brought to trial, convicted of the crime of voting —because she was a woman, and the word PERSONS mentioned in the 14th and 15th amendments to our Constitution *DID NOT MEAN WOMEN*.

It is a vital truth that the word PERSONS mentioned in our Constitution does not mean women, because the Constitution itself was written in the light of the OLD ENGLISH COMMON LAW which did not recognize women as PERSONS.

If she were alive today, Susan B. Anthony might vote, but she would still see 1000 legal discriminations against women upon various state statute books. This is because in all other legal respects EXCEPT THE RIGHT TO VOTE, women of U.S.A. still live under State Laws.

Let us remember that men are in charge of Congress. Today in the U.S. Senate there are 99 men and ONE women: Senator Margaret Chase Smith of Maine. (She became Senator on the death of her husband, Senator Smith.)

In the House of Representatives are 425 men and TEN women.

Perhaps we can excuse our Founding Fathers for leaving women out of the Constitution, the world being what it was then; but can we excuse today's Senators and Congressmen for KEEPING WOMEN OUT?

Of course we will not list all 1000 legal discriminations against women on various State Statute Books, but let us glance at a few.

WHAT OF DISCRIMINATION IN EDUCATION?

In 1958 the U.S. Supreme Court upheld the decision of the Texas Supreme Court in denying the admission of two women to the Texas A. and M. College, solely on the basis of sex.

In 1960 three women were denied admission there—they wanted courses in floriculture not given in other colleges.

The Texas A. and M. is SUPPORTED BY TAXES. (In payment of taxes there's no trace of sex discrimination.)

On February 6, 1964 the *Congressional Record* had an article that said qualified women had been refused admission to Virginia colleges at the rate of 7,000 a year since 1960. Thus, in the State of Virginia's tax-supported schools, 21,000 qualified women had been denied an education while men students were admitted.

WHAT OF DISCRIMINATION IN DIVORCE LAWS?

In Kentucky a husband may obtain a divorce on SUSPICION of misconduct on his wife's part. HE DOES NOT HAVE TO PROVE IT. She not only must prove he has been unfaithful, but also must prove that his unfaithfulness is habitual.

In Texas a man may win a divorce because of his wife's unfaithfulness, but she must prove he not only is unfaithful but also has abandoned her. If he continues to live with her, even though unfaithful, SHE MAY NOT SECURE A DIVORCE.

WHAT OF DISCRIMINATION IN MARRIAGE LAWS?

In many states a wife may not enter into a business contract without her husband's consent. She may not sign a promissory note, nor give a deed or mortgage without his sanction.

In Nevada and New Mexico when the husband and wife own common property, the husband may will away his half but while the husband lives the wife cannot leave one dollar of her half to anyone—not even to her own children.

WHAT OF DISCRIMINATION IN EMPLOYMENT?

Title VII of the 1964 Civil Rights Act forbids discrimination in employment on the grounds of race, creed, color, national origin or sex, but this has been carelessly enforced, and working women have been required to take their employment cases to court—an expensive procedure.

The State of Delaware has repealed all laws regulating working women so Title VII now governs there.

But all over the country protective legislation is being used as a tool to circumvent Title VII.

You know about protective legislation. It pretects women out of the better paying jobs and gives these jobs to men. It began in 1836 when the New England Association of Farmers and Merchants and other working men expressed the male viewpoint in a resolution which read: "WHEREAS LABOR IS A PHYSICAL AND MORAL INJURY TO WOMEN AND A COMPETITIVE MENACE TO MEN, we recommend legislation to restrict women in industry."

New York State passed a law forbidding women to work after midnight. This affected telephone operators, proofreaders, and waitresses. The latter lost the better tips—at night. Women who scrubbed offices at night were not affected.

If women work only eight daily hours, and men may work as long as they please, who collects the overtime? With millions of women now HEADS OF FAMILIES, how do you think they feel, having to watch men take home that overtime pay that would have bought better food, more food, for their children?

Protective legislation—health laws—should apply to both sexes.

You may say that the Supreme Court should today take a NEW LOOK at the Constitution and declare that women ARE Persons. But this is not legally possible because it is the INTENT of the lawmakers that counts; and it was the INTENT of the writers of the Constitution to leave women out because they were writing it in the light of the Old English Common Law wherein women were not considered to be persons.

And now we come to the solution of the problem of giving women 100 per cent protection of the Constitution, and that is the adoption of the Equal Rights for Women Amendment which reads: "EQUALITY OF RIGHTS UNDER THE LAW SHALL NOT BE DENIED OR ABRIDGED BY THE UNITED STATES OR BY ANY STATE ON ACCOUNT OF SEX."

The word "women" does not appear in the text of the amendment and women would be given no special privileges. The amendment merely forbids discrimination on the basis of sex, and special laws may still be enacted for citizens in need of special laws. No one today questions special laws for veterans, the blind, etc. Thus, under the amendment, women may still enjoy special laws for mothers, or mothers-to-be.

The National Woman's Party has long had as its sole aim the adoption of the Equal Rights Amendment, and other women's organizations, representing approximately ten million women, have endorsed the measure. Ten state legislatures have petitioned Congress for the amendment's adoption, and during the last Presidential campaign every Presidential candidate endorsed the amendment in writing. President Richard M. Nixon recently wrote: "It is my hope that there will be widespread support for the Equal Rights for Women Amendment to our Constitution, which would add equality between the sexes to the freedoms and liberties guaranteed to all Americans."

Many congressmen have promised to vote "YES" when the Equal Rights Amendment comes up for a vote in the House of Representatives, and many senators have endorsed it. Once the Amendment passes the House and Senate, it must be ratified by three quarters of the state legislatures. After that, our country's women will enjoy full citizenship.

LANGUAGE

Language . . .
Conceals and hides . . .
Confounds our listeners . . .
We often cloak our thoughts in a
Disguise.

DORTHINE BLASCH,
Phi Chapter Tau State.

WHO SHALL BE PRINCIPAL—A MAN OR A WOMAN?

(By John Hoyle)

Are men more capable administrators than women? This question is considered continually by superintendents, boards of education, teachers, and the public. The fact is, boards of education seem to favor men at both the high school and the elementary school level. Data reveal that while men constitute only 12 percent of the elementary teaching force, they account for 69 percent of the elementary principalships.[1]

Because of the recent increased trend toward employing men as elementary school principals, one might assume that men *are* better principals than women. However, certain research findings challenge this assumption. For example, studies by Wiles[2] and Grobman and Hines[3] reveal that women ranked significantly ahead of men as "democratic leaders." Hemphill, Griffiths, and Frederiksen substantiated the findings of the above studies and found that there probably is no reason to prefer men as principals.[4] These researchers indicated that if such interest as working with teachers and outsiders, being concerned with objectives of teaching, encouraging pupil participation, evaluating learning, and gaining positive reactions from teachers and superiors are important, then probably women should be favored, since women in their study possessed these interests to a significantly greater degree than did men.

One reason often mentioned for favoring men is the assumption that women teachers dislike working for women principals, and men teachers like it even less. In a survey by Barter, however, a group of teachers rated female and

---

[1] National Education Association, Research Division. "Status of Public-School Teachers, 1965." *NEA Research Bulletin* 43 : 67 ; October 1965.
  Among teaching elementary school principals in 1966-67, 36 percent were women and 64 percent were men ; the proportions among supervising principals were 22 percent women and 78 percent men ; the total sample showed 25 percent women and 75 percent men. See page 11 of *The Elementary School Principalship in 1968*, a research study published by the Department of Elementary School Principals, NEA, in June 1968.
  John Hoyle is Assistant Professor of Educational Administration, Texas Christian University, Fort Worth.
  Editor's Note : The question of whether men make better school administrators than women is hardly a new one. While in a so-called enlightened and progressive age the question would seem to be one we could solve by common sense, old traditions, prejudices, and shibboleths still persist. The author of this article has approached the problem on a more scientific basis, and has taken a look at a small sample of teachers and principals. The editors feel this approach marks an interesting contribution to the study of a question that warrants further exploration—including exploration of the possibility that women may not be as much interested in being principals today as they were at an earlier point in time.
[2] Wiles, Kimball, and Grobman, Hulda Gross. "Principals as Leaders." *Nation's Schools* 56 : 75 ; October 1955.
[3] Grobman, Hulda, and Hines, Vynce A. "What Makes a Good Principal?" *National Association of Secondary School Principals Bulletin* 40 : 5-16 ; November 1956.
[4] Hemphill, John K. ; Griffiths, Daniel E. ; and Frederiksen, Norman. *Administrative Performance and Personality.* New York : Bureau of Publications, Teachers College, Columbia University, 1962.

male principals as equal in ability and personal qualities.[5] The results indicated that while, in general, women teachers approved of women principals more than men teachers did, those male teachers who had taught in schools administered by women were more favorable to women principals than to men. Those who disapproved of female principals were men who had taught only under male principals.

In another study, Newell found that female elementary school principals showed more evidence of being aware of the cognitive factor of the learning process than did male administrators.[6] And finally, research of this type prompted McIntyre to assert that ". . . research does not show men to be superior to women in the principalship—in fact, the little evidence that we have suggests just the opposite conclusions."[7]

In an attempt to uncover a little more evidence about the male-female question, I recently conducted a study that compared the manner in which male and female principals make decisions or solve problems.[8]

The central purpose of the research reported here was to explore the relationship between sex and the five aspects of problem-attack behavior of selected elementary school principals.

To accomplish this purpose, data were gathered by administering Randall's *Problem-Attack Behavior Inventory* (PABI) to faculty members in 30 Texas suburban elementary schools.[9] The teachers were asked to describe the behavior of their principals in the handling of problems that arose in the schools. Their responses were based upon impressions they had formed about how frequently their principals engaged in the following five kinds of administrative behavior, as described in the revised form of PABI:

1. *Problem-Recognition Behavior:* the extent to which an administrator appears to perceive situations that are seen as problems by his staff.

2. *Problem-Analysis Behavior:* the extent to which an administrator appears to discover and examine responses to problem situations.

3. *Group Participation Behavior:* the extent to which an administrator encourages those with whom he works to use initiative to criticize and to involve themselves in solving school problems.

4. *Administrator-Action Behavior:* the extent to which an administrator acts on problem situations, including the quality of his actions.

5. *Administrator-Evaluation Behavior:* the extent to which an administrator reviews the results of his action.

In the study, 216 teachers described 21 male principals, and 98 teachers described 9 female principals. A comparison of the results revealed that teachers described female administrators as noticing potential problem situations (variable 1) and as reviewing results of action (variable 5) significantly more often than did male administrators. On other variables, differences were not significant.

In attempting to discuss the possible reasons for the above results, we might compare this study to the aforementioned study by Hemphill, *et al.*[10]

One explanation for Hemphill's conclusion is that, generally speaking, the female principals in his study had more years of elementary school teaching experience than the male principals, prior to assuming an administrative position.[11]

In the study reported here, 66.7 percent of the males had less than six years of elementary school teaching experience before becoming principals. Only one principal had less than two years of teaching experience.

Conversely, 88 percent of the female principals (eight out of nine) became principals after six or more years of elementary school teaching experience. In other words, the female administrators had had considerably more teaching ex-

---

[5] Barter, Alice S. "The Status of Women in School Administration." *Educational Horizons* 37 : 72-75 ; Spring 1959.
[6] Newell, Laura A. *A Study of Instructional Awareness of Elementary School Principals in Selected School Districts Throughout the United States.* Doctor's thesis. Auburn, Ala. : Auburn University, 1960. (Unpublished)
[7] McIntyre, Kenneth E. "The Selection of Elementary School Principals." *National Elementary Principal* 44 : 42-47 ; April 1965.
[8] Hoyle, John R. *Problem-Attack Behavior and Its Relationship to the Sex, Prior Teaching Experience, and College Preparation of Selected Elementary School Principals.* Doctor's thesis. College Station, Tex. : Texas A & M University, 1967. (Unpublished)
[9] Randall, Robert S. *The Development and Testing of an Instrument to Describe Problem-Attack Behavior of High School Principals.* Doctor's thesis. Austin, Tex. : University of Texas, 1965.
[10] See footnote 4.

perience in the elementary school, which may account for the "more often" behavior scores they received in terms of "recognizing potential problems" and "evaluating results of actions." One possible explanation, then, is that the experiences these women gained as teachers may have had an effect upon their behavior in problem situations after they became elementary principals.

Another possible explanation is that female principals may be more sensitive to "problems" of other women than male principals are. Also, since most of the teacher repondents in the study are women, they may have tended to describe their principals' behavior from a "female point of view."

But in spite of the research studies which extol the administrative skills of women elementary principals, the ratio of women to men administrators is continuing to decrease. It would seem that in light of the accumulating evidence, boards of education and suprintendents would do well to avoid discrimination on the basis of sex and look instead for the personal qualities and administrative skills that are needed in the particular leadership job to be filled.

SPEAKING OUT—LET'S DRAFT WOMEN, TOO!

(By Caroline Bird)*

Is the draft unfair? A number of critics have charged that it discriminates against Negroes, the poor, the uneducated, and particulary the high-school graduate who is through school in a neighborhood where the other boys are going on to college. Even if these charges are true, there is a greater inequity in the draft, one so big that nobody sees it. The draft is unfair to the whole male sex. Women are not drafted, and they should be.

When we talk about the obligation of men to bear arms in defense of their country, we have in the back of our minds a picture of a farmer leaving his plow in the field to shoulder a gun. Once it really was this way. In the Civil War, for instance, only one out of every 10 men did anything comparable to civilian work. But during World War II, the Pentagon is embarrassed to admit, military-manpower specialists figured that half the men in uniform had jobs that women could have done just as well as men. By 1960, a study showed, almost nine out of 10 servicemen were doing something that could have been a civilian job.

The citizen-soldier seldom has the rifle anymore, let alone the farm. In World War II, only one out of four in uniform served in what Pentagon manpower expert Harold Wool calls a "man-with-gun" job. Now only one in eight is in this category. One serviceman in eight is also needed just to keep the electronic hardware of the armed forces going.

The obligation to bear arms, in other words, is often not that at all. Instead, in the name of patriotism, most draftees are conscripted to do exactly what they did or might have done for a living back home—drive a truck, punch a Teletype, keep records, file letters, run a store, interpret foreign languages, do bookkeeping work or swab floors. The draft has become detached from battle and transformed into a means of shifting manpower from the civilian work force to the military work force. Since women are now a major part of the civilian work force, it is only common sense to declare that women should be called into service.

Even Pentagon traditionalists concede that a modern army moves on paperwork, and this involves abilities and experience on which women have a near-monopoly. In particular, women in civilian life dominate such jobs as computer programmer and data processor, which are vital to military operations. There are important military jobs men simply cannot do. For some reason, men cannot run a telephone switchboard. In World War I, Gen. "Black Jack" Pershing broke down and cabled Washington to send 100 French-speaking women telephone operators to save the sanity of the American Expeditionary Force in France. In World War II, at least one Air Force general publicly grumbled that his men would be a lot safer it he were allowed to take his women phone operators into battle areas. Mata Hari to the contrary notwithstanding, women make lousy spies, but for some reason they are extraordinarily good at making sense out of pictures taken from U-2 planes.

In spite of all the rich folklore which labels almost all jobs "his" or "hers," psychologists know pitifully little about what difference, if any, sex makes in aptitude for the work most people do today. But public policy is now clear. For nearly a year now Title VII of the Civil Rights Act of 1964 has forbidden employers to discriminate among their workers on the basis of sex (as well as race or religion) except where a bona fide sex qualification exists. There are unusual jobs, such as working in washrooms. Consistency demands that the armed forces abandon sex-typing of work that is now prescribed for private employers.

Equity demands that women be drafted for jobs they can do as well as men. Draftees often suffer simply because they must accept soldiers' pay while postponing a career. It does not make sense to demand this sacrifice of men while women are left free to demand whatever they can command in a shrinking labor market.

Drastic as it may sound, the idea of drafting women is not really so unusual. The crack Israel Army, for example, drafts all boys and single girls at 18 and gives them both basic training with weapons. Girls who marry during their draft terms—and three out of 10 do—go into the reserves. Pregnant women and mothers are excused, but women officers in the regular army get four months of fully paid leave beginning with the ninth month of pregnancy, much as some women in U.S. civilian employment now do. Israeli women no longer serve with men in fire fights as they did—and gallantly—during the height of the Arab war, because Arab soldiers would literally rather die than surrender to a woman. Now women are assigned work in administration, communications, the medical corps, and the education of newcomers to Israel. Commanders report higher morale where men and women soldiers work together.

The British drafted women along with men in World War II. Our forces, meanwhile, had so much trouble competing with war industry for workers that two of our most celebrated military leaders. Generals Dwight D. Eisenhower and Mark Clark, warned Congress that women would have to be drafted in future wars. The Women's Army Corps grew so desperate it spent an average of $125 to recruit each women. Pentagon staffers proposed a proclamation stating that military service is an obligation that "rests upon women as well as men."

During the Korean War, a women's draft very nearly happened here. Women were so afraid of ridicule and humiliation that they would not come to recruiting offices and had to be interviewed in their homes. But women were needed, and Washington planners debated tactics for getting them with as little public outcry as possible. In 1950 President Truman hinted that he was thinking of registering women as a first step in the event of an "emergency."

"All the social forces which make women hesitate to volunteer for military duty would vanish if women were drafted," World War II Wave Director Mildred McAfee pointed out in urging conscription for women. To this day, the reluctance of women to volunteer is cited in the Pentagon as proof that women should not be drafted because "they don't want to serve." The reasoning is parallel to the notion that racial integration was unnecessary because "Negroes don't want to go to school with white folks."

Today, all the Pentagon manpower specialists agree that we will *have* to draft women if we get into a major ground war—for instance, with the Communist Chinese. It is a hoary tradition at the Pentagon that public opinion is against drafting women except in the direst straits. Actually, public-opinion polls have rolled up respectable and sometimes majority votes for drafting women, depending on the military outlook of the moment and the way the question is worded.

Almost anyone you ask in Washington tells you that its someone else who stands in the way. Daniel Flood, Pennsylvania Democrat on the House subcommittee that handles the armed forces' appropriations, chimes in that "Congress won't stand for a draft of women now." The Selective Service Director, Lt. Gen. Lewis B. Hershey, says that "the public is still just not ready to see women as draftees, rained on, out in the cold, and getting killed. We might get to drafting women if we were near complete mobilization—say more than 12 million in the armed forces." What Hershey is reluctant to talk about is that he already *has* plans—classified, of course—for drafting women. Hershey goes on: "If Congress were to call me up and say, 'We're going to draft women,' I'm not going to just say, 'Huh . . . women?' as though it had never occurred to me."

If eventually, why not now? We now need three million in uniform, and a lot of people think we're going to need more. Draft calls currently running over 25,000 a month pinch our tight labor market. Waiting to draft women until we run out of men is like waiting to hire Negroes until all the white men have jobs. Discrimination is easier but just as objectionable when there are more qualified people than there are jobs, or more young men of draft age than the armed forces really need, or more qualified applicants for college than the colleges can take. What we do with the young people heading toward college and the draft today is just what we did with the young who queued up at the employment office during the Depression. Rather than let the power possibilities of this choice go to waste, we invent qualifications which protect the status quo. In an "easy labor market" you can, if you wish, insist on hiring a blue-eyed white male Protestant clerk who plays the cello you need to complete your string quartet. Under full employment, you find that the office work proceeds swimmingly with a brown-eyed Catholic Negro woman who has no musical talent of any kind. So long as we need no more than half of the boys coming of draft age every year, we prefer to take those who might otherwise be unemployed and defer those who manage to get good grades in college. We can, in other words, afford the luxury of discriminating on rather tenuous grounds. I submit that if we are willing to accept such gross inequity, it would make better sense to spread it as thin as possible.

As I've discovered, you can sometimes get a policymaker to admit that women could serve and women should serve. Then he leans back with a smile and says, "Of course, but it's not practical" If you ask him why, he laughs. Plato had the same experience when he advocated military service for women as well as men in *The Republic*, and he did not let the laughers get away with it. "In his laughter," Plato wrote sternly, "he himself is plucking the fruit of unripe wisdom, and he himself is ignorant of what he is laughing at."

The "practical" reason that seems most obvious to Pentagon manpower researchers is cost. Women simply must cost more than men to maintain. You have to put doors on the toilets, and women need bathrobes and lounge chairs. And if you have them on a military post, you've got to maintain a guard of men soldiers to keep off-duty GI's from breaking into the female quarters. In fact, however, a staff study of 1948 showed tht a Wac cost the Army $77 *less* a year than the man she replaced. Her clothes did cost more, but her food cost less, she smashed up less furniture, and she saved the Government the money that might have been spent on moving the man's dependents. What is truly impractical is the military folklore which says that all servicemen even the I.B.M. operators, must spend a lot of time marching up and down dusty fields and wasting ammunition on rifle ranges, and I trust that most female draftees could be spared foolishness of that kind.

For some reason, the idea of women in uniform produces highly emotional reactions and even fear. There were allegations that our women soldiers in World War II were issued contraceptives so that they could more readily bolster the morale of male soldiers. Some fear, in all sincerity, that military life will somehow "damage" women. To these objectors, Gen. Eisenhower had a notable remark:

"Like most old soldiers, I was violently against women soldiers," he testified at hearings on the bill to integrate the women's services in 1948. "I thought a tremendous number of difficulties would occur, not only of an administrative nature . . . but others of a more personal type that would get us into trouble. None of that occurred. In tasks for which they were particularly suited, Wacs are more valuable than men and fewer of them are required to perform a given amount of work. . . . In the disciplinary field, they were . . . a model for the Army. More than this, their influence throughout the whole command was good. I am convinced that in another war they have got to be drafted just like men." Unfortunately the bill that emerged from those hearings put a quota of two percent on women in military service.

In our military, the notion persists that women are nothing but defective men." Unfortunately the bill that emerged from those hearings put a quota of itary service." Gen. Hershey admits. "So could men in wheelchairs. But you couldn't expect the services to want a whole company of people in wheelchairs." The analogy is revealing—about the Selective Service experts. Confronted with a proposal that women be drafted, one of the manpower specialists wailed, "Think of the humiliation! What has become of the manhood of America?" I doubt that working alongside a woman draftee in a Pentagon office would do any more damage to American manhood than working beside a woman civilian on Madison Avenue or Michigan Boulevard. For that matter, I doubt that the American man is in such a precarious state of manhood that a woman's draft would destroy him.

The Case for Drafting All Boys—And Girls
(By Margaret Mead)

Young Americans in every part of the land are finding their voices. Whatever the issue, more and more of them—girls as well as boys—are declaring themselves. When they speak up it is most often to protest: "It isn't fair!"

This is a generation that does not readily accept things as they are. There are some young people, of course, who are merely restive—the black-helmeted boys who race into a town on their motorcycles and the boys and girls who converge in masses on holiday resorts. And some, like the students at an Eastern college who marched all day out of "general discontent," seem to be protesting mainly for the sake of protest.

But others, an ever-growing number, are concerning themselves seriously and vigorously with public issues. Through sit-ins, stand-ins, teach-ins, marches and demonstrations, on campus and off, they are debating and taking positions—a wide variety of positions—on civil rights, academic freedom and responsibility, the forms of voluntary service young people should be allowed to give, the kind of war they are willing or unwilling to support, whether those who are called upon to bear arms should not also have the right to vote, and above all, the inequities of the draft. Faced with adult responsibilities, they are protesting their status as nonadults. Confronted by problems of policy, they are demanding their right to take part in decisions that affect their lives and the lives of others, as students, as wage earners (or as uneducated and unemployable young people) and as parents and citizens. In short, they want a voice in the affairs of the country. Especially they want to be heard when, on any issue, they protest: "It isn't fair."

Today the focus of protest is the draft. The sense that what is happening in the draft isn't fair has made it the central issue on which a great many dissatisfactions converge. And the inequities of the draft may make it a stumbling block for a whole generation. The most obvious inequities are those that affect the lives of young men—not only the relatively small number who are called to military service but also those who are deferred, perhaps indefinitely, and those who are rejected permanently. But there are other inequities, less obvious but equally serious. For this system, because it concentrates on young men, sets girls and young women apart as if they did not exist. And because it concentrates only on military service, it is a threat to this generation's growing sense that what happens to any of them will affect the future of all of them.

It is significant that the strongest protests among young people against the present system do not come from those who have the least hope of preferment —the dropouts, the unskilled and those who have the brains but not the means to go to college or professional schools. Rather it is the students in our colleges and universities, those whom the present system most favors, who are most loudly protesting the essential unfairness of making their less-privileged age mates carry the heaviest burdens of hardship and danger. What we are seeing is not a widening rift between those who have some possibility of choice and those who have none. Instead, we are witnessing an upsurge of discontent among those most favored.

It is significant also that girls see the draft as an issue on which they too should take a stand, as they have on other contemporary issues. Together with boys, they have worked for civil rights, they have served in the Peace Corps and other voluntary organizations that allow them to give practical expression to idealism and they have joined actively in the dialogue on the issues of war and peace. All this has placed them in a different relationship to the young men of their generation even where, as in the draft, their interests and their very existence are disregarded.

The system of the draft thus brings to a head, as young people themselves see it, the question of whether it is fair to ask only a portion of a generation to give involuntary service to their country; whether it is equitable to exclude all the rest of that generation—all the girls, all the boys who lack the qualifications necessary to meet military requirements and all the boys who are exempted for reasons beyond their control.

And so a new question is raised, a question that many people are asking today: Would a universal national service be more equitable?

There are those who will object to any innovation. But for those who are sensitive to the long history of our American struggle to reconcile responsibility, privilege and freedom and for those who are tuned to the protesting voices of contemporary young Americans, the idea of universal national service will have a special appeal. By setting aside older ideas and instead shaping a program to our own expectations, we may transform a service asked of and given by all young people into something that is peculiarly American—a worthy sequel to our conception of universal free education for every child in the United States, regardless of race and color, creed and class.

Universal national service is still only an idea. But for a moment I should like to suppose . . .

Suppose *all* young people were required to register at the age of 18. Each one, girl and boy, would be given a series of educational and medical examinations that would place all young people within the whole group of their generation in the country. Each also would be given an opportunity to state the kind of service to the country he or she could in good conscience give. No one would be exempt—or disregarded—in the old sense. No one would be relieved of the obligation to give two years, let us say, to the country, working under direction and living on the same subsistence allowance as everyone else. But equally, no one would be excluded from the privilege of being individually and carefully assessed, helped and brought as close as possible to our best standards for education, skill, health, civic knowledge and responsibility. No one would be excluded from an opportunity to know and work with young people like and different from himself or herself. No one would be excluded from the experience of leaving home and the home neighborhood and discovering a new environment and a different set of demands and possibilities. No one would be excluded from the opportunity to develop a special talent merely because he or she lacked the expected foundation of knowledge or skill or even the awareness of how such a talent could be developed.

Those who did not know how to plan a trip or read a map or make up a budget or talk to a stranger or fill out a form or follow written directions would have a chance to learn. Those who had been overprotected, who had been in "good" schools since nursery-school days, associating only with other children exactly like themselves, studying until they felt that book knowledge was running out of their ears, would have a chance to discover new directions and work in new settings. By the time they are 18, many of our most privileged children have had 15 years of schooling without any chance to put their learning to work, while a very large proportion of our least privileged children have had to survive ten or more years of utterly unrewarding sitting in dreary classrooms, learning less and less, falling further and further behind, suffering defeat of hope and denigration of individuality. Both would profit by living and working within a new group of peers in an unfamiliar place, by the discovery that they had recognized rights and obligations and by the experience of finding out that they were neither exempt nor excluded from responsibility.

Universal national service would not mean that every boy and every girl would be set the same task. On the contrary, it would mean the mobilization on a national scale of a great variety of activities to meet the needs of our country and of our young people. It would fulfill our most basic obligations to our young men and women and provide them with appropriate means of giving service. It would open new doors for a great many. But it would not provide individual freedom of choice in any simple sense. At 18, young people are moving toward adult life; they themselves are asking for adult status. Combining all this would mean the development of a new sense of what is fair and equitable—for everyone.

Looking to the future, it would be necessary for some—boys and girls—to learn the skills essential to our industrial world and for some to begin the training required to produce the next generation of scientists, engineers, physicians, nurses, teachers and technicians. What we hoped to accomplish by deferring certain students from the draft—that is, to provide for the necessary quota of trained and qualified men—would still be important. But now we could include young women as well, setting goals for their achievement that few girls have had in the recent past. And those, boys and girls, who are excluded today from the exercise of their talents would be given a chance to find themselves. And we would still need to meet the requirements, different at different times, of our armed services. The difference would be that those who were selected to carry this responsibility would not be the *only* ones who were called on for service. Nor would we be faced by the all but insoluble dilemma of finding special ways of showing appreciation for those who volunteer and of compensating adequately those who are serving involuntarily.

However, it was organized in detail, universal national service would not absolve young men and young women from responsibility. All of them, whatever they were doing, would be committed for a certain time to some form of activity as citizens, full citizens, with a voice in what they were doing and responsibility for what they had in hand. Eighteen-year-olds, both the privileged and underprivileged, are unready for parenthood in a complex world. But they are ready for many forms of adult activity that involve the companionship of girls and boys as equals, as individuals, all of whom have a stake in what they are accomplishing. And all of them would benefit by the experience of a kind of life, for a limited period, in which obligation, privilege and responsibility were combined, in which no distinction was made between rights and duties as they took part in the very varied and necessary tasks of protecting, conserving and developing the country in which they expected to live as self-sustaining adults, free to make their own choices and decisions.

The current protest, "It isn't fair," has grown out of the uncertainties and inequities of segregating one ill-defined group in a whole generation. A universal national service may be the one equitable answer.

Appeals from the United States District Court for the Southern District of Indiana, New Albany Division

IN THE UNITED STATES COURT OF APPEALS FOR THE SEVENTH CIRCUIT
SEPTEMBER TERM, 1968—APRIL SESSION, 1969

No. 16624

THELMA BOWE, ET AL., PLAINTIFFS-APPELLEES V. COLGATE-PALMOLIVE COMPANY,
ET AL., DEFENDANTS-APPELLANTS

No. 16625

THELMA BOWE, ET AL., PLAINTIFFS-APPELLANTS V. COLGATE-PALMOLIVE COMPANY,
ET AL., DEFENDANTS-APPELLEES

No. 16626

THELMA BOWE, ET AL., PLAINTIFFS-APPELLANTS V. COLGATE-PALMOLIVE COMPANY,
ET AL., DEFENDANTS-APPELLEES AND INTERNATIONAL CHEMICAL WORKERS UNION,
LOCAL NO. 15, DEFENDANT-APPELLANT

No. 16632

GEORGIANNA SELLERS, ET AL., PLAINTIFFS-APPELLANTS V. COLGATE-PALMOLIVE
COMPANY, ET AL., DEFENDANTS-APPELLEES

SEPTEMBER 26, 1969.

Before CUMMINGS and KERNER, *Circuit Judges,* and WISE, *District Judge.**
KERNER, *Circuit Judge.* Plaintiffs are present and/or former female employees of defendant Colgate-Palmolive Company (Colgate) who were represented, for collective bargaining purposes, by defendant International Chemical Workers Union, Local No. 15 (Union) at Colgate's Jeffersonville, Indiana, plant. Plaintiffs sued Colgate and the Union under Title VII of the Civil Rights Act of 1964, 42 U.S.C. § 2000e *et seq.* charging that they were intentionally discriminated against by a system of job classification which deprived them of various opportunities in the plant and that they were subjected to discriminatory layoffs under a segregated plant seniority system based on the employees' sex.

Prior to trial, the court below required plaintiffs to elect whether they would proceed in this action or whether they would seek remedy under the collective bargaining agreement through arbitration. The court also refused to consider the claims of certain plaintiffs who had not filed charges with the Equal Employment Opportunity Commission (EEOC) and had not received notice of the right to sue from the EEOC, having determined that this action could not be maintained as a class action for purposes of applying a back pay remedy for the layoffs. After trial by the court without a jury, a memorandum opinion was filed which found for the Union in full, and for Colgate on all issues on the merits except as to certain layoffs under the segregated seniority lists in November, 1965. The

* Judge Wise is sitting by designation from the United States District Court for the Eastern District of Illinois.

crux of the lower court's opinion on the merits in its holding that Colgate acted reasonably in imposing a 35-pound weight-lifting limit on jobs which were open to females, thus foreclosing them from competing for jobs requiring lifting of more than 35 pounds. The facts are carefully set out in *Bowe* v. *Colgate-Palmolive Co.*, 272 F. Supp. 332, esp. 340-60 (S.D. Ind. 1967). Except for portions of the partial relief granted below, we reverse.

1. ELECTION OF REMEDIES

The first major issue for our consideration is whether the trial court acted properly in requiring plaintiffs to elect whether they would pursue their statutory remedy in this action or seek arbitration of grievances under the collective bargaining contract. Thus, the court required an election of remedies prior to any decision on the merits in either of the available fora.

The situation facing the trial court was one in which there exists concurrent jurisdiction under the statutory scheme and under the grievance and arbitration process for the resolution of claims against an employer and a union. The analogy to labor disputes involving concurrent jurisdiction of the N.L.R.B. and the arbitration process is not merely compelling, we hold it conclusive.[1]

While we recognize that there is a burden placed on the defendant who must defend in two different fora, we also note that there may be crucial differences between the two processes and the remedy afforded by each. Also, as with unfair labor practice cases, in a case involving an alleged breach of a contract brought before an arbitrator, the arbitrator may consider himself bound to apply the contract and not give the types of remedy which are available under the statute. Conversely, an action in court may not be able to delve into all the ramifications of the contract nor afford some types of relief available through arbitration, *e.g.*, back pay prior to the date of the statute. *Steelworkers* v. *American Int'l Aluminum Corp.*, 334 F. 2d 147 (5th Cir. 1964), and cases cited *supra*, note 1.

Moreover, in an action brought under Title VII, the charging party and suing plaintiff acts as a private attorney general who "takes on the mantel of the sovereign." *Jenkins* v. *United Gas Corp.*, 400 F. 2d 28, 32 (5th Cir. 1968). See also *Oatis* v. *Crown Zellerbach Corp.*, 398 F. 2d 496 (5th Cir. 1968).[2] When, as frequently happens, the alleged discrimination has been practiced on the plaintiff because he or she is a member of a class which is allegedly discriminated against, the trial court bears a special responsibility in the public interest to resolve the dispute by determining the facts regardless of the position of the individual plaintiff. *Jenkins*, *supra* at 33, n. 10. This is only fair to the defendant as it avoids forcing him to defend a multiplicity of actions.

Accordingly, we hold that it was error not to permit the plaintiffs to utilize dual or parallel prosecution both in court and through arbitration so long as election of remedy was made after adjudication so as to preclude duplicate relief which would result in an unjust enrichment or windfall to the plaintiffs. *American Int'l Aluminum*, *supra* at 152. *N.L.R.B.* v. *Geo. E. Light Boat Storage, Inc.*, 373 F. 2d 762, 767–68 (5th Cir. 1967).

2. WEIGHT-LIFTING RESTRICTION

Colgate uses an unusual system of plant-wide seniority due to the uncertainty from week to week as to which jobs in the plant will operate. Each week, every employee completes a job preference sheet for the following week with job assignments being made on the basis of seniority. The seniority system is bifurcated into separate eligibility lists for men and women. While men may bid for jobs plant wide, women are restricted to jobs which do not require lifting more than 35 pounds. The history and mechanics of this unusual system are fully set out at 272 F. Supp. 340–47. The Union also bears responsibility for this system since it continued to abide by it as enshrined in the contract in force on the effective date of Title VII and since it preserved some parts of the system in its 1966

---

[1] It should also be noted that other remedies may have been available to the plaintiffs here before the N.L.R.B. and in the courts under sections 10 and 301(a) of the Labor-Management Relations Act. *Cf. Local 357* v. N.L.R.B., 365 U.S. 667 (1961) ; *Smith* v. *Evening News Ass'n.*, 371 U.S. 195, 197-98 (1962) ; *Care·· v. Westinghouse Elec. Corp.*, 375 U.S. 261, 268 (1964) ; and *Humphrey* v. *Moore*, 375 U.S. 335 (1964).

[2] An analogous situation existed in *Newman* v. *Piggie Park Enterprises*, 390 U.S. 400 (1968).

contract with Colgate. However, as shown below, there is no liability on the part of the Union due to the failure of any of the plaintiffs to comply with the jurisdictional requisites for filing a suit against the Union.

The trial court carefully analyzed the various facts relating to the weight-lifting restriction and conclude that Colgate had acted reasonably and in the interest of the safety of its female employees in imposing the 35-pound restriction. 272 F. Supp. at 353–57, and 363–66. While this was a carefully reasoned and conscientious approach, we hold it error as it is based on a misconception of the requirements of Title VII's anti-discrimination provisions.

The trial court relied on 42 U.S.C. § 2000e–2(e) which permits discrimination in hiring by sex where sex "is a bona fide occupational qualification reasonably necessary to the normal operation of that particular business or enterprise" and § 2000e–3(b) which similarly permits discrimination in job advertisements where sex "is a bona fide occupational qualification for employment." The court also relied on § 2000e7 which states that the Act shall not be deemed to relieve those covered under it from any liability imposed by state law, except where such law would require the doing of "any act which would be an unlawful employment practice under this subchapter." Thus, the court succumbed to the erroneous argument that state laws setting weight-lifting restrictions on women were not affected by Title VII. While we agree with the court's noting of the EEOC's statement that it cannot be assumed that Congress intended ot strike down all such legislation,[3] we also observe that that statement was presented to the court out of its proper context. The EEOC guideline on sex as a "bona fide occupation qualification" (BFOQ) reads, in pertinent part, 29 C.F.R. §§ 1604.1 and 1604.2 (1968):

§ 1604.1.   Sex as a bona fide occupational qualification.

(a) The Commission believes that the bona finde occupational qualification exception as to sex should be interpreted narrowly. Labels— "Men's jobs" and "Women's jobs"—tend to deny employment opportunities unnecessary to one sex or the other.

(3) Most States have enacted laws or administrative regulations with respect to the employment of women. These laws fall into the general categories:

(i) Laws that require that certain benefits be provided for female employees, such as minimum wages, premium pay for overtime, rest periods or physical facilities;

(ii) Laws that prohibit the employment of women in certain hazardous occupations, in jobs requiring the lifting of heavy weights, during certain hours of the night, or for more than a specified number of hours per day or per week.

(b) The Commission believes that some state laws and regulations with respect to the employment of women, although originally for valid protective reasons, have ceased to be relevant to our technology or to the expanding role of the woman worker in our economy. We shall continue to study the problems posed by these laws and regulations in particular factual contexts, and to cooperate with other appropriate agencies in achieving a regulatory system more responsive to the demands of equal opportunity in employment.

(c) The Commission does not believe that Congress intended to disturb such laws and regulations which are intended to, and have the effect of, protecting women against exploitation and hazard. Accordingly, the Commission will consider limitations or prohibitions imposed by such state laws or regulations as a basis for application of the bona fide occupational qualification exception. However, in cases where the clear effect of a law in current circumstances is not to protect women but to subject them to discrimination, the law will not be considered a justification for discrimination. So, for example, restrictions on lifting weights will not be deemed in conflict with Title VII except where the limit is set at an unreasonably low level which could not endanger women.

(1) An employer, accordingly, will not be considered to be engaged in an unlawful employment practice when he refuses to employ a woman in a job in which women are legally prohibited from being

---

[3] See 30 Fed. Reg. 14926 (1695).

employed or which involve duties which women may not legally be permitted to perform because of hazards reasonably to be apprehended from such employment.

§ 1604.2 Separate lines of progression and seniority systems.

(a) It is an unlawful employment practice to classify a job as "male" or "female" or to maintain separate lines of progression or separate seniority lists based on sex where this would adversely affect any employee unless sex is a bona fide occupational qualification for that job. Accordingly, employment practices are unlawful which arbitrarily classify jobs so that:

(1) A female is prohibited from applying for a job labeled "male," or for a job in a "male" line of progression; and vice versa.

(2) A male scheduled for layoff is prohibited from displacing a less senior female on a "female" seniority list; and vice versa.

(b) A seniority system or line of progression which distinguishes between "light" and "heavy" jobs constitutes an unlawful employment practice if it operates as a disguised form of classification by sex, or creates unreasonable obstacles to the advancement by members of either sex into jobs which members of that sex would reasonably be expected to perform.

By way of further interpretation of its guidelines, especially § 1604.1(a)(3)(c) relating to weight-lifting limits, the EEOC has, in three separate cases, indicated that this guideline is not to be read as an approval of general weight-limits by sex in any state or even in a particular industry, but that consideration must be given on a highly individualized basis. It views such broad limitation as violative of its prohibition against the use of broad class stereotypes including those in which sex is the stereotyping factor.[4] In case Nos. CH 7–3–183, et al., August 31, 1967, the EEOC voided a 35-pound weight limit imposed by one employer on all women employees holding that "individuals [must] be considered on the basis of individual capacities and not on the basis of any characteristics generally attributed to the group." In case Nos. AU 68–10–209E, et al., July 24, 1968, the EEOC held that an agreement between an employer and union limiting females to jobs involving lifting weights of less than 55 pounds was based on a generic classification which was arbitrary and discriminatory and based on a "stereotyped characterization of the sexes," rather than consideration of individual capacities as to physical strength and particular job requirements. Finally, in Case Nos. CL–68–11–326E, et al. Sept. 26, 1968, fn. 1 (a case involving another major Indiana employer), the EEOC expressly stated its disagreement with the particular decision below.[5]

If anything is certain in this controversial area, it is that there is no general agreement as to what is a maximum permissible weight which can be safely lifted by women in the course of their employment. The states which have limits vary considerably. Most of the state limits were enacted many years ago and most, if not all, would be considered clearly unreasonable in light of the average physical development, strength and stamina of most modern American women who participate in the industrial work force. Almost all state limits are below the 33 to 44.1 pounds recommended by an investigatory committee of the International Labor Organization (I.L.O.) in March, 1964. Even those limits were rejected by the I.L.O. and the provision finally adopted in I.L.O. Convention No. 127 (June 28, 1967) simply states that no worker should transport loads "which, by reason of its weight is likely to jeopardize his health or safety" and that the maximum weight of loads for women "shall be substantially less than that permitted for adult male workers." At the same time, Recommendation 127 was adopted stating that the maximum load for an adult male should be 55 kg. or 121 pounds. While there was no agreement as to a maximum load for women, the I.L.O. experts individually suggested limits ranging

[4] 29 C.F.R. §1604.1(a)(1)(ii)(1968).
[5] It is also important to note that Indiana has no legislation of the type here discussed. The 35-pound weight-limit was arrived at by Colgate and sustained by the court below on the basis of a general analysis of legislation in other states. To the extent that the court relied on California's law, here assumed relevant due to the location of other Colgate plants in that state, we note with approval the decision in *Rosenfeld* v. *Southern Pac. Co.*, 293 F. Supp. 1219 (C.D. Calif. 1968), holding California's "hours and weights legislation" invalid as setting unreasonably low standards for women in violation of Title VII. We also note that the trial court may have been misled by Colgate into relying on an apparently non-existent limitation in New Jersey. See Brief of the EEOC at 43, n. 28 and Appendix A.

from 60.5 to 76.9 pounds, virtually twice the limit agreed to by the court below.

We agree with the Secretary of Labor insofar as he stated that it is best to consider individual qualifications and conditions, such as the physical capability and physiological makeup of an individual, climatic conditions, and the manner in which the weight is to be lifted.[6] *See also, Claudine B. Cheatwood* v. *South Central Bell Telephone & Telegraph Co.,* ____ F. Supp. ____ (M.D. Ala., Jul. 31, 1969). There is a significant difference in job requirements which must be considered just as carefully as the physiological capabilities of individual employees. Thus, there are probably very few plant workers (male or female) who could not lift a 38-pound case with a handle and move it 10 feet once during a shift. If, however, the case had to be moved further, or more frequently, or lifted to a shoulder-height shelf, the degree of exertion is increased and the number of those capable of performing it is diminished.

Accordingly, we hold that Colgate may, if it so desires, retain its 35-pound weight-lifting limit as a general guide-line for all of its employees, male and female. However, it must notify all of its workers that each of them who desires to do so will be afforded a reasonable opportunity to demonstrate his or her ability to perform more strenuous jobs on a regular basis. Each employee who is able to so demonstrate must be permitted to bid on and fill any position to which his or her seniority may entitle him or her. On remand, the court shall study the problem together with the parties and devise and adopt a system which will afford this opportunity to each employee desiring it.[7]

3. PROCEDURAL ISSUES

Colgate has raised some procedural issues which it urges would preclude recovery by at least some of the plaintiffs. The first issue related to the time sequence involved in filing suit and various formalities regarding the EEOC charge. Subsequently, this Court decided this issue in another Title VII case, *Choate* v. *Caterpillar Tractor Co.,* 402 F. 2d 357 (7th Cir. 1968). We accept Colgate's concession that *Choate* disposes of this issue adversely to Colgate and lays it to rest in this case.

Colgate also argued that there was a failure of necessary joinder in the actions below as none of its male employees were made parties to the action. The issue is frivolous. The Union was made a party and its duty was to represent the male employees as well as the famel employees.[8] There is nothing in the law which precluded the Union from recognizing the injustice done to a substantial minority of its members and from moving to correct it. This is an internal union matter which had to be resolved within the Union and did not require intervention by the employer. See *Humphrey* v. *Moore,* 375 U.S. 335 (1964).[9]

Colgate also argued that the trial court was correct in deciding not to issue a preliminary injunction against it to compel discontinuance of the discriminatory practices. We believe that this was error, in part. Had the court correctly perceived the meaning of BFOQ, it would have issued an injunction. However, it could not issue one against the discriminatory layoffs as the determination of this issue was dependent on the type of careful proofs adduced at trial and therefore not appropriate for pre-

---

[6] U.S. Dept. of Labor, *Teach Them to Lift* (Bull. No. 110, rev. ed. 1965). See also National Safety Council, *The Woman on the Job—Her Health and Safety,* 16–18 (1964), which states that it is better not to set definite group limits as there are too many variables. Each woman should be considered in relation to the particular job involved as the strength of women varies greatly and not even physical size can be taken as a guide, as there are many small women with high stamina who are accustomed to doing physical work.

[7] The court and parties may find it helpful to have a job study performed which would analyze the weight-lifting requirements of each job and then classify the jobs according to the degree of strength and stamina required. Under such a system, employees may be able to demonstrate their capacity at different levels and bid on those jobs at or below the level at which they qualified. For example, a job requiring the moving of a 50-pound case from the floor to a shelf four feet high at a distance of 10 feet and a frequency of five times per shift can be expressed in terms of the foot-pounds required to perform the task and an employee who qualifies for it may bid on all jobs at or below that level of exertion.

[8] In fact, since a majority of the Jeffersonville employees were male, it is not unreasonable to assume that the officers of the Union were elected by a majority of male members and would, therefore, be responsive to their interests.

[9] *Neal* v. *System Bd. of Adjustment,* 348 F. 2d 722 (8th Cir. 1965), relied on by Colgate is a case arising under the unique provisions of the Railway Labor Act and is not in point.

liminary injunctive relief under the peculiar facts of this case.

It is a jurisdictional prerequisite to the filing of a suit under Title VII that a charge to be filed with the EEOC against the party sought to be sued. 42 U.S.C. § 2000e5(e). This provision serves two important purposes. First, it notifies the charged party of the asserted violation. Secondly, it brings the charged party before the EEOC and permits effectuation of the Act's primary goal, the securing of voluntary compliance with the law. While we believe that the Union was not entirely blameless in permitting discrimination to exist and could have worked harder to eliminate the residual and continuing effects of the blatant prior discrimination, it is undisputed that at no time was the Union ever charged before the EEOC as a party in violation of Title VII. Accordingly, the Union cannot be held liable for any of the damages resulting from the discrimination and the trial court's determination in favor of the Union is affirmed.

4. CLASS ACTION AND REMEDY

Having determined that the court below erred in holding the weight-limit to be a BFOQ, the decision that the November layoffs were discriminatory is now more strongly supported. For the reasons stated below, and in this opinion as to the BFOQ, that part of the trial court's decision is affirmed.

However, the court committed error in determining that only those plaintiffs who filed a charge with the EEOC were permitted to recover back pay. It should have permitted recovery by the intervening plaintiffs and required the posting of a notice allowing any other similarly situated employee to apply to the court for appropriate relief.

A suit for violation of Title VII is necessarily a class action as the evil sought to be ended is discrimination on the basis of a class characteristic, i.e., race, sex, religion or national origin. In our view, it is indistinguishable on this point from actions under Title II relating to discrimination in public accommodations. In *Newman* v. *Piggie Park Enterprises, Inc.*, 390 U.S. 400, 401–02 (1968), the court held that since vindication of the public interest is dependent upon private suits, the suits are private in form only and a plaintiff who obtains an injunction does so "as a 'private attorney general' vindicating a policy that Congress considered of the highest priority." *Oatis* v. *Crown Zellerbach Corp.*, 383 F. 2nd 496, (5th Cir. 1968), and *Jenkins* v. *United Gas Corporation*, 400 F. 2d 28, 35 (5th Cir. 1968), hold similarly as to Title VII actions regarding racial discrimination. We agree with the Fifth Circuit and perceive no reason under the law or the cases why the same should not be true of Title VII actions against sex discrimination. *See also Quarles* v. *Philip Morris, Inc.*, 271 F. Supp. 842 (D. Va. 1967).

We are also unable to perceive any justification for treating such a suit as a class action for injunctive purposes, but not treat it so for purposes of other relief. The clear purpose of Title VII is to bring an end to the proscribed discriminatory practices and to make whole, in a pecuniary fashion, those who have suffered by it. To permit only injunctive relief in the class action would frustrate the implementation of the strong Congressional purpose expressed in the Civil Rights Act of 1964. To require that each employee file a charge with the EEOC and then join in the suit would have a deleterious effect on the purpose of the Act and impose an unnecessary hurdle to recovery for the wrong inflicted. We agree with the holding in *Oatis, supra* at 48, that:

". . . It would be wasteful, if not vain, for numerous employees, all with the same grievance, to have to process many identical complaints with the EEOC.

. . . The better approach would appear to be that once an aggrieved person raises a particular issue with the EEOC which he has standing to raise, he may bring an action for himself and the class of persons similarly situated. . . ."

To the extent that any *dicta* in *Hall* v. *Werthan Bag Corp.*, 251 F. Supp. 184 (M.D. Tenn. 1966), holds *contra*, we reject it.

Colgate argues that the language of 42 U.S.C. § 2000e–5(e) requires that each person seeking recovery must first file a charge with the EEOC and then formally join in or institute suit for recovery. This is not required in order to serve the policy behind that section. The purpose of the section (as observed above in discussing the Union) is to provide for notice to the charged party and to bring to bear the voluntary compliance and

338

conciliation functions of the EEOC. Also, as noted by this court in *Choate v. Caterpillar Tractor Corp.*, 402 F. 2d 357, 360 (7th Cir. 1968), and in *Cox v. United States Gypsum Co.*, 409 F. 2d 289, 291 (7th Cir. 1969), another important function of filing the charge is to permit the EEOC to determine whether the charge is adequate. Finally, the charge determines the scope of the alleged violation and thereby serves to narrow the issues for prompt adjudication and decision.[10] *Cf. Edwards v. North Amer. Rockwell Corp.*, 291 F. Supp. 199 (C.D. Calif. 1968).

It is apparent that each of these purposes is served when any charge is filed and a proper suit follows which fairly asserts grievances common to the class to be afforded relief in the court. There can be no claim of surprise in such a situation. Also, as held in *Miller v. Int'l Paper Co.*, 408 F. 2d 283, 285 (5th Cir. 1969: ". . . no procedural purpose could be served by requiring sources of substantially identical grievances to be processed through EEOC when a single charge would be sufficient to effectuate both the letter and spirit of Title VII." Wherefore we reverse the decision below on this point and hold that this suit may properly be treated as a class action under Title VII as to all forms of relief to which any and all members of the class may be entitled by virtue of Colgate's discriminating practices.

42 U.S.C. § 2000e–5(g) requires that if the court finds an intentional unlawful employment practice, it may enjoin the practice "and order such affirmative action as may be appropriate." This grant of authority should be broadly read and applied so as to effectively terminate the practice and make its victims whole. This was not done here. As held in *Jenkins, supra* at 33–35, the District Court when applying Title VII should, after a finding of an unlawful employment practice which is plant-wide in nature, actively make the court available to all those members of the injured class who may be entitled to relief. *Cf.* Fibreboard Paper Prods. Corp., 138 N.L.R.B. 500, 554–56 (1962), *enforced*, 379 U.S. 203 (1964). The full remedial powers of the court must be brought to bear and all appropriate relief given.

In the instant case, this requires that all those who were discriminatorily laid off be compensated at the highest rate of pay for such jobs as they would have bid on/and qualified for if a non-discriminatory seniority scheme would have been in existence. This relief should be made available to all who were so damaged whether or not they filed charges and whether or not they joined in the suit.[11] The court shall, on remand, also enter such appropriate injunctive orders as may be required to completely eliminate the discriminatory system and any residual effect.[12]

We have considered the few remaining lesser points and find no determinative issues among them. On the issue of proof of damage, we affirm the lower court's determination that sufficient proof was adduced to support the relief. The deduction of unemployment compensation was proper, being required by 42 U.S.C. § 2000e–5(g).

The case is remanded to the District Court for the Southern District of Indiana for further proceedings in conformity with this opinion.

AFFIRMED IN PART, REVERSED IN PART, MODIFIED AND REMANDED.

A true Copy :
   Teste :

Clerk of the United States Court of Appeals for the Seventh Circuit.

---

[10] Under the National Labor Relations Act, these latter two functions are performed by the N.L.R.B.'s Regional Director's staff. It would be anomolous indeed to require more of the untrained aggrieved party in EEOC proceeding or suit than is expected of the trained specialists on a Regional Director's staff.

[11] Given the court's finding as to Colgate's attendance at the pre-effective date EEOC conference, it is likely that Colgate was acting intentially as of the effective date of Title VII. If this is so, then all those who were on layoff prior to the effective date who were not recalled due to the discriminatory seniority system would also be entitled to relief for such loss as could be shown consistent with requirements of the act.

[12] The court should also ascertain the feasibility of computing the damage to those who, while not laid off, were denied the opportunity to bid on higher paying jobs for which they may have been qualified. We would view it as unjust to permit Colgate to profit from its own voluntary destruction of the crewing-up records.

EQUAL EMPLOYMENT OPPORTUNITY COMMISSION,
Washington, D.C., September 16, 1968.

In Reply Refer To: Case No. 68–10–219EU, Colgate Palmolive Company
Clarksville, Indiana, and Local #15, International Chemical
Workers Union, Jeffersonville, Indiana.

MRS. GEORGIANNA SELLERS,
New Albany, Ind.

DEAR MRS. SELLERS: The Commission has investigated your charge of
employment discrimination and has found reasonable cause to believe that an
unlawful employment practice within the meaning of Title VII of the Civil
Rights Act of 1964 has been committed. A copy of the decision is enclosed.
The Commission will attempt to eliminate this practice by conciliation as
provided in Title VII. You will be kept informed of the progress of conciliation efforts.

Sincerely yours,

ROBERT L. RANDOLPH, *Director of Compliance.*

[Enclosure]

EQUAL EMPLOYMENT OPPORTUNITY COMMISSION,
Washington, D.C.

Georgiana Sellers, Case No. CL–68–10–219EU. Lena Moore, CL–68–10–2207EU.
Ann Casey, CL–68–10–221EU. Charging Parties vs. Colgate Palmolive Com-
pany, Clarksville, Indiana, and Local #15, International Chemical Workers
Union, Jeffersonville, Indiana, Respondents.

Date of Alleged Violation: March 30, 1966 and continuing.

Date of Filing of Charge: October 3, 1967.

Date of Service of Charge: October 19, 1967 (Employer), December 19,
1967 (Union).

DECISION

Summary of charges

Charging Parties, all of whom are female, claim that Respondent Employer has violated Title VII, Section 704(a) of the Civil Rights Act of
1964. Charging Parties claim that since filing suit in Federal District
Court against Respondent Employer for an unlawful employment practice
in violation of Title VII, Respondent Employer has retaliated against and
harassed the Charging Parties by doing away with jobs for women, speeding up work lines, reprimanding Charging Party Moore on the basis of
false charges, and treating the Charging Parties with contempt and disrespect.

Charging Parties join the Union as a Co-Respondent because of the
Union's alleged failure to adequately represent the Charging Parties and
because of its alleged acquiescense in a discriminatory collective bargaining
agreement.

Summary of investigation

Respondent engages in the manufacture and production of over one
thousand household and toiletry products. The subject plant employs approximately 1400 persons of whom 300 are female.

Respondents were made defendants in a civil suit filed by the Charging
Parties and other female employees in the U. S. District Court, Southern
District of Indiana on March 30, 1966. This civil action was filed pursuant
to Section 706(e) of Title VII of the Civil Rights Act of 1964. The
District Court rendered a judgment of $28,440.80 in favor of the female
plaintiffs, but ruled that Respondent Employer could maintain a 35 pound
weight limitation with respect to its female employees. The plaintiffs have
appealed this decision.

Charging Parties allege that because of the filing of a charge with the
Commission and because of the filing of the civil suit, that Respondent
Employer has taken certain retaliatory measures in violation of Section
704(a) of Title VII. These alleged measures include an unjustified reprimand
against Charging Party Moore, the revision of the job content of various
jobs to include weight lifting and thereby to do away with many jobs
which females can perform, the speed up of work lines, and the creation
of an atmosphere which has put Charging Parties under severe nervous
strain.

The evidence sustains the allegation that Respondent has been doing
away with jobs which females can perform by revising the job content

of various job classifications to include weight lifting duty.[1]

It appears that this sudden revision of the content of various job classifications is being used as a means to eliminate female employees. This conclusion is supported by Respondent's apparent reluctance to reclassify jobs which have been traditionally staffed with males. Indeed, in response to an inquiry concerning the opening of more jobs to female employees, Respondent's Personnel Supervisor stated that:

"I do not believe in spending industrial engineering time and money in a finite work up of job contents to determine whether or not females may be assigned to jobs which male employees have consistently performed."

Yet it appears that Respondent has conducted a "finite work up" of those jobs which females have traditionally performed. There appears to be no justification for this disparate treatment.

The Union President admits that the Union has done nothing to prevent Respondent Company from revising the job content of these jobs to include heavy duty and thereby to exclude females. He cites the collective bargaining agreement in defense of the Union's inaction. This agreement gives the Company the right to "combine, discontinue, or add job classifications." The Union cannot justify its failure to defend its members on the basis of compliance with a collective bargaining agreement, when reliance on its provisions permits the employer to discriminate. Failure to represent its female employees on this issue is thus a violation of Title VII.

With regard to Respondent's use of the 35 pound weight limitation, the Commission maintains its position that the emphasis in hiring and job assignment must be on individual capabilities, not on broad group norms. The fact that some or indeed most females are incapable of performing a specific job does not justify excluding those who are capable. Unless sex is a bona fide occupational requirement for a given job, Respondent cannot arbitrarily exclude all females from this job without taking into consideration the particular capabilities of individual job applicants. The Commission believes that a uniform weight limitation is not such a bona fide occupational requirement.

Charging Parties allege that Respondent has often speeded up production lines to harass female employees. Respondent admits that its production lines are "speeded up or decreased as we see fit." Individual lines are controlled by Respondent's foreman. Union officials state that they do not doubt that line speed up is one of the forms of harassment used by Respondent Employer. In view of the other examples of harassment and in light of the Respondent's attitude with respect to its female employees[2] the Commission finds it reasonable to believe that this charge is true.

Charging Parties also allege that Charging Party Moore's reprimand was unjustified. Five female eye witnesses have made sworn statements supporting this contention. Respondent's foreman, the individual responsible for the reprimand, claims otherwise. The Union President stated that this foreman is impatient with both male and female subordinates. In the context of the atmosphere of harassment at the subject plant it would appear that Charging Parties claims seem likely to be valid. Furthermore, the Union's refusal to take the issue to arbitration was discriminatory. Respondent Union did process Charging Party Moore's grievance to the fourth step. The Union President said that the grievance was not referred to arbitration because it would cost $500.00 to do so. He claimed this cost was prohibitive in light of the $11,000 expended to defend the civil court action. Respondent Union cannot justify its refusal to take the issue to arbitration on this basis. Charging Party Moore's grievance should have been considered without regard to the civil action. Respondent Union's failure to do so is a violation of Section 704(a) of Title VII.

DECISION

Reasonable cause exists to believe that the Respondents are in violation of Title VII as alleged.

AUGUST 29, 1968.   MARIE D. WILSON, *Secretary.*

---

[1] The President of Respondent Union points out that the following jobs had been revised in this manner. (This list is suggestive not exhaustive):
Line 23—Case Taper Set Off—General Labor.
Line 25—Flap Folder—Finishing Labor.
Line 15—Two Jobs—Finishing Labor.
Line 22—Two Jobs—Finishing Labor.
Line 8—Case Maker Set Off—Finishing Labor.

THE SUBMISSIVE MAJORITY: MODERN TRENDS IN THE LAW CONCERNING WOMEN'S RIGHTS

Faith A. Seidenberg†

The popular assumption that the law is even-handed does not hold true in the area of women's rights. Under the guise of paternalism (and you notice the word refers to a father), women have systematically been denied the equal protection of laws. Recently, however, there has been an upsurge of the feminist movement, and men are being forced to take a second look at some of the paternalistic laws they have propounded. Although challenge to the laws adversely affecting women is presently at about the same stage that the civil rights movement occupied in the 1930's, in the last few years there has nevertheless been a small beginning towards equal rights.

I

CRIMINAL LAW

The idea that a "bad" woman is much worse than a "bad" man probably can be traced to the witch hunts that took place in the early days of the American Colonies; however, it survives to the present day. For example, it is a crime for a woman to engage in prostitution[1] but not for her customer to use her services. She is breaking the law, it seems, while he is only doing what comes naturally. However, in *City of Portland v. Sherill*[2] a city ordinance that punished women but not men who offered themselves for immoral purposes was held unconstitutional.

In addition, in several states higher penalties are imposed on a woman who commits a crime than on a man who commits the same crime.[3] The constitutionality of greater penalties for women was re-

---

† President, Syracuse Chapter of National Organization for Women. B.A. 1944, J.D. 1954, Syracuse University.

[1] *See* THE SOCIAL EVIL (Seligman ed. 1902); George, *Legal, Medical and Psychiatric Considerations in the Control of Prostitution*, 60 MICH. L. REV. 717 (1962).

[2] No. M-47623 (Circuit Ct., Multnomah County, Ore., Jan. 9, 1967).

[3] *E.g.*, Pennsylvania, Connecticut. *See* statutes upheld in *Ex parte* Gosselin, M1 Me. 412, 44 A.2d 882 (1945); Platt v. Commonwealth, 256 Mass. 539, 152 N.E. 914 (1926).

EDITOR'S NOTE: Portions of this article were reset for clarity.

cently challenged in two cases. In *Commonwealth v. Daniels*[4] a woman was first sentenced to a term of from one to four years for the crime of robbery; one month later the sentence was vacated and the defendant resentenced to up to ten years under Pennsylvania's Muncy Act.[5] The Muncy Act provided that a woman imprisoned for a crime "punishable by imprisonment for more than a year" should be sentenced to an indeterminate period of up to three years except when the crime for which she was sentenced had a maximum of more than three years, in which case she had to receive the maximum sentence. That is, for a crime carrying a sentence of one to ten years, a man might have been sentenced to one to four years, but a woman could only be sentenced to an indefinite term of up to ten years. The discretion of the trial judge to set a maximum term for a woman of less than the maximum for the crime involved was thereby eliminated. The Superior Court of Pennsylvania affirmed the trial court's action, holding that longer incarceration for women is justifiable because of "the physiological and psychological make-up of women . . . their roles in society [and] their unique vocational skills and pursuits . . . ."[6] Whatever their significance, these characteristics did not convince the Pennsylvania Supreme Court that the Muncy Act's classification was reasonable. The court held that women are entitled to the protection afforded by the equal protection clause of the United States Constitution and, since the maximum sentence is the real sentence, that a sentence of ten years for women as opposed to four years for men is unconstitutional.[7] In *United States ex rel. Robinson v. York*[8] a federal district court held a

---

[4] 210 Pa. Super. 156, 232 A.2d 247 (1967).

[5] PA. STAT. tit. 61, § 566 (1964), *as amended,* (Supp. 1969).

[6] 210 Pa. Super. at 164, 232 A.2d at 252. The philosophy of the statute is more cogently, if not convincingly, explained as follows:

There is little doubt in the minds of those who have had much experience in dealing with women delinquents, that the fundamental fact is that they belong to a class of women who lead sexually immoral lives....

[Such a statute] would remove permanently from the community the feeble-minded delinquents who are now generally recognized as a social menace, and would relieve the state from the ever increasing burden of the support of their illegitimate children.

Commonwealth v. Daniels, 210 Pa. Super. 156, 171 n.2, 232 A.2d 247, 255 n.2 (1967) (dissenting opinion). Oddly enough, the material quoted from the *Daniels* case was supplied by Philadelphia District Attorney Arlen Specter in a brief urging the *unconsti*tutionality of the Muncy Act.

[7] 430 Pa. 642, 243 A.2d 400 (1968). Shortly thereafter the Pennsylvania legislature enacted a statute that required the court to set a maximum sentence, but prohibited it from setting a minimum term. PA. STAT. tit. 61, § 566 (Supp. 1969).

[8] 281 F. Supp. 8 (D. Conn. 1968).

Connecticut statute[9] similar to the Muncy Act unconstitutional. The decision was appealed by the state's Attorney General, but he withdrew the appeal after the decision came down in the *Daniels* case. Sixteen women, who had already served more time than a man's maximum sentence, were released.[10]

Criminal abortion statutes[11] are another example of the law's discrimination against women. That a woman has a right to control her own body is perhaps an idea whose time has yet to come, but there is at least a glimmering in some legal minds. Most lawyers and legislators, if they are talking about the subject at all, are still talking in terms of abortion reform instead of abortion repeal.[12] They discuss a need for change, but they sound a cautious note.[13] One case moving against the prevailing winds, however, is *People v. Belous*,[14] recently decided in the Supreme Court of California. The defendant was convicted for performing an abortion, and an amicus curiae counsel argued that

> [t]he right of reproductive autonomy sought to be protected here is clearly more basic and essential to a woman's dignity, self-respect and personal freedom than those personal rights . . . for which Constitutional protection has already been afforded. Probably, nothing except death itself can affect a woman's life more seriously than enforced bearing of children and enforced responsibility for them for perhaps the remainder of her and their lives. The choice must be that of the woman unless some overwhelming state interest requires otherwise, and those state interests generally adverted to will be shown below to be significantly, for constitutional purposes, less important than the interest of the woman

---

9 CONN. GEN. STAT. ANN. § 17-360 (1958).

10 Middletown Press, Aug. 12, 1968, at 1, col. 1 (Middletown, Connecticut).

11 *E.g.*, CAL. PENAL CODE § 274 (West 1955). Prior to its liberalization in 1967, it was similar to statutes in 41 other jurisdictions. Leavy & Kummer, *Criminal Abortion: A Failure of Law*, 50 A.B.A.J. 52 n.2 (1964).

12 *But see* Brief for Appellant as Amicus Curiae at 37-38, People v. Belous, 71 Cal. 2d 996, 458 P.2d 194, 80 Cal. Rptr. 354 (1969), reporting that Father Robert Drinan, Dean of Boston College Law School, has come out for repeal on the grounds that it should be a matter of individual conscience, not law.

13 *See, e.g.*, L. KANOWITZ, WOMEN AND THE LAW: THE UNFINISHED REVOLUTION 27 (1969):

> Though very few people would urge the legalization of all abortions, the principle of legal equality of the sexes is an additional reason for extending the circumstances under which therapeutic abortions should be legally justified.

14 71 Cal. 2d 996, 458 P.2d 194, 80 Cal. Rptr. 354 (1969).

herself. That right should be protected to the fullest by a holding that no state interest can control this field.[15]

In New York two bills, one for reform of abortion[16] and one for repeal,[17] were before the state legislature in the spring of 1969. Only the former had any chance of passing. Had it not been for the National Organization for Women's coming out strongly in 1968 for abortion repeal,[18] followed by agreement by the State Council of Churches[19] and the American Civil Liberties Union[20] on this position, the bills would probably not have been considered at all. However, as is beginning to be seen in California, where the abortion laws were just reformed,[21] abortion reform is worse from the standpoint of freedom of choice for the woman than no reform at all.[22]

II

CIVIL RIGHTS

For untold years there have been so-called "protective" laws regulating the working conditions of women. Necessary changes are beginning to be made, but the progress is slow; even legal experts do not always recognize the full dimensions of the problem. One commentator, for example, has remarked of women's working laws:

> With regard to social policy, the initial reaction is that the modern woman should not be subjected to state protective restrictions on her right to work should she choose to experience the conditions from which she is being protected. However, it is clear that the extent to which sex differences constitute "discrimination" is a question of degree, depending upon what social mores it seems desirable to perpetuate. . . . [Here], *considerations of preserving femininity and motherhood appear.*[23]

---

[15] *Belous* Brief, *supra* note 12, at 10-11 (footnotes omitted).

[16] (1969) Assy. Int. No. 3473-A (Mr. Blumenthal).

[17] (1969) Assy. Int. No. 1061 (Mrs. Cook).

[18] *See* 2 Now ACTS 14 (Winter-Spring 1969).

[19] New York State Council of Churches Leg. Release No. 8 (Feb. 10, 1969).

[20] American Civil Liberties Union Release (March 25, 1968).

[21] CAL. PENAL CODE § 274 (West Supp. 1968).

[22] Two actions were just filed in New York to have that state's abortion statutes declared unconstitutional. N.Y. Times, Oct. 8, 1969, at 53, col. 1; *id.*, Oct. 1, 1969, at 55, col. 3.

[23] Oldham, *Sex Discrimination and State Protective Laws,* 44 DENVER L. REV. 344,

Unfortunately, this misses the point. The net effect of these laws is to limit the advancement of women in industry and, since women are everywhere the majority, to ensure that there is always a large supply of poorly-paid persons.

California has a particularly stringent system of governing women's employment. Section 1350 of the California Labor Code,[24] for example, prohibits an employer from employing women workers for more than eight hours a day or forty-eight hours a week. The effect of this restriction is to prevent women, solely because of their sex, from pursuing certain better-paid occupations, such as running test equipment, doing final assembly work, and working as supervisors, and from earning overtime pay in the positions they now hold. In addition, paragraph 17 of the California Industrial Welfare Commission's Order No. 9-68[25] not only regulates wages, hours, and working conditions of women and minors in the transportation industry but also limits the number of pounds a woman may lift to twenty-five.

This regulatory system was recently challenged. In *Mengelkoch v. Industrial Welfare Commission*[26] plaintiffs asked that a three-judge court be convened because the constitutionality of section 1350 was an important constitutional issue to be resolved. The request was denied. However, in a similar case, *Rosenfeld v. Southern Pacific Co.*,[27] the judge ruled in favor of plaintiff. This case concerned both section 1350 and paragraph 17. In it, plaintiff, a woman, applied for a job that had

---

375 (1967) (emphasis added). *But see* R. Seidenberg, *Our Outraged Remnant*, 6 PSYCHIATRIC OPINION, Oct. 1969, at 18:

> The exaggeration of the difference between the sexes has been used to justify misogyny. Our young people want to make it difficult to distinguish between the sexes to show that everything feminine is not contemptible. One can wear long hair proudly; to be taken for a woman is not something to despair. Make the sexes undifferentiated, and then, perhaps, the mythology of "feminine" and "masculine" will be revealed for what it really is—a ruse to keep women subjugated and to guarantee men an unearned superiority.

24 CAL. LABOR CODE § 1350 (West Supp. 1968):

> No female shall be employed in any manufacturing, mechanical, or mercantile establishment or industry, laundry, . . . cleaning and dyeing establishment, hotel, public lodging house . . . in this state, more than eight hours during any one day of 24 hours or more than 48 hours in one week . . . .
>
> Females covered by the Fair Labor Standards Act, however, are exempt from the prohibitions of § 1350. *Id.* § 1350.5.

25 CAL. ADMIN. CODE tit. 8, § 11460 (1968). The division of public welfare is given specific enforcement power of § 1350. CAL. LABOR CODE § 1356 (West Supp. 1968).

26 284 F. Supp. 950 (C.D. Cal.), *vacated,* 393 U.S. 993 (1968).

27 293 F. Supp. 1219 (C.D. Cal. 1968).

just opened up at the defendant company's facilities at Thermal, California. Although she was the most senior employee bidding for the position and was fully qualified, the company assigned a male with less seniority than plaintiff. The company never tested or evaluated plaintiff's ability to perform the work required, but argued that the appointment was within its discretion as an employer and, since plaintiff was a woman, that her assignment to the position would violate the California Labor Code. The court, however, held both that the California hours and weights legislation discriminates against women and is therefore unconstitutional and that defendant's refusal to assign plaintiff to Thermal was not a lawful exercise of its discretion as an employer.

Restrictions on the amount of weight a woman can legally lift[28] are under attack in other states. An employer's thirty-five pound limitation[29] was tested in *Bowe v. Colgate-Palmolive Co.*,[30] where the court held it legal and proper for an employer to fix a thirty-five pound maximum weight for carrying or lifting by female employees. In another case, *Weeks v. Southern Bell Telephone & Telegraph Co.*,[31] defendant company took the position that because the job of switchman required lifting weight in excess of thirty pounds, the legal limit in Georgia,[32] a woman could not hold the job. The company conceded that plaintiff had seniority over the male awarded the position and that she was paid $78 per week as opposed to the $135 she would receive if she were a switchman. The sole issue in the case was whether or not sex is a bona fide occupational qualification, entitling defendant to bar a

---

[28] The typical restriction to 30 or 35 pounds is ironic if the goal is to preserve the femininity of women laborers; mothers commonly lift their children until they are 6 or 7 years old, when they weigh at least 70 pounds.

[29] Originally instituted because of substantial female employment during World War II, this practice continued even when the men returned to work. Bowe v. Colgate-Palmolive Co., 272 F. Supp. 332, 340 (S.D. Ind. 1967).

[30] 272 F. Supp. 332 (S.D. Ind. 1967). The provision was also challenged in Sellers v. Colgate-Palmolive Co., — F.2d — (7th Cir. 1969), which held in favor of the plaintiffs.

The *Bowe* court did hold, however, that use of a seniority list segregated by sex, which resulted in certain female employees being laid off from employment while males with less plant seniority were retained, resulted in discrimination in violation of the 1964 Civil Rights Act. 272 F. Supp. at 359.

[31] 408 F.2d 228 (5th Cir. 1969).

[32] Rule 59, promulgated by Georgia Commissioner of Labor, pursuant to GA. CODE ANN. § 54-122(d) (1961): "[f]or women and minors, not over 30 pounds." A more flexible rule, setting no specific limitations, replaced Rule 59 in 1968. *See* 408 F.2d at 233.

woman, as such, from consideration for the job of switchman, her capacities notwithstanding. The lower court held for defendant, but the Fifth Circuit reversed, finding illegal discrimination based on sex.

Segregated "help wanted" advertisements are another aspect of discrimination against women. Although the Civil Rights Act of 1964 forbids most such ads to be placed in newspapers[33] and forbids discrimination by sex in employment, the Equal Employment Opportunity Commission guidelines[34] nonetheless allowed two columns classified by sex to stand in the newspapers. In July 1968, therefore, the National Organization for Women brought a mandamus suit against the EEOC to compel it to enforce the law as written. The court summarily dismissed the complaint, saying that obviously some jobs were better suited to men and others to women,[35] but the suit did cause the EEOC to change its guidelines to conform with the law.[36] The American Newspaper Publishers Association brought an action to enjoin enforcement of the guidelines;[37] both the district court and the court of appeals found for the EEOC. However, although the *New York Times* and some other New York newspapers have now desegregated their want ads, most newspapers around the country still refuse to abide by the law.

The public accommodations section[38] of the Civil Rights Act of 1964, unlike the employment section, does not forbid discrimination on account of sex. A test case[39] was recently brought in New York against a Syracuse hotel that does not allow women to sit at the bar unescorted, and the action was dismissed. The court emphasized, first,

---

33 Civil Rights Act of 1964, § 704(b), 78 Stat. 257, 42 U.S.C. § 2000e-3(b) (1964):

It shall be an unlawful employment practice for an employer, labor organization, or employment agency to print or publish or cause to be printed or published any notice or advertisement relating to employment by such an employer or membership in or any classification or referral for employment by such a labor organization, or relating to any classification or referral for employment by such an employment agency, indicating any preference, limitation, specification, or discrimination, based on race, color, religion, sex, or national origin, except that such a notice or advertisement may indicate a preference, limitation, specification, or discrimination based on religion, sex, or national origin when religion, sex, or national origin is a bona fide occupational qualification for employment.

34 31 Fed. Reg. 6414 (1965).

35 The court pointed out that secretaries are obviously female, despite the presence in front of the bench of the male stenographer.

36 29 C.F.R. § 1604.4 (1969).

37 American Newspaper Pub. Ass'n v. Alexander, 294 F. Supp. 1100 (D.D.C. 1968).

38 42 U.S.C. § 2000a (1964).

39 DeCrow v. Hotel Syracuse Corp., 288 F. Supp. 530 (N.D.N.Y. 1968).

that there was no state action, since the women who sat in at the bar were not arrested; and second, because the public accommodation law does not forbid discrimination on the basis of sex, that the hotel could discriminate if it so wished.[40]

The case was not appealed because the author, whose case it was, thought it would be relatively easy to obtain state action in an arrest. Accordingly, she and another member of the National Organization for Women sat in at several bars, including one in New York City that has not served women for the last one hundred and fourteen years. Although they suffered many indignities, they were not arrested. The author then decided to bring an action in a New York state court under a new section of the state civil rights law[41] that makes it illegal to refuse to serve a customer "without just cause." Summary judgment was granted to defendants and the case was dismissed. The author filed a third case, however, that was heard on August 6, 1969 and that was decided in favor of plaintiff.

III

PRIVATE LAW

Some colleges have strict rules covering the hours when coeds must be in their dormitories and an inflexible system of signing in

---

[40] *Id.* at 532. It is interesting to note that the court did not find the hotel's admitted discrimination offensive; this is in accord with public opinion. The *Syracuse Post-Standard* said in a lead editorial:

> The campaign waged for several months by the National Organization for Women (NOW) against Hotel Syracuse for its long-standing policy of refusing to serve drinks to unescorted women at the bar in the Rainbow Lounge has reached another absurd point.
>
> All sororities at Syracuse University have been asked to refuse to patronize Hotel Syracuse "because they discriminate against women at their bar," in a letter from Faith A. Seidenberg, one of three directors of the Central New York Chapter of NOW.
>
> . . . .
>
> Hotel Syracuse has had the no-unescorted-women-at-the-bar rule ever since Prohibition was repealed in an effort "to maintain the dignity of the room" and to discourage undesirables and wouldbe pickups from frequenting the Rainbow Lounge, which is at street level, just off the main entrance to the hotel.
>
> . . . .
>
> Hotel Syracuse should be commended for running a decent place, instead of being subjected to the repeated persecution of sit-ins and boycott efforts. Surely any women's rights group could find a better cause than this!

Syracuse Post-Standard, Nov. 8, 1968, at 12, col. 1.

[41] N.Y. CIV. RIGHTS LAW § 40-e (McKinney Supp. 1969).

and out.[42] Regulation is the product of the idea that a university stands *in loco parentis* to its students, an idea that is hopefully changing. After all, a married women of eighteen is considered to be "emancipated" from her parents under the law.[43] Why then is a college student living away from home not equally adult? But in any case, the rationale is not consistently applied; male students are not subjected to the same restrictions as women in the use of the dormitories, or even to the requirement that they live on campus. The Oneonta College curfew was challenged, but the case was dismissed on technical grounds without examination of the merits. Possibly because of the suit, however, the college voluntarily rescinded its curfew regulations,[44] so the students were the ultimate winners.

A double standard is also apparent in the law governing married women. Under present law, a married woman loses her name and becomes lost in the anonymity of her husband's name. Her domicile is his no matter where she lives,[45] which means she cannot vote or run for office in her place of residence if her husband lives elsewhere. If she wants an annulment and is over eighteen, in certain cases she cannot get one,[46] but her husband can until he is twenty-one.[47] In practice, if not in theory, she cannot contract for any large amount, borrow money, or get a credit card in her own name. She is, in fact, a non-person with no name.

Women receive little in exchange for this loss of status. Although in theory the husband and wife are one person, the relationship "has worked out in reality to mean . . . the one is the husband."[48] For example, husband and wife do not have equal rights to consortium,[49] the exclusive right to the services of the spouse and to his or her society, companionship, and conjugal affection.[50] Until re-

---

[42] *E.g.*, Syracuse University at Syracuse, N.Y. Letter sent to parents of freshmen, January 1969 (freshman curfew); State University of New York at Oneonta, Experimental Women's Hours Policy, spring semester 1968 (freshman curfew).

[43] *E.g.*, N.Y. DOM. REL. LAW § 140(b) (McKinney 1964).

[44] State University of New York at Oneonta, Experimental Women's Hours Policy (Rev. Sept. 1968).

[45] New York Trust Co. v. Riley, 24 Del. Ch. 354, 16 A.2d 772 (1940). *But see* N.Y. DOM. REL. LAW § 61 (McKinney 1964).

[46] *E.g.*, CAL. CIV. CODE §§ 56, 82 (West Supp. 1968).

[47] *E.g.*, *id.*

[48] United States v. Yazell, 382 U.S. 341, 361 (1966) (dissenting opinion).

[49] Burk v. Anderson, 232 Ind. 77, 81, 109 N.E.2d 407, 408 (1952) (dictum).

[50] Smith v. Nicholas Bldg. Co., 93 Ohio 101, 112 N.E. 204 (1915).

cently it was everywhere the law that only the husband could recover for loss of consortium, and this is still the law in about two-thirds of the states.[51] The major breakthrough came in 1950 in *Hitaffer v. Argonne Co.*,[52] which reversed the prevailing rule. In a more recent case, *Karczewski v. Baltimore & O.R.R.*,[53] the court concluded, "[m]arriage is no longer viewed as a 'master-servant relationship,' "[54] and in *Owen v. Illinois Baking Corp.*[55] the court held that denying a wife the right to sue for loss of consortium while permitting such suit to a husband violates the equal protection clause.[56]

The unreasonableness of denying an action for loss of consortium to the wife is well expressed by Michigan Supreme Court Justice Smith:

> The gist of the matter is that in today's society the wife's position is analogous to that of a partner, neither kitchen slattern nor upstairs maid. Her duties and responsibilties in respect of the family unit complement those of the husband, extending only to another sphere. In the good times she lights the hearth with her own inimitable glow. But when tragedy strikes it is a part of her unique glory that, forsaking the shelter, the comfort, and warmth of the home, she puts her arm and shoulder to the plow. We are now at the heart of the issue. In such circumstances, when her husband's love is denied her, his strength sapped, and his protection destroyed, in short, when she has been forced by the defendant to exchange a heart for a husk, we are urged to rule that she has suffered no loss compensable at the law. But let some scoundrel dent a dishpan in the family kitchen and the law, in all its majesty, will convene the court, will march with measured tread to the halls of justice, and will there suffer a jury of her

---

[51] *See* Moran v. Quality Alum. Casting Co., 34 Wis. 2d 542, 549-50 nn.15 & 16, 150 N.W.2d 137, 140 nn.15 & 16 (1968); Simeone, *The Wife's Action for Loss of Consortium—Progress or No?*, 4 St. Louis U.L.J. 424 (1957).

[52] 183 F.2d 811 (D.C. Cir. 1950).

[53] 274 F. Supp. 169 (N.D. Ill. 1967).

[54] *Id.* at 175. The court summarized the rationale of the prevailing rule:
The early status of women during the sixteenth and seventeenth centuries vitally affected the common law attitude toward relational marital interests. The wife was viewed for many purposes as a chattel of her husband, and he was entitled to her services in the eyes of the law. . . . The wife, however, as a "servant" was not entitled to sue for the loss of services of her husband, since in theory he provided none.
Id. at 171.

[55] 260 F. Supp. 820 (W.D. Mich. 1966).

[56] "To draw such a distinction between a husband and wife is a classification which is unreasonable and impermissible." *Id.* at 822.

peers to assess the damages. Why are we asked, then, in the case before us, to look the other way? Is this what is meant when it is said that justice is blind?[57]

Conclusion

In theory all persons should be equal, but in practice women are less "equal" than men. In all phases of life women are second-class citizens leading legally sanctioned second-rate lives. The law, it seems, has done little but perpetuate the myth of the helpless female best kept on her pedestal. In truth, however, that pedestal is a cage bound by a constricting social system and hemmed in by layers of archaic and anti-feminist laws.

---

[57] Montgomery v. Stephan, 359 Mich. 33, 48-49, 101 N.W.2d 227, 234 (1960), *quoted with approval*, Millington v. Southeastern Elev. Co., 22 N.Y.2d 493, 503-04, 239 N.E.2d 897, 900, 293 N.Y.S.2d 305, 309 (1968).

Are Married Women Competent to Manage Their Property?

(By Marguerite Rawalt*)

Single women enjoy equality of legal treatment with men in regard to property rights and contract law. When a woman marries, she forfeits such equality in one degree or another in practically every state in the Union. Do you know your rights to your earnings, to your separate property, to the matrimonial property?

The property rights of married women are fixed by the laws of the states as interpreted by the courts. Those laws fall into two categories, the common-law, patterned after old English common law, and the community property law which follows the Spanish Code.

In the common law states, each spouse has the right to his or her individual earnings and the property acquired therewith. What of the wife and mother who spends her life at work in the home and never has any outside earnings? All the matrimonial property belongs to the husband, and if he should die without a will, she has only a dower right, a claim to ⅓ the property for life. Children or others inheriting part ownership may go to court to value her interest and order its sale. Further, since all is legally owned by the husband, estate and inheritance taxes stand to be higher than if each owned ½, despite statutory marital deduction allowances, thus reducing the net estate to be passed to the survivors.

And in event of divorce, the wife must depend upon "settlements" worked out by jousting attorneys, with the husband's attorney working to have as much as possible of her settlement labelled alimony (rather than support) which then becomes wholly taxable to her and deductible by the husband for income tax purposes.

In the eight community property states, the principle is that husband and wife each owns an outright ½ of real property, acquired during marriage, even though the wife has no outside earnings. But in most of these jurisdictions, the husband, but not the wife, has sole management rights, exercise of which enables him to create debts against their property (even gambling debts) without knowledge or consent of his wife. Such rights extend to her earnings and to the income from her separate or inherited property in which he has no ownership. The persistence of the organized women of Texas in obtaining support of the State Bar Association, brought change of this law there. The new statute provides that "each spouse shall have sole management, control, and disposition of that community property which he or she would have owned if single" and for joint management of combined property.

Such provision is similar to the laws of Norway and Denmark. Sweden and the Federal Republic of Germany have a formula for equitable division of property upon termination of marriage which might well be adopted in our states. For example, upon termination of marriage, there could first be deducted from each spouse's property the debts of that spouse. Inherited or separate property would be excluded from the division. The remaining properties, the marital property, would then be divided equally between husband and wife.

Centuries ago, when women had no access to education and no experience in the business world, their need of "protection" from the unscrupulous perhaps justified restriction of their property rights, placed in control of their husbands. But today, we live in a world with 27,000,000 women working outside the home, participating in the affairs of the marketplace, able to read and write and to judge of motives of public trading.

The President's Commission on the Status of Women, appointed by President John F. Kennedy, reported to him in October, 1963, stating that one kind of legal disability for another limited the rights of married women *in every state*. Beginning in 1963, every state set up a State Commission on the Status of Women. Their reports contain studies, analyses and review of state laws which provide basic information as to the situation in each state.

In 1967, ten state Commissions recommended changes needed to protect the rights of a spouse in the property and earnings of the other. Five recom-

---

*Miss Rawalt served as a member of the President's Commission and of the Citizens Advisory Council on the Status of Women; also as Chairman of the Task Force on Family Law.

Miss Rawalt, an attorney, is past President of the Federal Bar, past National President of the Business and Professional Women's Clubs, past President National Women Lawyers, and past President of the D.C. Federation of Women's Clubs.

mended needed changes in inheritance laws. One pointed out need for equal rights for husbands by re-establishment of inheritance rights in the wife's estate. Random examples of inequitable laws included: (a) a second wife invested her outside earnings with the husband's in home and property; after 25 years, he died without a will, no children; his long estranged mother became entitled to a large share of the marital property; but if the wife had died first, ALL the property would have gone to the husband; (b) in community property states, court decisions have established that the wife cannot dispose of her half of the property but the husband can dispose of ALL of it; she cannot go into business with her own funds without his permission and signature; he can abandon her for years and return to claim half of whatever she may have acquired in the meantime; she cannot control investments made with income from her separate property; (c) in at least one jurisdiction, the husband is given divorce on grounds of· one act of adultery, but this will not suffice for a divorce sought by the wife; and if the husband kills a man "taken in adultery" with his wife, it is justifiable homicide, while in the reverse, the wife is charged with murder.

The Florida Supreme Court in 1944 pointed out the absurdity of treating a married woman as legally incompetent in these words:

". . . a woman's responsibilities and faculties remain intact from age of maturity until she finds her mate; whereupon, incompetency seizes her and she needs protection in an extreme degree. Upon the advent of widowhood she is reinvested with all her capabilities which had been dormant during her marriage, only to lose them again upon remarriage. Intermittently, she is protected and benefited accordingly as she is married or single."

The United Nations report on the Legal Status of Women sets forth two BASIC concepts of matrimonial property: (a) recognition of married women as independent persons before the law; and (b) recognition of the *economic partnership* involved in marriage and acknowledgement of the financial contribution of the wife who works only in the home.

The Citizens Advisory Council on the Status of Women (1963–1968) which succeeded the President's Commission on Status of Women, set up a special Task Force on Family Law, composed of law school professors, outstanding attorneys specializing in family law, sociologists. Many consultations with experts in the field were held. The property rights recommendation of the group, adopted by the Council was as follows:

"Marriage as a partnership in which each spouse make a different but equally important contribution is increasingly recognized as a reality in this country and is already reflected in the laws of some other countries. During marriage, each spouse should have a legally defined substantial right in the earnings of the other, in the real and personal property acquired through these earnings, and in their management. Such a right should be legally recognized as surviving the marriage in the event of its termination by divorce, annulment, or death. Appropriate legislation should safeguard either spouse and protect the surviving spouse against improper alienation of property by the other. Surviving children as well . . . should be protected from disinheritance."

What better C.I.P. Project could be undertaken than an authoritative "Know Your Property Rights" bulletin, on today's property rights of married women in your state? This would fill a needed service. It must be prepared from the negative viewpoint of disclosing the inequities, the legal handicaps on married women, rather than the viewpoint of sustaining existing laws. It must of necessity have lawyer guidance and reviews. Such accurate information will point the direction of future legislative changes. Your State Commission report should provide the starting point. Women of the Federation have the power to clear the path for themselves, and for millions of future young wives, by updating these laws to provide for a 50-50 economic partnership in marriage.

THE LIBRARY OF CONGRESS,
LEGISLATIVE REFERENCE SERVICE,
Washington, D.C., June 10, 1970.

To: Senate Constitutional Amendments Subcommittee.
From: American Law Division.
Subject: Women As Jurors On State Juries.

The fifty State survey presented below is submitted in response to your request for a determination as to whether there is any sex discrimination as to qualifications for serving on the juries of the various States, and as to what exemptions or excuses are specifically directed at women. It should be noted that provisions dealing with service depending on separate or adequate facilities for female jurors or with the procedure for claiming any allowed exemption or excuse have not been considered here. With regard to exemptions provided for women who have care of a child, we have included those States which phrase the exemption in terms of a "person" having care of a child. Likewise, although there are male nurses, included here are those States which provide an exemption from jury duty for nurses.

Since the Library of Congress has not yet received many of the laws enacted by the 1970 sessions of those State legislatures which met in 1970, they have not been included in this survey. However, it is possible that some of these States have acted in this area either by changing or adding to any of the provisions mentioned here.

A search of the laws of the fifty States appears to indicate that in all of the jurisdictions there is no distinction between males and females as to the basic qualifications for service on juries. With regard to whether women are permitted to serve on juries, one State, Washington, deserves a special discussion and treatment below. Of the other forty-nine States, twenty-six do not appear to have any distinction between males and females and to qualifications (although some affirmative act may have to be performed by a woman or a determination made by the body listing potential jurors before service may be allowed) and no specific exemptions are directed at females, and the remaining twenty-three States do not appear to have any distinction between males and females as to qualifications but contain specific exemptions or excuses for women or for female-dominated professions or categories.

NO DISTINCTION, NO FEMALE EXEMPTIONS

Alaska—Alaska Stats. §§ 09.20.010, 09.20.030.
Arizona—A.R.S. §§ 21.201, 21–202.
Arkansis—Ark. Stats. § 34–101 et seq. A provision that a woman was not compelled to serve as a juror against her will was repealed in 1969.
California—Code of Civil Proc. § 198 et seq.
Colorado—Col. Rev. Stats. § 78–1–1 et seq.
Delaware—10 Del. C. § 4504 et seq.
Florida—F.S.A. § 40.01 et seq.
Hawaii—Hawaii Rev. Stats. § 609–1 et seq.
Idaho—Idaho Code, § 2–201 et seq.
Illinois—S.H.A. ch. 78, § 1 et seq.
Indiana—Burn's Ind. Stats. § 4–7115.
Kentucky—Baldwin's Rev. Stats., §§ 29.025, 29.035.
Maine—14 M.R.S.A. § 1201 et seq.
Maryland—Ann. Code of Md., Art. 51, § 1 et seq.
Michigan—M.C.L.A. §§ 600.1306, 600.1307.
Mississippi—Code Miss. 1942, § 1762 et seq.
Nebraska—R.R.S. 1943 (R.S. Supp. 1967), § 25–1601 et seq. Particular exemptions provided for women repealed in 1967.
New Mexico—N.M. Stats. Ann. 19–1–1 et seq.
North Carolina—Gen. Stats. of N.C., § 9–1 et seq.
North Dakota—N.D. Cent. Code, 27–09–01 et seq.
Oregon—ORS § 10.010 et seq.
Pennsylvania—17 P.S. § 971 et seq.
South Dakota—SDLC 1967, § 16–13–1 et seq.
Vermont—Vt. Stats., Ann., T.12, App. VII, Rules 1 to 31.
West Virginia—West Va. Code § 52–1–1 et seq.; Const. Art. 3, § 21.
Wisconsin—W.S.A. 246.15, 255.01 et seq.

NO DISTINCTIONS, FEMALE EXEMPTIONS

Alabama—Code of Ala. Tit. 30, §§ 21.21(1). A female has a right to be excused for good cause shown in the discretion of the judge (§ 21).
Connecticut—C.G.S.A., § 51–217 et seq. Exemption, if desired, for any woman who is a trained nurse in active practice, an assistant in a hospital or an attendant nurse or who is nursing a sick member of her family, or who cares for one or more children under the age of 16 years (§ 51–218).
Georgia—Code of Ga. Ann., § 59–106 et seq. Excuse provided for a housewife with children 14 years or younger (§ 59–112(b)), and any woman who does not desire to serve may notify jury commissioner to that effect and her

name will not be placed in jury box (§ 59–112(d)).

Iowa—Iowa Code Ann., § 607.1 et seq. Exemption for registered nurses (§ 607.2(2)).

Kansas—K.S.A. 43–101 et seq. Duty of each township and city assessor to inquire of each woman elector whether she desires to be exempt from jury service (§ 43–117).

Louisiana—L.S.A.-R.S. 13:3055, 13:3056. A woman shall not be selected for jury service unless she has previously filed with the clerk of the court of the parish in which she resides a written declaration of her desire to be subject to jury service (13:3055).

Massachusetts—M.G.L.A. c. 234, § 1. Exemption for trained nurses, attendant nurses, mothers of children under 16 years of age or women having custody of such children, and women members of religious orders.

Minnesota—M.S.A. §§ 593.01 et seq., 628.49. A woman may be excused upon request in the discretion of the court (§ 628.49).

Missouri—V.A.M.S. § 494.010 et seq. Excuse provided for any woman who requests exemption before being sworn as a juror (§ 494.031(2)).

Montana—Rev. Codes of Montana, § 93–1301 et seq. Exemption provided for nurses engaged on a case of a "person" caring directly for one or more children (§ 93–1304(12)).

Nevada—NRS 6.010 et seq. Exemption for any woman for one year periods upon filing of a written statement claiming exemption (6.020(3)).

New Hampshire—RSA 500:1 et seq. Exemption provided for any woman who has care of one or more children under the age of twelve years if she so desires (500:1).

New Jersey—N.J.S.A. 2A: 69–1, 2A: 69–2. Exemption for any "person" who has the actual physical care and custody of a minor child.

New York—Judiciary Law, §§ 500 et seq., 590 et seq. Exemption provided for a woman (§§ 507(7), 597(7)).

Ohio—Page's Ohio Rev. Code Ann. § 2313.01 et seq. Exemption for registered nurses and nuns (§ 2313.34).

Oklahoma—38 Okl. St. Ann. § 28. Exemption, if claimed, for all women with minor children.

Rhode Island—Gen. Laws of R.I., 9–9–1 et seq. A woman can be excused upon notice (9–9–11).

South Carolina—Code of Laws of S.C., § 38–52 et seq. Excuse, declared by presiding judge, for any woman who has the legal custody and duty of care of a child under seven years of age.

Tennessee—Tenn. Code Ann. § 22–101 et seq. A woman has the option of serving or not when summoned to jury duty (§§ 22–101, 22–108).

Texas—Vernon's Ann. Civ. St. Art. 2133, art. 2135. Exemption for all females who have legal custody of a child or children under the age of sixteen (art. 2135(7)), and for all registered, practical and vocational nurses actively engaged in the practice of their profession (art. 2135(8)).

Utah—Utah Code Ann. § 78–46–1 et seq. Exemption for a female citizen who has the active care of minor children (§ 78–46–10(14)).

Virginia—Code of Va., § 8–174 et seq. Women are exempt (§§ 8–178(30), 8–182).

Wyoming—Wyoming Stats Ann. § 1–77 et seq. A woman may be excused from jury service "when household duties or family obligations require her absence" (§ 1–80).

WASHINGTON

The provisions of Washington relating to women serving on juries have been isolated here for separate treatment only because a reading of the pertinent provisions thereof makes it unclear as to which of the two categories mentioned above it belongs. In fact, a literal reading would appear to indicate that although women are qualified to be jurors, if they have an exemption, it is mandatory that they exercise it.

Prior to 1967, RCWA 2.36.080 provided an exemption for women. In a law approved March 15, 1967, this section was amended and no longer provides for an exemption for women. On March 21, 1967, the provision dealing with the drawing of jury lists was amended (RCWA 2.36.060), and this sentence can now be found therein: "Any woman who upon being listed upon the list as in this section provided shall claim her exemption to serve as a juror, shall not be listed in the preparation of the list of jurors."

DANIEL HILL ZAFREN, *Legislative Attorney*.

summary of
state labor laws
for women

MARCH 1969

UNITED STATES DEPARTMENT OF LABOR
WAGE AND LABOR STANDARDS ADMINISTRATION
WOMENS' BUREAU

SUMMARY OF STATE LABOR LAWS FOR WOMEN 1/

During a century of development, the field of labor legislation for women has seen a tremendous increase in the number of laws and a notable improvement in the standards established. Today the 50 States, the District of Columbia, and Puerto Rico have laws relating to the employment of women. The principal subjects of regulation are: (1) minimum wage; (2) overtime compensation; (3) hours of work, including maximum daily and weekly hours, day of rest, meal and rest periods, and nightwork; (4) equal pay; (5) fair employment practices; (6) industrial homework; (7) employment before and after childbirth; (8) occupational limitations; and (9) other standards, such as seating provisions and weightlifting limitations.

Although legislation in one or more of these fields has been enacted in all of the States, the District of Columbia, and Puerto Rico, the standards established vary widely. In some jurisdictions different standards apply to different occupations or industries. Laws relating to minors are mentioned here only if they apply also to women.

MINIMUM WAGE

A total of 36 States, the District of Columbia, and Puerto Rico have minimum wage laws with minimum rates currently in effect. These laws apply to men as well as women in 29 States, the District of Columbia, and Puerto Rico. In 7 States minimum wage laws apply only to women or to women and minors. An additional 3 States have minimum wage laws, applicable to females and/or minors, which are not in operation.

1/ As of December 1968.

In general minimum wage laws are applicable to all industries and occupations except domestic service and agriculture, which are specifically exempt in most States. The laws of 9 States--Arkansas, California, Colorado, Michigan, New Jersey, North Dakota, Utah, Washington, and Wisconsin--either set statutory minimum wage rates or permit a wage board to set minimum rates for both domestic service and agricultural workers. In Wisconsin wage orders cover both groups. The Michigan statutory rate applies to agricultural employees (except certain employees engaged in harvesting on a piecework basis) and domestic service workers, but is limited to employers of 4 or more. The Arkansas law is limited to employers of 5 or more and applies to agricultural workers, with some exceptions, whose employer used more than 500 man-days of agricultural labor in any 4 months of the preceding year. The New Jersey statutory rate applies to agricultural workers and excludes domestic service workers, but the law permits them to be covered by a wage order. California has a wage order applicable to agricultural workers, but has none for domestic service workers. The remaining 4 States--Colorado, North Dakota, Utah, and Washington--have no wage orders that apply to domestic service or agricultural workers.

Seven jurisdictions--the District of Columbia, Hawaii, Massachusetts, New Mexico, Oregon, Puerto Rico, and West Virginia--cover either domestic service or agricultural workers, but not both. West Virginia does not exclude domestic service workers as a group, but coverage is limited to employers of 6 or more. Some or all agricultural workers are covered under the minimum wage law or orders in the District of Columbia, Hawaii, Massachusetts, New Mexico, Oregon, and Puerto Rico.

Since the Federal Fair Labor Standards Act (FLSA) of 1938, as amended, establishes a minimum hourly rate for both men and women engaged in or producing goods for interstate commerce and for employees of most large retail firms and other specified establishments, as well as some workers in agriculture, State minimum wage legislation applies chiefly to workers in local trade and service industries.

Historical Record

The history of minimum wage legislation began in 1912 with the enactment of a law in Massachusetts. At that time minimum wage legislation was designed for the protection of women and minors, and did much to raise their extremely low wages in manufacturing (now covered by the FLSA) and trade and service industries. Between 1912 and 1923 laws were enacted in 15 States,[2] the District of Columbia, and Puerto Rico.

---

[2] One of these laws was repealed in 1919 (Nebraska); another, in 1921 (Texas).

Legislative progress was interrupted by the 1923 decision of the U.S. Supreme Court declaring the District of Columbia law unconstitutional, and no new minimum wage laws were passed during the next 10 years.

The depression years of the 1930's brought a revival of interest in minimum wage legislation, and 13 additional States and Alaska enacted laws.

In 1937 the U.S. Supreme Court upheld the constitutionality of the minimum wage law in the State of Washington, expressly reversing its prior decision on the District of Columbia law.

In 1941 Hawaii enacted a minimum wage law, bringing to 30 the number of jurisdictions with such legislation.

From 1941 through 1954 no State enacted a minimum wage law. However, there was a considerable amount of legislative activity in the States with minimum wage legislation on their statute books. In some States the laws were amended to extend coverage to men; in others, to establish or increase a statutory rate; and in still others, to strengthen the procedural provisions.

In the period 1955-66:

10 States--Delaware, Idaho, Indiana, Maryland, Michigan, New Mexico, North Carolina, Vermont, West Virginia, and Wyoming--enacted minimum wage laws for the first time, making a total of 40 jurisdictions with such laws.

7 States--Maine, New Jersey, New York, Oklahoma, Pennsylvania, Rhode Island, and Washington--and the District of Columbia, with wage board laws, enacted statutory rate laws, retaining, with the exception of Maine and Oklahoma, the wage board provision. The enactments in 5 States--Maine, New Jersey, Oklahoma, Pennsylvania, and Washington--and the District of Columbia also extended coverage to men.

4 States--Kentucky, Nevada, North Dakota, and South Dakota--amended their laws to extend coverage to men.

16 States--Alaska, Connecticut, Hawaii, Idaho, Maine, Massachusetts, Nevada, New Hampshire, New Mexico, New York, North Carolina, Rhode Island, South Dakota, Vermont, Washington, and Wyoming--amended their laws one or more times to increase the statutory rates.

2 States--Massachusetts and New Jersey--and the District of Columbia amended their premium pay requirements. Massachusetts amended its minimum wage law to require the payment of not less than $1\frac{1}{2}$ times an employee's regular rate for hours worked in excess of 40 a week, exempting a number of occupations and industries from the overtime provision. In New Jersey and the District of Columbia new statutory rate laws were enacted which included overtime pay requirements covering most workers.

Other amendments in a number of States affected coverage of the minimum wage laws, clarified specific provisions, or otherwise strengthened the laws.

In 1967:

1 State--Nebraska--enacted a minimum wage law for the first time, bringing to 41 the total number of jurisdictions having such laws. This law establishes a statutory rate applicable to men, women, and minors, and is limited to employers of 4 or more.

1 State--Oregon--with a wage board law applicable to women and minors, enacted a statutory rate law applicable to men and women 18 years and over.

1 State--New Hampshire--made its wage board provisions applicable to men.

1 State--Maryland--extended coverage by eliminating the exemption for employers of less than 7.

12 States--Connecticut, Delaware, Idaho, Indiana, Maine, Maryland, New Hampshire, New Mexico, Rhode Island, Vermont, Washington, and Wyoming-- amended their laws to increase their statutory rates.

2 States--California and Wisconsin--with wage board laws, revised wage orders, setting a single rate for all occupations and industries.

2 States--New Mexico and Massachusetts--extended coverage to some or all agricultural workers.

1 State--Michigan--amended its minimum wage regulations to decrease allowable deductions and strengthen enforcement.

In 1968:

1 State--Arkansas--with a statutory rate law applicable to females, enacted a new law establishing a statutory rate applicable to men, women, and minors, effective January 1, 1969.

1 State--Delaware--amended its law to set a minimum rate for employees receiving gratuities.

1 State--Pennsylvania--amended its law to increase the statutory rate and to require overtime pay.

Roster of Minimum Wage Jurisdictions

The 41 jurisdictions with minimum wage legislation are:

Alaska	District of Columbia	Louisiana 3/
Arizona	Hawaii	Maine
Arkansas	Idaho	Maryland
California	Illinois 3/	Massachusetts
Colorado	Indiana	Michigan
Connecticut	Kansas 3/	Minnesota
Delaware	Kentucky	Nebraska

3/ No minimum rates in effect.

Nevada	Ohio	Utah
New Hampshire	Oklahoma	Vermont
New Jersey	Oregon	Washington
New Mexico	Pennsylvania	West Virginia
New York	Puerto Rico	Wisconsin
North Carolina	Rhode Island	Wyoming
North Dakota	South Dakota	

Eight States, the District of Columbia, and Puerto Rico have laws that set a statutory rate and also provide for the establishment of occupation or industry rates based on recommendations of wage boards. Nineteen States have statutory rate laws only; that is, the rate is set by the legislature. Twelve States (including 3 with no minimum wage rates currently in effect) have laws that set no fixed rate but provide for minimum rates to be established on an occupation or industry basis by wage board action.

The following list shows, for the 41 jurisdictions, the type of law and employee covered:

1. Statutory rate and wage board law for:

   Men, women, and minors

Connecticut	New Jersey 4/	Rhode Island
District of Columbia	New York	Washington 4/
Massachusetts	Pennsylvania	
New Hampshire	Puerto Rico	

2. Statutory rate law only for:

   Men, women, and minors

Alaska	Maryland	South Dakota
Arkansas (eff. 1/1/69)	Nebraska	(14 years and over)
Delaware	Nevada	Vermont
Hawaii	New Mexico	West Virginia
Idaho	North Carolina	
Maine	(16 to 65 years)	

   Men and women

Indiana (18 years and over)	Oregon (18 years and over)
Michigan (18 to 65 years)	Wyoming (18 years and over)
Oklahoma (18 to 65 years)	

4/ Wage orders applicable to women and minors only.

3. Wage board law only for:

Men, women, and minors

Kentucky   North Dakota

Women and minors

Arizona   Kansas 5/   Utah
California   Minnesota   Wisconsin
Colorado   Ohio
Illinois 5/

Females

Louisiana 5/

OVERTIME COMPENSATION

Sixteen States, the District of Columbia, and Puerto Rico have laws or regulations, usually part of the minimum wage program, that provide for overtime compensation. These generally require the payment of premium rates for hours worked in excess of a daily and/or weekly standard. Premium pay requirements are both a deterrent to excessive hours of work and an impetus to the equitable distribution of work.

Statutory Requirements

Statutes of 10 States and the District of Columbia require the payment of 1½ times the regular rate of pay after a specified number of daily and/or weekly hours. Generally these statutes are applicable to men, women, and minors. The following list of jurisdictions with statutory overtime rates shows the hours after which premium pay is required:

	Daily Standard	Weekly Standard
Alaska	8	40
Connecticut		42; 40 (7/1/69)
District of Columbia		40
Hawaii		40

5/ No minimum rates in effect.

	Daily Standard	Weekly Standard
Idaho 6/	8	48
Maine		48
Massachusetts		40
New Jersey		40
Pennsylvania		42; 40 (2/1/69)
Vermont		48
West Virginia		48

Wage Order Requirements

Wage orders issued as part of the minimum wage program in 6 States and Puerto Rico require the payment of premium rates for overtime. Generally the orders provide for payment of $1\frac{1}{2}$ times, or double, either the minimum rate or the regular rate of pay for hours in excess of a daily and/or weekly standard. The following list of jurisdictions with wage orders that require overtime rates (for men, women, and minors unless otherwise indicated) shows the premium rate established and the hours after which the premium is payable. Most of the jurisdictions have issued a number of wage orders with varying standards for different occupations. The one shown is the highest standard of general application.

	Rate	Daily Standard	Weekly Standard
California 7/	$1\frac{1}{2}$ times the regular rate	8	40
	double the regular rate	12; 8 on 7th day	
Colorado 7/	$1\frac{1}{2}$ times the regular rate	8	40
Kentucky 8/	$1\frac{1}{2}$ times the minimum rate		44
New York	$1\frac{1}{2}$ times basic minimum rate		40
Oregon 7/	$1\frac{1}{2}$ times the minimum rate	8	40
Rhode Island	$1\frac{1}{2}$ times the minimum rate		45
Puerto Rico	double the regular rate	8	44

6/ The premium pay requirement is separate from the minimum wage program and is applicable only to women.

7/ Applicable to women and minors only. In California, minors under 18 limited to 8 hours a day, 6 days a week.

8/ Since the issuance of wage orders applicable to women and minors only, statutory coverage of the wage board program has been extended to men.

HOURS OF WORK

The first enforceable law regulating the hours of employment of women became effective in Massachusetts in 1879. Today 46 States, the District of Columbia, and Puerto Rico have established standards governing at least one aspect of women's hours of employment; that is, maximum daily or weekly hours, day of rest, meal and rest periods, and nightwork. Some of these standards have been established by statute; others, by minimum wage or industrial welfare order.

Maximum Daily and Weekly Hours

Forty-one States and the District of Columbia regulate the number of daily and/or weekly hours of employment for women in one or more industries. These limitations have been established either by statute or by order. Nine States--Alabama, Alaska, Delaware, Florida, Hawaii, Idaho, Indiana, Iowa, and West Virginia--and Puerto Rico do not have such laws; however, laws or wage orders in 5 of these jurisdictions--Alaska, Hawaii, Idaho, Puerto Rico, and West Virginia--require the payment of premium rates for time worked over specified hours.

Hours standards for 3 of the 41 States--Georgia, Montana, and South Carolina--are applicable to both men and women. In addition there are 3 States--New Mexico, North Carolina, and Washington--which cover men and women in some industries and women only in others.

The standard setting the fewest maximum hours which may be worked, in one or more industries, is shown for each of the 41 States and the District of Columbia.

	Maximum hours			Maximum hours	
	Daily	Weekly		Daily	Weekly
Arizona- - - - -	8	48	Georgia- - - - - -	10	60
Arkansas - - - -	8	(9/)	Illinois - - - - -	8	48
California - - -	8	48	Kansas 10/ - - - -	8	48
Colorado - - - -	8	--	Kentucky - - - - -	10	60
Connecticut- - -	8	48	Louisiana- - - - -	8	48
District of			Maine- - - - - - -	9	50
Columbia - - -	8	48	Maryland - - - - -	10	60

9/ A 6-day week limitation provides, in effect, for 48-hour workweek.

10/ Maximum hours standards set by Labor Commissioner under minimum wage program.

	Maximum hours				Maximum hours	
	Daily	Weekly			Daily	Weekly
Massachusetts -	9	48	Oklahoma - - - - -		9	54
Michigan- - - -	9	54	Oregon 11/ - - - -		8	40
Minnesota - - -	--	54	Pennsylvania - - -		10	48
Mississippi - -	10	60	Rhode Island - - -		9	48
Missouri- - - -	9	54	South Carolina - -		8	40
Montana - - - -	8	48	South Dakota - - -		10	54
Nebraska- - - -	9	54	Tennessee- - - - -		10	50
Nevada- - - - -	8	48	Texas- - - - - - -		9	54
New Hampshire -	10	48	Utah - - - - - - -		8	48
New Jersey- - -	10	54	Vermont- - - - - -		9	50
New Mexico- - -	8	48	Virginia - - - - -		9	48
New York - - - -	8	48	Washington - - - -		8	48
North Carolina-	9	48	Wisconsin- - - - -		9	50
North Dakota- -	8½	48	Wyoming 12/- - - -		8	48
Ohio- - - - - -	8	48				

A brief summary of the above table shows that in one or more industries:

Two States have a maximum of 8 hours a day, 40 hours a week.

Twenty-three States and the District of Columbia have set maximum hours of 8 a day, 48 a week, or both.

Eight States have a maximum 9-hour day, 50- or 54-hour week. (This includes Michigan with an average 9-hour, maximum 10-hour, day.)

Minnesota has no daily hours limitation in its statute, but limits weekly hours to 54.

Seven States have a maximum 10-hour day, 50- to 60-hour week.

However, many of these hours laws contain exemptions or exceptions from their limitations. For example:

Work is permitted in excess of the maximum hours limitations for at least some employees in 16 States if they receive overtime compensation: Arizona, Arkansas, California, Colorado, Kansas, Nevada, New Mexico, North Carolina, Oklahoma, Oregon, Rhode Island, South Carolina, Texas, Virginia, Wisconsin, and Wyoming.

11/ See footnote 10.

12/ If the 8 hours of work are spread over more than 12 hours in a day, time and a half must be paid for each of the 8 hours worked after the 12-hour period.

Four States (North Carolina, Oregon, South Carolina, Virginia) exempt workers who are paid in accordance with the overtime requirements of, or who are subject to, the Fair Labor Standards Act, the Federal minimum wage and hour law of most general application. Arizona exempts employers operating in compliance with the Fair Labor Standards Act, provided 1½ times the regular rate is paid for hours over 8 a day. California permits airline and railroad personnel and women protected by the Fair Labor Standards Act, with some industry exceptions, to work up to 10 hours a day and 58 hours a week if they are paid 1½ times their regular rate for hours over 8 a day and 40 a week. Kansas exempts most firms meeting the wage, overtime, and recordkeeping requirements of the Fair Labor Standards Act or comparable standards set by collective bargaining agreements. New Mexico exempts employees in interstate commerce whose hours are regulated by acts of Congress.

One State, Maryland, exempts employment subject to a bona fide collective bargaining agreement.

State agencies in Arkansas, Kansas, Massachusetts, Michigan, Minnesota, Oregon, Pennsylvania, and Wisconsin have broad authority to permit work in excess of the maximum hours limitations on a case-by-case basis; to vary hours restrictions by industry or occupation; or to regulate hours by requiring premium pay for overtime. Premium pay for overtime work is required by law or order regulating hours in Arkansas, Kansas, Oregon, and Wisconsin (page 9), and the minimum wage laws or orders of Massachusetts, Oregon, and Pennsylvania require premium pay for overtime work (page 7). Twenty-eight more States have specific exceptions to the hours restrictions for emergencies, seasonal peaks, national defense, and other reasons.

Some or all women employed in executive, administrative, and professional positions are exempt from hours laws limitations in 26 States and the District of Columbia.

Since 1963, 16 States (Arizona, California, Colorado, Illinois, Kansas, Maryland, Massachusetts, Michigan, Missouri, Nebraska, New York, North Carolina, Oregon, Pennsylvania, Virginia, Washington) and the District of Columbia modified their maximum hours laws or orders one or more times to permit work beyond the limits established by the maximum hours laws under regulated conditions, to exempt additional groups of workers from hours restrictions, or to establish administrative procedures for varying hours limitations. One State, Delaware, eliminated hours restrictions altogether.

In Michigan the State Occupational Safety Standards Commission has promulgated a standard which removes the limitations on women's daily and weekly hours of work, effective February 15, 1969, subject to modification by the State legislature.

Day of Rest

Twenty States, the District of Columbia, and Puerto Rico have established a 6-day maximum workweek for women employed in some or all industries. In 8 of these jurisdictions--California, Connecticut, Illinois, Massachusetts, New Hampshire, New York, Puerto Rico, and Wisconsin--this standard is applicable to both men and women. Jurisdictions that provide for a 6-day maximum workweek are:

Arizona	Massachusetts	Oregon
Arkansas	Nevada	Pennsylvania
California	New Hampshire	Puerto Rico
Connecticut	New Jersey	Utah
District of Columbia	New York	Washington
Illinois	North Carolina	Wisconsin
Kansas	North Dakota	
Louisiana	Ohio	

Of the remaining 30 States, 20 have laws that prohibit specified employment or activities on Sunday:

Alabama	Maryland	South Dakota
Florida	Mississippi	Tennessee
Georgia	Missouri	Texas
Idaho	New Mexico	Vermont
Indiana	Oklahoma	Virginia
Kentucky	Rhode Island	West Virginia
Maine	South Carolina	

Meal Period

Twenty-three States, the District of Columbia, and Puerto Rico provide that meal periods, varying from 20 minutes to 1 hour in duration, must be allowed women employed in some or all industries. In 3 States--Indiana, Nebraska, and New York--these provisions apply to men as well as women. Jurisdictions that provide for the length of the meal period by statute, order, or regulation are:

Arkansas	Massachusetts	Pennsylvania
California	Nebraska	Puerto Rico
Colorado	Nevada	Rhode Island
District of Columbia	New Mexico	Utah
Indiana	New York	Washington
Kansas	North Carolina	West Virginia
Louisiana	North Dakota	Wisconsin
Maine	Ohio	
Maryland	Oregon	

Combining rest period and meal period provisions, Kentucky requires, before and after the regularly scheduled lunch period (duration not specified), rest periods to be granted to females, and Wyoming requires two paid rest periods, one before and one after the lunch hour, to be granted to females employed in specified establishments who are required to be on their feet continuously.

Rest Period

Twelve States and Puerto Rico provide by statute or wage order for rest periods (as distinct from meal periods) for women workers. The statutes in 4 of these States--Alaska, Kentucky, Nevada, and Wyoming--cover a variety of industries (in Alaska and Wyoming applicable only to women standing continuously); laws in New York and Pennsylvania apply to elevator operators not provided with seating facilities. Rest periods in one or more industries are required by wage orders in Arizona, California, Colorado, Oregon, Utah, Washington, and Puerto Rico. Most of the provisions are for a 10-minute rest period within each half day of work. The North Dakota Manufacturing Occupation Order prohibits the employment of women for more than 2 hours without a rest period (duration not specified).

Arkansas manufacturing establishments operating on a 24-hour schedule may be exempt, when necessary, from the meal period provision if females are granted two 10-minute paid rest periods and provision is made for them to eat at their work.

Nightwork

In 18 States and Puerto Rico nightwork for adult women is prohibited and/or regulated in certain industries or occupations.

Nine States and Puerto Rico prohibit nightwork for adult women in certain occupations or industries or under specified conditions:

Connecticut	New Jersey	Puerto Rico
Kansas	New York	Washington
Massachusetts	North Dakota	
Nebraska	Ohio	

In North Dakota and Washington the prohibition applies only to elevator operators; in Ohio, only to taxicab drivers.

In 9 other States, as well as in several of the jurisdictions that prohibit nightwork in specified industries or occupations, the employment of adult women at night is regulated either by maximum hour provisions or by specified standards of working conditions. For example, in one State women and minors are limited to 8 hours a night.

California	New Mexico	Rhode Island
Illinois	Oregon	Utah
New Hampshire	Pennsylvania	Wisconsin

Arizona and the District of Columbia prohibit the employment of females under 21 years of age in night messenger service; the Arizona law also is applicable to males under 21.

EQUAL PAY

Thirty-one States have equal pay laws applicable to private employment that prohibit discrimination in rate of pay based on sex. They establish the principle of payment of a wage rate based on the job and not on the sex of the worker. Five States with no equal pay law have fair employment practices laws and the District of Columbia, an ordinance, that prohibit discrimination in rate of pay or compensation based on sex.

Historical Record

Public attention was first sharply focused on equal pay for women during World War I when large numbers of women were employed in war industries on the same jobs as men, and the National War Labor Board enforced the policy of "no wage discrimination against women on the grounds of sex." In 1919, 2 States--Michigan and Montana--enacted equal pay legislation. For nearly 25 years these were the only States with such laws.

Great progress in the equal pay field was made during World War II when again large numbers of women entered the labor force, many of them in jobs previously held by men. Government agencies, employers, unions, organizations, and the general public were concerned with the removal of wage differentials as a means of furthering the war effort.

During the period 1943-45 equal pay laws were enacted in 4 States-- Illinois, Massachusetts, New York, and Washington.

In the next 4 years 6 States--California, Connecticut, Maine, New Hampshire, Pennsylvania, and Rhode Island--and Alaska passed equal pay laws.

New Jersey enacted an equal pay law in 1952. Arkansas, Colorado, and Oregon passed such legislation in 1955.

In 1957 California amended its equal pay law to strengthen existing legislation, and Nebraska adopted a resolution endorsing the policy of equal pay for equal work without discrimination based on sex and urging the adoption of this policy by all employers in the State. Hawaii, Ohio, and Wyoming passed equal pay laws in 1959.

In 1961 Wisconsin amended its fair employment practices act to prohibit discrimination because of sex and to provide that a differential in pay between employees, when based in good faith on any factor other than sex, is not prohibited.

In 1962 Arizona passed an equal pay law, and Michigan amended its law (which previously covered only manufacture or production of any article) to extend coverage to any employer of labor employing both males and females.

During 1963 Missouri enacted an equal pay law, and Vermont passed a fair employment practices law which also prohibits discrimination in rates of pay by reason of sex.

Also in 1963 the Federal Equal Pay Act was passed as an amendment to the FLSA.

In 1965, 3 States--North Dakota, Oklahoma, and West Virginia--enacted equal pay laws, and 3 States with no equal pay law--Maryland, Nebraska, and Utah--passed fair employment practices laws which prohibit discrimination in compensation based on sex. Amendments in California, Maine, New York, and Rhode Island strengthened existing equal pay laws.

In 1966, 4 States--Georgia, Kentucky, Maryland, and South Dakota--enacted equal pay laws. Massachusetts enacted a law that provides equal pay for certain civil service employees.

In 1967, 2 States--Indiana and Nebraska--enacted equal pay laws.

Roster of Equal Pay States 13/

The 31 States with equal pay laws are:

Alaska	Maine	Ohio
Arizona	Maryland	Oklahoma
Arkansas	Massachusetts	Oregon
California	Michigan	Pennsylvania
Colorado	Missouri	Rhode Island
Connecticut	Montana	South Dakota
Georgia	Nebraska	Washington
Hawaii	New Hampshire	West Virginia
Illinois	New Jersey	Wyoming
Indiana 14/	New York	
Kentucky	North Dakota	

13/ Fair employment practices acts in 5 States with no equal pay law-- Idaho, Nevada, Utah, Vermont, and Wisconsin--prohibit discrimination in rate of pay or compensation based on sex. In the District of Columbia there is an ordinance prohibiting discrimination based on sex.

14/ Indiana included an equal pay provision in its amendments to the minimum wage law.

Equal pay laws in Colorado, Georgia, Indiana, Kentucky, Maryland, Montana, Nebraska, North Dakota, and Pennsylvania are applicable to public as well as private employment. (A Massachusetts law contains an elective equal pay provision, applicable to employees of cities or towns who are in the classified civil service; and a Texas law requires equal pay for women in public employment.) In 21 States the laws apply to most types of private employment; in general those specifying exemptions exclude agricultural labor and domestic service. The Illinois law applies only to manufacturing.

FAIR EMPLOYMENT PRACTICES

Title VII of the Federal Civil Rights Act of 1964 prohibits discrimination in private employment based on sex, in addition to race, color, religion, and national origin. Title VII covers private employment and labor organizations engaged in industries affecting commerce, as well as employment agencies, and applies to such employers and unions with at least 25 employees or members.

Thirty-seven States, the District of Columbia, and Puerto Rico have fair employment practices laws, but only 15 of the States and the District of Columbia include a prohibition against discrimination in employment based on sex. Prior to the enactment of title VII, the laws of only 2 States, Hawaii and Wisconsin, prohibited sex discrimination in employment.

The 37 States with fair employment practices laws are:

Alaska	Indiana	Missouri	Oklahoma 15/
Arizona	Iowa	Montana	Oregon
California	Kansas	Nebraska	Pennsylvania
Colorado	Kentucky	Nevada	Rhode Island
Connecticut	Maine	New Hampshire	Utah
Delaware	Maryland	New Jersey	Vermont
Hawaii	Massachusetts	New Mexico	Washington
Idaho	Michigan	New York	West Virginia
Illinois	Minnesota	Ohio	Wisconsin
			Wyoming

The 16 jurisdictions whose fair employment practices laws prohibit discrimination in employment based on sex are:

Arizona	Maryland	Nevada
Connecticut	Massachusetts	New York
District of Columbia	Michigan	Oklahoma 15/
Hawaii	Missouri	Utah
Idaho	Nebraska	Wisconsin
		Wyoming

15/ Effective May 16, 1969.

In 2 additional States--Alaska and Vermont--the fair employment
practices law prohibits discrimination based on sex, in wages only. In a
third State--Colorado--the law only prohibits discrimination based on sex
in apprenticeship, on-the-job training, or other occupational instruction,
training, or retraining programs.

OTHER LABOR LEGISLATION

Industrial Homework

Nineteen States and Puerto Rico have industrial homework laws or
regulations:

California	Michigan	Puerto Rico
Connecticut	Missouri	Rhode Island
Hawaii	New Jersey	Tennessee
Illinois	New York	Texas
Indiana	Ohio	West Virginia
Maryland	Oregon	Wisconsin
Massachusetts	Pennsylvania	

These regulations apply to all persons, except that in Oregon the
provisions apply to women and minors only.

In addition, the Alaska and Washington minimum wage and hour laws
authorize the issuance of rules and regulations restricting or prohibiting
industrial homework where necessary to safeguard the minimum wage rate
prescribed in the laws.

Employment Before and After Childbirth

Six States and Puerto Rico prohibit the employment of women in one
or more industries or occupations immediately before and/or after childbirth.
These standards are established by statute or by minimum wage or welfare
orders. Women may not be employed in:

Connecticut----- 4 weeks before and 4 weeks after childbirth
Massachusetts--- 4 weeks before and 4 weeks after childbirth
Missouri-------- 3 weeks before and 3 weeks after childbirth
New York------------------------- 4 weeks after childbirth
Puerto Rico----- 4 weeks before and 4 weeks after childbirth
Vermont--------- 2 weeks before and 4 weeks after childbirth
Washington------ 4 months before and 6 weeks after childbirth

In addition to the prohibition of employment, Puerto Rico requires the employer to pay the working mother half her regular wage or salary during an 8-week period and provides for job security during the required absence.

Rhode Island's Temporary Disability Insurance Act provides that women workers covered by the act who are unemployed because of sickness resulting from pregnancy are entitled to cash benefits for maternity leave for a 14-week period beginning with the sixth week prior to the week of expected childbirth, or with the week childbirth occurs if it is more than 6 weeks prior to the expected birth.

The New Jersey Temporary Disability Benefits Act provides that women workers to whom the act applies are entitled to cash payments for disability existing during the 4 weeks before and the 4 weeks after childbirth.

Also, the Oregon Mercantile Order recommends that an employer should not employ a female at any work during the 6 weeks preceding and the 4 weeks following the birth of her child, unless recommended by a licensed medical authority.

Occupational Limitations

Twenty-six States have laws or regulations that prohibit the employment of adult women in specified occupations or industries or under certain working conditions that are considered hazardous or injurious to health and safety. In 17 of these States the prohibition applies to women's employment in or about mines. (Clerical or similar work is excepted from the prohibition in about half of these States.) Ten States prohibit women from mixing, selling, or dispensing alcoholic beverages for on-premises consumption, and 1 State--Georgia--prohibits their employment in retail liquor stores. (In addition, a Florida statute authorizes the city of Tampa to prohibit females from soliciting customers to buy alcoholic beverages.)

The following States have occupational limitations applicable to:

Mines

Alabama	Maryland	Utah
Arizona	Missouri	Virginia
Arkansas	New York	Washington
Colorado	Ohio	Wisconsin
Illinois	Oklahoma	Wyoming
Indiana	Pennsylvania	

Establishments serving alcoholic beverages

Alaska	Indiana	Rhode Island
California	Kentucky	Wyoming
Connecticut	Ohio	
Illinois 16/	Pennsylvania	

16/ Illinois State law empowers city and county governments to prohibit by general ordinance or resolution.

Eleven States prohibit the employment of women in other places or occupations, or under certain conditions:

Arizona--In occupations requiring constant standing.
Colorado--Working around coke ovens.
Massachusetts--Working on cores more than 2 cubic feet or 60 pounds.
Michigan--Handling harmful substances; in foundries without approval of the Department of Labor.
Minnesota--Placing cores in or out of ovens; cleaning moving machinery.
Missouri--Cleaning or working between moving machinery.
New York--Coremaking, or in connection with coremaking, in a room in which the oven is also in operation.
Ohio--As crossing watchman, section hand, express driver, metal molder, bellhop, gas or electric meter reader; in shoeshining parlors, bowling alleys as pinsetters, poolrooms; in delivery service on motor-propelled vehicles of over 1-ton capacity; in operating freight or baggage elevators if the doors are not automatically or semiautomatically controlled; in baggage and freight handling; trucking and handling by means of handtrucks, heavy materials of any kind; in blast furnaces and smelters.
Pennsylvania--In dangerous or injurious occupations.
Washington--As a bellhop
Wisconsin--In dangerous or injurious occupations.

The majority of the States with occupational limitations for adult women also have prohibitory legislation for persons under 21 years. In addition, 10 States have occupational limitations for persons under 21 years only. Most of these limitations apply to the serving of liquor and to the driving of taxicabs, schoolbuses, or public vehicles; others prohibit the employment of females under 21 years in jobs demanding constant standing or as messengers, bellhops, or caddies.

Seating and Weightlifting

A number of jurisdictions--through statutes, minimum wage orders, and other regulations--have established employment standards for women relating to plant facilities such as seats, lunchrooms, dressing rooms, restrooms, and toilet rooms and to weightlifting. Only the seating and weightlifting provisions are included in this summary.

Seating.--Forty-five States, the District of Columbia, and Puerto Rico have seating laws or orders; all but one (the Florida law) apply exclusively to women. Delaware, Hawaii, Illinois, Maryland, and Mississippi have no seating laws or orders.

Weightlifting.--Ten States and Puerto Rico have statutes, rules, regulations, and/or orders which specify the maximum weight women employees may lift, carry, or lift and carry. Following are the standards established for weightlifting and carrying in the 11 jurisdictions. Some States have standards varying by occupation or industry and are, therefore, listed more than once.

Any occupation: "excessive weight" in Oregon; 30 pounds lifting and 15 pounds carrying in Utah; 35 percent of body weight, or 25 pounds where repetitive lifting in Alaska; 25 in Ohio; 40 in Massachusetts; 44 in Puerto Rico; 50 in California.
Foundries and core rooms: 25 pounds in Maryland, Massachusetts, Minnesota, and New York.
Specified occupations or industries (by orders): 25 pounds in California; 25 to 50 in Oregon; 35 pounds and "excessive weight" in Washington.

Women's Bureau publications on wages, hours, equal pay, and related subjects may be obtained:

At prices quoted, from the Superintendent of Documents, U.S. Government Printing Office, Washington, D.C. 20402--

State Minimum Wage Laws. Leaflet 4. April 1966. 5¢.
Analysis of Coverage and Wage Rates of State Minimum Wage Laws and Orders. August 1, 1965. Bull. 291. 1965. 40¢.
Fringe Benefit Provisions From State Minimum Wage Laws and Orders. September 1, 1966. Bull. 293. 1967. 55¢.
State Hour Laws for Women. Bull. 277. 1961. 35¢.
Equal Pay Facts. Leaflet 2. May 1966. 5¢.
1965 Handbook on Women Workers. Bull. 290. 1966. $1.00.

From the Women's Bureau, Wage and Labor Standards Administration, U.S. Department of Labor, Washington, D.C. 20210--

Labor Laws Affecting Women. (Specify State)
Labor Laws Affecting Private Household Workers. July 15, 1967.
Laws on Sex Discrimination in Employment. April 1, 1967.
What the Equal Pay Principle Means to Women. August 1966.
Weightlifting Provisions for Women by State. July 1966.
Why State Equal Pay Laws? June 1966.
Action for Equal Pay. January 1966.
Getting the Facts on Equal Pay. January 1966.

SUMMARY OF LEGAL ACTION IN 1969 AFFECTING STATE LABOR LAWS
FOR WOMEN

In the past year a number of significant judicial interpretations of Title VII of the Civil Rights Act of 1964 have been made. Of greatest importance were *Weeks* v. *Southern Bell Telephone and Telegraph Company*, decided March 4, 1969, by the Fifth Circuit Court of Appeals and *Bowe et al* v. *Colgate Palmolive Co.*, decided September 26, 1969, by the Seventh Circuit Court of Appeals.

The *Weeks* case included the following interpretation of bona fide occupational qualification:

We conclude that the principle of nondiscrimination requires that we hold that in order to rely on the bona fide occupational qualification exception an employer has the burden of proving that he had reasonable cause to believe, that is, a factual basis for believing, that all or substantially all women would be unable to perform safely and efficiently the duties of the job involved.

In the *Bowe* case, the court held that an employer could not refuse to assign women to jobs requiring the lifting of 35 pounds or more. Each employee, male and female, must be afforded a reasonable opportunity to demonstrate his or her ability to perform more strenuous jobs on a regular basis. The court further determined that all employees who had been discriminated against, not limited to those plaintiffs filing a charge with the Equal Employment Opportunity Commission, were entitled to redress including back pay. The court also held that the women could seek redress under Title VII *and* under the collective bargaining contract at the same time. It is ironic that the plaintiffs in these cases have yet to recover any damages, although many other women in other companies and in other establishments of the same company have benefited from the decisions.

A less favorable decision was rendered in the Fifth Circuit Court of Appeals in the case of *Phillips* v. *Martin Marietta Corporation.* The court held that an employer's refusal to hire women with pre-school age children was not a violation of Title VII. After the panel had made its decision, the Chief Judge of the Fifth Circuit asked for a rehearing *en banc* that is, a rehearing of the issue by all the judges in that circuit. The request was denied; the plaintiff petitioned the Supreme Court for a writ of certiorari; and the Solicitor General filed a brief for the U.S. as amicus curiae in behalf of the plaintiff. The Supreme Court on March 2, 1970, agreed to hear the case in the fall term.

The Equal Employment Opportunity Commission filed amicus curiae briefs in behalf of the plaintiffs in all three cases. The National Federation of Business and Professional Women's Clubs and the United Automobile Workers filed amicus curiae briefs in the *Bowe* case. The women in the *Bowe* and *Weeks* cases were represented by volunteer attorneys from the Human Rights for Women, Inc. and the National Organization for Women. The NAACP is counsel for Mrs. Phillips, who is white, in her appeal to the Supreme Court.

District Courts in California and Oregon have held that State labor laws applying only to women were superseded by Title VII of the Civil Rights Act. (*Rosenfeld* v. *Southern Pacific* and *Richards* v. *Griffiths Rubber Mills*). The Equal Employment Opportunity Commission filed amicus curiae briefs in both cases and with the appellate court in the *Rosenfeld* case, which has been appealed. Following the decisions in these cases, the Equal Employment Opportunity Commission, on August 19, 1969, revised its guidelines to state:

"Many States have enacted laws or promulgated administrative regulations with respect to the employment of females. Among these laws are those which prohibit or limit the employment of females, e.g., the employment of females in certain occupations, in jobs requiring the lifting or carrying of weights exceeding certain prescribed limits, during certain hours of the night, or for more than a specified number of hours per day or per week.

"The Commission believes that such State laws and regulations, although originally promulgated for the purpose of protecting females, have ceased to be relevant to our technology or to the expanding role of the female worker in our economy. The Commission has found that such laws and regulations do take into account the capacities, preferences, and abilities of individual females and tend to discriminate rather than protect. Accordingly, the Commission has concluded that such laws and regulations conflict with Title VII of the Civil Rights Act of 1964 and will not be considered a defense to an otherwise established unlawful employment practice or as a basis for the application of the bona fide occupational qualification exception."

Numerous other cases in a number of States are pending at the Federal district court level.

State courts in Wyoming and California have overturned State protective labor laws. In the Wyoming case, the Supreme Court held that a Wyoming law barring the employment of female bartenders was superseded by the State fair employment practices act. In the California case the Superior Court for Los Angeles County held that a California law prohibiting women from working as bartenders was invalidated by Title VII, the State is appealing the case.

The Attorneys General of South Dakota, Pennsylvania, Oklahoma, and Michigan in 1969 issued opinions that Title VII and/or their State fair employment practices legislation superseded their State's protective labor legislation. The Ohio Department of Industrial Relations announced that the department would not prosecute alleged violations of Ohio's protective laws in conflict with the guidelines of the Equal Employment Opportunity Commission until the Ohio General Assembly conformed the Ohio law with Title VII.

The Nebraska legislature repealed its State protective laws in the 1969 session. Tennessee and Maryland exempted establishments covered by the Fair Labor Standards Act (this type exemption would apply to most of the employers covered by Title VII). New Mexico exempted "any female who signs a written agreement to work more than 8 hours a day or more than 40 hours a week" provided time and one-half overtime is paid for hours over 40 a week. New York amended its laws to provide exceptions by the administering agency on application of the employer if the employee has voluntarily agreed, employment is not in violation of the collective bargaining agreement, and there are adequate safeguards for the health and welfare of women.

Prior to 1969, Delaware had repealed its laws and Virginia, North Carolina, Arizona, and California exempted women covered by the Fair Labor Standards Act from their hours laws. Arizona and California required overtime for hours in excess of 8 a day, and California restricted total hours to 10 hours a day and 58 hours a week for one employer.

The trend is thus clearly toward elimination of State labor laws applying only to women. A decision by the 9th Circuit Court of Appeals upholding the decision of the District Court in the *Rosenfeld* case would accelerate action.

SIGNIFICANT CHANGES IN STATE LABOR LAWS FOR WOMEN SINCE 1966

Repealed hours laws: Arizona; Delaware; Nebraska; New York (eff. 7/1/70); Oregon; Vermont.

Rulings by Attys. Genl. that State laws are superseded by Title VII or State Fair Employment Laws: District of Columbia; Michigan; Oklahoma; Pennsylvania; South Dakota; Washington.

Exemptions from hours laws of those covered by Fair Labor Standards Act or comparable standards—some include other conditions for the exception: California; Kansas; Maryland; North Carolina, Tennessee; Virginia.

No Prosecutions now because of uncertainty as to effects of Title VII: Ohio; North Dakota.

Exemption from hours law if employee voluntarily agrees: New Mexico. specific pound limit: Georgia.

Modification of weightlifting regulation to apply to men and to omit specific pound limit: Georgia.

Note: Michigan also withdrew a weightlifting regulation when it was discovered there was no statutory authority.

---

[2] During the course of the investigation it became clear that Respondent's officials were extremely hostile to these female employees. In addition to specific comments to that effect, Respondent refused to allow the investigator to speak to the Acting Foreman of Toilet Articles, the department in which most of the women are assigned.

Double Standard Between Men and Women in Employment Opportunities, Handling, Weight Lifting, Work Hours and Pay

Double Standard Between Men and Women in Employment Opportunities, Handling, Weight Lifting, Work Hours and Pay

Congress intended to eliminate sex discrimination when it enacted Title VII of the Civil Rights Act of 1964. A substantial amount of sex discrimination still continues, because the Equal Employment Opportunity Commission had, until lately, taken the position--like so many others-- that State restrictive laws on hours of employment and weight lifting by women qualify as "bona fide" occupational qualifications under Title VII of the Civil Rights Act of 1964.

Many of the women are still suffering from discrimination inflicted upon females with respect to their employment opportunities under the guise of state laws--including "bona fide restriction"--which limits women's work hours--without overtime pay--restricted working places, weight lifting, employment opportunities, handling and pay.

The Women's Liberation Movement has been harassing Governor Milliken in the newspapers and they have even been challenging their own husbands. Many women think they are on the wrong track with their demands for equal authority over tax returns and assembly lines.

The women's organizations allege that men treat women as sex objects and they are male dominated, and further that the world is male oriented with male supremacy. We see it in the newspapers, magazines and also in our own life. The Detroit W.L.M. (Women's League Movement) is planning a campaign converting men to their cause.

Many engineering students at Cass Tech have overthrown the school's ban on slacks in the classrooms. The Detroit W.L.M. called to show solidarity and many students of Cass came with slacks to class determined that it is wrong to require the wearing of a dress to be considered a lady; prostitutes wear dresses too. One man had a special thought of this opinion from the students. A male attending the Wayne State Free University Course on women's oppression brought the discussion to an abrupt stop with this statement, "A wife, as far as I'm concerned is nothing but a high-class prostitute. The only difference is she does it legal."[1]

The W.L.M. of Detroit says it wants nothing more than men and women to be recognized as people without any reflection or references to their sexual roles. The Women's Liberation Movement is going many steps further, saying they will free man too. "Not only women," explained Barbara Borris, "There are a number of men who do not want to play this sadistic dominant role they are cast in by society."[2]

The Civil Rights Act of 1964, Title VII, is specially designed to end discrimination against sex and to provide American citizens with equal employment opportunities regardless of their sex. The Civil Rights Act of 1964, became effective July 2, 1965, and July 2, 1968.

This provision could have far-reaching effects on the employment opportunities for females if not prior to the enactment all but a few states had

---

[1]"They Resent Male Domination", Detroit Free Press, 5-4-69

[2]"They Resent Male Domination", Detroit Free Press, 5-4-69

adopted laws supporting to protect women in employment. The state's legislation for protection of women in employment was recognized by the Supreme Court 1908. These state protection laws prohibit the employment of women in certain capacities, those which confer special benefits on women, laws which prescribe maximum daily and weekly hours for women, also prohibit night time employment of women. Certain state laws prohibit the employment of women in certain occupations, like bartenders, croupiers and dealers in playchambers in Las Vegas.

When the "EEOC" adopted its guidelines on discrimination against sex, it was hoping that the state protective laws would be over-ridden by the Civil Rights Act of 1964, Title VII.

The United Nations too, considered backing the rights of women. They had a document for years in preparation, which called on governments, organizations and individuals to work towards the goal for the equal rights for women. It was approved and voted in the General Assembly 111 to 0, eleven delegates were not present.

> "...Although the declaration does not require national ratification and does not have the binding legal effect of a treaty, its supporters hail it with varying degrees of enthusiasm as a statement of goals and say it may be persuasive in obtaining rights for women."[3]

With this the United Nations tried its best, but even it was not able to influence other nations. For example in West Germany the sexes have equal rights, but not in court procedures. The Detroit News of October 25, 1967, wrote about it in an article entitled, "Fraus [Frauen] Jailed, Men Fined."

---

[3] "U.N. 111 to 0 Backs Rights of Women", New York Times, 11-8-67.

Despite that they proclaim that equal rights are administered between both sexes in West Germany. It is not so! There the women's organization has filed a suit in the Supreme Court at Karlsruhe to get all female minor offenders out of jail. The suit is more or less an outgrowth of a bizarre shortage in jail cells for men, which was the reason that all male offenders were being excused from jail terms because there was no room for men, and the female offenders are directed to go to jail for precisely the same offenses for which the males are excused. The German woman is not only denied equality of rights under the action of waiving confinement for male offenders, but also illustrates an illogical fact, that women there are specially punished because they are more law abiding than German males. Otherwise, the women's jail would also not have any room for women offenders.[4]

It is not much better in other countries. For instance, the Detroit News had an article on March 20, 1969, "Women Still Unequal Sex, But Swedes Offer Remedy." "It is still primarily a man's world, United Nation's Secretary General U Thant has reported to the U.N...." (Manuscript has been submitted).

Similar instances are found in Switzerland, a country which always will stay out of trouble--sovereign--but in case of equal rights for women, it has no provisions to solve this big problem between the sexes. Some of the largest fortunes in Switzerland are in the hands of elderly widows. They are also Switzerland's largest taxpayers and do not even have the right to vote, which is a completely incorrect situation.

---

[4]"Fraus Jailed, Men Fined", Detroit News, 10-25-67.

"The league against voting rights for women organizes no
public lectures or demonstrations, makes no noise. 'We are
just here,' Mrs. Zwicky said in her view, 'A Woman's Family
Comes First.' Men are doing a good job of governing Switzerland.
We are envied all over the world. We as women may enter any
profession, any field of study, hold even such positions as that of
a judge or minister. We should continue to leave the political
decisions to men."[5]

This shows clearly that it is worse in Switzerland with respect to the

women's equal rights, but there is not any uproar or demonstration.

How are the equal rights of Michigan women" (The manuscript of

the Free Press Staff Writer, Jean Sprain Wilson, has been submitted.)

I believe that prejudice and discrimination against women in a certain

percentage is still severe and also admit that many women and women's or-

ganizations are too extreme in their demands, but that under any circumstances

a reasonable provision between the sexes has yet to be found.

I will begin with my first contention that there still exists prejudice

and discrimination against women, with Miss Pauline Dziob, a stewardess

aboard the Moore-McCormack Passenger Lines. She says, "They'll let us be

a waitress, stewardess and child attendant on the passenger ships, and that's

it." She is taking on the Maritime Union and the steamship line in her battle to

be certified a Yoeman. Last December, she was promoted to Yeoman to take care

of a vacancy because she says she is an expert typist and her work was found

satisfactory. She was kicked back to stewardess and replaced with an 18 year

old boy with no experience. This boy had, after two weeks quit to go to school.

---

[5]"Swiss Women Do Not Have Any Right To Vote",-Zurich, The Christian Science
Monitor, 7-18-67.

A Union official told her a Yeoman is a male position. I agree with Jean

Faust's opinion--she is the President of the New York Area Chapter, "Pauline

Dziob may make history as the woman who proved finally that blatent dis-

crimination based upon sex is as illegal and intollerable as discrimination

based upon race or religion."[6]

There is a very interesting case from Las Vegas, where a woman wants

to work as a croupier or dealer. The District Attorney, George Franklin, said

he would oppose changing the county ordinance. If women are to stand equal

with men, then they should be able to register for the draft and fight for their

country!

I'm shocked with this statement, because it is already a proven fact

that women were, and are, soldiers as in Russia and other countries. The

United States also has women engaged in the Army and we do not know yet

what may come in the future. Besides this, a woman in her motherhood is--

in her way--a soldier, risking her life and fighting under heavy pain for the

reproduction of her country. That not all women have children is balancing

the fact that not all men are drafted.[7]

One other case shows where women stand--" 'New' Women Vetoes

'Chicks Up Front.' " The Feminist Movement is giving a full report and we do

not have to add anything--it speaks for itself. (Article submitted).

---

[6] "National Maritime Union Contra Miss Dziob", The Christian Science Monitor, 10-10-67.

[7] "Men Resist Distaff Inroads at the Gambling Table", New York Times, 8-10-69.

When two union women wrangle over female work limits it is dreadful. On the one side is Mrs. Caroline Davis, Director of the U.A.W. Women's Department. She would like to have a maximum 54 hour work week. Mrs. Marguerite Wolfgang, Secretary of Local 705, Hotel, Motel and Restaurant Employees Union is on the other side. She favors retention of the law which comes in fact February 15. Mrs. Davis considers the limit of 54 weekly working hours contrary to Title VII of the Federal Civil Rights Act of 1964, illegal, and she thinks and feels that the Michigan law limiting the number of working hours may put women on an unfair disadvantage by women who like, and have, to work hard. Also, it is a disadvantage when women cannot and men can get promotions or job transfers, when being considered.[8] I'm completely on the side of Mrs. Davis, because if a woman does not want or does not have to have extra income then she does not have to work; but if a woman is in a bad situation, fighting for survival, she would not have a chance if Mrs. Wolfgang's decision, with limited worktime for women is enacted.

There is another factor that keeps women away from jobs--the lack of mobility of women in job changes. Mrs. Pat Hitt, the Undersecretary of the Department of Health, Education and Welfare, understands this problem well for the reason of her own experience. When she accepted her post and therefore became the first woman named to a major position in the U.S. Government, her husband, Robert Hitt, had to make the decision to leave his public relations firm in California and move [with her] to Washington. Pat Hitt says,

---

[8] "Two Union Women Wrangle Over Female Work Limit", Detroit News, 1-17-69.

"Availability is the key. When Mr. Richard Nixon appoints a man to a government post, there is generally no question about what the wife and children will do. They will accompany the man to his job. "

Senator Beebe says Mrs. Pat Hitt is the greatest in the V.I.D. She is of the opinion that more women should run for office, and also that more involvement in governmental work should grow. She is absolutely not satisfied with the number of women which are participating in governmental work.[9]

We can find sex discrimination in any field of occupation. A woman pilot takes her job flight to court. This is a 41 year old female pilot who had logged 10,000 hours as a pilot where she was rejected by an airline because of her sex.

Miss Jean Dietrich, of San Francisco, who had a student license when she was sixteen, now is licensed as a commercial multi-engine instrument and seaplane pilot. Miss Dietrich said the World Airway's Inc., Oakland, a big charter company, rejected her under the Civil Rights Act of 1964. The company's officers said it was not policy to hire women pilots. We had "Lindberg" and "Emilia Erhard" as flight pioneers--a male and a female. What is the difference? Society formed the opinion that "ONLY" men have the capacity and that is what has to be changed.

"Women's ordination gets a grudging lift" is a misleading title of one of the religious writer's articles. A Michigan Episcopalian Bishop Bennisow said in an interview:

---

[9]"Lack of Mobility Hurts Women's Job Changes", Detroit Free Press, 3-17-70.

"...That he had even greater doubts that the conference will
approve any recommendations regarding the ordination of women
to the Anglican or Episcopalian Priesthood....The Priesthood
has serious misgivings about the ordination of female Priests...."
Mrs. Ann Cheetham, British Lecturer, Journalist and Broadcaster,
said in an interview that she and a Protestant and Roman Catholic
colleagues had petitioned Elizabeth II, Queen from Britain, because
she is the dedicated, consecrated head of the church of England
and by the way, doing a good job of it."[10]

Queen Elizabeth II, herself is a female and therefore, no further comment

on this subject.

"University Sex Bias" and "Protesters Defend Woman Power" by Nicholas

von Hoffman, Guy Halverson and Lucia Mouat have written about the sex

discrimination, the cases in the University of Chicago. One of the persons in

question is Marlene Dixon. She has a Ph.D. in Sociology and the second is

Naomi Weisstein who took her Ph.D. at Harvard, where she reported things are no

better there. At first the students insisted the decision of uproar was based

strictly on Mrs. Dixon's radical political views. Lately, they have added that

it also is because she is a woman. Nancy Stokely, Senior in History, charged:

"Male chauvinism is an element in every University of Chicago course."

As always with political cases, a clear set of facts is next to impossible

to establish. Sociology is a highly inexact discipline where one man's

scholarship is another man's idea of pure, political propaganda. Discrimination

on the ground of sex is as hard to prove as discrimination on grounds of race

or religion. Determining the truth in a particular case is next to impossible. The

only way is to look at how an institution has performed over a period of

---

[10]"Womens Ordination Gets Grudging Lift", Detroit News, 8-13-68.

time, and if you do that with the University of Chicago, you begin to wonder if
Mrs. Dixon may not have a strong case, because the Sociology Department
kept women from the tenured, full faculty positions that begin with the Assistant
Professor. In Mrs. Dixon's general field of the Social Sciences, it is clear to
see, that women need not apply at Chicago. In the past 77 years the only female
professors were engaged in Anthropology, Political Science has had one, and
Psychology fourteen females. [11] [12] The truth alludes us, floating in the clouds
and will never be known. This repeats in all other occupations, in many
stronger than in others.

The "Legion of Angry Women" and "Would-be Astronauts" is the
climax of sex discrimination written about--the two page commitment of
happenings in selecting the astronauts. They interviewed eight of the
seventeen lady applicants. They were attractive, witty and intelligent with
a zest for adventure, share love of science, have the same dash, courage
daring and believe in it (that made the original seven first astronauts heroes).
The females tried to become scientists and astronauts--some could boast
scientific credentials and heroic exploits that would force any male astronaut
to look to his laurels. Mrs. Gladys A. Philpoyt of Sonnyvale, California,
said, "What can you do? It is a fact. It's a kind of discrimination that is
not spelled out."

Mrs. Abigail E. Beutler, Ann Arbor, Michigan, a special Physicist,
who aspires to rise above the laboratory, disagrees. She believes the ideal

[11] "University Sex Bids", Detroit News 3-2-69.

[12] "Protesters Defend Women Power", The Christian Science Monitor, 2-5-69.

lady astronaut in the screening board's mind, would be a Jackie Kennedy with a Ph.D. In the 1961 rejection of women NASA banished from space seventeen women applicants, including Jerri Cobb, at that time thirty-one, who has flown sixty-three types of aircraft, including jects. She had test-piloted conventional airplanes, but could not get accepted as a jet test pilot [woman], at the time she had logged more than 10,000 hours of flying time, compared with 5,100 for Astronaut Glenn and 2,900 for Astronaut Scott Carpenter. Glenn had no college degree, so the educational requirements had to be waived--then Glenn could become an astronaut. Cobb holds college degrees in addition to all her before maintained 10,000 flying hours and the different types of aircraft and jets she was flying. She demonstrated that she could hold her own in space. She breezed through three phases of astronaut testing, including the test in which she swallowed three feet of rubber hose. This woman astronaut had spent three hours in an isolated air-filled room to measure ability to remain alert without hallucinations in a weightless state. Mrs. Cobb took a far more rigorous test, submerging in body-temperature water in a shockproff, soundproof tank, which deprived her of sight, sound, hearing, smell, taste and feeling. She still hadn't reached her tolerance limit when she was pulled out after nine hours and forty minutes. At this point NASA abruptly halted her test with the explanation that it had no requirement for female astronauts.

Here is Russia teaching us a very good lesson!

The other rejected women are certainly the most impressive group of ladies there ever were. For example, Mrs. Elizabeth Suadra, 35, of Manhatten

Beach, California. She was the first girl ever to enter the University of Wichita, Aeronautic School, then transferred to California, where she earned her B.D. in 1959, and then got two consecutive American Emilia Erhard Fellowships which helped her to a Master's Degree in fluid mechanics and acoustics. She was even the author and co-author of two scientific papers dealing with such materials as changing the orbit plane of space vehicles with small amounts of power.

Gladys Philport, has had an equally dramatic career at Boston University where she picked up an undergraduate degree in Biology in 1960, her Master's Degree the next year and a Ph.D. in Histology and Cytology in 1963. At that time she was 34 years old and doing research in two areas of concern to our astronauts.

Another rejected applicant is Abigail Beutler, a divorcee, who is raising three children and has four degrees, but no Doctorate. She wants to believe it is the lack of the Ph.D. and not a prejudice that kept her out of a space capsule. [Glenn didn't even have a college degree]. She got her undergraduate degree in Physics at Radcliff in 1950, then three Master's Degrees. She worked for three years as a Research Analyst on guided missiles, another two years with the University of Michigan Radio Astronomy Observatory planning space probes of the planet Mars, and is now an Associate Research Physicist in the space Physics Research Laboratory at the University of Michigan.

Dr. Charlie Heyes, another rejected applicant, has been fighting all her life to do things men think they [women] cannot do.

Among other female "Flunk Outs" is Janner Trubath. She was the first woman graduate of Polytechnic Institute of Brooklyn.

Another is Mrs. Robinson Painter, 27 of Knoxville, Kentucky, who completed her Doctorate in Radiation Physics with an Atomic-Energy Commission Fellowship.

Dr. Linda Marie Hunter, 27, at the time she held a post Doctorate position in the Radiation Laboratory at the University of Notre Dame. She was the first woman to get a Ph.D. in Chemistry from Florida State.

These ladies yearn for space, but NASA says, "No!" [Because they are women!] Emily Kozakoff and Dr. Charlie (Marjorie) Haynes are among the rejected women applicants and many more who charge prejudice.[13]

These are a few outgrowths of the fact that men under all circumstances try and keep to the men the primary standing in the society, but they overlook completely the fact that this is more damaging than helpful. The Russians caught on earlier than the Americans. They had a female astronaut. Honorary President of the SWC--in Russia--is Valentina Tereshnova, the first woman space traveler, who orbited earth in 1963. The way the gifted women get their right place there is marvelous. This should give the Americans a lesson. Or are the Americans not able to design a spacesuit for females even thought the Russians could do it?

For the reason to compare the different countries with their action and handling of gifted women and women scientists I enclose a further manuscript,

---

[13] "Women Be Astronauts", Detroit Free Press, November 1967.

"Women, A Vast Underprivileged Class," by London Service Staff Writer, (Manuscript has been submitted).

The member of the Feminists accused the Labor Department of, "Trying to pull a very dirty trick on women." The Executive Order No. 11374 says, "There shall be no discrimination." The Labor Department is preparing now to amend it. "No discrimination" can not mean "That some discrimination is permissible." Should these guidelines pass, I think it would be a serious step backward for women in this country. By the provisions of guidelines women would not include in their benefits such things as pension plans and provisions, because an industry spokesman testified that if women were included in the pension plans it would be too costly. Why? This would not cost any more than the cost for men! If women hold the same positions, the same work and capacity and qualification and on the side of the women perhaps the same responsibilities towards her family. Why should the woman not get the full earnings of her work? Why should the industry, business or individual put "saved benefits" in their pocket and let women that provided the same work suffer? It would be slavery! And many business owners and managers would use these "slaves" [women] for their purpose--to get the same work done by the women for part of the normal pay for man. [14]

It should be considered very carefully what to do to avoid the use of the "bona fide" clause in a discrimination form, because it is so easy to use the "bona fide" limitation in the Title VII of the equal rights law of 1964, against

---

[14] "Labor Accused of Bias", Federal Times, 8-30-69.

the woman workers. Where is the line for disqualification of a certain job
for women?

Women eat and sleep with men and stay under the Constitution today
as--about where negroes were many, many decades ago--then according to
the President's Commission on the Status of Women the Supreme Court has
never accorded women the protection of the 14th Amendment. This is unfair
and shocking!

There are clouds of myths around us everywhere and we have to overcome
these. It is the idea that the women's place is in the home. Alright, one
woman needs to live by it, another does not. Who will dictate another person's life?

There is also an emotional resistance. I feel it, but cannot lay my
hands on it. A strange and mystic, psychological thing. For man it does
help his "ego" if there is someone of an inferior class. Let's keep it this
way--"That Woman!"

Women must be educated to know what is at stake and must be
included in the policies and all decisions. Our time has to solve such
emense problems. The biggest is "Peace on Earth". I do not know how it
will be done without the majority of human beings--the women!!!

"The high level government committee on the status of women has
practically ignored the issue of sex discrimination," says Representative
Martha W. Griffith. "The committee should be providing leadership in this
field, but I'm sorry to say, it has failed to do so."[15]

---

[15] "Sex Bias Law Ineffective", The Christian Science Monitor, 9-6-67.

The time in which we now live is too serious, and we women and men have to stay together to reach our goals of "Peace". Therefore, this is not a time to speak "frivolous" language and tear a woman down with threefold jokes and a really cultivated man would never do such a thing to a lady.

The following happened a couple of weeks ago. Mrs. Betty Friedan, who is President of the "National" Organization for Women, was invited to The Tiger Bay (all men) Club, in Miami, to give a speech. After Mr. Bergida, the host, got mad at Mrs. Friedan about her fee for the speech, he told a dirty joke, as Mrs. Fridan terms it. It referred to Mrs. Friedan's decision not to go to the "men's room". This happened before the whole club of all men! This was more than discrimination--why in the first place they invited her for this speech if not to create this situation? Where is their respect for women and the manners of men? What really do men think about women? I believe they don't know women at all. [16]

Not all women want to dominate their husbands or boy friends, and not all women want to be the head of the family even if they have to be for some logical reason. These thoughts leading the men are exaggerated from the mind of men who hate women and they in turn try to plant it in the minds of other men. The women do want to be equal if they qaulify for it. Most women love to be in the family under "his" wings and feel security, warmth and the sensation of life. She likes to snuggle into his body and let "him" take the leadership if he is able. Women love to get rosses--or even once in a while

[16]"Feminist, Male Club Clash Over Pay", Detroit Free Press, 3-19-70.

one rose--to assure them of tender understanding and romance. Women love to get doors held open for them and admiring glances that sweeps her off her feet and up to heaven. The women are hungry for it, and they get it so seldom. Do you not see that, you "majesty men"? We love lovesongs, poetry and being taken away to the dark jungle with vigor sense of blossom, but how many and how often do women get it? So many hearts are begging love, but are freezing in the dark night, in the desert of life. Why do you men not hear that? Why do you come and keep the last soul of a wife to retrieve her into the safety of your strong, warm arms and understanding instead of seeing only a second-class creature in her? A sex object for advertising and leasure hours in offices. Why do you not recognize the value of the woman as an equal human being?

We do not say all women are alike in qualifications, like men are not all alike in values. The women individual merit and potential should be the determining factor, but in spite of all, the women have to fight for equal standards between themselves and men. MEN AND WOMEN ARE EQUAL. The man himself has proved this to be true. For example in war times or other emergencies, women were badly needed in all occupations and did an equally good job to men's work, but after such time the women were kicked back because the men, ruling the earth, were back from their other duties. Until the laws and handling of women have not reached the right standings, the state laws and the "bona fide restriction" will not protect the women. They will rob the women of their jobs and earnings. If any individual woman desires a job, which is for another woman too much, it should not be denied her merely because most females could not qualify for it, and when a woman does her work well equal to a man in that position, she should get paid like a man, pension plans and retirement included.

Women try to pursuade the human race to change this situation immediately, but if this will not take place soon, nature will take care in a crude way and revenge, with which we all--men and women--would never be happy.

BIBLIOGRAPHY

Anderson, Jack, Legion of Angry Women, Detroit Free Press, November 1967.

Bamberger, Werner, Promotion Discrimination Alleged at State Hearing, New York Times, 4-22-69.

Carmody, Deirdre, Porley Studies Change Woman, New York Times, 11-26-67.

Emerson, Gloria, Vaste Male Conspiracy to Keep Women Inferiority, New York Times, 6-4-69.

Fogel, Helene, She Wins $885, And Makes History, Detroit Free Press, 8-25-68.

Frankel, Max, Johnson Sign Order to Protect Women in U.S. Jobs from Bias, New York Times, 10-14-67.

Friedan, Betty, Feminist, Male Club Clash Over Her Pay, Detroit Free Press, 3-19-70.

Glasek, Vera, No 14th Amendment for Women-Yet, Detroit News, 3-18-69.

Griffiths, Martha W., Sex-Bias Law Ineffective, Associated Press-Washington The Christian Science Monitor, 9-6-67.

Gurewitsch, Eleanor, Swiss Women Do Not Have the Vote, The Christian Science Monitor, Zurich, 7-18-69.

Halverson, Guy & Mouat, Lucia, Protesters Defend Women Power, The Christian Science Monitor, 2-5-69.

Hoffman, Von Nicholas, University Sex Bias, Detroit News, 3-2-69.

Jensen, Shirley, Plugs Hard for Women, Detroit News, 8-24-69.

Women A Vaste Underprivileged Class, Detroit Free Press, by London Express Service, 11-3-68.

May, Helen, Women's Group Opposes Rights Amendment, Detroit Free Press, 3-17-70.

Miller, Joy, National Maritime Union and Steamship Line-Contra Miss Dziob, Stewardess, The Christian Science Monitor, 10-10-67.

Miller, Joy, Protective Laws Are Under Fire, Detroit Free Press, 7-29-67.

Morris, Julia, They Resent Male Domination, Detroit Free Press, 5-4-69.

Nordin, D. Kenneth, Women Equal Rights, The Christian Science Monitor, 5-26-67.

Popa, A. Robert, Women Want Equality, But Not That Much, Detroit News, 11-27-68.

Popa, A. Robert, Two Union Women Wrangle Over Female Work Limit, The Detroit News, 1-17-69.

Bibliography - 2

Simachern, Harold, Women's Ordination Gets Grudging Lift, The Detroit News, 8-13-68.

Simachern, Harold (Staff Writers), Fraus Jailed, Men Fined, Bonn-West Germany, Detroit News, 10-25-67.

Simachern, Harold (Staff Writers), Woman Pilot Takes Job Fight to Court, Detroit News, 10-9-68.

Simachern, Harold (Staff Writers), Women Still Unequal Sex, But Swedes Offer Remedy, Detroit News, 3-20-69.

Simachern, Harold (Staff Writers), Women Pickets Demonstrate But Mrs. Nixon Denies Bias, Detroit News, 5-8-69.

Simachern, Harold (Staff Writers), Labor Accused of Bias, Federal Times, Washington 8-30-69.

Simachern, Harold (Staff Writers), Womens Salary Gains Held More Than Mens, New York Times, 8-4-68.

Simachern, Harold (Staff Writers), Men Resist Distaff Inroads at the Gambling Table, New York Times, 8-10-69.

Teltschm, Kathern, U.N. 111 to 0 Backs Rights of Women, (To End Discrimination) New York Times, 11-8-67.

Weigers, Mary, "New" Women Vetoes 'Chicks Up Front', Detroit News, 3-16-70.

Wiegers, Mary, Women's Lives - Neatly Labeled Roles, Detroit News, 3-17-70.

Wilson, Jean-Sprain, Lack of Nobility Hurts Women's Job Changes, Detroit Free Press, 3-19-70.

Wilson, Jean-Sprain, How Equal Are Rights of Michigan Women?, Detroit Free Press, 10-7-69.

AMERICAN WOMEN 1968
Citizens' Advisory Council
on the Status of Women

REPORT OF THE
TASK FORCE ON
FAMILY LAW
AND POLICY

CITIZENS' ADVISORY COUNCIL ON THE STATUS OF WOMEN
U.S. Department of Labor, Room 2131
Washington, D.C. 20210

Senator Maurine B. Neuberger, Chairman

Mrs. Ellen Boddy
Civic Leader

Mrs. Mary E. Callahan
Executive Board Member
International Union of Electrical,
  Radio, and Machine Workers
AFL-CIO

Mr. J. Curtis Counts
Vice President, Employe Relations
Douglas Aircraft Co., Inc.

Dr. Henry David, Executive Secretary
Division of Behavioral Sciences
National Academy of Sciences

Mrs. Elizabeth Wickenden Goldschmidt
Technical Consultant on Public Social
  Policy

Mrs. Anna Roosevelt Halsted
Civic Leader

Miss Dorothy Height
President
National Council of Negro Women

Mrs. Viola H. Hymes
Member, Minneapolis School Board
Former Chairman, Minnesota
  Governor's Commission on the
  Status of Women

Mr. Maurice Lazarus
Vice Chairman
Federated Department Stores

Dr. Richard A. Lester
Director of Graduate School and
  Associate Dean
Woodrow Wilson School

Miss Margaret Mealey
Executive Director
National Council of Catholic
  Women

Dr. Rosemary Park
Vice Chancellor
University of California

Miss Marguerite Rawalt
Attorney at Law
Former President, National
  Federation of Business and
  Professional Women's Clubs

Mr. Edward A. Robie
Vice President and Personnel
  Director
Equitable Life Assurance Society
  of the U.S.

Mrs. Mary Roebling
President and Chairman of the Board
Trenton Trust Company

Mr. William F. Schnitzler
Secretary-Treasurer, AFL-CIO

Dr. Anne Firor Scott
Associate Professor of History
Duke University

Dr. Caroline Ware
Consultant

Dr. Cynthia C. Wedel
Associate General Secretary
National Council of Churches

****

Staff

Mrs. Catherine East
Executive Secretary

Miss Mary Jane Christgau
Assistant to the Chairman

Mrs. Bertha H. Whittaker
Assistant to the Executive Secretary

Mrs. Betty T. Owen
Staff Assistant

Report of

the Task Force on . . .

FAMILY LAW AND POLICY

to the

CITIZENS' ADVISORY COUNCIL ON THE STATUS OF WOMEN

April 1968

TO OUR READERS:

This is the report of the Task Force on Family Law
and Policy, one of the four task forces charged by
the Citizens' Advisory Council on the Status of
Women early in 1967 with studying and making recommendations to the Council in specific areas. Members of the task forces were chosen for their special
competence in the subject area.

The Council considered recommendations of the Task
Force on Family Law and Policy at its meetings on
December 2-3, 1967, and April 26, 1968. The Council approved all of the recommendations except as
otherwise noted in the body of the report.

We are grateful to the task force for very constructive work and to the Justice Department for furnishing professional staff and other services.

The task force and the council are citizen groups;
therefore neither this report nor action on its
recommendations by the Council can be attributed
to any Federal agency.

                        Maurine B. Neuberger
                        Chairman
                        Citizens' Advisory Council
                          on the Status of Women

April 19, 1968

The Honorable Maurine B. Neuberger
Chairman, Citizens' Advisory Council
   on the Status of Women
Washington, D. C.   20210

Dear Senator Neuberger:

The Task Force on Family Law and Policy is pleased
to transmit to you the report of its findings and
recommendations.

We are grateful to Jacob L. Isaacs, Alvin L. Schorr
and Hyman Smollar, who met with the task force and
shared their expertise and professional experience
in the area of alimony and child support.

The task force is also grateful to the Women's
Bureau for furnishing information on various aspects
of family law, and particularly to Dominic Amadeo
for his study on domicile.

We hope this report will be useful to the State commissions on the status of women, and to other groups
and individuals concerned with family law and policy.

                    Sincerely,

                    Task Force on Family Law
                       and Policy

       (signed)   Marguerite Rawalt, Chairman
                  Joseph Goldstein
                  Hylan Lewis
                  Harriet F. Pilpel
                  Una Rita Quenstedt
                  Alice S. Rossi
                  Frank E.A. Sander
                  Howard Hilton Spellman
                  Robert S. Weiss

THE TASK FORCE ON FAMILY LAW AND POLICY

Miss Marguerite Rawalt
Attorney at Law
1801 - 16th Street, N.W.
Washington, D.C. 20009
Chairman of the Task Force
  and Member of the Council

Dr. Joseph Goldstein
Professor of Law
Yale University
New Haven, Connecticut 06520

Dr. Hylan Lewis
Professor of Sociology
Brooklyn College
Fellow, Metropolitan Applied
  Research Center
330 West 58th Street
New York, New York 10019

Mrs. Harriet F. Pilpel
Attorney at Law
Greenbaum, Woolf & Ernst
285 Madison Avenue
New York, New York 10017

Mrs. Una Rita Quenstedt
Domestic Relations Division
Office of the Corporation Counsel
451 Indiana Avenue, N.W.
Washington, D.C. 20001

Dr. Alice S. Rossi
Department of Social
  Relations
Johns Hopkins University
Baltimore, Maryland 21218

Dr. Frank E.A. Sander
Professor of Law
Harvard University
Cambridge, Massachusetts

Mr. Howard Hilton Spellman
Attorney and Counselor at Law
39 Broadway
New York, New York 10006

Dr. Robert S. Weiss
Lecturer in Sociology
Department of Psychiatry
Harvard Medical School
58 Fenwood Road
Boston, Massachusetts 02115

Miss Mary O. Eastwood
Attorney, Office of Legal
  Counsel
U.S. Department of Jusitce
Technical Assistant for the
  Task Force

CONTENTS

404

INTRODUCTION

The fundamental principle underlying the considerations of the Task Force on Family Law and Policy
is that men and women are entitled to equal rights
in regard to marriage and the family as well as in
all other aspects of American life. Although the
chief focus is on the rights, freedoms, and responsibilities of women, this report deals also with
those of men and of children, and in some instances
of government.

Included in this report are recommendations
and principles which are new to American law. Some
will no doubt be controversial. Others are not and
their implementation will involve simply removing
archaic discriminations which are holdovers from an
earlier day when women were regarded as economically-
dependent reproducers and there was little concern
for their human rights as persons.

This report does not purport to cover all
issues relating to family law and policy. Moreover, there is greater and sometimes disproportional
detail and specificity with respect to some aspects
covered than in others. On some subjects there are
firm recommendations; as to others the principles
or desired goals are simply stated. This "lack of
uniformity" in treating the various subjects is due
in part to the availability of information and
studies and to the special expertise which individual members brought to the task force.

I. MARRIAGE AS AN ECONOMIC PARTNERSHIP

In March, 1966, one third of married women living
with their husbands worked outside the home, contributing to the economic support of their families. 1/ A
much larger proportion of married women, of course, are
employed at some time during their married lives. On
the other hand, in many families the mother spends
almost all of her married life in homemaking and child
rearing.

State laws dealing with property rights as between
the spouses must be examined in light of the varied
family patterns in existence today; the law should operate fairly on both spouses, whether the work of the
wife is as homemaker or in a paid job or both.

There are two types of property systems in the
United States -- "common law" and community property.
In the 42 common law States and the District of Columbia, income and property acquired by each spouse
during marriage is owned separately by the spouse who
acquires it. In the remaining eight "community
property" States (Arizona, California, Idaho, Louisiana,
New Mexico, Nevada, Texas and Washington) income and
property acquired by each spouse during the marriage
is generally owned in common by husband and wife.

A. Management of Jointly Owned Property in Community
Property States

In community property States, even where the wife
works all or part of her married life as a housewife
and mother, rather than as a wage earner outside the
home, her contribution to the family is recognized
since she has an equal interest in the family income
and property. However, the Civil and Political Rights
Committee Report of the President's Commission on the
Status of Women pointed out that management control

1/ Working Wives -- Their Contribution to Family
Income, Women's Bureau, U.S. Department of
Labor, 1967.

of community property, acquired by either husband or wife, generally vests in the husband.

The income of a working wife as well as that of the husband becomes part of the community property and, under the traditional community property system is managed by the husband, with the wife having no say in how her income is to be spent.

Texas has recently eliminated this inequity to working wives by amending its community property laws to provide that "each spouse shall have sole management, control and disposition of that community property which he or she would have owned if a single person," and if community property subject to the management of one spouse is mixed or combined with that of the other spouse, it is subject to joint management unless the spouses agree otherwise. (Texas Rev. Civ. Stats., Art. 4621). This system of separate control of community property is similar to the system for management of matrimonial property adopted in Norway and Denmark.

B. Division of Property at Death of a Spouse in Common Law States

Unlike the traditional community property system which gives the husband power to manage his wife's income, the common law system of separate ownership allows each spouse to manage his own income and property. However, the principle of separate ownership of property by each spouse generally does not adequately recognize the contribution to the family made by a wife who works only in the home. In such case a wife does not have an opportunity to acquire earnings and property of her own.

The Report of the President's Commission on the Status of Women (American Women, page 47) directs the attention of State legislatures and other groups concerned with improving family law to the following statement:

"Marriage as a partnership in which each
spouse makes a different but equally important contribution is increasingly
recognized as a reality in this country
and is already reflected in the laws of
some other countries. During marriage,
each spouse should have a legally defined
substantial right in the earnings of the
other, in the real and personal property
acquired through those earnings, and in
their management. Such a right should
be legally recognized as surviving the
marriage in the event of its termination
by divorce, annulment, or death. Appropriate legislation should safeguard either
spouse and protect the surviving spouse
against improper alienation of property
by the other. Surviving children as well
as the surviving spouse should be protected
from disinheritance." (emphasis supplied)

Upon termination of marriage at the death of
a spouse, the property of both spouses could be divided according to a statutory formula. For example,
there could first be deducted from each spouse's
property, any of his or her debts. There could also
be deducted certain types of property -- the value
of property owned at the time of marriage, gifts
from third persons and inheritances, and any other
property which the spouses agreed to have deducted
by a marital property contract. The remainder,
after these deductions are made from each spouse's
property, could be added together and divided
equally between husband and wife. Similar formulae
have been adopted in Sweden and the Federal Republic
of Germany for equitable division of the spouses'
property upon termination of the marriage. The
task force believes that such a formula for property
division upon termination of marriage by death would
help to implement the above-quoted statement from

American Women and could be adapted to the separate property systems in the 42 common law States and the District of Columbia.

The foregoing discussion outlining a 50-50 formula for property division at the death of a spouse in common law States should not be confused with *inheriting* property from a spouse. If a State provided for such a property division upon the death of a spouse it would mean that the surviving spouse would own outright 50 percent of the marital property. After the division is made the inheritance laws would apply, but only to the deceased's 50 percent, of course.

C. Property Division Upon Divorce in Common Law States 1/

At the present time, the laws of some States (e.g., New York and New Jersey) do not authorize courts to divide property of the spouses upon divorce. Other States give the courts discretion to make a property division between the spouses. See, for example, Wisconsin Statutes Annotated, Sec. 247.26. 2/

1/ Under some circumstances the discussion in this section might also be relevant to cases of annulment and separate maintenance proceedings.

2/ However, the Wisconsin law does not apply equally to the spouses. In addition to providing for alimony for the *wife*, the court is authorized to "finally divide and distribute the estate, both real and personal, of the husband, and so much of the estate of the wife as has been derived from the husband, between the parties and divest and transfer the title of any thereof accordingly, after having given due regard to the legal and equitable rights of each party, the ability of the husband, the special estate of the wife, the character and situation of the parties and all the circumstances of the case; * * *."

The task force considered the question of whether the application of a statutory formula for dividing property of the spouses, such as described above (page 3) with respect to termination of marriage by death, would be desirable in cases of termination of marriage by divorce. For example, deductions of certain types of property (such as property owned by a spouse before marriage, gifts and inheritances) might be made from each spouse's property, the remainder added together and divided 50-50 between husband and wife. The laws of Germany and the Scandinavian countries provide for a system of property division upon divorce along these lines.

Some task force members believed that a fixed equal division of property upon divorce would not operate fairly in some cases, and that divorce courts should be given discretion to determine a different proportion for each spouse, based on consideration of such factors as the respective contributions (not limited to financial) each spouse made to the marriage, duration of the marriage, economic dependency and age of the spouses. On the other hand, with respect to property division at the death of a spouse, a fixed 50-50 formula would have some advantages. Unlike the case of death, a divorce proceeding is a two-party action with both spouses having an opportunity to show the respective contributions they have made to the marriage. Moreover, if a probate court had to consider and make a determination based on various factors in the marriage of a deceased person, it would delay the settling of estates.

D. Protection Against Disposition of Property to Defeat Spouse's Rights

If a legally defined right such as this equal division of the combined property of the spouses at the death of one spouse is given to each spouse, some legal control of disposing of property during the lifetime of the spouses would be necessary so

the husband (or wife) could not defeat the rights of
the other by selling or giving away all his property
while living. In order that restrictions on the
freedom to manage and dispose of one's property be
kept at a minimum, this legal control over disposing
of property could be limited to requiring the consent of the other spouse or of the court (1) to the
sale by the owner-spouse of the home, and (2) to
excessive gifts made from the kind of property which
would be combined and divided equally under the
above formula (i.e., this would not apply to gifts
from property owned before marriage or inherited
property).

E. Recommendations

In view of the foregoing problems under present
law, and some of the possible solutions adverted to,
as well as the need for further careful study of
these complex issues, the task force recommends that
the Council request some appropriate agency (such as
the American Law Institute, the American Bar Foundation or the Commissioners on Uniform State Laws) to
undertake a fundamental study of family property
interests. Pending the completion of such a study,
we recommend the following interim steps:

(1) The Council bring to the attention of State
Commissions on the Status of Women and other appropriate organizations in community property States the
recent Texas legislation described on page 3 of this
report.

(2) The Council bring to the attention of State
Commissions and other appropriate organizations the
desirability of empowering their courts to make discre-
tionary divisions of the property of the spouses in
matrimonial status actions (such as separation, divorce
or annulment), it being left to local determination what
types of property are to be subject to such division and
the criteria which are to govern.

II. FAMILY SUPPORT

A. The Question of Alimony

Some State laws permit divorce courts to grant alimony to the wife but not to the husband. More than one-third of the States permit alimony to be awarded to either spouse. The amount of the alimony, if any, awarded to a spouse is ultimately a question for determination by the court in light of the circumstances of the particular case, such as the economic needs of the spouses, duration of marriage and relative contributions to the marriage.

Consultations with experienced practitioners indicated that in the great majority of divorce cases, the amount of alimony and child support is determined by negotiation between the parties, with the court simply confirming the agreement. Often child support payments are camouflaged as alimony because of the impact of Federal income tax laws; taxes on alimony payments to an ex-wife are payable by her not the ex-husband, i.e., the total amount of alimony is subtracted from the ex-husband's income. The party which contributes more than one-half the support of a child may take the $600 dependency exemption for the child. In most cases the wife's income is less than that of the husband and she therefore pays taxes at a lower rate. As a result of lumping child support payments together with alimony and designating the total sum as alimony, the husband has a tax advantage and the wife may be able to negotiate a larger total payment. Because of these factors, although the laws on the books in some States favor women by permitting alimony for wives but not for husbands, this seeming inequity to men may be somewhat tempered by the law in practice.

If a system for division of property between husband and wife upon divorce such as outlined above were adopted, and if the family has sufficient property to divide, it would be possible to drastically reduce or eliminate alimony as continued support for an ex-spouse.

Whether, how much, and for how long alimony should be paid in a given case necessarily involves consideration of a variety of factors. The task force suggests the following as being among the criteria which are consistent with the economic partnership view of marriage.

1. In the traditional family, where the husband has been the chief source of income, the contribution of the wife to the economic partnership of marriage may have been great, as in a marriage of many years in which she was devoted to her family's well-being, or it may have been minimal, as in a marriage of brief duration. Alimony should recognize a contribution made by a spouse to the family's well-being which would otherwise be without recompense.

2. Alimony should provide recompense for loss of earning capacity suffered by either spouse because of the marriage. For example, where a wife interrupts her career because of homemaking and child rearing.

3. If either spouse upon divorce is in financial need, some continuing responsibility on the part of the other spouse to meet such need may be recognized for a period of time after the dissolution of a marriage. One of the

> determinants of the proper period may be
> the duration of the marriage; another
> might be whether the dependent spouse
> can or should establish some other means
> of support, and if so, the time likely
> to be required to do so.

Alimony payments are sometimes used as a means of redressing wrongs suffered by either spouse at the hands of the other. The spouse who is found at fault may be required to pay more or to accept less. This encourages actions for divorce or separation to explore the relative faults of the parties and is virtually certain to have undesirable consequences for any future relations between the couple. Alimony should not be used as a way of awarding compensation for damages.

B. Obligations for Support

1. **Spouse-spouse liability.** If marriage is viewed as a partnership between a man and a woman, then each spouse should be responsible for the other in accordance with need and ability to support. This general principle should be reflected in State laws dealing with support obligations for spouses. Some of the task force members believed that a husband should only be liable for the support of a wife who is unable to support herself due to physical handicap, acute stage of family responsibility or unemployability on other grounds. Other task force members believed that other factors may need to be considered in light of the general equities of the situation. A wife should be responsible for the support of her husband if he is unable to support himself and she is able to furnish such support.

The Council of State Governments list of "Basic
Duties of Support Imposed by State Law" 1/ indicates
that the following jurisdictions do not impose an
obligation on the wife to support a husband unable to
support himself: Alabama, Colorado, Florida, Georgia,
Hawaii, Indiana, Iowa, Kentucky, Maryland, Massachusetts, Mississippi, Missouri, Rhode Island, South
Carolina, Tennessee, Texas, Virginia, Washington,
and Wyoming. All jurisdictions make a husband liable
for the support of his wife, but without regard to
the ability of the wife to support herself.

2. Parent-child liability. As an extension of
the equal partnership principle of marriage, both
parents should be liable for the support of their
offspring, not merely the father. No distinction
should be made in the rights of legitimate and "illegitimate" children to parental support. The Council
of State Governments lists Colorado, Montana, Ohio,
and Rhode Island as requiring the father alone to
support legitimate children, and Alaska, Colorado,
Minnesota, Mississippi, Ohio and Rhode Island as
requiring the father alone to support illegitimate
children.

No distinction should be made in the rights of
boys and girls to parental support. The Council of
State Governments lists Arkansas, Idaho, Nevada,
North Dakota, Oklahoma, South Dakota and Utah as
giving girls a right to support up to age 18, and
boys to age 21.

The age at which a child's right to parental
support terminates varies from State to State; ages
18 or 21 are most often specified. The task force
believes that in general an adult should not be
legally liable for the support of other adults (other

1/   Information Manual on Reciprocal State Legisla-
      tion to Enforce the Support of Dependents (1964
      edition).

than spouses) and that the age at which legal liability for the support of a child terminates should be
no older than 21. However, with respect to a handicapped child over the legal age (or at any age),
further study is needed on the question of whether
the financial burden for providing proper treatment
and care for such a child should be on the parents
or whether the State should assume all or part of
this responsibility. Proper care for mentally or
physically defective children is often extremely
expensive and seriously affects the standard of
living of middle income, as well as poor, families.

Further study is also needed on the question
of whether children should be obligated by law to
support their parents. Requiring a person to support a parent can aggravate family hostilities and
can depress family income levels to the detriment
of his own children. A majority, but not all, of
the task force members favored repeal of laws requiring children to support their parents.

The Council of State Governments lists the
following jurisdictions as imposing legal obli-
gations on children to support their parents (see
note, page 10): Alabama, Alaska, California,
Connecticut, Delaware, District of Columbia, Guam,
Hawaii, Idaho, Illinois, Indiana, Iowa, Louisiana,
Maine, Maryland, Massachusetts, Michigan, Montana,
Nevada, New Hampshire, New Jersey, North Carolina,
North Dakota, Ohio, Oregon, Pennsylvania, Puerto
Rico, Rhode Island, South Dakota, Utah, Vermont,
Virginia, Virgin Islands, and West Virginia.

3. <u>Liability beyond the nuclear family</u>. The
basic unit in modern society consists of a man and
a woman and their dependent offspring. We are
increasingly an urban, mobile, technological society
and have witnessed over the past thirty years of

social security and welfare legislation a gradual
recognition of the changed nature of our family
system. Unemployment compensation, old age and
retirement benefits under social security are contemporary substitutes for responsibility that was
once defined as a "family matter," sometimes gen-
erously offered, sometimes with considerable reluctance and hardship.

Religious and moral values often guide individuals to assume voluntarily varying degrees of responsibility for parents, grandparents, siblings,
nieces and nephews. Where these obligations to
their kinsmen are voluntarily accepted by adults
without undue hardship to their primary obligations
to spouse and dependent children, these are admirable social acts of generosity. However, such support should be just this -- voluntary. If individuals are not themselves committed to a value that
extends obligations outside the primary family, or
if individuals cannot afford to lend financial support to kinsmen, they should not be subject to legal
pressure to assume such responsibilities.

The task force recommends that laws which require individuals to accept financial responsibility
for the support of siblings, grandparents, grandchildren or other extended kin be repealed.

The Council of State Governments list (note,
page 10) indicates the following jurisdictions as
imposing legal obligations to support extended kin:

Sibling support -- Alabama, Alaska, Colorado,
Illinois, Massachusetts, Montana, Nevada, Puerto
Rico, Utah, Virgin Islands, West Virginia.

Grandparents for grandchildren -- Alabama, Alaska, Colorado, Iowa, Louisiana, Montana, New Jersey, Rhode Island, Utah, Virgin Islands.

Grandchildren for grandparents -- Alabama, Alaska, Colorado, Iowa, Louisiana, New Jersey, Puerto Rico, Utah.

The task force recommends that the Council invite the attention of State Commissions on the Status of Women and other interested groups to the foregoing principles and recommendations with a view to reexamination and appropriate revision of laws pertaining to family support obligations.

C. Interstate Enforcement of Family Support Obligations

All of the States, the organized territories and the District of Columbia have enacted the Uniform Reciprocal Enforcement of Support Act or a similar law providing for both civil and criminal enforcement of support obligations across State lines.

Support obligations imposed by one State may be enforced against a parent in another State through reciprocal court proceedings in the two States. By far the greatest number of reciprocal actions involve cases where the mother and children reside in one State and the mother is seeking financial assistance for the children's support from the father who resides in another State. The parents may or may not be divorced.

The procedure is as follows: The mother may file a complaint in a court in the State where she resides. The county or city prosecuting attorney generally represents the complainant, at the request of the court. The complaint must state the name, and so far as known to the complainant-mother, the address and circumstances of the father and the children for whom support is sought. If the court finds that the complaint sets forth facts from which it may be determined that the respondent-father owes a duty of support and that the court of another State may obtain jurisdiction over the father, the court transmits copies of the complaint and other pertinent papers to the court of the father's State.

When the clerk of the latter responding court receives the documents, he dockets the case and notifies his county's (or city's) prosecuting attorney. The prosecuting attorney is required to use all means at his disposal to locate the respondent or his property.

If the responding court finds a duty of support, it may order the father to furnish support and subject his property to the support order.

The Uniform Act also provides for extradition of persons charged with the crime of failing to provide for the support of a dependent. In some States the law provides that civil proceedings such as described above must first be tried, or that it be shown that such civil proceedings would not be effective, before the Governor will turn over the respondent-father to the authorities in the mother's State.

The latter provision was added by 1958 amendments to the Uniform Act. The 1958 amendments also provided an additional civil procedure for cases in which the mother has previously obtained a support order, such as a child support order as part of a divorce decree. In such a case, she may simply register the

support order directly in the court of the State
where the father resides. The latter court may
confirm the support order and enforce it as if it
were an original order of that court. However,
more than half the States have not yet adopted
the 1958 amendments. The 1958 amendments also
provide that the Uniform Act may be used when the
parties are in the same State, but in different
counties.

Proceedings under State reciprocal enforcement of support laws do not always result in
child support payments. Some of the reasons
for lack of success under the laws are: (1) the
father cannot be located; (2) officials, particularly in the responding State where the obligor
resides, are not diligent in enforcing the law;
(3) the obligor-father simply does not have the
money to pay and perhaps has acquired a second
family.

1. Locating missing parents. The Council
of State Governments' Handbook of Administrative
Procedures under the Uniform Reciprocal Enforcement of Support Act includes an appendix listing
techniques and sources of information as to the
whereabouts of missing parents. To some extent,
certain Federal records may be used. For example,
regulations of the Secretary of Health, Education,
and Welfare permit disclosure of information from
Social Security records to local public welfare
officials about the whereabouts of parents who
have deserted their children. However, this applies only to cases where the children are eligible
for assistance under the aid to families with dependent children program.

District Directors of Internal Revenue are
permitted to advise whether or not a person has
filed an income tax return and, if so, the name

and address appearing on the return. (See 26
U.S.C. 6103(f)). Veterans' Administration regulations permit addresses of VA claimants to be
furnished only to police or court officials and
only in cases where there is an indictment against
the claimant or a warrant for his arrest. (38 CFR
1.518).

One of the requirements of State plans for
aid to families with dependent children is that
provision be made for prompt notice to law enforcement officials in cases where children have
been deserted or abandoned by a parent. (42 U.S.C.
602). The Department of Health, Education, and
Welfare requires State welfare departments to establish location services to assist in locating
persons liable for support in cases involving aid
to families with dependent children funds.

A New York law provides that the State Department of Social Welfare shall establish a
central registry of records for location of deserting parents of children who are recipients of
public assistance or likely to become in need of
assistance. The Department is authorized to obtain
information concerning the identity and whereabouts
of deserting parents from other agencies of the
State or political subdivisions (e.g., motor vehicle and tax records). Information is available
only to welfare officials and law enforcement
officials and agencies having jurisdiction in
support or abandonment proceedings. (McKinney's
Consol. Laws of N.Y., Soc. Wel. Law, sec. 372-a.)
Similar central location units have been set up
in a number of other States and some provide interstate assistance in locating deserting parents.

With respect to families receiving aid to dependent children funds, section 211 of the Social Security Amendments of 1967 (P.L. 90-248; 81 Stat. 821, 896) provides that the State agencies are to report to the Department of Health, Education, and Welfare names of missing parents who are not complying with a support order or against whom a petition for support has been filed. The names are then to be furnished to the Department of the Treasury which endeavors to ascertain the address of such parent from Internal Revenue Service files.

2. <u>Failure to enforce the law</u>. In some cases officials in the responding State simply do not follow through on reciprocal actions. This may be due to lack of appreciation of the importance of enforcing child support or a belief that efforts to enforce the parent's child support obligations would not result in payments and would be a waste of time. The Council of State Governments suggests that a district attorney in a State where an action is initiated who is not able to ascertain the status of a case in a court of the responding State should write to the "State information agent" of the responding State for assistance. The agency designated under the State reciprocal laws is usually either the State Welfare Department or the Attorney General's Office.

For a number of years, bills have been introduced in Congress to provide for enforcement of support orders in Federal courts and to make it a crime to move in interstate commerce to avoid compliance with support orders. See for example, H.R. 11633, 90th Cong., 1st Sess. (1967), a proposed "Federal Family Support Act." That bill would permit an obligee (usually the mother) to register her support order in a State or Federal court which has

jurisdiction over the obligor (usually the father).
The court could then bring contempt proceedings
against the obligor in the same manner as if the
original support order were its own order.   In
addition, each Federal district court would have
original jurisdiction, concurrent with the State
courts, of civil actions brought by a citizen of
another State to order a citizen of the State in
which the court is located to make support payments.   However, the complainant would have to show
that she had first exhausted remedies available in
the State courts.   The bill would also provide a
criminal penalty of a fine of $2500 or imprisonment
for three years or both for moving in interstate or
foreign commerce from a State in which proceedings
had been begun under the "Federal Family Support
Act."

Whether or not such legislation would benefit
mothers in obtaining financial assistance from
fathers for the support of their children would
depend in part on: (a) the extent to which procedures under the Uniform Reciprocal Enforcement
of Support Act fail to result in adequate support
payments for children; (b) the extent to which
lack of diligence on the part of State and local
officials is responsible for such failure; and
(c) whether Federal officials (U.S. attorneys,
U.S. marshals and F.B.I.) would likely be more
diligent in enforcing child support obligations.

D.   Inability to Pay

The mother more often has custody of the children by court order or by the fact of desertion of
the family by the father.   This means the mother
not only has the responsibility for the care and
upbringing of the children, but the entire burden
of their financial support as well.   When she
faces the added obstacle of sex discrimination

424

(and in the case of nonwhite mothers, racial discrimination) in employment and in job training, she may well find herself one of the 42% of families headed by women with annual incomes of less than $3000.

But where the father simply does not have the means to provide support, enforcement of support laws is no solution to the problem. A lower-income father may find himself in jail for being delinquent in making child support payments. This does not help the mother or the children and gives an otherwise law-abiding father a criminal record. Some public assistance agencies require an applicant for Aid to Families with Dependent Children to declare her willingness to file criminal non-support charges against the father. This is a degrading experience for both mother and father and creates further hostilities and bitterness between them, often to the detriment of the children.

The task force recommends the following:

1. That criminal enforcement of support should not be resorted to until after exhaustion of civil remedies. (The Uniform Reciprocal Enforcement of Support Act contains a provision to this effect.)

2. Public assistance agencies should not require that the granting of an application for AFDC assistance be conditioned upon willingness on the part of a parent to file a criminal non-support charge.

3. Such agencies should attempt wherever possible to negotiate support agreements rather than resort to court action.

4. The responsibility for enforcing the obligations of a spouse for child support should be the public assistance agency's or the appropriate law enforcement officer's, rather than the other spouse's.

In particular, a woman should not be required to appear in court as complainant against the father of her children should the latter fail to satisfy a court order to reimburse a public assistance agency. This task should be assumed by the agency.

The responsibility of child support should be shared by the parents. The amount of child support required of the parent who does not have custody should reflect this, as well as the capacity to furnish support, and the earnings and financial situation of the spouses. The level of child support and alimony together should take into consideration the principle that it is desirable for both husband and wife to maintain a reasonable standard of living. The level should also be such that it would enable both the parent having custody and the parent paying child support to remarry.

Where the income level of both families would be reduced below subsistence level, it should be supplemented by the government.

The task force supports the current study of the various possible methods of family income maintenance. The need for some system of insuring a minimum family income level, whether through the social security system, negative income tax or other legal machinery, is particularly acute in cases of broken families.

The task force recommends that the Council bring the foregoing principles and recommendations to the attention of the State Commissions on the Status of Women, State agencies administering Aid to Families with Dependent Children, appropriate law enforcement officials and other interested persons and groups.

III.

PROTECTION OF THE RIGHTS OF CHILDREN

A. Effect of Circumstances of Parents

The fact that a child's parents are not married to each other should not operate to deprive the child of rights accorded to "legitimate children." With respect to the right to inherit, the right to parental support and all other rights, the law should make no distinction among children in terms of the marital status of their parents.

Similarly, if a child is conceived by artificial insemination, this should not affect his legal rights in relation to his mother and her husband where the husband has consented.

B. Limitations by Reason of Age

The task force has suggested no older than 21 as the age at which a child's legal right to parental support should terminate. The support age is an age at which a right is cut off (i.e., the right to sue for parental support). Other age specifications in State laws are limitations on children. For example, the age when one can vote, enter into a contract, marry without parental consent, undertake certain employment, and obtain medical care without parental consent. In view of the downward trend in the age boys and girls mature, the task force recommends that all disabilities of minority be removed at least by

age 18. 1/ Further study should be made to determine in what areas the disabilities should be removed by an earlier age. There should be no distinction between girls and boys in the age at which
a disability is removed.

C. Child Custody and Visitation

At the dissolution of a marriage the custody
of the children should be awarded in accordance
with their best interests. This is the general
rule today. However, in some States, the mother
is automatically given preference in custody of
children of tender age. The task force believes
that there should be no automatic preference of
a parent on the basis of sex and that neither
the mother nor the father should have a superior
right to custody.

In today's mobile society, one of the most
difficult problems of family law is the removal
of children beyond the jurisdiction of the court
which determined custody and visitation rights,
defeating the interest of the other parent. A
committee of the National Conference of Commissioners on Uniform State Laws is currently working on a proposed "Uniform Child Custody Jurisdiction Act." For this reason, the task force
deferred consideration of this subject.

1/   The British Government recently announced plans
      to introduce legislation to lower Britain's
      legal age of majority from 21 years to 18,
      based on a study and recommendation of a par-
      liamentary committee, which gave as reasons
      for the recommendation, "better education of
      the young, their greater affluence and sophis-
      tication, and earlier physical maturity." (N.Y.
      Times, April 11, 1968, p. 47). The Government
      is giving further study to a recommendation
      that the minimum voting age be changed from 21
      to 20.

D. Legal Representation for Children in Domestic
    Relations Cases

Recent decisions of the United States Supreme
Court recognize the importance of the right of defendants in criminal proceedings to representation
by counsel. The Supreme Court has also held that
a child has a right to be represented by counsel,
and appointed counsel if he is unable to employ an
attorney, in a case where a court is empowered to
commit the child to an institution for delinquents.
In re Gualt, 387 U.S. 1, (1967). The importance of
legal representation for the poor in civil as well
as criminal matters is increasingly recognized in
our national policy as part of human rights.

Important decisions affecting the lives of
the children are made in connection with divorce
and separation proceedings, such as property
settlements, custody and visitation arrangements
and child support. Agreements and concessions as
between husband and wife may not always be in the
best interests of the children. In Wisconsin, the
practice is to appoint an attorney or guardian ad
litem for the children to represent their rights
as a third party in the case, where the circumstances of the case indicate the need. 1/

1/   The Wisconsin practice is recognized in court
     decisions but there is no specific legislation
     requiring appointment of attorneys for child-
     ren. See Hansen, "Divorce in Wisconsin," 38
     Wis. Bar Bull. 20 (1965); Children in the
     Courts, The Question of Representation (edit.
     by George C. Newman, Institute of Continuing
     Legal Education, Ann Arbor, Mich., 1967).

Children may be disadvantaged in a legal battle
where others concerned are represented by counsel.
The task force believes that some means should be
provided for protecting the interests of children
in domestic relations cases.

E. Inheritance Rights

The report of the President's Commission on
the Status of Women states that "surviving children as well as the surviving spouse should be protected from disinheritance." American Women, page
47. This might be implemented by a statutory
right of children to inherit a minimum proportion
of a parent's estate. In the case of small estates,
a minimum dollar amount could be specified in order
to protect the rights of children under a certain
age to continued support. Thus, only amounts above
the minimum could be willed to other persons. (It
may be noted that in some States provision is made
for payment of allowances for child support from a
decedent-parent's estate in certain circumstances.
See e.g., Florida Stats. Annot., sec. 733.20(j)).

The task force recommends that the foregoing
principles relating to protecting rights of children be brought to the attention of the State commissions on the status of women and other appropriate
groups. 1/

1/ Adopted by the Citizens' Advisory Council on
the Status of Women, but with an objection
by Anne Draper, AFL-CIO, as to a uniform age
for removing legal disabilities where child
labor laws are involved.

IV

PERSONAL RIGHTS RELATING TO PREGNANCY

A. Laws Penalizing Abortion

1. Problem definition and context.

The world's population explosion is one of mankind's most crucial problems.

It took from the beginning of man to 1830 to produce the first billion people on earth. It took only 100 years (1830-1930) to produce the second billion; the third billion took only 30 years, from 1930 to 1960; and it is now estimated by demographers that it will take only 15 years, from 1960 to 1975, to reach a world population of 4 billion. Some demographers estimate that even if all people had only the number of children they wanted, the population growth rate would be in excess of the needs or the capability of economic resources to sustain life in an increasingly industrialized urban world. 1/ From this perspective, long range population policy becomes a critical need in all countries in the world, yet few have done anything toward developing such a national population policy.

We must face the problem of how to stabilize the world population growth rate. This necessarily involves the question of what women do with their lives. Motherhood should not be the exclusive goal of women, for this encourages the view that the more children, the better the mother, as well as the view that no marriage is complete without a child. Praise and social approval for women with large numbers of children are no longer functionally appropriate to

---

1/ Kingsley Davis, "Population Policy: Will Current Programs Succeed?", Science, Nov. 10, 1967, Vol. 158, No. 3602.

an urban crowded society. This applies to economically well-to-do women as well as to poor women, to
women in the United States as well as to Latin
American and Asian women, to white women as well
as to black women.

Abortion as an alternative to other contraceptive methods is now primarily the pattern in Catholic
countries in which chemical and mechanical contraceptive devices have not been available, and in underdeveloped countries which have not yet had widespread
exposure to the ideas of birth control. In France,
the annual number of abortions equals the number of
live births. In Latin American countries, there is
an average of one abortion for every two live births.
In some countries, like Uruguay, the ratio is as high
as three abortions for every live birth. Recent support for family planning has only begun to affect
this high rate of abortion, and for many years to
come, will serve only a minimal role in stemming the
fantastic population growth of the South American
continent.

The majority of the women who have been helped
with contraceptive advice and devices in Asian
countries are women who have already borne five or
more children, and hence already have contributed
dangerously to the growth rate of their countries.

While it is extremely difficult to assess the
incidence of illegal abortions in the United States,
estimates range from 250,000 to over a million
annually. The vast majority of these cases are
married women who have attained the number of children they wish or can afford to care for.

The development of more efficient contraceptives may gradually reduce the incidence of unwanted pregnancies, but we are a long way from
this situation, for several reasons.

1. Not all women can use chemical or mechanical contraceptives for a variety of physical and medical reasons.

2. Not all women have access to contraceptive information and devices.

3. Even the pill, the most efficient contraceptive known to date, has a one percent failure rate. There are 25 million women in the United States between the ages of 15 and 44; only about 3 million of these women want to conceive in any given year, leaving 22 million women exposed to the risk of an unwanted pregnancy. Even if all these women could use the pill the failure rate of one percent could still yield as many as 220,000 pregnancies that were not wanted by the women. Research underway now toward the development of "morning after" pills is still a long way from realization.

The central ideology of the family planning movement over the past half-century has been the human right of a woman to determine the number of children she will have. This is also an important foundation for the ability of women to plan their lives to include active and meaningful participation in the world outside the family. In the United States, the family planning ideology has gained widespread acceptance, and most people would state as a corollary of this principle of human rights that every child should be born into a loving environment, a wanted child eagerly awaited by its parents. This is the most fundamental, best "headstart" a child can have, which no ameliorative headstart program, no adoption system for unwed mothers, no community mental health center, can begin to match. We must take the next step to the realization that no woman should be forced to be the unwilling parent of an unwanted child. The task force believes that it is from this perspective that any recommendation for abortion law reform should be viewed.

2. State law reform.

Forty-two States prohibit the performance of an abortion unless it is necessary to save the life of the pregnant woman (or, in the case of Connecticut, the life of the woman or the unborn child). In the remaining eight States (Alabama, California, Colorado, Maryland, Mississippi, New Mexico, North Carolina and Oregon) and the District of Columbia, abortions are permitted in certain other circumstances in addition to cases where abortion is necessary to save the woman's life. For example, Mississippi permits abortions where the pregnancy is the result of rape; California permits abortions where the physical or mental health of the woman is endangered, or in cases of statutory rape of a girl under 15 or where pregnancy is the result of forcible rape or incest. Colorado and North Carolina have recently enacted laws patterned after the American Law Institute's Model Penal Code, which would permit abortions in the following circumstances: continuance of the pregnancy would gravely impair the physical or mental health of the woman; the child would be born with grave physical or mental defect; the pregnancy resulted from rape, incest or other felonious intercourse, including illicit intercourse with a girl below the age of 16.

Bills to make abortion laws less restrictive were introduced in 30 States and were enacted in three (Calif., Colo., N.C.) in 1967. Mississippi amended its law in 1966. In 1968, Maryland amended its law to permit termination of pregnancies by licensed physicians in accredited hospitals, upon

434

written authorization of a hospital abortion review
authority, in situations where (1) continuation of
the pregnancy is likely to result in the death of
the mother, (2) continuation of the pregnancy would
gravely impair the physical or mental health of the
mother, (3) there is a substantial risk of birth of
a child with grave and permanent physical deformity
or mental retardation, and (4) the pregnancy resulted
from rape. Under the new Maryland law, a licensed
physician who performs an abortion in an accredited
hospital is not subject to criminal penalty, but if
he performs an abortion in violation of the new law,
his license may be revoked or suspended under the
same procedures for revocation or suspension of
licenses provided for unprofessional or dishonor-
able conduct. (H.B. 88, approved May 7, 1968).

Even if all States enacted the provisions of
the Model Penal Code, it is estimated that only
about 15% of the illegal abortions would ·fall
within the permitted classes of abortions and the
remaining 85% of abortions (170,000 to 850,000
per year) would continue to be subject to criminal
sanctions under State abortion laws.

The Task Force on Administration of Justice
of the President's Commission on Law Enforcement
and Administration of Justice stated in its report (The Courts, page 105):

>"Abortion laws are another instance
>in which the criminal law, by its fail-
>ure to define prohibited conduct care-
>fully, has created high costs for
>society and has placed obstacles in the
>path of effective enforcement. The de-
>mand for abortions, both by married and
>unmarried women, is widespread. It is

often produced by motives and inclinations that manifest no serious dangerousness or deviation from the normal on the part of the people who seek it. These factors produce the spectacle of pervasive violations but few prosecutions."

That task force concluded that "the time is overdue for realistic reexamination of the abortion laws."

From the experience of other countries it seems clear that what the law permits or does not permit in this area has little effect upon the incidence of abortion. When most abortions are illegal, women either resort to devious, exaggerated claims to obtain a legal abortion, or seek illegal abortions in secret and, for poor women especially, in medically unsafe conditions, or worst of all try to induce the abortion themselves. When abortions are legal, the incidence is about the same, the only difference being the greater health precautions followed in a hospital setting. Criminal abortion laws are generally not enforced and are indeed unenforceable, and when this is the case, it is wise "for the law to withdraw rather than have the majesty of the law brought into disrespect by open disobedience and unpunished defiance." (Robert Drinan, Dean of Boston College Law School, Washington Conference on Abortion, 1967).

Revision of State laws along the lines of the American Law Institute proposal would continue criminal penalties for some abortions while sanctioning others. The repeal of laws penalizing abortion may be more acceptable than the A.L.I. proposal to those who believe that all abortions are doctrinally immoral. As Dean Drinan stated:

436

> "A system of permitting abortion on request
> has the undeniable virtue of neutralizing
> the law, so that, while the law does not
> forbid abortion, it does not on the other
> hand sanction it, even on a presumably
> restricted basis."

It may be noted that there is very little difference
between Catholics and Protestants on attitudes toward
abortion law reform and there is increasing support
for liberalizing abortion laws. 1/

Proposals which permit abortions under certain
circumstances while penalizing all others deny the
right of a woman to control her own reproductive
life in light of her own circumstances, intelligence,
and conscience. Although governmental agencies and
the medical profession may offer service and counsel,
they should not exercise the power of decision over
the woman's personal right to limit the number of
children she will have, and her right to decide
whether to terminate a particular pregnancy she does
not wish to carry to term.

Convinced that the right of a woman to determine her own reproductive life is a basic human
right, the task force recommends that laws penalizing abortion be repealed and urges the Council
to encourage the State Commissions on the Status
of Women to assume responsibility for educating

1/   Alice S. Rossi, "Abortion Laws and Their Vic-
      tims," Trans-action, Sept. - Oct., 1966;
      Association for the Study of Abortion, 1967
      survey in New York State.

the public on this issue and in getting State legislatures to repeal criminal abortion laws. 1/

The repeal of criminal abortion laws would mean
that abortion would be treated in the same way as
other medical procedures. It would mean that abortions could be performed by physicians without penalty and it would virtually eliminate abortions by
unauthorized practitioners.

B. Federal Restrictions on Access to Birth Control
    Information and Devices

Section 1461 of Title 18, United States Code,
makes the mailing of obscene or crime-inciting
matter a Federal crime. Included in the prohibition are the mailing of articles and advertisements
of articles for preventing conception or producing
abortion. Section 1462 of Title 18 prohibits the
importation or transportation in interstate or
foreign commerce of such articles. Section 305(a)
of the Tariff Act of 1930, 19 U.S.C. 1305(a) prohibits the importation of any article for the pre-
vention of conception or for causing unlawful
abortion. These provisions are derived from the
Comstock Act, enacted by Congress in 1873.

1/ The Citizens' Advisory Council on the Status
    of Women adopted this recommendation in the
    following form:

    The Council recommends that laws making
    abortion a criminal offense be repealed
    and urges State commissions on the status
    of women to assume responsibility for edu-
    cating the public on this issue.

    Margaret Mealey, National Council of Catholic
    Women, and Mary E. Callahan, International Union
    of Electrical, Radio, and Machine Workers, dis-
    sented. Anne Draper, AFL-CIO, abstained. Miss
    Mealey's statement appears on page 60 .

The courts have interpreted these provisions as applying only where the Government can establish that the contraceptives are to be used for an unlawful purpose. In Youngs Rubber Corporation v. Lee, 45 F.2d 103, 108 (C.A. 2, 1930), the court stated that these laws are not violated unless there is shown "an intent on the part of the sender that the article mailed or shipped by common carrier be used for illegal contraception or abortion or for indecent or immoral purposes." In a 1936 case, United States v. One Package, 86 F.2d 737, 739 (C.A. 2), the court stated that the intent of the law "was not to prevent the importation, sale, or carriage by mail of things which might intelligently be employed by conscientious and competent physicians for the purpose of saving life or promoting the well being of their patients." See also, Consumers Union of the United States v. Walker, 145 F.2d 33 (C.A. D.C. 1944); United States v. Nicholas, 97 F.2d 510 (C.A. 2, 1938); Bours v. United States, 229 Fed. 960 (C.A. 7, 1915). In the Bours case, the court stated that a physician may lawfully use the mails to say that if an examination of a pregnant girl shows the necessity of an operation to save life he will operate, if this is his real position.

In 1965, the United States Supreme Court held that a Connecticut statute which prohibited the use of contraceptives was unconstitutional because it invaded the right to marital privacy. Griswold v. Connecticut, 381 U.S. 479.

Legislation has been proposed which would amend the above Federal statutes by deleting the words pertaining to preventing conception. See, for example, H.R. 7461, (amending Title 18) and H.R. 1259 (amending the Tariff Act of 1930), 90th Cong., 1st Sess. (1967). Under these proposals the prohibitions relating to articles for producing unlawful abortions would be retained.

The task force urges the Council to support the
enactment of this proposed legislation.

V. DIVORCE GROUNDS

A 1965 report of the United Nations on the dissolution of marriage 1/ illustrates the wide variation among the nations of the world on the availability of divorce. There is no divorce in the usual
sense in Argentina, Chile, Italy, San Marino, St.
Lucia (U.K.) and Spain. On the other hand, divorce
may be obtained by mutual consent of the spouses in
Belgium, Burma, Ceylon, Denmark, India, Japan, Lux-
embourg, Mexico, Pakistan, Thailand, and Yugoslavia. 2/
The USSR reported that grounds for divorce are not
enumerated in Soviet law. A marriage may be dissolved
"when the court, having examined all the relevant circumstances, concludes that the application for dissolution of the marriage has been made for carefully considered reasons and that family relations cannot be
restored." 3/

1/   "Dissolution of Marriage, Annulment of Marriage
      and Judicial Separation" United Nations E/CN.6/
      415/Add.2, Table I (Feb., 1965).

2/   Applies in Ceylon only for those under Kandyan
      and Muslim law; applies in India to marriages
      registered under the Special Marriage Act of
      1954.

3/   UN Report, Table I, note 5. The Report of the
      California Governor's Commission on the Family
      recommended elimination of specific grounds
      for divorce in that State and suggested that
      the standard for a decree of divorce be whether
      the particular marriage relationship has so far
      broken down that there remains no reasonable
      likelihood that the marriage can be saved.
      Commission Report, Dec., 1966, page 27.

- 34 -

The UN report also shows that in Ceylon
(Kandyan Law), India (Muslims), Iran, Iraq, Pakistan (Muslims), Aden (U.K.), and the British Sol-
omon Islands Protectorate, a husband may divorce
his wife by pronouncing "talak." Desertion by
the wife of the conjugal home for one night without a legitimate reason is grounds for divorce in
Cambodia, as is infliction of blows or wounds,
cruelty, or gross insults by the second wife toward
the first wife. In Burma a husband may obtain a
divorce if the wife is "like a master or an enemy."

There is also variation on the grounds for
divorce among the States of the United States.
The most common grounds for divorce under the
laws of the several States are as follows (based
on a 1967 tabulation by the Women's Bureau, U.S.
Department of Labor, see Appendix C):

> adultery -- 50 States and D.C.
> desertion -- 47 States and D.C.
> cruelty -- 45 States
> felony conviction or imprisonment --
>   45 States and D.C.
> alcoholism -- 41 States
> impotency -- 32 States
> nonsupport -- 30 States
> insanity -- 29 States
> separation or absence -- 25 States
>   and D.C.

Other grounds include pregnancy at marriage (13
States), drug addiction (12 States) and incompatibility (4 States).

The task force believes that there are several
principles which should guide revision of State
divorce laws:

1. Where it is contemplated that a marriage is to be broken, there should be a sufficient time lapse before a divorce is granted, regardless of the cause of the break-up, to permit the respective parties to reconsider, seek counseling if they wish, and perhaps change their minds.

2. Marriage is basically a private relationship which should not be manipulated by government, absent an overriding public interest.

3. The concept that there must be a guilty party to any divorce is unrealistic and unnecessarily creates hostility between the parties, which is often detrimental to their children.

In view of these principles the task force suggests, without making specific suggestions as to other, traditional grounds for divorce, that the bases for divorce should include the following: 1/

1. voluntarily living apart for one year;

2. where one party deserts, but the other party wishes to continue the marriage, the deserted party may obtain a divorce after a period of six months; the deserting party after 18 months. (Recognition in the law of a right of the deserting, as well as the deserted, party to obtain a divorce would make desertion a non-fault basis for divorce.)

1/ It should be noted that a divorce itself affects only the parties' marital status and not their support obligations.

Under this proposal, the time lapse required would enable the parties to reconsider and decide to stay married if they wished. The only fact which would need to be established for divorce would be the period of time of separation. There would be no requirement in the law that fault be established, and no requirement that the personal difficulties between the parties be laid before the court.

The availability of these grounds for divorce would have the virtue of not requiring that a marriage be opened up to public exposure. 1/ The United States Supreme Court has recognized marital privacy as a right entitled to constitutional protection from governmental interference. In striking down the Connecticut prohibition against the use of contraceptives, the Court stated:

> "Would we allow the police to search ·the sacred precincts of marital bedrooms for tell-tale signs of the use of contraceptives? The very idea is repulsive to the notions of privacy surrounding the marriage relationship.
> "We deal with a right of privacy older than the Bill of Rights -- older than our political parties, older than our school system. Marriage is a coming together for better or for worse, hopefully enduring and intimate to the degree of being sacred. It is an association that promotes a way of life, not causes; a harmony in living, not political faiths; a bilateral loyalty, not commercial or social projects. Yet it is an association for as noble a purpose as any involved in our prior decisions." Griswold v. Connecticut, 381 U.S. 479, 485-86 (1965).

1/   Similar considerations respecting invasions of privacy would apply as to separation proceedings.

If the grounds for divorce which require a showing of fault and assume a "guilty" party were eliminated, the doctrines of condonation 1/ and recrimination 2/ would become obsolete.

North Carolina, Ohio and District of Columbia laws presently permit a divorce for voluntary separation for one year. Hawaii provides a period of 6 months for desertion. Thus, the only new feature in the above proposal is permitting the deserting party to obtain a divorce.

The task force recommends that the Council bring the foregoing principles and suggestions to the attention of State Commissions on the Status of Women and other appropriate groups, particularly those which may be currently working on drafting a uniform divorce law.

VI. DENIAL OF RIGHTS OF MARRIED WOMEN BY OPERATION OF DOMICILIARY RULES

A person's domicile or legal residence can determine in which State he may vote, where he may run for public office, where he may serve on juries, where he is liable for taxes, and where his estate will be administered. The Civil and Political Rights Committee of the President's Commission on the Status of Women stated that the "traditional rule that the domicile of a married woman automatically follows that of her

---

1/ A spouse who has forgiven the other spouse's wrongdoing is precluded from obtaining a divorce on that basis.

2/ Countercharge by defendant in divorce action of wrongdoing by plaintiff as a defense to the divorce.

444

husband is inconsistent with the partnership principle of marriage and contrary to the universal
trend toward legal equality of men and women." In
its 1963 report, the Commission approved the committee's recommendation that "the law governing
domicile for purposes such as voting, holding public office, jury service, taxation, and probate
should be the same for married women as it is for
married men." American Women, page 47. The Commission also approved the Committee's recommendation for further study of "the effect of according
married women the same right as married men to
establish a separate domicile on marital status,
rights, and obligations, on alimony and support,
on custody and visitation of children." American
Women, page 48.

The Women's Bureau of the U.S. Department of
Labor has recently completed a comprehensive study
on State laws governing domicile of married women.
That study shows that in only five States (Alaska,
Arkansas, Delaware, Hawaii, and Wisconsin) a married
woman has the same right as a married man to have
her own domicile for all purposes without regard to
the domicile of her spouse. A married woman living
with her husband has the right, as does a married
man, to her own domicile for purposes of holding
public office in eight States (including the five
above), for jury duty, in seven States, probate in
eight, taxation in nine, and voting in 18. See
Appendix A.

The study revealed no problems in giving married women equal rights to establish domicile.
With respect to children, the traditional rule
that the domicile of the child also follows that
of the father, would need to be altered in the
case where the child's parents have different
legal domiciles, though living together. The
task force suggests that the child's domicile should
be in such case the place of the family residence.
(Where the parents are living apart, and the child
lives with the mother, his domicile is generally
that of the mother.)

The only other issue raised by the Women's
Bureau study is the effect of giving wives equal
rights to establish domicile on the common rule
that the unjustifiable failure or refusal to
accompany or follow the husband to a new domicile
amounts to desertion or abandonment, which may
constitute grounds for divorce for the husband.
This limitation on the availability of divorce
for husbands on the ground of "constructive desertion" by the wife's failure to follow does
not appear to be sufficiently important to justify discriminatory domiciliary limitations on
married women.

Accordingly, the task force recommends that
States which do not provide for equal rights for
married women and men to establish their own
domicile revise their laws. Particular attention
is invited to the laws of the five States (and
especially those of Arkansas) which the Women's
Bureau study indicates give married women the
same rights as married men with respect to domicile. These statutes are set forth in Appendix
A.

WOMEN AS PEOPLE, MOTHERS AND WIVES

Several recent studies raise serious questions
about traditional assumptions that a woman is happi-
est, most fulfilled, and makes the greatest contribution to society if she marries, has children, and
stays home to rear them, abdicating responsibility
for their economic support, and her own support, to
another person.

An analysis of French and Sherwood suggests
that individual self-identity is affected primarily
by what people do, and accordingly people change
with time in response to change in their activities.
Simply put, these psychologists suggest that people
become what they do. A married woman has three
primary family roles, as wife, mother and housekeeper. But she spends a great deal more time as
a housekeeper than she does as either a wife or a
mother. A married woman may have a doctorate

degree, a loving husband, and two bright energetic
children, but her major daytime activities revolve
about essentially a particular type of blue collar
work -- cleaning, cooking, laundering, mending,
etc. Bright and intellectually alert young American women undergo a subtle change during the two
decades of early and middle adulthood. By forty-
five years of age, many have lost the intellectual
alertness they showed at 25, for they have been
affected by the activities that filled those years.
They have "become" blue collar workers at some
fundamental level of self identification. There
is nothing inherently wrong or inferior with domestic labor if it is appropriate to the interest and
ability level of the individuals who engage in it.
It is a personal frustration, and a societal loss
to have a very large proportion of educated women
undergo such a depression from the potential they
showed in late adolescence. There may well be a
nostalgia for some past former self behind the
apologetic note educated homemakers show when they
identify themselves as "just a housewife."

Society has a legitimate and important interest in the proper rearing of future generations.
It has for too long been assumed, however, that
the necessary requirement to achieve this is the
confinement of women to the home in full time
responsibility for child rearing. In fact, recent
studies have shown that a full-time homemaker
spends relatively little time in interaction with
her children -- less than two hours per day including the time she spends with them while she attends
to other household duties -- and employed women
spend only 42 minutes less time with their children
than the full-time homemakers. 1/ If children spend

1/   Data from a study by the Survey Research Center
     at the University of Michigan, as summarized by
     Daryl and Sandra Bem in "Training the Women to
     Know Her Place", a paper presented at the 1967
     Delaware Governor's Conference on the Status of
     Women.

large portions of their days by themselves and with
their age peers, at school and in their neighborhood,
and married women spend the bulk of their days in
home maintenance rather than maternal duties, then
it is clear that our old assumptions about the necessity for women to be at home full time to adequately
rear the next generation have been false.

In a study by Gurin et al. 1/ the researchers
found a significant relationship between marital
status and individual self-esteem or self-worth,
happiness, worry, and active sociability. Single
men are less happy, less active and show lower
self-esteem than single women, but among the married, women are unhappier, have more problems,
feel less adequate as parents, have a more negative,
passive outlook on life and show a lower level of
self-esteem or self-worth than married men do.
Furthermore, married men showed no variation by age,
but married women showed lower self-esteem the older
they were, suggesting that men's self esteem is positively reinforced by marriage and their experience
in work during adulthood, but women's self-esteem is
lowered by their experience of marriage. It is not
marriage qua marriage that has this undesirable impact upon American women, but the restrictions of
their social roles after marriage and the content
of these roles as homemakers, mothers, volunteers
and often underpaid employees. We must face the
serious implication of these findings that American
women lose ground in personal development and self
esteem during the years of their married life,
whereas men do not. 2/

1/ Gurin, Gerold, J. Veroff, and S. Feld, Americans
    View their Mental Health, New York: Basic
    Books, Monograph Series No. 4, Joint Commission
    on Mental Illness and Health, 1960.

2/ Rossi, Alice, S., "Transition to Parenthood",
    Journal of Marriage and the Family, Vol. XXX,
    No. 1, February 1968, 26-39.

Implementation of the recommendations of this task force will contribute to the complex process needed to undo this unfortunate difference between the sexes. The removal of legal inequities, the extension to women of all the fundamental human rights denied to her under our current social institutions and laws, and a courageous attempt to develop new institutions needed in a complex urban society, will all stimulate social change that will assure a personally meaningful and socially useful life for both men and women.

APPENDIX A

STATE LAWS CONCERNING DOMICILE OF MARRIED WOMEN

A preliminary report of a study by the Women's
Bureau, U.S. Department of Labor

Separate Domicile For All Purposes

(1) Alaska Statutes, Title 25, § 25.15.110; Cramer v. Cramer
     379 F. 2d 95 (1963)
(2) Arkansas Statutes Annotated, § 34-1307, § 34-1308,
     § 34-1309
(3) Delaware Statutes, Title 13, § 1702
(4) Revised Laws of Hawaii, Title 33, § 323-4
(5) Wisconsin Statutes, § 246.15

Separate Domicile For Purposes of Divorce and When Not Living
Together For Just Cause

(1) Alabama--Hanberry v. Hanberry, 29 Ala. 719 (1857)
(2) Alaska Statutes, Title 9, § 09.55.170
(3) Arizona--Carlson v. Carlson, 256 P. 2d 249 (1953)
(4) Arkansas--McLauglin v. McLauglin, 99 S.W. 2d 571 (1937)
(5) California Statutes, Civil Code § 129
(6) Colorado Statutes, § 46-1-3
(7) Connecticut--Scott v. Furrow, 104 A. 2d 224 (1954)
(8) Delaware--Burkhardt v. Burkhardt, 193 Atl. 924 (1937)
(9) District of Columbia--McGrath v. Zander, 117 F.2d 649 (1950)
(10) Florida--McIntyre v. McIntyre, 53 So. 2d 824 (1951)
(11) Georgia Code Annotated, § 79-403
(12) Hawaii--Revised Laws of Hawaii, Title 33, § 323-4
(13) Idaho Statutes § 32-702; Radermacher v. Radermacher, 100 P.
     2d 955 (1940)
(14) Illinois--People v. Rose, 113 N.E. 2d 75 (1953)
(15) Indiana--Petty v. Petty, 88 N.E. 995 (1908)
(16) Iowa--Miller v. Miller, 206 N.W. 262 (1925)
(17) Kansas Statutes, § 60-1603
(18) Kentucky--Whitaker v. Stephens, 45 S.W. 2d 1045 (1932)
(19) Louisiana Civil Code, Article 142--Zinko v. Zinko, 12 So.
     2d 859 (1944)
(20) Maine Statutes, Title 19, § 581--Chirvis v. Chirvis, 184
     A. 2d 773 (1962)

450

Separate Domicile For Purposes of Divorce and When Not Living
Together For Just Cause--Continued

(21) Maryland--Sewell v. Sewell, 145 A. 2d 422 (1958)
(22) Massachusetts--Wiley v. Wiley, 103 N.E. 2d 699 (1952)
(23) Michigan--Bradfield v. Bradfield, 117 N.W. 588 (1908)
(24) Minnesota--Bechtel v. Bechtel, 112 N.W. 883 (1907);
      Statutes § 518.07, § 518.09
(25) Mississippi--Carter v. Carter, 90 So. 2d 529 (1957)
(26) Missouri--Phelps v. Phelps, 246 S.W. 2d 838 (1952)
(27) Montana--State v. District Court, 214 Pac. 85 (1923)
(28) Nebraska--Wray v. Wray, 31 N.W. 2d 228 (1948)
(29) Nevada--Barber v. Barber, 222 Pac. 284 (1924)
(30) New Hampshire-- Van Renesselaer v. Van Renesselaer,
      164 A. 2d 244 (1960)
(31) New Jersey--Antonelli v. Antonelli, 84 A. 2d 753 (1951)
(32) New Mexico Statutes, § 22-7-4
(33) New York Domestic Relations Code, § 230, § 231
(34) North Carolina Statutes, § 163-26; Rector v. Rector,
      120 S.E. 195 (1923)
(35) North Dakota Code, § 14-05-18
(36) Ohio--Armstrong v. Armstrong, 135 N.E. 2d 710 (1954)
(37) Oklahoma Statutes Annotated, Title 12, § 1272, § 1286;
      Bixby v. Bixby, 361 P. 2d 1075 (1961)
(38) Oregon--Volmer v. Volmer, 271 P. 2d 70 (1962)
(39) Pennsylvania--Harrison v. Harrison, 163 Atl. 62 (1932)
(40) Rhode Island--Brown v. Brown, 177 A. 2d 380 (1962)
(41) South Carolina--Cone v. Cone, 39 S.E. 648 (1901)
(42) South Dakota Code, § 14.0721
(43) Tennessee--Bernardi v. Bernardi, 302 S.E. 2d 63 (1956)
(44) Texas--Postle v. Postle, 280 S.W. 2d 633 (1955)
(45) Utah--State v. Morse, 87 Pac. 705 (1906)
(46) Vermont--Tower v. Tower, 138 A. 2d 602 (1957)
(47) Virginia--Humphrey's v. Humphrey's, 123 S.E. 554 (1924)
(48) Washington--McCallum v. McCallum, 279 Pac. 88 (1929)
(49) West Virginia Statutes, § 48-2-7, § 48-2-8(b); Gardner
      v. Gardner, 110 S.E. 2d 495 (1959)
(50) Wisconsin Statutes, § 246.15; Lucas v. Lucas, 28 N.W.
      2d 337 (1947)
(51) Wyoming Statutes, § 20-49

Domicile of Minor Children in Relation to Separate Domicile
For Married Woman Living With Husband

(1) Alabama--Cleckley v. Cleckley, 33 So. 2d 338 (1948)
(2) Alaska
(3) Arizona--In Re Webb's Adoption, 117 P. 2d 222 (1947)
(4) Arkansas--Johnson v. Turner, 29 Ark. 280 (1874)
(5) California--Guardianship of Brayeal, 254 P. 2d 886 (1953)
(6) Colorado Statutes, § 153-17-3
(7) Connecticut--Boardman v. Boardman, 62 A. 2d 521 (1949)
(8) Delaware Code Annotated, Title 13, § 1703
(9) District of Columbia--Oxley v. Oxley, 159 Fed. 10 (1947)
(10) Florida--Fields v. Fields, 197 So. 530 (1940)
(11) Georgia Code Annotated, § 79-404
(12) Hawaii
(13) Idaho--Duryea v. Duryea, 269 Pac. 987 (1928)
(14) Illinois--Owego v. Goodrich, 171 N.E. 2d 816 (1961)
(15) Indiana--Johnson v. Smith, 180 N.E. 188 (1932)
(16) Iowa--Hundorff v. Soureign, 129 N.W. 831 (1911)
(17) Kansas--Ex Parte McCoun, 150 P. 516 (1915)
(18) Kentucky--Abbott v. Abbott, 200 S.W. 2d 283 (1947)
(19) Louisiana Civil Code, Article 39
(20) Maine Statutes, Title 19, § 211
(21) Maryland--Glass v. Glass, 157 N.E. 621 (1927)
(22) Massachusetts
(23) Michigan--Hering v. Mosher, 107 N.W. 917 (1906)
(24) Minnesota--Larson v. Larson, 252 N.W. 329 (1934)
(25) Mississippi-Allen v. Allen, 136 So. 2d 627 (1962)
(26) Missouri--Dawson v. Dawson, 241 S.W. 2d 725 (1951)
(27) Montana
(28) Nebraska Statutes, § 68-115
(29) Nevada
(30) New Hampshire Statutes, § 460:12
(31) New Jersey
(32) New Mexico--Application of Lang, 193 N.Y.S. 2d 763 (1959)
(33) New York
(34) North Carolina
(35) North Dakota Code, § 54-01-26
(36) Ohio Code, § 3109.03
(37) Oklahoma--McKiddy v. McKiddy, 366 P. 2d 933 (1961)
(38) Oregon, 1960-62 Op. Att'y Gen. 30
(39) Pennsylvania--Alburger v. Alburger, 10 A. 2d 888 (1940)
(40) Rhode Island--Greene v. Greene, 133 Atl. 651 (1926)

Domicile of Minor Children in Relation to Separate Domicile
For Married Woman Living With Husband--Continued

(41) South Carolina--<u>Jackson</u> v. <u>Jackson</u>, 126 S.E. 2d 855(1964)
(42) South Dakota
(43) Tennessee--<u>Clothier</u> v. <u>Clothier</u>, 232 S.W. 2d 363 (1953)
(44) Texas--<u>Collins</u> v. <u>Land</u>, 213 S.W. 2d 265 (1948)
(45) Utah
(46) Vermont
(47) Virginia
(48) Washington
(49) West Virginia
(50) Wisconsin--<u>Carlton</u> v. <u>Carlton</u>, 74 N.W. 2d 340 (1956)
(51) Wyoming

Separate Domicile For Public Office When Married and Living
Together

(1) Alaska Statutes, Title 25, § 25.15.110; <u>Cramer</u> v. <u>Cramer</u>,
      379 P. 2d 95 (1963)
(2) Arkansas Statutes Annotated, § 34-1307, § 34-1308,
      § 34-1309
(3) Delaware Statutes, Title 13, § 1702
(4) Revised Laws of Hawaii, Title 33, § 323-4
(5) Maine Statutes, Title 21, § 242
(6) N. Jersey Statutes, § 37:2-3
(7) New York Domestic Relations Code, § 61
(8) Wisconsin Statutes, § 246.15

Separate Domicile for Jury Duty When Married and Living
Together

(1) Alaska Statutes, Title 25, § 25.15.110; <u>Cramer</u> v. <u>Cramer</u>,
      379 P. 2d 95 (1963)
(2) Arkansas Statutes Annotated, § 34-1307, § 34-1308, § 34-1309
(3) Revised Laws of Hawaii, Title 33, § 323-4
(4) Maine Statutes, Title 21, 242
(5) New Jersey Statutes, § 37:2-3
(6) Wisconsin Statutes, § 246.15

Separate Domicile For Probate When Married and Living Together

(1) Alaska Statutes, Title 25, § 25.15.110; Cramer v. Cramer
       379 P. 2d 95 (1963)
(2) Arkansas Statutes Annotated, § 34-1307, § 34-1308, § 34-1309
(3) California, In Re Wickes' Estate, 60 Pac. 867 (1900)
(4) Delaware Statutes, Title 13, §1702
(5) Florida Statutes, § 732.06, with nonresident husband
(6) Revised Laws of Hawaii, Title 33, § 323-4
(7) New Jersey Statutes, § 37:2-3
(8) Wisconsin Statutes, § 246.15

Separate Domicile For Taxation When Married and Living Together

(1) Alaska Statutes, Title 25, § 25.15.110; Cramer v. Cramer
       379 P. 2d 95 (1963)
(2) Arkansas Statutes Annotated, § 34-1307, § 34-1308, § 34-1309
(3) Delaware Statutes, Title 13, § 1702
(4) Florida--Judd v. Schooley, 158 So. 2d 514 (1963)
(5) Hawaii--Revised Laws of Hawaii, Title 33, § 323-4
(6) New Jersey Statutes, § 37:2-3
(7) New York Tax Code, § 611
(8) West Virginia Statutes, § 11-21-11
(9) Wisconsin Statutes, § 246.15

Separate Domicile For Voting When Married and Living Together

(1) Alaska Statutes, Title 25, § 25.15.110; Cramer v. Cramer
       379 P. 2d 95 (1963)
(2) Arkansas Statutes Annotated, § 34-1307, § 34-1308, § 34-1309
(3) California Statutes, Election Code, § 14289, § 14290 (If
       Separated)
(4) Connecticut, 29 Op. Att'y Gen. 280 (1950)
(5) Delaware Statutes, Title 13, § 1702
(6) Florida, 1952 Op. Att'y Gen. 107
(7) Revised Laws of Hawaii, Title 33, § 323-4
(8) Illinois, 1917 Op. Att'y Gen. 283
(9) Indiana Statutes, § 29-4803 (If Separated)
(10) Iowa--State v. Mohr, 199 N.W. 278 (1924)
(11) Maine Statutes, Title 21, § 242
(12) Massachusetts Statutes, Ch. 51, § 1; Constitutional
       Amendment - Article 3
(13) Michigan Statutes, § 6.1011; Constitution Article II, § 1

454

Separate Domicile For Voting When Married and Living Together--
Continued

(14) New Jersey Statutes, § 37:2-3
(15) New York Statutes, Domestic Relations Code, § 61
(16) North Dakota Code, § 54-01-26
(17) Wisconsin Statutes, § 246.15
(18) Wyoming Statutes, § 22-118.3

Separate Domicile For Miscellaneous Reasons When Married and
Living Together

(1) Alaska Statutes, Title 25, § 25.15.110; Cramer v. Cramer
     379 P. 2d 95 (1963)
(2) Arkansas Statutes Annotated, § 34-1307, § 34-1308, § 34-1309
(3) California Statutes, Welfare and Inst. Code, § 17103
(4) Delaware Statutes, Title 13, § 1702
(5) Revised Laws of Hawaii, Title 33, § 323-4
(6) Michigan Statutes, Relief Law, § 16.431
(7) Minnesota Statutes, Relief Law, § 261.07
(8) Nebraska Statutes, Relief Law, § 68-115
(9) Vermont Statutes, Title 33, § 741 (If Deserted)
(10) Wisconsin Statutes, § 246.15

Laws of States Which Give Married Women
Equal Domiciliary Rights

A L A S K A

All laws which impose or recognize civil disabilities
upon a married woman which are not imposed or recognized as
existing as to the husband are repealed. Thus, a married
woman has the same right to appeal in her own name alone to
call counts for redress that the husband has. Title 25 Sec.
25.15.110; Decker v. Kedly, 148 Fed. 68 (C.A. 9, 1906);
Cramer v. Cramer, 379 P. 2d 95 (1963).

The statutes of Alaska relating to the property rights
of married women have abolished the common law unity of husband and wife and, therefore, a conveyance to husband and
wife is a conveyance to two or more persons. Title 25 Sec.
10; Carver v. Gilbert, 387 P. 2d 928 (1963).

Divorce:

No person may commence an action for divorce until he
has been a resident of the State for at least one year before
the commencement of the action. Title 9, Sec. 09.55.140.

Residence means a place of abode, and within the meaning
of this section, it is the place where the person resides, and
has the same meaning as domicile. Wilson v. Wilson, 10 Alaska
616 (1945).

Where the wife is plaintiff in an action for divorce or
to declare void a marriage which was not solemnized in the
State, the residence of the husband in this State insures to
her benefit and she may institute the action if her husband
is at the time of its commencement qualified as to residence
to institute a similar action. Title 9 Sec. 09.55.150.

In actions for divorce, wives may acquire a separate
residence or domicile from that of the husband without
reference among other factors to misconduct or consent of
the husband. Title 9 Sec. 09.55.170.

Alaska-Divorce-Cont.

Where domicile is a statutory jurisdictional prerequisite, it is quote correct to say that jurisdiction for divorce is founded on this concept. It is quote another matter to flatly declare that there may be no other relation between a State and an individual which will create a sufficient interest in the State under the due process clause to give it power to decree divorces. Lauterbach v. Lauterbach, 392 P. 2d 24 (1964).

Infants:

Found nothing.

Jury duty:

No discrimination as to women -- they must be a citizen of the United States, and a resident of the State. Title 9, Sec. 09.20.010.

Probate:

Non-residents of the State are not qualified to act as executors or administrators. Title 13, Sec. 12.20.020.

Public Office:

Women have the same right to hold State appointed office as men, they only have to be citizens of the United States. Title 39, Sec. 39.05.010. (1965 Amendment). There is no discrimination as to women who run for office as candidates; however they must fulfill the qualifications of the statute. Title 15, Sec. 15.25.030.

Taxes:

There is a tax each taxable year upon the net income of every resident and non-resident individual. Title 43, Sec. 43.20.010. Resident as used in this chapter includes natural persons domiciled in the State. Title 43, Sec. 43.20.010.

Alaska-continued

Voting:

Is granted every citizen of the United States who meets
qualifications of Statute. Must have been a resident of the
State for one year and for thirty days a resident of the
election district. Constitution of Alaska, Article 5, Sec. 1.
Title 15, Sec. 15.05.010. The place where a man's family resides is presumed to be his place of residence, but a man who
takes up or continues his abode with intention of remaining
at a place other than where his family resides is a resident
where he abides. Title 15, Sec. 15.05.020.

A R K A N S A S

Any person who is a citizen of the United States may
become a resident and domiciled in the State. § 34-1301.

No person shall be admitted to become a resident
domiciled in the State who has not resided in the State
for at least thirty days preceding his application for
admission as a resident domiciled in the State. § 34-1307.

Any woman who marries a resident domiciled in Arkansas
does not become domiciled in the State by reason of her
marriage, but she may acquire such domicile by compliance
with the statutory requirements for State domicile. § 34-
1308.

A woman who has lost her domicile in the State because
of marriage to a citizen of another State may regain such
domicile by complying with the statutory requirements.
§ 34-1309.

Divorce:

The term residence as used in the divorce laws is
defined as meaning actual presence, and upon proof of
such, the party is considered domiciled in the State.
§ 13.1201.1. Thus, domicile or residence is sufficient

for jurisdiction in divorce cases. <u>Weaver</u> v. <u>Weaver</u>, 231 Ark. 341, 329 S.W. 2d 2/22 (1959); <u>Wheat</u> v. <u>Wheat</u>, 229 Ark. 842, 318 S.W. 2d 793 (1958). A wife may acquire a separate domicile from that of her husband and at that domicile she may institute proceedings for divorce. <u>McLaughlin</u> v. McLaughlin, 193 Ark. 207, 99 S.W. 2d 571 (1937).

Infants:

The domicile of the father is the domicile of the minor child. <u>Johnson</u> v. <u>Turner</u>, 29 Ar,. 280 (1874).

Jury Duty:

Arkansas Constitution - Amendment 8. Women shall not be compelled to serve on juries. No woman shall be compelled to serve on any jury against her will. § 39-112. Her refusal to serve may be made to the officer when serving the writ of summons, or when notifying her of her selection as a juror and not thereafter. § 39-113. However, nothing in this act shall be so construed as to prevent a woman, when summoned, from serving on a jury if she desires; providing however, that she can otherwise qualify as a juror as provided by law. § 39-114.

Probate:

No person is qualified to serve as domiciliary personal representative who is a nonresident of this State unless he meets all the following conditions: § 62-2201, § 62-3101, § 62-3104.

Public Office:

Arkansas Constitution - Article 8. No discrimination as to women who would want to run for office. However, they must possess the qualifications as an elector. Article 19, § 3. Sex shall not be a bar to the holding of any public office or civil office in this State. § 12-101.

Taxes:

Every word in the taxation section importing the masculine gender, shall extend and be applied to females as well
as males. § 84-101. The word resident means natural persons
and includes for the purpose of determining liability to the
tax imposed by this act upon or with reference to the income
of any taxable year, any person domiciled in the State, and
any other person who maintains a permanent place of abode
within the State and spends in the aggregate more than six
months of the taxable year within the State. § 84-2002.

Voting:

Arkansas Constitution - Article 3, § 1. Every citizen
of the United States of the age of twenty-one, who has resided in the State twelve months, in the county six months,
and in the precinct, town, or ward one month may vote.
Amendment 8 of Article 3, § 1. It is declared to be the
purpose of this amendment to confer suffrage equally upon
both men and women, without regard to sex.

D E L A W A R E

Though domicile and residence are sometimes used inter-
changeably in legislative expressions, the governing factor
in each case is the legislative intent. In Re Adoption of
Goodman, 121 A. 2d 676 (1956). A married woman follows and
has the domicile of her husband, if he has any within the
State; otherwise her own domicile at the time of marriage,
if she had any, shall not be lost or suspended by the marriage. Title 13, § 1702.

Divorce:

Wife may establish separate domicile for purposes of
divorce for cause or by mutual consent or understanding.
Burkhardt v. Burkhardt, 38 Del. 492, 193 Atl. 924 (1937).
Desertion or abandonment destroys the unity of the matrimonial domicile and empowers the innocent spouse to establish a separate domicile carrying with it the jurisdiction
of the marriage status and of the interest of the parties

460

in such status and such domicile is therefore sufficient for divorce purposes. Bond v. Bond, 41 Del. 153, 17 A. 2d 229 (1941). However, wife cannot acquire separate domicile for purposes of divorce on ground of desertion when she is guilty party. Feuerstein v. Feuerstein, 37 Del. 414, 183 Atl. 705 (1936).

Infants:

Legitimate children follow and have the domicile of their father, if he has any within the State, until they gain a domicile of their own; but if he has none, they shall, in like manner, follow and have the domicile of their mother, if she has any. Title 13, § 1703.

Jury Duty:

Women are subject to jury service on the same terms and conditions as men. All persons qualified to vote at the general election shall be liable to serve as jurors, other than the enumerated classes of professions or occupations for which exemption is allowed. Title 10, § 4504.

Probate:

Any executrix or administratrix, being a married woman, may act in such representative capacity as though she was a feeme sole, and the fact of marriage shall not give her husband any right to participate in any manner in the management direction and settlement of the estate of deceased. Title 13, § 12.

Public Office:

Delaware Constitution - Article 15, § 29. No citizen of the State shall be disqualified to hold and enjoy any office, or public trust, under the laws of this State by reason of sex.

Taxes:

Taxable means: - A natural person including a minor, with a gross income of $600 or more, who is a resident of the State or who has been a resident of the State at any

time during the income year. Each spouse in the case of a
married couple living together with a combined gross income
of $1,200 or more. Title 30, § 1101.

The word resident which defined as taxable an adult
person who is resident of State, is synonymous with domiciled. Mitchell v. Delaware State Tax Commissioner, 42
Del. 589, 42 A. 2d 19 (1945); Delaware Constitution:
Article 5, § 2. No discrimination as to women in regard
to suffrage franchise. Only need to be citizen of age
twenty-one, resident of State one year, and for last
three months a resident of the county and for the last
thirty days a resident of the hundred or election district
in which he may offer to vote.

H A W A I I

Hawaiian Constitution, Art. I, § 4. No person shall
be deprived of life, liberty, or property without due
process of law, nor be denied the equal protection of the
laws, nor be denied the enjoyment of his civil rights or
be discriminated against in the exercise thereof because
of race, religion, sex or ancestry.

The domicile of any woman whose domicile at the time
of marriage was in the State, shall not be held to be
changed by reason of marriage to a man whose domicile is
in some foreign State, district, territory, or county,
unless such woman after marriage assumes the actual domicile of her husband. Title 33, § 323-4. Thus, the common
law rules applies if she assumes her husband's domicile,
thereafter the domicile of the wife follows that of her
husband.

Divorce:

Found nothing.

Infants:

Found nothing.

Jury Duty:

   Hawaiian Constitution, Art. I, § 12. No person shall
be disqualified to serve as a juror because of sex. However, they must be a citizen of the United States and the
State, twenty years old, and posses qualifications for registration as a voter and have resided in the State for not
less than three years. Title 26, § 221-1.

Probate:

   Every executor or administrator appointed by any
court of the State shall be either an individual residing in the State or a trust company organized under the
laws of the State. Title 32, § 317-9.

   A married woman may be an executrix, administratrix,
guardian, or trustee, and may bind herself and the estate
she represents without any act or assent on the part of
the husband. Title 33, § 325-3.

Public Office:

   Men and women are subject generally to the same
legal qualification to determine eligibility for election, appointment, to public office and voting; - However, they shall be citizens of the United States and
residents of the States for three years. Title I, § 5-1.

Taxes:

   Men as well as women are subject to State income
taxes.

   Resident means, (a) every individual domiciled in
the State, and (b) every other individual whether domiciled in the State or not, who resides within the State.
Title 16, § 121-1.

Voting:

Hawaiian Constitution, Art. II, § 1. Voting franchise
is granted to every citizen of the United States, twenty-one
years old, who has been a resident of the State not less
than one year next preceding election. All above citizens
shall have registered as a duly qualified elector of the
precinct in which he resides. Title I, § 11-101.

W I S C O N S I N

Generally:

Women shall have the same rights and privileges under
the law as men in the exercise of suffrage, freedom of
contract, choice of residence for voting purposes, jury
service, holding office, and conveying property, care and
custody of children, and in all other respects. § 246.15.

Divorce:

In the absence of statutory provision, the common law
rule prevails that the domicile of the wife is that of her
husband.

Under the statute giving women the same rights and
privileges as men in enumerated respects, a wife may maintain a separate residence from that of her husband for
purposes of divorce. Norwithstanding the general rule
that the domicile of the wife follows that of husband, a
wife may acquire a separate domicile from that of her
husband if his misconduct has given her adequate cause
for divorce. Lucas v. Lucas, 251 Wis. 129 28, N.W. 2d
337 (1947).

Infants:

Domicile of minor child, with certain exceptions, is
that of its father. Cartlon v. State, 271 Wis. 465 74, N.W.
2d 340 (1956).

Jury Duty:

Women are eligible for jury service. However, any women drawn to serve as jurors may be excused to serve on request. § 6.015.

Public Office:

Women shall have the same rights and privileges under the law as men in holding office and in all other respects. § 6.015.

Voting and Taxation:

Women have the same rights and privileges under the law as men in the choice of residence for voting purposes. § 246.15; Constitution Article 3, § 1. When a woman residing in this State marries a man residing in another State, her voting residence automatically becomes that of her husband under the theory that a married women is presumed to intend to live with her husband not temporarily, but permanently. 17 Op. Att'y Gen. 489 (1928). Residence for voting purposes and tax situs of income is the same. Op. Att'y Gen. 92 (1943).

Statement of Council member Margaret Mealey, Executive
Director, National Council of Catholic Women,
on the abortion recommendation

The recommendation on abortion of the Task Force on
Family Law and Policy is unacceptable for a number
of reasons:

1. The report treats abortion as an alterna-
    tive to other methods of contraception or
    as a backstop for faulty contraception.
    The present discussion in the various
    States does not consider abortion as a
    method of contraception, but as an ad hoc
    response in very specific problem areas,
    and there is no unanimity as to whether
    it is even a suitable response in these
    cases.

2. In its heavy emphasis on assuring freedom
    of action to women in regard to child-
    bearing, the report continually overlooks
    the fact that present contraceptive laws
    provide great freedom to women without
    correspondingly endangering the life or
    right of the child in utero. One of the
    central legal problems of abortion law
    change is the dilemma of how society pro-
    tects the lives of unborn children if such
    life is made secondary to the personal
    decision of the mother or the physician.
    This report argues for total repeal of all
    laws - abortion on demand - and does not
    consider the welfare or rights of the
    infant.

3. The U.N. Declaration on the Rights of the
    Child maintains that special legal pro-
    tection should be given to children,
    before as well as after birth, because
    of the child's dependent status, and
    Society is expected to have stronger
    laws protecting the child because the
    child is unable to protect himself or
    herself. The Declaration restates and

makes specific application of the Declaration on Human Rights which holds that the right to life is an inalienable personal right. This is also the underlying philosophy of the American Constitution.

4. There is much in this report that is highly subjective, making it an argument that presents only one side of a complex controversy.

5. Virtually no consideration is given to the fact that parenthood is a responsibility of both husband and wife. Neither persons should be allowed unilaterally to terminate the life of the child. The concept of parental partnership requires that both partners support and complement each other. To make abortion a matter of decision for the woman alone can lead to a reversal of double-standard morality which destroys the partnership concept of the husband-wife relationship. Both husband and wife are expected to act responsibly, rather than seek escape at the expense of the child.

APPENDIX B
STATE MARRIAGE LAWS AS OF JULY 1, 1967
U.S. Department of Labor

State or other jurisdiction	Age at which marriage can be contracted with parental consent		Age below which parental consent is required		Common law marriage recognized
	Male	Female	Male	Female	
Alabama--------	17(a)	14(a)	21	18	*
Alaska---------	18(c)	16(c)	21	18	....
Arizona--------	18(c)	16(c)	21	18	....
Arkansas-------	18(c)	16(c)	21	18	....
California-----	18(a,d)	16(a,d)	21	18	....
Colorado-------	16(d)	16(d)	21	18	*
Connecticut----	16(d)	16(d)	21	21	....
Delaware-------	18(c)	16(c)	21	18	....
Florida--------	18(a,c)	16(a,c)	21	21	*
Georgia--------	18(c,f)	16(c,f)	19(f)	19(f)	*
Hawaii---------	18	16(d)	20	20	....
Idaho----------	18	16(d)	21	18	*
Illinois-------	18	16	21	18	....
Indiana--------	18(c)	16(c)	21	18	....
Iowa-----------	18(c)	16(c)	21	18	*
Kansas---------	18(d)	18(d)	21	18	*
Kentucky-------	18(a,c)	16(a,c)	21	21	....
Lousiana-------	18(d)	16(d)	21	21	....
Maine----------	16(d)	16(d)	21	18	....
Maryland-------	18(c)	16(c)	21	18	....
Massachusetts--	18(d)	16(d)	21	18	....
Michigan-------	(i)	16(c)	18	18	....
Minnesota------	18(a)	16(j)	21	18	....
Mississippi----	17(d)	15(d)	21	21	....
Missouri-------	15(d)	15(d)	21	18	....
Montana--------	18(d)	16(d)	21	18	*
Nebraska-------	18(c)	16(c)	21	21	....
Nevada---------	18(a,d)	16(a,d)	21	18	....
New Hampshire--	(k)	(k)	20	18	....
New Jersey-----	18(d)	16(d)	21	18	....
New Mexico-----	18(c)	16(c)	21	18	....
New York-------	16	16(d)	21	18	....
North Carolina-	16	16(c)	18	18	....
North Dakota---	18	15	21	18	....
Ohio-----------	18(c)	16(c)	21	21	*
Oklahoma-------	18(c)	15(c)	21	18	*
Oregon---------	18(j)	15(j)	21	18	....
Pennsylvania---	16(d)	16(d)	21	21	*
Rhode Island---	18(d)	16(d)	21	21	*
South Carolina-	16(c)	14(c)	18	18	*
South Dakota---	18(c)	16(c)	21	18	....
Tennessee------	16(d)	16(d)	21	21	....
Texas----------	16	14	21	18	*
Utah-----------	16(a)	14(a)	21	18	....
Vermont--------	18(d)	16(d)	21	18	....
Virginia-------	18(a,c)	16(a,c)	21	21	....
Washington-----	17(d)	17(d)	21	18	....
West Virginia--	18(a)	16(a)	21	21	....
Wisconsin------	18	16	21	18	....
Wyoming--------	18	16	21	21	....
District of Columbia-------	18(a)	16(a)	21	18	*

(a) Footnotes follow.

Physical examination and blood test for male and female		Waiting period	
Maximum period between examination and issuance of marriage license	Scope of medical examination	Before issuance of license	After issuance of license
30 da.	(b)	....	....
30 da.	(b)	3 da.	....
30 da.	(b)	....	....
30 da.	(b)	3 da.	....
30 da.	(b)	....	....
30 da.	(b)	....	....
40 da.	(b)	4 da.	....
30 da.	(b)	....	(e)
30 da.	(b)	3 da.	....
30 da.	(b)	3 da.(g)	....
30 da.	(b)	3 da.	....
30 da.	(b)	....	....
15 da.	(b)	....	....
30 da.	(b)	3 da.	....
20 da.	(b)	3 da.	....
30 da.	(b,h)	3 da.	....
15 da.	(b)	3 da.	....
10 da.	(b)	....	72 hrs.
30 da.	(b)	5 da.	....
......	.....	48 hrs.	....
30 da.	(b)	3 da.	....
30 da.	(b)	3 da.	....
......	.....	5 da.	....
30 da.	(b)	3 da.	....
15 da.	(b)	3 da.	....
20 da.	(b)	5 da.	....
30 da.	(b)	....	....
......	.....	....	....
30 da.	(b)	5 da.	....
30 da.	(b)	72 hrs.	....
30 da.	(b)	3 da.	....
30 da.	(b)	....	24 hrs.1
30 da.	(m)	(n)	....
30 da.	(o)	....	....
30 da.	(b)	5 da.	....
30 da.	(b)	72 hrs.(p)	....
30 da.(q)	(r)	7 da.	....
30 da.	(b)	3 da.	....
40 da.	(s)	....	(t)
......	.....	24 hrs.	....
20 da.	(b)	....	....
30 da.	(b)	3 da.(u)	....
15 da.	(b)	3 da.(p)	....
30 da.	(b)	....	....
30 da.	(b)	....	5 da.
30 da.	(b)	....	....
......	(o)	3 da.	....
30 da.	(b)	3 da.	....
20 da.	(b)	5 da.	....
30 da.	(b)	....	....
30 da.	(b)	3 da.	....

(*)   Common law marriage recognized.
(a)   Parental consent not required if minor was previously married.
(b)   Venereal diseases.
(c)   Statute establishes procedure whereby younger parties may obtain license in case of pregnancy or birth of a child.
(d)   Statute establishes procedure whereby younger parties may obtain license in special circumstances.
(e)   Residents, 24 hours; nonresidents, 96 hours.
(f)   If parties are under 19 years of age, proof of age and consent of parents in person required. If a parent is ill, an affidavit by the incapacitated parent and a physician's affidavit to that effect required.
(g)   Unless parties are 21 years of age or over, or female is pregnant, or applicants are the parents of a living child born out of wedlock.
(h)   Feeblemindedness.
(i)   No provision in law for parental consent for males.
(j)   Parental consent and permission of judge required. In Oregon, permission of judge required for male under 19 years of age or female under 17.
(k)   Below age of consent parties need parental consent and permission of judge.
(l)   Marriage may not be solemnized within 3 days from date on which specimen for serological test was taken.
(m)   Venereal diseases and mental incompetence.
(n)   Forty-eight hours if both are nonresidents of the State.
(o)   Feeblemindedness, imbecility, insanity, chronic alcoholism, and venereal diseases. In Washington, also advanced tuberculosis and, if male, contagious venereal diseases.
(p)   If one or both parties are below the age for marriage without parental consent.
(q)   Time limit between date of examination and expiration of marriage license.
(r)   Venereal diseases, feeblemindedness, mental illness, drug addiction, and chronic alcoholism.
(s)   Infectious tuberculosis and venereal diseases.
(t)   If female is nonresident, must complete and sign license 5 days prior to marriage.
(u)   Unless parties are 21 years of age or over

APPENDIX C
STATE DIVORCE LAWS AS OF JULY 1, 1967
U.S. Department of Labor

State or other jurisdiction	Residence required before filing suit for divorce	Adultery	Desertion	Mental and/or physical cruelty	Felony conviction or imprisonment	Alcoholism	Impotency	Non-support of wife	Insanity	Separation or absence
Alabama-----	(a)	*	1 yr.	*	*	*	*	* (b)	5 yrs.	......
Alaska------	1 yr.	*	1 yr.	*	*	*	*	*	18 mos.	......
Arizona-----	1 yr.	*	1 yr.	*	*	*	*	*	....	5 yrs.
Arkansas----	2 mos.	*	1 yr.	*	*	*	*	* (h)	3 yrs.	3 yrs.
California--	1 yr.	*	1 yr.	*	*	*	..	*	3 yrs.	......
Colorado----	1 yr. (j)	*	1 yr.	*	*	*	*	*	3 yrs.	3 yrs.
Connecticut-	3 yrs. (j)	*	3 yrs.	*	*	*	..	..	5 yrs.	7 yrs.
Delaware----	2 yrs. (j)	*	2 yrs.	*	*	*	..	*	5 yrs.	3 yrs.
Florida-----	6 mos.	*	1 yr.	*	..	*	*	..	....	....
Georgia-----	6 mos.	*	1 yr.	*	*	*	*	..	2 yrs.	....
Hawaii------	1 yr.	*	6 mos.	*	*	*	..	*	3 yrs.	3 yrs.q
Idaho-------	6 wks.	*	1 yr.	*	*	*	..	*	6 yrs.	5 yrs.
Illinois----	1 yr. (j)	*	1 yr.	*	*	*	*	..	....	....
Indiana-----	1 yr. (t)	*	2 yrs.	*	*	*	*	*	5 yrs.	....
Iowa--------	1 yr.	*	2 yrs.	*	*	*	..	..	....	....
Kansas------	1 yr. (w)	*	1 yr.	*	*	*	..	*	3 yrs.	......
Kentucky----	1 yr.	*	1 yr.	*	*	* (x)	*	..	5 yrs.	5 yrs.
Lousiana----	(aa)	*	....	..	*	..	..	..	....	2 yrs.
Maine-------	6 mos. (j)	*	3 yrs.	*	..	*	*	*	....	......
Maryland----	1 yr. (ad)	*	18 mos.	..	*	..	*	..	3 yrs.	18 mos.
Massachusetts	5 yrs. (j)	*	3 yrs.	*	*	*	*	*	....	......
Michigan-----	1 yr. (j)	*	2 yrs.	*	*	*	*	*	....	......
Minnesota----	1 yr. (j)	*	1 yr.	*	*	*	*	..	5 yrs.	2 yrs.q
Mississippi--	1 yr.	*	1 yr.	*	*	*	*	..	3 yrs.	......
Missouri-----	1 yr. (j)	*	1 yr.	*	*	*	*	..	......	......
Montana------	1 yr.	*	1 yr.	*	*	*	..	*	5 yrs.	......
Nebraska-----	2 yrs. (j)	*	2 yrs.	*	*	*	*	*	5 yrs.	......
Nevada-------	6 wks. (j)	*	1 yr.	*	*	*	*	*	2 yrs.	1 yr.
New Hampshire	1 yr. (j)	*	2 yrs.	*	*	*	*	*	......	2 yrs.
New Jersey---	2 yrs. (j)	*	2 yrs.	*	..	..	..	..	......	......
New Mexico---	1 yr.	*	*	*	*	*	*	*	5 yrs.	......
New York-----	1 yr.	*	2 yrs.	*	*	..	*	..	......	2 yrs.q
North Carolina	6 mos.	*	....	..	*	..	*	..	5 yrs.	1 yr.
North Dakota-	1 yr. (t)	*	1 yr.	*	*	*	..	* (h)	5 yrs.	......
Ohio---------	1 yr.	*	....	*	*	*	*	*	......	1 yr.
Oklahoma-----	6 mos. (w)	*	1 yr.	*	*	*	*	*	5 yrs.	......
Oregon-------	1 yr.	*	1 yr.	*	*	*	*	..	2 yrs.	......
Pennsylvania-	1 yr.	*	2 yrs.	*	*	..	*	..	....	......
Rhode Island-	2 yrs.	*	5 yrs. al	*	..	*	*	*	......	10 yrs.
South Carolina	1 yr.	*	1 yr.	*	..	*	..	..	......	......
South Dakota-	1 yr. (j)	*	1 yr.	*	*	*	..	*	5 yrs.	......
Tennessee----	1 yr.	*	1 yr.	*	*	*	*	*	......	2 yrs.ap
Texas--------	12 mos.	*	3 yrs.	*	*	..	..	..	5 yrs.	3 yrs.
Utah---------	3 mos.	*	1 yr.	*	*	*	*	*	*	3 yrs.q
Vermont------	6 mos. (ai)	*	3 yrs.	..	*	..	..	*	5 yrs.	3 yrs.
Virginia----	1 yr.	*	1 yr.	..	*	..	*	..	......	2 yrs.
Washington---	1 yr.	*	1 yr.	*	*	*	*	*	2 yrs.	2 yrs.
West Virginia	2 yrs. (j)	*	1 yr.	*	*	*	..	..	......	......
Wisconsin----	2 yrs.	*	1 yr.	*	*	*	..	*	......	5 yrs.
Wyoming------	60 days(j)	*	1 yr.	*	*	*	*	*	2 yrs.	2 yrs.
District of Columbia-----	1 yr.	*	1 yr.	..	*	..	..	..	......	1 yr.

(a) Footnotes follow.

Pregnancy at marriage	Drug addiction	Infamous crime	Bigamy	Fraud, force, or duress	Prior decree of limited divorce	Other	Period before parties may remarry after final decree	
							Plaintiff	Defendant
*	*				(c)	(d)	60 days (e)	60 days (e)
	*					(f)		
*		*				(g)	1 yr.	1 yr.
		*	*				(i)	(i)
	*				(c)			
		*		*		(c)		
			*			(k)	3 mos. (l)	3 mos. (l)
	*		*			(m,n,o)		
*				*		(o,p)	(l)	(l)
	*				(c)		(i)	(i)
						(r,s)		
		*	*				(u)	
		*						
* (v)							1 yr. (e,1)	1 yr. (e,1)
							60 days	60 days
*				*		(r,y,z)		
					(ab)		wife,10 mos.	wife, 10 mos.ac
	*							
						(ae)		
	*					(n)		(af)
					(c)		6 mos.	6 mos.
*	*		*			(o,p)		(ag)
*		*	*			(g,ah)		
							6 mos.	6 mos.
						(f)		
		*				(y,ai)		
							3 mos. (l)	3 mos. (l)
*						(f)		
*						(d)		
	*				(c)		(l)	(l)
			*	*		(n)	(aj)	
*				*		(f,n)	6 mos.	6 mos.
							6 mos.	6 mos.
			*	*		(o,ak)		(ac)
	*					(am,an)	6 mos.	6 mos.
	*							
								(ao)
*		*	*			(a,ak)		(ac)
							(aq)	(aq)
							3 mos. (l)	3 mos. (l)
						(as)	6 mos. (l)	2 yrs. (l)
*		*			(at)	(d,au)	(av)	(av)
				*		(aw)	6 mos.	6 mos.
	*						60 days	60 days (ax)
					(ay)		1 yr.	1 yr.
*		*				(g,ah)		
					(az)		6 mos.	6 mos.

*) Indicates ground for absolute divorce.
a) No specific period, except 1 year when ground is desertion or defendant is nonresident or 2 years if wife sues husband for nonsupport.
b) To wife, living separate and apart from husband, as resident of the State for 2 years before suit and without support from him during such time.
c) May be enlarged into an absolute divorce after expiration of 4 years; in Connecticut, any time after decree of separation; Hawaii, 2 years after decree for separate maintenance or from bed and board; Minnesota, 5 years after decree of limited divorce.
d) Crime against nature.
e) Except to each other.
f) Incompatibility.
g) Crime before marriage.
h) Also to husband in certain circumstances.
i) Final decree is not entered until 1 year after interlocutory decree.
j) Under certain circumstances a lesser period of time may be required.
k) Female under 16, male under 18, if complaining party under age of consent at time of marriage has not confirmed the marriage after reaching such age.
l) In the discretion of the court.
m) Habitual violent and ungovernable temper.
n) Defendent obtained divorce from plaintiff in another State.
o) Relationship within prohibited degrees.
p) Mental incapacity.
q) Under decree of separate maintenance.
r) Loathsome disease.
s) Attempt on the life of the spouse by poison or other means showing malice.
t) Five years if on ground of insanity.
u) Two years where service on defendant is only by publication.
v) Unless at time of marriage husl and had an illegitimate child living, which fact was not known to wi e.
w) Five years if on ground of ins..nity and insane spouse is in out-of-State institution.
x) If on part of the husband, accompanied by wasting of husband's estate to the detriment of the wife and children.
y) Joining religious sect disbelieving in marriage.
z) Unchaste behavior on part of wife after marriage.
aa) No statutory requirement for adultery or felony conviction; 2 years when ground is separation.
ab) Limited divorce may be enlarged into absolute divorce after 6 months for the party who obtained the limited divorce and after 9 months for the other spouse.

ac) When divorce is granted on ground of adultery, the guilty party cannot marry the accomplice in adultery during lifetime of former spouse.

ad) No specific period required, except 1 year if cause occurred out of State and 2 years if on ground of insanity.

ae) Any cause which renders marriage null and void from the beginning.

af) Not more than 2 years in court's discretion.

ag) When divorce is granted on ground of adultery, court may prohibit remarriage. After 1 year, court may remove disability upon satisfactory evidence of reformation.

ah) Husband a vagrant.

ai) Wife's absence out of State for 10 years without husband's consent.

aj) When husband is entitled to a divorce and alimony or child support from husband is granted, the decree may be delayed until security is entered for payment.

ak) Incapable of procreation.

al) Or a lesser time in court's discretion.

am) Void or voidable marriage.

an) Gross misbehavior or wickedness; loss of citizenship rights of one party due to crime; presumption of death.

ao) When divorce is for adultery, the guilty party cannot remarry except to the innocent spouse, until the death of the spouse.

ap) To husband for wife's refusal to move with him to this State without reasonable cause, and willfully absenting herself from him for 2 years.

aq) When divorce is granted on ground of cruelty, neither party may remarry for 12 months except to each other.

ar) One year before final hearing, and 2 years if on ground of insanity.

as) Intolerable severity.

at) A limited divorce granted on the ground of cruelty or desertion may be merged with an absolute divorce after 1 year.

au) Wife a prostitute prior to marriage.

av) When divorce is granted on ground of adultery, court may decree the guilty party cannot remarry. After 6 months the court may remove disability for good cause. Remarriage of either party forbidden pending appeal.

aw) Want of legal age or sufficient understanding.

ax) In court's discretion, guilty party may be prohibited from remarrying for a period not to exceed 1 year.

ay) Living entirely apart for 5 years pursuant to a judgment of legal separation.

az) Limited divorce may be enlarged into absolute divorce after 1 year. Also, absolute divorce may be granted for any cause arising after a divorce from bed and board, sufficient to entitle complaining party to an absolute divorce.

A MATTER OF SIMPLE JUSTICE

The Report of
The President's Task Force on
Women's Rights and Responsibilities

April 1970

MISS VIRGINIA R. ALLAN, CHAIRMAN
JUDGE ELIZABETH ATHANASAKOS   MISS DOROTHY HAENER
MRS. ANN R. BLACKHAM   MRS. LADDIE F. HUTAR
MISS P. DEE BOERSMA   MRS. KATHERINE B. MASSENBURG
MISS EVELYN CUNNINGHAM   MR. WILLIAM C. MERCER
ANN IDA GANNON, B.V.M.   DR. ALAN SIMPSON
MRS. VERA GLASER   MISS EVELYN E. WHITLOW

Presidential Task Force On Women's Rights And Responsibilities

WASHINGTON, D.C. 20210

December 15, 1969.

The PRESIDENT,
The White House, Washington, D.C.

DEAR MR. PRESIDENT: As President of the United States, committed to the principle of equal rights for all, your leadership can be crucial to the more than half our citizens who are women and who are now denied their full constitutional and legal rights.

The quality of life to which we aspire and the questioning at home and abroad of our commitment to the democratic ideal make it imperative that our nation utilize to the fullest the potential of all citizens.

Yet the research and deliberations of this Task Force reveal that the United States, as it approaches its 200th anniversary, lags behind other enlightened, and indeed some newly emerging, countries in the role ascribed to women.

Social attitudes are slow to change. So widespread and pervasive are discriminatory practices against women they have come to be regarded, more often than not, as normal. Unless there is clear indication of Administration concern at the highest level, it is unlikely that significant progress can be made in correcting ancient, entrenched injustices.

American women are increasingly aware and restive over the denial of equal opportunity, equal responsibility, even equal protection of the law. An abiding concern for home and children should not, in their view, cut them off from the freedom to choose the role in society to which their interest, education, and training entitle them.

Women do not seek special privileges. They do seek equal rights. They do wish to assume their full responsibilities.

Equality for women is unalterably linked to many broader questions of social justice. Inequities within our society serve to restrict the contribution of both sexes. We have witnessed a decade of rebellion during which black Americans fought for true equality. The battle still rages Nothing could demonstrate more dramatically the explosive potential of denying fulfillment as human beings to any segment of our society.

What this Task Force recommends is a national commitment to basic changes that will bring women into the mainstream of American life. Such a commitment, we believe, is necessary to healthy psychological, social, and economic growth of our society.

The leader who makes possible a fairer and fuller contribution by women to the nation's destiny will reap dividends of productivity measurable in billions of dollars. He will command respect and loyalty beyond measure from those freed from second-class citizenship. He will reaffirm, at a time of renewed worldwide emphasis on human rights, America's fitness for leadership in the community of nations.

His task will not be easy, for he must inspire and persuade government and the private sector to abandon outmoded attitudes based on false premises.

Without such leadership there is danger of accelerating militancy or the kind of deadening apathy that stills progress and inhibits creativity.

Therefore, this Task Force recommends that the President:

1. Establish an Office of Women's Rights and Responsibilities, whose director would serve as a special assistant reporting directly to the President.

2. Call a White House conference on women's rights and responsibilities in 1970, the fiftieth anniversary of the ratification of the suffrage amendment and establishment of the Women's Bureau.

3. Send a message to the Congress citing the widespread discriminations against women, proposing legislation to remedy these inequities, asserting Federal leadership, recommending prompt State action as a corollary, and calling upon the private sector to follow suit.

The message should recommend the following legislation necessary to ensure full legal equality for women:

    a. Passage of a joint resolution proposing the equal rights amendment to the Constitution.

    b. Amendment of Title VII of the Civil Rights Act of 1964 to (1) remove the burden of enforcement from the aggrieved individual by empowering the Equal Employment Opportunity Commission to enforce the law, and (2) extend coverage to State and local governments and to teachers.

    c. Amendment of Titles IV and IX of the Civil Rights Act of 1964 to authorize the Attorney General to aid women and parents of minor girls in suits seeking equal access to public education, and to require the Office of Education to make a survey concerning the lack of equal educational opportunities for individuals by reason of sex.

    d. Amendment of Title II of the Civil Rights Act of 1964 to prohibit discrimination because of sex in public accommodations.

    e. Amendment of the Civil Rights Act of 1957 to extend the jurisdiction of the Civil Rights Commission to include denial of civil rights because of sex.

    f. Amendment of the Fair Labor Standards Act to extend coverage of its equal pay provisions to executive, administrative, and professional employees.

    g. Amendment of the Social Security Act to (1) provide benefits to husbands and widowers of disabled and deceased women workers under the same conditions as they are provided to wives and widows of men workers, and (2) provide more equitable retirement benefits for families with working wives.

h. Adoption of the liberalized provisions for child care in the family assistance plan and authorization of Federal aid for child care for families not covered by the family assistance plan.

i. Enactment of legislation to guarantee husbands and children of women employees of the Federal government the same fringe benefits provided for wives and children of male employees in those few areas where inequities still remain.

j. Amendment of the Internal Revenue Code to permit families in which both spouses are employed, families in which one spouse is disabled and the other employed, and families headed by single persons, to deduct from gross income as a business expense some reasonable amount paid to a housekeeper, nurse, or institution for care of children or disabled dependents.

k. Enactment of legislation authorizing Federal grants on a matching basis for financing State commissions on the status of women.

4. The executive branch of the Federal government should be as seriously concerned with sex discrimination as with race discrimination, and with women in poverty as with men in poverty.
Implementation of such a policy will require the following Cabinet-level actions:

a. Immediate issuance by the Secretary of Labor of guidelines to carry out the prohibition against sex discrimination by government contractors, which was added to Executive Order 11246 in October 1967, became effective October 1968, but remains unimplemented.

b. Establishment by the Secretary of Labor of priorities, as sensitive to sex discrimination as to race discrimination, for manpower training programs and in referral to training and employment.

c. Initiation by the Attorney General of legal actions in cases of sex discrimination under section 706(e) and 707 of the Civil Rights Act of 1964, and intervention or filing of amicus curiae briefs by the Attorney General in pending cases challenging the validity under the 5th and 14th amendments of laws involving disparities based on sex.

d. Establishment of a women's unit in the Office of Education to lead efforts to end discrimination in education because of sex.

e. Collection, tabulation, and publication of all economic and social data collected by the Federal government by sex as well as race.

f. Establishment of a high priority for training for household employment by the Secretary of Labor and the Secretary of Health, Education, and Welfare.

5. The President should appoint more women to positions of top responsibility in all branches of the Federal government, to achieve a more equitable ratio of men and women. Cabinet and agency heads should be directed to issue firm instructions that qualified women receive equal consideration in hiring and promotions.

Respectfully submitted,

Virginia R. Allan

VIRGINIA R. ALLAN, *Chairman.*

Elizabeth Athanasakos	Dorothy Haener
Ann R. Blackham	Patricia Hutar
P. Dee Boersma	Katherine B. Massenburg
Evelyn Cunningham	William C. Mercer
Ann Ida Gannon, B.V.M.	Alan Simpson
Vera Glaser	Evelyn E. Whitlow

Contents

October 1, 1969.

The White House

The President today announced the establishment of the Task Force on Women's Rights and Responsibilities, with Miss Virginia R. Allan, former President of the National Federation of Business & Professional Women's Clubs as the Chairman. The task force will review the present status of women in our society and recommend what might be done in the future to further advance their opportunities.

The members of the Task Force on Women's Rights and Responsibilities are:

MISS VIRGINIA R. ALLAN
Executive Vice President
Cahalan Drug Stores, Inc.
Wyandotte, Michigan

HON. ELIZABETH ATHANASAKOS
Municipal Court Judge and Practicing
  Attorney
Fort Lauderdale, Florida

MRS. ANN R. BLACKHAM
President
Ann R. Blackham & Company
Winchester, Massachusetts

MISS P. DEE BOERSMA
Student Gov't. Leader
Graduate Student
Ohio State University
Columbus, Ohio

MISS EVELYN CUNNINGHAM
Director, Women's Unit
Office of the Governor
New York, New York

SISTER ANN IDA GANNON, B.V.M.
President
Mundelein College
Chicago, Illinois

MRS. VERA GLASER
Correspondent
Knight Newspapers
Washington, D.C.

MISS DOROTHY HAENER
International Representative
Women's Department, UAW
Detroit, Michigan

MRS. LADDIE F. HUTAR
President
Public Affairs Service Associates, Inc.
Chicago, Illinois

MRS. KATHERINE B. MASSENBURG
Chairman
Maryland Commission on the Status of
  Women
Baltimore, Maryland

MR. WILLIAM C. MERCER
Vice President, Personnel Relations
American Telephone & Telegraph Co.
New York, New York

DR. ALAN SIMPSON
President
Vassar College
Poughkeepsie, New York

MISS EVELYN E. WHITLOW
Attorney at Law
Los Angeles, California

Office of Women's Rights and Responsibilities

It Is Recommended That the President Establish an Office of Women's Rights and Responsibilities, Whose Director Would Also Serve as a Special Assistant Reporting Directly to the President.

The goal of equality for women is tied to that of a better world for all. The Task Force strongly urges that this objective be given the visibility and priority of entrusting it to an official at the President's right hand.

There has been no individual or office at a sufficiently high level to assume effective overall responsibility for Federal legislative and executive action in the area of equal rights and responsibilities for women, or to set an example for State and local governments.

Establishment of this office in the White House with an adequate staff would offer concrete evidence that the President of the United States is committed to the urgent need for action and is assuming leadership.

The Director of the Office of Women's Rights and Responsibilities would coordinate recruitment and urge consideration of qualified women for policy-level Federal positions.

She would seek new ways to utilize the female sector for the national benefit and to engage women in the hard tasks, challenges, decisions, and experiences through which capabilities are stretched and leadership is developed.

As the President's representative she would seek to inform leaders of business, labor, education, religion, State and local governments, and the communications media on the nature and scope of the problem of sex discrimination, striving to enlist their support in working toward improvement.

(1)

She would chair the interdepartmental committee comprised of top level representatives of those departments and agencies with programs and functions significantly affecting women's rights and responsibilities.

The Interdepartmental Committee would review and coordinate Federal programs for the purpose of assessing their impact on women and girls and would recommend policies and programs to Federal agencies and to the President. It would oversee implementation of the President's program for equal opportunity in the Federal service.

She would serve as executive secretary of the advisory council on women's rights and responsibilities, which serves as a link and a clearinghouse between government and interested private groups. The Council should be comprised of men and women broadly representative of business, labor, education, women's organizations (youth and adult), and State commissions on the status of women.

The Task Force commends to this Office for early consideration a number of important problems, on which the task force did not make recommendations for lack of time or lack of jurisdiction. They are listed in Appendix A.

White House Conference on Women's Rights and Responsibilities

It Is Recommended That the President Call a White House Conference on Women's Rights and Responsibilities in 1970, the Fiftieth Anniversary of the Ratification of the Suffrage Amendment and Establishment of the Women's Bureau.

Major objectives would be to bring together a representative group of the Nation's men and women

- to encourage American women to participate more fully in American life and leadership; to create an awareness of their responsibilities as citizens;
- to examine present laws and mores that influence or determine the status of women;
- to educate women on a positive course of action for achieving equal rights and responsibilities.

The Director of the Office of Women's Rights and Responsibilities, with the advice of the Presidential Advisory Council referred to in Recommendation 1, would plan the structure and program of the conference.

Topics for discussion would include among others: education (including continuing education), counseling, abortion, childhood education and care, women in politics, employment, legal discrimination, volunteer careers, the creative women, women in tomorrow's world, consumer protection, and women as catalysts for peace.

A plan of this nature emphasizes positive action by the President and demonstrates a genuine awareness of the problems facing women. Coupled with corrective legislative action, it would be a deterrent to the radical liberation movements preaching revolution.

Message to Congress
Proposing Legislation

It Is Recommended That the President Urge Passage of the Equal Rights Amendment to the Constitution.

The proposed Equal Rights Amendment reads as follows: "Equality of rights under the law shall not be denied or abridged by the United States or by any State on account of sex."

Passage of the so-called "Equal Rights Amendment" would impose upon women as many responsibilities as it would confer rights. The task force views this objective as desirable.

It is ironic that the basic rights women seek through this amendment are guaranteed all citizens under the Constitution. The applicability of the 5th and 14th amendments in parallel cases involving racial bias has been repeatedly tested and sustained, a process which has taken years and has cost millions of dollars.

The Supreme Court, however, has thus far not accorded the protection of those amendments to female citizens. It has upheld or refused to review laws and practices making discriminatory distinctions based on sex.

These include the practice of excluding women from State universities, a law requiring longer prison sentences for women than for men for the same offense, and a law prohibiting women from working as bartenders (but not in the less lucrative jobs as waitresses in bars).

At the State level there are numerous laws regulating marriage, guardianship, dependents, property ownership, independent business ownership, dower rights, and domicile, which clearly discriminate against women as autonomous, mature persons.

A number of discriminatory State laws have in the past four years been declared unconstitutional by the lower courts, but no case has reached the Supreme Court.

A constitutional amendment is needed to secure justice expeditiously and to avoid the time, expense, uncertainties, and practical difficulties of a case-by-case, State-by-State procedure.

Some effects of passage of the equal rights amendment:

> It would guarantee women and girls admission to publicly sup-ported educational institutions under the same standards as men and boys, but it would also require women to assume equal responsibility for alimony and support of children (within their means, as is the standard applied to men). Women presently bear these responsibilities in some States, but not in all.
>
> It would require that women not be given automatic preference for custody of children in divorce suits. The welfare of the child would become the primary criterion in determining custody.
>
> It would require Federal, State, and local governments to grant women equal opportunity in employment.
>
> It would render invalid any current State laws providing longer prison sentences for women than for men for the same offense.
>
> It would impose on women an obligation for military service. They would not be required to serve in functions for which they are not fitted, any more than men are so required.
>
> Once the equal rights amendment is ratified, the burden of proving the reasonableness of disparate treatment on the basis of sex would shift to the United States or the State. Presently the burden is on the aggrieved individuals to show unreasonableness.

The mere passing of the Amendment will not make unconstitutional any law which has as its basis a differential based on facts other than sex. It will, in the broad field of rights, eliminate discrimination. It would make unconstitutional legislation with disparate treatment based wholly or arbitrarily on sex.

Past opposition to the Equal Rights Amendment has been based to a considerable extent on the fact that it would invalidate State laws regulating the employment of women only. Since these laws are disappearing under the impact of Title VII of the Civil Rights Act of 1964 and State fair employment laws, opposition will be much less and may evaporate in the light of information developed at hearings.

The Equal Rights Amendment has been endorsed by Presidents Eisenhower, Kennedy, Johnson, and Nixon.

5

Title VII of the Civil Rights Act of 1964 Should Be Amended To:

Remove the burden of enforcement from the aggrieved individual by empowering the Equal Employment Opportunity Commission to enforce the law, and
Extend coverage to State and local governments and to teachers.

Title VII of the Civil Rights Act of 1964 has made significant gains in promoting nondiscriminatory practices in industry in hiring and promotions. However, the enforcement provisions of Title VII are inadequate. They place the main burden of enforcement on the individual complainant. The Equal Employment Opportunity Commission's authority is limited to conciliation efforts.

Less cooperation can be anticipated in arriving at a satisfactory resolution of a discrimination complaint when there is knowledge that the Commission's power is merely exhortative. Conciliation efforts have been unsuccessful in more than half the cases in which the Commission found that discrimination had occurred.

In addition, the Commission should be budgeted to provide an adequate staff of investigators, field officers, and other professionals to carry out its responsibilities.

Two bills in Congress would give the Commission enforcement powers. Both would relieve the individual complainant of the burden he now bears in most cases. The Administration bill (S. 2806) would confer upon the Commission the authority to institute enforcement actions in the Federal district courts. S. 2453 also removes the burden of enforcement from the complainant by providing an interim administration proceeding before it or an employer would have recourse to court action.

While the Task Force agreed that the Commission should have enforcement authority, most members were not prepared to choose between the two methods.

With respect to part 2 of the recommendation, Title VII exempts from coverage States and their political subdivisions [see subsection 701(a), (b), (c), and (h)].

Section 702 exempts educational institutions with respect to the employment of individuals to perform work connected with the educational activities of such institutions.

There seems no reason to exempt State and local governments. As representatives of all the people, they are under an obligation to provide equal employment opportunities.

There is gross discrimination against women in education. For example, few women are named school principals. In the school year

1966–67 75% of elementary school principals were men. In 1964–65 men held 96% of the junior high school principal positions while a survey of high school principals for the academic year 1963–64 showed 90% to be men.[1] There is a growing body of evidence of discrimination against women faculty in higher education.

Title IV and Title IX of the Civil Rights Act of 1964 Should Be Amended To Authorize the Attorney General to Aid Women and Parents of Minor Girls in Suits Seeking Equal Access to Public Education, and To Require the Office of Education To Make a Survey Concerning the Lack of Equal Educational Opportunities for Individuals by Reason of Sex.

Discrimination in education is one of the most damaging injustices women suffer. It denies them equal education and equal employment opportunity, contributing to a second class self image.

There have been enough individual instances and limited surveys publicized recently to make it apparent that substantial discrimination does exist. For example, until forced to do so by legal action, the New York City Board of Education did not admit girls to Stuyvesant High School,[2] a specialized high school for science with a national reputation for excellence. Legal action recently has forced the State of Virginia to admit women to the University College of Arts and Sciences at Charlottesville.[3]

Higher admission standards for women than for men are widespread in undergraduate schools and are even more discriminatory in graduate and professional schools. For this reason counselors and parents frequently guide young women into the "feminine" occupations without regard to interests, aptitudes and qualifications.

Only 5.9 percent of our law students and 8.3 percent of our medical students are women,[4] although according to the Office of Education women tend to do better than men on tests for admission to law and medical school.

Section 402 of Title IV, passed in 1964, required the Commissioner of Education to conduct a survey of the extent of discrimination because of race, religion, color, or national origin. Title IV should be amended

---

[1] Research Division, National Education Association.
[2] *De Rivera* v. *Fliedner,* Sup. Ct. N.Y. Civil Action, 00938–69. Resolved by administrative appeal.
[3] *Kirstein et al* v. *University of Virginia,* E. C. Va. Civil Action No. 22069–R.
[4] Executive Secretary, Association of American Law Schools, 1968. Association of American Medical Colleges, 1967.

7

to require a similar survey of discrimination because of sex, not only in practices with respect to students but also in employment of faculty and administration members.

Section 407 of Title IV authorizes the Attorney General to bring suits in behalf of persons denied equal protection of the laws by public school officials. It grants no new rights. While no case relating to sex discrimination in public education has yet reached the Supreme Court, discrimination based on sex in public education should be prohibited by the 14th amendment. The President's Commission on the Status of Women took this position in its 1963 report to the President.[5] Section 902 of the Civil Rights Act authorizes the Attorney General to intervene in cases of this kind after a suit is brought by private parties. Both section 407 and section 902 should be amended to add sex, and section 410 should be similarly amended.

Title II of the Civil Rights Act Should Be Amended To Prohibit Discrimination Because of Sex in Public Accommodations.

Title II of the Civil Rights Act of 1964 provides that "All persons shall be entitled to the full and equal enjoyment of the goods, services, facilities, privileges, advantages, and accommodations of any place of public accommodations, as defined in this section, without discrimination or segregation on the ground of race, color, religion, or national origin."

Injunctive relief is provided for persons whose rights are violated, and the Attorney General is authorized to initiate suits in patterns or practice cases and to intervene in suits filed by individuals.

Discrimination because of sex is practiced primarily in restaurants and bars. While the Task Force does not consider this the most injurious discrimination against women today, it is wrong in principle.

The State of Pennsylvania and the City of Pittsburgh have amended their human rights legislation to prohibit discrimination because of sex in public accommodations.

The Task Force recommends amendment of sections 201(a) and 202 by adding "sex," between "religion" and "or."

---

[5] President's Commission on the Status of Women, *American Women,* p. 45, 1963.

8

The Civil Rights Act of 1957 Should Be Amended To Extend the Jurisdiction of the Civil Rights Commission To Include Denial of Civil Rights Because of Sex.

The Civil Rights Commission is authorized by section 104 of the Civil Rights Act of 1957, as amended (42 U.S.C. 1975c) to

- study and collect information concerning legal developments which constitute a denial of equal protection of the laws under the Constitution because of race, color, religion, or national origin or in the administration of justice;
- appraise the laws and policies of the Federal government with respect to equal protection of the laws under the Constitution because of race, color, religion, or national origin or in the administration of justice;
- Serve as a national clearinghouse for civil rights information.

The Commission is also authorized to investigate deprivation of voting rights because of race, color, religion, or national origin; but this function is of little concern in sex discrimination since there is apparently no concerted effort to deprive women of their voting rights.

Deprivation of equal educational opportunity and enforcement of laws prohibiting sex discrimination in employment are of great concern, however. The hearings and reports of the Civil Rights Commission would help draw public attention to the extent to which equal protection of the laws is denied because of sex. A clearinghouse for civil rights information is also needed.

Perhaps the greatest deterrent to securing improvement in the legal status of women is the lack of public knowledge of the facts and the lack of a central information bank.

For example, laws in Connecticut and Pennsylvania requiring longer prison sentences for women than for men for the same offense were declared unconstitutional in 1968.[6] There is now no Federal organization with responsibility for exploring and publicizing the extent to which this and other inequalities in the criminal law and practice, such as those involving abortion, exist in the United States.

"Sex" should be inserted after "religion" wherever the word appears in section 104(a) of the Civil Rights Act of 1957, as amended, including paragraph (1) relating to voting rights. While there may be no problem with respect to voting rights, an overall pattern of prohibiting discrimination based on sex should be consistently sought.

---

[6] *Daniels* v. *Pennsylvania,* 232A, 2d 252; *U.S. ex rel Robinson* v. *York,* 281 F. Supp. 8(D. Conn. 1958).

9

The Fair Labor Standards Act Should Be Amended To Extend Coverage of Its Equal Pay Provisions (i.e., the Equal Pay Act of 1963) to Executive, Administrative, and Professional Employees.

The original legislative proposal for an equal pay law, as drafted by the Labor Department, did not exempt executive, professional, and administrative employees. At no point in the legislative process was it proposed to make such an exemption.

When the Congress decided that the equal pay requirement should be administered by the Wage and Hour and Public Contracts Divisions of the Labor Department, the equal pay bill was made an amendment to the Fair Labor Standards Act which the Department administers. The exemptions of the Fair Labor Standards Act then automatically applied to the equal pay provisions. One exempt category covers executive, administrative, and professional employees.

Women in professional, executive, and administrative positions have the protection of Title VII of the Civil Rights Act of 1964, which prohibits discrimination in employment because of sex, as well as because of race, color, religion, or national origin. Title VII, however, does not permit a complainant's identity to be withheld from the employer, as it can be under the Fair Labor Standards Act.

This is particularly important to women who have achieved professional, executive, and administrative positions, which they are very reluctant to endanger. Such women do not have the protection against reprisal provided by union contracts. Furthermore, Title VII at present includes no enforcement authority for the administering agency.

Thirty-six thousand other women (and a few men) have been awarded $12.6 million in wages since the law went into effect in 1964, including $4.6 million awarded 16,000 employees in the 1969 fiscal year.[7]

It would be necessary to amend section 13 of the Fair Labor Standards Act (29 U.S.C. 213) so that this exemption of section 13 does not apply to section 6(d).

---

[7] Unpublished figures from Wage and Hour and Public Contracts Divisions, U.S. Department of Labor, 1969.

10

The Social Security Act Should Be Amended To:

Provide benefits to husbands and widowers of disabled and deceased women workers under the same conditions as they are provided to wives and widows of men workers, and

Provide more equitable retirement benefits for families with working wives.

The emergence of a new pattern of family economic interdependence has been accompanied by an awareness of inequities in the social security program as they apply to families where the wife works.

Under current law a wife or widow receives a benefit based on her husband's earnings without meeting any test of dependency. A husband or widower of a woman worker is entitled to a benefit only if he proves he receives one-half or more of his support from his wife.

The family protection provisions of the social security program were based on the sociological conditions and climate of the 1930's. In 1940, 14.7 percent of married women were in the labor force; in 1968 the percentage had increased to 38.3 percent. In these families the wives contributed on the average 26.6 percent of the family income. In 25.6 percent of such families, the wives contributed 40 percent or more of the family income. In most of the families where the wife was in the labor force, the husband's yearly income was below $7,000.[8] The percentage of two-income families is increasing and more and more frequently the family standard of living is based on two incomes.

The death or disablement of a wife in a two-income family will leave the husband with increased responsibility for the children and less income with which to meet the needs. With almost two-fifths of all husband-wife families following a new pattern of economic interdependence, it is time for the social security program to adapt to the new sociological conditions and climate. Changes to recognize the new-type family began with a series of amendments in 1950 which provide benefits to children of working women under the the same conditions as for children of working men.

---

[8] Unpublished data from Bureau of Labor Statistics, U.S. Department of Labor.

Social Security Act provisions for automatic benefits for wives of retiring male workers lead to a second type of inequity. In 1939, a benefit was provided for the wives of retiring men workers—on the assumption that the wives were dependent and it cost more for a family to live than for a single person. If the wife is entitled to a benefit based on her own earnings, she has to choose between the two. In 1950 this benefit was provided for dependent husbands of women workers. The benefit for wife or dependent husband is 50 percent of the worker's benefit with a maximum of $105 per month.

Thus a wife who has worked for many years and contributed to the social security system may receive no larger benefit than if she had never worked. For example, a wife who never worked under social security would get a wife's benefit of $105 at age 65 if her husband had the maximum average monthly earnings of $650. If the same wife had worked and paid contributions on average monthly earnings of $120, she would be entitled at age 65 to a benefit of $81.10, plus an additional wife's benefit of $23.90, for a total benefit of $105—the same as if she had not contributed to the social security system.[9]

The present provisions also result in situations where a retired couple who have both worked receive less in benefits than a couple where only the husband worked and had the same earnings as the combined earnings of the working couple. If, for example, only the husband had worked and had average earnings of $650 a month—$7,800 a year—the benefits paid to the couple at age 65 would be $323 ($218 to the husband and $105 to the wife). By contrast, if the husband and wife each had average earnings of $325 a month, or $3,900 a year—combined annual earnings of $7,800—their benefits will be lower—$134.30 each, or a total of $268.60.[10]

Proposals for giving greater recognition to working wives' social security contributions have been made by the Social Insurance and Taxes Committee of the President's Commission on the Status of Women [11]; by the Citizens' Advisory Council on the Status of Women [12]; and by Congresswoman Martha Griffiths in H.R. 841.

---

[9] Citizens' Advisory Council on the Status of Women, *Report of Task Force on Social Insurance and Taxes,* p. 70, 1968.

[10] Ibid, p. 72.

[11] President's Commission on the Status of Women, *Report of Committee on Social Insurance and Taxes,* p. 36, 1963.

[12] See 8 above, p. 77.

The Administration Should Urge Congress To Adopt the Liberalized Provisions for Child Care Proposed in S. 2986 for Inclusion in the Social Security Act (Section 437 of Title IV). The Administration Should Also Support Authorization of Federal Aid for Child Care for Families Not Covered Under the Family Assistance Plan, With at Least a Modest Appropriation in 1970.

Lack of adequate child care facilities has been found to be a major deterrent to solution or even significant progress in providing greater education opportunities for children, reducing the welfare burden, giving greater dignity and self-respect to mothers on welfare, filling critical manpower needs in shortage occupations and providing real freedom of choice in life style for women.

Every Federal and State study of the status of women has referred to the necessity for expanding child care facilities.

Department of Labor manpower experts cite lack of child care as the most serious single barrier to job training or employment for low-income mothers.

Our national goal should be:

1. A system of well-run child care centers available to all pre-school children. Although priority would be given the needs of low-income working mothers, the facilities should be available to middle income mothers who wish to use them.
2. After-school activities for school-age children at all economic levels who require them.

The National Advisory Council on Economic Opportunity estimated this year that 700,000 migrant children need day care. Only 13,000 spaces are available.

The Council found that 1,373,000 economically deprived children could have benefited from participation in full-time Head Start programs. Only 213,000 spaces were funded this year.[13]

The Task Force endorses the Administration's plan for increasing facilities for care of pre-school and school age children, with priority for low-income and welfare families.

In addition, we recommend that the Administration support legislation to authorize Federal grants for developing child care facilities for families at all income levels, with at least a modest appropriation.

---

[13] Office of Economic Opportunity, *Continuity and Change in Antipoverty Programs,* Second Report of National Advisory Council on Economic Opportunity, 1969.

The funds would be used to construct child care centers, expand existing care programs, renovate facilities, assist States in improving their licensing standards, train professional and sub-professional staff, research, food programs, and a comprehensive study of existing child care programs at Federal, State, and local levels.

H.R. 469 and H.R. 466 Should Be Enacted To Guarantee Husbands and Children of Women Employees of the Federal Government the Same Fringe Benefits Provided for Wives and Children of Male Employees in Those Few Areas Where Inequities Still Remain.

A number of the laws and regulations governing fringe benefits of Federal employees are, like the social security program, based on the assumption that a wife is dependent on her husband except in those few cases where he is unable to work when it is recognized that he may be dependent on her. The facts demonstrate that in the 38.3 percent [14] of all husband-wife families where the wife works, there is interdependency, and the dependency concepts applicable to the traditional family are not viable (see recommendation 3(g) for additional relevant facts).

Under the civil service and foreign service retirement systems, for example, the surviving husband of a deceased woman employee is not eligible for an annuity unless he is incapable of self-support because of physical or mental disability and has received more than half his support from the deceased woman [15] employee. The surviving spouse of a deceased male employee is automatically eligible for an annuity.

There are inequities in quarters' allowances for employees serving overseas and in eligibility free attendance at dependents' schools.

There are similar differences in treatment of military personnel.

To correct these inequities the Interdepartmental Committee on the Status of Women considered and endorsed H. R. 643 introduced by Congresswoman Griffiths in the 90th Congress. This bill had been drafted by the Civil Service Commission at the request of the Congresswoman.

H.R. 469 of the 91st Congress is identical to H.R. 643, and H.R. 466 would correct the same problems in the military personnel systems.

---

[14] Unpublished data from the Bureau of Labor Statistics, U.S. Department of Labor.
[15] 5 U.S.C. 8341 and 22 U.S.C. 1082.

The Internal Revenue Code Should Be Amended To Permit Families in Which Both Spouses Are Employed, Families in Which One Spouse Is Disabled and the Other Employed, and Families Headed by Single Persons, To Deduct from Gross Income as a Business Expense Some Reasonable Amount Paid to a Housekeeper, Nurse, or Institution for Care of Children or Disabled Dependents.

This proposal differs from present provisions of law in the following respects:

The present deduction is a personal deduction from taxable income. It is of no benefit to the taxpayer for whom the standard deduction (now generally 10 percent of gross income up to a maximum of $1,000) is more advantageous than itemizing allowable deductions for charitable contributions, interest on mortgages and loans, medical expenses, taxes, and casualty losses. Taxpayers who are not homeowners are not likely to have enough personal deductions to exceed the standard allowance; therefore, they receive no, or a very reduced, benefit from a personal deduction. The Task Force believes it would be more equitable and more rational to deduct the expenses from gross income as a business expense.

Under present law a husband-wife family benefit from the deduction only if their income does not exceed $6,600 with one dependent or $6,900 with two or more dependents. The Task Force proposal eliminates this limitation on income. There is no income limitation on the single head of household, and there seems to be no good reason for limiting the deduction to low-income husband-wife families.

The present law does not permit single men with disabled dependents in their care (such as parents) to take this deduction although single women in the same situation are covered. The Task Force believes both should be covered.

The present law does not allow men or women with disabled spouses requiring care at home or in an institution to benefit from this deduction. Such a couple can deduct only expenses for care of "dependents," which by definition does not include spouses. This also seems irrational and inequitable and the Task Force believes that if care of the disabled spouse is necessary to enable the other spouse to be gainfully employed, the expenses of such care typically should be deductible to the same extent that expenses for care of "dependents" is deductible.

The existing law limits the deduction to $600 for one dependent and $900 for two or more. The Task Force finds that corrective action is needed, but additional economic data would be required to establish the level of deduction.

Legislation Should Be Proposed Authorizing Federal Grants on a Matching Basis for Financing State Commissions on the Status of Women.

Since 1962 every State, the District of Columbia, Puerto Rico, the Virgin Islands, and several cities have established commissions on the status of women. Although most were unfunded or inadequately funded, 38 commissions or successor bodies are still functioning. These 38 do not include women's divisions created by statute in Louisiana and New Jersey, which are not yet operational. The Governor of Ohio also has recently issued an executive order establishing a yet to be staffed women's unit in the State government. Other governors are committed to reactivating their State commissions.

In most of the States the commissions are still independent bodies. In a few States, a women's unit, usually with a citizens' advisory committee, has been established in a permanent part of the State structure— in the Governor's office, the Department of Human Rights, the Department of Community Affairs, the Employment Security Department, or the Labor Department.

Few commissions have received sufficient staff assistance or funds to carry out their programs as recommended in the *Handbook for State and City Commissions on the Status of Women,* prepared by members of the 1967 Midwest Regional Conference of State Commissions.[16] The need cited there include: a headquarters office with funds for a chairman or executive secretary, phone, files, postage, office supplies and equipment, transportation to meetings and conferences, surveys and pilot projects, and publication of reports.

Only seven of the commissions receive any regular State appropriations—Alaska, $5,000; California, $44,210; Illinois, $5,000; Kentucky, $25,000 (plus $15,000 grant for a research project); Maine, $2,000; Michigan, $11,500; and North Carolina, $3,000. The New York Women's Unit in the Office of the Governor is best staffed, having 11 salaried employees.

The many positive contributions of the commissions in a variety of fields are documented in progress reports of the Federal Interdepartmental Committee on the Status of Women and in reports of conferences of the commissions, all available from the U.S. Department of Labor, Women's Bureau.

---

[16] University Extension, The University of Wisconsin, *Handbook for State Commissions on the Status of Women,* 1968. Available from Women's Bureau, U.S. Department of Labor.

Their durability under adverse circumstances and through changes in State administration further demonstrates that they are needed and useful. With the growth of commissions on university campuses, the State groups will have another function—to give technical assistance to the younger women and to see to it that the concerns of university commissions are effectively brought to the attention of the Governors and State legislatures.

The Task Force recommends that one of the first assignments of the Office of Women's Rights and Responsibilities be to develop a legislative proposal for Federal grants to State commissions and to State government units having the same functions. The grants should be made under standards that will encourage growth of university commissions.

Policy of Executive Branch Respecting Sex Discrimination

The Executive Branch of the Federal Government Should Be as Seriously Concerned With Sex Discrimination as Race Discrimination and With Women in Poverty as Men in Poverty.

The testimony and published data received by the Task Force indicate that long-established policies of Federal agencies base their efforts to alleviate poverty and discrimination on the assumption that race discrimination is more inflammatory than sex discrimination.

Sex bias takes a greater economic toll than racial bias. The median earnings of white men employed year-round full-time is $7,396, of Negro men $4,777, of white women $4,279, of Negro women $3,194. Women with some college education both white and Negro, earn less than Negro men with 8 years of education.[1]

Women head 1,723,000 impoverished families, Negro males head 820,000. One-quarter of all families headed by white women are in poverty. More than half of all headed by Negro women are in poverty. Less than a quarter of those headed by Negro males are in poverty. Seven percent of those headed by white males are in poverty.[2]

The unemployment rate is higher among women than men, among girls than boys. More Negro women are unemployed than Negro men, and almost as many white women as white men are unemployed (most women on welfare are not included in the unemployment figures—only those actually seeking employment.)[3]

Unrest, particularly among poor women and college girls, is mounting. Studies show that 39 percent of the rioters in Detroit were women and in Los Angeles 50 percent were women. The proportion of women

---

[1] U.S. Department of Commerce, Bureau of the Census: CPR–60, No. 60, Table 11 and Table 4.

[2] U.S. Department of Commerce, Bureau of the Census: CPR–60, No. 55.

[3] U.S. Department of Labor, Bureau of Labor Statistics, *Employment and Earnings*, Vol. 15, No. 7, January 1969, Table A–1.

among the arrestees was 10 and 13 percent, respectively.[4] Welfare mothers are using disruptive tactics to demand greater welfare payments. Radical women's groups, some with a philosophy similar to that of the Students for a Democratic Society are mushrooming on college campuses.

Essential justice requires the Federal government to give much greater attention to the elimination of sex discrimination and to the needs of women in poverty. The following specifications are recommended as a beginning.

The Secretary of Labor Should Immediately Issue Guidelines To Carry Out the Prohibition Against Sex Discrimination in Employment by Government Contractors, Which Was Added to Executive Order 11246 in October 1967, Became Effective October 1968, but Remains Unimplemented.

The first Presidential executive order prohibiting discrimination in employment by employers operating under Government contracts was issued in 1941. Each Administration has continued its existence in various ways. Organizations and women's groups have been on record supporting the inclusion of the word "sex" in this order since its inception. This pressure was persistent and it grew in numbers over the years.

The 1963 report of the President's Commission on the Status of Women took cognizance of this problem but recommended its correction by a separate executive order stating the principle of nondiscrimination but without the enforcement possible under the executive order covering other phases of discrimination.[5] A minority report was issued by a member of the Committee on Private Employment of the President's Commission on this recommendation.[6] The President never acted upon the recommendation.

The Commission also recommended:

> . . . appropriate Federal, State, and local officials in all branches of government should be urged to scrutinize carefully those laws, regulations, and practices which distinguish on the basis of sex to determine whether they are justifiable in the light of contemporary conditions and to the end of removing archaic standards which today operate as discriminatory.[7]

---

[4] Fogelson and Hill, *Who Riots? A Study of Participation in 1967 Riots,* July 1968. Published in *Supplemental Studies for The National Advisory Commission on Civil Disorders,* p. 233.
[5] President's Commission on the Status of Women, *American Women,* p. 30, 1963.
[6] President's Commission on the Status of Women, *Report of the Committee on Private Employment,* 1963.
[7] President's Commission on the Status of Women, *American Women,* p. 45.

After Title VII of the Civil Rights Act of 1964 clearly established that sex discrimination in employment was contrary to public policy, the executive order on government contracts was revised and reissued on September 24, 1965, as Executive Order 11246 without prohibiting sex discrimination.

Not until two years later, after extensive concern had been expressed by women's groups and other organizations, was the order amended to prohibit sex bias. The effective date was October 17, 1968, one year after the date of issue, to permit the Labor Department adequate time for developing policy.

It was not until January 17, 1969, that *proposed* guidelines were issued, with interested persons allowed 30 days in which to comment. Many women's groups and organizations responded with impatient requests for immediate issuance. After some time oral hearings were scheduled for August 4, 5, and 6, 1969. Women's groups and organizations, ranging from radical to conservative, testified. All urged immediate implementation of the sex discrimination provision of Executive Order 11246.

It is imperative that revised and updated guidelines be issued immediately and the Executive Order vigorously enforced.

The Secretary of Labor Should Establish Priorities as Sensitive To Sex Discrimination as To Race Discrimination in Manpower Training Programs and in Referrals To Training and Employment.

A disadvantaged individual for manpower program purposes, "is a poor person who does not have suitable employment and who is either (1) a school dropout, (2) a member of a minority, (3) under 22 years of age, (4) 45 years of age or over, or (5) handicapped." [8]

Being female is not considered to be as much of a handicap as belonging to a minority group, despite economic data clearly indicating the contrary (see the economic data with recommendation 4).

The definition of "disadvantaged individual" would not include a white woman on welfare unless she were a school dropout, under 22 years of age, 45 years of age or over, or handicapped. This definition clearly needs to be revised to include all women who are poor and who do not have suitable employment.

In the on-the-job training programs conducted under the Manpower Development and Training Act only 31.7 percent of the 125,000 trainees

---

[8] U.S. Department of Labor, Manpower Administration Order 1–69 of January 16, 1969.

in fiscal year 1968 were women. The on-the-job training is particularly important because the placement rate is higher than for institutional training programs.[9]

In the JOBS (Job Opportunities in the Business Sector) program, only 24 percent of those hired were female. This program is for the disadvantaged only. As of November 1968, 54,000 employee-trainees were in projects funded by the Labor Department.[10]

Of the 33,000 enrollees in the Job Corps in June 1968, only 29 percent were female.[11]

Young men have the additional advantage of military training, with 100,000 below-standard young men receiving training every year, in addition to the training the military provides for poor young men who meet the normal standards.[12]

The Government's failure to accord a higher priority to training of women either in civilian or military programs is unjust and is socially very costly.

The number of unemployed young women, age 16 to 24, has risen from 268,000 in 1947 to 697,000 in 1968. (The unemployment rate for young women has increased while decreasing for young men in this age range.[13])

Without any question the growing number of families on Aid to Families with Dependent Children is related to the increase in unemployed young women. For many girls living in very poor or disorganized families, the inability to find a job means turning to prostitution or other crime—or having a child to get on welfare. Potential husbands do not earn enough to support an unemployed wife.

The stability of the low income family depends as much on training women for employment as it does on training men. Only through employment of both partners can such families move into the middle class.

The task force expects welfare rolls will continue to rise unless society takes more seriously the needs of disadvantaged girls and young women.

---

[9] U.S. Department of Labor, *Statistics on Manpower: A Supplement to the Manpower Report of the President,* Tables F–2 and F–5, March 1969.

[10] U.S. Department of Labor, *Manpower Report of the President,* p. 94, January 1969.

[11] See footnote 9 above, Table F–15.

[12] See footnote 10, p. 119.

[13] See footnote 9 above, p. 18, Table A–12.

The Attorney General Should Initiate Legal Actions in Cases of Sex Discrimination Under Sections 706(e) and 707 of the Civil Rights Act of 1964, and Intervention or Filing of Amicus Curiae Briefs in Pending Cases Challenging the Validity Under the 5th and 14th Amendments of Laws Involving Disparities Based on Sex.

Although the Justice Department has participated in more than 40 cases of racial bias, it has not intervened in behalf of an individual discriminated against because of sex, except in one case on a procedural point.

The Justice Department, likewise, has not given aid in any case in which women are challenging the constitutionality of State laws discriminating on the basis of sex—with one exception *White* v. *Crook*.[14] in which race discrimination was also a factor.

A former Attorney General, who was a member of the 1963 President's Commission on the Status of Women, not only signed the commission's report but sponsored the following recommendation:

> Early and definitive court pronouncement, particularly by the U.S. Supreme Court, is urgently needed with regard to the validity under the 5th and 14th amendments of laws and official practices discriminating against women, to the end that the principle of equality become firmly established in constitutional doctrine.
>
> Accordingly, interested groups should give high priority to bringing under court review cases involving laws and practices which discriminate against women.[15]

Women will be skeptical of the Administration's commitment to equality as long as the Justice Department refuses to act.

The Commissioner of Education Should Establish a Women's Unit in His Office To Lead Efforts To End Discrimination in Education Because of Sex.

Discrimination in education is so widespread that we believe a special unit in the Office of the Commissioner is needed to focus public and agency attention on the facts and effects of discrimination against women in education.

---

[14] 251 F. Supp. 401.
[15] President's Commission on the Status of Women, *American Women,* page 45, 1963.

The percentage of graduate degrees awarded women is lower than in 1930, when women received 40 percent of all masters degrees. They received 34 percent in 1966. Fifteen percent of doctors degrees in 1930 wen to women, but only 12 percent in 1966.[16] University commissions on the status of women organized by women students are surveying the numbers of women students and faculty members and finding strong evidence to support their personal observations. Other evidences of discrimination are stated under recommendation 3(c).

Functions of the unit should include the following:

- to collect data now available on the status of women and girls as students and as faculty and administration in secondary schools and schools of higher education and to plan and coordinate a survey to fill the gaps;
- to give technical assistance to State and university commissions on the status of women and to other organizations actively concerned with status of women in education;
- to invite such organizations as the Association of American University Professors, American Council on Education, Association of American Colleges, and the Association of Governing Boards of Colleges and Universities to cooperate in identifying and securing corrective action on discrimination against women as members of faculty and administration;
- to work with Federal, State, and local officials, with professional organizations, and with the Parent-Teachers Association to improve the quality of counseling of girls and women;
- to become a clearinghouse of information on women in education and counseling needs of women;
- to speak for the needs of disadvantaged girls within the educational community; to lead efforts to break down the legal and attitudinal barriers to all types of vocational training for girls; to encourage establishment of vocational training in household skills;
- to see to it that counseling institutes sponsored by the Office of Education include a substantial segment on the special counseling needs of women, needs growing out of societal attitudes and institutions that constrict the aspiration of girls and keep from them knowledge of the great choice of roles open to them;
- to find means of assuring that the financial needs of part-time students are given appropriate priority in allocation of money available for financial assistance.

[16] Women's Bureau, U.S. Department of Labor *Fact Sheet on Trends in Educational Attainment of Women,* April 1968.

As a result of the testimony of numerous witnesses, which provided convincing evidence of discrimination against women as students and as faculty and which included many specific suggestions for governmental leadership action, the Task Force concluded that the Office of Education should have a women's unit, whose director would report to the Commissioner, to give leadership to public and private efforts to eliminate discrimination in education.

All Agencies of the Federal Government That Collect Economic or Social Data About Persons Should Collect, Tabulate, and Publish Results by Sex as Well as Race.

Government studies, publications and press releases frequently obscure the degree of economic handicap women suffer and its consequences. Sometimes results of studies are published for males only or for males and females combined. Sometimes the data are structured so as to ignore gross differences by sex.

For example, the Bureau of the Census published a summary of major highlights of the March 1969 Current Population Survey.[17] The following tables do not include data by sex: "Median Earnings in 1968 and 1967 by Occupation of Longest Job During Year—Civilian Males 14 Years Old and Over with Earnings" (page 5), "Persons Below the Poverty Level by Color: 1959–1968" (page 6), and "Percent Distribution by Years of School Completed for Persons 20 Years Old and Over" (page 9). A table on page 4 "Median Family Income of Negroes as a Percent of White Family Income" should have included median family income by race of families headed by women and families headed by men.

While later detailed publications will include data by sex and race, the summary will be the publication most useful to the general public. When its tables do not include sex breakdowns, one has to dig into a number of detailed publications in order to get the most basic kinds of data relating to sex discrimination.

Another example of ignoring the economic situation of women is "Welfare Reform Charts: 1969 Legislative Recommendations" published by the Department of Health, Education, and Welfare.[18] Although almost two-thirds of the adult poor are women and although a much higher pro-

---

[17] U.S. Department of Commerce, *Selected Characteristics of Persons and Families: March 1969,* Series P–20, No. 189, August 18, 1969.
[18] U.S. Department of Health, Education, and Welfare, *Welfare Reform Charts, 1969 Legislative Recommendations,* October 1969.

portion of those adults on welfare are women, the publication never mentions this fact or even uses the word "women."

One item in this publication reads "There are over one million families headed by fathers who are working full time and earning less than the average AFDC–UF payment for families without other income." The number of such families with women heads should have been given as well.

Although one of the key features of the proposed family assistance plan is a great expansion in day care centers to make it possible for mothers to get training and employment, there is no chart on day care and none relating to training and employment of women.

The Equal Employment Opportunity Commission, the agency charged with enforcement of legislation forbidding discrimination in employment, has published a three-volume report [19] based on a survey of numbers of persons employed in the private sector by industry, occupation, sex, and race. One can examine this whole report and never find a table or narrative statement that compares the employment situation for white men, Negro men, white women, Negro women. There are not even any tables comparing white women with white men or Negro women with Negro men.

The tables are all based on comparisons of minority men with white men, minority women with white women. The underlying assumption of this appears to be that sex differences in industry and occupational distribution of white men and white women are insignificant or perhaps that these differences do not result from discrimination. It is submitted that this assumption begs the question, because it is only from such facts that the discrimination if any can be spotted and then analyzed.

An analysis of the data by Princeton University, under a grant from the Commission and the Department of Labor, used an extraordinarily sophisticated and confusing methodology, which obscured sex discrimination in employment. Much emphasis is given this analysis in the report.

The Princeton group constructed "an index to show the relative standing of each racial group based on how many were employed in low- or high-paying occupations". [20] Actually they constructed two indexes—one for males and one for females. The "standing" of Anglo males was arbitrarily given a value of 100 and minority males were compared. In separate tables Anglo females were assigned an index of 100 and minority group females were compared with the Anglo females. This methodology

---

[19] Equal Employment Opportunity Commission, *Equal Employment Opportunity Report No. 1: Job Patterns for Minorities and Women,* 1968.

[20] Ibid, page 6 of Volume 1 of Equal Employment Opportunity Commission Report.

avoids acknowledging that in all earnings information, whether overall, by occupation, or by education, white women rank below Negro men and way below white men. For the report to be a proper foundation upon which to base an opinion the standing of Anglo females to Anglo males and minority males and of minority females to Anglo males and minority males should be set forth.

All statistics on employment published by any Federal agency should show breakdowns by race and sex for every factor analyzed. Study designs should be based on the principle that sex discrimination is illegal and immoral.

The Secretary of Labor and the Secretary of Health, Education, and Welfare Should Give Training for Household Employment a High Priority in Manpower Training.

Through the leadership of the Women's Bureau, a National Committee on Household Employment was established in 1965. Seven experimental and demonstration training programs have been funded in Alexandria, Virginia; Boston, Massachusetts; Chicago, Illinois; Manhattan, Kansas; Philadelphia, Pennsylvania; Pittsburgh, Pennsylvania; and New York, New York.

The following results are reported: improvement in the attitude and performance of workers and the regularity of their employment, increased wage potential, and better employee and employer attitudes and satisfaction. Employer training has been included in some programs and it is recommended for inclusion in all programs.

The Task Force recommends making such programs widely available under the Manpower Development and Training Act and the Vocational Education Act.

Funds should be earmarked by the Secretary of Labor from the national account (unallocated reserve) of the Manpower Development and Training Act budget.

The Committee establishing guidelines under the Cooperative Area Manpower Planning System (CAMPS) should be directed to give a high priority to such training.

State employment service offices should be required to give more attention to placement of household workers and determining manpower needs for household employment.

The Commissioner of Education should encourage the States to provide for training in household employment and home-related arts in their secondary and post-secondary training programs.

We recommend that consideration be given by curriculum planners in the Departments of Labor and Health, Education, and Welfare to including training in driving and home maintenance and upkeep, outside and inside. Elderly couples and individuals are an increasing market for household services, and need services of this kind, as do families with working mothers. Training in such skills would enable the employee to earn higher wages.

Equalization of Policy-Making Responsibility in the Federal Government

The President Should Appoint More Women to Positions of Top Responsibility in All Branches of the Federal Government, To Achieve a More Equitable Ratio of Men and Women. Cabinet and Agency Heads Should Be Directed To Issue Firm Instructions That Qualified Women Receive Equal Consideration in Hiring and Promotions.

Wise utilization of the Nation's human resources dictates that the responsibilities of leadership in America be distributed more equitably between our men and women citizens.

The United States has not capitalized fully on the skills, abilities, and special insights of women, particularly at the leadership level. When half the population is rendered virtually non-contributory in fashioning policy, the loss of balance and perspective is self-evident, tragic, and wasteful.

Shutting out any group stifles its urge to contribute, depresses its concept of self worth, and ultimately discourages the striving for excellence.

Where so large a proportion of citizens is involved, the damage to national pride and achievement can be far reaching and can call into question the Administration's basic fairness.

The present pace of appointments of women to high Federal positions should be accelerated, to reflect their numerical strength more realistically, and as an incentive and symbol of the Administration's commitment.

To do so, the President and his Cabinet should place stronger emphasis on appointments based on merit rather than sex, and wherever possible urge the private sector to follow suit.

In making appointments the "showcase" approach or tokenism should be avoided. Women should not be confined to the so-called distaff area but brought into the dynamics of policy development.

The existing bank of qualified women economists, lawyers, politicians, jurists, educators, scientists, physicians, writers, and administrators has the intellectual capacity to meet the most exacting demands.

Under present social and economic attitudes, relatively few of these professionals have been accorded the same public recognition as similarly qualified men, but they can and should be located.

The direction of a program staffed by volunteers often develops administrative and managerial skills of a high order.

For this reason standards and asumptions regarding the qualifications of women for high office should be reassessed with a view to capitalizing on these assets.

When the other recommendations in this report are implemented hopefully they will serve to reduce roadblocks now hampering women at lower levels, thus speeding an upward flow of talent and offering more choice to government talent scouts when women are sought for leadership roles.

Minority Views of Dorothy Haener on Extension of Fair Labor Standards Act

I am strongly of the opinion that this Task Force should have adopted the following recommendation:

> The Fair Labor Standards Act should be amended to extend its coverage, without exceptions, to every job within the reach of Federal authority. In particular, household workers and all other low-paid workers in the United States should be paid not less than the Federal minimum wage.

As recently as February 1968, an estimated 10 million workers in this country earned less than $1.60 an hour. Most of these workers were in agriculture, retail trade, and the services—particularly domestic service. Of the estimated 2.2 million employees in domestic service—the overwhelming majority of whom are women—86 percent, or more than 4 out of every 5 workers earned less than $1.00 an hour.

In considering the plight of these low-paid workers, it should be kept in mind that even in the case of persons covered by the Federal minimum wage of $1.60 an hour, an individual working full time, on the basis of a 40-hour week, earns only $3,328 a year.

These figures are well below the present poverty income level of $3,600 per year for a family of four as defined by the Department of Agriculture for "emergency or temporary use when funds are low." It would appear reasonable that the employer through adequate wages rather than the taxpayer should be expected to support the estimated 10,000,000 *working poor* who make less than $1.60 an hour. Even $1.60 an hour ($3,328 per year) is far below the $5,550 guaranteed income recommended for a family of four by President Nixon's recent White House Conference on Food, Nutrition, and Health.

The efforts of the Women's Bureau to give proper status and dignity to household employees through training and better working conditions would be aided greatly by coverage of employees under the Federal Fair Labor Standards Act. The lack of coverage under this and other labor standards legislation is one of the factors denying household employment appropriate dignity and status, as well as better pay and working conditions.

The Task Force cannot justify failure to take action on "lack of time or jurisdiction." The Task Force discussed on several occasions the question of Federal minimum wage. At least two recommendations were presented to the Task Force dealing with this question. A number of speakers in their presentations discussed minimum wage, and one speaker was specifically invited to speak to the Task Force on this subject.

The recommendations of the Task Force dealing with poverty make it self evident that the Task Force could not have made those recommendations without considering the problem of minimum wage. On a task force dealing with women's rights and responsibilities, it would seem one of the basic responsibilities is to speak for those who don't have a voice to speak for themselves.

I am of the firm opinion that the knowledge brought by the speakers, the discussions the Task Force had, and the knowledge generally available was fully sufficient for the task force to have taken a position.

In an effort to be reasonable in my proposed recommendation I did not include an increase in the minimum wage to $2.00 an hour.

Had I any anticipation at all that the Task Force would not adopt the recommendation, I would have included an increase in the minimum.

Comment of The Chairman Regarding Minority Statement

At many points in its deliberations, the Task Force did consider the massive problems of the "working poor". Several of the recommendations made in the report specifically attack certain of these problems. Extension of the Federal minimum wage to all workers is a complex matter of such pervasive effects throughout the national economy that the Task Force did not feel it was ready to make a specific recommendation without further intensive study.

APPENDIX A

Problems Commended for Early Consideration to Director, Office of Women's Rights and Responsibilities.

1. Extension of Federal Fair Labor Standards Act, particularly to household employees.
2. Methods of changing attitudes.
3. Abortion.
4. Social security benefits for women divorced after fewer than 20 years of marriage, for dependents of single persons, and for aged widows and widowers.
5. Civil service classification standards for "women's" occupations in the Federal service.
6. Deterrents to training of women employees of the Federal government.
7. Inequities in the unemployment insurance system.
8. Reemployment after childbirth and insurance against medical expenses and lack of income.

APPENDIX:

HOUSE AND SENATE FLOOR DEBATE

In 1970 both houses of Congress debated House Joint Resolution 264, which called for the Equal Rights Amendment to the Constitution. The House of Representatives did so on August 10, the Senate on October 7, 8, 9, 12, 13, 14. Reprinted here is a segment of the House floor debate and portions of the October 12 Senate floor debate. The complete House debate may be found in the *Congressional Record,* Vol. 116, Part 21, 91st Congress, 2nd Session, pp. 27999–28037. The complete Senate debate may be found in the *Congressional Record,* Vol. 116, Part 26, 91st Congress, 2nd Session, pp. 35448–35475, pp. 35623–35628; Vol. 116, Part 27, pp. 35943–35968, pp. 36265–36278, 36448–36451, p. 36832, and pp. 36862–36866.

HOUSE FLOOR DEBATE

MOTION OFFERED BY MRS. GRIFFITHS

Mrs. GRIFFITHS. Mr. Speaker, pursuant to the provisions of clause 4, rule XXVII, I move that the House proceed to the immediate consideration of House Joint Resolution 264.

The SPEAKER. The question is on the motion offered by the gentlewoman from Michigan (Mrs. GRIFFITHS).

The motion was agreed to.

The SPEAKER. The Clerk will report the joint resolution.

The Clerk read as follows:

H.J. RES. 264

Resolved by the Senate and House of Representatives of the United States of America in Congress assembled (two-thirds of each House concurring therein). That the following article is proposed as an amendment to the Constitution of the United States, which shall be valid to all intents and purposes as part of the Constitution when ratified by the legislatures of three-fourths of the several States:

"ARTICLE —

"SECTION 1. Equality of rights under the law shall not be denied or abridged by the United States or by any State on account of sex. Congress and the several States shall have power, within their respective jurisdictions, to enforce this article by appropriate legislation.

"SEC. 2. This article shall be inoperative unless it shall have been ratified as an amendment to the Constitution by the legislatures of three-fourths of the several States.

"SEC. 3. This amendment shall take effect one year after the date of ratification."

The SPEAKER. The gentlewoman from Michigan is recognized for 1 hour.

Mrs. GRIFFITHS. Mr. Speaker, I yield myself such time as I may consume, and I ask that I be notified when 10 minutes have passed.

Mr. Speaker, this is not a battle between the sexes—nor a battle between this body and women. This body and State legislatures have supported women. This is a battle with the Supreme Court of the United States.

Mr. McCORMACK. Mr. Speaker, will the gentlewoman yield?

Mrs. GRIFFITHS. I yield to the gentleman from Massachusetts.

Mr. McCORMACK. Mr. Speaker, this is a resolution which is very historic. It is

515

one that is aimed at an unintentional injustice on the part of most persons. My friend, the gentleman from New York, said we cannot change nature. This resolution does not undertake to change nature, but certainly it changes conditions. Many years ago we had the fight for women's suffrage—and what a fight that was. This is simply another historic step in connection with a sound and virile America where the injustices, unintentional in most cases and in the minds of most persons, are removed by this amendment.

I am glad to join with the gentlewoman from Michigan in urging passage of this joint resolution.

Mrs. GRIFFITHS. Thank you, Mr. Speaker. You are the fairest Speaker we have ever had.

There never was a time when decisions of the Supreme Court could not have done everything we ask today. In 1872, the Supreme Court denied a woman the right to practice law in Illinois; and reaffirmed the decision in 1894, although the Court struck down the California ordinance and extended the protection of the 14th amendment to male alien Chinese laundrymen in 1886 and in 1948 ruled a State statute invalid which denied a Japanese resident, ineligible for citizenship, a commercial fishing license.

In invalidating an Arizona statue in 1915, and thus extending the protections of the 14th amendment to an alien Austrian cook, the Court said:

It requires no argument to show that the right to work for a living in the common occupation of the country is the very essence of the personal freedom and opportunity that it was the purpose of the amendment to secure.

In 1938 the Court forced the admission of a Negro to the University of Missouri law school, and in 1960 refused the same protection to three Texas women who applied to the Texas A. & M. College for the purposes of studying floraculture, courses offered at no other school in the State of Texas.

In 1961, the Court ruled that the systematic exclusion of women from a jury was perfectly all right, although they had long ago decided that Negroes could not be excluded.

Fortunately, a three-judge Federal court in Alabama has recently held that the State law excluding women jurors was in violation of the 14th amendment. Let me repeat again and again that the States, their legislatures and frequently their courts or Federal district courts have shown more sense than the Supreme Court ever has.

Any stockholder can demand an accounting from a corporation; but a woman seeking a divorce in Louisiana in 1967, who asked an accounting of community property from her husband was denied it by the supreme court of Louisiana and the Supreme Court of the United States when they denied her the right to appeal on the basis that she was being deprived of her property without due process of law.

The Court has held for 98 years that women, as a class, are not entitled to equal protection of the laws. They are not "persons" within the meaning of the Constitution.

What will be the effect of the amendment?

The amendment would restrict only governmental action, and would not apply to purely private action. What constitutes "State action" would be the same as under the 14th amendment and as developed in 14th amendment litigation on other subjects. In 1964 Civil Rights Act granted far more rights to women and other minorities than this amendment ever dreamed of. That act applies against private industry. This amendment applies only against government.

Special restrictions on property rights of married women would be unconstitutional; married women could engage in business as freely as a member of the male sex; inheritance rights of widows would be same as for widowers.

Women would be equally subject to jury service and to military service, but women would not be required to serve—in the Armed Forces—where they are not fitted any more than men are required to so serve.

The real effect before this amendment is finally passed would probably be to permit both sexes to volunteer on an equal basis, which is not now the case.

Where the law confers a benefit, privilege or obligation of citizenship, such would be extended to the other sex, i.e. the effect of the amendment would be to strike the words of sex identification. Thus, such laws would not be rendered unconstitutional but would be extended to apply to both sexes by operation of the amendment. We have already gone through this in the 15th and 19th amendments.

Examples of such laws include: minimum wage laws applying only to women; laws requiring lunch periods and rest periods only for women; laws which permit alimony to be awarded under certain circumstances to wives but not to husbands would permit the Judge to determine who gets the alimony. Social security and other social benefits legislation which give greater benefits to one sex than the other would extend the benefits to the other sex.

Any expression of preference in the law for the mother in child custody cases would be extended to both parents—as against claims of third parties. Children are entitled to support from both parents under the existing laws of most States. Child support laws would be affected only if they discriminate on the basis of sex. The amendment would not prohibit the requiring of one parent to provide financial support for children who are in the custody of the other.

Where a law restricts or denies opportunities of women or men, as the case may be, the effect of the equal rights amendment would be to render such laws unconstitutional.

Examples are: hours and weight lifting laws but four States have repealed "so-called" protective legislation which restricts women: Delaware has repealed all restrictive legislation in 1967, and there has never been a lawsuit. The idea that this would cause unlimited lawsuits is ridiculous. Georgia has repealed its hours law. Oregon and Vermont have repealed their hours laws. Fifteen States have declared such laws unenforceable either through action of their supreme court or by some official of the government: Arizona, District of Columbia, Maryland, Kansas, New Mexico, Michigan, New York, North Carolina, Ohio, Oklahoma, Pennsylvania, South Dakota, North Dakota, Tennessee, Virginia, and Wyoming.

And let me say that there has never been an hours law which keeps a woman from working more than 40 hours a week. This is just not true. The law prohibits an employer from employing her. She can work 16 hours a day, and there is nobody that protects that woman—certainly not the AFL-CIO.

Separation of the sexes by law would be forbidden under the amendment except in situations where the separation is shown to be necessary because of an overriding and compelling public interest and does not deny individual rights and liberties.

For example, in our present culture the recognition of the right to privacy would justify separate restroom facilities in public buildings.

The amendment would not change the substance of existing laws, except that those which restrict and deny opportunities to women would be rendered unconstitutional. In all other cases, the laws presently on the books would simply be equalized, and this includes the entire body of family law. Moreover, this amendment does not restrict States from changing their laws. This law does not apply to criminal acts capable of commission by only one sex. It does not have anything to to with the law of rape or prostitution. You are not going to have to change those laws.

Forty-seven years ago the passage of this amendment would have been earth-shaking; but that was a different world. Today, we are fellow immigrants in a strange new world—30 million women are working. The census has shown that the poverty stricken families of men show upward mobility; but not the poverty stricken families headed by a woman.

It is past time that we consider these facts and that we begin the removal of any legal discrimination against women; as we are attempting to removal legal discriminations against all other minorities.

I urge you to vote for the previous question.

The SPEAKER pro tempore (Mr. HOLIFIELD). The gentlewoman from Michigan has consumed 12 minutes.

Mrs. GRIFFITHS. Mr. Speaker, at this moment I yield, for the purposes of debate only, 15 minutes to the gentleman from New York (Mr. CELLER).

Mr. CELLER. Mr. Speaker, I yield 7 minutes to the gentleman from Ohio (Mr. McCULLOCH).

Mr. McCULLOCH. Mr. Speaker, I yield 5 minutes to the gentleman from California (Mr. WIGGINS).

Mr. GROSS. A point of order, Mr. Speaker.

The SPEAKER pro tempore. The gentlewoman from Michigan has yielded 15 minutes to the gentleman from New York (Mr. CELLER). The gentleman from New York has control of his 15 minutes. He may yield to the gentleman from Ohio, and the Chair will notify the gentleman from New York when the gentleman from Ohio has consumed 7 minutes.

The gentleman from New York must remain on his feet, and he may yield to whomever he wishes.

Mr. CELLER. That I will do, Mr. Speaker.

Mr. McCULLOCH. That will do also, Mr. Speaker.

I now yield 5 minutes to the gentleman from California (Mr. WIGGINS).

PARLIAMENTARY INQUIRY

Mr. GROSS. Mr. Speaker, a parliamentary inquiry.

The SPEAKER pro tempore. The gentleman will state his parliamentary inquiry.

Mr. GROSS. Mr. Speaker, my parliamentary inquiry is this: May the gentleman yield to a third party?

The SPEAKER pro tempore (Mr. HOLIFIELD). The Chair will state that he may do so only by unanimous consent.

Mr. GROSS. I thank the Speaker, and that is what I thought.

The SPEAKER pro tempore. Is there objection?

PARLIAMENTARY INQUIRY

Mr. GERALD R. FORD. Mr. Speaker, a parliamentary inquiry.

The SPEAKER pro tempore. The gentleman will state his parliamentary inquiry.

Mr. GERALD R. FORD. As I recollect, Mr. Speaker, the gentlewoman from Michigan (Mrs. GRIFFITHS) yielded to the gentleman from New York only for the purpose of debate.

The SPEAKER pro tempore (Mr. HOLIFIELD). That is right.

Mrs. GRIFFITHS. That is right.

Mr. GERALD R. FORD. Now, if the gentleman from New York yields time to any one or more Members, is he yielding solely on that basis as well?

The SPEAKER pro tempore (Mr. HOLIFIELD). The Chair will state that would be the situation.

Mr. GERALD R. FORD. In other words, the gentleman cannot yield for any other purpose except debate?

The SPEAKER pro tempore (Mr. HOLIFIELD). The Chair will state that that is a correct interpretation of the situation.

Mr. GERALD R. FORD. I thank the Speaker.

Mr. CELLER. Mr. Speaker, I yield 5 minutes to the gentleman from California (Mr. WIGGINS).

The SPEAKER pro tempore. The gentleman from California (Mr. WIGGINS) is recognized for 5 minutes.

Mr. WIGGINS. Mr. Speaker, the question is: Shall this House recommend to the States for their ratification an amendment to the U.S. Constitution providing, in essence, that—

Equality of right . . . shall not be denied . . . on account of sex?

We are being asked, Mr. Speaker, to amend the Constitution and to do so after 60 minutes of controlled debate without the benefit of hearings before any committee of this House. In short, we are being asked to forgo our legislative responsibilities because it would be the gallant and gentlemanly thing to do.

It is possible to be for equality of rights under the law as between the sexes and still to resist the steamroller with which we are confronted today. I deeply regret that my committee has not held hearings on this measure, but its failure to do so should not be the excuse for compounding its error by hasty, ill-considered action today.

It is not too late to correct the mistakes of the past and I hope that the Members will avail themselves of that opportunity by recommitting this resolution to the Judiciary Committee with instructions that prompt hearings be held.

Are such hearings necessary? Of course they are.

The American Bar Association and distinguished constitutional scholars should be invited to testify. To date we have heard mostly from women's groups, whose objectivity on this issue may be suspect.

The attorneys general from the various States should be invited to testify concerning the impact of this amendment upon State laws, particularly property laws and the laws governing decedents' estates. It takes no great imagination to believe that comprehensive estate plans based upon established property rights may be profoundly affected by this amendment.

The Justice Department should be required to detail the many—perhaps hundreds —of Federal laws which be affected by our actions.

Perhaps even sociologists should be invited to comment upon the change in our social structure which is implicit in this amendment.

And, finally, perhaps all of us should like the opportunity to reflect upon whether the continued recognition in appropriate cases that men are men and women are women remains in the national interest.

It is not necessary to adopt this amendment to reach economic discrimination which is the heart of the problem. I strongly urge my colleagues—of both sexes— not to insert blindly words into our Constitution without a full understanding of their import. The Members should support a responsible motion to recommit requiring prompt hearings.

Mr. DENNIS. Mr. Speaker, will the gentleman yield?

Mr. WIGGINS. I yield to the gentleman.

Mr. DENNIS. It has been said that this amendment would make a profound social change, and I would just like to ask the gentleman if he does not agree that when we are considering an amendment, which according to the gentlewoman from Michigan will submit woman to military draft, that that certainly entails possibilities of a very profound social change in this country.

Mr. WIGGINS. Indeed, it does and it is certainly not the kind of change that we are to acquiesce in on the basis of 60 minutes of debate.

Mr. McCULLOCH. Mr. Speaker, will the gentleman from California yield for a question to the chairman of the Committee on the Judiciary?

Mr. WIGGINS. I yield to the gentleman.

Mr. McCULLOCH. Could the chairman state his intention with respect to the scheduling and holding of hearings by the Committee on the Judiciary on this proposal?

Mr. CELLER. As I already announced, hearings before the full Committee on the Judiciary are scheduled to begin on September 16. Shortly thereafter the committee would report to the House.

Mr. WIGGINS. I will say in conclusion that the chairman of our full committee, the distinguished gentleman from New York, has personally promised me, and I am sure he would extend the same promise to every Member in this Chamber, that the Committee on the Judiciary will hold hearings and that at the conclusion of those hearings, which will be in this session of the Congress, the issue will be brought before the full committee for prompt disposition in a normal and orderly way.

Mr. CELLER. Mr. Speaker, I yield 2 minutes to the gentleman from Ohio (Mr. McCULLOCH).

Mr. McCULLOCH. Mr. Speaker, never since I have been a Member of the Congress has a proposal to amend the Constitution of the United States been treated so cavalierly. Of course, I know there are strong forces for such consideration where the gentler sex is concerned. But, Mr. Speaker, I am fearful of the changes in basic property and human rights that a quick proposal to amend the Constitution across the board, as proposed in this legislation, might bring about.

Mr. Speaker, I do not rise in opposition to House Joint Resolution 264. My opposition is only to passage at the present time. To adopt this constitutional amendment without adequate hearings and debate would raise more questions than it would answer, and would be a most irresponsible act by this great legislative body. I would like to discuss just a few of the questions that this proposal presents.

The argument has been made that the equal rights amendment would add nothing to the equal protection clause of the 14th Amendment since the language of the two is substantially the same. In the past, courts have at times upheld laws which treated women differently on the theory that women, as a class, were different and that such distinctions were reasonable. In recent years, however, a variety of laws has been successfully challenged as working an arbitrary discrimination between the sexes.

For example, it has been held that a policewoman has a right to take the examination for the rank of sergeant, *Shpritzer* v. *Lang*, 17 N.Y.S. 2d 265 (1962)—dictum as to equal protection issue; that limits on the weight an employee may lift must be applied on an individual basis and not on the basis of sex, *Bowe et al.,* v. *Colgate Palmolive Company,* 416 F. 2d 711 (7th Cir. 1969); that a State may not exclude women from jury service, *White* v. *Crook,* 251 F. Supp. 401 (M.D. Ala., 1966); and that a State law may not provide for longer prison terms for women than for men for the same crime, *Commonwealth* v. *Daniel,* 430 Pa. 642 (1968), *U.S. ex. rel. Robinson* v. *York,* 281 F. Supp. 8 (D. Conn., 1968).

While some argue that the amendment is little more than an unnecessary gesture, Professor Freund contends that it "would set up a constitutional yardstick of absolute equality between men and women in all legal relationships," the effect of which would be an inflexibility, rigidity and above all confusion in numerous areas of the law; 96 CONGRESSIONAL RECORD 865, 1950. If there is to be absolute equality of the sexes, our selective service law would have to be revised to accommodate lady draftees. The entire structure of our family and domestic relations law as developed by the 50 States, especially those provisions giving preferential treatment to women, would be thrown into turmoil.

In the area of employment, the States have over the past century built up a large body of law designed to protect women in areas such as minimum wages, hours of work, weightlifting limitations, and other employment practices. An example which shows how much these laws are rooted in history is the first enforceable law regulating the hours of employment of women, which became effective in Massachusetts in 1879. The equal rights amendment might well strike from the statute books many of these laws. In order to illustrate the broad sweep of the laws which might be affected I insert at the conclusion of my remarks an excerpt from the "1969 Handbook on Women Workers," prepared by the Women's Bureau of the Department of Labor, which indicates statistics and identifies the number of States which have labor legislation designed to protect women.

If the amendment is to be given this broad construction—a point by no means resolved—we will, in effect, be restructuring a very basic portion of the social fabric of this country. I would not attempt to say whether this would be wise or if wise, whether those changes affecting areas of essentially local concern such as family law should be effectuated at the Federal level. What I can say with certainty is that the matter merits more than the very brief debate available today.

Probably the area of greatest legitimate concern is that of discrimination by sex in employment. Yet the rulings of the Equal Employment Opportunity Commission under title VII of the 1964 Civil Rights Act have attacked the various discriminatory practices complained of. The real problem is that the EEOC has no enforcement powers. Perhaps what is needed, rather than the pious language of a constitutional amendment, is the grant of real power to the EEOC to protect the right of all Americans—regardless not only of sex, but of race, color, religion or national origin—to fair and equal treatment in securing employment.

Another problem is that the Equal Rights Amendment, if adopted, would be the first constitutional amendment to grant to the States, as well as to Congress, authority to implement the amendment by appropriate legislation. The situation is complicated by the doctrine of *Katzenbach* v. *Morgan,* 384 U.S. 641 (1966), that the Supreme Court will uphold any statute of Congress enacted to vindicate 14th Amendment rights if it can "perceive a basis" for such action by Congress. Presumably, the Court will have to uphold any State statute if it can "perceive a basis" by which such statute vindicates rights granted by the equal rights amendment. The questions which would be raised by this result concerning the supremacy clause and the notion of federalism are difficult to define, let alone answer.

If my remarks have demonstrated anything, Mr. Speaker, it is that House Joint Resolution 264 needs more detailed study. It is my hope that the House will not preclude such study by approving this resolution on a wave of emotion.

EQUAL RIGHTS FOR MEN AND WOMEN

The ACTING PRESIDENT pro tempore. Under the previous order, the Chair lays before the Senate the unfinished business, which the clerk will state.

The assistant legislative clerk read the title, as follows:

A joint resolution (H.J. Res. 264) proposing an amendment to the Constitution of the United States relative to equal rights for men and women.

The Senate proceeded to consider the joint resolution.

Mr. BYRD of West Virginia. Mr. President, I suggest the absence of a quorum.

The ACTING PRESIDENT pro tempore. The clerk will call the roll.

The assistant legislative clerk proceeded to call the roll.

Mr. BYRD of West Virginia. Mr. President, I ask unanimous consent that the order for the quorum call be rescinded.

The ACTING PRESIDENT pro tempore. Without objection, it is so ordered.

Mr. ERVIN. Mr. President, the most compassionate prayer ever uttered was the prayer spoken by the lowly Man of Galilee when He was hanging upon the cross at Calvary. He looked upon those who were crucifying Him, and prayed this prayer in their behalf:

Then said Jesus, Father, forgive them; for they know not what they do.

This is the most compassionate of all prayers, as recorded in the 34th verse of the 23d chapter of the Gospel according to Luke.

It is not my purpose to be sacrilegious in any respect, but I say with all sincerity that those who advocate the adoption of the equal rights amendment stand in need of this prayer, because they do not know what they do.

I would say, furthermore, Mr. President, that those who occupy the state of ignorance as to what this amendment would be interpreted to mean, like the Senator from North Carolina, also stand in need of a prayer of this nature. Frankly, I do not know what the Supreme Court is going to say this amendment means; and when I say that, I put myself in the same state of ignorance which embraces every other Member of the Senate who is going to be called upon to vote upon the proposed amendment and every Member of the House of Representatives who already has voted upon the proposed amendment.

A very significant remark was made by Robert Sherrill, a correspondent for the Nation, in an article published in the New York Times a few days ago on this precise point.

Mr. Sherrill said—and he said quite truthfully—

The equal-rights amendment's journey down the corridors of Congress has so far been an impressive demonstration of what can be achieved through almost total ignorance. No one in Congress can make even a reasonably good case as to the amendment's probable effect on laws covering such matters as wife support, child support, military conscription, and property division.

Not withstanding the fact that no one can safely predict what this amendment will be interpreted to mean in the event it is submitted by Congress to the States and ratified by the States, we have insistent demands that we immediately vote, in our present state of ignorance, on this amendment.

In other words, we are urged to act in haste and let the wives, the mothers, the working women, and the widows of America lament the probable consequences of this amendment in leisure.

One of the difficulties incident to present-day legislation arises from the fact that before a Member of Congress can educate Congress, he has to educate the news media of the country and depend upon the news media of the country to educate the Members of Congress. The New York Times of Saturday, October 10, 1970, published an editorial indicating that the news media of the country are about to become educated with respect to this amendment. The New York Times made some very cogent observations concerning this amendment and concerning the total ignorance as to its future interpretation on the part of Congress, on the part of its proponents, and on the part of the country generally. It makes some comments on the fact that this amendment has been traveling to and fro in Congress for 47 years and that nobody has attempted to make a complete study as to its probable interpretation and as to its probable consequences. So the New York Times, in this editorial, warns Congress not to be in any haste to submit this amendment to the States for ratification or rejection.

Despite this fact, we have in respect to this amendment, during the current session of Congress, a virtually unprecedented effort to prevent any study of this amendment being made by any congressional committee. There were no hearings upon this amendment in the House of Representatives, and the House of Representatives voted on this amendment after some 60, 65, or 70 minutes of debate. It voted upon this amendment upon the assertion, which has been repeated on the floor of the Senate, that the Supreme Court of the United States has never held that a woman is even a person within the meaning of the 14th amendment. I do not think that a more extravagant and a more insupportable assertion than that has ever been made. The strange thing about it is that to prove the truth of that assertion, those who make it refer to the case of *Hoyt* v. *Florida,* 368 U.S. 57. This very case says this:

Several observations should initially be made. We, of course, recognize that the Fourteenth Amendment reaches not only arbitrary classes of exclusions from jury service based on race or color but also all other exclusions which single out any class of persons for different treatment not based on some reasonable classification.

What that means in plain English is that the 14th amendment prohibits a State from making any legal distinctions between one group of persons, whether they be men, women, or children, and another group of persons, whether they be men, women, or children, unless that distinction is based upon a reasonable classification. I expect later to make further allusions to the Hoyt case.

At this moment, I should like to call attention to the fact that some leaders of our women's organizations are flatly opposed to the submission of the proposed amendment to the States for ratification or rejection. . . .

Mr. President, it was stated on the floor of the Senate last week by the Senator from Indiana that any reasonable man could read the amendment and determine what it means. I consider the Senator from Indiana to be a reasonable man. He was queried as to the meaning of the amendment by the junior Senator from Missouri (Mr. EAGLETON), and the Senator from Indiana admitted, in reply to interrogatories propounded to him by the Senator from Missouri, that he would have to leave some of the questions asked him by the Senator from Missouri to the courts for decision and for that reason was unable to answer them.

Well, let us see whether the statement that all reasonable men can understand exactly what the amendment means is supported by the facts.

As Gov. Al Smith of New York was wont to remark, "Let's look at the record."

One of the most knowledgeable men in the United States on this subject is Prof. Paul A. Freund. He teaches constitutional law at Harvard Law School. He has this to say about the amendment:

That the proposed equal rights amendment would open up an era of regrettable consequences for the legal status of women in this country is highly probable. That it would open up a period of extreme confusion in constitutional law is a certainty . . . The amendment expresses noble sentiments, but I'm afraid it will work much mischief in actual application. It will open a Pandora's box of legal complications.

Professor Freund testified before the Judiciary Committee in opposition to the amendment and pointed out many of the dire consequences which could ensue if the amendment should be submitted by Congress to the States and ratified by the States.

I digress here to note—as I have said before—that there have been more obstacles thrown in the way of an intelligent understanding of the amendment in this session of Congress than has ever characterized consideration of any other legislative proposal during the 16 years I have been privileged to be a Member of the Senate.

I have already stated that there were no hearings in the House and that the consideration of the amendment in the House was for approximately 60, 65, or 70 minutes, or thereabouts; but when the amendment came to the Senate, the amendment was stopped at the desk and placed on the Calendar for immediate consideration without any committee hearings and without any committee consideration, notwithstanding that the rules of the Senate contemplate that proposals to amend the Constitution shall be referred to the Judiciary Committee and considered by that committee, and that the Senate should have a report and recommendation from the Judiciary Committee with respect to proposed constitutional amendments before the Senate votes upon such constitutional amendments.

After this proposed amendment was passed by the House and placed on the Senate Calendar, instead of being allowed to take its normal course and being referred to the Judiciary Committee for study and report, the overwhelming majority of the Judiciary Committee, with one member opposing and one member abstaining, adopted a request of the Senate leadership in which they asked the Senate leadership to permit the amendment to take its regular course and be referred to the Judiciary Committee for study and report to the Senate prior to its consideration by the Senate. That request has been ignored by the Senate leadership.

Notwithstanding the fact that the resolution has never been referred to the Judiciary Committee for study and report, the Judiciary Committee held hearings on a companion measure introduced by the Senator from Indiana, and received the testimony of such knowledgeable persons as Prof. Paul A. Freund, Philip B. Kurland, Mrs. Myra Wolfgang, Mrs. Mary Dublin Keyserling, and others.

Unfortunately, the testimony taken by the Judiciary Committee has just been printed and Senators have not yet had an opportunity to avail themselves of the advice which that testimony affords them concerning the dangers of this particular proposed amendment.

I respectfully submit that instead of trying to hurry Senate action on this proposal, we should strive to have intelligent action rather than hasty action, and should at least postpone consideration of the measure until Senators have an opportunity to study the testimony just made available to Members of the Senate.

This is the first time in my experience as a Member of the Senate that it appears the proponents of such an important matter as a proposed constitutional amendment seem to want the Senate of the United States to legislate in darkness rather than in light.

I mentioned a moment ago that Prof. Paul A. Freund, of the Harvard Law School, is a reasonable man, that he has studied the proposed amendment, and that he has warned the Senate against approving it in its present form, not only during the hearings held by the Judiciary Committee during this year, but as far back as 1953.

Prof. Philip Kurland, professor of constitutional law at the University of Chicago and editor of the annual publication known as the Supreme Court Review, had this to say concerning the proposed amendment:

H.J. Res. 264 is in keeping with much of the temper of our times that demands instant and simplistic solutions to complex problems, that assumes that the cure for such problems is the utterance of the magic word "equality," and that the proper governmental agency for effecting the cure is the judiciary.

The following is a release by the Women's Bureau of the Department of Labor in February 1970 concerning the proposed amendment. Presumably the Women's Bureau of the Department of Labor is staffed by women, and presumably those women are intelligent and are capable of expressing an opinion in respect to this question. Here is what the release says:

There are a great many questions concerning the equal-rights amendment, but very few answers.

The editor of the Wall Street Journal, who is known to me to be a highly intelligent man, notwithstanding the fact that his father tried, very unsuccessfully, to teach me some Latin many years ago, when I was a student at the University of North Carolina at Chapel Hill, had this to say about the proposed amendment:

We are all for ladies, but even so, before we write some new words into the Constitution, it'd be nice to know what they really do mean.

A number of the intelligent women whom I named a moment or so ago as being opponents of the proposed amendment are affiliated with labor unions which are collective bargaining agents for women who work in the industries of America. The AFL-CIO has joined them in opposition to the amendment, as is reflected by a statement made by Andrew J. Biemiller, legislative director of the AFL-CIO. This is what Mr. Biemiller said:

A myriad of legal relationships in every area of life . . . might be affected by the equal rights amendment, with uncertain and possibly inequitable results in particular situations where identity of treatment might not yield true equality of treatment between the sexes.

Prof. Soia Mentschikoff, of the Chicago Law School, had this to say about the amendment:

The ligation could be endless. The courts would have to decide whether sex can ever be a reasonable classification.

Mr. President, I have read some of the documents which have been issued in support of this amendment. With all due respect to those who wrote them, I would have to say that the documents exhibit symptoms of intellectual schizophrenia.

These articles start out with a flat assertion that the equal rights amendments will abolish every existing Federal or State law which makes any legal distinction between men and women and that it will render the Congress and the legislatures of all 50 of the States powerless at any time in the future to enact any new laws which make any legal distinction between men and women.

After making these assertions, however, the writers of this propaganda recognize that they are trapping themselves in their own words. So they proceed in the documents they have prepared to contradict themselves.

They recognize that under the assertions they have made, they are asking the Congress of the United States and the legislatures of all 50 States to give up their power to enact laws which recognize that the good Lord made physiological and functional differences between men and women and to forget that rational action on the part of Congress and the 50 States requires them to enact such laws.

Then they proceed to assert in contradiction of what they have already said that laws which are beneficial to women will not be affected by this amendment although the amendment, they reiterate, is designed to make identical legal beings of men and women. In so doing, the writers of this propaganda emulate the example of the man in Aesop's Fable who blew both hot and cold with the same breath.

Another reasonable person, who opposes this amendment is Cernoria Johnson, Washington Director of the National Urban League. Cernoria Johnson has this to say about the amendment:

The Urban League is not in favor of current proposals which could eliminate protective standards for women or which might adversely affect their economic welfare, health, privacy or special responsibilities as mothers.

Prof. James J. White of the Law School of the University of Michigan said this in his testimony before the Committee on the Judiciary:

If I were a Senator, my reaction would be that I would vote against H.J. Res. 264 and I would seek to accomplish the goals by additional legislation. . . . It would be great for lawyers, though.

Glen Alison, Washington director, National Association of Social Workers, said this about the amendment:

The Equal Rights amendment could alter legal, economic, and other relationships between men and women. These are complex issues affecting the basic tenets of our society, which do not lend themselves to the blunderbuss approach of the Equal Rights Amendment.

In August of this year the New York Times made editorial comment on this amendment, in which it deplored the hasty manner in which it had been considered in the House of Representatives. In the editorial the New York Times said:

The clear responsibility of the Senate is to give the amendment the thorough analysis it never got in the House. The Constitution and the rights of women are both too important for any further playing to the ladies' gallery.

Mrs. Leonard H. Weiner, national president, National Council of Jewish Women, had this to say concerning the proposed amendment:

The effect of the Equal Rights Amendment upon our law proposes a great many questions to which the proponents have given no answers. . . . The Amendment is not the proper vehicle for the elimination of whatever discriminations against women might still exist.

Mrs. Norman F. Folda, national president, National Council of Catholic Women, had this to say:

We are opposed to the passage of the Equal Rights Amendment because it will jeopardize many socially desirable laws necessary for the maintenance and strengthening of the family structure.

Miss Evelyn Dubrow, legislative representative, International Ladies' Garment Workers' Union, had this to say about the amendment:

Under the proposed (Equal Rights) Amendment, a number of essential legislative safeguards of women's rights as industrial citizens would be wiped out. This should not be permitted to happen.

Miss Dubrow is the legislative representative of an organization which represents thousands of women who are employed in industry. She says, and quite correctly, that the amendment would destroy many safeguards which have been adopted by legislative bodies on both the national and the local level for the protection of women's rights.

During my opening remarks I mentioned the fact that an editorial in the New York Times of October 10, 1970, had warned Congress against hasty action on this amendment. The New York Times pointed out that society does make many discriminations against women. It points out that many of these discriminations have their origin outside of the law and owe their existence solely to the practices of our society. It also points out that certain Federal legislation, such as the Civil Rights Act of 1964 and the equal pay law, which was made part of the Fair Labor Standards Act and certain Executive orders have done much to relieve legal discriminations against women, and it adds that more can be done by legislation, but that enforcement of the laws already on the books at least is necessary. . . .

Mr. ERVIN. Mr. President, this amendment deserves thorough study. It deserves consideration by the Senate Judiciary Committee. I propose, after the recess, to make a motion that this amendment be permitted to take the regular normal course pointed out by the Senate rules for constitutional amendments, and that it be referred to the Senate Judiciary Committee so that that committee, which is composed entirely of lawyers, can express to the Senate an opinion concerning the amendment.

I return now to the case of *Hoyt* v. *Florida,* 368 U.S. 57. This case makes as clear as the noonday sun in a cloudless sky that the statement that the Supreme Court has never held that women are persons within the purview of the 14th amendment is totally insupportable. This case arose in Florida. A woman was convicted of the second degree murder of her husband by a jury composed entirely of men. It eventually reached the Supreme Court of the United States upon her allegation that the State of Florida excluded women from service upon juries in State courts and that she was a person within the purview of the 14th amendment, and that by reason of the exclusion of women from juries by the State of Florida in State trials, she had been deprived of the equal protection of the laws under the provision of the 14th amendment which says, in substance, that no State shall deny to any person within its jurisdiction the equal protection of the laws.

The Supreme Court recognized that she was right in one respect, and that was that the 14th amendment covers with the shield of its protection all human beings, whether they be men or women or children. It rejected her appeal, however, on the ground that the State of Florida did not exclude women from juries, and that, she had not been denied the equal protection of the laws. . . .

Mr. ERVIN. Mr. President, what did the Hoyt case hold? The Hoyt case held that, under the equal protection clause of the 14th amendment every State law which makes any legal distinction between men and women is unconstitutional unless it is based on some reasonable classification.

Stating the proposition in another way, the Hoyt case held that the equal protection clause of the 14th amendment invalidates every State law that treats men and women differently unless the difference in treatment is based upon some reasonable classification.

The Supreme Court pointed out in the Hoyt case that the laws of Florida did not exclude women from service upon grand and petit juries in that State; that the laws of Florida made both men and women eligible to serve upon grand and petit juries in the courts of Florida; that the laws of Florida did make a legal distinction between men and women in respect to their obligation—not their eligibility, but their obligation—to serve on grand and petit juries in the courts of the State;

that this distinction lay in the fact that the laws of Florida provided that no woman should be compelled to serve upon a jury unless she notified the appropriate clerk of the court having jurisdiction in the area of her residence that service on the jury was compatible with her other obligations; that in the event she so advised the clerk of the court, she would be summoned to serve on grand and petit juries just as men were summoned; and that this difference in treatment of men and women in respect of jury service was reasonable because it took into consideration certain functional differences made by nature and society between men and women.

Some of the proponents of the pending amendment deplore this decision. This attitude rises out of the fact that there seems to be quite a difference of opinion between some of the proponents of the amendment, and those women who have assumed voluntarily the role of wives or the role of mothers, and those women who have assumed involuntarily, on account to their economic status, the role of workers in industry, and those women who have involuntarily assumed, by reason of the deaths of their husbands, the role of widows.

Under Florida laws, any business or professional woman is perfectly free to inform the clerk of the court of the jurisdiction in which she resides that service upon State juries will not conflict with her personal obligations, and thereby make it obligatory for herself to serve upon such juries in the same manner in which men are required to serve on such juries. Why the proponents of the amendment insist that homemakers should be compelled by law to leave their homes to serve on juries, that mothers should be compelled by law to neglect their children to serve on juries, and that working women should be compelled by law to leave their jobs to serve on juries, and why widows should be compelled by law to do their bidding, in this respect, is something I am incapable of comprehending.

It may be that in their view the courthouse has become more important than the home, and that in consequence they disagree with this observation made by the Supreme Court of the United States in the Hoyt case:

In neither respect can we conclude that Florida's statute is not "based on some reasonable classification," and that it is thus infected with unconstitutionality. Despite the enlightened emancipation of women from the restrictions and protections of bygone years, and their entry into many parts of community life formerly considered to be reserved to men, woman is still regarded as the center of home and family life. We cannot say that it is constitutionally impermissible for a State, acting in pursuit of the general welfare, to conclude that a woman should be relieved from the civic duties of jury service unless she herself determines that such service is consistent with her own special responsibilities.

Florida is not alone in so concluding. Women are now eligible for jury service in all but three States of the Union. Of the forty-seven States where women are eligible, seventeen besides Florida, as well as the District of Columbia, have accorded women an absolute exemption based solely on their sex, exercisable in one form or another. In two of these States, as in Florida, the exemption is automatic, unless a woman volunteers for such service. It is true, of course, that Florida could have limited the exemption, as some other States have done, only to women who have family responsibilities. But we cannot regard it as irrational for a state legislature to consider preferable a broad exemption, whether born of the State's historic public policy or of a determination that it would not be administratively feasible to decide in each individual instance whether the family responsibilities of a prospective female juror were serious enough to warrant an exemption.

Likewise we cannot say that Florida could not reasonably conclude that full effectuation of this exemption made it desirable to relieve women of the necessity of affirmatively claiming it, while at the same time requiring of men an assertion of the exemptions available to them. Moreover, from the standpoint of its own administrative concerns the State might well consider that it was "impractical to compel large numbers of women, who have an absolute exemption, to come to the clerk's office for examination since they so generally assert their exemption." . . .

Appellant argues that whatever may have been the design of this Florida enactment, the statute in practical operation results in an exclusion of women from jury service, because women like men, can be expected to be available for jury service only under compulsion.

That last statement represents the attitude and reveals the reason why some militant proponents of the pending amendment want to compel all women to have to serve on juries, why they want homemakers to have to leave their homes and go to the courthouse for jury services, and why they want mothers to have to forsake their children and go to the courthouse, either to serve on juries or to ask the court for an excuse from service for their children's benefit.

The Supreme Court pointed out that 17 States have laws of this nature, and I would predict that the proponents of this amendment are not going to be very successful in persuading the legisuatures of those 17 States to ratify an amendment which would outlaw their handiwork in enacting jury laws of this nature, and which would forever prohibit them, at any time in the future, from enacting any laws which take into consideration that there are functional differences between men and women which justify legislative bodies to make distinctions of the kind made in the Florida jury laws.

Mr. BAYH. Mr. President, will the Senator yield?

Mr. ERVIN. Yes.

Mr. BAYH. I have listened with a great deal of interest to the usual eloquence of my friend from North Carolina. I should like to make just one brief observation: I take issue with the Supreme Court's decision in Hoyt not because it protects women from being required to serve on juries against their will but, rather, because that even women who want to serve on juries, women who want to take advantage of their constitutional right, have to go to special pains in order to serve under the Florida statute. The Florida statute at issue in Hoyt did not require that a woman could be excused by saying, "I object. Remove me from this obstacle." Quite the contrary, the Florida statute said that any woman who wanted to serve on a jury had to leave her home or business and "register" with the clerk of court. I think this is wrong.

Mr. ERVIN. The Senator from Indiana is absolutely wrong as to what the statute requires. It does not say that she has to leave her home and go to the court. She can use her finger to dial the clerk's office and tell him over the telephone that she wants to serve, and it will not take more than 30 seconds to do it. All she need say is, "I am longing to serve on the jury."

Mr. BAYH. She has to make a special effort.

Mr. ERVIN. That is a terrible effort, is it not?

Mr. BAYH. Why should she not be treated as men, equally, under this particular statute?

Mr. ERVIN. Because there is an old Spanish proverb which says that an ounce of mother is worth a pound of priest. She should not be required to leave her children, who need her far more than the court does.

Mr. BAYH. It seems to me that if the Senator from North Carolina is going to be consistent—and he usually is—the proper statute would say that that woman could dial the telephone and say, "Relieve me from the burden of serving." Why should she have to telephone and say, "Treat me like a first-class citizen; stop treating me like a second-class citizen"?

Mr. ERVIN. This statute says, "Treat me like a mother, whose first obligation is to her children." That is what the statute says. It treats her like a mother.

Mr. BAYH. Mothers also happen to be citizens; and I do not see why they should be treated different from men conditions at home allow them to serve. Yet the Florida statute does this, and the Supreme Court has sustained it.

Mr. ERVIN. The Florida statute says to a mother, "If you feel that serving on a jury is consistent with the performance of your duty as a mother, all you have to do is to dial the clerk of the court and tell him so, and then you will be summoned to leave your children and serve on the jury." It gives the mother an option. But the statute recognizes that there are persons above all others whom the Lord God Almighty appointed to look after their little children during their maturing years. In effect, the Florida Legislature says to mothers. "You can be the judge of whether or not you want to serve on a jury and whether or not you think your service on the jury will be consistent with your duties as a mother. If so, then you can serve, and all you have to do is to dial the clerk's office and tell him so."

I believe in doing something special for mothers. The Senator from Indiana may believe that mothers should be treated just like everybody else, but I do not believe that, because I find a response in my heart for these words of Rudyard Kipling:

If I were hanged on the highest hill,
Mother o' mine, O mother o' mine!
I know whose love would follow me still,

> Mother o' mine, O mother o' mine!
> If I were damned of body and soul,
> I know whose prayers would make me whole,
> Mother o' mine, O mother o' mine!

I disagree fundamentally with my friend, the distinguished Senator from Indiana. I believe in giving a little special consideration to the mothers of our Nation. I do not believe I would want to classify them with the general run of society and drag them to the court houses to serve on juries when they feel that their duty is to their children whom the good Lord has given them.

Mr. BAYH. Mr. President, will the Senator yield?

Mr. ERVIN. I yield.

Mr. BAYH. Perhaps the great poet Kipling would turn over in his grave at this thought. But if we are going to be consistent, he ought to add one more line to that marvelous verse, which would read something like this:

> If I would serve in the court house tall,
> I would have to give the clerk a call.

In other words, if I am a mother or if I am a woman, I am going to have to do something special in order to have the chance to serve on a jury.

I suggest to the Senator from North Carolina that the Senator from Indiana has as much love for his mother and respect for motherhood as anybody else. But no one should be relegated to second-class citizenship just because one is a mother. If she wants to serve on a jury, she should not have to go to the special effort which the Florida statute requires.

Mr. ERVIN. When I think of the tears mothers shed for us and the prayers they utter for us and the love they extend to us, I am not much impressed by the concern of the Senator from Indiana that it is a great imposition to a mother who would rather serve on a jury than look after her children to require her to dial a telephone and tell the clerk of the court that she thinks she ought to be compelled to serve on a jury even if she has to neglect her children.

Mr. BAYH. I appreciate the Senator from North Carolina yielding to me.

What we are trying to stress in this equal rights amendment is as much symbolic as it is real. It deals not only with statutes like that in Florida but also with the fact that, according to the Supreme Court of the United States, when Hoyt was decided, there were still three States that would not let women serve on juries at all. Today women are doing the same kind of work but receiving significantly less than men. There are still institutions of higher learning which require girl students to score significantly higher on entrance tests before they will let them in. Some States today require women, even if they are the sole support of their children, to get court orders before they can go into business. The amendment deals with this type of problem, our treating women as second-class citizens.

Mr. ERVIN. I would say to the Senator from Indiana that if he objects only to the jury laws of three States, he should work on the State legislatures which enacted those laws to get them to repeal those laws and get them to make women eligible for jury service, instead of advocating a constitutional amendment to drag mothers to the courthouse in legal chains, against their will to the neglect of their children. I submit that such a course of action would be preferred above imposing upon mothers of the other 47 States burdens they deem incompatible with their duty to provide nurture for their small children.

Mr. COOK. Mr. President, will the Senator yield?

Mr. ERVIN. I yield.

Mr. COOK. Will the Senator explain to me, with more than 30 million women in the United States working every day, why a man who is tapped to serve on jury duty receives far less compensation to serve on the jury than he takes home from his work, while the more than 30 million American women who work do not have to be worried about that? They can stay right there, unless they want to take a reduction in their daily salary, and then they can go to the courthouse and say, "I'm a working mother"—or a working woman—"and I want my name on the list; and if you want to call me, go ahead." Otherwise, every man is eligible to serve and must serve, even if he is the one and only breadwinner, and he is asked to serve for $5 a day or $7.50 a day. Yet the 30-odd million women who work in the

United States need not have that problem to face.

Mr. ERVIN. I would suggest to the Senator from Kentucky that he ask that question of the President of the National Council of Negro Women, the vice president of the United Farm Workers Organizing Committee, the former Director of the Women's Bureau of the U.S. Department of Labor—

Mr. COOK. I thought the Senator would give me the answer.

Mr. ERVIN. Just a minute—or the executive director of the National Council of Catholic Women, or the former chairman of the California Advisory Commission on the Status of Women, or the general secretary of the National Consumers League, or the former administrator of the Social Rehabilitation Service of the U.S. Department of HEW, or the former member of the President's Commission on the Status of Women, and all the other women whose names I have mentioned as being strong opponents of this proposal.

The ACTING PRESIDENT pro tempore (Mr. METCALF). Under the previous agreement, the time has now arrived to consider the question of agreement to the amendment of the Senator from Alabama (Mr. ALLEN), which was modified, and when reprinted as modified was printed as amendment No. 1047, which the clerk will state.

The assistant legislative clerk read the amendment as follows:

On page 1, line 3, beginning with the word "That" strike out everything down through line 7 and insert in lieu thereof the following: "That the articles set for in sections 2 and 3 of this joint resolution are proposed as amendments to the Constitution of the United States, and either or both articles shall be valid to all intents and purposes as part of the Constitution if ratified by the legislatures of three-fourths of the several States within seven years after being submitted by the Congress to the States for ratification".

On page 1, between lines 7 and 8, insert the following:
"SEC. 2. The first article so proposed is the following:"
On page 2, after line 7, insert the following:
"SEC. 3. The second article so proposed is the following:
"ARTICLE —

"A State shall have the absolute right to assign students to the public schools it operates by a freedom of choice system. A freedom of choice system means a system for the assignment of students to public shcools and within public schools maintained by a school board operating a system of public schools in which the public schools and the classes it operates are open to students of all races, creeds, and national origins, and in which the students are granted the freedom to attend public schools and classes chosen by their respective parents from among the public schools and classes available for the instruction of students of their ages and educational standings."

The ACTING PRESIDENT pro tempore. The time for the consideration of this amendment is controlled. Who yields time?

Mr. ALLEN. Mr. President, I yield myself 7 minutes.

The ACTING PRESIDENT pro tempore. The Senator from Alabama is recognized for 7 minutes. . . .

Mr. ALLEN. Mr. President, in offering the amendment, there is no disposition on the part of the Senator from Alabama to interfere in any way with a final vote on House Joint Resolution 264, the equal-rights-for-women amendment.

In March of last year, the junior Senator from Alabama introduced Senate Joint Resolution 80, which provides for submitting a constitutional amendment that would have the effect of returning the public schools of the Nation to State and local governments. That amendment has reposed in the Subcommittee on Constitutional Amendments for more than 18 months, from March 1969 up to the present time.

Thus, on Thursday last, when amendment No. 1042 was submitted by the junior Senator from Alabama, it was his hope that we would add this amendment to the amendment sought to be submitted by House Joint Resolution 264. It would be an additional amendment to be submitted by the same measure and would in no way supplant or be in lieu of the equal-rights-for-women provision.

There is no need to have 100 separate resolutions in order to submit 100 separate constitutional amendments. It would be possible, theoretically, to submit by the same measure two, four, ten, a dozen, or a hundred proposed constitutional amendments. So there is no disposition on the part of the junior Senator from Alabama to hold up a vote on the main question. He merely seeks to have a vote on this great school issue.

On the last legislative day, Friday of last week, the junior Senator from Alabama offered a modification of his amendment. It has been printed as amendment No. 1047. Actually it is not a separate amendment. It is the same amendment which has been modified. Instead of providing for a complete return of the schools to the States and for supplanting the Federal courts with State courts as the final arbiter of rights, privileges, and immunities of citizens with respect to school matters, it provides for leaving jurisdiction with the Federal Courts, with the Supreme Court to be the final arbiter. But the modification does allow a State the absolute right to set up a freedom-of-choice system for the operating and management of its public schools.

Mr. President, the Supreme Court of the United States has not held that freedom of choice plans are, per se, unconstitutional. It has held in at least one case that where the freedom of choice plan did not result in the degree of desegregation, that degree being unspecified, but the degree of desegregation that the Supreme Court thought should take place, then that plan was stricken down. But freedom-of-choice plans as such have not been ruled unconstitutional by the Supreme Court of the United States.

Mr. President, all the amendment would do would be to send out to the States, along with the equal rights for women amendment, an amendment providing for freedom of choice—yes, equal rights—for school children, as well as equal rights for women. The number of States that the consideration of the respective amendments by the States would not be in any way connected. In other words, all States might ratify the equal rights for women amendment and it would become a part of the Constitution, having been ratified. But that would have no effect on the freedom-of-choice amendment. That would have to stand on its own and receive the approval of 38 States.

This is not a sectional issue. It would provide any State in the Union with the right to set up a freedom of choice plan.

We need this amendment in Alabama and the South to allow us to have the same rights, privileges, and immunities in Alabama and the South that are now enjoyed in other sections of the country. So it would take the express authorization of 38 States of the Union for this freedom-of-choice option on the part of the States to become a part of the Constitution. It would not be a sectional matter, it would require a three-fourths majority of the States. It would not require any State to institute a freedom-of-choice plan. It would allow the freedom-of-choice plan, as defined in the modification, to be set up by any State that saw fit to do so. Then the Federal court, with the Supreme Court being the final arbiter, would then have jurisdiction to determine whether in its application a true freedom of choice is being provided.

It would in no way interfere with the jurisdiction or the role of final arbiter of the Supreme Court.

Mr. President, I hope that the amendment will be adopted and that it will become part of House Joint Resolution 264, and that, by a two-thirds vote, both amendments to House Joint Resolution 264 will be submitted by the Congress to the States and that at least 38 of the States will ratify both amendments. . . .

Mr. NELSON. Mr. President, over 50 years ago, thousands of women across the Nation were engaged in a political fight to secure the right to vote. My mother was among those women.

They won the power of the ballot in the 19th amendment to the Constitution and, with that, American women thought they were well on the way to eliminating discrimination based on sex.

Any objective evaluation of the current situation must conclude that the power of the ballot box has not solved the problem. In fact, in many ways there is more discrimination now than there was then.

A half century ago the country was rural, leisure time was limited, society lacked mobility, and most jobs were unskilled manual labor. Women who wanted employment became teachers or nurses, if they desired to work in a professional field. About the only other employment opportunities open to them were clerical, stenographic, domestic, and miscellaneous unskilled labor positions.

Vast changes in the past half century have created a demand for a great variety of talents and skills. The number of women, both single and married, who wish to enter the job market has been expanding rapidly for more than a quarter century.

However, women find widespread discrimination in getting admitted to professional schools to attain the kind of education they must have, and they find discrimination in the jobs they are offered when they finish school. Once employed, they find their opportunities for advancement limited.

The discrimination extends from law firms to educational institutions, Government jobs of all kinds, and to all private and nonprofit organizations.

It is a widely followed custom that certain jobs are earmarked for women. There is even a common descriptive term, "woman's work." The best positions—supervisors, managers, and executives, are for men. For example, although the American school system has more women than men teachers, the men outnumber the women in reaching the highest positions.

A 1968 study of the Federal Government showed that of the 667,234 women employed at that time, 80 percent were in the bottom six grades, and the majority worked in clerical and lower-grade technician jobs. Only 1 percent of the women held jobs in the top six grades.

Equally discriminatory is the question of salary. Where women perform the same or equivalent work as men, it is still a common practice to pay them a lower salary.

In 1968, women working full-time earned, on the average, 58 percent as much as their male counterparts. For each specific field, the figures are similar. In sales work, the median income for women was $3,461, and for men, it was $7,351.

Overall, 8 percent of the men holding jobs in the country earned salaries of $15,000 or more, as compared with 0.4 percent of the women working full-time. At the other end of the scale, 20 percent of the women workers earned below $3,000, while only 7.5 percent of the men were in this category.

Even with full equality under the law, the economic forms of discrimination will not soon come to end. But like achieving woman suffrage, achieving legal equality will be another great advance in the right direction.

Equal rights is a concept that is not limited to one issue or one class of people. It is universal, and it means allowing all human beings, men and women alike, the best possible chance to guide their own destinies and to choose a way of life they find personally fulfilling.

We now have an opportunity, in the equal rights for women amendment, to provide the women of this Nation with an effective means of protecting their legal rights and opposing still-existing forms of legal discrimination.

In principal, the Constitution guarantees equal rights to all citizens as a birthright. Therefore, such an amendment should not be necessary. But experience has shown that equal rights have never been a reality, and that the courts can be agonizingly slow in extending even the clear-cut provisions of the 14th amendment to the people for whom they were intended.

In my opinion, this amendment is necessary and long overdue, in guaranteeing the women of this country full citizenship and full participation in modern life which has been so affected by sweeping technological and social changes.

I strongly support House Joint Resolution 264, and I would hope that the Senate will pass the measure without amendment.

The PRESIDING OFFICER. The question is on agreeing to the amendment of the Senator from Alabama. On this question the yeas and nays have been ordered, and the clerk will call the roll.

The legislative clerk called the roll.

Mr. SPONG (when his name was called). On this vote I have a pair with the distinguished Senator from Minnesota (Mr. MONDALE). If he were president and voting, he would vote "nay." If I were at liberty to vote, I would vote "yea." I withhold my vote.

Mr. BYRD of West Virginia. I announce that the Senator from Nevada (Mr. CANNON), the Senator from Tennessee (Mr. GORE), the Senator from Oklahoma (Mr. HARRIS), the Senator from Indiana (Mr. HARTKE), the Senator from Massachusetts (Mr. KENNEDY), the Senator from Montana (Mr. MANSFIELD), the Senator from Minnesota (Mr. MCCARTHY), the Senator from Wyoming (Mr. MCGEE), the Senator from Minnesota (Mr. MONDALE), the Senator from Utah (Mr. MOSS), the Senator from

Rhode Island (Mr PASTORE), the Senator from Rhode Island (Mr. PELL), and the Senator from Texas (Mr. YARBOROUGH), are necessarily absent.

I further announce that, if present and voting, the senior Senator from Rhode Island (Mr. PASTORE), the junior Senator from Rhode Island (Mr. PELL), and the Senator from Oklahoma (Mr. HARRIS) would each vote "nay."

Mr. GRIFFIN. I announce that the Senators from Vermont (Mr. AIKEN and Mr. PROUTY), the Senator from Hawaii (Mr. FONG), the Senator from Arizona (Mr. GOLDWATER), the Senator from New York (Mr. GOODELL), the Senator from Maryland (Mr. MATHIAS), the Senator from California (Mr. MURPHY), the Senator from Oregon (Mr. PACKWOOD), the Senator from Illinois (Mr. SMITH), and the Senator from Texas (Mr. TOWER) are necessarily absent.

The Senator from South Dakota (Mr. MUNDT) is absent because of illness.

The Senator from Utah (Mr. BENNETT) is detained on official business.

If present and voting, the Senator from New York (Mr. GOODELL), the Senator from South Dakota (Mr. MUNDT), the Senator from Illinois (Mr. SMITH), and the Senator from California (Mr. MURPHY) would each vote "nay."

On this vote, the Senator from Texas (Mr. TOWER) is paired with the Senator from Maryland (Mr. MATHIAS). If present and voting, the Senator from Texas would vote "yea" and the Senator from Maryland would vote "nay."

The result was announced—yeas 17, nay 57, as follows: . . .

So Mr. ALLEN's amendment (No. 1047) was rejected.

Mr. BAYH. Mr. President, I move that the Senate reconsider the vote by which the amendment was rejected.

Mr. GRIFFIN. Mr. President, I move to lay that motion on the table.

The motion to lay on the table was agreed to.

INDEX OF INCLUSIONS

This index lists all the items included in this edition with the exception of the oral testimonies. The parenthetical number refers to the page in the GPO edition; the number following refers to the page in this volume. The titles of statements and prepared testimonies have been simplified.

INDEX OF OMISSIONS

Listed here are items in the original GPO editions that have been omitted from this volume. The parenthetical number refers to the page in the GPO edition. The titles of items have been simplified for easy reference.

INDEX OF PERSONS AND ORGANIZATIONS

This index includes the names of individuals who testified, submitted statements, or wrote articles and the names of organizations they represented. Only those whose material appears in this edition are included.

538

DATE DUE

DEMCO